The European Women's History Reader

The
European Women's
History Reader

Edited by

Fiona Montgomery and
Christine Collette

 Routledge
Taylor & Francis Group

LONDON AND NEW YORK

First published 2002 by Routledge
2 Park Square, Milton Park, Abingdon, Oxon, OX14 4RN

Simultaneously published in the USA and Canada
by Routledge
711 Third Avenue, New York, NY 10017

Routledge is an imprint of the Taylor & Francis Group, an informa business

Individual chapters © the original copyright holders

Typeset in Perpetua and Bell Gothic by
HWA Text and Data Management, Tunbridge Wells

British Library Cataloguing in Publication Data
A catalogue record for this book is available from the British Library

Library of Congress Cataloging in Publication Data
The European women's history reader / [edited by] Fiona Montgomery, Christine
Collette.
        p. cm.
    Includes bibliographical references and index.
        1. Women – Europe – History.   I. Montgomery, Fiona.   II. Collette, Christine
HQ1587.E983 2001
305.4´094–dc21
        2001041991

ISBN 0–415–22081–5 (hbk)
ISBN 0–415–22082–3 (pbk)

Contents

Acknowledgements

The editors and publishers wish to thank the following for their permission to reproduce copyright material.

Excerpt from Natalie Zemon Davis's '"Women's History" in Transition: The European case' is reprinted from *Feminist Studies*, Volume 3, No 3/4 (Spring/Summer 1976), by permission of the publisher, Feminist Studies Inc; excerpt from *Journal of Women's History* reproduced by permission of Indiana University Press; excerpts from Karen Offen's 'Defining Feminism' originally published in *Signs* Volume 14, No 1 (Fall, 1988), reproduced by permission of the University College of Chicago Press and the author; Chapter 2 'A lop-sided view: feminist history or the history of women?' by Deborah Thom from *Critical Feminism* edited by Kate Campbell, Open University Press, 1992, reproduced by permission of the author and Open University Press; excerpt from June Purvis's *Women's History: Britain 1850–1945* reproduced by permission of Taylor and Francis Books Ltd; 'Mary Wollstonecraft and the Wild Wish of Early Feminism' by Barbara Taylor, from *The History Workshop Journal*, Volume 33, pp. 197–219 (1992), reproduced by permission of Oxford University Press; excerpts from *Wollstonecraft's Daughters* by Clarissa Campbell Orr, 1996, Manchester University Press, Manchester, UK, reproduced by permission of Manchester University Press; 'The Struggle over the Gender Division of Labour, 1780–1826' reproduced from *The Struggle for the Breeches: Gender and the Making of the British*, by Anna Clark, Rivers Oram Press, London, 1995, reproduced by permission of Rivers Oram Press Ltd; 'Women's Work, Gender Conflict, and Labour Markets in Europe, 1500–1900' by Katrina Honeyman and Jordan Goodman from *Economic History Review* XLIV 4 (1991), reproduced by permission of the authors; excerpts from Maxine Berg's 'What Difference did Women's Work Make to the Industrial Revolution' from the *History Workshop Journal* (1993), reproduced by permission of Oxford University Press and the author; excerpts from Sally Alexander's 'Women, Class and Sexual Differences' from the *History Workshop Journal* Volume 17 (1984), reproduced by permission of Oxford University Press and the author; excerpt from Ann Goldberg's 'The Eberbach Asylum and the Practice(s) of Nymphomania in Germany, 1815–1849' from *Journal of Women's History*, reproduced by permission of Indiana University Press; excerpt from Jutta Schwarzkopf's *Women in the Chartist Movement* (Macmillan, 1991), reproduced by permission given by author who held copyright; excerpts from Catherine Hall's 'The Early Formation of Victorian Ideology' from *White, Male and Middle Class: Explorations in Feminism and History* (1992), pp. 75–92, reproduced by permission of Blackwell Publishers, Taylor and Francis Inc and the author; excerpts from Judith A. DeGroat's 'The Public Nature of Women's Work: Definitions and Debates During the Revolution of 1848' from *French Historical Studies* Volume 20, No 1 (Winter, 1997). Copyright 1997, Society for French Historical Studies. All rights reserved. Reproduced by permission of Duke University Press; 'The Rhetoric and Iconography of Reform: Women Coal Miners in Belgium, 1840–1914' by Patricia J. Hilden from the *Historical Journal* Volume 34, No 2 (1991), pp. 411–436, reproduced by permission of Cambridge University Press and the author; 'Pregnant, Single, and Far from Home: Migrant Women in Nineteenth-Century Paris' by Rachel G. Fuchs and Leslie Page Moch, from *American Historical Review* Volume 93, No 4 (October 1990), pp. 1007–1031, reproduced by permission of the American Historical Association and the authors; excerpts from Judith R. Walkowitz's 'Male Vice and Feminist Virtue: Feminism and the Politics of Prostitution in Nineteenth Century Britain' from the *History Workshop Journal*, Volume 25 (1982), reproduced by permission of Oxford University Press and the author; excerpt from Lorraine Coon's 'Neglected Sisters of the Women's Movement' from *Journal of Women's History*, reproduced by permission of Indiana University Press; 'Martyrs or Matriarchs' by Lynn Abrams, originally published in the *Women's History Review* and reproduced with permission of the author; *A History of their Own: Women in Europe from Prehistory to the Present*, Volume II, by Bonnie Anderson and Judith Zinsser (1990), pp. 367–370, reproduced by permission of Penguin UK; 'Womanly Duties' by Seth Koven and Sonya Michel, from the *American Historical Review*, Volume 95, No 4 (October 1990), pp. 1076–1108, reproduced by permission of the authors; 'Madeleine Pelletier (1874–1939): The Politics of Sexual Oppression' by Claudine Mitchell, from the *Feminist Review* No 33, (Autumn 1989), pp. 72–92, reproduced by permission of the *Feminist Review* and the author; excerpts from Margaret H. Darrow, 'French volunteer nursing and the myth of war experience in World War I' from the *American Historical Review*, Volume 101, No 1 (February 1996), pp. 80–106 reproduced by permission of the author; 'The Modernisation of Russian Motherhood, 1917–1937' by Elizabeth Waters, from *Europe-Asia Studies* Volume 44, No 1 (1992), pp. 123–135, reproduced by permission of Taylor and Francis Ltd; 'Men Against Women on the Shop Floor in Early Soviet Russia' by Diane P. Koenker, from the *American Historical Review*, Volume 100, No 5 (December 1995), pp. 1438–1464, reproduced by permission of the author and the American Historical Association; 'Man's Demonstrations and Women's Protest' by K. Hagemann, from *Gender and History*, Volume 5 (1993), pp. 101–119, reproduced by permission of Blackell Publishers Ltd; 'They didn't want women back in that job' by Penny Summerfield, from *Labour History Review* (1998), reproduced by permission of Edinburgh University Press; 'The Continuum of Sexual Violence in Occupied Germany, 1945–1949' by Hsu-Ming Teo, from the *Women's History Review* (1996), pp. 191–218, reproduced by permission of the author and Triangle Journals Ltd.

Every effort has been made to obtain permission to reproduce copyright material. If any proper acknowledgement has not been made, we would invite copyright holders to inform us of the oversight.

Introduction

■   Fiona Montgomery and Christine Collette

THIS READER IS INTENDED TO PROVIDE the basis for informing students of the major themes in the modern history of women in Europe. Commentaries at the start of each section point to the issues addressed. Many journal articles are reproduced in full and where this is the case footnotes are supplied. Book and article extracts are also given. Each extract /article has stood the test of time and provides an in-depth view of its subject. Together, they demonstrate the lines historians have taken over the last thirty years and the challenges posed by new lines of enquiry. Much of the work on the history of women has been inspired by feminist interest and throughout the *Reader*, both feminisms and feminists are the subject of discussion. This introduction briefly deals with the historiography that has informed the *Reader*, a discussion fully developed in the first, historiographical section. It then outlines the major historical movements which form the basis for the chronological arrangement of the *Reader*. Finally, suggestions for a thematic reading are given.

I

As the first section of this Reader shows, the writings about women's roles in the historical process over the last three decades have developed along a number of lines. Beginning from a position of invisibility and under the influence of the 1960s second wave feminists, the first challenge was to restore women to the historical process. It asked such questions as who were the great female thinkers and actors in history? The search for the missing women was sometimes referred to as 'contribution' or 'topping up' history, that is, it added women to the historical process without requesting any changes in traditional accounts of that process. In some cases this was accompanied by seeking to add men of colour to the jigsaw of history. At the same time a broadening of interest in social history was taking place generally. Thus areas which had previously been seen as ahistorical such as the family became the legitimate concern of history.

The rise of feminism however meant an upsurge in interest from self-confessed feminist historians who wanted to study minorities, as oppressed, and women, as subordinate groups. In addition they posed questions which challenged the historical process itself such as why has women's work been marginalised? They wanted to study women on their own terms and were concerned not simply with adding but also with rewriting the whole historical process. Women made history: they were the subject not just the object of the historical process. In the same way as E. D. Genovese pointed out that while slaves had been the object of persecution this was not a barrier to their creating history as subjects in their own right.[1]

This initial phase of feminist history, then, involved a focus: identifying women's oppression. This was not a blanket approach but varied with the political orientation of the author. Thus feminists who identified as Marxist took a Marxist approach, socialist feminists sought to explain the workings of capitalism and patriarchy and were particularly interested in women's working experiences. This was evidenced in Sally Alexander's and Anna Davin's introduction to the *History Workshop Journal*. Claiming a place for feminism they took issue with what they saw as Labour history's preoccupation with working-class waged men's labour and castigated social history for taking 'for granted sexual divisions at work, in the home, or in political and cultural life'.[2] Alexander and Davin reinforced the belief that the work of feminist historians was not 'simply to slot women in wherever they had been left out'.[3] Women were workers too; capitalism depended just as much on the unpaid work of women in looking after the welfare of the workers as well as creating the labour force in the first place. They confidently asserted, 'By bringing women into the foreground of historical enquiry our knowledge of production, of working class politics and culture, of class struggle, of the welfare state, will be transformed'.[4]

Such confidence however, seemed sadly misplaced, for a mere two years later Eric Hobsbawm in the very same journal claimed that industrialisation tended to make:

> marriage and the family the major career of the working-class woman who was not obliged by sheer poverty to take other work. In so far as she worked for wages before marriage, she saw wage-work as a temporary, though no doubt desirable phase in her life. Once married, she belonged to the proletariat not as a worker, but as the wife, mother and housekeeper of workers.[5]

Sally Alexander, Anna Davin and Eve Hostettler immediately replied pointing out that Hobsbawm, as a labour historian was continuing to ignore women's paid work and unpaid work within the home; that he was not questioning the limitation of his evidence and that he was denying women their potential for taking part in class struggle.[6]

For radical feminist historians however patriarchy was *the* enemy and sexuality a prime concern. And this in turn led to further debate, initially between Alexander and Taylor, on the one hand, arguing for patriarchy as a useful framework for analysing oppression[7] and, on the other, Sheila Rowbotham who argued 'There are times when class or race solidarity are much stronger than sex-gender conflict'.[8] Meanwhile, Black feminists sought to explain and articulate the experience of women of colour and the operation of racism and imperialism. A political perspective became a necessary part of historical writing.

Essentialism, treating all women alike, and as conforming to a white middle-class stereotype, was shown to be inadequate and differences between women were celebrated.

By the 1980s women's agency had replaced notions of women as victim as the motivating force in feminist research.[9] 'Women's history' was seen to be a term downgrading women's experience and failing to claim the ground from a feminist approach. 'Feminist history' was then more usually referred to. Gender as an analytical tool was increasingly used to replace the more anodyne term 'woman'.[10] Gender systems as primary categories of historical analysis were recognised. Women were no longer the victims of historical events and historical analyses, but were now active historical participants. All of this represented a challenge to the disciplines. Current definitions such as the misleading 'universal' suffrage, applied to the *male* were shown to be inadequate and overdue for reappraisal.

Meanwhile Women's Studies was developing within Academia as a separate discipline.[11] 'Women's history' was no longer taught as an add-on to the history curriculum but as a valuable component of the multi-disciplinary remit of Women's Studies. In turn this impacted on traditional 'malestream' history. For instance Christopher Hill, the renowned historian of the English Civil War wrote:

> One of the things which I am most ashamed is that for decades I proudly illustrated the spread of democratic ideas in 17th century England by quoting the ringing Leveller declarations, "the poorest he that is in England hath a life to live as the greatest he", "every man that is to live under a government ought first by his own consent to put himself under that government". Every he? Every man? What about the other 50 per cent of the population? I suppose in one sense I noticed the absence of women from these statements; but I somehow assumed that they had to be taken for granted in 17th century England. But if we are to understand that society we have to ask why it was taken for granted – not only by men, but by the Leveller women who canvassed, agitated, petitioned, leafletted and lobbied for the vote for their menfolk and apparently never even thought of asking for it for themselves. Once we ask that question, other questions are opened up...[12]

Historical questions now had to account for gender, ethnicity, class. This in turn meant new understanding of men and masculinity. This is particularly noticeable in the world of paid employment. Once the construction of the male breadwinner and the assumption of unpaid domestic labour is analysed then the whole nature of economic organisation has to be scrutinised.

A number of new journals were born: *Gender and History* (1989), *Journal of Women's History* (1989), *Women's History Review* (1992) were prime examples and many of the contributions to this Reader are culled from these excellent publications. The editorial commentaries of each journal also depicted the various strands in historical thinking.

Gender and History sought to bring

> to the study of history the centrality of gender relations and to the study of gender a sense of history ... we seek to examine all historical social relations from a

feminist perspective, to construct a comprehensive analysis of all institutions that take their gender specific characters into account. In addressing men and masculinity as well as women and femininity, the journal will illuminate the ways in which societies have been shaped by the relations of power between women and men.[13]

This would involve not simply research on women and gender but also 'on how other divisions – of race, class, religion, ethnicity, and sexual orientation – have redounded on both ideas about gender and the experience of women.'[14]

The *Journal of Women's History* rather ambitiously questioned 'whether women's history will remain simply a subfield of the discipline waiting to be integrated into the mainstream or whether it is now in the process of becoming an alternative form of history ... The restructuring of history itself may well be on their [Gerda Lerner and others] minds.[15]

Women's History Review's aims in 1992 were to publish,

new, scholarly and interesting work in women's history that furthers feminist knowledge ... our primary focus is on women. We wish to encourage research on all aspects of women's lives, from a range of feminist perspectives. Thus we are keen to attract articles that explore the diversity and commonalities of women's experiences and that draw upon analyses concerned with sexual orientation, 'race', ethnicity, social class, nationality, disability, age and religion. ...

We also hope that *Women's History Review* will become a forum for debate about theoretical and methodological issues. Thus we wish to encourage dialogue about the nature of such topics as women's history, feminist history, gender history, black women's history and lesbian history, and about the relationship, for example, between feminist theory and women's history or post-modernism and women's history – indeed, a whole range of controversial themes. Part of our aim is to widen the study of women's history and to encourage contributions from a number of disciplines such as women's studies, history, cultural studies, sociology, literature, politics, anthropology, social policy, social administration and philosophy.[16]

These issues are further developed in section one, historiography.

II

The broader remit of history enabled different appreciations to be made of change through time. This Reader takes a chronological approach to allow transnational comparisons. The history of Europe is a complex one: its existence as an entity has been, and is, a matter of controversy. Its boundaries are as fluid as are those of the various states within it. Thus the article by Honeyman and Goodman is one of few whose remit has been European wide.[17] More usual has been work on one European country, with references to the same issues in other countries. Major changes in political, social and economic development were, however, experienced contemporaneously throughout much of the European continent. The section on the late eighteenth century represents the development of the concept of the nation state, hitherto extant only in the minds of the political philosophers. Some of this debate is reflected, together with its impact on women. In the nineteenth century, the Napoleonic wars affected Europe's geography as much as the process of industrialisation. As the section on the nineteenth century shows, the nation-state developed at a different rate in the component parts of Europe. The European Empires were dismantled by the First World War and the political and social changes thereafter. The final section on the twentieth century reflects these issues. In each section, the impact of specific women on great movements are examined, for instance, Mary Wollstonecraft's and Albertine Necker de Saussure's relationship to the Enlightenment, women Chartists and suffragists, Madeleine Pelletier's contribution to twentieth-century feminism.

III

While the Reader has a strong chronological approach, it also provides a good overview of industrialisation. As changes in work patterns and conditions and in the labour movement have been a major factor in the chronological account, they feature strongly in the Reader. In addition, the Reader gives a good overview of perceptions of motherhood, prostitution and sexuality, and deals with violence and war. For those who wish to take a thematic approach, the following suggestions may be helpful:

Work patterns and conditions, and labour movements:

1   Anna Clark, *The Struggle for the Breeches.*
2   K. Honeyman, and J. Goodman, 'Women's Work, Gender Conflict, and Labour Markets in Europe, 1500–1900'.
3   Maxine Berg, 'What Difference did Women's Work Make to the Industrial Revolution'.
4   Sally Alexander, 'Women, Class and Sexual Difference in the 1830s and 1840s'.
5   Jutta Schwarzkopf, extract from *Women in the Chartist Movement.*
6   J. DeGroat, 'The Public Nature of Women's Work: Definitions and Debates during the Revolution of 1848'.
7   P. J. Hilden, 'The Rhetoric and Iconography of Reform: Women Coal Miners in Belgium, 1840–1914'.
8   L. Coons, '"Neglected Sisters" of the Women's Movement: The Perception and Experience of Working Mothers in the Parisian Garment Industry, 1860–1915'.
9   K. Hagemann, 'Men's Demonstrations and Women's Protest: Gender in Collective Action in the Urban Working-Class Milieu during the Weimar Republic'.
10   Penny Summerfield, '"They didn't want women in that job": the Second World War and the Construction of Gendered Work Histories'.

Perceptions of motherhood, prostitution, sexuality:

1   A. Goldberg, 'The Eberbach Asylum and the Practice of Nymphomania in Germany, 1815–1914'.

2   Catherine Hall, 'The Early Formation of Victorian Domestic Ideology'.
3   R. Fuchs and L. P. Moch, 'Pregnant Single, and Far From Home: Migrant Women in Nineteenth-Century Paris'.
4   J. Walkowitz, 'Male Vice and Feminist Virtue: Feminism and the Politics of Prostitution in nineteenth-century Britain'.
5   L. Coons, '"Neglected Sisters" of the Women's Movement: The Perception and Experience of Working Mothers in the Parisian Garment Industry, 1860–1915'.
6   S. Koven and S. Michel, 'Womanly Duties: Maternalist Politics and the Origins of Welfare States in France, Germany, Great Britain and the Untied States, 1880–1920'.
7   L. Abrams, 'Martyrs or Matriarchs? Working-class Women's Experience of Marriage in Germany before the First World War'.
8   E. Waters, 'The Modernisation of Russian Motherhood, 1917–1939'.
9   H.-M. Teo, 'The Continuum of Sexual Violence in Occupied Germany, 1945–1949'.

Violence and war:

1   M. H. Darrow, 'French Volunteer Nursing and the Myth of War Experience in World War I.
2   Penny Summerfield '"They didn't want women in that job": the Second World War and the Construction of Gendered Work Histories'.
3   H.-M. Teo, 'The Continuum of Sexual Violence in Occupied Germany, 1945–1949'.

Feminism and feminists:

1   Part one.
2   Barbara Taylor, 'Mary Wollstonecraft and the Wild Wish of Early Feminism'.
3   Clarissa Campbell Orr, 'A Republican Answers Back: Jean-Jacques Rousseau, Albertine Necker de Saussure, and Forcing Little Girls to be Free'.
4   C. Mitchell, 'Madeleine Pelletier (1874–1939): The Politics of Sexual Oppression'.

Citizenship and class:

1   Barbara Taylor, 'Mary Wollstonecraft and the Wild Wish of Early Feminism'.
2   Clarissa Campbell Orr, 'A Republican Answers Back: Jean-Jacques Rousseau, Albertine Necker de Saussure, and Forcing Little Girls to be Free'.
3   Jutta Schwarzkopf, extract from *Women in the Chartist Movement*.
4   Bonnie Anderson and Judith Zinsser, *A History of Their Own*.
5   C. Mitchell, 'Madeleine Pelletier (1874–1939): The Politics of Sexual Oppression'.
6   D. P. Koenker, 'Men against Women on the Shop Floor in Early Soviet Russia: Gender and Class in the Socialist Workplace'.

It has been our privilege to revisit the seminal works incorporated into this Reader. We hope it will provide both the student of history and the general reader food for thought not only in its richness of detail about European women's lives from the late eighteenth century, the pageant of *hiercheuses*, *plumassieres*, nurses, garment workers, and politicians who fill its pages, but in the story it tells of the development of the history as a discipline. Women constructed Europe through their work and their ideas, and women reclaimed their right to their part in the telling of its story. We celebrate them.

Notes

1   E. D. Genovese, *Roll Jordon Roll: the World the Slaves Made* (London,Deutsch,1975)

2   *History Workshop Journal*, 1,1976, p. 4.

3   *Ibid.*, p. 5.

4   *Ibid.*

5   Eric Hobsbawm, 'Man and Woman in Socialist Iconography' *History Workshop Journal* 6,1978, p. 131.

6   Sally Alexander *et al.*, 'Labouring Women: a Reply to Eric Hobsbawm' *Ibid.* 8, 1979, pp. 174–82.

7   Sally Alexander and Barbara Taylor, 'In Defence of Patriarchy' in Sally Alexander, *Becoming a Woman and Other Essays in Nineteenth and Twentieth Century History* (London, Virago, 1994).

8   Sheila Rowbotham quoted in Alexander, *Becoming a Woman*, pp. 366–7. See also Sheila Rowbotham, 'The Trouble with Patriarchy' in Raphael Samuel (ed) *People's History and Socialist Theory* (London, Routledge and Kegan Paul, 1981) pp. 364–9.

9   See e.g. Judith M. Bennett, 'Feminism and History', *Gender and History* 1, 1989, pp. 251–72.

10   To follow the debate on gender see, Gisela Bock, 'Women's History and Gender History. Aspects of an International Debate', *Gender and History* 1, 1989, pp. 7–30.
     Joan Scott, *Gender and the Politics of History*, (New York, Columbia University Press, 1988).
     Joan W. Scott, 'Gender: a Useful Category of Analysis', *American Historical Review* 91, 1986, pp. 1053–76.
     Joan Hoff, 'Gender as a Post-modern Category of Paralysis', *Women's History Review* 3, 1994, pp. 149–68.
     Joan Hoff, 'A Reply to my Critics', *Women's History Review* 5, 1996, pp. 25–30.

11   F. A. Montgomery and C. Collette, *Into the Melting Pot: Teaching Women's Studies in the New Millennium* (Ashgate,1997).

12   Christopher Hill quoted in Rosalind Miles, 'Margins of Gain and Loss', *Times Higher Education Supplement*, 12 October 1990.

13   *Gender and History* 1, 1989.

14   *Ibid.*

15   *Journal of Women's History*, 1989.

16   *Women's History Review* 1, 1, 1992, p. 7.

17   Katrina Honeyman and Jordon Goodman, 'Women's Work, Labour Markets and Gender Conflict in Europe 1500–1900', *Economic History Review* 44, 1991, pp. 608–28.

PART ONE

Historiography

I N THIS SECTION EACH ARTICLE is a product of its time – together, they show the development from second wave to third wave feminism. Natalie Zemon Davis gives a typical second wave account of the rediscovery of feminist forebears and of the ways in which women have been included in writings on late eighteenth century/nineteenth century social history. She reminds us that it was not just that women were hidden from history but that histories of women were needed. Even when a breakthrough occurred it was lost. Thus pioneering historians such as Alice Clark and Eileen Power, wrote to a standard that was not again achieved for another fifty years; they went to the sources, were aware of essentialism, realised women were reflected through male eyes and were not victims. As with so much of women's experience, however this was not developed but simply disappeared from view.

Sonya Rose points out that feminist scholarship in the 1970s developed the concept of gender; this was the next step, recognising the social as well as biological construction of sexual difference and moving to consider gender relations. This led to new debates and the discussion of new methods of analysis including poststructuralism, postmodernism and Black feminist criticism. Rose ends by showing that 'differences can be the basis of community rather than a source of divisiveness'.[1]

The short extract from Karen Offen demonstrates the ways in which the history of feminism 'poses essential questions for the political and intellectual history of Europe and the modern world and again reinforces the need for attention on gender'.[2] Demonstrating the increasing interest in sexuality, a prime concern of the women's movement, she also deals with lesbianism.

Deborah Thom's article is the cornerstone of the whole section. She takes 'examples from work written mostly by British historians about Britain to describe the influence of a political movement that is also a discourse – feminism – on a discourse that has political implications – history'.[3] Thom concludes, 'feminism has given history ... pearls.'[4]

June Purvis, writing twenty years later than Natalie Zemon Davis discusses the developments Davis had foreshadowed, dealing not only with the 'new' feminist history but also the poststructuralist approach of the third wave. She examines the second wave feminist link with socialism and how that was reflected in groundbreaking journals like *History Workshop*. Purvis explains that she founded her own journal in order to give voice to the concerns of radical feminists and to reflect a diversity of feminist views.

Making the point that women's history is not necessarily feminist and defining feminist history as; 'history that is informed by the ideas and theories of feminism'[5] she also brings in ethnicity and lesbian feminism – reflecting not only the diversity of feminist history but the diversity of subject matter, Purvis both deals with difference and acknowledges common ground.

Notes

1   Rose, p. 18 below.
2   Offen, p. 25 below.
3   Thom, p. 28 below.
4   Ibid., p. 42 below.
5   Purvis, p. 45 below.

Chapter 1

Natalie Zemon Davis

■ from ' "WOMEN'S HISTORY" IN TRANSITION: THE EUROPEAN CASE', *Feminist Studies* 3 (3/4), Spring/Summer 1976, pp. 83–103

I F CERTAIN WAYS OF CONCEIVING women's history are very old, transitions in that subject have also occurred well before our time. I am thinking of the work of late eighteenth- and nineteenth-century writers in expanding the boundaries of social history so as to include subjects in which the activities of women, or of women and men together, could not fail to be considered explicitly: studies of the labouring poor, of the past and present of prostitution, and of private law; and collections by antiquarians and folklore societies of old customs and rites in regard to marriage and other stages of life.

More important, however, was the gradual realisation that the institution of the family and the relations between the sexes should not be perceived as essentially unchanging features of the European past. Rather they had varied appreciably, along with political, economic, or cultural changes.

[…]

I can find no better way to introduce and assess our own current 'transition in women's history' than to examine two of the best products of that earlier achievement. One of them is *Working Life of Women in the Seventeenth Century* (1919) by the Fabian socialist Alice Clark, research student at the London School of Economics. The other work is *La femme et le féminisme en France avant la Révolution* (1923) by the French Jew Léon Abensour, who intended, as he said, 'to take female activity of the eighteenth century away from the level of anecdote and scandal and place it in the mainstream of history'.[…]

What then did Clark and Abensour do and how would we do it differently? In the first place, they went to the sources – not just to the printed courtesy books, the pamphlets on the female sex, the agricultural manuals and the letters and memoirs of aristocratic women, but also to archival materials: local judicial, financial, and administrative records and, for the English historian, local account books as well. However much the written records of pre-industrial Europe may under-represent the female (along with the peasant, the poor, the illiterate, and the young of both sexes), Clark and Abensour were rightly dazzled by the wealth of the material they found on women of all classes; and they had not even yet turned to the marriage contracts, wills, parish and hospital records which nourish so much of the research of social historians today.

Second, Clark and Abensour did not refer generally to 'women' when a process or event they were describing involved only one social group. Clark spelled out the differences among her working women, from midwives and merchants through agricultural labourers, while Abensour gave separate consideration to the women of the courtly and provincial nobility, of the 'bourgeoisie' and of artisanal and peasant families.

Third, neither historian assumed that laws regarding marriage, guild regulations, informal prescriptions, rules of social intercourse, and other 'images' of women necessarily showed what female behaviour was really like. Indeed, a major argument of Abensour was that the legal tutelage of propertied women to their husbands in the eighteenth century and their legal exclusion from most forms of politics were in fact undermined by the considerable informal power that aristocratic women possessed in private life and in political discussion and patronage.

Next, both historians had some kind of theory to account for the changing relations of women to power, work, and property. Clark's view was by far the more interesting. A woman's independence, she thought, was a function of the full realisation of her productive powers, biological, educational, and economic.
[...]

Clark's view continues to be helpful in understanding the withdrawal of middle-class women from work outside the home and the eventual constriction of opportunities for women in industry. It was also a surprising anticipation of recent studies of the impact of so-called modernisation on the economic position of women in black Africa.

And finally, in my observations on Clark and Abensour, they respected their subjects, treating them neither as passive victims of historical injustice nor as constant heroines struggling to change society.
[...]

These are solid achievements in these books of fifty years ago. We are all disappointed that some of our present-day production in women's history still does not match them in methodology and analysis. Nevertheless, the last fifteen years have seen improvement in the study of sex roles. Let me consider a few of the ways we would want to rewrite Clark and Abensour. Neither of them devoted any attention to the demographic questions about which the French and English schools of population study have now told us so much — about life expectancy, age at marriage, rates of fertility, intervals between births, patterns of geographical mobility, and the like. Clark would indeed have had to modify her argument about the productive power of seventeenth-century working women, for it rested on the explicit assumption that their rate of fertility was *the same* as that of aristocratic women.
[...]

[...] we want to reckon more than they did. To their impressionistic sampling of, say, wages or numbers of parish schools, we are finally adding statistics not only on demography, but on the sex variable in migration, in crime, and in literacy, to mention only a few.
[...]

[...] these older works on women offered little or nothing about their sexual or erotic activity. Abensour was perhaps trying to break with the old tradition of scandalous anecdote. Clark, in a book on the working life of women, did not say a word about prostitution, her omission perhaps explained by the particularly moralistic character of her feminism. At any rate, these matters engage us a great deal nowadays, for what they can tell us both about intimate relations between and within the sexes and about patterns of culture and social organisation more generally [...] On attitudes toward homosexuality and lesbianism and on the laws regarding adultery, we still need a set of well documented monographs. The same is true for the history of prostitution.

[...]

Finally, in contrasting the work of Clark and Abensour with what I take to be our best present course, I think our goals are or should be more general and more sweeping than theirs. They wrote mostly about women; so too do we, to rectify the deep and long-lasting bias of the historical record. They wanted to make the relations between the sexes more just; so, too, do many of us, though it is no more true today than in the nineteenth century that all practitioners of women's history have the same political hopes. But it seems to me that we should be interested in the history of both women and men, that we should not be working only on the subjected sex any more than an historian of class can focus exclusively on peasants. Our goal is to understand the significance of the *sexes*, of gender groups in the historical past. Our goal is to discover the range in sex roles and in sexual symbolism in different societies and periods, to find out what meaning they had and how they functioned to maintain the social order or to promote its change. Our goal is to explain why sex roles were sometimes tightly prescribed and sometimes fluid, sometimes markedly asymmetrical and sometimes more even. [...]

Especially important, the study of the sexes should help promote a rethinking of some of the central issues faced by historians – power, social structure, property, symbols, and periodisation.

The nature of power: as with work on the lower classes, slave populations and peasants, work on relations between the sexes makes the location of power a trickier business than when one is looking at governments, parties, factions, and clientage systems. [...]

The nature of social structure: all the recent debates on the criteria for social stratification and on societies of orders as opposed to societies of classes have been concerned to locate males as heads of families on some kind of one- or two-dimensional chart. The contribution of women to that position, when it is considered at all, is usually confined to the advantages or disadvantages that dowry and family alliances may bring. [...]

Third, the study of gender groups extends notions of property and exchange to a new good – sex – ordinarily property and exchange in women. How and why these function in the European case is still far from clear.

Chapter 2

Sonya O. Rose

■ 'INTRODUCTION TO DIALOGUE: GENDER HISTORY/ WOMEN'S HISTORY: IS FEMINIST SCHOLARSHIP LOSING ITS CRITICAL EDGE?', *Journal of Women's History*, 5 (1), 1993, pp. 89– 101

THERE HAS NEVER BEEN A PERIOD when feminists have been unified around a single analytical frame. As a number of scholars have pointed out, disunity has marked feminism throughout history.[1] Major fault lines have formed and reformed over the very subject matter of feminist analysis—the category women.[2] The four essays that follow assess the implications of recent directions in feminist history, including the turn to gender history, but especially the emphasis on difference in feminist analysis.

A significant achievement of feminist scholarship in the 1970s was the development of the concept of gender signifying the social rather than the biological construction of sexual difference. Another major accomplishment was the revelation that the relations between women and men varied historically and cross-culturally. As historians became increasingly interested in these relations and structures, many began to focus on the subject of gender itself. They argued that to focus only on women instead of on gender relations was to reinforce the idea that only women have gender, which "ironically privileges the man as unproblematic or exempted from determination by gender relations."[3] Many feminist historians have shifted their primary focus from examining women's lives to demonstrating the centrality of gender to various arenas of social life.[4]

Not everyone has greeted this turn to gender with unqualified approval. Some have worried that a focus on gender—on men as well as women and on the ways that gender is intrinsic to all social relations—has deflected historians from the feminist movement's primary political goals of unmasking oppression and enhancing the potential for emancipatory politics.[5] Arguing that feminist history should be concerned with the issue of women's oppression which has been sidestepped by the recent focus on gender, Judith Bennett, for example, proposed that historians rethink the concept of patriarchy in order to bring "moral and political commitment" back into women's history.[6]

More problematic for women's history than the gender turn have been the challenges that were implicit in feminist history as it developed and that were quite explicit in the divisions among women themselves. These center on the issue of *difference*; not *the* differences between women and men, but the differences that the term *women* obscures and mystifies.

Two quite distinct critiques of feminist analysis centering on the issue of difference have led to vexing questions about the subject matter of women's history and the methods of feminist analysis. One comes from postmodernism, particularly in its French post-structuralist guise. In history this critique has been made most influentially by Joan Scott.[7] The other comes from various black and Third World theorists and critics.

Joan Scott, like other feminist theorists and historians who focus on gender, maintains that "gender is a constitutive element of social relationships based on perceived differences between the sexes."[8] In addition she states, "gender is a primary way of signifying relationships of power," suggesting that the "gender question in feminism" is about discourse and how it creates meaning.[9] Scott argues that French post-structuralism, especially the method of deconstruction, is well suited for use by historians who are concerned with examining the meanings generated through language, and it is this focus she maintains that is necessary for feminist historical analysis to advance.[10] Scott contends that post-structuralism offers feminists a radical epistemology that relativizes "the status of all knowledge, links knowledge and power, and theorizes these in terms of the operations of difference."[11]

The appropriate objects of study, according to Scott, are epistemological categories. She writes, "The story is no longer about the things that have happened to women and men and how they have reacted to them; instead it is about how the subjective and collective meanings of women and men as categories of identity have been constructed."[12] For Scott and other post-structuralists, identity or subjectivity itself, is radically de-essentialized. Rather than stemming from one's being or experience, post-structuralists conceptualize subjectivity as a position in a discursive field. In her more recent writings, Scott has questioned historians' focus on experience altogether, because she maintains that experience is not the authentic source of human agency, but rather it is itself discursively produced. There is no experience outside of the ways that language constructs it.[13]

Scott's ideas have had an enormous impact on many feminist historians, and increasingly the terms *discourse* and *text* and a focus on language and the production of meanings are appearing in their scholarship. Although feminist historians before Scott examined discourses and explored the social constructions of gender, she has stimulated substantial debate by challenging scholars to become overtly analytical in their work, to focus their studies on texts using the tools of deconstruction, and to adopt a postmodernist epistemology.[14] While some historians have welcomed this program, others have expressed their scepticism or out-and-out hostility to it.[15]

A second major assault on the foundations of feminism has come from the writings of women of color. In a continuing explosion of historical scholarship and theoretical writings, they have critiqued feminist scholarship, expressing their experience of exclusion—from the academy, from circles of white feminist scholars and activists, as well as from the versions of women being reclaimed by white Western women's historians.[16] Collectively, the writings on and by women of color dispute the validity of many of the analyses of women's experiences, showing them to have been studies, not of American women, but of white and often middle-class women in the United States. For instance, they challenge the notion that women in the nineteenth century were enshrined in a "cult of domesticity";[17] they dispute feminist accounts of patriarchal family structures and their consequences for women; they bring into feminist historical consciousness a new awareness and appreciation of the community bonds among women; and contest the idea that all women have been deprived of a public voice in their communities.[18] By focusing on the differing historical experiences of Third

World women, the writings of women of color have, in short, challenged the idea that there is something that can be identified as "women's experience."

A pivotal idea running through the various strands of black and Third World feminist thought is that race, gender and class are interlocking and interdependent formations of domination, and that these dimensions of social life are experienced simultaneously.[19] One is not a woman at one moment in time, and an African American or white Canadian the next.

This scholarship joins postmodernist feminism in fracturing the unitary historical subject of feminism. Much of the work by women of color, however, challenges the very form of theorizing engaged in by self-consciously postmodernist writers. A number of African-American theorists have argued that narratives are central components of theory.[20] Stories, rather than abstract theoretical statements, are to be trusted as core belief.[21] Like post-modernists, these feminist theorists maintain that there can be no politically neutral and all-knowing standpoint from which to generate objective knowledge. However, in contrast to deconstructionist post-modernism, they argue that their theories and analyses are grounded in both experience and action.[22] When compared with the writings of many postmodernist feminists, the feminist analyses by women of color are often deliberately political and are oriented to empowering the people of their communities and to dismantling structures of domination.[23]

Although post-structuralist, postmodernist analyses and the theories created by women of color differ substantially in their form and substance, both challenge the enterprise of women's history by raising questions about the subject of historical scholarship, its methods, and its purpose and politics. The essays in this dialogue address this challenge.

Kathleen Canning, Anna Clark, and Mariana Valverde consider issues raised by post-structuralism. Rather than rejecting the linguistic turn, they respond to it in creative ways, and indicate how they apply their understandings of language, meaning, and subjectivity or identity in their own empirical work. Kathleen Canning explores the controversies among German feminist historians over new directions in feminist inquiry. Her discussion illuminates the markedly different trajectories of scholarship in Germany as contrasted with the United Kingdom and North America. She raises thought provoking questions about the implications of the post-structuralist critique of subjectivity and experience for German historical practice. In her discussion, Canning demonstrates the importance of coming to terms, both theoretically and empirically, with the issue of historical agency and rethinking the analytical categories of discourse and experience and their relationship. She formulates her own understanding of identity as the location in which subjects link experience and discourse. In doing so, she suggests subjects create their own meanings and sometimes resist those that are dominant. It is in this way that they become historical agents.

Anna Clark contends that gender analysis is a step forward in feminist history, because it can make evident different forms of male power, and it can incorporate sexual orientation as a historical dynamic. She situates her own uneasiness with contemporary feminist history in particular aspects of postmodernism, especially in those strands influenced by Foucault. She is particularly concerned with the problem of linking the exercise of power to the instability of meaning created by the play of difference in language and the idea that subjects are created discursively. By turning to history itself, Clark challenges some of the under-standings about gender and language in post-structuralism. She suggests, for example, that the idea of gender as constituted by a binary opposition between the masculine and the feminine was an historical construction rather than being a timeless artifact of the operation of language. In order to conceptualize how language is linked to power and political struggle,

Clark prefers the term *rhetoric* to the concept of discourse.[24] Rhetoric, she suggests, implies a dialogue between and among social actors who are attempting to persuade one another.

Mariana Valverde parts company from Canning and Clark by more fully embracing post-structuralism, especially its theory of subjectivity. While Valverde faults Joan Scott for being overly enamored with deconstruction, she applauds post-structuralism for conceptualizing both discourses and subjectivities as fragmented and multiple. She suggests that historical agency resides in how "the constant work of reproducing the discursive structures subjectively, often subverts and fractures those very structures." Furthermore, Valverde maintains that gender history can be critical history if feminist historians take as their subject the analysis of gender formations, by which she means studying how "the two genders are formed and reformed, renegotiated, contested." Like Joan Scott, Valverde insists that it is crucial that feminist historians "remember the need for a philosophical critique of the formation of the categories whose history we study qua historians."

Each of these three essays suggest how feminist history can move forward by encompassing some if not all of the suppositions of post-structuralism. Clark and Canning are both concerned with the problem of agency, especially how subjects can "talk back" or can exercise power, and they wish for a concept of subjectivity that is not fully determined in and by discourses. Valverde, in contrast, is not at all troubled by the notion that subjectivities are formed through discourse. She conceptualizes historical agency as the process by which subjects, using multivalent language, both reproduce and challenge dominant meanings. Each of them provides imaginative ways of thinking about some of the problems for feminist history posed by post-structuralism, but they omit direct consideration of two issues. The first concerns how language and meaning are linked to other social practices, and the topic of gender as a *social* as well as linguistic relation. I believe that we need to incorporate some kind of sociological vision along with post-structuralist literary theory in our historical analysis. Possibilities for doing this include adapting some of the ideas informing British cultural studies;[25] attending to the work of sociologists who specifically attempt to deal with the problem of linking the concepts of structure and agency,[26] as well as to the writings of feminist sociologist Dorothy Smith.[27]

Feminist politics is the second issue that is unexplored in the three essays on post-structuralism and feminist history. To what extent does a turn toward more consciously theoretical or analytical feminist history deflect attention from concern with structures of domination and with building solidarities among diverse individuals and groups of women? This is the subject of Marcia Sawyer's essay. She asks how feminist theory can be altered so that it contributes to ending the racist practices of white women?

Sawyer focuses her attention on what she perceives to be white Western feminists' continuing reluctance to deal with their own racism, and the resulting moral bankruptcy of white, middle-class versions of feminism. She reminds us of the racist legacy of nineteenth-century feminism, and calls attention to the continuation of Enlightenment ideas among feminists who maintain a mind/body/spirit split that she argues contributes to the difficulty of "coalition building among women of different colors and nationalities." But before it is even possible to contemplate coalition building, Sawyer argues, white academic women need to confront their own racism, as well as to better understand both how being white has privileged them, and the incredible costs of racism borne by women of color. Difference to Sawyer means something distinct from the fractured identities of post-structuralist thinking and from the idea that language is structured through difference.

Writing about white academic women's new appreciation of difference Bell Hooks says:

> The upshot of all this has been the unprecedented support among scholars and intellectuals for the inclusion of the Other—in theory. Yes! Everyone seems to be clamoring for "difference," only few seem to want any difference that is about changing policy or that supports active engagement and struggle.... Too often, it seems, the point is to promote the *appearance* of difference within intellectual discourse, a "celebration" that fails to ask who is sponsoring the party and who is extending the invitations. For who is controlling this new discourse? Who is getting hired to teach it, and where? Who is getting paid to write about it?[28]

Can the new post-structuralist discourse of difference become a vehicle for an inclusive feminist politics?[29] As Marcia Sawyer asks, "Can feminist theory address any of this? Can white academic feminists create a theory that helps them with self-recovery and self-awareness?"

Where do we begin? Marcia Sawyer suggests and Bell Hooks advocates that white feminist historians incorporate race into their analysis, and that they do so by interrogating whiteness.[30] Such studies would not only reveal the historical consequences of race for whites, but by confronting the ways that our own personal identities have been insidiously molded by race, they might also stimulate our anger.[31]

To fully comprehend difference, including the different ways that people experience oppression, we may need to develop a theoretical analysis of embodiment. Elizabeth Spelman writes, "We cannot hope to understand the meaning of a person's experiences, including her experiences of oppression, without first thinking of her as embodied, and second thinking about the particular meanings assigned to that embodiment."[32] Without retreating into essentialism, we may have to rethink the concept of experience for as Iris Marion Young argues,

> Describing the processes of social life from the point of view of the subject brings to language the hurts and harms of oppressive structures, and only such experiential description can do so.... Experience names a moment of creative agency in social processes, which cannot be finally totalized or categorized by the dominant oppressive structures. Describing kinds of oppression, the experience of oppression, and the creative agency of the oppressed can help form resistance and envision alternatives.[33]

Such a rethinking might begin by examining the acknowledged role of experience and action in black and Third World feminist thought.[34]

Finally, the points at which black feminist thought and post-structuralist feminism meet suggest that difference can be the basis of community rather than a source of divisiveness. Recently, Joan Scott has proposed that to build community, it is necessary to recognize that differences "are what we have most in common"; "community is a strategically organized set of relationships"; and that "conflict and contest are therefore inherent in communities of difference."[35] As Audre Lorde has put it, "Certainly there are very real differences between us of race, age, and sex. But it is not those differences between us that are separating us. It is rather our refusal to recognize those differences, and to examine the distortion which result from our misnaming them and their effects upon human behavior and expectation."[36]

These and other writers suggest that solidarity is a fragile accomplishment born of conflict, contest, and struggle.

Notes

1 See, for example, Teresa de Lauretis, "Upping the Anti (Sic) in Feminist Theory," in *Conflicts in Feminism*, Marianne Hirsch and Evelyn Fox Keller (New York and London: Routledge, 1990), 255–270.

2 As Ann Snitow has eloquently and compellingly asserted, tension over the problem of identity —the issue of needing to act as women while refusing to be "woman"—has been at the core of feminism itself. Ann Snitow, "A Gender Diary," in *Conflicts in Feminism*, ed. Marianne Hirsch and Evelyn Fox Keller (New York and London: Routledge, 1990), 9–43. For other vigorous analyses of this problem see Judith Butler, *Gender Trouble: Feminism and the Subversion of Identity* (New York and London: Routledge, 1990); Mary Poovey, "Feminism and Deconstruction," *Feminist Studies* 14, no. 1 (1988): 51–65, who assesses the utility of deconstruction as a theory and method for feminism, and Denise Riley, *"Am I That Name?": Feminism and the Category of "Women" in History* (Minneapolis: University of Minnesota Press, 1988). Black and Third World women have continually critiqued the vision of women created in white Western feminism. See, for example, the essays in Bell Hooks, *Ain't I a Woman: Black Women and Feminism* (Boston: South End, 1981); Gloria T. Hull, Patricia Bell Scott, and Barbara Smith, eds, *All the Women Are White, All the Blacks Are Men, But Some of Us Are Brave* (Old Westbury, N.Y.: Feminist, 1981); Phyllis Marynick Palmer, "White Women/Black Women: The Dualism of Female Identity and Experience in the United States," *Feminist Studies* 9, no. 1 (1983): 152–155; Bernice Johnson Reagon, "Coalition Politics: Turning the Century," in *Home Girls: A Black Feminist Anthology*, ed. Barbara Smith (New York: Kitchen Table: Women of Color, 1983), 360.

3 Jane Flax, "Postmodernism and Gender Relations in Feminist Theory," in *Feminism/Postmodernism*, ed. Linda Nicholson (New York and London: Routledge, 1990), 45. Joan Scott has made a very forceful argument about the necessity for gender analysis in history. Joan W. Scott, "Gender: A Useful Category of Historical Analysis," in *Gender and the Politics of History* (New York: Columbia University Press, 1988), 28–50.

4 Examples include: The essays in *Work Engendered: Toward a New History of American Labor*, ed. Ava Baron (Ithaca: Cornell University Press, 1991); Mary H. Blewett, *Men, Women, and Work: Class, Gender, and Protest in the New England Shoe Industry, 1780–1910* (Urbana: University of Illinois Press, 1988); Kathleen Canning, "Gender and the Politics of Class Formation: Rethinking German Labor History," *American Historical Review* 97, no. 3 (1992), 736–769; Leonore Davidoff and Catherine Hall, *Family Fortunes: Men and Women of the English Middle Class, 1780–1850* (London: Hutchinson, 1987); Elizabeth Faue, *Community of Suffering and Struggle: Women, Men and the Labor Movement in Minneapolis, 1915–1945* (Chapel Hill and London: University of North Carolina Press, 1991); Sonya O. Rose, *Limited Livelihoods: Gender and Class in Nineteenth-Century England* (Berkeley and Los Angeles: University of California Press, 1992).

5 See, for example, Elizabeth D. Genovese, *Feminism Without Illusions: A Critique of Individualism* (Chapel Hill and London: University of North Carolina Press, 1991), 145. For a discussion of differences between gender history and women's history, see Louise M. Newman, "Critical Theory and the History of Women: What's At Stake in Deconstructing Women's History," *Journal of Women's History* 2, no. 3 (1991): 58–68; and the comment by Lise Vogel, "Telling Tales: Historians of Our Own Lives," *Journal of Women's History* 2, no. 3 (1991): 89–101.

6 Judith Bennett, "Feminism and History," *Gender and History* 1, no. 3 (1989): 251–272.

7 Joan Wallach Scott, *Gender and the Politics of History*.

8 Joan W. Scott, *Gender and the Politics of History*, 42.

9   *Ibid.*

10   *Ibid.*, 7–9.

11   *Ibid.*, 4. What makes post-structuralism especially useful, Scott maintains, is that it insists that meanings are always unstable, and so implies that it is politics, or "the play of force" that gives meanings their appearance of solidity. However, Scott's theoretical emphasis appears to be on "the play of force" in language itself, rather than on social relations of power and their consequences.

12   *Ibid.*, 6.

13   Joan W. Scott, "The Evidence of Experience," *Critical Inquiry* 17 (Summer 1991): 773–797.

14   What postmodernist feminists share is a critique of Enlightenment thought that assumes human beings to be autonomous, stable selves who are capable of producing objective, rational analysis, and of discovering generalizable truths, yielding knowledge that exhaustively and completely explains history. Enlightenment ideas, and the knowledge generated with these ideas as a foundation, imagine that it is possible to know the truth about the world from an archimedian or God's eye view. Postmodernism eschews the idea that there is timeless, context-free knowledge. Any attempt to theorize the foundations of human existence and use them to explain history are acts of power that pretend to be objective and politically neutral. Heterogeneity, multiplicity, difference are the stuff of history. For discussions of feminist postmodernism from a variety of points of view see Linda Nicholson, ed., *Feminism/Postmodernism* (New York and London: Routledge, 1990).

15   For critical reviews of Scott's book, *Gender and the Politics of History*, see the previously cited reviews by Linda Gordon and Catherine Hall, and Claudia Koonz's critique in *Women's Review of Books* 6, no. 4 (1989): 19–20. Other critical comments on Scott's ideas include those by Bryan D. Palmer, *Descent into Discourse: The Reification of Language and the Writing of Social History* (Philadelphia: Temple University Press, 1990), 172–185; Christine Stansell, "A Response to Joan Scott," *International Labor and Working Class History* 31 (Spring 1987): 28–30; and Louise A. Tilly, "Gender, Women's History, and Social History," *Social Science History* 13, no. 4 (1989): 439–462. The use of literary analysis in history and the focus on representation more generally has stimulated lively debate and serious critique. See the discussions by Judith Walkowitz, Myra Jehlen, and Bell Chevigny in "Patrolling the Borders: Feminist Historiography and the New Historicism," *Radical History Review* 43, no. 1 (1989): 23–43; Judith Lowder Newton, "History as Usual/Feminism and the 'New Historicism'," in *The New Historicism*, ed. H. Aram Veeser (New York and London: Routledge, 1989), 152–169.

16   Historical works include Paula Giddings, *When and Where I Enter: The Impact of Black Women on Race and Sex in America* (New York: Bantam, 1984); Evelyn Nakano Glenn, *Issei, Nisei, War Bride: Three Generations of Japanese American Women in Domestic Service* (Philadelphia: Temple University Press, 1986); Darlene Clark Hine, *Black Women In White: Racial Conflict and Co-operation in the Nursing Profession, 1890–1950* (Bloomington and Indianapolis: Indiana University Press, 1989); Deborah G. White, *Ar'n't I A Woman?* (New York: W.W. Norton, 1985). Theoretical works and collections include: Patricia Hill Collins, *Black Feminist Thought: Knowledge, Consciousness, and the Politics of Empowerment* (London: Routledge 1990); Angela Y. Davis, *Women, Race and Class* (New York: Random House, 1981); Evelyn Brooks Higginbotham, "African-American Women's History and the Metalanguage of Race," *Signs* 17, no. 2 (1992): 251–274; Bell Hooks, *Feminist Theory from Margin to Center* (Boston: South End, 1984); Bell Hooks, *Yearning: Race, Gender, and Cultural Politics* (Boston: South End, 1990); Aida Hurtado, "Relating to Privilege: Seduction and Rejection in the Subordination of White Women and Women of Color," *Signs* 14, no. 4 (1989); Audre Lorde, *Sister Outsider: Essays and Speeches* (Freedom, Calif,: Crossing Press, 1984); Cherrie Moraga and Gloria Anzaldua, eds, *This Bridge Called my Back: Writings by Radical Women of Color* (New York: Kitchen Table: Women of Color, 1983); Chandra Talpade Mohanty, Ann Russo and Lourdes Torres, eds, *Third World Women and the Politics of Feminism* (Bloomington and Indianapolis: Indiana University Press, 1991); Barbara Smith, ed., *Home Girls: A Black Feminist*

Anthology (New York: Kitchen Table: Women of Color, 1983); Hortense Spillers, "Interstices: A Small Drama of Words," in *Pleasure and Danger: Exploring Female Sexuality*, ed. Carole S. Vance (London: Routledge and Kegan Paul, 1984, reprinted 1989), 73–100. Their work, and a concern about integrating race and gender is reflected in the scholarship of several white Western feminists including: Christie Farnham, "Sapphire? The Issue of Dominance in the Slave Family," in *"To Toil the Livelong Day": America's Women at Work, 1780–1980*, ed. Carole Groneman and Mary Beth Norton (New York: Cornell University Press, 1987): 68–83; Elizabeth Fox-Genovese, *Within the Plantation Household* (Chapel Hill: University of North Carolina Press, 1988); Jacqueline Dowd Hall, "The Mind that Burns in Each Body: Women, Rape, and Racial Violence," in *Powers of Desire: The Politics of Sexuality*, ed. Ann Snitow, Christine Stansell, and Sharon Thompson (New York: Monthly Review, 1983), 329–349; Dolores E. Janiewski, *Sisterhood Denied: Race, Gender and Class in a New South Community* (Philadelphia: Temple University Press, 1985); Jacqueline Jones, *Labor of Love, Labor of Sorrow: Black Women, Work and the Family from Slavery to the Present* (New York: Basic Books, 1985); Suzanne Lebsock, *The Free Women of Petersburg: Status and Culture in a Southern Town, 1784–1860* (New York: W.W. Norton, 1984); Elizabeth V. Spelman, *Inessential Woman: Problems of Exclusion in Feminist Thought* (Boston: Beacon, 1988).

17 For an overview of this and other findings, see Patricia Hill Collins, *Black Feminist Thought*, esp, chapters 3, 4, 6 and 7. Also see the review essay by Elizabeth Brooks Higgenbotham, "Beyond the Sound of Silence: Afro-American Women's History," *Gender and History* 1, no. 1 (1989): 50–67.

18 See, for example, the work of Cheryl Townsend Gilkes, "Building in Many Places: Multiple Commitments and Ideologies in Black, Women's Community Work," in *Women and the Politics of Empowerment*, eds Ann Bookman and Sandra Morgen (Philadelphia: Temple University Press, 1988); Patricia Hill Collins, *Black Feminist Thought*, chapter 7.

19 See, for example, Patricia Hill Collins, *Black Feminist Thought*, 16. Bell Hooks, *Feminist Theory*, chapter 1; Evelyn Brooks Higgenbotham, "African-American Women's History"; Deborah K. King, "Multiple Jeopardy, Multiple Consciousness: The Context of a Black Feminist Ideology," in *Feminist Theory in Practice and Process*, ed. Micheline R. Malson, *et al.*, (Chicago and London: University of Chicago Press, 1989), 75–106; Audre Lorde, "An Open Letter to Mary Daly," in *Sister Outsider*, 94–97; Elizabeth Spelman, *Inessential Woman*.

20 See, for example, Barbara Christian, "The Race for Theory," in *Gender and Theory; Dialogues on Feminist Criticism*, ed. Linda Kauffman (Oxford and New York: Basil Blackwell, 1989), 225–237.

21 Patricia Hill Collins, *Black Feminist Thought*, 210. For examples of autobiographical narratives that are also consciously theoretical see the superb books by Patricia J. Williams, *The Alchemy of Race and Rights* (Cambridge, Mass. and London: Harvard University Press, 1991); and Carolyn Steedman, *Landscape for a Good Woman: A Story of Two Lives* (London: Virago Press, 1986).

22 Patricia Hill Collins, for example, maintains that Afrocentric feminist epistemology is rooted in the everyday experiences of African-American women. *See Black Feminist Thought*, 208–212. Also see Bell Hooks who argues regarding the critique of essentialism in postmodernist theories, "An adequate response to this concern is to critique essentialism while emphasizing the significance of 'the authority of experience'." *Yearning*, 29.

23 A major criticism by several scholars about postmodernist feminism is that it does not provide a basis for feminist politics. See, for example, Christine Di Stefano, "Dilemmas of Difference: Feminism, Modernity, and Postmodernism," in *Feminism/Postmodernism*, ed. Linda J. Nicholson, 63–82; Susan Bordo, "Feminism, Postmodernism, and Gender-Scepticism," in *Feminism/Postmodernism*, ed. Linda J. Nicholson, 133–157. Several writers who either identify themselves with postmodernism, or whose work falls under that loose umbrella term, are specifically concerned with developing feminist theory and analysis that can address political issues. See, for example, Linda Alcoff, "Cultural Feminism Versus Post-Structuralism: The Identity Crisis

in Feminist Theory," in *Feminist Theory in Practice and Process*, ed. Micheline R. Malson, *et al.*, esp. 318–326; Nancy Fraser and Linda J. Nicholson, "Social Criticism without Philosophy: An Encounter between Feminism and Postmodernism," in *Feminism/Postmodernism* ed. Linda J. Nicholson, esp. 34–35; Nancy Fraser, *Unruly Practices: Power, Discourse and Gender in Contemporary Social Theory* (Minneapolis: University of Minnesota Press, 1989); Regenia Gagnier, "Feminist Postmodernism: The End of Feminism or the Ends of Theory?," in *Theoretical Perspectives on Sexual Difference*, ed. Deborah L. Rhode (New Haven and London: Yale University Press, 1990), 21–30.

24 Regenia Gagnier also has suggested the utility of rhetorical analysis in examining working-class autobiographies. See, *Subjectivities: A History of Self-Representation in Britain, 1832–1920* (New York: Oxford University Press, 1991), 3–5; 40–42.

25 From the writings of Antonio Gramsci, *Selections from the Prison Notebooks* (New York: International, 1971); and the work of Raymond Williams. See especially Raymond Williams, *Marxism and Literature* (Oxford: Oxford University Press, 1977). Also see Stuart Hall, "The Rediscovery of 'Ideology': Return of the Repressed in Media Studies," in *Culture, Society and the Media*, ed. Michael Gurevitch, *et al.* (London: Methuen, 1982), 56–90; and "The Toad in the Garden: Thatcherism among the Theorists," in *Marxism and the Interpretation of Culture*, eds. Cary Nelson and Lawrence Grossberg (Urbana and Chicago: University of Illinois Press, 1988), 58–74.

26 For example, Anthony Giddens, *The Constitution of Society* (Berkeley and Los Angeles: University of California Press, 1984); *Social Theory and Modern Sociology* (Stanford, Calif.: Stanford University Press, 1987); and "Structuralism, Poststructuralism and the Production of Culture," in *Social Theory Today*, ed. Anthony Giddens and Jonathan Turner (Stanford, Calif.: Stanford University Press, 1987), 195–223; Pierre Bourdieu, *Outline of a Theory of Practice* (Cambridge: Cambridge University Press, 1987); and the very helpful essay by William H. Sewell, Jr., "A Theory of Structure: Duality, Agency, and Transformation," *American Journal of Sociology* 98, no. 1 (1992): 1–29. Regenia Gagnier has found such theorists—whom she calls "practice theorists"—helpful in approaching the issue of subjectivity or agency in her analysis of British working-class autobiographies. See, *Subjectivities*, 8–11. For a useful application of such "practice" theory to theorizing gender see R.W. Connell, *Gender and Power* (Stanford, Calif.: Stanford University Press, 1987).

27 See, especially, Dorothy Smith, *The Everyday World as Problematic* (Boston: Northeastern University Press, 1987); and Dorothy Smith, *The Conceptual Practices of Power* (Boston: Northeastern Press, 1990).

28 Bell Hooks, *Yearning*, 54.

29 For a rigorous assessment of the political implications of deconstruction that is sensitive to issues of race, see Mary Poovey, "Feminism and Deconstruction," esp. 61–63.

30 Hooks, *ibid.*, 54; 165–171. Anne Russo also makes this point. See Ann Russo, " 'We Cannot Live Without Our Lives': White Women, Antiracism, and Feminism," in *Third World Women*, ed. Chandra Talpade Mohanty, Ann Russo and Lourdes Torres (Bloomington and Indianapolis: Indiana University Press), 299–301. Toni Morrison provides one model for understanding the centrality of race in American consciousness in her *Playing in the Dark: Whiteness and the Literary Imagination* (Cambridge: Harvard University Press, 1992). Catherine Hall's new work examines the importance of race for the construction of Englishness. See her collection of essays, *White, Male and Middle Class: Explorations in Feminism and History* (Cambridge: Polity, 1992), 25–30; and chapters 9 and 10. Also see Richard Roediger, *The Wages of Whiteness: Race and the Making of the American Working Class* (London: Verso, 1991). The work of anthropologist Anne Stoler is focused on such an analysis of gender, race, and national identity. See, for example, Anne L. Stoler, "Making Empire Respectable: The Politics of Race and Sexual Morality in Twentieth-Century Colonial Cultures," *American Ethnologist* 10, no. 4 (1989): 634–660; and "Sexual Affronts and Racial Frontiers: European Identities and the Cultural Politics of Exclusion in Colonial Southeast Asia," *Comparative Studies in Society and History* 34, no. 3 (1992): 514–

551. Also see, Antoinette Burton, "The Feminist Quest for Identity: British Imperial Suffragism and 'Global Sisterhood', 1900–1915," *Journal of Women's History* 3, no. 2 (1991): 46–81; Janaki Nair, "Uncovering the Zenana: Visions of Indian Womanhood in Englishwomen's Writings, 1813–1940," *Journal of Women's History* 2, no. 1 (1990): 8–34; Mariana Valverde, " 'When the Mother of the Race Is Free': Race, Reproduction and Sexuality in First-Wave Feminism," in *Gender Conflicts: New Essays in Women's History*, ed. Franca Iacovetta and Mariana Valverde (Toronto: University of Toronto Press, 1992), 3–26.

31 For an important discussion of anger, see Audre Lorde, "The Uses of Anger: Women Responding to Racism," in *Sister Outsider*, 124–133. Also see Bell Hooks, *Feminist Theory*, esp. 56–65.

32 Elizabeth V. Spelman, *Inessential Woman*, 129–130. Teresa de Lauretis suggests that feminist theory is "a developing theory of the female-sexed or female-embodied social subject, whose constitution and whose modes of social and subjective existence include most obviously sex and gender, but also race, class, and any other significant sociocultural divisions and representations; a developing theory of the female-embodied social subject that is based on its specific, emergent, and conflictual history." Teresa de Lauretis, "Upping the Anti (sic)," 267. Kathleen Canning also has suggested the importance of developing a theory of identity based on the non-discursively constituted female body. Kathleen Canning, "Contesting the Power of Categories: Discourse, Experience and Feminist Resistance," paper presented to Comparative Study of Social Transformations Conference, "Power: Thinking Through the Disciplines," University of Michigan, Ann Arbor, and forthcoming in *Signs*.

33 Iris Marion Young, *Throwing Like a Girl and Other Essays in Feminist Philosophy and Social Theory* (Bloomington and Indianapolis: Indiana University Press, 1990), 13–14. Also see Donna J. Haraway, "Situated Knowledges: The Science Question in Feminism and the Privilege of Partial Perspective," in *Cimians, Cyborgs, and Women: The Reinvention of Nature* (New York: Routledge, 1991), 183–202, and the conceptualization of "experience" by Teresa de Lauretis, *Alice Doesn't: Feminism, Semiotics, Cinema* (Bloomington: Indiana University Press, 1984), chapter 6.

34 See, for example, Bell Hooks, *Yearning*, 23–31; Chandra Talpade Mohanty, "Cartographies of Struggle, Third World Women and the Politics of Feminism," in *Third World Feminism*, ed. Chandra Talpade Mohanty, Ann Russo and Lourdes Torres, 32–39; Patricia Hill Collins, *Black Feminist Thought*, 22–23; 208–212. One direction that such a rethinking may lead is suggested in Patricia Hill Collins' "outsider-within" and "both-and" perspectives. *Ibid.*, 11–13; 225–226; 232–235. Elizabeth D. Genovese suggests a similar approach borrowing the concept of "twoness" from W. E. B. DuBois which she would make the basis for a new common ground for feminism. Elizabeth D. Genovese, *Feminism Without Illusions*, 139–141.

35 Joan W. Scott, "The New University: Beyond Political Correctness," *Perspectives* 30, 7 (1992): 18.

36 Audre Lorde, "Age, Race, Class and Sex: Women Redefining Difference," in *Sister Outsider*, 115. Also see Bell Hooks, "Sisterhood: Political Solidarity Between Women," in *Feminist Theory*, esp. 62–65.

Chapter 3

Karen Offen

■ from 'DEFINING FEMINISM: A COMPARATIVE HISTORICAL APPROACH', *Signs,* 14 (1), Fall 1988, pp. 142–153

[…]

THE HISTORY OF FEMINISM is inextricable from the time-honored concerns of historiography: politics and power. Hence, the history of feminism poses essential questions for the political and intellectual history of Europe and the modern Western world, just as women's history poses essential questions for its social and economic history. Throughout Europe and the Americas, the history of feminism – both in the growth of theory and in political practice – has become increasingly and inextricably entwined with the controversies surrounding the growth and elaboration of secular nation states, industrial capitalism, and war and peace among nations.

However, at the same time, our understanding of politics and power must be expanded by attention to gender. The new history of politics and power must henceforth comprehend the arguments and efforts of relational feminists to influence government-enacted protective legislation for women workers and state-sponsored maternity benefits; it must include the development of housewives' unions and demands for the compensation of housework as well as unions for employed women and equal pay for equal work; and it must include all political efforts to elaborate the welfare state so as to serve women's needs as wives and mothers (e.g., payment of family allowances to *mothers*, establishment of child-care facilities, movements for improved housing, and the like), as well as efforts to eliminate state control of women's bodies (e.g., contesting anti-abortion laws and regulated prostitution) and to end the so-called white slave trade; and it must include efforts to alter men's more violent habits by attacking alcoholism and wife-beating and by contesting war and promoting peace. Relational feminism informed most activities of the women's movements of France, England, the Scandinavian states, Germany, and other European nations; moreover, it characterized virtually all the reform efforts during the Progressive Era that have heretofore been labelled 'social feminism' by historians of the United States.

Between 1890 and 1920, however, the aims and goals of relational and individualist approaches appeared increasingly irreconcilable, as different groups of women began to articulate differing claims. The feminist family tree stands revealed as a two-forked tree, with many smaller branches. Especially in England and the United States, individualist feminism gained momentum as increasing numbers of highly educated, single women intent on achieving personal autonomy became visible for the first time, the participation of married women in the industrial labor force became a political issue, and – most significantly – birthrates began to fall. Following the Russian Revolution of 1917 and the development of a strong anticommunist reaction in the United States during the 1920s, feminist intellectuals veered sharply in the direction of downplaying sex differences.

In European circles – and to some extent, in Anglo-American circles – the quest for 'equal rights' sufficient to realize an individual woman's autonomy, a self-reliance asserted rhetorically as a self-contained ideal, seemingly without reference to societal purpose or relationship to others, provoked controversy and dissent. European critics of individualist feminism, echoing Tocqueville's more general concerns about individualism, filed charges of 'egoism' against women they thought to have adopted a male model as the human norm. [...]

Feminism emerges as a concept that can encompass both an ideology and a movement for sociopolitical change based on a critical analysis of male privilege and women's subordination within any given society. As the starting point for the elaboration of ideology, of course, feminism posits gender, or the differential social construction of the behavior of the sexes, based on their physiological differences, as the primary category of analysis. In so doing, feminism raises issues that concern personal autonomy or freedom – with constant reference to basic issues of societal organization, which center, in Western societies, on the long-standing debate over the family and its relationship to the state, and on the historically inequitable distribution of political, social, and economic power between the sexes that underlies this debate. Feminism opposes women's subordination to men in the family and society, along with men's claims to define what is best for women without consulting them; it thereby offers a frontal challenge to patriarchal thought, social organization, and control mechanisms. It seeks to destroy masculinist hierarchy but not sexual dualism. Feminism is necessarily pro-woman. However, it does not follow that it must be anti-man; indeed, in time past, some of the most important advocates of women's cause have been men. Feminism makes claims for a rebalancing between women and men of the social, economic, and political power within a given society, on behalf of both sexes in the name of their common humanity, but with respect for their differences. The challenge is fundamentally a humanistic one that raises concerns about individual freedom and responsibility, the collective responsibility of individuals to others in society, and modes of dealing with others. Even so, feminism has been, and remains today, a political challenge to male authority and hierarchy in the most profound sense; 'the ultimate vision,' as Claire Moses has argued, 'is revolu- tionary.' I would substitute the word 'transformational,' which carries fewer connotations of physical violence. As a historical movement in the Western world, the fortunes of feminism have varied widely from one society to another (from England, France, and the Scandinavian nations, on the one hand, to the Iberian peninsula and the Balkans on the other), depending on the possibilities available within a given society for the expression of dissent through word or deed.

Based on this definition of feminism, I would consider as feminists any persons, female or male, whose ideas and actions (insofar as they can be documented) show them to meet three criteria: (1) they recognize the validity of women's own interpretations of their lived experience and needs and acknowledge the values women claim publicly as their own (as distinct from an aesthetic ideal of womanhood invented by men) in assessing their status in society relative to men; (2) they exhibit consciousness of, discomfort at, or even anger over institutionalized injustice (or inequity) toward women as a group by men as a group in a given society; and (3) they advocate the elimination of that injustice by challenging, through efforts to alter prevailing ideas and/or social institutions and practices, the coercive power, force, or authority that upholds male prerogatives in that particular culture. Thus, to be a feminist is necessarily to be at odds with male-dominated culture and society.

The specific claims that have been made by feminists at particular times and in specific places in European history include arguments for ending the maligning of women in print, for educational opportunity, for changes in man-made laws governing marriage, for control of property and one's own person, and for valuation of women's unpaid labor along with opportunities for economic self-reliance. They also include demands for admission to the liberal professions, for readjustment of inequitable sexual mores and ending prostitution, for control over women's health, birthing, and childrearing practices, for state financial aid to mothers, and for representation in political and religious organizations (symbolized in Western societies not only by the vote but also by access to public office). Such claims can all be seen as culturally specific subsets of a broader challenge to male pretensions to monopolize societal authority, that is, to patriarchy. At the same time, each of these claims addresses a structural issue, a problematic practice with political dimensions, which transcends the boundaries of the Western world and is applicable to the experience of women in other societies. [...]

Chapter 4

Deborah Thom

■ 'A LOP-SIDED VIEW: FEMINIST HISTORY OR THE
HISTORY OF WOMEN?' in Kate Campbell (ed.) *Critical Feminism,*
Open University Press, Milton Keynes, 1992, pp. 26–51

THERE IS AN IRONY IN DISCUSSING FEMINISM in a series called *Ideas and Production* because the relationship between women, ideas and production has been so overdetermined by women's role in reproduction. Feminism is, especially, but not only, about women, but it is primarily the activity of giving them a voice, an access to power hitherto denied. It therefore includes many different sorts of political argument; it encompasses Mary Wollstonecraft's feminism, her 'wild wish' that women should no longer be subordinated to their bodies and the passions which their bodies encouraged in them;[1] the existential determinism of de Beauvoir's 'second sex';[2] Christabel Pankhurst's radical feminism which placed women's interests against heterosexual sex,[3] and the contemporary argument of suffragists, that women's sex or sexuality was an irrelevance compared to their lack of citizenship.[4] Hence the ambiguity in my title and in the project of juxtaposing feminism and history. The place to find the value in that juxtaposition is in an understanding of the differences in feminism as expressed throughout its history rather than in tracing similarities, or assuming homogeneity.

Both feminism and history are social products themselves and participants in both activities produce ideas in a way which is in part determined by their circumstances. Changes in the sets of ideas are common to intellectual and political life - in other words they need to be perceived historically themselves. There are a hundred years at least of the regular production of feminist ideas, many more of women's reflection upon their social position and its determinants. Most people who have reflected on such matters have been women (as is generally the case in histories of the experience of being oppressed, those most interested in the analysis are those most partisan in the politics). Beyon d that there are very few things that feminists have in common apart from an unease with things as they are, and therefore a common problem of the construction placed on things as they were. They share also a sense of critique, of making that unease which is fundamental to their activity general among practitioners of history. But they are divided about the importance of differences and the political significance of difference. From this division follows the division between those who study women and those who study womanhood.

The 'fair' sex *or* the argument has two sides

There is a simple divide between historical theorists on the position of women. On the one side are those who argue that women are simply citizens (or not), differentiated as men are by race, class, region, religion and occupation, so that there is no more a subject 'women's history' than there is a subject 'men's history'. History is always a particular history, with a hierarchy of significance headed by visible structures of power which are described as such by contemporaries – monarchs and parliaments – and any other set of interests is secondary. Typical of such historians is Lord Elton, who has dismissed women's history as part of his general attack on social history. Such an attack is founded on a real theoretical position, which is that to prioritize gender as a division in society is a mistake.[5] Allied to this position – although politically opposed to it – is one which also gives precedence in the discussion to the dominant attitudes of the day. It similarly takes the conceptual structures of an epoch and emphasizes gender within them. What it shares then with the traditional historians like Elton is a central concern with power – but to discourse is given the dominant role in inscribing power relations in a society, among which *for women* their gender plays a leading part. Joan Scott is perhaps the major exponent of this in general accounts of gender and history.[6]

On the other side (which unites two very disparate tendencies) are those who argue that for women the most important thing is their gender, the *common* experiences deriving from the rhetorical construction of womanhood, and the legal, social and economic disadvantages of womanhood. In particular, they see sex and motherhood as the proper subjects of history. This approach unites the social historian of women and the feminist who may not share a politics as a result but who do share a focus on the structures of gender which prioritizes the body, lived experience and the commonality of women's lives. To say then that this divide is simple is not to say that it is meaningless, but it is no more useful a description of the historical enterprise than to say that all history is or is not about the divisions caused by ethnicity. It is interesting precisely in its variability. Gender, like ethnicity, does derive from the subject's innate corporeal qualities – however subsequently determined by social agencies – but the meaning of gender, like the meaning of ethnicity, can only be located historically. In raising questions about history I am not doing the synthetic task of summarizing the many works on history that have already been produced. Jane Lewis did this excellently in her contribution to Dale Spender's *Mens' Studies Modified* (1981) at a time when the volume of work was more manageable than it is now a decade later, so although this is a historicist account it is a very sketchy one which has the intention of demonstrating the persistence of certain fundamental questions involved in the project of thinking politically about women. Specialist journals, academic appointees, courses and fields of study all indicate that the question of studying women historically is not whether it should be done but how.

Feminism has made a major contribution to history, but feminists have not always gained from history the political advances they hoped to make. Crudely, that feminists want emancipation is undeniable – but whether they get it by writing about women or womanhood is not always clear. I am going to take examples from work written mostly by British historians about Britain to describe the influence of a political movement that is also a discourse – feminism – on a discourse that has political implications – history. Nowhere has it been more widely recognized than in feminist contributions to history that the history the historian writes is the history of her own times. Since women's participation in public life is of comparatively recent date it is not surprising that in accounts of the history of history women hardly appear until the nineteenth century. The writing of history demands certain material conditions which effectively excluded all but a handful of women in Britain until then. Theorists of women's position did exist and often wrote with reference to the past, but none of them explicitly wrote history. That is to say that the production of history is a luxury to those who are subordinated and most women, however powerful in the domestic sphere or as political figures by birth, were subordinated both socially and legally – much less likely to have an education or even functional literacy than their brothers. The art of writing history was in some ways thought of as inappropriate for those few women who lived by their pens, and those fewer still who wrote on the situation of women. As Mary Astell, the conservative political theorist and advocate of the improvement of women's lives and education, observed with some irony,

> They allow us plays, poetry and romances, to divert us and themselves, and when they would express a particular esteem for a woman's sense, they recommend history; tho' with submission History can only serve us for amusement and a subject of discourse. For tho' it may be of use to the men who govern affairs, to know how their fore-fathers acted, yet what is this to us, who have nothing to do with such business?[7]

It was no part of Astell's enterprise to propose any new way in which History might be written. Even so she was critical of those rare accounts of the 'great and good actions of women' dealt with by the remark, 'That such women acted above their sex. By which one must suppose they would have their readers understand, that they were not women who did those great actions but that they were men in petticoats.'[8] Her acuteness of observation and her wit give Astell a high place in the annals of thinkers about the position of women, but she was not part of a movement for change, so that, although her work inspired some contemporary enthusiasm and her writings and life were recorded, she left no followers or school. Her understanding was critical and thus valuable as understanding of the social order of her day. It did not inspire much history, except in the late twentieth century when she has become another subject of study herself.

This account will deal, then, with feminist writing arising from feminist movements, and try to place it in the material construction of the day in order to trace the varying ways in which history has been altered by feminists and by feminism. I start with the simplest pair of positions which represent feminism, around which two poles the rest must revolve, here ignoring chronology. The second section makes a quick chronological survey of the relationship between feminism and history. The third looks at some recent writings to demonstrate the extent and the limits of the mutual interdependence of history and feminism.

Male oppressor, woman victim

One feminism argues that gender is not a historical construction but an essential – the feminism of radical feminists such as Andrea Dworkin. For her, gender relations are always structured by one simple central ahistorical fact – men oppress women. The agency of that oppression is heterosexual sexual intercourse.[9] This position has been newly inflected by Catherine Mckinnon in an analysis of women and the state.[10] Hers is a bracing and rigorous account of the reason why women continue to be subordinated in the USA despite a materially rich society and a quite complex legislative programme of equal opportunity. A forerunner of this position is Christabel Pankhurst, a leader of suffragette agitation with her mother, Mrs Emmeline Pankhurst, in the years 1900–1914. She argued in 'The Great Scourge and How to End it'[11] that the solution to sexually transmitted disease – which she saw as one of the main weaknesses of the society of her day, in itself an oppressor of women – was 'Votes for Women and Chastity for Men'. Implicit in this position is the same location of oppression in the difference between male and female desire, which is read off from a biological difference – of internal and external genital organs – as a representation of power relations. An edifice of verbal and visual rhetoric was created by the activities of Pankhurst's followers in the Women's Social and Political Union which sold postcards of Saint Christabel, emphasizing the martyrdom of the female activist, particularly the hunger-striker; used the image of Joan of Arc, virginal soldier-martyr; and maintained that all women were oppressed by the existence of female prostitution which began with the deflowering by rape of a child sold into 'white slavery'. Chastity for men would of course ultimately mean chastity for women – and in many ways the account is one which argues for celibacy. The rhetoric of this debate downplays sex between women since the arguments are essentially heterosexual in structure, in Dworkin's version of the 1980s and Pankhurst's of the 1910s, as they assume that power in sex is between the two genders, not individual participants irrespective of gender.[12]

The history that comes from this viewpoint shares several features with the work of the French theorist Michel Foucault.[13] It foregrounds the discourse of a society rather than some democratic notion of the practices of the majority; it removes some historical questions entirely. History is inescapably general, individual agents are merely creatures of the discourse of their times. It turns the historian's attention to sex and sexuality, where gender is most closely inscribed on to individuals. This radical feminist tradition has generated much work which contends that the project of historical explanation must include domains previously excluded as private, in particular arguing that discourse about sex constitutes an important domain of power. This feminism has been influential in two ways: firstly in recognizing the way in which women are particularly constrained by the law as heterosexual sexuality is controlled through the regulation of the deviant female rather than through men; secondly in maintaining that women themselves prioritize the life they lead as sexed beings.[14]

Women's concern with sexuality led to one great and successful campaign to change a law, the campaign against the Contagious Diseases Act in the 1870s. This was organized by a woman, Josephine Butler, who used to great effect the horrifying demonstration of the impact on women of sexual morality's double standard. In the course of her campaign she spoke in public about the effects of sexually transmitted disease on women's bodies. This was not so unusual in the discourse of evangelists who fulminated against sex; what was unusual was the way in which she waved the speculum that doctors used on prostitutes during their compulsory vaginal examination under the Acts. This was, as she pointed out, instrumental rape. The example is interesting because it raises the issue of the way in which discourse about sex and the double standard offers ambiguous support for a feminist project; and also the way in which religion is yoked to constructions of the social in the nineteenth century, makings its concept of social explanation different from ours.

Butler herself was interested in the historical roots of women's position, but not in doing history. That as an activity was inspired by the suffrage activists of the United States who were looking for examples of women's sense, civic virtue and strength of mind and character. In newspapers, pamphlets and books great women were described and rescued from obscurity, so too were the exemplary lives of the suffering. The genre was not new, it is characteristic of the evangelist tracts of the period 1820 to 1860. Popular history of the turn of the century followed a life-and-achievements model both in structure and narrative, and of course much of the popular fiction was about young women because so much of it was for young women. What feminism contributed was the sense that these achievements were representative of a sex and not of those who were unlike the rest of their sex. Such writings were always caught between the exemplary and celebratory nature of the genre and the need to explain the continuing subordination of all women, partly on the basis of the wrongs done to women, partly on the basis of the achievements of a few women who tried to right the wrongs.

Feminism as critique

One of the problems for the historian motivated by feminism is the contradiction between how women are and how they might be. Perhaps the earliest feminist discourse that confronted this issue over history was that of Mary Wollstonecraft, not just in her *A Vindication of the Rights of Women* but in her published accounts of the French Revolution and her educational manuals as well as her novels. She attacked the societies of her own day for avoiding real historical understanding in favour of essentialism, which she summed up in the attitude that 'Women ought always to be subjected because she has always been so' (*A Vindication*, p. 69). However she pointed out too that women were not, in the society of her day, equipped to achieve all the things of which they could be capable, for the mind will ever be unstable that has only prejudices to rest on, and the female virtue of obedience needed to be replaced by intransigence – 'when forebearance confounds right and wrong it ceases to be a virtue'. Wollstonecraft's argument against women's subordination was that it was based upon the effect of passion which disturbed the order of society. She wanted to demonstrate that it was the superior ordering of society that an educated womanhood would achieve: an individual woman would acquire 'the dignity of conscious virtue' and in so doing would become a 'better wife and mother'. In this way she made a set of political arguments about women as a wasted resource, as misused potential, that rested on the tension between what was and what could be, but also recognized and prioritized difference. She was arguing that women should escape the tyranny of the emotional life because it weakened them and thus society. Bitterly she pointed out that often a 'neglected wife was the best mother'. There is thus a double tension between the interests of men and women, and between the interests of women's particular social role and their universal humanity.

In her texts Wollstonecraft constantly exploited the notion that the personal is the political but she also sought to undermine it, because she saw that as a part of women's burden. Denise Riley has pointed to these tensions at the heart of Wollstonecraft's writing and her political project as a whole, in *Am I That Name?* (1988). She has also argued that this paradox is an essential component of any speaking on the subject 'woman'. It is and remains the central question in any discussion of the analysis embodied in any feminist writing or discourse. But it is not the only subject that feminism has brought to history, since history as wrought by feminism has not been just about how women are spoken of but how they act or how they speak of themselves – which may well be at variance with their ascribed behaviour. Wollstonecraft could say that women had always been subjected – but she felt no need to describe that subjection historically as differentiated. Her problem was to overcome the Rousseauan belief in a state of nature at all, to claim that gender relations were culturally determined, and to predict that only women's own activity could overcome this determination. Hence the impact of Enlightenment thought was to emphasize activity and activism, to look to the successes who escaped from subjection as an inspiration for all.

Stories we tell ourselves

Heroism was the dominant mode of historical explanation in the period in which women were challenging for power in Parliament. Hence the historic figures of interest to suffrage activists were usually those whose heroism had been of an unusual kind. The archetype for suffragettes was Joan of Arc. She was virginal, militant and embodied suffering for a cause. Christabel Pankhurst called her forces 'the women's army', and demanded the sacrifice of 'normal' expectations, either of marriage and children, or of a career in those occupations opening to women (something perhaps forgotten by later commentators). Joan of Arc had been a soldier and a martyr, whose cause had been challenged but who had not ultimately wavered. She represented the discipline that was needed to maintain an illegal set of activities in a small oganization operating in secrecy. She also represented some of the more dubious pleasures of self-sacrifice. There were other exemplars of women who were seen as early activists for a cause they had construed in other ways. The search for the exemplary was a task requiring historical skills but more often than not these skills were not used. History was the maintenance of a collective narrative, a skein in which new brightly coloured threads could be woven, in which the history of women joined that of the nation, democracy and the English common law as a slow glorious unfolding towards an improving present. What was distinctive about this feminist version of Whig history was the way in which these accounts, these empowering stories, celebrated new values. Biography of Joan of Arc was joined by biography of Elizabeth Fry (the Quaker prison reformer), accounts of Florence Nightingale's contribution to nursing, descriptions of the female monarchs who had held power and exercised it – Elizabeth I and Boadicea. However the implications of these popular studies were ambiguous. The suffragettes could argue that these histories demonstrated women's strength, civic virtue and abandonment of self in the interests of the greater good.

Opponents could argue these were the qualities which made them exceptional and the lack of these qualities was more evident in women in general than in men. They could also argue that the separation of public from private was unassailed by these few women in public life. If women's real claim to be participants in the public sphere was based on their mothering experience or capacities, most women would always wish to make that a priority in their lives so that these exceptions only proved the rule. History was always a minority interest among the feminists of the period 1900–1914, partly perhaps because of the necessary emphasis on political action rather than reflection or study, partly because writing history, finding out sources, learning the investigative skills required, understanding a period – all require time and money to sustain. Woolf's plea for a new history of women in *A Room of One's Own* specifically requested this new history from some student of Girton or Newnham, the few women who had access to the resources needed to write new history rather than re-write the old. 'What we want', she wrote,

> is a mass of information; at what age did she marry; how many children had she as a rule; what was her house like; had she a room to herself; did she do the cooking; would

she be likely to have a servant? All these facts lie somewhere, presumably, in parish registers and account books; the life of the average Elizabethan woman must be scattered about somewhere, could one collect it and make a book of it. It would be ambitious beyond my daring, I thought, looking about the shelves for books that were not there, to suggest to students of those famous colleges that they should rewrite history, though I own it often seems a little queer as it is, unreal, lop-sided; but why should they not add a supplement to history? calling it of course, by some inconspicuous name so that women might figure there without impropriety?[15]

Woolf's writing of social commentary was rediscovered by feminists of the 1970s, and her plea has been frequently cited. I will address the question of whether it has been answered – as Joan Scott says that it has – later; what I want to address for now is the nature of the plea itself. Woolf was a sponsor of the organization for working-class women who worked in the home, the Women's Cooperative Guild. This organization was set up in 1894 by Mrs Lawrenson, the wife of a Woolwich vicar, to stop women – who controlled domestic expenditure – from undermining their husbands' cooperative movement by buying goods more cheaply elsewhere. Very quickly these maternalist intentions were themselves undermined by the organization's members who turned it into a campaigning movement which addressed matters of concern to themselves far beyond the shop door – maternity, education, the vote and, most contentiously of all, birth control and divorce. Divorce was a subject of such delicacy that their support for divorce law reform cost them the financial support of the Cooperative Union, the umbrella movement for all local co-ops. In short this organization, which was the women's political body with which Woolf most associated herself (while recognizing the profound differences that lay between herself and these women), was one which advocated the writing of a new politics in women's interest – particularly that of the working-class woman who worked in her own home.

They also argued for the use of new evidence in furtherance of their political demands. Their two most influential books, which were collectively written – *Maternity: Letters from Working Women* and *Life As We Have Known It* – argued that their experience of life was an unheeded source of information which should be given greater political influence. The unedited words of these women were therefore seen as more truthful and more powerful than the careful, artistic productions of those professional authors – such as Woolf – who supported them. In these books were raw details of everyday life that were in a sense being spoken aloud for the first time. Women described their confinements, the need to work immediately after them, the resort to abortifacients when pregnancy was intolerable and the physical details of childbirth in overcrowded homes without adequate hot water. All of this added up to make an extremely powerful case for maternity benefit payable to the mother; but it also added up to a new claim for reportage, for the authenticity of experience which Woolf longed for. This experience provided a powerful argument about women, who were thus located in the domestic by their own defenders. The novelty of this reporting is that it is introduced by writers but not mediated very much through the construction of a narrative which they put on the material. This is their own work, albeit less innocent of literary technique than the presentation implied, since the soliciting of reports had set the terms of the narrative. This makes all the more remarkable their assured handling of concepts previously used to place women in public discourse as victims.

Feminists contributed another technique which prioritized experience in the period of suffrage agitation, the social survey work best represented by the Fabian Women's Group.

Sally Alexander has described their work in the introduction to a set of papers edited from the pamphlets they produced. They looked at the lives of women and portrayed their findings statistically with a range of empirical data and often novel methodology. In writing *Round About a Pound a Week* Mrs Pember Reeves described the daily struggle to maintain respectability in working-class Lambeth. She demonstrated how women coped with inadequate income, large families and poor housing. The conclusion of the study was that political commentary which deplored the inadequacies of the working-class mother was misconceived; it was only due to her competence that these families kept going at all.

These writers were not historians, they were polemicists. But they were developing a newly politicized sense of narrative which, in describing the lives of women, constituted evidence to indicate that in many ways Woolf's plea was neither so novel nor so long in being met as historians of the history of women have argued. It was no accident that Virago's reclamation of works of the past as history should have started with many of these texts, themselves now primary sources for historians. They too are subject to the paradox of the history based on experience – which is the nature of the project. Much of this description is exemplary. It shows the efforts women make and the difficulties they contend with, but there always remains the centrality of their experience as potential or actual mothers to their political claims. The account is always based on the experience of the majority of British women – heterosexual, white, working-class.

Difference celebrated

The First World War and the ten years after it saw a burgeoning of books about the position of women and the development of women's history by both professionals and amateurs. This distinction is worth attending to because publishers distinguish between the popular and the academic, with the idea of who the reader is affecting the marketing. Much history of this period was written as biography. The notion that this was an appropriate form for women's accounts of their lives was already well established. What this period showed was that Mary Astell's rueful recognition of the exclusion of women from the public concerns of history was being seen not as a disadvantage but an alternative. War itself emphasized this with what both historians and some of their contemporaries saw as a profound divide between the military and the Home Front. Separate spheres were here being written into history, and proving fruitful as a means of exploring new areas of historical investigation. Biography is often an opportunity to explore the insight of feminism and anti-feminism alike that for women the domestic, the gender-related world of love, children and the home seems more important than Parliament and court. The narrative is shaped by the genre and inherently foregrounds the personal. It is also inherently celebratory and exemplary. At the same time many of these histories can be woven together to form one history, a history of an entire gender recorded in a series of anecdotes or vignettes. Many women who worked as professional writers found this a lucrative way of maintaining an interest in the affairs of women, many feminist activists turned to instant history as a way of earning a living.[16]

Feminist authors increasingly turned to history as they constructed an explanation of the subjection of women which could be inserted into the discourses of the day. From 1913 to 1930 there was indeed a very large number of books published with titles including the word 'woman' or, more likely, if by feminists, 'women'. Most of them were not of the 'men in petticoats' variety at all. But they were most assuredly of the great deeds and actions type.

In the post-war years feminist activists of the suffrage agitation still had to fight for the vote because it had only been granted to women over thirty in 1918. Many of their actions have been described as decline, as the failure of feminism – although Jane Lewis for some time has been arguing that there is no failure here, only the reordering of feminist movements.[17] The splits observed by historians of suffrage, looking for one continuous 'movement', can easily be seen as an expansion of political activism – specialization not retrenchment. While some individuals were exhausted by the struggle for the vote and the exigencies of life in wartime many others took the skills they had learned fighting for the vote into new fields – pacifism, sex reform, education, trade unionism. Those commentators who wrote about women tended to shift their attention towards the lives of the poor, the mute, mothers and workers who most suffered from the over-determination involved in describing them by the name of woman. The classic figure of the period is not Joan of Arc as before the war, it is Gorky's *Mother*. The feminist culture which has been most radically critical of the gender divisions of its day had been the suffragette movement; in the post-war period, it became the socialist feminists who looked to the infant Bolshevik state for their model of utopianism. History was thus very much engaged with questions of class and production, and feminism with the lives of working-class women and reproduction. The slogan of the campaigners who fought against the spectre of maternal mortality (which had not yet declined nearly as fast as that other great indicator of social health, infant mortality) used to argue that it was 'four times more dangerous to bear a child than to go down a coal mine'. Political activism for feminists moved away from Parliament and into everyday life. The Workers Birth Control Group included writers like Naomi Mitchison and Dora Russell, both of whom 'used' history to demonstrate the contingency which altered women's lives – in other words to make arguments for recognizing the variability of human lives, human potential for change and the creative relationship possible between human beings and nature.

Women in production

Only a few women writers began to seek to do a new sort of history. Ivy Pinchbeck published *Women Workers and the Industrial Revolution* in 1930, which was the best work of its kind. Her work fitted into a tradition in English socialism – of analysis of the 'English people' – dating back to the 1880s. In this, change rather than stability was the subject of investigation: assessing its effect on the poor was a way of making more important the social rather than the national idea of the people. There was a radical claim (not stated very emphatically) which argued that the female part of the people was as important as the male. In other words this is critical history in a way that much of the earlier, more celebratory accounts of the particularity and gender-determined nature of women in society had not been. History should, she argued, be revised. The importance of women's entry into political life and production was as great in assessing the impact of new forms of society as that of men. Although Josephine Butler has written about women's work in 1869, and Barbara Drake had produced some excellent analysis in 1919 for the report of the War Cabinet Committee on Women in Industry[18] on the historical explanations of women's subordination in the workplace, neither had done any historical investigation and the history and research in their work were profoundly utilitarian. Pinchbeck did not know what she would find in historical investigations, while earlier polemicists went to history with the intention to prove a case. Hence her work represents a new development in methodology – an implicit assumption that women have made a contribution to civil society and that it should be investigated, rather than that they should be described as they are described by their contemporaries. History, then, should be about the lives of women as they were rather than the concepts of gender as used about them: women not Woman or womanhood were the subject of history. The sources of the account were not new, and like contemporaries who developed labour history she found much material in the publicly available domain of official records. She was not interested in private data or life inside the home. The assumption was that women had been participants in the world of production and that this was worthy of analysis and record – as it had been to contemporary commentators.

But the further assumption was that women had entered the important area of life through industrialization – had, as it were, entered history properly for the first time. The argument owed a great deal to Russia, and in particular to propaganda of the early days of the Bolshevik state when, as Lenin had argued, the 'woman question' would be answered by the entry of women into productive labour. That is, if women did what men did the historic division between the sexes would no longer be of any economic or social consequence. Other Bolshevik theorists in the 1920s, especially Alexandra Kollontai, had recognized the need for that model to be modified by addressing the question of whether it was not also necessary for men to do what women do – although the way it worked in practice was to suggest that all tasks should be socialized, removed from the home. These suggestions met with less enthusiasm and the organized attack on feminism, the economic crisis and the retreat from some of the early programmes ensured that such experiments as had been (like communal kitchens, public laundries, creches) were soon abandoned.[19]

In the 1970s, in the USA, Joan Scott and Louise Tilly did the same sort of synthetic collation of social history in their account of the transition to modern industrial society. Their book's title – *Women, Work and Family* – precisely delineates the concerns of this group of professional women's historians. They had worked in academic life for some time and under pressure from the forces for change in their own lives had begun to rethink professional practice. Joan Kelly summed up such a personal history in her posthumously published essay: 'The change I went through was kaleidoscopic. I had not read a new book. I did not stumble upon a new archive. No new piece of information was added to anything I knew …' But the history she had been doing was 'partial, distorted, limited, and deeply flawed by these limitations.'[20]

These women worked as academics in the United States, and the change in their focus of concern, seen in the new woman-centred history they began to write, partly evolved from the demands of their students, as well as their own re-reading of the sources they had been using. They were all thus involved in a dual professional innovation. They prioritized women but in so doing they prioritized the social as well. Much of their work indeed has been subsumed in accounts of the new social history being created in this period. Socialism or Marxism had inspired a similar emphasis on social change and many of the historians of the 1970s were socialists who began to criticize the sex-blind nature of the movements in which they operated politically, and to experience women's politics through consciousness-raising groups both in the USA and the UK. Sheila Rowbotham, who worked outside conventional academic teaching in adult education, wrote *Hidden from History*, published in 1974, partly to contribute to debates already underway within socialist feminism about the nature of women's contribution to past struggles, partly to explain her dissatisfaction with the role afforded them in struggles in the present.

History, which had been obscured by ignorance and negligence among historians, also demonstrated that both the processes of record and the selection of issues obscured women. They were hidden by those who wrote down the information which became the sources, and then buried even deeper by the disinclination of historians to ask about their contribution. Rowbotham was interested in sources not widely available, many of them in the public domain but not seen as of central importance. She wrote about women who contributed to Radical Dissenting groups — socialist suffragists, pacifists, birth-controllers, communitarians. All these women had attempted to attack the structures which oppressed women and had generated new politics themselves in so doing. She revealed new heroines, traditions within which the women's movement could place itself, heartening stories to inspire future political and historical work. She also revealed the persistent repetition of such discovery and forgetting of women's radical movements.

Rowbotham's work thus related to — while not fully supporting — the other conceptual framework which inspired much history in the 1970s, patriarchy. How far, women historians wanted to ask, was such neglect a piece of deliberate — if not either articulated or conscious — behaviour by men? As Jane Lewis wrote of this history — in *Men's Studies Modified* — a focus on women was a reordering of the priorities of history, an essentially radical act. As the book's title indicated, history along with all the other disciplines discussed would be altered simply by thinking more about women. However the structures of the account would not necessarily alter if neither sources nor questions modified the general social picture. Discussing the nature of the institutional framework by which, despite individual achievements or the effectiveness of groups of women, women in general remained subordinated, was thus involved in moving to new questions raised by trying to put women into history. This meant not centring the discussion on women themselves, not celebrating women but deploring men or more abstractly theorizing patriarchy. Thus, as Joan Kelly argued, new subjects of interest would be investigated. 'Patriarchy', she wrote in 1976, 'is at home at home. The private family is its proper domain.' Woolf's hope for an understanding of women was thus reinforced by those who wished as she did to know more about the experience of womanhood in the past in order to attack the institution of patriarchy.

Intellectual work in the late 1970s became much more separate from political struggles than it had been in the early 1970s (or alternatively, political struggle was more likely to be academic work). Women's studies courses began to appear in British universities, new journals based in the academy came to join polemical and other feminist journals. As *m/f* started publication in the late 1970s and attacked the concept of patriarchy, writers elsewhere were attempting to elaborate their descriptions of patriarchy and explain its persistence despite feminism and formal legal equality in equal pay and equal opportunities legislation of 1975 and 1976. Feminism was even less a unity than it had been in the 1910s when the division was about tactics, not about structures. However such a division was productive of much debate on domestic labour, legal status, motherhood, education and work outside the home. Most of this described the lives of working-class women. Very little of this writing was innovative in method or material, much of it was written not by historians but by economists and sociologists. This meant that it was conceptually rigorous and sophisticated but it was often based on public documents such as parliamentary commissions of enquiry — as if these were themselves not in need of critical attention. For example, to assume that the account of women's labour in mining given in the parliamentary commissions is neutral, gender-blind in the way it portrays women in mining is, as Angela John has argued, to ignore one of the fundamental revisions that feminist history should have created in the use of official texts by any historian.[21] Much of the historical work produced by writers grappling with the questions of domestic labour, of unionization and socio-legal constraints on women's success thus slotted into a debate which inspired investigative research projects – which take time to complete.

Gender and deconstruction

But in what sense did this change in academic history bring change in methodology or a change in sources consulted? Much of the work published in the 1980s was secondary in type – rather than being devoted to new archives or styles of historical writing it reordered the old. (New techniques concentrating on experience – oral history, collective biography – were characteristic of feminist history but not peculiar to it.) There was thus a profound interrogation, deconstruction and critique of influential historical works, particularly in social history. This process has continued up until the present with illuminating results especially in Joan Scott's *Gender and the Politics of History* (1988). She criticized some historians who have claimed support for feminist ideals, especially the group who produce *History Workshop*, for simply failing to see the implications of some of the things they are saying. Does this represent a rupture between feminist historians or a fruitful development which should stimulate new work? In many ways the concentration on discourse by most contemporary feminists writing history is a blind alley in the practice of history because it is so self-referential within history itself. To undertake an historical account of the state of feminism which would do justice to this shift would be difficult, but several main factors would seem to be: the development of interdisciplinary and other courses in women's studies in the UK, which necessarily involves a lot of overview work preparing lectures for students and introducing them to the field; greatly diminished time for original research; and the stage of academic life that many eminent women have reached – wanting to take stock, look backwards and sum up the experiences of their working lives. Secondly, less material considerations lead to the elaboration of theory that is based not on new historical studies but critiques of men's work – mainly the development in social and political theory of the work of the French theorists Michel Foucault, Jacques Derrida and Jacques Lacan.

Why have feminists been so much more deferential to these theorists – who all write mostly about male lives, desires and speech – than to their feminist, or female heirs? The theoretical contribution of deconstruction to the study of texts has been profound, and historians study texts, and lives described as texts. However the nature of the historical project is to use a variety of sources to create a text in the history they write. Hence the mediations of any one point of view in the time that has elapsed, the nature of the social context in which the view was produced, and the fate which the view-point endured through the accidents of survival into the present are an essential part of the historical assessment. There are historians who write about 'experience' as the authentic representation of the 'real;' but most do not. Feminist accounts of the discourse of a day have to assess competing descriptions of a life or a phenomenon. But to assume that they are not different one from the other is to disempower women as historical and political agents. If accounts of women are merely ventriloquism when they are by women, the assumption that it is possible to act as a feminist appears to be discountenanced. If the path of French theoreticians is followed and their assumption that feminine writing and female language have to be developed to create a humane and womanly world then women are excluded from the language of common humanity and thus from power. Hence the conclusion that such work in effect reaches – that historical study gives us only the world of the dominant male voice, produces critical commentary on texts, but does not produce history.[22] The history that disdains the texts which are not about individual subjects – the data on maternal mortality, for example – is intrinsically denying the material. The history which recognizes that the data is produced and reproduced by men and women in different ways is only doing the basic job of questioning the sources. I return to the slogan of the 1920s, that it was 'four times more dangerous to bear a child than to go down a coal mine'. The statistic is dubious but the politics are interesting. Lady Rhondda wanted women to be able to mine, maternalists wanted to protect mothers: both could exploit the slogan.

The ideas that did resonate and inform were those which directed the historian's attention to the nature of the text and the nature of the subjectivity of the woman who looked at the text. Hence Sally Alexander was able to use the central Lacanian theme of women as 'lack' to look at both absences and presences in public discourse, to articulate the shaping principles of nineteenth-century women's descriptions of their role as heart of a heartless world. But this concept of men as 'labour', women as 'love', is one that is there in the materials of historical study – it is the systematic recognition of that presence that is new.[23]

I share Linda Gordon's question as to how far the history produced by some work of textual analysis which queries the notion of historical agency is new or different, except in the nature of its subject.[24] I share her doubts too about the evidence of productivity in feminist history – looking at the volume of critique and seeing this as the production of theory. Such scepticism is not of the value of this work which focuses on texts and on discourses – it is valuable and it helps understanding – but it is a doubt as to the need for this to be all that goes on in the name of feminism. This doubt is created by the self-referential nature of the critique, as if the real force for women's oppression is the latest argument in a historical journal, when in fact the problems for most women, especially for feminists, may well lie in the field of political campaigning where history's lesson is only that women need always to defend their advances because they are rarely left alone to enjoy them undisturbed. Or, in other words, that the immediate needs and demands of feminism cannot be said to be necessarily linked to the historical project as they were until the mid 1970s. The study of women in history – which was mostly initiated by feminism – has been detached from the political project of feminism as it has developed its own structures, its own leaders and bureaucracy. In England there are now the journals *Gender and History, and Women's History Review*, there are several newly created professors who are pleased to call themselves specialists in women's history, several postgraduate courses in the field and numerous ones in undergraduate and adult education. Weber was quite right to see such processes as advances towards modernization – I in no way wish to suggest they are to be deplored – but they do of course lead to divergences among those pursuing the subject, feminist history.

One difference lies between those who study women's history and those who study gender. Among the latter are two of the leading names in feminist history – Leonore Davidoff and Catherine Hall – who produced in their book on the Victorian family and industrialization (*Family Fortunes*) an extremely powerful synthesis of their own researches in Birmingham and East Anglia and the secondary reading on the period which accounted for the development of the theories and practices of gender held by the Georgian and Victorian middle class. To adapt Marx, they show very clearly how women 'make their own history but not in circumstances of their own choosing.' Some of the history they relate refers in passing to women who had pronounced ideas about change in the position of women, and they hint, as other historians of the early Victorians have, that in many ways the elaboration of sexual difference was precisely the force which did most to undermine its dominance in the construction of the political order. This argues that to understand the history of feminism we need to look at what women think and do, not only at what is thought about and done to them.

What then is the sort of work being produced on the history of feminism? How feminist is it? Certainly the slow, arduous process of historical investigation is beginning to use or generate new data, and in so doing is filling in some of the absences from history of the past. The political claims of its practitioners are though less bold, more within the field of professionalism in history than politics. No longer is it necessary to write either as if all women were frustrated feminists prevented by men from realizing their 'true' natures, or as if those women who were feminists were deviant, 'women in trousers' rather than 'men in petticoats'. Feminists were very much like activists in other fields, subject to the structures and constraints of their own time, perhaps more critical of some of the dominant modes of thought, but not immune to them in a sort of 'sentimental priesthood', which was what Helena Swanwick argued in 1913 that they were seen to be becoming.

If historians of gender wished to account for the fact that most women live with men as well as other women and children, and that the negotiation of those relationships is as much a matter for the women as the men, historians of women have had to investigate the ways in which women rule other women, and reinforce oppressive attitudes and practices, particularly in societies with highly defined separate roles for classes, creeds or colours as well as genders. Hence the continuing interest in women's political organizations where womanhood is a central concern. Three recent books have looked at feminism as a movement. Sandra Stanley Holton's *Feminism and Democracy* (1986) investigates the political theory of militant and constitutional campaigners for the vote and concludes eloquently that they shared much in political philosophy and were mutually reinforcing in their campaigns. Philippa Levine's *Victorian Feminism* argues that women activists before the vote had an elaborate politics and strategy which should not be subordinated to the tracing back of suffrage agitation; Hal Smith's collection, *British Feminism in the Twentieth Century* (1990), emphasizes that this is not a single force waxing and waning but one which must be seen in its plurality. These books are all based on new sources, go beyond the public data of journals, books and official publications, and continue to make clear the error of the 1970s feminists who arrogantly lumped together this rich and varied past as 'first-wave' feminism.

Patricia Hollis looked at another sort of women's activism in her study of women who were active in local government after they won the right to vote and to stand for office in 1894. Her *Ladies Elect* looks at these energetic, successful local politicians who did so much to shape the institutions with which we all live. As in all these empirical studies the theoretical claims are not strongly stated but the reader should be able to see very clearly that they share a rejection of assumptions that women are a unitary category, that women are victims, that womanhood as a concept determines – rather than that their own activity shapes – their lives.

The debate between Linda Gordon and Joan Scott in *Signs* over the nature of the historian's enterprise has summarized the main divide on difference in stark detail. Gordon accuses Scott of neglecting material realities and divisions between women as demonstrated by looking at their experience of everyday life; Scott feels that Gordon is uncritical of the extent to which women's representation of their own experience is mediated through their habitation of the discourses of their own day. This is in part an argument about method. Does the historian look at endless minutiae of material existence, like Gordon's court proceedings, or does she look at what people write about women, or sex, or about power, like the essays collected by Higonnet and others in the collection on the Two World Wars called *Behind the Lines* (which had a foreword by Scott). This looks at the construction of discourses of gender, but very little at lives or experience. Gordon's comment that writers of history are still treating lives as texts without independent moral judgements of the status of the texts is probably correct, but equally problematic is Gordon's own use of the concept of social control which she attacks as denying her subjects historical agency – when, as Joan Scott argues, it might be better to theorize agency as itself a discursive effect. The dispute ends with Scott accusing Gordon of 'resisting' theory but concludes with the comment that

> it is the nature of feminism to disturb the ground it stands on, even its own ground; the resistance to theory is a resistance to the most radical effects of feminism itself. Such resistance then is a sign not of decline or disarray but of the vitality of this critical movement.[25]

There is a strong sense in this exchange of the more-political-than-thou attitude characteristic of debates within feminism. Nevertheless the recognition of intellectual difference is a sign of strength, of firm location of feminism in the academy of history. In the United States feminist historians were to be found on both sides in the Seears case (brought under anti-discrimination legislation) in which one side used the arguments of sexual difference to justify unequal treatment, the other argued that these were rationalizations of oppression and should be contradicted, not supported, in the interests of women.

The women who write women's history or feminist history are many. Woolf's plea for a history less lop-sided has begun to be met. But do women figure there without impropriety? There is a sense in which they do not yet do so. It is only when women figure in all the courses of history that, it seems, feminism will have achieved success by becoming a part of the norms of historical investigation, and that is a long way off. There remains a paradox at the heart of the relationship between feminism and history – that to prioritize the simple, single divide of gender is to make visible the one feature of life that may systematically oppress women or, if celebrated as an alternative view of the hierarchy of power, disempower them in a world of common humanity. To talk of woman is to hide the individual woman or to reduce her to what is the lowest common denominator in her life and that of others. Woolf's ironical plea for discretion is perhaps a double-edged reminder of how femininity and feminism can so easily be confused; how what *should be* is affected by what *is* and what *was* but not, ultimately, determined by them. Feminist writers of the past illuminate many of the options that face women writers of history in the present, but the material base of producing history is much broader than before, so is the institutional support. Still, the claim by Liz Stanley that all women produce theory is clearly true – we all have stories we tell of our own lives, our place in society and that of other names we call ourselves and others. However neither all women nor all feminists produce history. With cuts in part-time educational provision and educational resources like archives and libraries, that is increasingly in the UK something done by professionals – that is, in the academy.

In conclusion, are there no doubts about the validity of the whole enterprise? Would women do better just to get on with doing history competently and professionally as we know they can, and would that be enough? No, because the central concern of feminism, which is to explain and thus undermine the oppression of women, in no sense can be guaranteed by the fact that a woman is doing it. That is a problem of the assumption that there is any correlation between gender and political attitude. Of feminist history as an enterprise then there are few doubts; of its non-identical twin women's history there are. Without an assumption of value, of political purpose, there seems little point in simply knowing more and more about women, but then that is to go, as the question of what history is *for* usually does, beyond the frame of inquiry. Feminism has given history an enormously improved understanding of one of the fundamental divides in society; the one between the sexes, and it has given an improved understanding of why it is that a divide is also a structure of dominance; and that uncomfortable truth means that the impropriety remains, the grit which continues to produce pearls. The tension remains between a history which raises the question of one fundamental difference between the two sexes and how that discourse works, and a history which looks at women and their experience of differences – but only histories which allow for both will gain from the twin insights feminism has brought to history; either alone will remain a little lop-sided.

Notes

The place of publication is London unless indicated otherwise.

1   Wollstonecraft, M. (1792). *A Vindication of the Rights of Women*, J. Johnson.
2   de Beauvoir, S. (1969). *The Second Sex*. Harmondsworth, Penguin.
3   Pankhurst, C. (1 913). 'The Great Scourge and How to End It'. Published by E. Pankhurst.
4   Fawcett, M.G. (1920). *The Woman's Victory and After*. Sidgwick and Jackson.
5   Elton, G. (1984). *The History of England*. Inaugural lecture delivered 26 January 1984, Cambridge, Cambridge University Press.
6   Scott, J.W. (1988). *Gender and the Politics of History*. Columbia University Press.
7   Mary Astell, (1700). *Some Reflections upon Marriage*, (p. 88), quoted in Perry, R. (1976). *The Celebrated Mary Astell*. University of Chicago Press, p. 9.
8   Mary Astell, (1705), *The Christian Religion as Professed by a Daughter of the Church of England*, (p. 293), quoted in Perry (1976).
9   Dworkin, A. (1987). *Intercourse*. Secker and Warburg.
10 Mackinnon, C. (1989). *Towards a Feminist Theory of the State*. Harvard University Press.
11 Pankhurst, C., in Sheila Jeffreys (ed.) (1988). *The Sexuality Debates*, Routledge and Kegan Paul.
12 Tickner, L. (1987). *The Spectacle of Women: Imagery of the Suffrage Campaign*. Chatto and Windus.
13 Foucault, M. (1979). *The History of Sexuality*. Trans. R. Hurley. Allen Lane.
14 Such historians include: Sheila Jeffreys, *The Spinster and Her Enemies* (1985) and *The Sexuality Debates* (1988); Jeffrey Weeks, *Sexuality* (1986); Lilian Faderman, *Surpassing the Love of Men* (1981). See also Jane Lewis, *Labour and Love* (1986), especially the chapter by Lucy Bland; and Judith Walkowitz, *Prostitution and Victorian Society* (1980).
15 Virginia Woolf, 'Life as We Have Known It', quoted in Joan Scott (1988), p. 15.
16 Dodd, K. *Women's Studies International Forum*, vol. 13, 1/2, 1990, has written recently on the partisan nature of Ray Strachey's *The Cause*; also in this category should come Sylvia Pankhurst's own histories of the period, *The Suffragette Movement* (1932) and *The Home Front* (1931), and Vera Brittain's *Testament of Youth* (1933) which fictionalized diary information. These represent

the problem of evidence that 'experience' poses in that all texts are mediations – but this is a problem in any historical investigation.

17 Jane Lewis, 'Beyond sufferage: English feminism in the 1920s', *The Maryland Historian*, 7, Spring, 1975.

18 Josephine Butler, (1869). *Womens' Work and Woman's Culture*. Macmillan. Drake, B. Historical Survey to the Report of the War Cabinet Committee on 'Women in Industry', Parliamentary Papers, 1919, Cmd 139.

19 Stites, R. (1978). *Womens' Liberation in Russia*, Princeton University Press; Edmondson, L. (1984). *Feminism in Russia*, Heinemann.

20 Joan Kelly also came from the tradition of American Marxism, see further her account in the posthumously published essays *Women, History and Theory*, (1984), Chicago University Press.

21 John, A. (1984), *By the Sweat of their Brow*, Routledge and Kegan Paul; and reply to Jane Humphries in the long-running debate between Humphries and other socialist feminists on the question of the family wage (which here reflects a difference about sources), in *Feminist Review*, 1981, 7 and 9, Spring and Autumn.

22 Swindells, J. (1985). *Victorian Writing and Working Women*. Cambridge, Polity. In opposition to this view see, Stanley, L. 'Recovering women in history from feminist deconstructionism', *Women's Studies International Forum*, 13, 1/2, 1990, p. 155: 'people not as they *really* but actually are constructed and construct themselves' is how she sums up this standpoint, or as a 'materially experientially grounded epistemology'.

23 Sally Alexander. (1987). Unpublished paper delivered at *History Workshop* Conference.

24 Gordon, L., in T. de Lauretis (ed.) (1988). *Feminist Studies/Critical Studies*. Basingstoke, Macmillan.

25 L. Gordon and J. Scott reviewing each other's books in *Signs*, Summer 1990, pp. 848–860; the quotation is from Scott, p. 860.

Chapter 5

June Purvis

■ from 'FROM "WOMEN WORTHIES" TO POST-STRUCTURALISM? DEBATE AND CONTROVERSY IN WOMEN'S HISTORY IN BRITAIN' Chapter 1 of *Women's History: Britain 1850–1945,* Taylor and Francis, London, 1995, pp. 6–15

The "new" feminist women's history

BY 1969, THE SO-CALLED 'SECOND WAVE' of the organized women's movement in Western Europe and the USA had begun, and sparked off renewed interest in women's history. As feminists in the late 1960s and early 1970s met in women's consciousness-raising groups, they discussed and analyzed the subordination, oppression and inequalities that they felt and experienced as 'women'. In particular, in Britain, many feminists involved in left wing politics were disillusioned with the way they were treated by the male left and with the male bias of Socialism/Marxism. Juliet Mitchell epitomized this feeling of discontent in her widely read essay, 'Women: the longest revolution' – 'In the Marxist meetings on the politics of the Third World, in the University common rooms I frequent, where were the women? Absent in the practices and in the theories'. The invisibility generally of women in history, whether written from a socialist, liberal or mainstream perspective, was highlighted in Sheila Rowbottom's influential text *Hidden from history: 300 years of women's oppression and the fight against it.* Published in 1973, this book is regarded as the 'taking-off point' for women's history in Britain. Feminists 'set the pace' of this development, defining the field of activity and mapping out the main directions of research. Women's history thus developed separately from mainstream history as taught in higher education, and still has an indirect relationship with it today. In particular, some scholars will not accept the academic status of women's history. Professor Geoffrey Elton, for example, refers to the 'non-existent' history of ethnic entities and women; Ronald Hyman in *Empire and sexuality, the British experience,* speaks of 'the poverty of feminism' for historical work, asserting that feminist scholars display both a 'hostility to sex' and a 'dogma' about the supposedly 'pervasive violence against women by men', views which he labels 'sour and immature' and 'feminist hysterics'. By 1986 and 1990 respectively, when these male historians made those remarks, the division between women's history and feminist history was well marked, a development that was becoming evident in the 1970s.

Generally, *women's history* takes women as its subject matter and may be written by men (who cannot be feminists but may be sympathetic to, and supportive of, the women's cause) and women, alike. Women's history is not, therefore, necessarily feminist history, despite the fact that the links between the two have been strong. Indeed, some men writing women's history are decidedly anti-feminist. For example, David Mitchell's biography of Christabel Pankhurst, a leader, of the WSPU in Edwardian Britain, is renowned for its misogyny. His final chapter, where he compares Christabel's feminism, with 'the wilder rantings' of well-known feminists of the 1970s such as Kate Millet, Ti-Grace Atkinson and Germaine Greer is even titled 'Bitch power'. Furthermore, some women writing women's history, such as Elizabeth Roberts, wish to distance themselves from the label 'feminist'. Roberts, in an oral history of the daily lives of working-class women in three Lancashire towns in the late-nineteenth and early-twentieth centuries, explored a number of key themes – youth, work and leisure; marriage; women as housewives and managers; and families and neighbours. She stressed, however, that although she began and ended her research 'as a feminist', some feminists may be disturbed to find that her study does not seek to investigate patriarchy or male oppression of women. 'The patriarchal model tends to stress the negative aspects of women's lives,' she asserted, 'and thus, I believe, distorts the true picture at least in the area I studied'. Consequently, Roberts does not see her book as 'an obviously feminist history.'

As these examples illustrate, the terms, 'women's history' and 'feminist history' are not interchangeable. Feminist history is history that is informed by the ideas and theories of feminism and when the subject of study is women we should strictly use the term *feminist women's history*. However, feminists also research other topics, such as men, masculinity and the male world; when this is the case, the more general term *feminist history* should be used. However, not all writers follow these strict conventions, and so one frequently finds these terms used interchangeably with *women's history* and with each other.

In Britain, then, the growth of feminist women's history in the 1970s was intertwined with the politics of the women's liberation movement, and especially with socialist feminist historians such as Sheila Rowbotham, Sally Alexander, Anna Davin, Barbara Taylor, Jill Norris and Jill Liddington, who at that time were not employed full time in higher education and were connected with the socialist publication *History Workshop Journal* (HWJ). That the 'marriage' between Socialism and feminism was not very satisfactory was evident in the first issue of HWJ, where an editorial on 'Feminist history' pointed out that as recently as 1971, when the suggestion had been made at a History Workshop meeting, that people working on women's issues should meet later in the day, there was a roar of laughter. 'We know that women's history still has to be argued for,' it was tactfully pointed out by Alexander and Davin. Furthermore, they went on to define feminist women's history from a socialist perspective.
[...]

[...] socialist feminist historians at this time were working within paradigms constructed by influential male socialist historians, such as E.P. Thompson, who wished to write a 'history from below' rather than a history of elites and of constitutional matters. A concern with writing a 'history from the bottom up' led to a focus on the lives of working-class rather than middle-class women, and with an analysis that attempted to integrate both social class and gender divisions [...]

'Patriarchy', which usually referred to male domination and to the power relationships by which men dominated women, was criticised by Rowbotham as a term that implied a universal, transhistorical, fixed structure rooted in biological differences between men and women, suggesting a single determining cause of women's subordination. Alexander and Taylor, on the other hand, defended its usefulness, especially as a theoretical tool for explaining women's oppression.

[…]

Strong links with socialist history are also evident in the specialised journal, *Gender and History*, which, as its name implies, takes 'gender' rather than 'women' as its key focus of analysis. Whereas 'sex' refers to the biological differences between men and women, 'gender' commonly refers to the socially conditioned behaviour of men and women, and the ways in which 'masculinity' and 'femininity' are socially and culturally constructed (this broad distinction is usually upheld in the social sciences although 'sex', 'gender' and 'sexuality' interact in complex ways). It is this broad meaning of gender that *Gender and History* upholds.

[…]

Unlike socialist feminist historians in the 1970s and 1980s, radical feminist writers in Britain researching women's past often came from disciplines other than history, such as education and sociology, and were working within a women-centred paradigm derived from the emerging, multidisciplinary field of women's studies. Women's studies, like the 'new' feminist women's history, grew out of the second wave women's movement, and developed in the 1970s as a 'recuperative action' to challenge the silencing, stereotyping, marginalization and misrepresentation of women prevalent in malestream academic fields. Key figures in Britain in radical feminist women's history during the 1980s were Dale Spender, Elizabeth Sarah and Sheila Jeffreys, for whom patriarchy and sexual politics, rather than capitalism and class relations, were the key sources of women's oppression.

[…]

[…] radical feminists tend to investigate in history a different range of issues from those studied by socialist feminists, namely men's control over the production of knowledge; men's control over women's bodies; male violence towards women; personal relationships between men and women in courtship, in marriage and in parenthood; women's friendships; and sexuality. Yet radical feminism remained very much a 'minority voice' in feminist women's history in Britain despite its much more pervasive influence within the broader field of women's studies.

It was partly for this reason that I decided to launch in 1992 the new journal *Women's History Review*, since, as I stated in the editorial of our first issue, I hoped to attract 'a range of feminist perspectives', including the more radical.

[…]

The way in which feminist women's history in Britain was formed and shaped by some of the key concerns outlined here was not, of course, divorced from debates and issues within the women's movement generally. And as that movement in Britain became more fragmented during the 1980s, awareness grew of how the divisions between the usual 'big three' feminist perspectives of socialist, radical and liberal feminism, excluded other feminisms. In particular, black and lesbian feminists raised key questions about racism and heterosexuality, pointing out how their experiences as women had been marginalized in both feminist theory and practice. At the same time that this fragmentation was taking place, women's studies was becoming a major growth area in higher education – although women's history was much less rarely taught, and often located within women's studies and sociology rather than in history departments. But as the differences between women began to be voiced, women's studies and women's history became much more separate from feminist political struggles than had been the case earlier, when the commonalities that all women shared were emphasized. Indeed, fears were expressed that with the 'institutionalization' of women's studies, feminist knowledge was being tamed and incorporated within essentially unchanged systems.

[…]

Feminist women's history and post-structuralism

In 1988, two influential books appeared which argued that a post-structuralist approach could transform feminist women's history through focusing on gender (defined in a different way from that which we have considered previously) rather than on women, and through deconstructing the term 'women' and concentrating on the differences between women rather than what they have in common. Joan Scott's *Gender and the politics of history* emphasized the importance of studying the differing social meanings of gender through an analysis of language and discourse (ways of thinking and talking about the world) rather than the material reality that happens to people. The story, she asserted, is no longer 'about the things that have happened to women and men and how they have related to them: instead it is about how the subjective and collective meanings of women and men as categories of identity have been constructed.' For Scott, then, gender in this post-structuralist sense refers to abstract representations of the differences between men and women created by society, representations we can find through studying texts. Later, Scott further elaborated on the term 'experience', pointing out that although historians can never recapture it in the sense of lived reality, it is a word we cannot do without; however, the closest she came to defining 'experience' was to say that it is a 'linguistic event' that 'doesn't happen outside established meanings' – in other words, there is no experience outside the ways that language constructs it. Denise Riley, who worked with Scott as a post-doctoral research student, objected to what she saw as an unchanging essentialism in the category 'women' across different historical epochs, as if it had a common meaning throughout history. She argued, instead, that we see 'women' as a 'volatile collectivity in which female persons can be very differently positioned, so that the apparent continuity of the subject of women isn't to be relied on'.

[…]

[…] some gender history has made important contributions to our understanding of women in history. This is especially so in Britain, where the North American distinction between gender history and women's history is less well marked and where the term 'gender' has been used more in the traditional social science sense. But the gender historians making such a contribution tend to be grounded in feminist politics rather than abstract poststructural theorizing. As Catherine Hall, an eminent British gender historian, has commented, feminists do not need poststructuralism to develop gender as a category of analysis – it emerged out of years of work in consciousness-raising groups and out of years of studying malestream histories. Neither can one deny, I would claim, the importance of studying different meanings of the term 'women' in different historical epochs. However, post-structural feminists tend to ignore the fact that differences between women, especially of social class and marital status, have been researched by feminist historians for some years. To study women *as* women is not to claim, as post-structuralists assume, that all women's shared experiences have been experienced equally; as Liz Stanley, among others, has pointed out, the category 'women' has a number of multiple fractures based on differentiation by 'race', ethnicity, social class, marital status, sexual orientation, culture, religion, ablebodiedness and age. What is important is for feminist women's historians to research and explore women's differences while also acknowledging and recognizing the common ground of these female genders against male genders.

PART TWO

Late Eighteenth Century

THE LATE EIGHTEENTH CENTURY WAS A TIME of great social, political and economic upheaval. Revolutions in America (1776) and France (1789), giving birth to declarations of the Rights of Man, critiques of the Divine Right of Kings and debates on the nature of citizenship, were enacted against the background of emergent industrialisation. Within this ferment of revolutionary ideas, gender issues started to bubble to the surface. Rights of Man, however, were just what the words implied: rights for *men*. Mary Wollstonecraft, one of the last Enlightenment, and first Feminist, philosophers challenged the political philosophy of Rousseau, whose Social Contract was limited to Rational Man. Rousseau was quick to attack social injustices but ignored the most glaring: that of the lack of rights for women. Mary Wollstonecraft had witnessed the French Revolution at first hand and joined in the debate on the Rights of Man; but she passionately advocated the Rights of Women also. These were not simply to encompass political rights, but also rights within the domestic familial sphere. Thus her writings argued for a less corrupt social order in which all tyranny, not just that of political rulers, but also that of patriarchal heads of households, would be things of the past.

Barbara Taylor's article is an interesting historical document, illustrating the rediscovery by 'second wave' feminists of their foremothers. Taylor was an editor of *History Workshop Journal*, itself a forerunner in that it had challenged 'malestream' history by including 'feminist' in its title. She sought to confront and illuminate established views of Mary Wollstonecraft's ideas, appreciating Wollstonecraft's position in European history, and her importance for feminists today. This article is important not merely as a means of bringing Wollstonecraft's views to a wider public, but also because it contains a 'consideration of what it means to describe feminism as (in Alexander's words) the "politics of sexual difference"'.[1] Thus it encompasses a discussion of the view of the French feminist philosopher Julia Kristeva, including her influential notion of 'female time' and the authority of the author: 'women are never heard'.[2] Taylor points out that Wollstonecraft was already anticipating some of Kristeva's points: 'The desire of being always women is the very consciousness which degrades the sex.'[3] Why then, when Wollstonecraft's writings were so ahead of her time was she neglected? Taylor shows how Wollstonecraft's reputation changed with the political climate. Her image of 'liberated womanhood' with its sexual licence once meant that her views became tainted: 'feminism in the pre-Victorian period had a marked strain of sexual libertarianism running through it which proved a distinct embarrassment to their successors'.[4]

As Taylor establishes the need for a rigorous understanding of Wollstonecraft's feminism, Clarissa Campbell Orr sets her in the context of a continuum of feminist thought, discussing the work of Abertine Necker de Saussure. De Saussure dealt with the themes Wollstonecraft thought important but was more of a pragmatist, her aim being 'social cooperation'. Her writings were based on her childhood experiences in Geneva which dated from the same period as *The Social Contract*. Orr discusses the beginnings of a 'cult of motherhood' in this period. She shows that the family was assigned as women's place, but that revolutionary Jacobinism 'was destructive of [this] very sphere'.[5] Genevan society, however, with its Calvinist background of sexual morality for *both* men and women had many of the rights for which women in other countries were striving. Women could be educated and get divorced on the same grounds as men, while it appears that birth control was also practised thereby saving women from the ravages of endless pregnancies and childbirth. De Saussure, therefore was by no means untypical of Genevan women at this time. She was able to engage in philanthropic work, which Orr describes as 'as convenient border zone between the public state and the private home'.[6] This was to become a theme of women's activity in the nineteenth century.

De Saussure came from a background of educational reform. Like Wollstonecraft, she took the view that women's different educational attainments resulted from the fact that women did not receive the same opportunities as men. She did not envisage marriage as the be-all and end-all of women's existence; nor did she think that women should be educated to please men. Again like Wollstonecraft she knew that single women would have to maintain themselves.

The problem for women, however, was, that while women of the working classes had always worked, it was men who had the 'property of skills'. Women were seen as an economic threat to the artisan's status and way of life. The question of women and work has occupied much historical writing. Debates have been concerned with 'continuity' or 'change' as the main factor influencing women's experiences of work. Anna Clark discusses industrial and class development through the perspective of gender, thus her analysis involves both capitalism and patriarchy. She engages with the Thompsonian thesis of the workers' 'moral economy', their struggle to retain the working practices of the eighteenth century in a changing economic climate. The 'fraternal male bonding' of the early unions excluded women, so that their actions, even if successful in the short term, were missing the real chance of success by not uniting in a common working-class cause with women.

Notes

1   Taylor, p. 54 below.
2   Ibid., p. 53 below.
3   Ibid., p. 52 below.
4   Ibid., p. 56 below.
5   Campbell Orr, p. 71 below.
6   Clarissa Campbell Orr (1966) *Wollstonecraft's Daughters*, Manchester University Press, Manchester, p. 64.

Chapter 6

Barbara Taylor

■   'MARY WOLLSTONECRAFT AND THE WILD WISH OF
EARLY FEMINISM', *History Workshop Journal*, 33, Spring 1992,
pp. 197–219

'**A** WILD WISH HAS JUST FLOWN** from my heart to my head, and I will not
stifle it, though it may excite a horse-laugh. I do earnestly wish to see the distinction
of sex confounded in society, unless where love animates the behaviour.'[1]

The wild wish – to confound, confuse the distinction between the sexes – is here expressed
in the wild words of Mary Wollstonecraft's *A Vindication of the Rights of Woman* (1792), 'the
founding text of Anglo-American feminism'.[2] In case we think this wish is wild in another
sense – that is, beyond the author's intentions or responsibility – let us move a little further
along in the text: 'This desire of being always women, is the very consciousness which
degrades the sex. Excepting with a lover, I must repeat with emphasis ... It would be well
if they were only agreeable or rational companions.'[3]

The chapters from which these quotations are drawn are respectively titled 'The State
of Degradation to which Woman is Reduced' and 'Writers Who Have Rendered Women
Objects of Pity'. The state of degradation is the feminine state, the position to which women
are consigned through the designs and designations of male desire. The male writer whose
objectifying desire is the principal target of Wollstonecraft's polemic is her mentor, Rousseau.
And the wild wish to muddle up the distinction between the sexes is also a wish to confuse
Rousseau's words with her own so that within this particularly belligerent lover's discourse
the living, loving woman not only of necessity has the last word over the dead male beloved,
but also achieves for herself the authority of Author from the position of Woman. 'I am now
reading Rousseau's Emile' she wrote in a letter in 1787: 'he chuses (sic) a *common* capacity
to educate – and gives us a reason, that a genius will educate itself'.[4] Six months later in
another letter she described her first novel, *Mary: a Fiction*: 'a tale, to illustrate an opinion of
mine, that a genius will educate itself'.[5] It was 'Rousseau's opinion respecting men' which
she 'extend(ed) to women' she wrote in *A Vindication of the Rights of Woman*,[6] in the midst of
her extended quarrel with him which occupies so much of the text. 'I have always been half
in love with him' she confided in 1794.[7]

But if the feminine 'half' of Wollstonecraft loved Rousseau, the masculine 'half' clearly identified with him: from which part does the feminist philosopher speak? 'Born a woman' ... I feel more acutely the various ills my sex are fated to bear' the heroine of her final novel exclaims;[8] yet in the *Vindication* Wollstonecraft refused to present her own female fate as a legitimate ground for feminist protest: 'I plead for my sex, not for myself ...' Despite her sex she could and would speak; *against* her sex she spoke also, sometimes with a misogynist intensity which appals the modern reader; and *for* her sex, for their place as moral subjects and equal citizens she raised a voice which still echoes within feminist discourse. But *as* her sex she could never speak: for when women's sex talks, women are never heard. But if this is so, what do we make of the crucial qualification contained in both quotations given above: 'I do earnestly wish to see the distinction of sex confounded ... *unless where love animates the behaviour*' ... '*excepting with a lover.*' Why does the wild protest stop there – if it does? That it does not, that it is in fact within the domain of sexual love itself that the wish is formulated and exercises greatest force, is the argument I want to develop here. And it is in Wollstonecraft's impassioned dispute with Rousseau, I intend to show, that her critique of sexual passion finds its voice. 'I love his paradoxes' Wollstonecraft wrote of Rousseau,[9] and not the least paradoxical aspect of this encounter between the notorious exponent of female subordination and his most famous feminist opponent is how within it a critical theory of sexuality and sexual difference began to be forged.

In making this argument I am in effect testing it out on the readers of *History Workshop Journal*, as it involves preliminary formulations of ideas which will be developed in a book on Wollstonecraft's feminism, to be published by Virago. As an editor of *HWJ* I have often urged other would-be contributors of 'Work in Progress' pieces to stick their necks out and present arguments for which I suppose the word 'half-baked' is apposite, that is, ideas which need more time in the intellectual cooker yet are hopefully of interest at a provisional stage. Also, the assumption behind our 'Work-in-Progress' pieces is that the *process* by which historians do what we do is also of interest, and for this reason I have tried to share some of the questions through which I have been addressing the wild hopes of England's foremost feminist.

* * *

In 1992 *A Vindication of the Rights of Woman* is two hundred years old. It was on 3 January 1792 that Wollstonecraft handed the last pages of her manuscript to the printer, having just dashed off a note to her friend William Roscoe in which she announced that the book was done. 'I am dissatisfied, with myself,' she told him, 'for not having done justice to the subject ...' She was right; she hadn't; nor in fact has anyone since. But her contribution was crucial, so crucial that for over two centuries the *Vindication* has been widely regarded as the intellectual manifesto of western feminism. Particularly in this century, the book has been constantly cited as the pioneer text; its author applauded/condemned as the first modern feminist theorist. Yet despite the almost legendary status which Wollstonecraft has acquired, the actual content of her feminism has, until recently, been curiously under-explored. The arguments of the *Vindication* itself – complex, fragmented, in part derivative and yet strikingly innovative – are only now coming under close scrutiny; her other works (which include two novels, a reply to Burke's *Reflections on the Revolution in France* and a history of the French Revolution) attracted little serious attention until the early 1980s. This is, of course, a fate suffered by many popular ideologues, whose ideas are considered significant less in themselves than in their political effects. But in Wollstonecraft's case it has been exacerbated by two factors. The first has been the convergence around her of a cluster of stereotypes – powerful images of dissident womanhood – which have served to conceal more than they reveal. Mary Wollstonecraft as a symbol of female freedom has tended to overshadow her texts. The second, connected, factor has been the standard interpretation of feminism as an ideological off-shoot of the liberal tradition. The aspirations expressed in the *Vindication*, so the usual argument runs, represent simply an extension to women of the individualist, natural rights principles of middle-class progressivism as a whole. As one commentator puts it, Wollstonecraft's book was the 'first substantial treatise' to 'apply the ideas of individualism to the position of women in society'.[11] Feminism, in other words, was a sub-discourse within the libertarian language of an emergent bourgeoisie. The failure to consider closely Wollstonecraft's own words follows from and reinforces this position.

In fact the central preoccupation of the *Vindication* is not with the position of middle-class women as subordinate members of a newly ascendant class, nor even (despite its title) with the entire sex's lack of legal, political or economic rights – indeed, after an opening salvo fired against sexual reactionaries in the French Convention,[12] these issues are barely mentioned. Rather, as I have indicated, the book is a complex, often contradictory study of womanhood itself; an intricate exploration of the 'distinction of sex' and its implications for women's subjective and social experience. If it can be said to be a political text, it is so by virtue of the way feminism redraws the boundaries of political discourse to encompass issues of personal relations and emotional experience. 'Feminism', Sally Alexander has written, 'has been the principal contender in struggles for the reorganisation of sexual difference and division, and hence the social meaning of womanhood …':

> Feminism looks outward at the social forms of sexual division and the uneven destinies which claim the two sexes, but the critical look becomes an enquiry into the self and sexual difference and asks – 'what am I as a woman, and how am I different from a man?' No social relationship is left unturned, if only by implication, in this endeavour.[13]

This deeply subversive project inevitably exceeds, and potentially transforms, its original political setting. Re-interpreting the historiography of feminism in this light will, I believe, provide us with a very different view of its character as a radical tradition. I want to explore this point via a detour away from Wollstonecraft to a wider – and at this point, very speculative – consideration of what it means to describe feminism as (in Alexander's words) the 'politics of sexual difference'.

* * *

In a 1979 article, 'Women's Time', Julia Kristeva suggested a periodisation of the development of nineteenth- and twentieth-century Western feminist politics into three phases.[14] The first democratic phase, evolving within the 'egalitarian and universalistic spirit of Enlighten-ment Humanism', climaxed in the great suffrage struggles of the late nineteenth and early twentieth centuries. The ideological strength of feminism in this phase, Kristeva argued, was derived from an identification with the 'logical and ontological values of a rationality dominant in the nation-state', a rationality which – in its construction of the genderless citizen as the active subject of political history – excluded 'when necessary … the attributes traditionally considered feminine or maternal in so far as they are deemed incompatible with insertion in that history'.[15] This egalitarian refusal of the feminine was in its turn refused, Kristeva claims, by the post-1968 wave of feminist militancy which not only affirmed a female counter-identity but, in its radical manifestations, made this counter-identity the basis of a female counter-society 'constituted as a sort of alter ego of the official society, in which all real or fantasied possibilities for *jouissance* ('pleasure', 'fulfilment') take refuge'.[16] From out of and against both these preceding generations of feminist aspirations – aspirations toward insertion into the male order on the one hand, and toward the institution of a female counter-order on the other – Kristeva in her turn lauds the ambition of the (then) most recent grouping of *avant-garde* feminists who 'having started with the idea of difference' are attempting to break free of the 'very dichotomy man/woman as an opposition between two rival entities' which should now be understood, she argues, as 'belonging to *metaphysics*'. 'What can "identity", even "sexual identity", mean in a new theoretical and scientific space where the very notion of identity is challenged?' she demands.[17] Moving beyond either a refusal or celebration of 'woman' as a fixed social and psychic category, Kristeva adjures us to take the struggle over sexual difference back to the site on which that difference is first installed: to the construction of personal identity itself. The dissolution of gender hierarchy at a social level can only occur when the fluidity and instability of gender difference at the level of the individual subject is acknowledged and valorised by women and men alike. This is the hope, the wish that she wills for a rising generation of women, with new time on their hands.

This provocative account offers more than a chronology. The varieties of feminism which Kristeva describes are not phases within a staged development (as she herself recognises), but co-exist as ideological moments across the entire history of feminist thought. The point needs more emphasis, however, than Kristeva gives to it. The idea of an early feminist politics which entirely identified its aims with the defining logic of the bourgeois democratic order (as in Kriteva's account of first-phase feminism) is mythical; nor, on the other hand, has there ever existed a 'women-identified' feminism (even in its most separatist versions) capable of wholly refusing that logic. And finally, what Kristeva identifies as the most recent and subversive of feminist possibilities – the impulse to reach past our experience as the oppressed sex toward the interrogation and re-definition of sexual identity itself – has in fact always been present, if only as a half-articulated wish, within feminist discourse. 'This desire of being always women, is the very consciousness which degrades the sex,' Wollstonecraft writes: 'Expecting with a lover … it would be well if they were only agreeable or rational companions.'

Not three phases of feminism, then, but rather three impulses simultaneously at play across the entire field of feminist endeavour: toward masculine identification; toward feminine identification; and toward the transgression/supersession of the categories, masculine/feminine. The specific dynamic of feminism is to be found in the complex interplay of these impulses, just as the heterogeneity of the feminist tradition can be linked to the relative primacy of one or other of these impulses within different periods or styles of feminist politics. Inscribed within a politics of gender, in other words, are the shifting sexual identifications through which gender difference itself is always constructed; and it is in the light of these identifications that the question of how to interpret ideological affinities between feminism and other emancipationist discourses can best be answered.

In making this argument I am taking up the type of psychoanalytic perspective, from which, as Jane Flax puts it, 'the tensions and repressions often found within feminine identities appear to be reflected and played out in feminist discourse'.[18] These 'tensions and repressions', I am suggesting, are those described by Freud as integral to the process whereby little girls are 'made' out of psychically genderless neonates: the turbulent Oedipal transition in which a girl's identifications with her mother and father are formed and re-formed through complex configurations of need, desire, fantasy. To be a woman, to be a man, to be both, to be neither: even when warring aspirations settle down into a pattern which can be lived with (or not, as the case may be) those wishes remain; they cannot be fully extinguished; they are integral to that rather crazy, never finished business of becoming a woman. Wild wishes are the stuff of which we are made.

This area of discussion is one of the liveliest in feminist theorising today; all I can do here is gesture toward it and then outline how these wishes were manifested in the writings of one feminist, how in Wollstonecraft's feminism we can see at work those 'tensions and repressions', and transgressive aspirations, which are at the heart of feminism's complex agenda.

* * *

What Wollstonecraft actually said, I noted above, has been heavily overshadowed by what she came to represent: both the woman and her words locked in a matrix of ascribed meanings which together created a caricature of liberated womanhood. The construction of this mythic Wollstonecraft actually began even before the publication of the *Vindication*. Having first come into the public eye as the author of an impassioned defence of the French Revolution, by 1791 Wollstonecraft already had a reputation as an insurrectionist, the English equivalent of the 'revolutionary harpies of France, sprung from night and hell'.[19] 'The female advocates of Democracy in this country, though they have had no opportunity of imitating the French ladies in their atrocious acts of cruelty; have yet assumed a stern severity in the contemplation of those savage excesses ...', ran one anti-Wollstonecraft tract.[20] The publication of the *Vindication of the Rights of Woman* in the same year as the second part of Thomas Paine's *Rights of Man* only served to strengthen the connection. Viewed through the smoke of the Bastille, Wollstonecraft loomed like a blood-stained Amazon, the high priestess of 'loose-tongued Liberty' whose views 'if received, must overturn the basis of every civilised State'.[21] Walpole's view of her as a 'hyena in petticoats'[22] was shared not only by male anti-feminists but also by many influential women, including the Evangelical writer, Hannah More, who was prepared to condemn Wollstonecraft's book without having read it. 'There is something fantastic and absurd in the very title,' she told Walpole, adding that in her view 'there is no animal so much indebted to subordination for its good behaviour as woman'.[23]

As in most late eighteenth-century writings, 'good behaviour' here meant sexual propriety, and it was on this score above all that Wollstonecraft finally stood condemned – less in her own lifetime, fortunately, than immediately after, when her husband, William Godwin, chose to publish a memoir in which he revealed not only her sexual relations with him prior to their marriage but also her previous liaisons with the artist Henri Fuseli and the American radical, Gilbert Imlay, by whom she had an illegitimate daughter.[24] Her impassioned and increasingly frantic attempts to keep the errant Imlay by her side; her suicide attempts when she failed; her second pre-marital pregnancy (this time by Godwin, with the child who was to become Mary Shelley) – all came into view under the distorting glare of her authorial fame, turning her (as one newspaper put it) into a 'philosophical wanton, breaking down the bars intended to restrain licentiousness'.[25]

In fact Wollstonecraft's behaviour, although certainly heterodox, was by no means unique within the Anglo-French radical intelligentsia to which she belonged. And in general, as I have shown in my study of the Owenite socialists,[26] feminism in the pre-Victorian period had a marked strain of sexual libertarianism running through it which proved a distinct embarrassment to their successors. Wollstonecraft in particular created a delicate problem for nineteenth-century feminists, most of whom viewed her personal career with deep distaste. To Harriet Martineau, for example, Wollstonecraft's sexual history was not only deplorable in itself, but also contaminated her writings and diseased her politics. 'I could never reconcile my mind to Mary Wollstonecraft's writings, or to whatever I heard of her':

> Women who would improve the condition … of their sex must, I am certain, be not only affectionate and devoted, but rational and dispassionate, with the devotedness of benevolence, and not merely of personal love. But Mary Wollstonecraft was, with all her powers, a poor victim of passion, with no control over her own peace, and no calmness or content except when the needs of her individual nature were satisfied. I felt … in regard to her, just what I feel now in regard to some of the most conspicuous denouncers of the wrongs of women at this day; – that their advocacy of Woman's cause becomes mere detriment, precisely in proportion to their personal reasons for unhappiness, unless they have fortitude enough … to get their own troubles under their feet, and leave them wholly out of the account in stating the state of their sex.[27]

The dilemmas of the female sex, in other words, can only be addressed politically by those untroubled women who realise that 'women, like men, can obtain whatever they show themselves fit for' and that whatever a woman can do, 'society will be thankful to see her do, – just as if she were a man'. To Martineau and other feminists, both of her day and after, Mary Wollstonecraft had lived and spoken too much of the 'wrongs of women'.

By the hundredth birthday of the *Vindication*, however, some feminists were determined to reclaim Wollstonecraft as a pioneer for The Cause. Millicent Garrett Fawcett wrote an introduction to the 1891 edition in which she made the startling claim that, contrary to popular belief, Wollstonecraft had been a paragon of domestic virtue and an exemplary advocate of Women's Duty.[28] Here was a Wollstonecraft, one feels, who would have been presentable at any 1890s Liberal Party Conference – particularly since Fawcett's interpretation of the *Vindication* omitted any mention of its sexual themes, viewing it rather as a strictly liberal-rights argument for female equality. We can see Fawcett's point: if Wollstonecraft was to be accorded a place in the pantheon of radical intellectuals, she had to be drawn into the liberal democratic canon. And so she was, not only by Fawcett but by most subsequent interpreters. It is an interpretation, however, which both misunderstands eighteenth-century progressive politics and neglects the specificity of feminist ideology. The question of Wollstonecraft's relationship to the various traditions which are usually lumped together under the category of 'liberalism' is a complex one, to be explored in detail elsewhere. But here it is important to see how certain elements within these traditions shaped what I have described as the moment of masculine identification within her feminism, the points at which woman's self-identity is found not in difference but in similitude, in living her social experience (in Martineau's words) 'just as if she were a man'.

* * *

As a political ideologue, Wollstonecraft's place was within what Franco Venturi has dubbed the 'utopian' wing of eighteenth-century progressivism – that visionary, world-regenerating brand of democratic radicalism (deeply influenced by Rousseau) which reached a highpoint in the 'Jacobin' circle to which Wollstonecraft belonged. '*Had we a place to stand upon, we might raise the world*', Paine quoted Archimedes in his *Rights of Man*,[29] and for himself and his associates, including Wollstonecraft, revolutionary France seemed to be that place. 'The french revolution', Wollstonecraft wrote enthusiastically in 1793, 'is a strong proof of how far things will govern men, when simple principles begin to act with one powerful spring against the complicated wheels of ignorance.'[30] The 'simple principles' which she has in mind were those which had inspired an entire generation of French and English radicals: the natural right of every individual to political and social self-determination; the evils of autocratic government, hereditary privilege, and unearned wealth; the perfectibility of human nature and human institutions; and – above all – *égalité* as the foundation for a new morality within human relations. 'Virtue can only flourish among equals …' 'My opinion, indeed, respecting the rights and duties of woman seems to flow naturally from these simple principles,' she explained at the beginning of the *Vindication*.[31]

The application of these principles to women was not entirely new. From the seventeenth century onward, libertarian opposition to the oligarchic state had provided a few women with a platform – albeit an extremely narrow one – from which to raise their own demands as rational members of the *polis*. When combined, as popular reformation in Britain almost invariably was, with radical Protestant claims for the equality of all true believers, such ideals laid the foundation for a concept of human nature as, in its essence, genderless. Both reason and soul had 'nothing of sex in them', as some leading progressive theorists argued. Furthermore, those differential capacities which did mark out the sexual distinction provided no legitimate foundation for differential power, as the natural rights theorist, Pufendorf, argued in 1673:

> although, as a general thing, the male surpasses the female in strength of body and mind, yet that superiority is of itself far from being capable of giving the former authority over the latter. Therefore, whatever right a man has over a woman, inasmuch as she is his equal, will have to be secured by her consent, or by a just war.[32]

'*If all Men are born free,*' Mary Astell demanded in 1700, 'how is it that all Women are born slaves? As they must be if … subjected to the … arbitrary Will of Men … ?'[33] The question was echoed several decades later by Lady Mary Wortley Montagu, whose answer to it dramatically demonstrated the subversive possibilities implicit in Pufendorf's earlier argument. As 'there is no real difference between Us and the Men with regard to virtue' she claimed, so there must be no difference with regard to political and social rights:

> Our right is the same with theirs to all *public employments*; we are endow'd, by nature, with geniuses at least as capable of filling them as theirs can be; and our hearts are as susceptible of *virtue* as our heads are of the *sciences*. We neither want *spirit*, *strength*, nor *courage*, to *defend* a country, nor prudence to rule it.[34]

'Our souls are as perfect as theirs,' she insisted, as Wollstonecraft was to do a half-century later. But in fact neither soulfulness nor reason was recognised as a criterion for equal rights outside the social contexts in which these attributes displayed themselves, that is, outside the authority relations of a society whose fundamental political units were not righteous individuals but patriarchal, property-holding households. There was, according to J.G.A. Pocock, a 'male bias' across the entire spectrum of progressive opinion which 'bordered on the absolute':

> To qualify for equality and citizenship, the individual must be master of his own household, proprietor along with his equals of the only arms permitted to be borne in

wars which must be publicly undertaken, and possessor of property whose function was to bring him ... independence ... [35]

Ostensibly universal categories, in other words, were heavily invested with specific class and gender content; humanity was indeed mankind; and egalitarian demands were restricted to those who could display their civic virtue through virile activity. 'Is it not the good son, the good husband, the good father, who makes the good citizen?' Rousseau demanded. And thus 'the *rights* of humanity have been ... confined to the male line from Adam downwards,' as Wollstonecraft noted,[36] a wry comment on the patrilineage of the political discourse into which feminists had somehow to intervene. So clearly gendered was the concept of the free citizen that Wollstonecraft's own attempts to employ it on women's behalf constantly drew her away from a discourse of humanity to one of masculine identification. Since 'the attainment of those talents and virtues, the exercise of which ennobles the human character' had been largely confined to men, 'wish with me, that [women] may every day become more and more masculine', she demands of her readers, adding that '*rational* men will excuse me for endeavouring to persuade [women] to become more masculine and respectable ...'[37]

The term 'masculine' was only a 'bug-bear' she later insisted, but in fact it was much more than that – as her own personal and political career testified. The relationship of middle-class women to the nascent bourgeois order, if not placing them in an oppositional position, certainly relegated them to a marginal one. Without property or political rights, barred from the academies of higher education and from most professions, lacking any independent legal identity, women could in fact be said, as Wollstonecraft has one of her fictional heroines say of herself, to be 'without a country'. Wollstonecraft's own struggles – to survive financially in a job market virtually closed to poor women of genteel backgrounds; to assert her personal independence in a middle-class culture which encouraged independent enterprise in its menfolk and condemned it in women; to raise egalitarian political and social claims on behalf of herself and other women – all these marked her out, not as a good British bourgeois, but as an alien, an importer of French Jacobinical ideals, a foreigner in her own land and – above all – a foreigner to her sex, to her womanhood. Men could be citizens, entrepreneurs, legislators, labourers; women were – in every area of life and law – the 'sex', and it was no accident that the title of one of the most popular of the many anti-Wollstonecraft texts published at the time was 'The UnSex'd Females'.[38] It was impossible for women to speak *as* citizens without speaking *against* their womanhood – and thus it is against womanhood and for masculinity that Wollstonecraft is so often forced to speak.

It is in this way that feminists are continually returned, again and again, to the question of sexual difference itself. Women may attempt to raise claims as citizens, or workers, or God's elect but they are always, inevitably, drawn back to their womanhood. 'I shall first consider women in the grand light of human creatures who, in common with men, are placed on this earth to unfold their faculties', Wollstonecraft declares, and only 'afterwards I shall more particularly point out their peculiar designation'.[39] But in fact it is what is 'peculiar' about women – the peculiarity of femininity – which is the subject of virtually her entire *oeuvre*. What basis for freedom lies within womanhood itself – within the particularity, the peculiarity of femaleness? How can the fact of femininity be re-negotiated, re-asserted in women's favour?

1970s and 1980s radical feminism, as Kristeva argued, produced one answer to this in an idealised notion of female counter-identity in which all that is desired or desirable – all corporeal, spiritual and social possibilities – were placed on the feminine side of the sexual axis. Behind this contemporary ideal lies a vision of an authentic womanhood which needs only to be released from the debasing, distorting femininities imposed on it by a patriarchal society in order to recognise and speak itself. This deeply utopian aspiration has proved a tremendously potent force within feminism, not only within recent radical feminist theorising, but within all feminist thought from Wollstonecraft onward. It arises within what I have described as the moment of feminine identification: the moment when feminists look not past but toward each other for an idea of feminine possibility. What is very often seen, however, is not the difficult ambivalences of women's relationships as they are actually lived but rather *imagos* of ideal sororial and maternal relations. Thus Wollstonecraft continually identified friendship between women as a paradigm of unconditional love,[40] and the attitude toward women in her writing became much more sympathetic after she herself became the mother of a daughter. Her posthumously published novel, *Maria*, is – among other things – an extended account of good and bad mothering in which the attributes of the good mother (selflessness, pity, compassion) become the hallmarks of a natural, undeformed woman-hood.[41] The authentic female identity is rediscovered in authenticated forms of female love. It is this kind of loving which is usually sharply counterposed in her writings to the profoundly inauthentic experience of erotic love.

The argument oscillates to and fro, veering between, on the one hand, idealisations of male virtue, enterprise, genius ('I have been led to imagine that the few extraordinary women … were *male* spirits')[42] with a corresponding denigration of the feminine, and, on the other hand, an equally idealising view of specific forms of womanliness. And beyond both of these fantasised positions within and across the sexual divide, there is another – a wild wish to refuse the division itself, to see the 'distinction of sex confounded'. Except, as she 'repeats with emphasis', 'where love animates the behaviour'. But the qualification is in fact little more than a politic gesture toward romantic sensibilities, for love, it seems, is at the heart of the problem. 'To speak disrespectfully of love is, I know, high treason against sentiment and fine feelings …' an early passage in the *Vindication* defiantly opens;[43] but treason, after all, is hardly the sort of thing a revolutionary democrat balks at, and so page after page of the book provides a shockingly harsh critique of sexual love as a source and site of female oppression. Lust and love, Wollstonecraft argues, have deformed and depraved relations between the sexes to the point where all human integrity is sacrificed. Women are made 'systematically voluptuous' in order to become 'contentedly slaves of casual lust … standing dishes to which every glutton may have access.'[44] 'I cannot discover why … females should always be degraded by being made subservient to love or lust.'[45]

This anti-eroticism is present in all of Wollstonecraft's writings, but is most fiercely and systematically expressed in the *Vindication* – a text which, in Cora Kaplan's words, 'offers the readers a puritan sexual ethic with such passionate conviction that self-denial seems a libidinised activity'.[46] The language in which this ethic is articulate, however, is simultaneously dogmatic, tentative, haranguing, hesitant; in other words, deeply contra-dictory, as reflected particularly in the multiplicity of terms – appetite, instinct, passion, lust, desire, sensation, love, voluptuousness – which she uses sometimes interchangeably, sometimes in direct opposition to each other. As a biological instinct, the sexual urge is proclaimed to be both depraved and yet wholly natural (natural, note, in both women and men): this apparent contradiction is partially resolved, however, in classical puritan fashion. Sex is a natural and legitimate drive, Wollstonecraft argues, when – and only when – its aim is reproduction:

> Nature must ever be the standard of taste, the gauge of appetite – yet how grossly is nature insulted by the voluptuary. Leaving the refinements of love out of the question; nature, by making the gratification of an appetite … a natural and imperious law to preserve the species, exalts the appetite and mixes a little mind and affection with a sensual gust. The feelings of a parent mingling with an instinct merely animal, give it dignity …[47]

Sexual indulgence merely for its own sake, however, is wanton lasciviousness – even within marriage.

> In order to fulfil the duties of life, and to be able to pursue with vigour the various employments which form the moral character, a master and mistress of a family ought not to continue to love each other with passion. I mean to say that they ought not to indulge those emotions which disturb the order of society, and engross the thoughts that should otherwise be employed. … I will go still further, and advance, without dreaming of a paradox, that an unhappy marriage is often very advantageous to a family, and that the neglected wife is, in general, the best mother …[48]

How are we to understand this sharply censorious tone? 'Why is A Vindication so suffused with the sexual, and so severe about it?'[49]

Throughout the course of the seventeenth and eighteenth centuries there had emerged within British genteel culture a concept of the feminine which was wholly sexualised. Anatomy was not merely female destiny, it set all the boundaries of feminine duty; virtue in a woman had only one meaning and as the fate of Clarissa Harlowe showed, it was not even dependent on her conscious will. 'The business of a woman's life is sex,' Rousseau wrote, while Richardson has Clarissa's rapist state the matter with brutal clarity when, following Milton, he describes women simply as 'the sex'. A flood of didactic literature poured from the pens of popular writers advocating a style of womanhood so steeped in the feminine, so excessively assertive of sexual difference, that to the modern reader it smacks of parody. If women had an identity at all, it seemed to be located in their genitals: certainly everything else about a woman, even her capacity to think, was determined by her sex.

At the opening of the Vindication Wollstonecraft indicated that her book was written against this background chorus of prescriptive writings on women's conduct, authored mostly by men who 'considering females rather as women than human creatures, have been more anxious to make them alluring mistresses than affectionate wives and rational mothers', or 'to render them the insignificant objects of male desire …'.[50] The chapters which follow contain an extended quarrel with these men – Drs Gregory and Fordyce, Lord Chesterfield, but above all with Wollstonecraft's erstwhile mentor, Rousseau, whose voice is almost as prominent at many points in the text as Wollstonecraft's own. The aim of all these moralists, Wollstonecraft indicates, was to educate their female readers into a code of conduct which they deemed 'modest' – a term which when examined closely can be seen to imply acute sexual self-consciousness conveyed through a display of sexual ignorance so excessive that it served both as advertisement and provocation. The classic account of the modest female was provided by Rousseau, in his fictional portrayal of the young Sophie – bride-to-be of the exemplary boy-citizen, Emile.

> Her dress is extremely modest in appearance, and yet very coquettish in fact: she does not make a display of her charms, she conceals them; but in concealing them, she

knows how to affect your imagination. Everyone who sees her will say, There is a modest and discreet girl; but while you are near her, your eyes and affections will wander all over her person, so that you cannot withdraw them; and you would conclude, that every part of her dress, simple as it seems, was only put in its proper order to be taken to pieces by the imagination.[51]

Sophie, as Rousseau unnecessarily adds, has 'the art of pleasing men' — the art to which all other aspects of her life are subordinated. She treads, in fact, that fine line between overt erotic enticement and propriety which was the essence of feminine 'sensibility'. Viewing herself through the male gaze, Sophie produces herself only as an object of carnal scrutiny, never as the active subject of her own desires. Yet that these desires were at least present, if inactive, Rousseau — in common with other moralists of the period — had no doubt. The idea that women were the more carnal sex, the inveterate nibblers at forbidden apples, had of course been a central feature of Christian dogma, and it remained entrenched within eighteenth-century social theory. Women's 'first propensities', Rousseau insists, reveal an excess of 'sensibility' which is 'easily corrupted or perverted by too much indulgence'. In savage society this immoderate carnality is of little consequence, but in civil society it must be restrained lest it lead to an amoral anarchy destructive of family life, patrilineage and ultimately the *polis* itself. Women must therefore be 'subject all their lives to the most constant and severe restraint, which is that of decorum'. 'They must be trained to bear the yoke from the first, so that they may not feel it, to master their own caprices and to submit themselves to the will of others.' Rousseau acknowledges the artificiality of these constraints while at the same time insisting on their necessity for the sex whose original and eternal wrongdoing must not be allowed to poison the rest of society. 'The life of a good woman is reduced, by our absurd institutions, to a perpetual conflict with herself: but it is just that this sex should partake of the sufferings which arise from those evils it hath caused us.'[52]

These typical passages of Rousseauite sexual philosophising are quoted, in a growing crescendo of rage, by Wollstonecraft. 'And why is the life of a modest woman a perpetual conflict?' she finally demands, and then goes on to answer that it is the 'very system of education' which Rousseau advocated for women that makes it so: 'when sensibility is nurtured at the expense of the understanding, such weak beings must be restrained by arbitrary means, and be subjected to continual conflicts; but give (women's) activity of mind a wider range, and nobler passions and motives will govern their appetites and sentiments ...'[53] All the self-indulgent sensualism, the mindless love of pleasure and the narcissism with which Rousseau invests Sophie are, Wollstonecraft agrees, characteristic of most women (particularly women of the leisured landed class) but against this naturalist explanation she insists that this version of femininity is the 'effect of habit' rather than 'an undoubted indication of nature':

The absurdity ... of supposing that a girl is naturally a coquette ... is so unphilosophical, that such a sagacious philosopher as Rousseau would not have adopted it, if he had not been accustomed to make reason give way to his desire or singularity, and truth to a favourite paradox.

'I have, probably,' she goes on, 'had an opportunity of observing more girls in their infancy than Jean-Jacques Rousseau' — including, she adds, herself.[54] On this basis she later offers her own account of how, in her words, 'females are made women of when they are mere children':

Everything that they see or hear serves to fix impressions, call forth emotions, and associate ideas, that give a sexual character to the mind. False notions of beauty and delicacy stop the growth of their limbs and produce a sickly soreness, rather than delicacy of organs; and thus weakened … how can they attain the vigour necessary to enable them to throw off their factitious character? … This cruel association of ideas, which everything conspires to twist into all their habits of thinking, or, to speak with more precision, of feeling, receives new force when they begin to act a little for themselves; for they then perceive that it is only through their address to excite emotions in men, that pleasure and power are to be obtained.[55]

Left to herself, she goes on to say, a small girl will 'always be a romp', uninterested in dolls or small boys ('girls and boys … would play harmlessly together, if the distinction of sex was not inculcated long before nature makes any difference').[56] There is 'no sex to her mind', nor is her mind on sex unless 'improper education … by heating the imagination' calls forth 'the desire connected with the impulse of nature to propagate the species' prematurely. And it is precisely this which happens all the time, through false ideas and false habits, transforming female children of nature into little 'coquettes', 'the insignificant objects of male desire'.

Let us pause here to underline the scale of Wollstonecraft's achievement: what she has produced is an account of female sexuality based on a clear distinction between gender as a biological fact (when 'nature makes (the) difference') and the inculcated eroticism which she identifies as contemporary feminine subjectivity. It is the latter, this sexed self-identity, which Wollstonecraft declares, again and again, to be artificial, cultural, transmutable. The capacity to breed and mother is a fact of nature; the eroticised woman, however, is a product of culture; she is, in Wollstonecraft's term, 'factitious', a creature of cultural fictions. Moreover, not only is she herself a corrupt artefact of 'civilisation' but she is also responsible for spreading the contaminating influence of sexual vice throughout society. Steeped in inauthenticity, trained to be the objects of male desire, women learn to 'glory in their subjection' and to make of it a phoney empire of sexual conquest. Plunged into endemic 'sexual warfare', they wield the only weapons available to them – their talents in seduction:

> women are made systematically voluptuous, and though they may not all carry their libertinism to the same height, yet this heartless intercourse with the sex, which they allow themselves, depraves both sexes, because the taste of men is vitiated; and women, of all classes, naturally square their behaviour to gratify the taste by which they obtain pleasure and power.[57]

Elsewhere Wollstonecraft lays the blame for this situation squarely on the shoulders of men, whose greater susceptibility to 'the appetites' leads them to enslave women to their carnal needs. But the rhetorical weight of her condemnatory language lies heaviest on women themselves, on their depraved sensuality. There were many reasons for this. Envious antagonism toward the leisured ladies who had employed her as a companion or governess was one; writing from within the terms of her male opponents, with their overweening emphasis on the feminine erotic, was another. In addition, the harsh tone in which Wollstonecraft criticised sexualised femininity owed at least some of its severity to other discourses of social criticism. The fundamental opposition in the *Vindication* is between men and women, but this division is mapped onto others – the 'unnatural distinctions' of wealth and rank – which stood condemned within a large body of radical social theory. Wollstonecraft uses these theories (particularly those of Rousseau and Adam Smith) to produce a sociology of gender in which the position of women is seen as analogous to that of the idle rich. 'Women, in general, as well as the rich of both sexes, have acquired all the follies and vices of civilisation, and missed the useful fruit'.[58] Like the rich, women are granted privileges based not on what they do but simply on what they are; deprived of genuine rights and responsibilities, they make do instead with the temporary power of sexual conquest which earns them lives of 'false refinement', 'luxurious indolence' and 'enervating pleasure'. The language is redolent of republican disdain for the vices of the aristocracy. Luxury, eroticism and a narcissistic femininity are linguistically aligned: 'Confined ... in cages like the feathered race, they have nothing to do but to plume themselves, and stalk with mock majesty from perch to perch. It is true they are provided with food and raiment, for which they neither toil nor spin; but health, liberty, and virtue are given in exchange.'[59]

The vivid portrait clearly refers to women of wealthy backgrounds. But by Wollstonecraft's day the ideal it portrayed, the cult of the leisured lady, had moved downward into her own class, with – in her view – corrosive effects on traditional middle-class virtues of private respectability and public service. At one level the *Vindication* can be seen as a protest against this development – a rearguard defence of the eighteenth-century bourgeois 'goodwife' against the encroaching figure of the idle woman. From another direction it can be viewed as contributing to the development of the particular form of strident sexual puritanism which blossomed fully in the Victorian age. Both interpretations are certainly partially correct, since the late eighteenth century was a period of contestation over gender definitions within the middle class. The *Vindication* firmly placed itself within that contest. Since 'the instruction which has hitherto been addressed to women, has rather been applicable to *ladies* ... I pay particular attention to those in the middle class, because they appear to be in the most natural state'.[60] In fact, however, it is 'ladies' who still dominate the text, with ordinary middle-class women appearing infrequently and working-class women only as servants or 'the poor'. Nonetheless, Wollstonecraft's analysis certainly appears to be – does she not say so? – class-based. Most readings of the *Vindication* assume this, and then draw a direct connection between her class orientation and her sexual politics.

According to Cora Kaplan, for example, the *Vindication* is 'arguably as interested in developing a class sexuality for a radical, reformed bourgeoisie as in producing an analysis of women's subordination'.[61] In her influential essay Kaplan argues that Wollstonecraft's refusal of the erotic had its roots in the revolutionary class ideology of the bourgeoisie, in which was centrally inscribed an opposition between reason and passion, social order and sexual anarchy. The key figure here, as Kaplan notes and as we have already seen, was Rousseau whose 'radical project for the education and adult gender relations of an enlightened bourgeoisie ... depended for its success on the location of affection and sexuality in the family':

> The struggle between reason and passion has an internal and external expression in Rousseau, and the triumph of reason is ensured by the social nature of passion. Since male desire needs an object, and women are that infinitely provocative object, the social subordination of women to the will of men ensures that containment of passion. In this way Rousseau links the potential and freedom of the new middle class to the simultaneous suppression and exploitation of women's nature.[62]

The control and containment of sexuality in the family was essential not only to the maintenance of a patrilineal system of property inheritance but – of more fundamental importance for Rousseau – to the nurturance of those public sentiments and social virtues which made an orderly political existence possible. In the construction of the civic personality, sexuality had no legitimate place except in the carefully regulated production of new little citizens – all else, in Rousseau's words, was 'unredeemable chaos'.

Wollstonecraft was indeed deeply influenced by this position, as her reiterated evocation of the ideal citizen-mother (rational, industrious, and – above all – a companion to her husband rather than a lover) demonstrates. Yet there is more at stake in her sexual theorising than this. 'A wild wish has just flown from my heart to my head …' she writes, 'I do earnestly wish to see the distinction of sex confounded in society, unless where love animates the behaviour.' To confound the sexual distinction: here is the impulse, and far from exempting sexual love from her ambitions it is in fact there – in the realm of the erotic – that the impulse operates with greatest force. Commentators who view Wollstonecraft's feminism merely as an offshoot of a class-based democratic radicalism, and her sexual theory as essentially in service of bourgeois reformism, have forgotten that feminism has its own wild wishes, its complex agenda which Wollstonecraft helped to shape. 'It is the desire of being always women that degrades the sex', she tells us – and this *above all* with a lover, for it as the subjects and objects of libidinal love that women find themselves trapped within the feminine. Read through her anti-eroticism, Wollstonecraft's wish for a 'revolution in female manners' becomes the wild hope for a revolution of sexual subjectivity which will transform – at times she even hints supersede – gender as a psychological reality as well as a cultural force. 'Men are not always men in the company of women, and women would not always be women, if they were allowed to acquire greater understanding …'

This last quote is Wollstonecraft's direct re-working of a statement by Rousseau in which he is commenting on the difference between the sexes. 'A male is only a male now and again,' he writes, whereas, 'the female is always a female …'.[63] Passing over for a moment his assumption that sexual difference is invariably asymmetrical, let us look more closely at the extraordinary idea that precedes it: men are only men 'now Wollstonecraft's formulation: 'the sexual distinction which men have so warmly insisted upon, is arbitrary …',[64] a product of 'local customs' rather than nature. How did this idea emerge?

In the chapter of the *Vindication* titled 'Parental Affection' Wollstonecraft refers to Rousseau's famous distinction between *amour de soi* and *amour propre* – love of self and self-love – arguing that whereas the first is a 'natural and reasonable' emotion the second is a perverse selfishness which distorts all human relations. She mentions the distinction only in passing, yet many elements of it enter into her own account of feminine self-identity. As in Rousseau, so in Wollstonecraft the clamouring ego of *amour propre*, the civilised self, is seen as a mask over the face of the authentic self: the mask of culture and gender.

In the state of nature, according to Rousseau, the distinction between the sexes is merely lived rather than thought. Every individual, in his words, is a 'world unto himself', knowing only the instinctive needs of self-preservation (*amour de soi*). In this primordial, pre-cultural and pre-linguistic state there is no distinction made between self and other at all. The only emotion experienced is that of compassion, and empathetic pity based on identification (Rousseau continually describes the mother-child bond as the ideal relationship based on compassion). Sexual relations occur outside sentiment or emotion, within the realm of animal instinct and sensation which is pre-reflective and arbitrary as to its object:

this Rousseau dubs 'physical love' so to distinguish it from object-orientated erotic love, which he calls 'moral love'.

In men, the transition from physical to moral love is effected through the operations of the imagination. 'Imagination, which causes so much havoc among us, does not speak to savage hearts. Everyone waits peacably for the impulsion of nature, yields to it without choice ... and the needs satisfied, all desire is extinguished.'[65] But alas for this tranquil state: gradually men develop the capacity to compare one woman to another, and in doing so generate a fantasy of the ideal love object. Women, or rather images of women, thereby incite in men amorous passions 'in excess of man's power of satisfying those passions' – and it is in the gap between what may be gratified (the instinctive demands of physical love) and what is wanted (the idealised objects of moral love) that insatiable desire arises. It is this desire which forces men into speech (to state their desires) and into the ferocious sexual rivalry which inaugurates the life of the acquisitive ego: *amour propre*. It is also the point of entry into civil society, into the realm of law, prohibition, taboo, which must be entered if men are not to annihilate each other in the unrestricted warfare of competing sexual claims.[66]

It is through the operations of fantasy, then, that the eroticised self is created; the instinctual savage becomes the desiring subject yearning for ideal objects of love. Natural man gives way to social man, his sexuality shaped in a cultural psycho-drama. And natural woman? 'The consequences of sex,' Rousseau writes, 'are wholly unlike for man and woman.'

> The male is only a male now and again, the female is always a female, or at least all her youth; everything reminds her of her sex; the performance of her functions requires a special constitution.[67]

In women, in other words (in fact in Wollstonecraft's words), the 'sexual overwhelms the human character'. Men enter culture; women remain imprisoned in the realm of nature, locked inside primitive emotional and bodily states. Or so Rousseau mostly wants to claim – except when other ideas abruptly emerge. For the women who populate Rousseau's narratives also possess, in his words, 'vivid imaginations', including even the docile little Sophie who in a bizarre episode in *Emile* abandons the position of sexual object for that of a fantasising, impassioned subject whose own erotic object choice is the mythic Telemachus. No mere mortal man will do for little Sophie, and so like her creator she retreats from the banality of the real to love of the ideal, leaving her parents distraught and Rousseau in authorial difficulties, apparently bemused as to how to handle his rebellious heroine. Finally, in what must be one of the more peculiar moments in the early history of the novel, Rousseau takes himself directly into his narrative in order to retrieve his little model lady.

> Must I continue this sad story to its close? ... Must I portray the unhappy girl, more than ever devoted to her imaginary hero ... descending into the grave ...? No ... Let us give Emile his Sophie; let us restore this sweet girl to life and provide her with a less vivid imagination and a happier fate. I desired to paint an ordinary woman, but by endowing her with a great soul, I have disturbed her reason. I have gone astray ...[68]

And so Sophie is whipped back into line (and marriage to Emile) only to re-appear, her great soul intact, as the heroine of Wollstonecraft's first novel and the focus of the extended encounter with Rousseau which runs throughout her writings. In women, as in men,

Wollstonecraft argues, desire arises from the 'heated imagination' which paints for itself 'grand ideal objects of passion' and enslaves women to these objects, as they are themselves enslaved by the objectifying images men construct of them. It is not only as the targets of male desire but as the creators of their own erotic fantasies that women become absorbed into the sensual:

> taught to look for happiness in love, (women) refine on sensual feelings, and adopt metaphysical notions respecting that passion, which lead them shamefully to neglect the duties of life, and frequently … plump into actual vice.[69]

In her final, unfinished novel, *Maria, or The Wrongs of Woman*, the eponymous heroine falls in love: 'Maria's imagination found repose in portraying the possible virtues the world might contain. Pygmalion formed an ivory maid, and longed for an informing soul. She, on the contrary, combined all the qualities of a hero's mind, and fate presented a statue in which she might enshrine them' – with, according to the various endings Wollstonecraft drafted, tragic results.[70] In women, as in men, sexual love and the subjectivity moulded by it are imaginative artefacts: if men may be men only 'now and again', so also may women – the possibility of one immediately suggests the possibility of the other. 'Men are not always men in the company of women,' Wollstonecraft recapitulates Rousseau, 'nor would women always remember that they are women, if they were allowed to acquire more understanding.' If little Sophies must be hammered into the shape of women, then certain forms of womanhood may be abandoned – but with them must go not only the male desires which shape Sophie but her own fantasising eroticism likewise. And so the heroine of Wollstone-craft's first novel, *Mary: a Fiction*, written as a direct rejoinder to Sophie's fate, is entirely a-sexual, possessing a compassionate soul and a lively imagination which in her case, however, is fixed not on men but on God. And having created her fictional Mary, Wollstonecraft cannot resist presenting her to Rousseauite Man, represented as a poetic genius given over to cynical libertinism. The two characters meet:

> he found she had a capacious mind, and that her reason was as profound as her imagination was lively. She glanced from earth to heaven, and caught the light of truth. Her expressive countenance shewed what passed in her mind, and her tongue was ever the faithful interpreter of her heart; … [In] Mary's company he doubted whether heaven was peopled with spirits masculine; and almost forgot that he called the sex 'the pretty play things that render life tolerable'.[71]

But the price the fictional Mary pays for this splendid moral victory is an unhappy marriage (in which she felt a 'terrible sickness' whenever her husband made sexual approaches), a Platonic affair with, predictably, a dying man, and her own premature ascent into that realm 'where there is no marrying or giving in marriage'. And the pessimistic scenario does not alter much in Wollstonecraft's later texts – certainly not in the *Vindication* and not even in her final writings, produced after several love affairs.[72] The cost of womanhood was high – but high also the price of refusing it. Too high for Wollstonecraft herself, who could no more deny her sensuality than repress her intellect – yet the dilemma which she posed loses none of its significance through her own inability to resolve it. For as long as female self-hood is forged within structures of sex-based subordination – so long as the sexual distinction is in fact a site of division and opposition – so long must women's sexual subjectivity be a central site of feminist politics. That recognition is at least part of the legacy Mary Wollstone-craft has left to us.

My thanks to Jinty Nelson, Sally Alexander and Lyndal Roper for comments and advice, and to so many good friends for making the (eventual) writing of this essay possible.

Notes

1 Mary Wollstonecraft, *A Vindication of the Rights of Woman, with Strictures on Political and Moral Subjects* (1792), 1978, p. 147.
2 Cora Kaplan, 'Wild Nights: Pleasure/Sexuality/Feminism', in her *Sea Changes*, 1986, p. 34.
3 Wollstonecraft, *Vindication*, p. 199.
4 Letter from Mary Wollstonecraft to Everina Wollstonecraft, 24 March 1787, in Ralph M. Wardle (ed), *The Collected Letters of Mary Wollstonecraft*, 1979, p. 145.
5 Letter form Mary Wollstonecraft to the Reverend Henry Dyson Gabell, 13 September 1787, in Wardle, *Letters*, p. 162.
6 Wollstonecraft, *Vindication*, p. 103.
7 Letter from Mary Wollstonecraft to Gilbert Imlay, 22 September 1794, in Wardle, *Letters*, p. 263.
8 Mary Wollstonecraft, *Maria, or the Wrongs of Woman* (1798), 1975, p. 131.
9 Letter to Everina, 24 March 1787, in Wardle, *Letters*, p. 145.
10 Letter from Mary Wollstonecraft to William Roscoe, 3 January 1792, in Wardle, *Letters*, p. 205.
11 John Calvert, *Feminism*, 1982, p. 6.
12 Wollstonecraft began the *Vindication* with an open letter to Talleyrand in which she expressed her disappointment at the continued exclusion of women from political power in France, and her hope that her book would influence legislators to revise the constitution in women's favour.
13 Sally Alexander, 'Women, Class and Sexual Difference', *History Workshop Journal*, issue 17 (1984), p. 130.
14 Julia Kristeva, 'Women's Time', in Toril Moi (ed), *The Kristeva Reader*, 1986, pp. 186–213.
15 *Ibid.*, p. 194.
16 *Ibid.*, p. 202.
17 *Ibid.*, p. 209.
18 Jane Flax, *Thinking Fragments: Psychoanalysis, Feminism, and Postmodernism in the Contemporary West*, 1990, p. 179.
19 Edmund Burke, *A Letter from the Right Honourable Edmund Burke to a Noble Lord*, 1796, p. 21.
20 Richard Polwhele, *The Unsex'd Females*, (1793) 1800, p. 12.
21 *The Monthly Visitor*; quoted in Claire Tomalin, *The Life and Death of Mary Wollstonecraft*, 1974, p. 290.
22 Ralph Wardle, *Mary Wollstonecraft, a Critical Biography*, 1951, p. 159.
23 D.M. Stenton, *The English Woman in History*, 1957, p. 313.
24 William Godwin, *Memoirs of the Author of a Vindication of the Rights of Woman*, 1798.
25 R.M. Janes, 'On the Reception of Mary Wollstonecraft's *A Vindication of the Rights of Woman*' in *The Journal of the History of Ideas*, vol. 39, no. 2 (1978), p. 298.
26 *Eve and the New Jerusalem: Socialism and Feminism in the Nineteenth Century*, 1983 (reissued 1991).
27 Harriet Martineau, *Autobiography* vol. 1, (1877) 1983, p. 400.
28 Millicent Garrett Fawcett, Introduction to Wollstonecraft, *Vindication*, 1891.
29 Thomas Paine, *Rights of Man* (1791–2), 1977, p. 181.
30 Mary Wollstonecraft, *An Historical and Moral View of the French Revolution*, 1795, p. 20.

31 Wollstonecraft, *Vindication*, p. 85.

32 Samuel Pufendorf, *On the Law of Nature and Nations*, (1673) 1934, bk 6, ch 1, p. 853; quoted in Mary Lyndon Shanley, 'Marriage Contract and Social Contract in Seventeenth Century English Political Thought', in J. Bethke Elshtain, *The Family in Political Thought*, 1982, p. 89.

33 Mary Astell, *Reflections Upon Marriage*, 1700; quoted in Juliet Mitchell, 'Women and Equality', in J. Mitchell and A. Oakley (eds), *The Rights and Wrongs of Women*, 1976, p. 387.

34 Sophia, a Person of Quality (Lady Mary Wortley Montagu), *Woman not Inferior to Man*, 1739, p. 60.

35 J.G.A. Pocock, 'Cambridge Paradigms and Scotch Philosophers: a study of the relations between the civic humanist and the civil jurisprudential interpretation of eighteenth-century social thought', in E. Hont and M. Ignatieff (eds), *Wealth and Virtue: the Shaping of Political Economy in the Scottish Enlightenment*, 1983, pp. 235–6.

36 Wollstonecraft, *Vindication*, p. 185.

37 *Ibid.*, pp. 80–3.

38 Polwhele, *Unsex'd Females*.

39 Wollstonecraft, *Vindication*, pp. 80–1.

40 Wollstonecraft's passionate attachment to her friend Fanny Blood provided her with a model of reciprocal female devotion. At the same time, however, her attitude toward other women could be domineering and intolerant, as her letters indicate and as at least one woman who knew her in her Paris years (Madeleine Schweitzer) testified (see Margaret George, *One Woman's 'Situation': a Study of Mary Wollstonecraft*, 1970, for a thoughtful discussion of Wollstonecraft's complex feelings towards women).

41 Wollstonecraft, *Maria*.

42 Wollstonecraft, *Vindication*, p. 119.

43 *Ibid.*, p. 110.

44 *Ibid.*, p. 248.

45 *Ibid.*, p. 110.

46 Kaplan, 'Wild Nights', p. 36

47 Wollstonecraft, *Vindication*, p. 248.

48 *Ibid.*, p. 114.

49 Kaplan, 'Wild Nights', p. 35.

50 Wollstonecraft, *Vindication*, pp. 79, 83.

51 Jean-Jacques Rousseau, *Emile* (1762), quoted by Wollstonecraft, *Vindication*, pp. 185–6.

52 These passages from *Emile* are quoted by Wollstonecraft in chapter 5 of the *Vindication* (titled 'Writers who have rendered women objects of pity').

53 Wollstonecraft, *Vindication*, pp. 178–9.

54 *Ibid.*, pp. 127–8.

55 *Ibid.*, pp. 220–1.

56 *Ibid.*, p. 129.

57 *Ibid.*, p. 249.

58 *Ibid.*, p. 151.

59 *Ibid.*, p. 146.

60 *Ibid.*, p. 81.

61 Kaplan, 'Wild Nights', p. 35.

62 *Ibid.*, p. 40.

63 Wollstonecraft, *Vindication*, pp. 229n–30; Rousseau, *Emile*, English ed. 1918, p. 324.

64 Wollstonecraft, *Vindication*, p. 318.

65 Jean-Jacques Rousseau, *Second Discourse* (1755), New York, 1964, p. 136; quoted in J. Schwartz, *The Sexual Politics of Jean-Jacques Rousseau*, 1984, p. 14.

66 *Ibid.*, part two.

67 Rousseau, *Emile*, p. 324.

68 *Ibid.*, p. 368.
69 Wollstonecraft, *Vindication*, p. 306.
70 Mary Wollstonecraft, *Maria, or the Wrongs of Woman* (1798), 1975, p. 49 and pp. 151–4.
71 Mary Wollstonecraft, *Mary: a Fiction* (1788), 1980, p. 54.
72 Wollstonecraft's attitude toward sexuality in Maria is more nuanced than in the *Vindication*, probably in response to her own sexual experience. She still tended to view female eroticism as essentially tragic in its consequences for women, but much less reprehensible in itself. This shift is not surprising when one reads the letters she was writing to Godwin at the time: 'If the felicity of last night has had the same effect on your health as on my countenance, you have no cause to lament your failure of resolution,' she wrote on November 13, 1796, 'for I have seldom seen so much live fire running about my features as this morning when recollections – very dear, called forth the blush of pleasure, as I adjusted my hair.'

Chapter 7

Clarissa Campbell Orr

■ from 'A REPUBLICAN ANSWERS BACK: JEAN-JACQUES ROUSSEAU, ALBERTINE NECKER DE SAUSSURE, AND FORCING LITTLE GIRLS TO BE FREE' Chapter 2 of *Wollstonecraft's Daughters*, Manchester University Press, Manchester, 1966, pp. 61–70

HISTORIANS WHO HAVE EXAMINED in recent years the relationship of the French Revolution to questions of gender have agreed that the republican culture which emerged after the failure of a liberal, constitutionalist project to create a parliamentary monarchy (1789–92) was in many respects inimical to women. The direct political activism of the women's clubs was brought to an end by their closure in 1793. Jacobin republican culture was essentially masculinist, even misogynist. Central to its critique of the Ancient Régime was its belief that women had exercised undue influence in salon and boudoir over the cliques and secret factions inherent in Court-centred politics. Political power must instead be accountable to the sovereign people; words and deeds must be intelligible, transparent, incorruptible. Men must be citizens, acting heroically in the public sphere, reviving the civic virtue of the classical republic and if necessary dying for it. Women must acknowledge masculine authority both by exclusion from the public sphere and in deference to the male head of household in the private sphere. Yet the celebration of Roman models of patriotism which endorsed the sacrifice of family – of sons, husbands and fathers – to the needs of the *patrie* meant that Revolutionary republicanism was destructive of the very sphere, the family, assigned to women. This may have been one reason why French women in the Restoration continued to find republicanism unattractive; if it refused them citizenship, it also conceded them little real power in the private sphere.

A central strand of this republican ideology was of course derived from Rousseau, and it must be recognised how ambivalent was his message to and about women. It is evident that men and women felt liberated through their identification with his fictional characters and their emotional dilemmas, and that the cult of sensibility enabled women to see themselves as the heroines of their own life-dramas.

[...]

Rousseau believed it was essential to remodel motherhood, and the cult of natural motherhood and closer family affection indeed became fashionable even among the French Court whose values he had rejected.

[...]

Feminist historians have been divided over whether this cult of motherhood was ultimately to women's disadvantage or advantage. An emphasis on the importance of motherhood could and did lead to arguments for the better education of women precisely so that they could be better mothers; but this still tended to their exclusion from the civic sphere. The social contract was essentially between men. Wollstonecraft's own personal response to Rousseau led her to a rejection of Rousseauesque sensibility in favour of egalitarian rationalism. She was to conclude that motherhood necessitated participation in the public sphere for women as citizens: this, rather than her emphasis on the rationality of women was the measure of her radicalism.

[…]

Necker de Saussure's republican outlook therefore represents a different republican tradition from that of the Jacobins; it was one which was liberal, religious in an ecumenical not a dogmatic way, and one which believed that girls needed to be taught self-reliance and certain degree of autonomy even within the structure of marriage and family.

[…]

There were therefore spaces for women to be active socially, culturally, and to some extent intellectually, in Geneva's liberal republican society in a way that a Rousseausque/Jacobin republican culture would not have tolerated. True, there was no Court to act as a magnet for ambition and faction, no decadent monarchy, no *Parc aux Cerfs* supplying nubile girls for Louis XV, or *Petit Trianon* to amuse Marie Antoinette. But Genevan women were no domestic ciphers.

[…]

Women in Geneva were not able to participate directly in the political process, but in such an oligarchic system, politics was essentially about family concerns and strategies. Being *au fait* with public issues was tantamount to being familiar with the interests and deeds of one's father, husband, brother, son and so on; there was less of a disjunction between public and private spheres.

[…]

But it would I suggest be mistaken to regard her relative emancipation as characteristic of any but the elite few; rather, it represented a difference of degree, not kind, of freedom enjoyed by most Genevan women. The work of social historians suggests a pattern of intellectually developed, essentially sensible, and practically competent women similar to that associated in England with the Unitarian circles who were such an inspiration to Mary Wollstonecraft.

[…]

Women as well as men were able to initiate divorce, on the same grounds: adultery, desertion, and frigidity or impotence; and because a man leaving Geneva would lose his civic rights, it may have been that women felt they had less to lose in regularising their position.

[…]

These trends in Genevan society seem to have been little altered by the French occupation. In the Restoration epoch women were characterised by their intellectual interests, their role as social and moral educators, and their philanthropic activity. They were valued for their relational capacity, certainly – for being wives, mothers and daughters; but Genevan society preferred to see men also acting in a family context.

Albertine Necker de Saussure's recipe for the upbringing of girls is consistent with the social and cultural context sketched here of Genevan society. Her women would fulfil their religious, familial and social obligations, but they would so do in a self-possessed manner scarcely imagined by Rousseau. The advice she gives suggests that she wished to strike a balance between teaching them to be unselfish, and fostering their ability to make independent judgements. This advice was rendered in the context of a theory of historical progress characteristic of the Enlightenment.

[…]

Albertine Necker de Saussure certainly believed that in the past, social attitudes were detrimental to women's dignity, and that traces of this remained in women's sense of themselves:

> Whence then arises that lamentable alloy by which beings, evidently intended for better things, are so frequently debased? It seems to us that it is attributable in great measure to a cause of very remote date: to that degrading yoke of servitude so long imposed on them by men … its effects still remain – the trace of them is deeply impressed on the manners, the opinions, and even the thoughts of women. They have blindly adopted those humiliating maxims which it should have been their object to subvert.
>
> […]

But modern society, Necker de Saussure argues, is still flawed in its treatment of women: men still tend to regard women as their property, not persons in their own right who may have other talents to fulfil, in addition to their roles as wives and mothers. For Necker de Saussure, women cannot be exclusively defined by their relational capacities. Although in her view men and women have distinct natures, they also have gifts that are similar, including intellectual attributes. Difference of attainment is due solely to different education, not differential capacity.

Necker de Saussure's [sic] strongly criticised an education for women designed solely to meet masculine requirements: 'his object has been to render woman an instrument either for the gratification of his passions, or the advancement of his interests.' The result is that his aims are defeated: 'in vain will he be continually changing his system, and require from education by turns a mistress, an artist, or a housekeeper; he will never gain a wife, a companion, a being truly formed to be the charm and comfort of his life.'

Marriage is a likely and natural state for all women, but it is by no means the be-all and end-all of their lives. Their upbringing should be designed to develop their own individual potential as persons and moral beings, as well as equip them to enter into relations with others, and be trained to educate their own children. This sense of identity is also necessary because some women may not marry, and even the majority who do will in the end need to find resources to meet widowhood and old age. The outer limit of Necker de Saussure's vision therefore includes the single women who may have to earn her own living and will need a sense of her worth.

Like many liberals, she did not envisage a fundamental revision of structures and institutions. She wanted to change attitudes, so that while society has the same forms, it was animated by a different spirit. This may make her sound essentially conservative, but it may be argued that because she wants to alter the way women see *themselves,* her prescriptions are far more radical and comprehensive than if she had called for an enlargement of women's social and economic opportunity, without first reaching to the core of their internalised habits of deference and self-deprecation.

In sum, she wanted to foster in a young woman 'a happy mixture of humility and dignity'. Admittedly her sphere will be that of private life; her special influence will be the family; but consistent with Geneva's view of the significance of family life, 'to perfect, to animate, to embellish and sanctify private life' is no mean task, but 'a great and exalted object'.

[...]

Chapter 8

Anna Clark

■ from 'THE STRUGGLE OVER THE GENDER DIVISION OF LABOUR, 1780–1826', Chapter 7 of *The Struggle for the Breeches: Gender and the Making of the British Working Class*, Rivers Oram Press, London, 1995, pp. 119–120, 140

ONE DARK GLASGOW EVENING IN DECEMBER 1809, a few dozen cotton weavers left their wives and children toiling over looms and hurried down dank steps into the back room of a spirit cellar. This was no ordinary evening of drinking and carousing, but a special meeting of the Incorporated Weavers of Glasgow to discuss how to regain the prosperity they had once enjoyed. Following artisan tradition, they resolved to restrict the trade to those who had served an apprenticeship and joined their association. Yet they faced a dilemma. Although the organized weavers ornamented their membership tickets with female figures of Britannia and Justice, they could not decide whether to permit women in their association or to attempt to prohibit them from weaving. Perhaps the married men whose families depended on their wives' and daughters' labor objected to efforts to ban them from the loom, while the bachelors belligerently protested that these females undercut a single man's wage. Unable to agree, the weavers simply postponed the discussion – but in bleak January, snowy February, and rainy March, they could never resolve the issue and reconcile family needs with trade union strategy.

The weavers were drawing upon a long tradition of artisans combining into a trade union to restrict the unapprenticed – especially women – from working in their craft. They justified their efforts through the notion of 'property in skill', clearly assumed to be a masculine quality of honor. However, during the Napoleonic wars, their ability to keep out unskilled workers eroded. Thousands of men were pressed into the navy or joined the militia, then flooded back into the labor market as the fighting waxed and waned. While some trades suffered from the blockade, others boomed with the demand for military material such as uniforms. During labor shortages, manufacturers encouraged artisans and textile workers to teach their daughters and wives skills such as shoemaking and weaving, extolling the opportunity to bring more cash into the family. But when unemployment again loomed, employers impatient with their proud mechanics plotted to replace them with docile females on new machines or subdivided labor processes.

In response, workers organized to defend the 'moral economy' of their trades against the onslaught of deskilling, mechanization, fluctuating wages, and the decline in apprenticeship. Strikes against women workers, who were often used to introduce machinery and to replace apprenticed workmen, was one of their chief tactics. Between 1806 and 1811, hatters, calico printers, tailors, and framework knitters all struck against women in their occupations, and warpers, weavers, and cotton spinners also expressed concern over this competition. When these strikes failed to hold back the tide of deskilling, workers petitioned Parliament to improve their lot. In 1813, various trades organized to petition Parliament against the proposed repeal of the Statute of Artificers, which would end the legal requirement of apprenticeship. They defended the honor and pride of their skill and called on the government to regulate the balance of interests between masters and men. When workers argued that employers who hired unapprenticed workers robbed them of what they began to call their 'property in skill,' they invented a rhetoric to 'articulate what they had always assumed'. But strikes and parliamentary agitation eventually failed as tactics to keep women and other unskilled workers out of artisan and textile occupations.

Until the 1820s, artisans and textile workers found it difficult to formulate convincing replies to these accusations. References to drinking and debauchery hit close to home, for the carousing that bonded male workmates no doubt deterred many wives from supporting strikes. When masters claimed they should be able to employ poor women to save them from the streets, in response artisans could only bluster about their right to their trade. Organized workers did not yet demand a breadwinner wage in order to protect their wives and daughters from the contamination of wage labor.

[...]

To be sure, workers in the first two decades of the eighteenth century [sic nineteenth century] laid the groundwork for the later trade union movement. They formed powerful combinations which often defeated employers, and they began to create the infrastructure for the working-class movement as a whole. This period witnessed innovative instances of cross-occupational solidarity, including the campaign for a weavers' minimum wage that was supported by other artisans, the apprenticeship campaign of 1813, and the Lancashire strikes of 1818. But organized workers had not yet gained a sense of class consciousness. A large number of British workers shared the experiences of insecurity if not poverty, deskilling and unemployment, but many still did not perceive that they had interests in common with other proletarians. While workers often expressed resentment of their profiteering masters, they did not see themselves as locked into two antagonistic classes. Instead, they wished for a return to the days when masters and men shared culture, community, and craft rewards. More important, they were divided among themselves. In many instances, the organized artisans would welcome a man only if he was 'not a companion of the low and vulgar part of the community'. Traditional artisans in particular limited their organizations to the pub and workshop, determinedly excluding women and therefore limited their community base. Textile workers were sometimes able to draw men, women, and children together in a kin, neighborhood, and workplace community solidarity, but even then their actions pitted one group of workers against others who were more marginal and vulnerable. Frustrated by increasingly futile actions and weak industrial discourses, working people often concentrated on radical political actions, which developed a more inclusive rhetoric and forms of mobilization at an earlier date than trade unions.

PART THREE

Nineteenth Century

THIS VERY LARGE SECTION reflects the importance of the social, political and economic changes taking place in Europe. The nineteenth century was shaped by the dual revolutions occurring in industry and politics. As working patters and practices changed, they impacted not only on relationships between men and women but also between classes. Conditions for women lagged significantly behind those of men. Working practices became overtly gendered and ideas about 'skill' became imbued with notions of masculinity. While working-class men began to campaign for their political rights in movements such as Chartism – the British movement which aimed at radical political reform including universal *manhood* suffrage – women's role was restricted to a subordinate position, that of supporting the men's struggle.

Furthermore, across Europe women's sexuality was constrained, restricted and regulated. Women therefore were seen as potential threats to both men's economic status and to the moral standing of society. In addition as the century developed, so too did ideas of the nation-state and perceptions of national characteristics impacted on constructions of gender. Starting in 1500, the first article, Honeyman and Goodman, here reproduced in full, gives an overview of these changes.

Maxine Berg, in an article which has become a classic, discusses how new technologies and division of labour became gendered in industrialising Britain. Following on from this, the meaning of femininity is considered by Sally Alexander. This discussion is developed by the fascinating article on a neglected topic by Ann Goldberg. The treatment of nymphomania in German insane asylums reveals the ways in which what was seen as unacceptable female behaviour was regulated and 'helped construct a bourgeois normative ideal of womanhood: women were to be fragile, passive, modest, submissive and maternal'.[1]

Turning to politics an extract from Jutta Schwarzkopf's seminal work, *Women in the Chartist Movement* shows that 'women's special task is seen to consist in lending male Chartists the moral support deemed indispensable to the victory of the movement'. Nevertheless it was 'the first step ... into the public arena' for some women.[2] Schwarzkopf compares the view of some Chartists that women were intellectually able with the perception of female identity expounded by the growing Evangelical movement. Catherine Hall further comments on Evangelical images of women showing how these were crucial to 'The increasingly important Victorian middle-class ideal of womanhood – "the angel in the house"'.[3] She concludes that 'The bourgeois ideal of the family became a part of the dominant culture and, by the 1830s and 1840s, was being promoted through propaganda as the only proper way to live'.[4] This ideal influenced the nature of women's working lives as de Groat, Hilden, and Fuchs and Moch show. However the ideal was far from the reality in that working-class women could not afford the luxury of remaining in the domestic sphere but had to take part in public work. Nevertheless, as Hilden shows, Belgian moralists, legislators and industrialists were only too keen to intervene in their female workforces' perceived sexual excesses. In Belgium, as Hilden writes, women's hard manual labour was socially acceptable in contrast to many European countries where protective legislation for women was successfully introduced. Hilden records the way in which Belgian miners' unions began to organise the increasing number of women coal miners 'both by creating separate women's sections in each union and by organising mixed sex unions'.[5] The 'potentially independent' women of the Belgian coal mines contrast with the vulnerable women from rural France who arrived in Paris seeking work. Fuchs and Moch point to 'a clear link between migration to the city and sexual vulnerability'.[6]

Walkowitz takes attitudes to female sexuality further by discussing prostitution in nineteenth-century Britain. Concluding this section, Coons reveals how the strength of the domestic ideology, a theme running throughout this section, moulded the experiences of working mothers in the Parisian garment industry. She shows that in nineteenth-century France motherhood '...became the duty and *raison d'être* of women and their ultimate reward as well'.[7] However, underlining the point made in earlier articles that the image and reality were far apart, the birth rate in France continued to fall. Thus homework was seen as a solution to women's need to work, but not outside the home, but this was one of the most exploited areas of the labour market. Feminist responses were ambiguous even socialist feminists 'stopping short of denouncing home industry'.[8]

Notes

1   Goldberg p 109 below.
2   Schwarzkopf p 114 below.
3   Hall p 120 below.
4   Ibid p 123 below.
5   Hilden p 144 below.
6   Fuchs and Moch p 153 below.
7   Coons p 188 below.
8   Ibid p 194 below.

Chapter 9

Katrina Honeyman and Jordan Goodman

■ 'WOMEN'S WORK, GENDER CONFLICT, AND LABOUR MARKETS IN EUROPE, 1500–1900' *Economic History Review,* XLIV (4), 1991, pp. 608–28

T HE POSITION OF WOMEN in the labour markets of Europe from the middle ages to the beginning of the twentieth century has been the subject of a substantial and vital research effort in recent years.[2] In this area of enquiry, as so often in the social sciences, greater certainty surrounds what happened than why it happened. The central problem in the history of women's work is to explain the nature of and changes in the gender division of labour and the persistence of women in the lowest paid, least stable, and most unrewarding occupations.[3] A wealth of detail is presented in recent research on working women in the past which suggests a framework for its analysis. The three main features of this framework can be identified as follows. The first involves an escape from the periodization prevalent in social and economic history which is inappropriate to the history of women's work and has previously resulted in faulty and misleading assumptions. The most serious of these misconceptions has been the attempt to explain the origins of women's oppression within the context of the emergence of industrial capitalism. The best research of recent years has clearly revealed that labour markets in which women face discrimination are of very long standing and were not the creation of the forces of industrialization.[4]

The second component suggests an emphasis on periods of gender conflict as of crucial importance. It is by focusing on such crisis periods, which might arise for a number of reasons, that a clearer appreciation of the causes of a particular gender division of labour can develop. Two particularly intense periods of gender conflict in the workplace were manifest in Europe: from the late fifteenth to the end of the sixteenth century, and from the early nineteenth century.[5] Both episodes apparently occurred because artisans and other skilled men believed their position of economic strength and thus patriarchal power to be under threat. The outcomes in both cases included a more clearly specified gendering of jobs, new restrictions on the employment of women, and a reduction in the value placed on women's work associated with a greater emphasis on their domestic position in the family.

The third feature of this framework concerns the nature of patriarchy and its institutions especially in times of exceptional crisis.[6] It is now more readily accepted than in the past that the economic, political, and social subourdination of women has been at least partly determined by patriarchal forces, although too general a usage of patriarchy as an explanation has weakened its potential as a tool of analysis. Patriarchy can be defined as a pervading societal system or set of institutional arrangements which accept, reinforce, or structure male hegemony. There is nothing 'natural' about this system. Patriarchy is a construct, real and imagined. What is relevant in the present context is that patriarchy may seem inevitable because for long periods its forces are inactive and apparently invisible (and sometimes even denied), and its presence is affirmed only when threatened. It is at this point of 'active' patriarchy that its characteristics become open to examination.

By considering the recent contributions to the literature within the framework as outlined, it is hoped to show that significant progress has been made towards an understanding of the long-established gender division of labour and to indicate how it may be extended by further empirical investigations.

I

In early modern European cities occupational categories for men and women were already differentiated and there was a dual or segmented labour market.[7] Men's work comprised the primary labour market. Jobs were skilled, or perceived as such; they conferred a high degree of status and they were well rewarded both financially and in non-monetary ways. In workshop production, the locus of artisanal labour, wages formed the lesser part of the payment for work; of greater importance were customary rights to advanced payments and credit, widespread systems of subcontracting, and payments in food and lodgings. Social rewards, status, esteem, independence of supervision, dignified treatment, and mobility were part and parcel of this world.[8] Craftsmen more often resembled independent business-men than workers. In the building industry in early modern England, for example, craftsmen not only supplied their own raw materials, but earned a significant proportion of their income from a variety of economic sources.[9] Evidence from Parisian workshops in the eighteenth century points to a similar conclusion.[10]

The characteristics of women's work already conformed to those of a secondary labour market where employment was largely unskilled, of low status, poorly paid, casual, seasonal, and irregular. Working women operated within a narrow occupational structure, were generally more prone than men to long periods of underemployment and unemployment, and enjoyed few of the security buffers built into men's work. In industrial activities women were more dependent upon monetary wage payments than were men. With little other compensation, women workers were particularly vulnerable to the vagaries of the early modern economy. This reinforced the irregular rhythm of work.

Although a dual labour market clearly existed in the early modern economy, its origin is difficult to trace. It seems clear, however, that while the nature of men's work remained constant, fundamental changes in women's employment patterns occurred in the late middle ages. We turn, therefore, to the mechanisms by which women's position in the labour market became secondary. The transformation of women's work began in towns where women became excluded from crafts and skilled work and were relegated to low paid and low productivity employment. Prior to this subourdination, medieval urban women were relatively well represented in a variety of high-status occupations, though the pattern of their work was by no means uniform across Europe.[11] In some northern European cities, such as Bruges, Leiden, and Douai, women figured prominently in the manufacture of high-quality woollen cloth, filling managerial and other esteemed occupations. In other cities, however, such as Cologne, Florence, and Paris, women were less conspicuous in such positions or were entirely barred from them. Similarly, women participated in long-distance trade and in craft activities in London and Cologne but not in Paris and Venice. The explanation for this disparity is not entirely clear, but it is certain that medieval guilds were not always hostile to women; girls were apprenticed and women occupied official positions in many guilds. In Paris and Cologne, moreover, some guilds were run exclusively by women though membership was open to both sexes.[12]

In northern European cities, women appear to have occupied high status positions in the labour market chiefly in those economic activities where production was organized on the basis of family units; that is, where family members shared in the production of goods and services for the market rather than selling their labour.[13] High status derived mainly from the independence associated with access to raw materials and control over distribution. As the family production unit began to lose its hold over market production in Leiden, Cologne, Douai, and Frankfurt from the late fifteenth century, the position of women in the labour market declined noticeably. Organizational changes in the economy of these cities weakened the family production unit as it strengthened other modes of production, notably small commodity production and capitalist production. The main victims of these changes were women who, finding their access to high status positions increasingly restricted, retreated from market production altogether. Economic forces were clearly at work, but they were not the primary cause of the changes in women's work experience. The patriarchal order, increasingly under threat from the participation of women in market production, ensured that these economic changes were distributed differentially between men and women. The exclusion of women from high status positions in turn served to reinforce patriarchy within changed economic circumstances.[14]

Organizational changes in industrial production were certainly responsible for some changes in the working experiences of women but a much more gender-inspired movement was on its way led by urban craft guilds. Their strategy was to attack women directly as workers. This onslaught took several forms. Some guilds chose to pursue a policy of barring women from participation in their affairs. In some cities, this exclusion was achieved in incremental stages while in others, women were simply forced out. In fifteenth-century Leiden, for example, women were completely excluded and the guilds became male preserves. In Cologne, where women had actively participated in the guilds during the middle ages, their passage into marginality was less direct and immediate yet equally effective. By the late fifteenth century, almost all of the city's guilds had become male preserves with the exception of a few whose activities, such as needlework, embroidery, and belt-making were becoming defined as women's work.[15]

Another recourse was the imposition of a gender identification of work activities within individual guilds. In early modern German towns, for example, it became common for the tailors' guild to restrict the kind of work that seamstresses were allowed to do. In general, seamstresses were relegated to working with old, used, or cheap cloth while male tailors reserved the right to all other types. The bleaching and dyeing trades also distinguished minutely between men's and women's work, the latter being confined to small or used articles. In hatting, male guild members sought to bar women totally from making hats but when this failed, they settled for a compromise whereby women were confined to the least prestigious work of veil making, and hat repair.[16]

Evidence from a number of European economies, however, indicates that the most common form of attack was completely to close women's access to particular trades. Wherever this happened the result was the same: the range of occupations open to women became severely restricted; and because those that were available became defined as women's work, they normally ceased to be attractive to men. In Geneva, the marginality of women in the city's guild system had become well established by the mid sixteenth century. Few women remained in the skilled trades; their work identity was generally weak and their wages were particularly low. Apprenticeships for girls were confined to a narrow range of trades, such as those of laundress and seamstress and, overall, girls accounted for only a small proportion of the total number of apprentices. Women were found in domestic service, watchmaking, textile production, and working as seamstresses and laundresses, but rarely elsewhere.[17] In Frankfurt, Strasbourg, Nuremburg, Meningen, Stuttgart, and Munich, women were also excluded form a large number of crafts and, more generally, from the world of work. Male workers attempted to reduce competition for jobs by singling out and removing women. Journeymen demanded restrictions on women's work, even in instances where this worked against their own economic interests. Wives were prevented from earning decent wages and widows, who had been given unrestricted rights to carry on their former husband's shop in early German guild ordinances, found these curtailed.[18] In Augsburg, for example, widows were not permitted to keep apprentices, and in general, there was a growing hostility towards women operating independently of their men.[19]

Guilds did not, however, confine themselves simply to restricting the kinds of work women could practise; they also sought to define the proper spheres of productive and unproductive work in gender terms alone. In central Europe during the seventeenth and eighteenth centuries, conflict arose between guilds and household production units over the definition of productive work.[20] Guildsmen feared that rural household production, which could produce goods at lower cost than urban artisans, would undermine their monopoly position. Guilds had previously been hostile to rural production, but after the middle of the seventeenth century, their attack was directed as much at women as producers as at rural household production. Guildsmen, therefore, sought to debar the household from the market economy and, thereby, women from productive work. Gender, rather than industrial organization, became the determining factor. In future, esteemed productive work was to be a male sphere and domestic duties a female and less respected one.

The identification of gender as the criterion in deciding work values is also evident in the rhetoric of guilds and city councils in early modern Germany. Prohibitions on women's work were argued on the ground of gender alone. Some city councils seem to have been unashamedly hostile to women workers but were restrained in their desire to exclude women from the labour market altogether because of the likelihood of their becoming a burden. Low paid casual occupations were tolerated for this reason. Journeymen, too, took advantage of the chorus of anti-female rhetoric by successfully appropriating productive tasks which had previously been the responsibility of the master's wife and daughter.[21]

The origins of the guilds' hostility to women are still very poorly understood. That it was part of a complex process is beyond doubt, but its precise location is unclear. Guilds, for example, were involved in an intense political struggle with the state and guild monopolies over a wide variety of industrial work were themselves being attacked. On the other hand, women were also the target of both spiritual and secular authorities; institutions such as marriage and the family were subject to profound transformation. Whatever the explanation for the hostility, its impact on working women was straightforward, Some urban women retreated from the labour market altogether, and presumably found some refuge in the home; others, however, swelled the casual and irregular labour market and gravitated towards the distributive trades as well as towards large-scale, non-artisanal industrial production.[22] In the Florentine wool and silk industries, for example, women formed the majority of the workforce, appropriating tasks such as weaving which had earlier been male preserves; in the Bolognese silk industry all of the weavers were women. In both cases, the preponderance of women workers can be explained by the exclusion of women from artisanal trades and by the fact that the output of these industries consisted of simple cloths requiring little skill or capital.[23] By contrast, the silk industries in Lyons, Genoa, and Venice produced rich and complicated cloths and the vast majority of weavers were male.[24]

There was nothing inherently female or male about any activity, nor were the categorizations static; what identified gender and work was the intersection of the economic and gender systems. In the period from the late fifteenth century to the middle of the seventeenth, guilds, and through them, male artisans, were instrumental in creating an altered ideology of gender and work. The idea and reality of female artisan which was common in the middle ages became untenable in the early modern period. The privileges, the work identity, and the customary rights, trappings of artisanal work values, became the exclusive domain of skilled men. By setting artisanal work apart from work in general, guildsmen were also equating women with the unskilled—a critical signpost for the future. It is true, of course, that many working women were in occupations unrepresented by guilds, but the important point is that it was the guild which provoked gender conflict in the workplace.

The exclusion of women from a wide range of industrial occupations was an urban phenomenon. The countryside seems to have been devoid of the kind of hostility towards working women that existed in the towns.[25] The boom in the demand for rural industrial labour beginning in the late sixteenth and early seventeenth centuries swelled the number of women working in industrial production.[26] It is very likely that women's labour was critical to the expansion of rural industrial production, especially that of textile manufacture.[27]

By the late seventeenth century, women's work in urban Europe had settled into a new pattern. No longer associated directly with the artisanal trades, women were now confined to a narrow band of industries consisting primarily of textile manufacture and the clothing trades. Outside industry, the chief areas of women's work were retailing and domestic service.

II

Despite the changes in industrial organizations that occurred in nineteenth-century Europe with their attendant pressures on employment patterns, the position of women in the labour market remained fundamentally the same. The functions performed by men and women within the pre-factory manufacturing sector persisted in the nineteenth century but not without intervening upheaval. The possibility of restructuring gender relations in the labour market was momentarily indicated by changes in production methods, but ultimately men retained their monopoly of the more rewarding occupations.[28] Female labour played a critical role in the expansion of the various processes of industrial capitalist production.[29] While the factory was the most striking feature of nineteenth-century industrial transformation and depended heavily on women workers, cheap female labour was also used in the expansion of domestic service,[30] as the basis of some new urban and rural trades, and in the proliferating urban sweatshops of late nineteenth-century Europe.[31] Women, therefore, provided much-needed flexibility within the context of innovation, while men steadfastly maintained their domination of better-paid occupations and traditional crafts.[32]

From as early as the 1820s, but also during the later nineteenth century, gender relations in the labour market were temporarily disrupted. Anti-female sentiments, akin to those prominent in early modern guild politics, resurfaced. While the rhetoric and the exclusionary strategies were redolent of an earlier age, the gender conflict of the nineteenth century embraced novel social concerns. The marital status of women took on a new significance as protective legislation, the cult of the family wage, and the ideology of domesticity interacted to emphasize gender inequality in the labour market and to establish a hierarchical structure of employment that persists to the present. Thus, in nineteenth-century European labour markets, as married women became more overtly marginalized, young women and single women predominated in the visible urban trades. In the textile factories, for example, they commonly accounted for the bulk of the unskilled workforce,[33] and they dominated domestic service occupations and some sectors of garment-making in the towns and cities of England, France, Italy, and Germany.[34]

Later in the nineteenth century, the service sector provided new openings, particularly for unmarried women. Single women found work in the department store, which appeared in the larger European cities in response to the growth of consumerism. These new retail outlets provided employment on a grand scale; the Bon Marché in Paris, for example, employed 2,500 sales assistants in the 1880s and the Louvre, 3,500–4,000 in 1900.[35] Although some men were employed in these stores, women were much preferred because of their cheapness, because they were sober and polite, and because they were considered to be docile. The work was unskilled and low paid, and for women was usually curtailed on marriage.[36] The introduction of the typewriter in the last quarter of the nineteenth century restricted clerical occupations and also provided new opportunities for women. Male workers gained from this change, however, for, while women were allocated low status secretarial jobs, men moved into high status office work in banks and insurance companies.[37] The majority of female clerical occupations were reserved for the unmarried, and in most European offices, a marriage bar operated until well into the twentieth century.[38]

Married women's employment followed an altogether different pattern. The precise nature of their work is, however, difficult to ascertain. Many married women did not enter the official statistics (or other records) precisely because of their location in the secondary labour market and because their work was irregular, casual, and sometimes only semi-legal.[39] In many parts of industrial Europe, women tended to withdraw from the more visible areas of waged work—the factory and the workshop—upon marriage, and seek employment that could accommodate household responsibilities.[40] In Britain and Germany, this trend began before the mid nineteenth century, while in France the social and political pressures discouraging the gainful employment of married women began to emerge later in the century.[41]

Married women workers in nineteenth-century Europe were so concentrated in urban domestic industry that it is no exaggeration to speak of its feminization as one of the principal components of European industrialization.[42] They clustered in the clothing industry, in various forms of retail trading, and in menial occupations (like laundressing) that resembled household chores, a pattern reminiscent of the early modern period. The making of clothes, for example, had long been an important component of women's work and in most large cities of industrial Europe, the practice of the handicraft trades of plain sewing, shirtmaking, and button stitching apparently proved the salvation of women with family responsibilities in need of an income.[43] Plenty of such work existed and it was rare to find a clothing firm that did not employ many women at home in addition to those in the factory or workshop.

From the 1830s onwards, the numerous occupations subsumed within the general description of clothing employed thousands of women in the major European cities. Sweated labour either in the home or in what were euphemistically termed family workshops (sweatshops) prevailed in all the needleworking trades, where women worked irregularly for little reward.[44] The greater part of this workforce consisted of married women. In Berlin in 1887, for example, 75 per cent of all homeworkers were married, widowed, or separated women,[45] with an identical proportion of these categories employed as outworkers in Hamburg in 1913.[46] The introduction of the sewing machine considerably extended the possibilities for sweatshop and homeworking employment for women. Not only did it allow women to reconcile domestic functions with wage earning, and to comply with the late nineteenth-century moralists' feminine ideal, but it permitted the clothing manufacturers to make full use of a cheap and flexible labour force at a time when the expansion in the demand for ready-to-wear clothing placed great pressure on existing methods of production and suggested greater subdivision of tasks.[47]

The garment industries of Paris, Hamburg, and London were typically organized on the basis of outwork (or a refined putting-out system) making use of the large female labour force available in the fast expanding cities.[48] The system was capable not only of mass output, but also of the rapid expansion and contraction crucial in a trade where extreme seasonal fluctuations in demand occurred.[49] This was the case in the clothing industry generally and in women's fashions in particular. The women who dominated the labour force in this sector suffered very irregular employment.[50]

A clear, yet complex gender division of labour existed in the nineteenth-century European garment trades which distinguished workers both by the tasks they performed and by the location in which they performed them. The vast majority of outworkers were women, and those men that did enter the sweating sector did so as managers and middlemen.[51] Men monopolized such skilled work as remained within the scope of the generally unskilled ready-to-wear sector. Specializing in tailoring and the production of outerwear, men worked in small workshops and abhorred the practice of homeworking.[52] Women, by contrast, operated mainly in the mass production sector, at home, making women's garments, underwear, millinery, and standard workmen's clothes.[53] Outwork and homework also interacted with larger scale production in other sectors of the clothing trade. In the Parisian flowermaking trade, for example, which was partially mechanized, a large part of the production process was carried out in the homes of individual workers or in small workshops. As in other trades, a clear division of labour existed, whereby men were responsible for the dyeing and cutting, while women specialized in shaping and branching that required more manual dexterity.[54]

While homeworking suited the needs of many women, it did not end men's antipathy towards low-paid female labour. Indeed, in some instances, particularly in the early nineteenth century, skilled craftsmen were angered by the competition of cheaper and less skilled female domestic labour. In the early 1820s, tailors in the Saxon city of Naumburg an der Saale believed their families' livelihoods to be threatened and their own training undermined by the work of seamstresses engaged in dressmaking in their own homes.[55] Similarly, journeymen tailors in London in the 1830s accused sweatshop women of undercutting their product and of lowering their living standards.[56]

The expansion of domestic work, an integral component of nineteenth-century European industrial development, was the result both of married women's need to find socially and politically acceptable employment and of the increasing subdivision of tasks within the factory production. Mechanization in one part of the work process, for example, often generated the growth of homework in another;[57] and the growth of large factories could give rise to a division of labour that included (unskilled) tasks that could be performed easily by hand or by small machines at home. By making use of a plentiful supply of cheap female labour in a domestic setting, the capitalists not only reduced their labour costs by 25–50 per cent on factory levels,[58] but also diluted the power of the artisan by interfering in the continuous struggle between men and women for job recognition. Thus the greater division of labour served to intensify the gender segregation of the workforce and further confirmed the position of the primary and secondary labour markets.[59]

Working women were therefore employed, as before, in less skilled and lower paid occupations than the majority of men irrespective of the nature and location of their work. Thus, young single women who performed similar tasks to their male counterparts in factories were as disadvantaged as their married sisters who operated from home or in domestic-like environments in occupations that were almost exclusively 'female'. That women's position in the labour market remained subourdinate in the context of economic and industrial change was by no means automatic, but was more the result of a number of powerful interacting forces that emphasized women's domestic role and men's position as family breadwinners. These forces were patriarchal in character, and include the ideology of domesticity,[60] state protective legislation,[61] the widespread demand for the family wage, and the craftsman's successful efforts to monopolize technology and skill.

III

The hierarchical division of labour was confirmed in the nineteenth century after a brief interlude when, in some industries, notably textiles, greater employment opportunities were created for women by changes in the organization and technology of production and were supported by capitalist interests.[62] As artisans had used their control over the guilds in the late medieval and early modern period to resist women's encroachment on skilled and well-paid occupations, so skilled men in nineteenth-century Europe, fearful of an erosion of their position at work and at home, employed a range of restrictive practices for similar ends. Their actions included the manipulation of the very techniques that might potentially have undermined their own position: the deskilling implicit in the new technology itself was compounded by the threatened introduction of cheap and 'less skilled' female labour. Through the activities of the trade unions to which skilled men had enforced a restricted entry from the beginning of the century, they achieved control over the use of technical innovations, enhancing their own position and extending the inequality between men's work and women's work. One of the results of their actions was a 'gendering' of machinery: particular technologies commonly became associated with one sex only.[63] Men monopolized the bulk of nineteenth-century inventions,[64] while some machines, such as the typewriter, and to a lesser extent the sewing machine, became the preserve of women. Integral to the gendering of technology was a gendering of skill, such that skilled work became associated only with male machines, while 'women's machines' were confined to low-paid, unskilled, and exploitative occupations.[65] Thus, by restructuring notions of skill, craftsmen both avoided much of the deskilling potential of the new technology and further strengthened the perception of their own work as skilled and that of women as unskilled.

This general pattern (subject to variation among industries and techniques) was the outcome of a series of individual struggles between men and women for control over technology and thus of skilled employment. The most widely cited examples of such struggles, over the mule in cotton spinning,[66] and the compositing machine in the printing industry,[67] reveal the mechanisms by which machines were monopolized and skill was reconstructed within a novel framework. The introduction of the self-actor in the 1830s removed all technical barriers to the use of unskilled labour on the mule, but despite the efforts of many cotton factory masters to introduce willing female labour, the mule craft unionists closed ranks and successfully repelled the challenge to their position.[68] Among other tactics they persuaded the employers that they would relieve them of some of the task of controlling the labour force.

By careful redefinition, mule spinning remained a skilled job, largely entrusted to male hands. Although the new spinning system required a different range of tasks, skilled craft status persisted, not for technical reasons (though sometimes mechanical adjustment was required) but because the operator assumed responsibility for the management of the labour process and for quality control.[69] The ability to supervise had earlier been established as a skill to which only men had access, and by arguing that this was an essential component of the new system, the craftsmen retained control over employment. In cotton spinning, a hierarchical gender division of labour was established where mule spinning was male and skilled, while women, using older techniques, performed the unskilled work. The gender of the actor, more than the technology itself, determined the status of the work.[70]

Gender conflict within the traditionally male-dominated printing trade similarly inverted the potential impact of technical development. The late nineteenth-century introduction of an American invention represented a major leap forward in compositing which both removed the physical restraints on the employment of women in this stage of the production process and reduced the necessary level of skill. The male printers' antipathy towards the proposed introduction of cheaper female labour was revealed in both France and Britain through the immediate and concerted actions of the male craft unions.[71] In France, the Couriau affair illustrated both the level of hostility aroused and the effectiveness of male solidarity;[72] while in Britain, the eventual monopoly of the new technology and the retention of skill by the male printers was facilitated by the poor organization of the print manufacturers.[73] Neither women nor employers resisted the long-established might of the craftsmen and, despite the temporary appearance of female compositors in Scotland, their proportion ultimately changed little in either Britain or France.[74]

Whatever the gender association of a new technology, it served to raise the level of male skill relative to that of women. The sewing machine was quickly identified with women and the growth of unskilled, casual sweated labour, and homeworking.[75] It exemplified the position of women, especially married women, in late nineteenth-century industrial Europe.[76] It provided women with the opportunity to integrate wage earning with domestic functions and thus to conform to the ideology of domesticity; and as a domestic technology, it served to emphasize the hierarchical gender division of labour and especially women's position as marginalized and casual workers.[77] Women's monopoly of the use of the typewriter forced a restructuring of skilled activities and a heightening of the gender division of labour within clerical work. Categories previously occupied by men became filled by women and redefined as unskilled, as men moved into newly created skilled jobs.[78]

Nineteenth-century technology was far from neutral in its influence on gender divisions in the workplace. Through machinery, jobs were constructed with the gender of their occupants in mind, ensuring that women were crowded into low paid jobs which emphasized their previously established gender role as supplementary wage earners.[79] The process was frequently activated by skilled male unionists responding to a perceived threat of cheap female competition with its potential for weakening patriarchal authority. The institutional environment supported the male cause, as the ultimate goal of the skilled men—the removal of women from the labour market—found a parallel in the concerns of other social groups. Patriarchal forces underpinned women's subourdinate position in the labour market and were particularly manifest in the actions of the state.

IV

The proletarianization of female labour in nineteenth-century Europe provoked extensive debate about the position of women in the economy. In Britain in the 1840s and in France and Germany towards the end of the century, the visible participation of women in the labour market was considered a problem both morally and because it challenged patriarchal power.[80] A range of possible solutions was discussed, including the total elimination of women's wage labour, equal pay, and sex segregated spheres of work. The most popular answer, however, was protective legislation which attempted to restrict female and child labour in factories and mines. Such legislation was introduced in Britain in 1842, in Germany in 1891, and in France in 1892.[81] It was designed to reinforce the position of women as wives and mothers and certainly helped further to marginalize women's position in the labour market.[82] German factory inspectors at the turn of the twentieth century, for example, waxed lyrical at the success of their labour legislation in returning women to the home.[83] Thus, as women were squeezed out of employment in the public arena, they were forced either into purely domestic activities or into homeworking or sweatshop employment. Though it has been argued that domestic work was a means by which factory owners in late nineteenth-century France could avoid the restrictions imposed by law, it is as likely that the legislation itself provided the capitalist with the opportunity to remove women from the factory into the more economical environment of the sweatshop.[84] Although protective legislation established a precedent for improved working conditions for all workers, it was more significant in driving a wedge between men's work and women's work in industry. It excluded women from competition in important arenas of production and offered them little alternative but to work in unprotected places where gender conflict was minimal.[85]

The marginalization of female labour, an essential factor in the making of the modern family, was compounded by the persistent advocacy of the family wage.[86] That the norm of a breadwinner wage did not become a reality before 1914, does not detract from its signi-ficance in the nineteenth century as a principle that tended to undermine women's position in the labour market.[87] The idea of an individual male breadwinner earning sufficient to maintain a wife and children emerged in most parts of Europe during the course of the nineteenth century in parallel with an emphasis on women's domestic role, reducing their economic value and encouraging the diffusion of the 'ideal' bourgeois family form. This family wage was an unrealistic goal for the majority of working people, yet it was supported by most—women as well as men—and became a plank of male union wage demands. Men believed that with the introduction of a breadwinner wage, women's involvement in the labour market would be reduced. They would thus be less likely to compete for scarce jobs and to drive down the price of labour. As a result, men's position in the labour market would be greatly improved, not only absolutely but also in relation to the power of the employers.[88] The attainment of the family wage would also strengthen patriarchy, since a dependent and full-time housewife provided men with power and privileges in both the home and the workplace.[89]

The concept of the family wage, which originated with skilled workmen, also found support in the state, among capitalists, and in the middle class.[90] Pressure for its introduction grew in Britain from early in the nineteenth century, but emerged on the continent only from 1850. In France, where more women remained in paid employment upon marriage than in most other industrial European economies, the perception of working women as a problem and of the threat of their labour to the skilled working man arose relatively late.[91] It was not until the 1880s and 1890s that male unionists began to press for a family wage,[92] and middle-class concern over the well-being of children heightened demands for women to return to home duties with the financial support of a bread-winning husband.[93]

From the early nineteenth century the concept of the breadwinner wage and the bourgeois family gained currency, aided by changes in work practices, of which the most important was the decline of family hiring and subcontracting.[94] Consequently, women became employed as individuals, competing with men in the labour market and earning an independent wage.[95] This threat to the job security of skilled workers was antithetical to the patriarchal environment that had existed virtually unchallenged since the earlier period of upheaval in the sixteenth century. The pressure placed on patriarchy by nineteenth-century industrial developments reawakened the need to reinforce—if not redefine—patriarchal structures. In the nineteenth century, patriarchy became associated with many separate but related issues which, as they undermined women's economic role and emphasized their domestic responsibilities, strengthened the power of fathers and husbands both in the labour market and at home.[96] The growth of feminism, of anti-feminism, and of the politics of fertility control, all of which became central issues in the late nineteenth and twentieth centuries, need to be seen in this context.

By the outbreak of the First World War, European working women were burdened by actions of the state and by a pernicious domestic ideology which confined them to traditional areas of employment. Occupations in the new industries of the late nineteenth and early twentieth centuries, such as engineering, car manufacture, steel, chemicals, and electricity, which had grown directly out of the anti-female artisanal sector, were effectively closed to women.[97]

V

In recent years it has become clear that such periods of transition in European history as the Reformation, the industrial revolution, and the rise of capitalism are of limited relevance to historians of women's work.[98] While industrialization affected the structure of the gender division of labour, it was not responsible for instigating women's subordinate position in the labour market.

The most profitable current approach to an analysis of this subordination stems from Hartmann's pathbreaking discussion of the relationship between patriarchy and capitalism. She identified two systems underlying the pattern of women's work—the economic and what has been called the sex-gender system.[99] Historically, these systems have interacted, sometimes in opposition and confrontation, at others in unison, to create a specific gender division of labour. Economic forces influence the nature of women's employment within a particular sex-gender system.

The sex-gender system and its principal component, patriarchy, remain in the background so long as changes within the economic system do not impinge on the operation of the system. But when changes in women's economic position threaten to upset the equilibrium of the sex-gender system, the response of the patriarchal component is to establish a new set of rules defining the acceptable gender division of labour in the workplace. The momentous historical episodes of confrontation between these systems have been few but protracted. Only two have occurred between the middle ages and the twentieth century.

One of the main conclusions to emerge from recent publications is that female work patterns and domestic preoccupations—the dialectic of production and reproduction—were not solely or primarily determined by economic forces but by complex relationships between patriarchy and economic materialism. Pleas for further research into the nature and operation of patriarchy are commonplace, but it must be emphasized that patriarchy should be examined within historically specific situations.[100] The most rewarding of these are likely to be major periods of confrontation when actions determined by patriarchy were most clearly revealed.[101] There may indeed be, as Bennett suggests, 'many histories of many patriarchies',[102] but this would not preclude the identification of the most salient features of patriarchal forces and the deconstruction of the sex-gender system.

University of Leeds
University of Manchester Institute of Science and Technology

Notes

1 We should like to thank Peter Earle for his valuable comments on an earlier version of this article.
2 The most recent general treatment of the history of European women is Boxer and Quataert, *Connecting spheres*. See also Hanawalt, *Women and work*; and Bridenthal, Koonz, and Stuard, *Becoming visible*. Earlier surveys and general studies include Tilly and Scott, *Women, work and family*; Hufton, 'Women in history'; Scott, 'Women in history'.
3 This article focuses on the literature on women in industrial occupations. The problem of women in agricultural work has been largely excluded on the grounds that to do it justice would require a far longer essay. Notes 25–7 refer to some of the literature on this.
4 Bennett, 'History'; Thomas, 'Women'.
5 Gender conflict in the workplace can be argued to be a continuous feature of the politics of work. By isolating two momentous instances of such conflict, we are not denying this, but it is during these episodes only that fundamental changes in the pattern of women's employment occurred.
6 An approach supported by, among others, Bennett, 'Feminism', pp. 263–4.
7 There is a large literature on dual labour markets and labour market segmentation but nothing which explicitly treats the subject historically. See for example Sullivan, *Marginal workers*; Reich, Gordon, and Edwards, 'A theory'; Cain, 'Challenge'. For criticisms and applications to the problems of women's work see Blau and Jusenius, 'Economists' approaches', pp. 190–8; Walby, *Patriarchy at work*, pp. 80–5.

8 An assessment of the various forms of labour payments and their change over time is needed. Useful insights are, nevertheless, available. See, for example, Sonenscher, *Work and wages*; idem, 'Journeymen'; idem, 'Weavers'; idem, 'Work and wages'; Rule, *Labouring classes*; Hobsbawm, *Labouring men*, pp. 344–70. In sixteenth- and seventeenth-century England, wage earners were generally assumed to be paupers and regarded as unfree; see Hill, 'Pottage for freebourn'.

9 Woodward, 'Wage rates'.

10 Sonenscher, 'Work and wages'.

11 The use and meaning of status in occupations is discussed in Howell, *Women, production*, p. 24. For the position of women in medieval Europe see idem, 'Women, the family'; Bennett, *Women*; Jacobsen, 'Women's work'. For a dissenting voice, see Kowaleski and Bennet, 'Crafts, gilds and women'.

12 Howell, 'Women, the family', p. 200; Wensky, 'Women's guilds'; idem, *Stellung der Frau*.

13 Howell, *Women, production*, pp. 24, 27–8. Howell uses the term 'family production unit' with a similar meaning to the 'family economy' as defined by Tilly and Scott, *Women, work and family*, p.12.

14 Howell, *Women, production*, pp. 174–83.

15 Howell, 'Women, the family', pp. 202–13.

16 Wiesner, *Working women*, pp. 178–80.

17 Monter, 'Women in Calvinist Geneva', pp.199–204. See also Snell, 'Apprenticeship of women'.

18 Wiesner, *Working women*, pp. 3, 157.

19 Roper, 'Work, marriage and sexuality', pp. 62–81

20 The following is based upon Quataert, 'Shaping of women's work', pp. 1122–35.

21 Wiesner, *Working women*, pp. 11–35, 194–8. See also Roper, 'Women, marriage and sexuality', pp. 16–81.

22 Wiesner Wood, 'Paltry peddlers'; Wiesner, 'Spinsters and seamstresses', pp. 203–5; idem, 'Women's work', pp. 67–9.

23 Brown and Goodman, 'Women and industry'; Poni, 'Proto-industrialization', p. 313; Goodman, 'Tuscan commercial relations', pp. 337–8.

24 Davis, 'Women in the crafts'; Garden, *Lyon et les lyonnais*, pp. 225–8; Massa, *La 'fabbrica'*; Rapp, *Industry and economic decline*, p. 28.

25 This is partly explained by the absence of guild control over rural industrial production. Historians disagree, however, over the precise nature of gender divisions in rural industrial production. See, for example, Berg, *Age of manufactures*, pp. 129–58; Hufton, 'Women and the family'; idem 'Women without men'; Gullickson, 'Sexual division of labour'; idem, *Spinners and weavers*, pp. 52–3; Snell, 'Agricultural and seasonal unemployment'; Roberts, 'Sickles and scythes', pp. 18–9; Wrigley, 'Men on the land', p. 336; Boxer and Quataert, *Connecting spheres*, pp. 42–4. These stress the existence of clear divisions. Medick, 'Proto-industrial family economy', pp. 61–3 and Quataert, 'Combining agrarian and industrial livelihood', p. 151 argue for a neutral situation. Much work remains to be done.

26 There is now an enormous literature on the expansion of rural industry in early modern Europe. The field is surveyed in Clarkson, *Proto-industrialization*. For market conditions and background to these developments see Goodman and Honeyman, *Gainful pursuits*. Agricultural regions most favoured for the expansion of industrial production were those with a large landless or land-poor population. See Gullickson, 'Agriculture and cottage industry'; Quataert, 'New view'; Gullickson, *Spinners and weavers*; Holmes and Quataert, 'Approach to modern labour'; Quataert, 'Combining agrarian and industrial livelihood'. Many young women who would earlier have migrated to towns in search of industrial work and apprenticeships, now remained at home contributing to the family economy. See Snell, 'Apprenticeship of women'; Berg, *Age of manufactures*, p. 155; Monter, 'Women in Calvinist Geneva', p. 200; Carmona, 'Economia toscana', p. 38. In addition, if young, unmarried women remained in the countryside until they married, they tended to continue to work in the same employment when married—see,

for example, Gullickson, *Spinners and weavers*, pp. 129–61 and Hufton, 'Women, work and marriage'. This may account, in part, for the generally stagnant populations of European industrial cities; de Vries, *European urbanization*; Hohenberg and Lees, *Urban Europe*, pp. 106–36. The importance of young unmarried women in the labour force during the transition to factory production of textiles has been emphasized for Europe, the United States, and Japan. See Tilly and Scott, *Women, work and family*, pp. 151–6; Goldin and Sokoloff, 'Relative productivity'; Saxonhouse and Wright, 'Two forms'.

27 The best account is given by Gullickson in *Spinners and weavers*, pp. 46–85; idem, 'Agriculture and cottage industry'; idem, 'Proto-industrialization'.

28 This pattern is still not fully accepted. Although early or more traditional historians strongly believed that new opportunities, or even emancipation for women, accompanied nineteenth-century industrial change (for example George, *England in transition*; Pinchbeck, *Women workers*; and Landes, *Unbound Prometheus*), the weight of opinion is now on the side of those (like Richards, 'Women in the British economy') who argue for a decline in women's economic position. Many of this latter group also favour the notion that before the capitalist era, women had enjoyed a golden age of economic opportunity, as suggested by the work of Clark, *Working life*. On the golden age see Hanawalt, *Women and work*, pp. vii–xviii and Bennett, 'History that stands still'.

29 For the use of women's labour and the persistence of hand and intermediate techniques as an alternative to or in association with mechanization see Berg, *Age of manufactures*, pp. 145–51 and idem, 'Women's work, pp. 76–7. The role of children, particularly in the early factories, has recently been questioned by Freudenberger, Mather, and Nardinelli, 'New look'. See also Heywood, *Childhood*, pp. 97–145.

30 Tilly, 'Paths of proletarianization'; idem, 'Family, gender and occupations'.

31 Schmiechen, *Sweated industries*.

32 They continued to use the apprenticeship system, but, increasingly, they prevented women gaining access to the newest technology, and thus, commonly, to the best jobs; Rule, 'Property of skill'; Humphries, 'Sexual division of labour'.

33 Richards, 'Women in the British economy', p. 346; Tilly and Scott, *Women, work and family*, p. 82. The preponderance of young, unmarried females in cotton factories is also indicated in Hall, 'Home turned', pp. 24–5. The work of Hilden, *Working women*, pp. 278–9, however, shows that in the late nineteenth century, in the mill towns in the Nord, well over half of all women workers who married remained in employment. Why the Nord diverged from the general pattern is not at all clear.

34 Scott and Tilly, 'Women's work', p. 39.

35 McBridge, 'A woman's world', p. 65.

36 Ibid., pp. 670–1, 679.

37 Davies, 'Woman's place'; Zimmeck, 'Jobs for the girls', pp. 159–60.

38 It was the mid 1930s before married women were employed in the British Civil Service; see Zimmeck, 'Strategies and strategems', pp. 903–4, 922–4. On clerical work in the postal services in Germany, France, and England see Nienhaus, 'Technological change'.

39 This feature of under-recording in the official sources is illustrated in many studies, including Alexander, *Women's work*, pp. 11–4, 49–64; Roberts, *Women's work*, pp. 17–22; Scott and Tilly, 'Women's work', p. 40; John, *Unequal opportunities*, introd., pp. 36–41.

40 Typically at home and frequently jobs like sewing or clothes washing that resembled household chores.

41 According to Offen, 'Feminism, antifeminism', p. 183, 40 per cent of the female French labour force in 1901 were married; Hilden, *Working women*, pp. 278–9, estimates the equivalent figure for the Nord to be 58 per cent in the same year.

42 Franzoi, '…With the wolf', pp. 149, 154; Boxe and Quataert, eds, *Connecting spheres*, p. 101. See also Boxer, 'Protective legislation', pp. 47–51; Jordan, 'Exclusion of women'.

43 Franzoi, '…With the wolf', pp. 149–50.

44 Alexander, *Women's work*, pp. 30–40; Boxer, 'Protective legislation', pp. 45–7.

45 Hauser, 'Technischer Fortschritt', p. 163.

46 Dasey, 'Women's work', p. 243.

47 Perrot, 'Femmes et machines', pp. 12–3.

48 Hohenberg and Lees, *Urban Europe*, pp. 175–247.

49 Dasey, 'Women's work', pp. 232–4.

50 Ibid., pp. 238, 243; Hauser, 'Technischer Fortschritt', p. 163.

51 Hauser, 'Technischer Fortschritt', p. 160 and Dasey, 'Women's work', p. 235, although this was not true of the male immigrant workers, mostly Jews, in late nineteenth-century British cities who tended to be confined, or often associated with sweated, unskilled work; see Schmiechen, *Sweated industries*, pp. 32–7, 189; Bythell, *Sweated trades*, p. 175.

52 Scott, 'Men and women', p. 70.

53 Dasey, 'Women's work', p. 235.

54 Boxer, 'Women in industrial homework'.

55 Quataert, 'Shaping of women's work', pp. 1122–3.

56 Alexander, *Women's work*, pp. 31–2; Taylor, *Eve*, pp. 101–17.

57 A widely recorded phenomenon; see for example, Rendall, *Origins of modern feminism*, pp. 171–3; Tilly and Scott, *Women, work and family*, pp. 123–36.

58 Boxer, 'Protective legislation', p. 49.

59 Rendall, *Origins of modern feminism*, pp. 155–8.

60 Boxer, 'Protective legislation', p. 47; Hall, 'Early formation'. See also Rose, 'Proto-industry', p. 191.

61 The French legislation of 1892, which was supported by a further act of 1900, is discussed in Boxer, 'Protective legislation', pp. 46–7. A similar chronology applied to Germany. In Britain, state intervention in women's work began rather earlier, with the Mines Act of 1842. The significance of this is considered in Humphries, 'Protective legislation' and John, 'Colliery legislation'. According to Schmiechen, *Sweated industries*, pp. 134–60, the Factory and Workshop Acts of 1891 and 1895 may have helped to drive productions into domestic and other unregulated conditions of labour.

62 There is little doubt that the majority of capitalists preferred to employ women (and would have done so to a greater extent in the absence of male resistance).

63 Rose, '"Gender at work"', p. 119 and *idem*, 'Gender segregation', pp. 172–3 make explicit reference to the gendering of machines in the English midlands hosiery industry in the nineteenth century and it is implicit in much other writing on nineteenth-century capitalism. Such allocation of machines to particular genders may well have existed before the nineteenth century, but very little evidence on this subject is available.

64 Most notably the self-acting mule in cotton spinning and the compositing machine in the printing trade which will be discussed below.

65 Except where they were used by men, for example, when skilled male tailors used the sewing machine.

66 Most of the detailed research on this has focused on Britain, but evidence indicates parallels elsewhere; Lazonick, 'Industrial relations'; Freifeld, 'Technological change'; Valverde, 'Giving the female'.

67 See Cockburn, *Brothers* and *Machinery of dominance*, pp. 15–43 for an overview. In France, the Couriau affair—a dispute in the printing industry—sent ripples through the entire French labour movement. This is extensively discussed in the literature, notably by Sowerwine, 'Workers and women'. See also Boxer and Quataert, eds, *Connecting spheres*, p. 185.

68 Until the early nineteenth century, women and men had commonly engaged together in union activity. Beginning in the 1820s, women were denied access as to unions skilled male unionists practised exclusionary tactics; Rose, 'Gender antagonism'; Jordan, 'Exclusion of women'.

69 Freifeld, 'Technological change'; Rose, 'Gender segregation', pp. 173–4. The monopoly of supervision by men had been generally established well before the nineteenth century, although there is some evidence that in France, it was not unusual to see women supervising men at the end of the eighteenth century; Perrot, 'Femmes et machines', p. 8.

70 This is discussed by Lazonick, 'Industrial relations'; Freifeld, 'Technological change'; Valverde, 'Giving the female', pp. 621–5.

71 Boxer, 'Foyer or factory', p. 192.

72 Sowerwine, 'Workers and women', pp. 427–41. The meaning of the Couriau affair is subject to debate—the protagonists are discussed in ibid., pp. 412–4. See also Boxer and Quataert, eds, *Connecting spheres*, p. 185.

73 Cockburn, *Brothers*, pp. 28–9.

74 Ibid., pp. 23, 26–31; Sowerwine, 'Workers and women', p. 415.

75 While higher, indeed skilled, status was accorded to work performed by men using the sewing machine.

76 Perrot, 'Femmes et machines', pp. 7, 12–3, 15–7; Hauser, 'Technischer Fortschritt', pp. 157–63; Offen, '"Powered by a woman's foot"'; Offen, 'Feminism, antifeminism', p. 183; Dasey, 'Women's work', p. 228.

77 It even became an 'instrument of women's servitude' as suggested by Boxer, 'Protective legislation', p. 49.

78 Davies, 'Woman's place', pp. 248–59; Zimmeck, 'Jobs for the girls', pp. 159–60.

79 Rose, '"Gender at work"', pp. 118–28.

80 Implicit in a good deal of the literature; Boxer, 'Protective legislation', pp. 45–7; Hilden, *Working women*, p. 165; and Seccombe, 'Patriarchy stabilized'.

81 John, 'Colliery legislation'; Boxer, 'Protective legislation'.

82 Ibid.; Rose, 'Proto-industry', p. 191; Seccombe, 'Patriarchy stabilized', pp. 63–4, 73–4.

83 Quataert, 'Source analysis', p. 120.

84 Boxer, 'Protective legislation', pp. 49–50.

85 Ibid., p. 55.

86 Ibid., p. 47.

87 Mark-Lawson and Witz, 'From "family labour"', p. 154.

88 Seccombe, 'Patriarchy stabilized', p. 55.

89 Ibid., pp. 58–9; Rose, '"Gender at work"', pp. 125–6.

90 Seccombe, 'Patriarchy stabilized', pp. 65–74. Murray, 'Property and patriarchy', however, considers that the historical structuring of property along gender lines (for reasons of kinship) would have given rise to the male breadwinner ideology.

91 Hilden, *Working women*, pp. 278–9.

92 This coincided with the death of feminism in socialism which had occurred in Britain in the 1830s; Boxer, 'Foyer or factory', p. 199. See also Offen, 'Depopulation, nationalism'; idem, 'Defining feminism'.

93 Offen, 'Feminism, antifeminism', p. 183.

94 The exclusion of women from the workplace was often argued on economic grounds, that is that women competed for jobs with men and drove down the wages for all; Boxer, 'Foyer or factory', pp. 196–8.

95 Seccombe, 'Patriarchy stabilized', p. 66.

96 Including skilled male unionism, the family wage, a domestic ideology, the notion of the bourgeois family, and protective legislation.

97 See for example, Jordan, 'Exclusion of women'; Stockmann, 'Gewerbliche Frauenarbeit'; Wecker, 'Frauenlohnarbeit'; Burdy et al., 'Rôles, travaux et métiers'. A useful survey of women's work in Germany can be found in Fout, 'Working-class women's work'.

98 See the documents by Thomas, 'Women and capitalism'; also Shorter, 'Women's work'; Bennett, 'History that stands still'.

99 Hartmann, 'Capitalism patriarchy'. See also Neuschel, 'Review'; Seccombe, 'Patriarchy stabilized'; Rose, '"Gender at work"', pp.119–20; Howell, *Women, production*, pp. 27–46, 178–83; Walby, *Patriarchy at work*, pp. 5–69.

100 The best discussion of the trouble with patriarchy can be found in Walby, *Patriarchy at work*, pp. 22–37. The most recent historical work which stresses this approach can be found in Howell, *Women, production*. See also n.99 above as well as Davis, 'Women in the crafts', pp. 71–2; Rose, 'Gender segregation', pp. 178–80; Hilden, 'Class and gender'. One well-discussed exception is Stone, *Family, sex and marriage*, pp. 151–218. See also Hanley, 'Family and state'.

101 Bennett, 'Feminism', pp. 263–4.

102 Ibid., p. 262

Footnote references

Secondary sources

Alexander, S., *Women's work in nineteenth-century London: a study of the years 1820–50* (1983).

Bennett, J.M., 'History that stands still: women's work in the European past', *Feminist Stud.*, XIV (1988), pp. 269–83.

Bennett, J.M., 'Feminism and history', *Gender & Hist.*, I (1989), pp. 251–72.

Bennett, J.M., *Women in the medieval English countryside* (New York, 1987).

Berg, M., *The age of manufactures, 1700–1820* (1985).

Berg, M., 'Women's work, mechanisation and the early phases of industrialisation in England', in P. Joyce, ed., *The historical meanings of work* (Cambridge, 1987), pp. 64–98.

Blau. F.D. and Jusenius, C.L., 'Economists' approaches to sex segregation in the labour market: an appraisal', *Signs*, I (1976), pp. 181–99.

Boxer, M.J., 'Foyer or factory: working class women in nineteenth-century France', *Proc. Western Soc. French Hist.*, II (1975), pp. 192–206.

Boxer, M.J., 'Women in industrial homework: the flowermakers of Paris in the Belle Epoque', *French Hist. Stud.*, XII (1982), pp. 401–23.

Boxer, M.J., 'Protective legislation and home industry: the marginalization of women workers in late nineteenth-century France', *J. Soc. Hist.*, XX (1986), pp. 45–65.

Boxer, M.J. and Quataert, J.H., eds, *Connecting spheres* (New York, 1987).

Bridenthal, R., Koonz, C. and Stuard, S., eds, *Becoming visible: women in European history* (Boston, 1987).

Brown, J.C. and Goodman, J., 'Women and industry in Florence', *J. Econ. Hist.*, XL (1980), pp. 73–80.

Burdy, J.-P., Dubesset, M., and Zancarini-Fournel, M., 'Rôles, travaux et métiers de femmes dans une ville industrielle: Saint-Étienne, 1900–1950', *Le Mouvement social*, 140 (1987), pp. 27–53.

Bythell, D., *The sweated trades* (1978).

Cain, G.G., 'The challenge of segmented labour market theories to orthodox theory: a survey', *J. Econ. Lit.*, XIV (1976), pp. 1215–57.

Carmona, M., 'Sull'economia toscana del cinquecento e del seicento', *Archivio Storico Italiana*, CXX (1962), pp. 32–46.

Clark, A., *Working life of women in the seventeenth century* (1919).

Clarkson, L., *Proto-industrialization: the first phase of industrialization?* (1985).

Cockburn, C., *Brothers: male dominance and technological change* (1983).

Cockburn, C., *Machinery of dominance* (1985).

Dasey, R., 'Women's work and the family: women garment workers in Berlin and Hamburg before the First World War', in R.J. Evans and W.R. Lee, eds, *The German family: essays on the social history of the family in nineteenth and twentieth century Germany* (1981), pp. 221–55.

Davies, M., 'Woman's place is at the typewriter: the feminization of the clerical labour force', in Z. Eisenstein, ed., *Capitalism, patriarchy and the case for socialist feminism* (New York, 1978), pp. 248–66.

Davis, N.Z., 'Women in the crafts in sixteenth-century Lyon', *Feminist Stud.*, VIII (1982), pp. 47–80.

De Vries, J., *European urbanization, 1500–1800* (1984).

Fout, J.C., 'Working-class women's work in imperial Germany', *Hist. Eur. Ideas*, 8 (1987), pp. 625–32.

Franzoi, B., '"… With the wolf always at the door…": women's work in domestic industry in Britain and Germany', in M.J. Boxer and J.H. Quataert, eds, *Connecting spheres* (New York, 1987), pp. 149–54.

Freifeld, M., 'Technological change and the "self-acting" mule: a study of skill and the sexual division of labour', *Soc. Hist.*, XI (1986), pp. 319–43.

Freudenberger, H., Mather, F.J. and Nardinelli, C., 'A new look at the early factory labour force', *J. Econ. Hist.*, XLIV (1984), pp. 1085–90.

Garden, M., *Lyon et les lyonnais au xviiième siècle* (Paris, 1975).

George, D., *England in transition* (Harmondsworth, 1931).

Goldin, C. and Sokoloff, K., 'The relative productivity hypothesis of industrialization: the American case, 1820 to 1850', *Qu. J. Econ.*, XCIX (1984), pp. 461–87.

Goodman, J., 'Tuscan commercial relations with Europe, 1550–1620: Florence and the European textile market', in *Firenze e la Toscana dei Medici nell'Europa del'500*, 3 vols (Florence, 1983), I, pp. 327–41.

Goodman, J. and Honeyman, K., *Gainful pursuits: the making of industrial Europe, 1600–1914* (1988).

Gullickson, G.L., 'The sexual division of labour in cottage industry and agriculture in the Pays de Caux: Auffay, 1750–1850', *French Hist. Stud.*, XV (1981), pp. 177–99.

Gullickson, G.L., 'Proto-industrialization, demographic behavior and the sexual division of labour in Auffay, France, 1750–1850', *Peasant Stud.*, IX (1982), pp. 106–18.

Gullickson, G.L., 'Agriculture and cottage industry: redefining the causes of proto-industrialisation', *J. Econ Hist.*, XLIII (1983), pp. 831–50.

Gullickson, G.L., *Spinners and weavers of Auffay* (Cambridge, 1986).

Hafter, D.M., 'The programmed brocade loom and the decline of the drawgirl', in M.M. Trescott, ed., *Dynamos and virgins revisited: women and technological change in history* (Metuchen, 1979), pp. 49–66.

Hall, C., 'The early formation of Victorian domestic ideology', in S. Burman, ed., *Fit work for women* (1979), pp. 15–32.

Hall, C., 'The home turned upside down? The working class family in cotton textiles, 1780–1850', in E. Whitelegg, ed., *The changing experience of women* (Oxford, 1982), pp.17–29.

Hanawalt, B., ed., *Women and work in pre-industrial Europe* (Bloomington, 1986).

Hanley, S., 'Family and state in early modern France: the marriage pact', in M.J. Boxer and J.H. Quataert, eds, *Connecting spheres* (New York, 1987), pp. 53–63.

Hartmann, H., 'Capitalism, patriarchy, and job segregation by sex', *Signs*, I (1976), pp. 137–69.

Hauser, K., 'Technischer Fortschritt und Frauenarbeit im 19. Jahrhundert: zur Sozialgeschichte der Nähmaschine', *Geschichte und Gesellschaft*, IV (1978), pp. 148–69.

Heywood, C., *Childhood in nineteenth-century France* (Cambridge, 1988).

Hilden, P., 'Class and gender: conflicting components of women's behaviour in the textile mills of Lille, Roubaix and Tourcoing, 1880–1914', *Hist. J.*, XXVII (1984), pp. 361–85.

Hilden, P., *Working women and socialist politics in France, 1880–1914: a regional study* (Oxford, 1986).

Hill, C., 'Pottage for freebourn Englishmen: attitudes to wage labour in the sixteenth and seventeenth centuries', in C.H. Feinstein, ed., *Socialism, capitalism and economic growth* (Cambridge, 1967), pp. 338–50.

Hobsbawm, E.J., *Labouring men* (1964).

Hohenberg, P.M. and Lees, L.H., *The making of urban Europe, 1000–1950* (Cambridge, Mass., 1985).

Holmes, D.R. and Quataert, J.H., 'An approach to modern labour: worker peasantries in historic Saxony and the Friuli region over three centuries', *Comp. Stud. Soc. & Hist.*, XXVIII (1986), pp. 191–216.

Howell, M.C., 'Women, the family economy and the structure of market production in cities in northern Europe during the late middle ages', in B. Hanawalt, ed., *Women and work in pre-industrial Europe* (Bloomington, 1986), pp. 198–222.

Howell, M.C., *Women, production and patriarchy in late medieval cities* (Chicago, 1986).

Hufton, O., 'Women and the family economy in eighteenth-century France', *French Hist. Stud.*, IX (1975), pp. 1–22.

Hufton, O., 'Women, work and marriage in eighteenth-century France', in R.B. Outhwaite, ed., *Marriage and society: studies in the social history of marriage* (1981), pp. 186–203.

Hufton, O., 'Women in history: early modern Europe', *P. & P.*, 101 (1983), pp. 125–41.

Hufton, O., 'Women without men: widows and spinsters in Britain and France in the eighteenth century', *J. Fam. Hist.*, IX (1984), pp. 255–76.

Humphries, J., 'Protective legislation, the capitalist state and working class men: the case of the 1842 Mines Regulation Act', *Feminist Rev.*, VII (1981), pp. 1–33.

Humphries, J., '"…The most free from objection…": the sexual division of labour and women's work in nineteenth-century England', *J. Econ. Hist.*, XLVII (1987), pp. 929–49.

Jacobsen, G., 'Women's work and women's role: ideology and reality in Danish urban society', *Scand. Econ. Hist. Rev.*, XXXI (1983), pp. 2–20.

John, A.V., 'Colliery legislation and its consequences: 1842 and the women miners of Lancashire', *Bull. John Rylands Lib.*, LXI (1978), pp. 78–114.

John, A.V., *Unequal opportunities* (Oxford, 1986).

Jordan, E., 'The exclusion of women from industry in nineteenth-century Britain', *Comp. Stud. Soc. & Hist.*, XXXI (1989), pp. 273–96.

Kowaleski, M. and Bennett, J.M., 'Crafts, gilds, and women in the middle ages: fifty years after Marion K. Dale', *Signs*, 14 (1989), pp. 474–88.

Landes, D., *The unbound Prometheus* (Cambridge, 1969).

Lazonick, W., 'Industrial relations and technical change: the case of the self-acting mule', *Cambridge J. Econ.*, III (1979), pp. 231–62.

McBride, T., 'A woman's world: department stores and the evolution of women's employment, 1870–1920', *French Hist. Stud.*, X (1978), pp. 664–83.

Mark-Lawson, J. and Witz, A., 'From "family labour" to "family wage"? The case of women's labour in nineteenth-century coalmining', *Soc. Hist.*, XIII (1988), pp. 151–74.

Massa, P., *La 'Fabbrica' dei velluti genovesi* (Genoa, 1981).

Medick, H., 'The proto-industrial family economy', in P. Kriedte, H. Medick and J. Schlumbohm, eds, *Industrialization before industrialization* (Cambridge, 1981), pp. 38–73.

Monter, E.W., 'Women in Calvinist Geneva (1550–1800)', *Signs*, VI (1980), pp. 189–209.

Murray, M., 'Property and "patriarchy" in English history', *J. Hist. Sociol.*, 2 (1989), pp. 303–27.

Neuschel, K., 'Review', *Signs*, XIV (1988), pp. 209–13.

Nienhaus, U.D., 'Technological change, the welfare state, gender and real women. Female clerical workers in the postal services in Germany, France and England, 1860 to 1945. Report on a research project in progress', *Internationale wissenschaftliche Korrespondenz zur Geschichte der deutschen Arbeitsbewegung*, 23 (1987), pp. 223–30.

Offen, K., 'Depopulation, nationalism and feminism in fin-de-siècle France', *Amer. Hist. Rev.*, LXXXIX (1984), pp. 648–76.

Offen, K., 'Defining feminism: a comparative historical approach', *Signs*, XIV (1988), pp. 119–57.

Offen, K., '"Powered by a woman's foot": a documentary introduction to the sexual politics of the sewing machine in nineteenth-century France', *Women's Stud. Internat. Forum*, XI (1988), pp. 93–101.

Offen, K., 'Feminism, antifeminism and national family politics in early Third Republic France', in M.J. Boxer and J.H. Quataert, eds, *Connecting spheres* (New York, 1987), pp. 177–86.

Perrot, M., 'Femmes et machines au XIXᵉ siècle', *Romantisme*, XLI (1983), pp. 5–17.

Pinchbeck, I., *Women workers in the industrial revolution* (1930).

Poni, C., 'Proto-industrialization, rural and urban', *Review*, IX (1985), pp. 305–14.

Quataert, J.H., 'A new view of industrialization: "protoindustry" or the role of small-scale, labour-intensive manufacture in the capitalist environment', *Internat. Labour & Working-Class Hist.*, 33 (1988), pp. 3–22.

Quataert, J.H., 'A source analysis in German women's history: factory inspectors' reports and the shaping of working-class lives, 1878–1914', *Central Eur. Hist.*, 16 (1983), pp. 99–121.

Quataert, J.H., 'Combining agrarian and industrial livelihood: rural households in the Saxon Oberlausitz in the nineteenth century', *J. Fam. Hist.*, X (1985), pp. 145–62.

Quataert, J.H., 'The shaping of women's work in manufacturing: guilds, households and the state in central Europe, 1648–1870', *Amer. Hist. Rev.*, XC (1985), pp. 1122–48.

Rapp, R.T., *Industry and economic decline in seventeenth century Venice* (Cambridge, Mass., 1976).

Reich, M., Gordon, D.M. and Edwards, R.C., 'A theory of labour market segmentation', *Amer. Econ. Rev.*, LXIII (1973), pp. 359–65.

Rendall, J., *The origins of modern feminism: women in Britain, France and the United States, 1780–1860* (1985).

Richards, E., 'Women in the British economy since about 1700: an interpretation', *Hist.*, LXIX (1974), pp. 337–57.

Roberts, E., *Women's work, 1840–1940* (1988).

Roberts, M., 'Sickles and scythes: women's work and men's work at harvest time', *Hist. Workshop*, VII (1979), pp. 3–29.

Roper, L.A., 'Work, marriage and sexuality: women in Reformation Augsburg' (unpub. Ph.D. thesis, Univ. of London, 1985).

Rose, S.O., '"Gender at work": sex, class and industrial capitalism', *Hist. Workshop J.*, XXI (1986), pp. 113–31.

Rose, S.O., 'Gender segregation in the transition to the factory: the English hosiery industry, 1850–1910', *Feminist Stud.*, 13 (1987), pp. 163–84.

Rose, S.O., 'Gender antagonism and class conflict: exclusionary strategies of male trade unionists in nineteenth-century Britain', *Soc. Hist.*, XIII (1988), pp. 191–208.

Rose, S.O., 'Proto-industry, women's work and the household economy in the transitions to industrial capitalism', *J. Fam. Hist.*, 13 (1988), pp. 181–93.

Rule, J., *The labouring classes in early industrial England, 1750–1850* (1986).

Rule, J., 'The property of skill in the period of manufacture', in P. Joyce, ed., *The historical meanings of work* (Cambridge, 1987), pp. 99–118.

Saxonhouse, G. and Wright, G., 'Two forms of cheap labour in textile history', *Res. Econ. Hist.*, supp. 3 (1984), pp. 3–31.

Schmiechen, J., *Sweated industries and sweated labour* (1984).

Scott, J.W. and Tilly, L.A., 'Women's work and the family in nineteenth-century Europe', *Comp. Stud. Soc. & Hist.*, XVII (1975), pp. 36–64.

Scott, J.W., 'Women in history: the modern period', *P. & P.*, 101 (1983), pp. 141–57.

Scott, J.W., 'Men and women in the Parisian garment trades: discussions of family and work in the 1830s and 1840s', in P. Thane *et al.*, eds, *The power of the past* (Cambridge, 1984), pp. 67–93.

Seccombe, W., 'Patriarchy stabilized: the construction of the male breadwinner wage norm in nineteenth-century Britain', *Soc. Hist.*, XI (1986), pp. 53–76.

Shorter, E., 'Women's work: what difference did capitalism make?', *Theory & Soc.*, III (1976), pp. 513–27.

Snell, K.D.M., 'Agricultural and seasonal unemployment, the standard of living and women's work in the south and east, 1690–1860', *Econ. Hist. Rev.*, 2nd ser., XXXIV (1983), pp. 407–37.

Snell, K.D.M., 'The apprenticeship of women', in *idem, Annals of the labouring poor: social change and agrarian England, 1660–1900* (Cambridge, 1985), pp. 270–319.

Sonenscher, M., 'Weavers, wage-rates and the measurement of work in eighteenth-century Rouen', *Text. Hist.*, 17 (1986), pp. 71–8.

Sonenscher, M., *Work and wages* (Cambridge, 1989).

Sonenscher, M., 'Work and wages in Paris in the eighteenth century', in M. Berg, P. Hudson and M. Sonenscher, eds, *Manufacture in town and country before the factory* (Cambridge, 1983), pp. 147–72.

Sonenscher, M., 'Journeymen, the courts and the French trades, 1781–1791', *P. & P.*, 114 (1987), pp. 77–109.

Sowerwine, C., 'Workers and women in France before 1914: the debate over the Couriau affair', *J. Mod. Hist.*, LV (1983), pp. 411–41.

Stockmann, R., 'Gewerbliche Frauenarbeit in Deutschland, 1875–1980: zur Entwicklung des Beschäftigtenstruktur', *Geschichte und Gessellschaft*, 11 (1985), pp. 447–75.

Stone, L., *The family, sex and marriage in England, 1500–1800* (1977).

Sullivan, T.A., *Marginal workers, marginal jobs* (Austin, 1978).

Taylor, B., *Eve and the New Jerusalem* (1983).

Thomas, J., 'Women and capitalism: oppression or emancipation?', *Comp. Stud. Soc. & Hist.*, XXX (1988), pp. 534–49.

Tilly, L.A., 'Paths of proletarianization: organization of production, sexual division of labour, and women's collective action', *Signs*, VII (1981), pp. 400–17.

Tilly, L.A., 'Family, gender and occupations in industrial France: past and present', in A.C. Rossi, ed., *Gender and the life course* (New York, 1985), pp. 193–212.

Tilly, L.A. and Scott, J.W., *Women, work and family* (New York, 1978).

Valverde, M., '"Giving the female a domestic turn": the social, legal and moral regulation of women's work in British cotton mills, 1820–1850', *J. Soc. Hist.*, 21 (1988), pp. 619–34.

Walby, S., *Patriarchy at work* (Cambridge, 1986).

Wecker, R., 'Frauenlohnarbeit—Statistik und Wirklichkeit in der Schweiz an der Wende zum 20. Jahrhundert', *Schweizerische Zeitschrift für Geschichte*, 34 (1984), pp. 346–56.

Wensky, M., 'Women's guilds in Cologne in the later middle ages', *J. Eur. Econ. Hist.*, XI (1982), pp. 631–50.

Wensky, M., *Die Stellung der Frau in der stadtkölnischen Wirtschaft im Spätmittelalter* (Cologne & Vienna, 1980).

Wiesner, M.E., 'Spinsters and seamstresses: women in cloth and clothing production', in M.W. Ferguson, M. Quilligan and N.J. Vickers, eds, *Rewriting the Renaissance: the discourses of sexual difference in early modern Europe* (Chicago, 1986), pp. 191–205.

Wiesner, M.E., *Working women in Renaissance Germany* (New Brunswick, 1986).

Wiesner, M.E., 'Women's work in the changing city economy, 1500–1650', in M.J. Boxer and J.H. Quataert, eds, *Connecting spheres* (New York, 1987), pp. 64–74.

Wiesner Wood, M., 'Paltry peddlers or essential merchants: women in the distributive trades in early modern Nuremberg', *Sixteenth Century J.*, XXI (1981), pp. 3–13.

Woodward, D., 'Wage rates and living standards in pre-industrial England', *P. & P.*, 91 (1981), pp. 28–46.

Wrigley, E.A., 'Men on the land and men in the countryside: employment in agriculture in early nineteenth-century England', in L.M. Bonfield, R.M. Smith and K. Wrightson, eds, *The world we have gained* (Oxford, 1986), pp. 295–336.

Zimmeck, M., 'Jobs for the girls: the expansion of clerical work for women, 1850–1914', in A.V. John, ed., *Unequal opportunities* (Oxford, 1986), pp. 153–77.

Zimmeck, M., 'Strategies and stratagems for the employment of women in the British Civil Service, 1919–1939', *Hist. J.*, XXVII (1984), pp. 901–24.

Chapter 10

Maxine Berg

■ from 'WHAT DIFFERENCE DID WOMEN'S WORK
MAKE TO THE INDUSTRIAL REVOLUTION?', *History Workshop
Journal*, 35, Spring 1993, pp. 22–40

T HE EXTENT TO WHICH WOMEN'S employment opportunities in industry
waxed or waned over the course of the eighteenth and early nineteenth centuries varied
according to the industry, region, town, rural community, and time period chosen. Women's
employment opportunities were also women's labour-force participation rates in rapidly
changing or traditional activities. Women's labour-force participation has therefore been
cut off from the whole discussion of productivity change, shifts of labour and incomes
between sectors and output growth in the period. Male occupational structures, on the
contrary, have formed the basic building block of all these macro-economic estimates.
[...]
   The relative place of the textile industries needs to be set in the context of wider
industrial output. The textile industries as a whole contributed 45.9 per cent of value added
in British industry in 1770 and 46 per cent in 1831. What had changed over the period was
the contribution of the individual industries. Cotton's place grew from 2.6 per cent to
22.14 per cent, and wool's declined from 30.6 per cent to 14 per cent. But the gender
division of the workforce did not change: it remained predominantly female throughout
the period. In 1770 fourteen men were needed to make twelve broadcloths, but an additional
seventeen women and twenty-seven children were also required. In the Yorkshire worsted
manufacture, female spinners outnumbered woolcombers and weavers by three to one.
The linen industry contributed more to value added in 1770 than did the iron industry, and
only approximately 2 per cent less than it did in 1831. Adam Smith calculated that in
addition to flax growers and dressers, three or four spinners were necessary to keep one
weaver in constant employment. Silk contributed 4.4 per cent of value added in 1770, the
same proportion as coal; by 1831 the position of coal was more important at 7 per cent, but
equally silk's had grown, after a dip, to 5.1 per cent. This too was a women's industry. In
1765, the proportion of women and children to men in the London trade was fourteen to
one; and there were 4,000 in the Spitalfields trade. In addition to this the industry was
scattered by the late eighteenth century over twenty counties and fifty towns, with one mill
in Stockport employing 2,000. Women were employed in both the throwing and the weaving

sections of the industry, including large numbers of colliers' wives in the suburbs of Coventry. These were 'women's industries', though they also of course employed smaller proportions of men in branches such as weaving. Even in face of the technological innovation and factory organization that raised some of them by the early nineteenth century into 'dynamic' industrial sectors, they remained women's industries. For many 'dynamic' sectors, it was the distribution of the female labour force, not the male, which counted.

The cotton industry, the key 'dynamic' sector credited with much of the productivity increase of the industrial sector, employed higher proportions of women and children than of men in factories in both the eighteenth and the early nineteenth century. The few large-scale cotton mills of the eighteenth century employed roughly equal proportions of men and women, and of adults and children. The cotton factory labour force of 1818 showed that women accounted for a little over half of the workforce, and children accounted for a substantial proportion. In Scotland, these proportions were even more marked. Women and girls made up 61 per cent of the workforce in Scottish cotton mills; outside of Glasgow, the women were even more prominent, for they were also employed in throstle spinning and in spinning on short mules.

Too much emphasis has been given in histories of women's work to the factories, whereas only a small amount of industry was organized in this way in the eighteenth and early nineteenth centuries. Dynamic industries might also, however, be organized as work-shops or as dispersed or subcontracted units. Innovation in markets, distribution networks and division and specialization of labour were equally important ingredients to a progressive industrial sector.

Other textile industries employing high proportions of women were lacemaking and stocking knitting, two decentralized or putting-out industries. Lacemaking was exclusively a female trade.

[…]

Thus when we talk of industry in the eighteenth and early nineteenth centuries, we are talking of a largely female workforce. Of course there were many other predominantly male industries which also contributed substantial proportions of value added: the leather trades, building and mining. But these are also classic examples of traditional industries which underwent very little innovation over the period. Indeed the building trades and shoemaking were sponges for casual surplus labour.

To be sure, there were a number of such traditional industries which absorbed excess female labour, but many of these had declined in the eighteenth century; hand spinning and knitting were notable examples. But in some regions these had been replaced by other newer manufactures – flax spinning in Scotland, silk throwing in Essex, and jennyspinning in Lancashire. In many cases, these new industries absorbed much less women's labour than had the former local industries. Women not reabsorbed into new industries were left unemployed, or moved into the fastest-growing occupational category of all, domestic service.

[…]

Those industries at the forefront of technological and organizational innovation were also mainly industries employing women's labour. Why was this the case at a time when there was so much disguised and real unemployment among male workers in the industrial sector? The usual reason given for the employment of women rather than of men in industry is cheap labour. Women had lower wages than men, and were therefore substituted where the opportunity arose. New industries would, therefore, seek out locations where there was female unemployment, and so acquire traditionally cheap labour at an even greater discount.

But this analysis is not sufficient if we assume a labour-surplus economy. If there was male unemployment, and wages at the margin at only a subsistence level, why did not entrepreneurs seek out male labour? There is evidence of stable if not falling male wage rates for the period up to 1820. There are, of course, no long-term wage trends for women, but it is generally assumed that women by custom received one third to one half the wage of men. This in itself might be enough to induce a substitution of female for male labour. But there is more data available at the regional level to indicate other factors at play. We know that there were big regional differences in male wages. But so there were too for female wages.

Relatively high earnings for women in manufacturing were to be found in areas of the North and the Midlands where textiles, metalwares and potteries were expanding rapidly; and also in some southern agricultural areas where lacemaking, straw plaiting and silk spinning were growth industries. *Relative* is just as it says – women's wages were nearly always lower than men's wages in any branch of manufacture. In most cases they were also lower than the lowest local male wages, those of male agricultural labourers. But in the newer, expanding industries some women's wage rates were at least equal to those received by local male agricultural labour, and sometimes much higher. It must also be remembered that wages were not earnings. High earnings required not just high wage rates, but steady employment over the week, the seasons and the economic cycle. Earnings for women were also tied to family contributions, especially from children, and to future work expectations. 'Apprentice-ship', training or experience divided the wages of young learners from the piece rates of older tradeswomen. And equally high-wage teenage labour could be a short-lived experience in the range of a woman's lifetime earnings. All of these factors must be considered to provide a profile of trends in women's earnings over the Industrial Revolution.
[…]

Low wages were clearly not the only reason for employing women in new industries. Indeed most of these occupations were gender-segregated, at least for time and place, though these gender divisions were subject to change. In the short run, and with no other contiguous changes, there was little possibility of substituting female for male labour as wage differentials changed.

The lacemaking industry is a good example. Far from being an industry developed on the feminization of poverty, it promoted the independence of women as wage earners. Wages in the seventeenth and early eighteenth century were high, higher than those for wool spinners and much higher than those for local male agricultural labour. Yet despite the evident prosperity of this occupation for a time, men were not employed in it, neither did they seek to enter it. It was not wages which determined this gender divide, but the organizational and technological attributes of a women's workforce. The reason for this gender division did not lie in any physical attribute such as steady application or small fingers. For men were tailors, jewellers and makers of watch parts and scientific instruments. Old men and boys in some rural areas were also to be found stocking knitting by hand.

When women workers were introduced in new industries or new settings, they usually entered these along with a whole range of organizational and technological changes. A simple example was their entry into power-loom weaving. These new labour forces, technologies and organization associated together to yield substantially higher rates of profit than had been possible in other industries or under earlier manufacturing regimes.
[…]

It is evident in Britain that women and children were simply assumed to be the key workforce to be targeted with any novelty in manufacturing methods. Machines and processes were invented with this workforce in mind. New techniques in calico printing and spinning provide classic examples of experimentation on a child and female workforce. In calico printing, processes were broken down into a series of operations performed particularly well by teenage girls who contributed manual dexterity (learned already at home) with high labour intensity. The spinning jenny was first invented for use by a young girl, its horizontal wheel making it uncomfortable for an adult worker to use for any length of time. Girls (and boys as well) were, as is well known, widely employed with the newer textile technologies in the silk and cotton industries. They were used in the silk throwing mills, where they were taken on from the ages of 6 to 8, 'because their fingers are supple and they learn the skills more easily'. A cotton mill at Emscote was reported to have dismissed girls after their apprenticeship because their fingers were too big to go between the threads. Patents and contemporary descriptions of new industries frequently pointed out the close connection between a particular innovation and its use of a child or female labour force. The economist Dean Tucker, in 1760, described as the key attribute of the division of labour in the Birmingham trades the use of child assistants as an extra appendage of the worker; this use also trained these children to habits of industry. It was widely held at the time that machines for stamping and piercing in the small metal trades extended the range of female employment, especially that of young girls. Girls were specifically requested in advertisements in Birmingham's *Aris's Gazette* as button piercers, annealers and for stove and polishing work in the japanning trades.

Josiah Wedgwood reported to the Children's Employment Commission in 1816 that girls were employed in 'painting on the biscuit' mainly, but they also paint upon the glaze and after the second dipping. They work with a camel hair pencil in painting patterns upon the ware, sitting at the table.' [*sic*] The hand-made nail trade relied largely on the labour of women and children. An early nineteenth-century innovation, the 'oliver' or foot-operated spring hammer, allowed a smith to work single-handed, but was responsible for all kinds of deformities in the teenage girls who used it.

These are just some examples of the ways in which new technologies and divisions of labour were introduced, then described by contemporaries in terms of the gender and age of the workforce using them. Such gender-typing of innovation would probably have entailed two explanations. The first is that manufacturers and inventors saw the technical and profit-making advantages in using a new workforce which could be integrated with the new techniques, in such a way as to bypass traditional artisan customs and arrangements. If these latter arrangements were left in place while new techniques were introduced, the likely result was resistance by producers to the new technology. Contemporary manufacturers furthermore believed that women and girls had a greater 'natural' aptitude for the manual dexterity and fine motor skills required by the new techniques, and that 'female' ways of working together were more amenable to division of labour than were 'male' work cultures.

The second way of looking at this gendered technology is that inventions and new working methods in manufacture were rather public affairs in the eighteenth century. The advantages of new projects in the seventeenth century, and of new manufacturing enterprises in the eighteenth century, were frequently presented to the state or to local communities in terms of their capacities for providing employment. Though the real point of such innovation was to save labour, if it was to be profitable, nevertheless it was politically expedient to present technologies in terms of the female and child labour they would employ, rather than the male labour they would save. The concerns of Poor Law authorities for providing manufacturing employment for women and girls, as well as industrial training for young girls in spinning and lace schools, reflected concerns not just over poor rates, but over illegitimacy and in some areas the high proportion of single women among the poor. These concerns were also related to the differential effects of changing agricultural practices and declining opportunities in rural domestic industry on the gender division of the labour market. New methods were making sharp inroads on women's work in pastoral agriculture, dairying and hand spinning. Robert Allen estimates the proportionate reduction of women's employment in agriculture in the South Midlands to be much higher than that of men or boys.

[…]

It seems that the new industries of the eighteenth century and their innovations can be presented either as moulders of a new type of industrial workforce, or as a sponge for a traditionally cheap and even more available source of labour. What role did women and girls play in these new industries?

Labour-supply factors no doubt played a part in the characteristics of the industrial labour force in the eighteenth century. Women went in large numbers to many 'traditional' female manufactures such as needlework, just as men flocked to the building trades and shoemaking. Demographic change over the course of the eighteenth century was introducing new age and gender balances in the workforce. Children aged five to fourteen comprised approximately one-sixth of the population in the 1670s and one-quarter in the 1820s. This compares with only 6 per cent in 1951. The young were thus both a potential source of labour, and the source of a high dependency ratio in society. Gender balances were also skewed towards women until late in the eighteenth century. Pamela Sharpe has shown recently the extent to which sex ratios in Colyton moved in favour of women throughout the seventeenth and the first half of the eighteenth century, and less so in the later eighteenth century. Women married late, and there were higher numbers of spinsters and widows in the population than there were to be in the early nineteenth century. Close associations between spinsterhood, poverty and illegitimacy prevailed over the century in Colyton. Celibacy peaked at approximately one-quarter of groups reaching marriageable age in the 1670s and 1680s, and fell thereafter, until it started to rise again in the 1780s.

[…]

While wages for women in the newer industries could well be respectable, and, as demonstrated, were sometimes higher than those for men in agricultural labour, they were also volatile, or the wages of relatively brief 'golden ages'. As such, single women and widows were certainly able to take the opportunity of an independent subsistence for a time in many of these industries, but this good fortune might be precarious and was frequently short-lived.

Where women worked within a family economy their low or fluctuating wages could become the deciding factor between crisis and stable or improving conditions for families. Even limited earnings, if pooled within a family economy, could help to put together a subsistence. This subsistence was most often based not on the traditional model of the family enterprise, but on individuals within a family or household working at a variety of activities and for a range of different employers. The female silk weavers of Bedworth, Hillfields and Nuneaton in Warwickshire were the wives of miners; the female chain and nailmakers of the Black Country were the wives and daughters of ironworkers.

Estimates for industrial productivity have thus far been based only on data for male labour and wages. This wage data indicates stable or falling real wages at least until 1820, although there was considerable regional variation. These trends in income levels have been associated with overall slow rates of growth in productivity, and especially of industrial productivity.

But the inclusion of women's wage rates and labour-force participation could make a substantial difference to these trends. Low male wage rates where family incomes were at stake had the effect of encouraging high rates of female labour-force participation. Among very poor families, all women and children did any work they could find; among those who were poor, but could eke out a living, the earnings of the household head, rather than female market wages, provided the major determinant of female participation rates.

[...]

What effect did this combination of female labour supply and gender-based industrial expansion have on women's employment and incomes? While high proportions of the labour force employed in manufacturing were female, especially in the newer textile industries, it is also evident that the employment provided by industry was not sufficient to the task of soaking up the surplus labour left in the wake of demographic and agricultural change.

Note: figures and tables have been omitted.

Chapter 11

Sally Alexander

■ from 'WOMEN, CLASS AND SEXUAL DIFFERENCE IN THE 1830s AND 1840s: SOME REFLECTIONS ON THE WRITING OF A FEMINIST HISTORY', *History Workshop Journal*, 17, Spring 1984, pp. 125–6

[...]

IT IS IMPOSSIBLE EVER TO GOVERN SUBJECTS rightly, without knowing as well what they really are as what they only seem; which the *Men* can never be supposed to do, while they labour to force *Women* to live in constant masquerade.
Sophia, *Woman not Inferior to Man*, 1739

This desire of being always woman is the very consciousness that degrades the sex. Excepting with a lover, I must repeat with emphasis, a former observation, – it would be well if they were only agreeable or rational companions.
Mary Wollstonecraft, *A Vindication of the Rights of Woman*, 1792

Throughout history, people have knocked their heads against the riddle of the nature of femininity –

[...] Nor will you have escaped worrying over this problem – those of you who are men; to those of you who are women this will not apply – you are yourselves the problem.
Sigmund Freud, *Lecture on Femininity, 1933*, Standard Edition, vol xxii

For a long time I have hesitated to write a book on woman. The subject is irritating, especially to women; and it is not new. The voluminous nonsense uttered during the last century seems to have done little to illuminate the problem. After all, is there a problem? And if so, what is it? Are there women, really? One wonders if women still exist, if they will always exist, whether or not it is desirable that they should, what place they occupy in this world, what their place should be.
Simone de Beauvoir, *The Second Sex*, 1949

1. The problem: woman, a historical and political category

The problem: woman, the riddle: femininity have a capricious but nevertheless a political history. Capricious because they surface at different moments among different social milieux, within diverse political movements; and a history in the sense that the social conditions and political status of women have undergone changes which may be traced, and with them some of the shifts in the meanings of femininity. As we become acquainted with the historical range and diversity of women's political status and social roles, the enigma itself occupies a different place. It is removed outside history to some other realm beyond the reach of social analysis or political theory. Since there can be no aspect of the human condition which is not social where could that other place be?

If the meaning of femininity, the political implications of Womanhood have at moments in the past 300 years been contested, then it must be that what they represent is not some eternal and universal essence of woman, but the difficulty of the sexual relation itself between women and men; which is always a social ordering, and one where the unconscious and its conflicting drives and desires presses most urgently on conscious behaviour, where political thought, though most capable of producing principles of equality and justice in its delineations of the proper relations between the sexes, nevertheless cannot always anticipate or circumscribe the urgency of those conflicts as they are lived.

Feminism, the conscious political movement of women, has been since the 17th century the principle [sic] contender in the struggles for the reorganization of sexual difference and division, and hence the social meaning of womanhood. If feminism's underlying demand is for women's full inclusion in humanity, (whether that inclusion is strategically posed in terms of equal rights, socialism or millenarianism) then the dilemma for a feminist political strategy may be summed up in the tension between the plea for equality and the assertion of sexual difference. If the sexes are different, then how may that difference (and all that it implies for the relative needs and desires of women and men) be represented throughout culture, without the sex that is different becoming subordinated.

History offers many symptoms of this difficulty; from the sixteenth century Royal Edicts which prohibited women's public gossip, to the nineteenth century House of Commons references to women as 'the sex' or feminism as the 'shrieking sisterhood'. Whether dismissed as a 'monstrous regiment', 'set of devils' or a 'menace to the Labour movement', feminism both arouses sexual antagonisms and invokes a threat which cannot be explained with reference to the demands of the women's movements – nothing if not reasonable in themselves. By suggesting that what both feminism and femininity stand for is not Woman – who like Man is no more nor less than human – but the social organisation of sexual difference and division, I am refusing to abandon femininity to an enigma/mystery beyond history. But then the problem becomes how to write a history of women and feminism which engages with those issues.

[…]

Chapter 12

Ann Goldberg

■ from 'THE EBERBACH ASYLUM AND THE PRACTICE(S) OF NYMPHOMANIA IN GERMANY, 1815–1849', *Journal of Women's History*, 9, 4 Winter 1998, pp. 35–48

[…]

IN THE EBERBACH CASE HISTORIES, it was nymphomania, not hysteria, that predominated in medical representations of female sexual maladies, appearing – either its symptoms or diagnosis – in the case files of almost one-third of the female patients. Hysteria could be and was diagnosed in lower-class women (at Eberbach and elsewhere), but since the eighteenth century its cultural association with privilege (as a fashionable pathological by-product of luxury, leisure, and 'civilization' in elite women) seemingly did not lend itself well to educated physicians and officials speaking and thinking about lower-class female sexual deviancy. By contrast, nymphomania – an illness of transgression, eruption, excess, strength, and passion – did. At Eberbach, it was seen disproportionately in lower-class women from peasant families of small landholders and the rural proletariat, a group which, while typical of early-nineteenth-century asylum patients, has received no systematic treatment in the study of gender and madness.

Neither the word nor the concept of nymphomania was new in the nineteenth century. The image of dangerously oversexed females stretches back centuries, as do the diagnoses of such female illnesses associated with pathologically out-of-control sexuality as uterine fury and, since the late seventeenth century, nymphomania. New in the nineteenth century was the institutionalization of nymphomaniacs in insane asylums. This became possible for the first time in early-nineteenth-century Germany (and elsewhere in Europe and the United States) with the founding of the first specialized medical institutions for the treatment of mental illness. The Eberbach asylum (1815–1849), located in a former Cistercian monastery in the western German state of Nassau, was in most ways typical of those asylums at the forefront of innovation in Germany. A public asylum, administered jointly by the jurist civil servant Philipp H. Lindpaintner and the house physician Ferdinand W. Windt, Eberbach employed a number of therapeutic treatments aimed at mental cure – ranging from the psychological techniques of 'moral treatment' to an array of mechanical instruments, baths, and medications for shocking or soothing an over-heated or understimulated mind via the body.

Nymphomania was not a preexisting illness awaiting its treatment in the new asylums. As clinical diagnosis, it was rather a creation of medicine itself and the asylum system, which recoded into the terms of pathological genitals a huge range of female sexual (and nonsexual) transgressions. Before the advent of the nineteenth-century mental hospital, women with very similar social profiles and behavioral characteristics as Eberbach's nymphomaniacs (for example, sexually promiscuous women) were treated as delinquents and disciplinary problems, not medical cases. These women were either incarcerated as 'lecherous women' in prisons and workhouses or fined and left in the custody of their families. [...]

Since nymphomania was defined not in terms of specific acts but as a state of being – of overexcitation – it had the effect of bringing together the most disparate behavior into a causal unity and thereby sexualizing a vast range of seemingly contradictory symptoms. This can be seen in the following description of a nymphomaniac patient:

> Previously she was well-behaved and modest. Now she is in a state in which there is no sign of shame or morality. She takes her clothes off, throws them to the earth, rolls on the ground, hits out, disobeys the attendant....In conversation she lapses into convulsive laughter or breaks out into the most frightful swearing. At the sight of a man she goes into raptures, approaches with great trust, and betrays here all too well the fire which has ignited the passions.

The 'fire' was the physiological process occurring in the genitals, and it is this inner condition that unifies the wildly different acts and moods of this woman – rage, insubordination, humor, and seduction. In this and many other cases, the symptoms of nymphomania could thus extend far beyond the realm of overt and 'excessive' sexuality. Indeed, a bodily state of excited genitals required no outward sexuality to be 'seen' as long as some indication in the woman's past or near present (illegitimate children, work in a bordello, masturbation) indicated the possibility of an original 'unnatural' sexual stimulation or frustration.

The ability to see nymphomania, therefore, required a specific body of medical 'knowledge' and the middle-class conceptions of femininity and sexuality which underpinned theories of the illness. For, if the nymphomania concept sexualized an enormous range of female behavior, the Eberbach cases show that it also pathologized precisely those traits that were being excluded from the norms of bourgeois femininity: aggression, passion, immodesty, and strength. Nymphomaniacs were not only immodestly overt in their sexual desires, but were women who openly and forcefully expressed a range of emotions. Nymphomania was a question of loud and foul mouths, unruliness and open defiance, and of 'coarse,' 'uncouth,' 'impudent,' and 'insubordinate' females. Adjectives of aggressivity, such as 'demanding,' 'pushy,' 'forward,' and 'fresh,' constantly appear in these cases – which may or may not relate to sexual matters. Elisabeth G., for example, the adulterous wife of a poor boot cleaner, is said not just to have engaged in an affair with a former employer but to have 'obtrusively approached him' herself. Sexual arousal in women is set against the duties of wife and mother. It leads to a concentration on the meeting of one's own needs and desires, and therefore destroys the ideal of self-sacrifice enshrined in the bourgeois concepts of modesty and female honor.

In this way, within the supposedly neutral terms of science, nymphomania, like other contemporary 'female illnesses,' was based on and helped construct a bourgeois normative ideal of womanhood: women were to be fragile, passive, modest, submissive, and maternal.

This ideal was made an essential component by which a woman's health and potential release from the asylum were determined. Further, medical writers explained the vulnerability of women to sexual illnesses and the greater frequency of sex obsession in women (as compared to nymphomania's male counterpart – satyriasis) by what they saw as woman's special nature and function: her attachment to family and thus the great importance of love in her life, her weak nerves, and the dominance of the reproductive organs over her body and mind. A series of normative and precautionary statements on gender and the social role of women were hereby embedded in the nymphomania diagnosis. Weak-nerved and delicate women at the mercy of their emotions and reproductive organs belong at home as wives and mothers and require protection and surveillance to ensure against the potentially disruptive forces of a latent sexual voracity.

Doctors' greater tendency to diagnose nymphomania in lower-class patients was in part the result of the application of these ideals of womanhood to their peasant patients, whose body gestures and physical appearance shaped by lives of hard physical labor hardly conformed to the bourgeois model of modesty/health/femininity. This standard appeared in the medical comments on lower-class nymphomaniacs as 'coarse,' 'sensual,' 'ill-bred,' and 'without upbringing and feeling for decorum and law.'

The idea that women from the lower strata of society suffered from pathological sexuality took on added force given the close association between lower-class sexuality and the 'social question' in the *Vormärz* period (1815–1848). This association became a staple theme of the pauperism debate and the basis of state public policies aimed at restricting and containing what, in Malthusian terms, was perceived as an out-of-control sexuality creating over-population and hence mass poverty. The perception of the danger and excess of the genitals of lower-class women embodied these concerns, for it was precisely these sexually overexcited women whose immoral behavior was supposedly causing the rising illegitimacy rates, threatening to deplete local poor-funds, and both reflecting and helping to cause the hungry, lawless, and dangerous state of the lower orders.
[…]

[…] all this occurred in a situation where sex became one medium of (mis)communication between doctor and patient about a range of issues – power, identity, freedom, and daily existence within the asylum. From this perspective, one begins to see that the alleged lust of 'nymphomaniacs' had a certain meaning and aim, one that had very little to do with bodily sexual urges as such.

Katharina J., a poor, widowed, peasant woman had been incarcerated both in prison and in Eberbach for her intransigent and violent demands for the return of her home, which had been auctioned against her will to a local official. In 1827, when a medical civil servant went to examine her at home two months after her first release from Eberbach, he encountered an unexpected display of affectionate and seductive behavior.

> I found her at home alone. Immediately at my entrance she received me, as earlier, with her wordless smile, and to my question where and how she has been living up to now, I received no other answer than this senseless smiling. All of a sudden, she saw my signet ring and asked me for it. My silver-studded whip likewise appealed to her. I let her take hold of it in order to see what she wanted to do with it; and with amorous glances and smiling countenance, she drew it softly over my back. To the question what she wanted on the 25th and 26th in G., particularly at the government office, she smiled at me, and before I knew it, embraced and kissed me with the answer: 'that's

what I wanted to give him.' This embrace and kiss was supposedly not meant for me but for a certain individual in G. at whose home she explained she will live in the future … It clearly follows from the above that the widow J. has fallen into insanity which seems to have taken on an amorous [*verliebt*] tendency.

[…]

[…] seduction was perhaps the only way of exercising a measure of control over the man, by playing with the one quality both doctor and patient possessed that crossed and potentially leveled class differences: sexuality. Rather than uncontrolled genital eruptions, sexuality was a kind of language to be manipulated for specific purposes; it was the vehicle of (mis)communication between doctor and patient, the boundaries and terms of which Katharina aptly expressed in the image of the whip and the caress.

If in Eberbach much of what was labeled 'nymphomaniacal' contained components of aggressive, angry behavior, it is because most of these women were extremely angry as a direct result of their incarceration. While there were indigent and formerly abused patients accepting of the care they received at the asylum, most of the women diagnosed as nymphomaniacs were enraged at their incarceration and desperate to get out. They called Eberbach a 'prison,' complained about the 'injustice' of their confinement, and issued threats of legal proceedings. These battles with the asylum could be furiously maintained over years, and there were also a number of escape attempts — some patients exerting enormous energy and ingenuity in this enterprise.

As in Katharina's case, one of the driving forces behind 'shameless,' 'sexual' behavior in these women was not desire but rage. Lodged as they are among notations on insubordination and escape attempts, it is hard not to see 'shamelessness,' 'impudence,' and the provocative sexual talk and behavior some female patients engaged in as extensions of battles against the asylum. In a setting where 'proper,' 'feminine' behavior was rigidly enforced, and where, for example, patients could be punished with solitary confinement for 'slovenliness' or swearing, 'shamelessness' was (whether intentional or not) an act of insubordination. Given the sexual prudery of the asylum staff, certain sexually explicit acts and speech by their patients — such as stripping, simulating coitus, and 'telling lecherous tales' — appear as outright provocations. Certainly, patients noticed doctors' horrified reactions — the fact that the behavior was often so 'scandalous' it could 'not be described.' The context of the medical notations surrounding such behavior and the whole course of an individual patient's 'career' in the asylum support the idea that 'scandalous' was often precisely the intent of such acts.

The behavior of Barbara N. provides a case in point. At the time of admission, quiet and sad from homesickness and worrying about her children, she began searching for ways to escape. Locked away from her home and family, forced to work and obey, and punished when she did not, Barbara N. became increasingly enraged — hitting the staff, refusing to work, demanding to go home, and 'raving.' Running parallel to rage, sexual desire appears as the second motif in the notations. At first, 'liking to talk of handsome men, [by whom] she wishes to be touched,' her behavior later reached, according to the doctors, the 'highest degree' of nymphomania. In the intervals between 'running around to every door to … flee,' she made a great display of her sexuality: 'letting herself fall to the floor, and rubbing her bottom around on the stones to satisfy [*sic*] the sex act'; masturbating to the point that 'she injures her genitals'; or, 'at the sight of men, uncovering herself in the most lecherous way.' Was there a connection between the woman locked away desperately seeking to escape and the woman 'plagued' with sexual desire? Dr. Windt, the house physician, thought so: 'The constant aimed for restraint of her wild desires [with the straitjacket] roused her to the greatest wrath, and limited the sexual excitation just as little as the medication.' Here, Barbara's sexual provocation became the medium in which a power struggle between patient and asylum – between freedom and restraint – was played out, and where sexuality was fed by rage. If there was one clear message from Barbara's behavior in her years at Eberbach, it was an unrelenting and furious desire to escape. She even succeeded once, jumping through a window of the solitary confinement building.

Patients could also use seduction and flirtation to meet certain needs within the asylum world. For many patients, an attitude of outrage and absolute rejection of the asylum eventually gave way to accommodation. When and if an inner assimilation occurred, the issues for patients changed from escape or revenge to negotiating their material and psychological needs within the rules and norms of the system. These desires were practical, such as receiving more and better food, avoiding work, and, most important, avoiding punishment or any number of 'therapeutic treatments' that amounted to the same thing. Negotiations were also related to meeting emotional and social needs – recognition, respect, and attention, for instance. Given that in all such cases, the opinion that mattered most came from the male staff with its decision-making authority (in the adjudicating of patient-attendant quarrels, meting out punishment and treatment, and altering a patient's daily schedule or place of residence within the asylum), it should be no surprise that female patients tried out the force of their sex appeal. In, for example, the case of Christina D., a former servant, she seems to have used seductive behavior as a plea (or ploy) for attention and care. The word 'mannstoll' (man crazy) appears for the first time within a register entry describing Christina as 'often simulating illness, full of demands to change her situation.' Later entries include that she: 'demands better care and service' and 'believes she is neglected and not duly regarded.'

Viewed as communicative and strategic acts taking place within a specific social context (the power dynamics of the asylum and the doctor-patient relationship), nymphomania thus reveals the ways in which female patients sought to manipulate the asylum and resist its power. Indeed, nymphomania was constructed by the asylum precisely in and through these acts of resistance. The production of 'sexuality' through acts of resistance is seen in a closer examination of one of the most common nymphomaniacal acts: stripping. Poorer patients most frequently used this method of resistance, a fact reinforcing the disproportionate use of the nymphomania diagnosis in lower-class women. However, the connection between poverty and stripping lay not in a shared lower-class pathology (however defined), but in a particular relationship that poor patients had to clothing.

In case files, the term usually used for stripping (sich entblössen) is ambiguous and seems to have encompassed two different behaviors: uncovering the body, usually in the gesture of raising the skirt (den Rock aufheben); and fully removing the clothes or undressing (sich auskleiden). Pulling up the skirt as a female gesture of shaming and blaming the observer stretches back centuries (in ancient mythology, medieval iconography, folklore, and modern protests), and it appears in the tactics of certain asylum patients in battles they waged against the institution. The act of stripping, often combined with destroying the clothes, had quite a different set of meanings. While the doctors saw such acts in reference to the unclothed body, the sources suggest that the patients regarded the acts as referring to the clothes themselves and the symbolic meanings attached to them. In other words, the act of stripping was not about exposing the (gendered) body (as in lifting the skirt), but of ridding the self of the clothing; and its meaning was not in the theme of sex, or for that matter a physiological process of sexual excitement, but in the social and symbolic context and function of clothing within the asylum order.

This implication and the struggle surrounding it had largely to do with a patient's social identity. Clothes were symbolic of the person; they stated who one was and where one belonged within a familial and societal hierarchy. In the asylum, where the patient had been severed from his or her home and past identity, and where identity itself was called into question and reworked by the institutional regime, clothing took on enormous symbolic significance. As something closely associated with social identity, and one of the few (if not sole) possessions of patients, clothing became a focal point of (mis)communication and struggle between patient and asylum staff about who the patient was, how and who was to define her, and the place she held within the asylum.

The loss of one's past identity, and the confusion, fear, and anger that the onslaught of the asylum's regime provoked is captured well in the statements of two nymphomaniacs: both poor, one a former servant and the other a former day laborer. Anna S. 'asserts that she is simultaneously in N. [her home] and here, which is however impossible,' and later she states that 'she is not [Anna S.]; she [Anna] has long been buried. But who she is, she does not know.' No longer being Anna S. referred to the person 'who was,' as she claimed, 'the prettiest girl in the world and could have made an extraordinarily lucrative marriage.' This was at best an exaggeration, but her point about the loss of one's past hopes is clear. Being an inmate of the asylum made one into another person, even if one was not sure who that person was. This transformation occurred because commitment to the institution meant the loss of reputation and honor – the qualities necessary for establishing an adult social identity as a married woman in the community.

[…]

One need only compare the lengthy lists of clothing middle-class patients brought to the asylum with the short and meager lists of their lower-class counterparts to see that it would have been particularly (if not exclusively) poorer patients like Margaretta K. who were subject to wearing the asylum uniform. And it was also these poorer patients who most frequently turn up in the asylum notes detailing acts of stripping and tearing up their clothes.

[…]

The ability to wear one's own clothes allowed a patient to retain a part of her past identity and thus avoid, if only symbolically, the complete absorption of the self into the asylum regime. By contrast, wearing the clothes of the asylum signified precisely what one refused to accept: the role and life of the inmate. It fixed the self in the identity of inmate perhaps as much as any other daily event of asylum life.

[…]

Finally, clothes were symbols of one's class position – both in the outer world and within the asylum. Lower-class women rejected clothes 'not good enough' for them, or demanded 'better' clothes like those of the higher-classed patients. The desire for status and material gain which clothing symbolized in the outer world also applied to the world of the asylum, where the patient's class determined very different types of treatment.

[…]

Chapter 13

Jutta Schwarzkopf

■ from 'CHARTIST WOMEN IN PUBLIC POLITICS', in Chapter 6 of *Women in the Chartist Movement*, Macmillan, London, 1991, pp. 174–218

1. The extension of domestic responsibilities into the public arena

THE FIRST STEP OUT INTO THE OPEN for many Chartist women consisted in an extension of their domestic responsibilities into the public arena. There were various ways in which Chartism sought to mobilise specifically female skills to further its aims.

Although favouring female political involvement, Chartists did not expect women to support the movement in the same way as men. Thus the Hull WMA [Working Men's Association] appealed to the men and women of Hull:

> Men and women of Hull – We ask you to join with us in our effort to obtain freedom and happiness for the masses – we call upon the men to join in holy brotherhood with us as members of the Working Men's Association – we call upon the women to cheer us on with the smiles of their approbation, and to encourage us with their support.

The women's special task was seen to consist in lending male Chartists the moral support deemed indispensable to the victory of the movement. Again and again they were called upon along the following lines: 'Lend us then your powerful assistance, animate us in the glorious struggle, cheer us by your approbation, enliven us by your presence, and we cannot, we will not fail of success.' Women were exhorted to lend men moral support by 'smiling them on to victory', as the standard phrase went, thus doing for the movement at large what every woman was supposedly accustomed to do at home, namely to cater for her family's psychological needs.

The large number of fairly well endowed Chartist funds – most of which were set up for the relief of Chartist prisoners' families ... owed their existence to women's ability to economise, even though the actual donation might have been made in the husband's name or in that of a male association. Frequently, however, women themselves featured as contributors, especially to funds set up for the relief of Chartist prisoners' families.

The difficulty working-class women had in eking donations out of a scanty income is demonstrated by the actual amounts given. The high average percentage (13 per cent) of female contributions in aid of the 'Welsh widows' amounted to a meagre total of £4. 14s. 9½d.

Women's lack of financial power was taken into account by the movement. As Caroline Maria Williams, a Bristol Chartist, had done in 1842, so the executive of the Defence Fund – set up in 1848 to cover the cost of procuring legal defence for imprisoned Chartists – suggested that women should sell handmade articles of needlework for the benefit of this fund. Significantly, the male executive took the occasion to assign a political meaning to the employment of specifically female skills in a typically female setting by arguing:

> Indeed this work of benevolence seems peculiarly adapted to, and should call forth the energies of the female mind; for what more noble and pleasurable enjoyment can a woman find, after the performance of her domestic duties, than in exercising her talents in the formation of some useful or fancy article, consoled by the reflection that her industry will counteract the venomenous [sic] sting of tyranny, dry the widows' and orphans' tears, and shed the sunshine of the heart upon the house of the desolate.

Chartist women were not the first to engage in activities geared towards the relief of the families of political activists. In July 1832, a number of politically active London women had formed themselves into a group called 'The Friends of the Oppressed'. They had aimed at giving moral and financial support to the families of political prisoners, especially those involved in the struggle for a free press. This kind of activity arose out of women's awareness of the plight of a family deprived of the male breadwinner's earnings. By alleviating the sufferings of the families thus afflicted, these women helped sustain political movements by easing male activists' anxiety for the survival of their families in the event of imprisonment.

In their capacity as the chief purchasers for their families, women employed the tactic of exclusive dealing to put pressure on the newly enfranchised shopkeepers either to vote for Chartist candidates at elections or to donate to the movement's funds. Robert Lowery devoted an entire pamphlet to this issue. Predictably enough, he began by reminding his readers of the treachery he found the middle-class shopkeepers guilty of through their conduct in 1832. In that year the Reform Act had been passed, the result of a campaign uniting the unenfranchised working and middle classes, from which the latter alone had benefited. Lowery proceeded to argue that shopkeepers' prosperity, and thereby ultimately their franchise, depended on the spending power of their working-class clientele, a power currently curtailed by heavy taxation. Thus he argued an identity of interests between shopkeepers and Chartists, which, once perceived, would, he hoped, convert the former to the Charter.

Lowery then focused on the moral power underlying exclusive dealing. He was convinced that this practice would unite the working class by a double tie, principle and self-interest. Moreover, it would get them used to habits of regularity in their plans, and this, along with their determination in carrying these out, was sure to topple tyranny. Rigorously applied, he maintained, exclusive dealing would, by ultimately pulling the financial base out from under the middle class's feet, turn them into working people and thus enhance the power of the working class.

Lowery realised that the carrying out of this plan would not be feasible without women's co-operation, and he therefore appealed to them:

> Women of Britain! On your co-operation much depends; without your aid we cannot be successful! You have the laying out of our wages....Remember that no woman is worthy of the name of a working-man's wife, who will lay out his hard-earned wages in the shops of those who insult him and deny him his political rights.

This passage is remarkable for the underlying awareness of the highly political significance of everyday tasks such as shopping. Such awareness, which (as shown above) was not confined to Lowery, eased women's entry into the movement by imbuing their housewifely duties with political meaning and placed them in a key position with regard to at least this Chartist tactic.

Although Lowery's claims as to the ultimate effects of exclusive dealing were somewhat exaggerated, the practice proved effective in the short run, for shopkeepers in working-class districts were in fact unable to afford losing their clientele. The amount of pressure exerted on them aroused a great deal of concern among the authorities.

The practise [*sic*] of exclusive dealing was confined to the early period of Chartism. This may be attributable to the shift of female support, ... Nevertheless, the tactic's previous success motivated attempts to revert to it at later stages. The political analysis underlying this tactic also survived. As late as in the summer of 1848, the female Chartists of Bethnal Green reiterated Lowery's argument of the identity of interests between shopkeepers and the working class in an appeal to the former to join the Chartist ranks.

Vincent, while also advocating exclusive dealing in an address to the women of the west of England, advised them to abstain additionally from all excisable articles and 'to do all in their power to deprive the government of money'. He himself in fact acted on this principle. [...]

Without the efforts of its female membership, the Chartist movement would never have become renowned for its well-developed social life, which was made up of countless tea and dinner parties, picnics, soirées and similar events. On these occasions, a committee was usually formed to see to the necessary catering arrangements.

Apart from providing food, the catering involved decorating the room in which the gathering was to take place. To this end, women not only used flowers abundantly, but also hung up portraits of their Chartist champions or caps of liberty to point to the political context in which the social occurred. The women's efforts were duly acknowledged, usually by proposing a toast along the lines of: 'The Tea Committee, thanks to them for their labours'.

By getting up these socials, women not merely brought to bear on Chartism the domestic skills they had acquired in their homes, but also imbued them with their own sense and understanding of female political involvement. Conversely, by attributing political significance to women's domestic skills, Chartism enabled women to participate in the movement without, however, opening up forms of activity that transgressed the boundaries of female domestic responsibilities. The movement's insistence on the manifold ways in which women might utilise the fulfilment of domestic tasks to further the Chartist cause certainly enabled Chartism to tap a larger pool of potential female support. Simultaneously, though, it confined women to a secondary role within the movement.

2. Female Chartists' appearance in public

Boosting Chartist ranks

[...]
Female Chartist petitioners thus stood in a tradition in which women had appealed to parliament for help whenever they had believed the integrity of their families to be under extreme pressure. Significantly, women made up a relatively larger proportion of signatories in areas where the Anti-Poor Law campaign had taken hold and where there existed precedents for female petitioning ...

Rioting

At least verbally, female Chartists occasionally declared themselves to be prepared to resort to violence in order to attain the Charter, or to condone what came to be called 'physical force'. The female Chartists of Ashton, while stating their abhorrence of bloodshed, quoted the Bible in justification of violent opposition to severe oppression.
[...]

Learning and teaching

The Chartist view of female intellectual abilities stood in stark contrast to the increasingly dominant Evangelical image of woman. This conceived of the sexes as essentially different, as antipodes, with women embodying emotions, men rationality. Men were characterised by physical and mental strength, an ambitious and enterprising spirit, courage, activity and perseverance, ability for close and comprehensive reasoning, all of which woman lacked. She, on the other hand, was construed as tender, compassionate, gentle, disinterested, conscientious, pious, contented, gay, cheerful, all of which qualities she was said to possess to a greater degree than man. Woman's mind, like her body, was chiefly characterised by weakness, rendering her prone to failings and surely unfitting her for any kind of serious application. The mental powers woman was believed to possess were all geared towards alleviating the sorrows and anxieties besetting the lives of her fellow-beings.

The female character, as conceived of by the Evangelicals, was so artificial as to require careful education for its creation. The emphasis was on moral education as opposed to the development of the intellect. This would bring out the spirit of devotion — that necessary requisite of femininity — ensure woman's acceptance of her proper sphere, and guard against presumption.

Chartist educational efforts have to be viewed against the notoriously deficient facilities available at the time for the education of women, particularly in the working class. Women rarely had equal access to available forms of adult education. It was at least the partial knocking down of such barriers that 'Sophia' had in mind when proposing that women be admitted to Mechanics' Institutes' lectures and reading rooms, 'of course, under severe restrictions, and altogether separate from the youths'. She called for the recognition of women's right to attend lectures on any subject, but particularly those dealing with the human frame, education and the right treatment of children. This was because she considered women to be entitled to knowledge on everything to do with children's minds and persons. Moreover, she advocated lectures be followed by discussion and suggested that lectures concerning women in particular be delivered by female speakers.

Despite the variety of forms of female adult education provided, the course-content was remarkably uniform, encompassing the three R's, sewing, cooking and some limited general knowledge. On the whole, the curriculum was geared towards improving women's domestic and child-rearing skills, thereby reinforcing the sexual division of labour within the working-class family.

This was the professed intention of Chartist educationalists, who maintained that the instruction of women must not estrange them from their domestic duties, which, troublesome as they might be, were considered an integral part of women's lives. Thence the emphasis on the following demand: *'Female education cannot be complete without a thorough knowledge of domestic arrangements.'* 'Sophia', like many other Chartist women, considered it to be their particular duty to prove that their education would not only not interfere with their attendance to domestic matters, but actually improve it.

[...]

Contributing to the Chartist press

The Chartist press received a large number of contributions from women, either in the form of articles, or, more often, in that of letters to the editor. Their exact scale can only be guessed at, for almost any proportion of the contributions that were only initialled or submitted entirely anonymously may have been of female origin.

The obstacles female contributors had to surmount, in terms of both literacy and conventions, are illustrated by the following opening to a letter sent by a working woman to the editor of *The National Association Gazette*. She self-consciously apologised for all grammatical and orthographical mistakes and implied that, had the paper not previously inserted contributions from other women and were her own long-standing adherence to Chartism not likely to induce the editor to leniency, her courage would have failed her. Her letter began thus: 'Please to excuse all faults, and put this letter in your *Gazette*. Myself and husband are both Chartists, and read your paper every week; and we have seen there [sic] letters from women, therefore I thought you would put in mine.'

[...]

Joining Female Chartist Associations

Apart from sexually mixed ventures, the Chartist movement provided the framework for women's structured participation with the founding of FCAs, which were exclusively female, at least in terms of membership. A total of just under one hundred and fifty of these have been found to exist at least at some stage of English Chartism between 1838 and 1852. This amounts to about one-ninth of the number of WMAs listed by Dorothy Thompson for the years 1839, 1841, 1842, 1844 and 1848.

The life-cycle of FCAs also showed a different pattern from those of their male counterparts. The latter had their climax in the years 1839 to 1842. Numbers had dropped down markedly by 1844, but had picked up considerably by 1848. Yet in that year, the number of WMAs was only half that in 1839.

[...]

The strongholds of FCAs were to be found in the heartlands of Britain's textile industry. The bulk of them clustered in Yorkshire, which was closely followed by Lancashire, including the northern half of Cheshire. FCAs thus mirrored the geographical pattern of female Chartism already outlined [...]. In areas where women's support of Chartism was very strong anyway, there was consequently an increased likelihood of their formalising their commitment to the movement by founding one of its female branches.

Membership of FCAs varied over time as well as according to the size of the population in a given locality. Birmingham, a comparatively large town, had, unlike London, only one central FCA boasting at one stage over 1300 members. This was quite exceptional, for the average FCA numbered between thirty and fifty women.

From among the female committee members whose names were reported in the Chartist press, the overwhelming majority (sixty-one) were married, while only nineteen were single. It would appear that being married helped to enhance a woman's status, thus increasing her willingness to stand for, and that of others to elect her into, office. The City of London FCA was unique in being exclusively organised by single women.

Furthermore, FCAs seem to have afforded several generations of women from one family scope for political activity.

[...]

The means of exerting political influence that were employed by FCAs were modelled on those of their male counterparts. FCAs would participate in Chartist demonstrations parading their own banners, which expressed specifically female concerns. Banners bearing inscriptions such as 'our children cryeth [sic] for Bread' or 'Mothers, claim the Rights of your children' emphasised that it was in order to safeguard their children's interests that many women had come into Chartism.

[...]

FCAs were very important in boosting contributions to the Chartist funds and also actively supported Chartist prisoners, be it by petitioning on their behalf or by collecting useful articles.

[...]

Clearly the members of FCAs formed an inner core of supporters, whom many other women sympathetic to the cause would join for special events or in times of great activity nationally. This accounts for the certain degree of overlap between activities listed as those of FCAs in this section, but also considered (in the subsections above) as activities engaged in by individual women.

Chartist leaders also perceived the vanguard function of FCAs by hoping they would win non-organised women over to Chartism.

[...]

FCAs were rooted in the tradition of sexually segregated organisation both within trade unions and political campaigns. With the spread of waged labour, followed by the introduction of factories, which heavily relied on a female workforce, conditions of work and pay had begun to affect male and female workers alike and had inspired resistance regardless of sex.

In the early stages of workplace organisation, exclusion on grounds of sex was not always total. Within trades employing a sexually mixed workforce, combinations had reflected this, even where women's status as secondary workers had long been established.[...]

Chapter 14

Catherine Hall

■ from 'THE EARLY FORMATION OF VICTORIAN
DOMESTIC IDEOLOGY', Chapter 3 of *White, Male and Middle Class:
Explorations in Feminism and History*, Polity, London, 1992, pp. 75–90

THE VICTORIAN MIDDLE-CLASS IDEAL of womanhood is one that is well documented – the 'angel in the house', the 'relative creature' who maintained the home as a haven, is familiar from novels, manuals and even government reports. There is plenty of evidence to suggest that by the 1830s and 1840s the definition of women as primarily relating to home and family was well established. But what were the origins of this ideal? 1780–1830 has been called the period of the making of the industrial bourgeoisie. That class defined itself not only in opposition to the new proletariat, but also to the classes of landed capitalism – the gentry and the aristocracy. Their class definition was built not only at the level of the political and the economic – the historic confrontations of 1832 and 1846 – but also at the level of culture and ideology. The new bourgeois way of life involved a recodification of ideas about women. Central to those new ideas was an emphasis on women as domestic beings, as primarily wives and mothers. Evangelicalism provided one crucial influence on this definition of home and family. Between 1780 and 1820, in the Evangelical struggle over anti-slavery and over the reform of manners and morals, a new view of the nation, of political power and of family life was forged. This view was to become a dominant one in the 1830s and 1840s. The Evangelical emphasis on the creation of a new life-style, a new ethic, provided the framework for the emergence of the Victorian bourgeoisie. [...]

Central to the Evangelicals' attempt to reconstruct daily life and create a new morality with liberal and humanist parameters on the one hand (the attack on slavery), yet buttressed by social conservatism on the other (the reform of manners and morals), was the redefinition of the position of the woman in the family. The Evangelical attempt to transform daily life was based on the belief in the universality of sin and the need for constant struggle against it. A primary arena of this struggle must be the home and family. The Evangelical ideal of the family and the woman at home was developed well before the French Revolution. Cowper, for example, 'the poet of domesticity', was writing in the 1780s. But it was the debate about the nature and the role of women, produced by the Revolution, which opened the floodgates of manuals from Evangelical pens. Mary Wollstonecraft's *Vindication of the Rights of Women* was first published in 1792 – before the tide had really been turned in England by the Terror. Hannah More was appalled by the book and she became the major protagonist of an alternative stance.

[…]

The Evangelicals pilloried aristocratic ideals of women – they attacked as inadequate the way in which women were educated and the refusal to take them seriously. They denounced the double standard and championed the value of a good marriage. They drew on the eighteenth-century debate about women – they admired Richardson and agreed with the early Cobbett about, for example, the unfortunate aping of their betters by aspirant farmers' wives. They were responding again to the major social transformation which was taking place in England as a result of the development of capitalism. They were concerned with the problem of defining for the middle ranks a way of life best suited to their affluence and leisure. By the 1780s existing material conditions enabled many more women to forgo employment – and a 'lady of leisure' enjoyed the hallmark of gentility. As Pinchbeck has demonstrated, the number of well-to-do women in mercantile and commercial ventures was dropping. How were these women, with their new-found wealth and time, to behave? And who was to provide the model? Hannah More, Gisborne, Wilberforce, Mrs West, Mrs Sherwood and many others were adept and successful in assuming the role of mentors.

Evangelicalism has been described as 'the religion of the household' and it is clear that the notion of home and family was central to their religious views. Cowper refers to:

Domestic happiness, thou only bliss
Of paradise that has survived the Fall.
[…]

Within the household it was quite clearly established that men and women had their separate spheres. Hannah More defined certain qualities and dispositions as 'peculiarly feminine'. Cultural differences were seen as natural. Women were naturally more delicate, more fragile, morally weaker, and all this demanded a greater degree of caution, retirement and reserve. 'Men, on the contrary, are formed for the more public exhibition on the great theatre of human life'; men had grandeur, dignity and force; women had ease, simplicity and purity. This absolute distinction between men and women is repeated time and again in Evangelical writing.

Evangelicals expected women to sustain and even to improve the moral qualities of the opposite sex. It is at this level that the Evangelicals offered women an area of importance which, therefore, holds within itself considerable contradictions. Women, it was believed, could act as the moral regenerators of the nation. They occupied a key position in the struggle to reform and revive the nation. Women in the home could provide, as it were, a revolutionary base from which their influence could shine forth: 'If our women lose their domestic virtues, all the charities will be dissolved, for which our country is a name so dear. The men will be profligate, the public will be betrayed, and whatever has blessed or distinguished the English nation on the Continent will disappear,' wrote a friend to More, congratulating her on her book on female education. That book, published in 1799 in the wake of the moral panic, exhorted women to play their part in the struggle for national survival. They were being offered a field where they could be allowed to wield some power and influence within the moral sphere. They could play an important part in the reform of manners and morals. Wilberforce made a similar plea for women's support in *Practical*

Christianity. He argued that women were especially disposed to religion; this was partly because their education was limited and they were not exposed to the moral dangers of the classics. The woman, therefore, had the particular duty of encouraging her husband's religious sensibilities: 'when the husband should return to his family, worn and harassed by worldly cares or professional labours, the wife, habitually preserving a warmer and more unimpaired spirit of devotion, than is perhaps consistent with being immersed in the bustle of life, might revive his languid piety.' Women had open to them a most noble office: 'we would make them as it were the medium of our intercourse with the heavenly world, the faithful repositories of the religious principle for the benefit both of the present and the rising generation.' Because the major problem in England was seen by the Evangelicals as being the prevalent state of religious and moral decadence, this emphasis on the religious power of the woman considerably modified their emphasis elsewhere on subordination. In a later period, Victorian feminists like Mrs Jameson were to build on this contradiction.

The good Evangelical woman had recognizable characteristics: she was modest, unassuming, unaffected and rational. ('Rational' was used as the opposite to 'sentimental' or 'subject to violent feeling'.)

[...]

The right choice in marriage was seen as vital to a good Evangelical life. Since the religious household was the basis of Christian practice, it was essential to find the right partner.

[...]

The unmarried woman had to do what she could; basically, Evangelical writing on women assumed marriage and the family. Within marriage it was quite clear that the wife was subordinate to her husband – it was not a question open to 'speculative arguments'. Faithful and willing obedience on the part of the wife was essential, even in cases of domestic management. The first set of duties – looking after the home and family – was, in St Paul's terms, 'guiding the house'. The superintendence of domestic management is clearly demarcated from doing the work itself; there was an absolute assumption that servants would be available. Domestic management required regularity of accounts and the proper care of money. Home should be seen as the wife's centre. There she could influence to the good her children, her servants, and her neighbours. It is in the home that 'the general character, the acknowledged property, and the established connections of her husband, will contribute with more force than they can possess elsewhere, to give weight and impressiveness to all her proceedings'. Women were consequently advised not to leave home too much – it was only there that they could achieve moral excellence.

[...]

If women were to be able to exercise a proper moral influence, they must be well educated. A clear distinction was made between the education of the daughters of the poor and those of the upper and middle classes. The daughters of the poor should be trained as servants or as good wives; the emphasis in their schooling should be on industry, frugality, diligence and good management. The daughters of the well-to-do, on the other hand, should be educated for moral excellence, and that meant that the traditional girls' training which they had been receiving was quite inadequate. To be able to dress well, to dance and play the piano, was not enough. 'The profession of ladies,' wrote More, 'is that of daughters, wives, mothers and mistresses of families.' They should, therefore, be trained for that. Given these considerations, there was much to be said for educating girls at home. A mother was the best person to train her daughter. The purpose of that training was not to enable women to compete with men, but to prepare them in the best possible way for their relative sphere. Mothers were responsible for the children of both sexes in infancy, for their daughters until they left home. The Evangelicals stressed the importance of parental responsibility and the religious implications of good motherhood. The fathers took especial responsibility for their sons, but often had very close domestic ties with their daughters as well.

The Evangelical ideology of domesticity, it has been argued here, was not an ideal constructed for others, but an attempt to reconstruct family life and the relations between the sexes on the basis of 'real' Christianity. The Puritans had developed many similar views on marriage in an earlier period. The two groups shared the experience of living through a period of very rapid social, political and economic change; the articulation of their response was in religious terms, but it cannot be understood outside the particular historical conjuncture. Changing ideas about women and the family must be seen in relation to changes in the mode of production and in the social relations of production and reproduction. The Puritans and the Evangelicals shared a need to build a protected space in a hostile world, from which the great campaign of evangelization could be securely launched. The home was an area which could be controlled and which was relatively independent of what went on outside. The home did provide a haven. The expansion of capitalist relations of production in the late eighteenth century meant that homes were increasingly separated from workplaces, although this was a lengthy process and, in some trades, family workshops survived for a very long time. It has also been suggested that domestic demand for such items of household utility as china provided one of the main factors in the industrial 'take-off' at the end of the eighteenth century. In other words, the emergence of a particular kind of home was directly related to the expansion of productive forces. But the way that home was realized, lived in and experienced within the middle ranks was crucially mediated by Evangelicalism. [...]

[...] The bourgeois ideal of the family became a part of the dominant culture and, by the 1830s and 1840s, was being promoted through propaganda as the only proper way to live. In the government reports of that period, working wives and mothers are presented as something unnatural and immoral. Working-class women were castigated for being poor housewives and inadequate mothers. If married women were to enter paid employment, they should not be seen; they should work at home. They should not flaunt their independence as the mill girls did. It is worth noting that the early campaigns to improve the working conditions of women focused on the factory system and the mines and did not come to grips with more hidden areas, such as the sweated trades. The bourgeois family was seen as the proper family, and that meant that married women should not work. The ideology of the family thus obscured class relations, for it came to appear above class. That ideology also obscured the cultural definition of the sexual division of labour, since the split between men and women came to be seen as naturally ordained. Nature decreed that all women were first and foremost wives and mothers.

Chapter 15

Judith A. DeGroat

■ from 'THE PUBLIC NATURE OF WOMEN'S WORK:
DEFINITIONS AND DEBATES DURING THE REVOLUTION
OF 1848', *French Historical Studies*, 20 (1), Winter 1997, pp. 31–47

O N 21 MAY 1848 THE REVOLUTIONARY government held a festival in Paris
[*Fête de la Concorde*] to celebrate the Republic and to gather French citizens in a display
of harmony and unity. A major feature of the parade was a band of five hundred young girls,
dressed in white and crowned with oak leaves, who sang the 'Hymn of the Girondins'.

The presence of these working-class girls received considerable attention in press
accounts and memoirs of the event, especially given both the circumscribed role they played
in the overall festivities and the participation of other groups of women. Some accounts
were favorable in their discussion of the girls; most were not. Commentators used gendered
terms; their praise or criticism reflected their awareness of current, and competing, norms
of female sexuality. Based on an assessment of the girls' suitability to represent the Republic,
journalists, government officials, and observers from both the left and the right judged
them to be either virginal or corrupt. These critics also noted without much comment the
appearance of other women in the choirs and in delegations from female trades. [...]
Women's presence in the political arena was unsettling in a time that had begun to define
public space as masculine.
[...]

[...] Women worked throughout the Parisian handicraft sector: in the furniture, print,
chemical, and luxury trades as well as in garment and textile production. It is important to
note women's vital presence in the other trades of the capital, a presence well established
since the eighteenth century. By 1848, for example, one-quarter of the wood gilders (*doreurs
sur bois*) in the Faubourg St. Antoine were women; female upholstery workers (*tapissières*)
made up half the trade's workforce. Women composed a significant part of the workforce
in the luxury trades such as fancy work with feathers (*plumassières*) and in particular dominated
artificial-flower making (*fleuristes*). Already considerable in the eighteenth century, the female
component constituted 40 percent of the workforce in the Parisian manufacturing sector at
midcentury.

While the participation of women in the Paris trades was not new, the responses to
their activities reflected a sharpened attention to their presence in the labor force. Although

sweated home work employed increasing numbers of women throughout this period, more than half of female wage labor took place in the city's workshops. The expansion of subcontracting in the Paris trades during the 1830s and 1840s had drawn largely on the female labor force, which challenged the dominance of male artisan *corporations* in the handicraft sector. These men responded unfavorably to what they termed unfair competition from unskilled female labor. Working-class men, joined by socialist writers, simultaneously regarded women workers as economic competitors and as victims of bourgeois sexual exploitation. The editors of the working men's journal *L'Atelier* reported with approbation the strikes of male workers against shops that hired women even as they extolled the purity and endurance of their women in the face of sexual and economic exploitation by the bourgeois classes. Louis Blanc and other socialist writers contributed to the portrait of wage competition, shattered families, and women forced to 'choose between prostitution and hunger.' *L'Atelier*'s editors summed up the official working men's view on the subject of women's wage labor: 'Woman was not made to manufacture our products or to occupy our factories, she must devote herself to the education of her children, to the cares of her household.'

Sharing a concern for the working-class family, political economists and social reformers upheld women as the saviors of men. Unlike Blanc and other socialists, however, many middle-class men were unconvinced that working-class women participated equally in the cult of true womanhood that increasingly enshrined their bourgeois sisters. Working mothers and wives, employed in workshops and factories at low wages, contributed to the growth of the French manufacturing economy; at the same time, they raised fears of uncontrolled female sexuality. While acknowledging the necessity of female wage labor, even political economists warned of the dire social consequences of the sexual promiscuity of the workplace, their term for the character of the workshops that employed both women and men. In addition, reformers such as Honoré Frégier warned of women who corrupted young female apprentices in the workshops of Paris by 'their base inclination, their immorality, and their excesses.' This supposed affinity for sexual corruption extended into the home. Among others, A. J. B. Parent Duchâtelet, the epoch's authority on prostitution, and Théodore Fix, a leading political economist, joined Frégier in a chorus that denounced the debauched working-class mother who destroyed her family through neglect. Still, most authors held out hope of the salvation inherent in working-class motherhood. Bourgeois writers went to great lengths to avoid direct confrontation with the contradictions presented by their representations of the woman worker, just as working-class spokesmen did. Thus, the debate over female labor that pervaded the public discourse of the July Monarchy was dominated by the conflicting images wielded in the struggle between bourgeois and working-class men.

Women's participation in and, at times, instigation of strikes and other labor actions put forward their own definitions of female labor. One of the earliest strikes in the July Monarchy began as a walkout of twenty women in the hat trade. These fur cutters left their shop and called out the women in a neighboring shop, owned by a Madam Badeuil, to protest a wage cut that they charged was the result of colluding *patrons*. The National Guard arrested five women, four of whom were subsequently convicted of illegal coalition. A year later a strike started by a group of shawl cutters challenging the introduction of cutting machines led to a week-long revolt in Montmartre; authorities swiftly shifted their attention away from the women, arguing that the instigators had to have been men disguised as women. During the trial of the nine women arrested for coalition, press accounts expressed surprise that such feminine creatures, rather than those with 'male and marked traits, the strong voice of a hussy,' could be responsible for 'a revolt in skirts.' In the politically volatile year of 1834 — which resulted in the suppression of much working-class activism until 1848 — female and male wood gilders struck the *patron* of a furniture shop who had contracted prison labor; six women and seventeen men were sentenced to prison for illegal coalition. In this case the women's activism was dismissed as being influenced by their husbands' politics. Female labor activism revealed women's determination to have a voice in their work and their lives; the representations of that activism in the press and in government reports equally revealed the discomfort and ambivalence generated by such acts.

Working women's very active presence in the events of the Revolution of 1848 continued a tradition begun in 1789 and revived in 1830; it also contributed to the conflicting images attributed to them. Well before the *fête* of 21 May, women had participated in the revolt that overthrew Louis Philippe, had demanded inclusion in the formation of the Luxembourg Commission to study the labor question, and had formed political clubs to further female political and economic emancipation. Fur cutters and artificial-flower makers petitioned for government assistance for individual female trades. More successfully, unemployed women demonstrated for the establishment of *ateliers de femmes*, a program which had already been established for the male unemployed in the early days of the revolution. On 29 March, the mayor of Paris, Marrast, announced the opening of workshops in which women would sew shirts for National Guard. A. Duclerc, the functionary in charge of the workshops, was soon deluged with demands from women who wished to take their work home so that they could tend to their household as well as to their wage-earning work. In addition, workers, including the former *saint simonienne* Desirée Gay, challenged male officials' assumption that all women knew how to sew; they continued to press the government to provide useful employment for women of all trades. As a result of their activism, women found themselves caricatured in the right-wing press as mannish and desexed, as foolish young things easily led by others, or as raging viragos. Many writers on the left, while acknowledging the tireless labor of the working-class housewife, also continued their portrayal of the working woman as solely a sexual victim of the *patron*. By the time of the Festival of Concord, then, a variety of images and definitions of working women and their labor existed.

[...]

Other groups of women also prepared to participate in the festival parade. Those female trades accepted within the organization of Parisian handicrafts appeared as part of the presentation of artisan *corporations*, national guards, and soldiers: makers of plumes and of artificial flowers, porcelain painters, and upholsterers were to be part of the *corps d'état*. These trades were important elements in luxury and furniture production, which were themselves key sectors of the expanding manufacturing economy of the capital. Women's work in these occupations was also established within a sexual division of labor that accepted them as female trades. [...] the intricate work of constructing flowers and feathered ornaments had been part of this tradition since the eighteenth century, as had women's work in ceramics and areas of the furniture trades. No reports indicate women's presence among the wood gilders' *corps*. Although certainly part of the trade, *doreuses* were also viewed with hostility by the male leaders of the trade and may not, for that reason, have been included in the festival contingent. The presence of women from the predominantly female trades would not have provoked the hostility generated by male artisans' fears of competition.

The garment and textile trades, the largest employers of female labor in manufacturing, were also not represented. Although accepted as women's work, women's employment in these trades generated resentment among several artisan *corporations*, particularly the tailors, as unfair competition for male wages. Garment work was also considered the least skilled of female occupations; certainly, it was among the lowest paid. In addition, the concern generated by female wage labor in the early nineteenth century focused on urban seamstresses and textile factory operatives. Villermé's study of the condition of workers in the northern textile centers frequently cited female mill hands as a major cause of moral decline. The employment of women in the shops and garrets of the urban needle trades had acquired a disreputable reputation. The rise of sweated home work merged in some minds with clandestine prostitution and led seamstresses to be deemed sexually corrupt by bourgeois social observers. Central to the economic transformation that France was currently experiencing, women in garment and textile production were also the repository for anxieties generated by industrial capitalism. The government, to avoid controversy with this very public festival, carefully selected the representatives of working women.

In the same way, members of the women's national workshops met resistance to their request to be represented in the festivities. Women had already fought to get the government to acknowledge that the right to work included women as well as men; the *ateliers des femmes* were set up one month after those for men. Since the establishment of the workshops, the workers and individual mayors had fought with Duclerc, the director of the women's shops, for materials, equipment, and pay. Additionally, the women launched a successful effort to be allowed to take their work home in order to combine their household and wage-earning responsibilities. As described by Desirée Gay in the journal *La Voix des femmes*, battles raged over Duclerc's efforts to eliminate from the workshops those he deemed 'undeserving.' The women also charged him with administrative waste, which prevented the employment of additional women. The *ouvrières* also demanded that the work provided be expanded to include women whose skills did not include needlework. Women lost this battle. Fifty years earlier, spinning had been defined as women's work; *ateliers de filatures* were the charity workshops of the 1790s. The transformation of manufacturing had transformed the image of the woman worker into that of seamstress. Duclerc and those he represented would not take seriously requests for employment from copper burnishers, bookbinders, and artificial-flower makers to provide them with work in their trades.

[…]

The five hundred young girls dressed in white were the focus of accounts of women's participation in the festival parade. The republican press was favorable in its response. In these accounts, the girls represented purity, innocence, and patriotism, traits well received by the assembled populace.

[…]

The other female participants remained almost unnoticed in discussions of the festival. Few appeared to have observed the delegation from the women's national workshops. Some viewers noted the female *corporations*, but the presence of these women did not generate either the praise or the hostility provoked by the young girls in white. The material reality of mid-nineteenth-century Parisian society included working women, as sweated home workers and in the workshops of the crafts. At the same time, their existence was problematic for that society, all the more so because of women's activism since the outbreak of the Revolution. For the most part, adult female workers were mothers. They were also a direct reminder of the social and economic transformation that France was experiencing. Working women represented the exploitation of female and child labor, the subsequent profits of manufacturing entrepreneurs and the growth of the dangerous classes, more populous and stirred to revolutionary fervor. The government carefully stage-managed the representations of female labor in the parade and sought to avoid reminders. Observers acquiesced as they lost sight of these women workers amid the fraternal confusion of the festival. As Gay Gullickson argues, 'The way men have demonstrated their mastery of the revolution has often been by mastering the representation' of women. Both sides of the revolutionary conflict in late May 1848 had an interest in constructing a particular image of the Parisian working woman.

The young girls in white represented working-class womanhood to all who attended the *fête*. The planners of the festival carefully chose them from working-class backgrounds; there was no reason for anyone to question their social status. There, however, consensus ended, for the spectators gave very different meanings to what they saw. For some, the young women were the heart of the popular festival, the white of their gowns a symbol of their purity and their simplicity, which in turn represented the purity of the people, the true hearts of the Republic. For others, these symbols revealed what frightened them about working-class women: a sexuality that was not controlled. The very public activity of these young women mocked, for these witnesses, the chastity implied in their dress. They, in turn, scorned not only the girls' virginity but also their beauty, their femininity, their ability to participate fully in this political and public event. At the same time, the appearance of five hundred working-class girls underscored the implications inherent in the establishment of the democratic and social Republic called for by workers and socialists. Class politics certainly added another dimension to the representation of the working women in the Festival of Concord. Divisions between left and right, between those who supported the Republic and those who did not, can be read in the critiques of the young girls dressed in white. It should be noted, however, that the voices of working-class men in the dialogue surrounding the *fête* were few, perhaps silenced by the abolition of the Luxembourg Commission or perhaps by their own contradictory images of working-class womanhood. Other, related aspects of this festival also bear further scrutiny that would deepen this analysis, such as the question of masculine identity and its representations at the time. What this preliminary sketch suggests, however, is that the public events of the Revolution and women's participation in them are very rich areas for the study of the meanings given to women's activities at a very particular point in history.

Chapter 16

Patricia J. Hilden

■ 'THE RHETORIC AND ICONOGRAPHY OF REFORM: WOMEN COAL MINERS IN BELGIUM, 1840–1914', *Historical Journal*, 34 (2), 1991, pp. 411–36

R EFLECTING ON THE DEVELOPMENT of industrial capitalism in Europe, Antonio Gramsci wrote:

> It is worth drawing attention to the way in which industrialists ... have been concerned with the sexual affairs of their employees and with their family arrangements in general. One should not be misled ... by the 'puritanical' appearance assumed by this concern. The truth is that the new type of man demanded by the rationalization of production and work cannot be developed until the sexual instinct has been suitably regulated and until it too has been rationalized.[1]

In nineteenth-century Belgium, industrialists, legislators, and bourgeois reformers were not merely concerned with the sexual and family arrangements of coal miners. Throughout the decades following independence in 1830, all three groups engaged in enthusiastic efforts to intervene in the sexual lives of those who mined Belgium's coal. The effort was a lengthy one. Not until the early years of the twentieth century were the laws in place, that successfully eliminated what reformers had seen as the dangerously unrestricted sexual life of an underground world in which women and men, boys and girls, toiled together.

In addition to widespread concern about the purported sexual stimulation of underground labor, many reformers found several other motives for concerning themselves with the nature of coal production as it was practised in Belgium. For one thing, unlike other key industries such as textiles, the coal industry had changed very little since the twelfth century. This longevity meant both that the traditions of the industry were deeply entrenched and that few Belgians (perhaps only the inhabitants of rural Flanders) were unaware of the nature of mine work in their coal fields. Thus public appeals to reform – or to rationalize – industrial production that were focused on altering the private morals of workers were most likely to find sympathy if they cited the well-known case of coal mining.

One key aspect of mining traditions was peculiarly troublesome to reformers who grew increasingly anxious over the course of the nineteenth century to impose bourgeois standards on the working class. This was the nature of women's work. In the Belgian mines, women's work was less clearly segregated by sex than it was elsewhere in industrializing Europe. Women and men, girls and boys, frequently did the same work. For example, all these groups broke and loaded the newly-cut coal, and women, girls and boys together had the primary responsibility for transporting it to the surface. Thus females of all ages shared with males all the hardest work, and the terrible dangers of mining coal. The fact that Belgium's women worked underground, in an industry increasingly associated solely with working class masculinity (as any reading of Emile Zola's *Germinal* or George Orwell's later *Road to Wigan pier* will readily demonstrate) meant that bourgeois efforts to rationalize both the work process and the private lives of coal miners were rather different from those employed elsewhere. Efforts to change the Belgian coal mining work-force into a 'modern' (i.e. male) one, necessitated propaganda directed at changing the public view of women coal miners from a positive one to one that aroused sufficient public distress to persuade reluctant liberal legislators to restrict female work underground (as was done in Britain in the 1840s). The nineteenth century thus witnessed sustained efforts on the part of reformers and some legislators, as well as certain far-sighted industrialists, to convince Belgians that bourgeois standards of behavior and morality must be imposed – by legislation, if necessary – on the inhabitants of coal mining districts. From the 1840s, they focused their arguments on gender – first on the imagined dangers of the confusion of gender roles, and second on the sexual licence which 'naturally' resulted from the constant physical proximity of the males and females underground. Most reformers favored a solution based on a clear sexual division of labor which would restrict women workers to the surface of coal mines, leaving men and boys working alone underground.

There were two kinds of arguments adduced to support such a reform: first, many argued that working in the dimly-lit underground world of the coal mine encouraged sexual licence. Others insisted that women's constant close contact with men altered both their physiognomies and their personalities. In other words, both women's purportedly masculinized bodies and their womanly participation in public life – in strikes, in demonstrations, and in the social life after working hours of the ubiquitous café-bars – were direct results of the unseemly mixing of the sexes in the mines. In the minds of most bourgeois reformers, 'moral' women belonged only in their 'proper' domestic sphere: that is, in what one recent writer has called 'that sphere of sexual containment *par excellence*' – the home.[2]

In Belgium, however, removing working class women from mining (as well as from all Belgium's major industries) would have had two deleterious effects. First, it would have imposed an extraordinary hardship on working class families in a society virtually without public social welfare institutions. Second, and doubtless more important, it would have created a massive economic problem for industrialists because of industrial Wallonia's labor shortage. Thus efforts to encourage working women to emulate their bourgeois sisters by retreating into the domestic sphere and assuming an existence entirely devoted to male family members, faced considerable opposition. Indeed, bourgeois family values had so little effect on the lives of the Belgian working class that the socialist deputy, Lucie Dejardin, recalled her youthful family life in a coal mining town at the end of the nineteenth century with irony. 'Thanks to the beautiful principle of liberty of work', she wrote, 'Belgium presented, until the end of the nineteenth century, a spectacle rare in Europe, of the perfect family life: father, mother, and children in the depths of the mine.' The historian Henri Pirenne similarly characterized working class life in nineteenth-century Belgian coal towns. Writing of the 1840s, he observed, 'As for the women, excepting the few days when their annual lying-in keeps them at home, they spend their lives as their husbands and children do … in the mines'.[3]

Thus it was unlikely that reformers would succeed in transforming Belgian mining women into the privatized, sexually 'pure' domestic creatures idealized by much of bourgeois society. The requisite innocence of sexuality, of men, of politics, or of industrial work was denied them. Without it, their gender identity never developed the degree of separateness commonly associated with women of the middle and upper classes. By contrast, in Britain, Belgium's nearest economic rival, reformers were successful in restricting women to surface work in the coal mines by the end of the 1840s, a reform thought to lead the women closer to their proper spheres. In addition, British married women tended increasingly to leave all mining work, even that restricted to the surface. Thus British coal mining quickly became identified with proletarian masculinity. So complete was this transformation, that even those women who continued to work in various heavy, dirty jobs around the coal mines effectively vanished from public view. By the end of the nineteenth century, the English word 'miner' connoted both various admirable physical attributes and a distinct gender identity.[4]

It is worth noting, too, that the departure of married women from British coal mining was duplicated in most other heavy industries in Britain. Thus the Victorian ideology of women's proper place reflected some degree of working class reality. The British, therefore, were largely successful in 'rationalizing' workers' private lives, in which women existed within the reproductive sphere, isolated from the public world of work and politics.[5]

In Belgium, however, attempts to rationalize – or to control – the working and private lives of coal miners were doomed to failure as a centuries-old, mixed sex tradition in Belgian coal mining was reluctant to die of its own accord. Nevertheless, the public's image of Belgian women coal miners did not remain static over the course of the nineteenth century. But rather than vanish into a slightly disreputable, seldom-recalled past, as, they did in Britain after legislation drove them out of the mines, Belgian women miners were gradually assimilated to the young country's developing national identity – an identity that began to emerge in the decades after independence. There were many features of women coal mine workers that rendered them ideal symbols of this emergent national identity. Typically they were young, physically strong, stoical and hard-working. All these elements shaped the ways in which Belgians began to talk about themselves as a nation different from the other nations of industrializing Europe.

The vehicle for the transformation of women coal mine workers into national icons was art. In the final quarter of the nineteenth century, a group of painters and sculptors emerged whose socialist sympathies turned their attention towards workers of all kinds. For this group, the women miners – now called by a generic term, 'hiercheuse' [6] – provided an unusually ideal subject. The nature of their work, together with their positive notoriety, made them the perfect heroine of labor who could stand proudly, side-by-side with other Belgian worker-heroes, such as the Antwerp dockers or the highly-skilled iron workers. (It is interesting to note that those workers upon whom so much of Belgium's economic prosperity rested, the textile workers, never elicited the public approbation reserved for some other workers.)

The work of these artists was enthusiastically supported by the growing socialist party (founded in 1885). Leaders of the *Parti ouvrier belge* were, in fact, unique among leaders of Second International parties in their conviction that art was of particular importance in arousing class consciousness. The Belgian party sponsored many lecture series aimed at teaching workers about art; they gave further evidence of their belief in the importance of art by commissioning paintings, sculptures and even buildings. (The Maison du Peuple in Brussels was designed, for example, by the *art nouveau* architect, Victor Horta.) And of course art for the proletariat, often became art of the proletariat, in which workers as subjects played a prominent role. Not surprisingly, therefore, the *hiercheuse* became one of the most frequently painted, sculpted, and later photographed workers in Belgium from the 1880s onward.[7] Hundreds of portraits of *hiercheuses*, at work, at rest, sometimes at play, turned female coal miners into a national icon. Displayed publicly all over the country, the *hiercheuse* became to some extent, at least – Belgium's unique *Marianne*.

In this unusual transformation of real subjects into an artistic image, the sexuality of the 'real' *hiercheuses* – imagine to be particularly uncontrolled underground – was tamed, not by forcing women miners into the separate world of the home, or even by restricting them to surface work, where the light of day might prevent untoward sexual promiscuity, but rather by aestheticizing them into a-sexual, pre-pubescents. In other words, virtually every portrait of these *hiercheuses* shows a youthful figure almost entirely lacking overt female sexual characteristics. Thus did the artistic imagination succeed in reducing the perceived threat of Belgium's most visible, and purportedly most militant working women. It was a transformation that found no parallels in neighboring countries. Indeed, in Britain, by comparison, the artistic imagination found one of two stereotypes with which to portray working class women: the highly sentimentalized mother-saints who were poor, but honest, replicas of their bourgeois sisters, or the equally sentimentalized, undomesticated fallen women, beloved of the pre-Raphaelites. (Of course, the latter stereotypes did show up in some Belgian painting of the time, but they were far outnumbered by the *hiercheuses*.)[8]

The story of this transformation of women coal miners from a dual role as the *bête noir* of mid-century reformers, on the one hand, or the ideal proletarian woman beloved of industrialists and economic liberals on the other, into an icon of Belgian and socialist labor is complex. It begins in the public debate over protective labor legislation, launched in the 1840s. This debate focused on women's work in the coal industry, doubtless because both the nature of the world and its venue seemed most vulnerable to public sentiment.

The debate engaged four issues of interest to historians. First, its early rhetoric was clearly borrowed from France and reflected the extent to which French influence still dominated Belgium's intellectuals, even after independence. (If there was any residual Dutch influence – and this is debatable – it was restricted to the primarily agricultural, Dutch-speaking region of Flanders.) It is possible to trace the post-independence development of an indigenous political rhetoric by examining the gradual disappearance of French ideas from Belgian reformers' arguments.

Second, the terms of the debate, including its internal contradictions, underscore the uniqueness of gender relations within the mining labor force, as compared with, for example, the textile workers. The easy familiarity between men and women coal miners so shocked many bourgeois opponents of women's work that they insisted that Belgian mining turned the natural world inside out as well as upside down. Mikhail Bakhtin's remarks about the lengthy historical past of fears about the underground world, or for that matter Jane Harrison's observations about the gender significance of the underground in Greek religious beliefs, both suggest that the world below the ground has long served as a locus of sexual fears[9] – fears abundantly evident in the discourse of nineteenth-century Belgian reformers. Thus most of the latter argued that not only were human beings threatening the 'natural' spatial order by working deep below ground, but they were also challenging the psychological order, by mingling women and men together in what most agreed was more properly a male world.

Third, in mid-century, when Belgians were in the process of creating a new nation after centuries of occupation, the importance of maintaining post-revolutionary order was crucial. Although the 1840s and 1850s presented little evidence that social disorder was imminent (indeed, Belgium was uniquely calm in 1848) the *fear* of social unrest shaped much political language. (Then too, many non-mine-owning industrialists had an interest in convincing liberal legislators to continue to intervene in controlling their *potentially* restive work force as a further means of creating a 'modern', disciplined working class.)

Finally, the ineffectiveness of the proponents of protective labor legislation highlighted Belgium's differences from other industrializing countries. In contrast to most of the rest of industrial Europe, Belgian women's hard manual labor had long been an accepted fact of life. Working women's visibility (in a small, densely-populated country) as well as the general public's acceptance of women's work, prompted many observers, both foreign and domestic, to conclude – in the words of one 'In Belgium, women do all the work'.[10] And it was true that without women's labor, few of Belgium's key industries would have enjoyed an adequate domestic supply of labor. Thus women worked not only in the coal mines, but also in textile mills, in glass-works, in armaments manufacture, on the docks, in brick-yards, in chemical factories, and so on.

The debate over legislative restrictions on women's work thus unfolded in the very special context of Belgian economic and social life. Not surprisingly, its rhetoric was replete with contradiction, and sometimes a high degree of sheer muddle. Before beginning to disentangle the elements of this debate, however, it is important to identify the women workers who were its objects.

In Belgian coal mines, women and girls (i.e., those under 18) comprised about one-tenth of the underground work force. At the height of adult women's employment below ground, between 1860 and 1889, there were probably about 11,000 women working below ground, together with about 100,000 adult men. (Of course, many thousands more women worked at the surface, where the ratio of women to men was smaller.)[11] Although the figures here are just as unreliable as they were for French employment in the same era, for example, it is clear that substantial numbers of women were working together with men underground, though their tenure at work was likely to be shorter than most men's, and usually more sporadic (although both men and women were prone to taking informal leaves of absence from the mines every spring when work was available outdoors in the brick-yards of Wallonia and Flanders).[12]

Women and girls did a variety of jobs inside the mines. In the larger mines, their work was usually identified as 'women's work'. The sexual division of labor was considerably less clear in smaller mines, where work depended upon a more improvised working process. Generally speaking, women did the hardest, dirtiest, most dangerous work (as many mine visitors noted). Essentially they were responsible for moving the coal from the coal face to the surface. This meant that they also had to break the large chunks of newly cut coat into moveable, sortable pieces. They loaded the broken pieces either into sacks which they tied to their heads and dragged to the surface, or later, into carts which they pushed and pulled to the surface. (In the more prosperous mines, iron rails were laid to aid their efforts. In newer mines, galleries were increasingly enlarged to allow ponies to replace the *hiercheuses*. But the oldest mines were too deep to allow such a change.)

At the surface, women's work still involved moving the coal about the mines, loading and unloading the heavy iron wagons, weighing them, sorting the coal, and then loading the train cars waiting to take the coal away. The worst work of all — usually, but not always reserved for elderly or incapacitated women — was that of the '*glaneuses*'. These gleaners worked on the towering, slippery black slag heaps that surrounded every coal mine, picking usable coal from the waste. In most mines, these were self-employed local women, whose rights to glean were recognized by mine owners. The most fortunate of these women (who were often helped by those of their children who were too young to go down the mines) found enough coal both to provide for their own needs and to sell in nearby towns and villages.

The only work that was exclusively men's work was that of cutting the coal itself. Even here, however, gender distinctions were sometimes blurred. When the Victorian Arthur Munby visited Charleroi in 1865, he was told by one male miner about some women 'getters', one of whom, 'a strong, young woman', 'did it as well as a man'.[13]

These, then, were Belgium's women coal miners. Their numbers show, of course, that not all women in coal regions worked in the mines. And indeed, there were alternative occupations available for working class women, though few that paid as well as mining. Still, it was coal that shaped the lives of all the inhabitants, male and female, of coal villages and towns — whether they kept the café-bars in which miners of both sexes socialized after work, or whether they worked as *boteresses*, carrying coal and other goods from city to city on their backs. And even for those women whose working lives were spent working at some occupation other than coal mining or its ancillaries, it was likely that some time in their lives they would go down the mines.[14]

And thus it was the women of the *pays noir* who became the targets of reformers in the 1840s. The main thrust of these reformers' arguments against women working in coal reflected, as I have said, French gender discourse, which in the early nineteenth century came from the French romantics. In this rhetoric, 'nature', which had been the bestower of reason during the enlightenment, became the repository of human emotion. For romantics, 'true' nature existed only in the primitive state; human intervention always deformed the original system. Virtue was achieved only by returning to the original condition.

For working women, this meant withdrawing from the 'unnatural' industrial world, and returning to the virtuous domestic sphere, where their 'true natures' could perform their natural function: reproduction. *Production* — the active intervention of human beings in nature — was reserved for males. In a state of nature, men were active, women passive.

One Belgian reformer argued that coal mining — perhaps the most active human intervention in the natural world — was thus ideally suited to men. In 1846 he wrote:

Man needs to use his force to confirm his sense of it to himself everyday, through acts displaying it. Sedentary life bothers him; he springs outward; he defies the open air's asperity. Heavy and painful labors are those he prefers. His energetic self-confidence braves all dangers. He likes to consider nature in general, and the beings around him in particular only in terms of the power he can exercise upon them.[15]

Coal mining, for this observer, was the 'natural' male occupation. For women, however, it was quite the contrary. Because females were naturally passive beings, wresting coal from the earth (the 'female' element which in this case gave birth to a product seized and owned by males) ran counter to the natural course of things. Given the context of the Belgian labor market, however, this writer was not anxious to argue in favor of driving women out of industry altogether. Rather, he insisted that there *was* a 'natural' place for women industrial workers, and that was the factory. 'The cloistered life of the factory', he argued, suited women's nature because of its 'monotony and tranquillity', which, 'distanced it ... from the tumultuous life outside'.[16] Thus it was not necessary to exclude women from industry altogether; they must only be 'cloistered' away from the sexually dangerous, hot, dark world of the mines. Behind what were indeed the high brick walls of textile or glass mills, separated into clearly defined women's work, proletarian women could go about their more passive sexually quiescent work, in a venue reminiscent of Belgium's *béguinages*.[17]

In that same year, 1846, a Liège doctor added his voice to the debate. He wrote:

> The constitutional weakness ... of the woman oppose[s] her introduction into the mines ... where she often develops the seed of demoralization which ends by leading to ... physical disorganization ...[18]

Thus the passive receptacle 'introduced' by some other agent into the mines, could nurture there a different seed from that nature assigned – and by so doing, could 'disorganize' the natural system.

These early arguments fell on deaf legislative ears. Indeed, the numbers of women coal miners continued to increase through the 1850s. Thus frustration heightened the tone of reformers' rhetoric, and women's sexuality became more overtly the subject of bourgeois concerns. In fact, by the mid-50s, many were warning that coal mining not only disordered nature but that it also turned women workers into 'half-men', or even, at the most extreme, '*hommes-femmes*'.[19]

As the rhetoric grew more extreme, so women's participation in social unrest increased, thus bolstering the case of opponents of women miners. Throughout the 1850s, the latter were blamed for every illegal 'coalition', and every strike. (One mining engineer, however, dismissed the importance of coal miners' unrest by noting that most strikers were only women, and, in his words, 'women have a natural tendency to scream in a crisis'.[20])

By the 1860s, social disorders had increased enough to arouse significant public concern. And the man who immediately capitalized on that concern to try to rally opinion behind his efforts to exclude women from coal mining was francophiliac doctor, Hyack Kuborn, who was president of the Royal Academy of Medicine. Kuborn – like many of his medical colleagues – was particularly fond of quoting the French ideologue, Pierre-Jean-George Cabanis, as well as the French romantic historian, Jules Michelet.[21]

In the opening years of the 1860s, Kuborn's voice dominated the opposition to Belgium's *hiercheuses*. He rested his arguments on a peculiarly dated – indeed, medieval – cosmology. To Kuborn, the world was a vast organism; in its primitive 'natural' state, the organism rested in a state of equilibrium. Within this larger organism were millions of tiny micro-organisms, each a human body. These micro-worlds were equally susceptible to disequilibrium. Moreover, both the macro- and microworlds were naturally closed systems. Any external influence could shift the system into imbalance.[22]

Each human body also had its own economy – and for Kuborn, it was primarily a sexual economy.[23] According to him, woman's body (the singular is apposite here) followed one principle: *mulier propter uterum id est quod est* – 'Woman is her uterus'. 'There', Kuborn wrote, 'is the immutable characteristic which marks all woman's nature.' Her sole destiny was 'displayed in every fibre of her body'. It was 'to menstruate, to generate, to secrete milk'.[24]

Thus was woman's biology her destiny. But further, Kuborn insisted that this biology also created woman's personality. The uterus gave woman 'exquisite sensibility, mobility of impressions, and tender feelings'. It also rendered her naturally compassionate, timid, patient and self-abnegating.[25]

In contrast to this inward-turning female, the male (whose personality's organic source – the penis – was never directly mentioned in Kuborn's work) was 'proud, powerful, commanding'. He possessed 'persistent energy', and was, therefore, 'a creature destined to thought, to physical struggles, to danger'. In Kuborn's cosmology, man was the actor, the dominator of the natural world while woman was the object, acted upon but never acting. He summarized woman's role in these words: 'Her role lies (*gésir*) in the great reproduction act; she is (following Galen) the "*dépôt du germe*".' Kuborn's choice of words underscored his conviction that females were totally passive creatures. Not only was woman the site where a man's seed germinated, but she awaited this seed with extraordinary passivity: Kuborn's verb – *gésir* – means either to lie helpless or to lie dead.[26]

Needless to say, women who rejected nature's dictates, especially those who were so flagrant as to undertake coal mining, risked throwing the whole world into disequilibrium. Kuborn's evidence? Every woman coal miner – each a micro-world – showed signs of physical deformation. These '*germes de famille*' in Kuborn's interesting phrase, were 'in constant contact with men, exposed to all men's dangers, far from the bosoms of their families, dressed in men's clothes'. (This fear of the broad effects of clothing exchange had its roots in the Bible. In Deuteronomy 22:15 the warning is clear: 'The woman shall not wear that which pertaineth unto a man ...') As a result of their proximity to men and their unwomanly clothing, these women acquired some of men's characteristics, though none of the positive ones. Women miners, he argued, 'lost their breasts'.[27] (One might point out that Amazons, distinguished in ancient mythology by the absence of one breast, were much on the minds of French colonialists because of their fear of the notorious women's army of Dahomey, who were often called 'Amazons' in French military rhetoric.[28]) In addition, women miners were driven to invade what Kuborn considered to be man's social realm, the café-bar, where passers-by could even see the unnatural women smoking pipes. The situation was so bad, Kuborn insisted, that some passers-by could not even distinguish the women from the men. In short, Kuborn concluded, somewhat hysterically, a woman coal miner was 'a hideous being, a virago'. (This kind of rhetoric was not limited to Belgium, of course. Gill Burke has shown that many verbal attacks on women tin mine workers in Cornwall accused them of being 'mannish Amazons', and Claire Moses has published a group of satirical portraits of French women's rightists in 1848 which also feature 'unnatural' women dressed in 'men's clothes'.[29])

Kuborn did not content himself with these attacks; he also blamed the mine strikes of 1868 on these deformed women. 'It is they', he complained, 'who provoke the most in popular agitations, in revolts, in strikes.' He continued:

See these mannish women with their flabby breasts and wide-set haunches, with their knowing walk and their harsh speech, [their] insolent looks and bold gestures, it is they who... at Marchienne, at Chatelineau, seize the riot banner and carry it along, singing, at the head of a wild crowd, breathing forth dissension, urging men on to pillage. And [the men], mistakenly ashamed at finding themselves outstripped by the women, end up committing the worst excesses![30]

Like a twisted version of Delacroix's personified Liberty, Belgium's women strikers thus achieved a full-blown, disreputable sexuality via sagging breasts and broad pelvises. Dragon-like, these women 'breathed' (soufflant) discord, luring men to the destruction of the social order. A colleague echoed Kuborn's opinion of the strikers' transformation from an unnatural worker into a militant: 'the miner's daughter', he wrote, 'becomes an ungovernable shrew, and more often than not, the most ardent to urge violence in a riot, the most unconquerable and the most cruel in these scenes of disorder'.[31]

Another writer offered a similar description of women miners, but added an explanation for their behavior. In the mines, he wrote, 'women's nature becomes impregnated with a coarseness altogether too masculine'. Moreover, working underground a woman gained:

> the most detestable education, the grossest language, the basest manners. Woman goes there to cast off the principal qualities that distinguish 'le sexe'; there she contracts men's habits, the allures of independence and liberty which later become the cause of disputes, of quarrels, and even of acts of violence. Earning a rather high wage, she becomes prodigal, and no longer knows the value of money. Habituated to going out every day, her house's interior becomes a burden ...[32]

These observations not only mirrored Kuborn's convictions about women's primarily reproductive nature, but they also added a second fear that runs as a sub-text through much of this debate: that is, that once women were 'impregnated' with independence, they became addicted to it, so that they were no longer content with their 'proper' sphere. The discord this was supposed to occasion was, of course, that which was thought to result from a male worker's insistence that a woman agree to fulfil her domestic 'duties', which normally included acting as his unpaid servant. The observers here, it is important to note, were not male workers. Rather they were members of the middle class, whose wives, mothers and daughters no doubt remained isolated in their proper domestic sphere. (Gill Burke has also shown that independent working women in Cornwall elicited similar fears amongst bourgeois men.[33])

This fascination with the sexuality and potential gender transformation of the underground world of coal mining was not limited to opponents of women's work. Indeed, some defenders of that work expressed themselves in language very like that of Kuborn and his colleagues. One pharmacist, for instance, insisted '... the female miners are not unchaste but only coarse ... little by little, by prolonged contact, they contract the scabrous language of male workers who, for them, have lost their sexuality and are only comrades'. Furthermore, he wrote, the 'men's clothing' worn by women miners was not a bad thing, but rather a means of protecting women's virtue. In his words, the woman miners' trousers were 'sordides et ensevilies dans l'ordure' — an interesting turn of phrase that means 'disgusting' and 'buried' (or 'shrouded') in filth (or 'excrement' or 'lewdness').[34]

Both opponents and proponents of women's coal mining were clearly fascinated by the imagined world of the coal mines, as well as by the congeries of negative images associated with the industrial world throughout the nineteenth century.[35] Moreover, the image of disease ('scabrous' language was 'contracted'), as well as the images of death and female sexuality, together suggested the extent to which women coal miners stimulated male bourgeois fears.[36]

The strength of these fears helps explain the unambiguously negative resolution passed by the Royal Academy at the end of the 1860s which resoundingly condemned women's work in coal mining, and called for its immediate end.

Again, however, these would-be reformers met only frustration. In fact, the only immediate result of the publication of the Academy's report was the emergence into the debate of several proponents of women's continued work in coal mining. Among these defenders of the *hiercheuses* were those who continued to argue from the point of view of women's physical appearance – and sexual state – as well as a new group who called themselves 'social scientists', and who reasoned from what they insisted were scientific facts.[37]

The former group's rhetoric tended to depend upon paternalistic notions of workers' 'otherness', as well as upon a condescending infantilization of women workers. Characteristic of the language of these men were the words of two doctors from coal country, who wrote, 'Our girls are gay, free, saucy, impertinent even, but usually only when they are in groups. On Sundays they promenade together in the commune, or go together to the little fetes, laughing, dancing, singing, gambolling ... returning in the same company'.[38]

The social scientists had a spokesperson among Belgium's doctors. He was Martin Schoenfeld, who had practised amongst coal miners most of his working life when he first involved himself in a debate with Kuborn. So strongly did he disagree with his colleague in the Royal Academy that he wrote a lengthy minority report. When Kuborn refused to allow it to be entered into the Academy's minutes, Schoenfeld published it at his own expense, in 1870.

Schoenfeld began by attacking Kuborn's methods, which he insisted depended not on scientific observation, but rather on prejudice. Neither Kuborn, nor the French authorities he was fond of quoting had ever visited a mine. With considerable sarcasm, Schoenfeld admired Kuborn's 'really very marvellous telescope', which allowed him to see miners from a very great distance. Still more wonderful was the *'lunette d'approche'* of the French politician, Jules Simon, who, all the way from Paris, 'sees what goes on inside our mines in order to approve the conclusions of the report'.[39]

Schoenfeld argued that contrary to the report's conclusions, 'the vast majority of women miners are in no way physically deformed by their work', nor were they 'in the condition of beasts'. Rather, their appearance conformed to the 'normal human exterior'. Furthermore, even their reproductive lives showed no signs of the deformation upon which Kuborn and his colleagues insisted. Not only did women coal miners suffer no more in childbirth than did women working in other industries, but in some cases had fewer problems than did other *ouvrières*.[40]

Furthermore, Schoenfeld accused Kuborn and the others of hiding their real motives for opposing women's work in the mines. They were not really concerned about the physical and moral well-being of coal miners, Schoenfeld argued, but rather terrified of women's collective drive toward independence. In other words, he wrote, the male bourgeoisie was increasingly fearful that working women's economic independence might lead them to demand those civil rights denied them in Belgium's constitution. Thus Schoenfeld wrote:

> The equality of rights inscribed in our constitution contrasts markedly with the inequality of the conditions we see; because from the point of view of equality and of civil liberties, women are rather badly treated and we see that women's emancipation and their participation in political life are on the agenda for those who occupy themselves with social science.

Schoenfeld went on with a lengthy discussion of women's rights in the U.S.A. – the country, in his words, 'of new times and new mores'. He concluded:

> I content myself to think that the place of woman, especially in purely industrial localities, is everywhere where she can honorably earn her daily bread and that of her family...[41]

Schoenfeld's views might well have been dismissed as the ravings of a radical had they not found echoes amongst workers in mining regions. But they did. Despite the widespread Proudhonism of many Walloon workers of the time, which denied women their equality with men one Liège workers' newspaper, *L'ami du peuple*, reported in 1873, 'Next to the *Association Internationale des Travailleurs* stands the *Internationale des Femmes* ... Woman has the right, along with man, to emancipate herself morally and materially'.[42] Given the extent of unrest in working class areas in these years – and despite the continuing reassurance of many male workers' expressed hostility to women's work – it was not surprising that Schoenfeld's work was controversial. At the same time, there was one group whose self-interests were served by Schoenfeld's work, and they were quick to support his positive view of women coal miners, though not his call for women's emancipation. These were the coal owners, who also published a report critical of Kuborn's.[43]

The owners agreed with Schoenfeld that if the doctors had visited a mine they might have had more credibility. Instead, they characterized the Academy's report as highly imaginative but totally inaccurate. A visit to a mine, even a short one, would have shown the Academy's doctors that the promiscuous sexual activity they imagined was a physical impossibility given the tiny space in which the miners worked. Moreover, miners had no time to indulge in sexual activity, even had they wanted to. Everyone underground was hard at work throughout a given shift, pausing only to eat. Then, too, Belgian miners – who worked in some of the most dangerous coal mines in the world – were highly superstitious, and unwilling to act in any way that might tempt fate.[44]

Furthermore, the owners argued that Belgian women miners in no way resembled the deformed androgynous characters depicted by the would-be reformers. Instead, they wrote: 'foreigners who are not used to seeing women working in the mines are struck by the air of health and good humor of most of our mining women.'[45] (On the other hand, one of the most famous foreign visitors to Belgium's mines was far from as sanguine about his experiences as the mine owners' claim would suggest. Victor Hugo characterized Liège coal-mining as 'the hell of women ...'.[46]) In contrast to 'their' women, the owners suggested that Belgians look at a group of women who *were* 'deformed' by their lives. These were the women of the United States, deformed not by work but rather by idleness, They wrote that American women were 'entirely confined to the domestic hearth'. 'To precisely this', they added, 'is attributed the degeneration of the race ... to the forced repose that one considers today among us as a panacea destined to rid us at once of physical and social evils.'[47]

Neither side prevailed however. Not until the great general strikes of 1886 terrified the voting public into keeping the liberals out of office in favor of a catholic conservative government did legislative intervention in the mining industry begin to be a possibility. At the same time, two other changes were occurring which also helped alter the role of women coal miners in public discourse. Firstly, the Belgian nation reached a point in its development where a national identity began to emerge – and it was an identity based on those characteristics that made Belgium unique in Europe: its industrial success, its status as the 'workshop of Europe'. Moreover, most Belgians recognized that their country's place at the forefront of continental industry depended upon the vast pool of industrial workers, whose strength, courage and discipline made continued economic progress possible.

Second, the Belgian working class became organized. And among the leaders of the new socialist movement, as noted above, were many artists, who sought subjects for their increasingly political art. Following in the footsteps of the French realists, many socialist painters began to depict 'real' people. In the Belgian world of the 1880s and 1890s, their favorite subjects were workers.[48]

These developments – the quest for a distinctive national identity and the creation of proletarian icons – together with a conservative legislature's willingness to impose restrictions on women's underground work, provided the context for the final 'rationalization' of Belgium's *hiercheuses*. From highly sexual, independent and militant beings, the *hiercheuses* were 'tamed' into one of two types. In most artists' eyes they became a-sexual, almost androgynous pre-pubescent youths. Hundreds of paintings and drawings and sculptures showed *hiercheuses* as boyish figures, whose sexuality, if present at all, was still latent. A smaller number of works 'tamed' the threat of the *hiercheuses* by sentimentalizing them, either as very young girls or as very old hag-like women. In the case of the former, the theme was the 'loss of childhood', achieved by posing a lovely young child against the horrifyingly black, looming world of the coal mine. In the latter, the theme was Macbethian. Artists depicted old women, clothed in filthy rags, limbs deformed into claws.

The most prolific of the painters who created Belgium's icons of labor was Constantin Meunier. One contemporary suggested the way in which Meunier's work transformed the adult *hiercheuses* though not into entirely a-sexual characters. He described one of Meunier's many sculptures in these words:

> I know a work which is, perhaps, the most agreeable of Meunier's. It represents a young *hiercheuse*, who throws out her chest deliciously, her hands on her hips, with a boyish grace. Beneath the trousers and the twill jacket ... one devines the colorations, one suspects the nascent forms of puberty, ready to blossom. She has the charm of a rosebud which will burst tomorrow out of its fragile cover ...[49]

Whatever this writer's fantasies of the incipient sexuality of Meunier's *hiercheuse*, his observation of the boyishness of the figure would have served for any of Meunier's hundreds of depictions of these women miners. All were young and boyish, in demeanour, in feature, in pose. All wore the uniform – white jackets and knee-length trousers, dark stockings, wooden sabots, indigo blue headscarves. Most carry the tools of the *hiercheuses'* trade: a shovel and lamp. A few are shown at work, pushing the heavy coal carts around a mine. Some are on a break, chatting with other *hiercheuses* or male miners, or resting alone, gazing dreamily into the distance.

In addition to using only young, physically immature female models (which in turn show that Meunier worked with studio models rather than from life) the artist added to the impression of female youth by his placement of male miners' figures in those works that included workers of both sexes. In every case, the male miners were clearly adults. They are shown visibly tired, usually stooped over or crouching next to young girls who stand upright without any signs of exhaustion.[50]

One interpretation of Meunier's iconography might be that the painter was deliberately marginalizing these boyish young women from the real, active working life of the mine. Their signal lack of exhaustion, their cleanliness, their apparent insouciance all contrast sharply with the grizzled, dirty, tired 'real' men miners. In most of Meunier's paintings, male miners are clearly symbols of exploitation – clearly victims of their work. The females, on the other hand, appear as decorations, separate from the dirt of the mine.

Meunier's sculptures, however, suggest a second interpretation. In the dozens of bronze *hiercheuses* Meunier produced before his death in 1904, there is none that suggests anything but independence and spirit, as well as youth. All are shown erect, posed with one hand on a hip, one leg thrust forward, the body curved, the chin pointed upward with an insolent expression. All these figures suggest workers proud of their work and far from overwhelmed by it. On the other hand, Meunier's '*mineurs*' are completely overcome by their work. Most of his male figures stoop, crouch and huddle, as they do in his paintings. From faces black with coal dust, the figures' eyes stare wide-eyed, but unseeing. Their mouths hang open with tiredness. In one rare erect figure, Meunier shows a miner who is far from the upright, proud *hiercheuses*. Instead, this *mineur* stands slightly stooped, bare-chested, bare-footed. His feet are so oversized that they suggest those of a beast rather than of a man. The enormous protruding toes of the figure cling to an uneven rock formation, suggesting an inhuman relationship with the rocky earth.[51]

On the other hand, there is a male figure amongst Meunier's works that closely replicates those of his *hiercheuses*. He is an Antwerp docker. Hand on one hip, a leg thrust forward, eyes cast upward into the middle distance, chin upright, the docker is the very image of labor's ideal hero: independent, strong, proud. Like the *hiercheuses*, this docker is fully clothed, including his characteristic headgear. Whereas Meunier's male miners are clearly meant to evoke pity, the docker and the *hiercheuses* represent entirely (and clearly idealized) positive ideas about the grandeur and dignity of labor.

Finally, in Meunier's best-known painting, the '*Retour des Mines*', which today hangs in the Fine Arts Museum in Brussels, he has again set the *hiercheuses* off from the four male miners who accompany her. The two who walk next to the *hiercheuse* walk stooped, their faces in shadow, their axes carried both over a shoulder and clutched, in exhaustion, to the chest. Of the five figures in the picture, only the *hiercheuse* is fully shown. Of the others, who are missing either tops of heads or feet, only one has an entire head. Finally, the only light in the picture falls on the *hiercheuse*'s face, highlighting her separateness from the others.

Again, the singling out of the female figure in this painting suggests Meunier's wish to separate the young woman from her male comrades – though in this case, rather than suggesting her marginality, he seems to be showing the resilience of her youth. Then, too, the painting hints at what was, in fact, the reality: that women coal miners were vanishing from the real world while the men worked on – indeed, in increasing numbers. In other words, just as Meunier was 'discovering' the *hiercheuses*, they were disappearing – often only to surface work, but nevertheless, out of the underground world so redolent of bourgeois fears earlier on. By the end of the 1880s, the numbers of women working underground was declining rapidly. Not only did a newly-catholic legislature pass restrictive legislation (which took effect in 1892), but some mines began to employ pit ponies to replace the women and children who had transported coal to the surface. These ponies evoked no public outcry, and they never went on strike. Moreover, their morals were hardly at risk underground. Thus women and girls began to vanish from the world underground, until there were only about 100 women still working below the ground in 1914.[52] Meunier's female miner, then, was virtually a symbol of a vanished past.

Their disappearance from the mines in no way stimulated their disappearance from the art world, however. Indeed, the *hiercheuses* quickly found other portraitists. In fact, from

1880 onwards, hundreds of portraits of the *hiercheuses* flooded the market. So vast was the output, and so popular the subject, that today no municipal museum (including those in Flanders, where no coal was ever mined) is without its *hiercheuse*. In coal cities such as Charleroi, Liège, Mons, and so on, the museums are full of pictures of *hiercheuses*. In Charleroi's *Université de Travail*, moreover, a group of stained glass windows honoring local workers includes several *hiercheuses*.[53]

The first series of portraits to follow Meunier's early works were painted by the French woman, Cécile Douard, who had come from Paris to study in the Borinage. Her work began to appear in the 1890s, and, in fact, was chosen by a national women's committee to illustrate a report sent from Belgium to the Chicago Exposition's women's pavilion, in 1893.[54] Her depictions of *hiercheuses* resemble Meunier's in her use of very youthful figures, dressed in the standard uniform. Unlike Meunier, however, Douard painted from sketches made underground. Her figures are also considerably less idealized.[55] Her subjects are shown moving, working, acting. Well-developed muscles flex and relax in her work as the *hiercheuses* break coal, load it, and strain to push the heavy coal carts up steep underground inclines. Even in her paintings of women waiting their turn to go down into the mines, Douard shows her subjects in action – leaning together, talking, touching each other, and so on. Unlike Meunier's idealized, static figures, Douard's appear to be alive. Moreover, she did not limit herself to the most attractive of the women in the coal world. Instead, she painted many portraits of the most tragic figures of the coal mines: the *glaneuses*, who labored endless hours on the high, slippery, filthy slag heaps gathering remnants of usable coal and placing them in heavy burlap sacks which they then carried – tied to their foreheads – to nearby towns and cities for sale. Douard's huge canvases show these women as hag-like creatures, whose hands have become claws, and whose feet are shod in flapping rags. Her pallet for these paintings was grim and dark, reflecting the hellish world of Belgium's *glaneuses*.

Despite the greater realism of Douard's work, however, she, too, contributed to the aestheticization of Belgium's vanishing women coal miners. Her *hiercheuses* were all young, healthy, attractive and independent – very far from the deformed, highly-sexed or totally masculinized women presented by bourgeois reformers earlier in the century.

Douard and Meunier were followed by dozens of artists and photographers who found in the disappearing *hiercheuses* an ideal subject for their depictions of Belgium's industrial world. One Liège photographer, Gustave Marissiaux, who made his early reputation as the highly romantic photographer of beauty spots (e.g. Venice at dusk, or scenes of classical ruins, draped in vines and lit by full moons) startled the public with a large exhibit of his mining photographs in 1905.[56] The exhibit's featured attractions were his many photographs of women mine workers – all highly romanticized (i.e. all clean, all extraordinarily beautiful), all carefully posed against the black, looming iron machinery of the coal mine. His subjects, who were all at work on the surface, had relinquished the *hiercheuse* uniform, though not the name. His female subjects all wore the skirts and blouses, covered by a wide apron, that was everywhere typical of working class European women. When they finished work, or when the weather demanded it, his subjects donned the dark-colored shawls that also identified them as working class women.[57]

Many other painters joined Meunier and Douard in depicting Belgium's vanishing women coal miners. Pierre Paulus, Henri Marechal, Armand Rassenfosse, Alex-Louis Martin, Marius Carion, Léon Vandenhouten and Xavier Méllery all produced pictures of women coal miners during the years before the war.

(Interestingly, both Rassenfosse and Marechal painted some portraits of *hiercheuses* as partly-nude trollops, suggesting that the time-honored image of the sexually promiscuous working women continued to thrive in Belgium. Indeed, like their 'de-sexing' in androgynous portraits, the *hiercheuses'* transformation into prostitutes also had the effect of diluting the importance or threat of their political behavior.[58]) Most of these paintings showed the *hiercheuses* larger than life, younger than reality, and always extremely attractive. Their artistic transformation from the viragos or men–women of the mid-nineteenth century was thus complete by 1900. From then on, they were readily assimilated into the uniquely Belgian image of industrial workers.

One example of the extent to which the *hiercheuses* took their place in the pantheon of national symbols was the journal of a Liège-area literary avant-garde group, 'La Jeune Wallonie', which in 1906 chose a Pierre Paulus picture of a *hiercheuse*, posed standing on a slag heap, with a coal mine in the background pouring smoke into the sky, for its *logo*. Every monthly issue of 'Young Wallonia' thus showed its self-image to be that of a young *hiercheuse*.

There were other groups for whom an idealized *hiercheuse* became a symbol. In addition to these kinds of uses of women miners, however, there were also many photographs of Belgium's vanished *hiercheuses* printed on menu cards for the endless banquets beloved of the Belgian provincial bourgeoisie. A banquet's menu was often printed just above a tiny photograph of a group of coal miners – or, indeed, of any other group of Belgian industrial workers. Thus did the flourishing, prosperous bourgeoisie celebrate itself in this world where, ironically, Karl Marx and Friedrich Engels had been stimulated to write *The Communist Manifesto* in 1849!

The culmination of this process whereby Belgium's *hiercheuses* became part of a romanticized national image was probably the production of a vast canvas painted in the mid-1930s which hangs today in Charleroi's *Musée des Beaux-Arts*. Painted by Edmond Dumont, this wall-sized canvas, titled '*Fleur du Terril: Hiercheuse*' (Flower of the Slag-Heap: *Hiercheuse*), features a woman coal worker dressed as an eighteenth-century shepherdess. Her coal bucket, used to carry her gleanings, closely resembles a milk bucket. No dirty coal mars its pristine state. Her dress, of a light blue fabric, floats gently on a breeze, which also ruffles the grasses and flowers growing on the slag beneath her feet. Her hair also blows gently, below her flowered scarf. She smiles pensively, between the traditional rosy cheeks. She stands posed against a soft pastel sky, in which clouds drift. No sign of coal mars the bucolic scene. In fact, if it were not for the title card hanging to the right of the canvas, few would see it as other than an extremely banal picture of a rural woman, perhaps a dairy maid. By the 1930s, then, Belgium's *hiercheuses* had entirely departed reality. This one did not even represent a lost industrial past. Rather, she symbolizes a pre-industrial, rural world. [59]

Although Belgian artists were in the process of altering public perceptions of women coal mine workers, the 'real world' of working class politics continued to address the problem of including these women, who still worked in their thousands at the surface of the mines. Among male workers, both negative Proudhonist attitudes and more positive ones continued to vie for dominance in union and political movements. The voices raised in favor of women mine workers included one male miner who recalled that in his youth at the turn of century the special work relations of the Borinage had shaped the way men treated women. He noted that a male 'Borain' never used the possessive form when speaking of 'his companion'. Rather, he spoke of 'the woman of the house'. If he forgot, and said 'my wife' or 'my companion' he was quickly reminded by his comrades of both sexes of how pretentious such usages sounded – as if a woman 'belongs to him'.[60]

A second man, who had been the leader of the national miners' union for nearly half a century, observed that in the 1890s 'one became a miner, according to the sacred expression, from father to son, and ... from mother to daughter'.[61] By the end of the century, moreover, miners' unions were engaged in a serious campaign to organize women members, both by creating separate women's sections in each union and by organizing mixed sex unions.[62] The regional federation of Liège published this policy statement in 1910: 'The provincial *syndicat* has for its field of action the entire province. It affirms, moreover, from its first article that it includes the *ouvrières*, the *ouvriers*, and the machinists of all categories, both underground and at the surface of coal and other mines in the province of Liège.'[63]

Of course these were socialist unions and union leaders. Considerable hostility to women workers remained among male catholic workers who, in 1905, according to one historian of Church-sponsored unions, feared both the growing Belgian feminist movement and the possibility of women's suffrage because, they feared 'pipe-smoking women in trousers'.[64]

However, even the most sympathetic male unionists, or even the most committed *hiercheuses*, could not halt the gradual disappearance of most women from work underground. By 1914, the handful still laboring below the surface were without economic significance. As for their political and social significance, however, these continued to exist far beyond the limits of mining regions. Thanks to countless artists, the *hiercheuses* were transformed from fearsome, unnatural women, targets of bourgeois reformers' wrath, into icons of industrial labor who helped romanticize the dangerous but necessary world of coal mining at the same time they helped the Belgian bourgeoisie assimilate women industrial workers into a key aspect of the national identity. Because Belgium's working women could not realistically be driven into the private, unthreatening world of pseudo-bourgeois domesticity, they had to be 'tamed' in some other manner. In the case of the *hiercheuses*, the process was accomplished in two ways: by artists, who by exaggerating their youth, their independence and their a-sexuality, both de-sexed this most-threatening group of women workers (at least for most observers) and by legislators, who altered the gender balance in the coal mines in order to restrict women to the considerably less dramatic world of surface work. Indeed, women's above-ground work in the Belgian context, at least, was almost acceptably 'women's work': cleaning and sorting the coal, loading it into baskets, and even shovelling were acts not dissimilar to those performed for centuries by women agricultural workers. As for gleaning, that too had its rural, ancient associations, however different were the towering dirty mountains of slag from the harvested fields of a Belgian autumn. (Linking women's work in industry with some form of 'traditional' women's work was a process long-utilized by textile mill owners to arm themselves against the criticism that they were tearing women from their homes and exploiting them in mills. Again, although factory textile production bore virtually no relation to the domestic production of yarn, thread and cloth, it was still possible to stimulate a collective memory of 'women's work', carding and spinning in her home to deflect criticism of the industrial reality.)

Gramsci's observations that the 'sexual question' would be full of 'unhealthy charac-teristics' until women attained both consciousness and genuine independence certainly held true amongst the bourgeoisie nineteenth-century Belgium. Moreover, the 'puritanical' interest shown by bourgeois reformers in the sexual characteristics of miners was indeed indicative of their desire to control the reproductive, as well as the productive, lives of the working class.

However, the 'solution,' to the problem of controlling potentially independent working women used elsewhere in some parts of Europe – i.e. removing married women from the public work-world and containing them in the domestic sphere — was not available in Belgium. Therefore, a unique process occurred which had the effect of 'rationalizing' women coal miners' private and public lives, both by turning them into iconic a-sexual figures and by legislating them into less fantasy-stimulating work at the surface of coal mines.

Even given the ubiquity of public portraits of the *hiercheuses*, public interest in them waned rapidly as their history was gradually forgotten in the years after 1914. So rapid was their disappearance from public consciousness, in fact, that by the close of the First World War, few outside the coal cities of Liège and Charleroi, or the smaller towns of the Borinage, had more than the vaguest memory of the women who bhd helped mine Belgium's coal for so many centuries. The explanation for this change was two-fold. First, legislation had effected a total sexual division of labor that restricted women to work at the surface. This quickly became their 'correct' place — so much so that the term *hiercheuse* was usually used to describe them. Second, as Belgium increasingly became part of Europe, the overt hostility to women's mine work (as well as to women's industrial work of all kinds) prevalent in most other European countries began to characterize Belgian discourse as well. The story of this latter process lies outside the scope of this essay. However, two documents offer a glimpse at the change. In the first, the Belgian miners' union newspaper, *L'Ouvrier Mineur*, which began publication in 1903, the origins are clearly shown in the debate in the international miners' union over women's mine work. This debate shows a persistent attempt on the part of miners' representatives from Germany and Austria (the two European countries where women still worked in coal) to persuade the Belgians to join their attempts to throw women out of coal mining altogether. Their arguments — grounded in a visceral hatred of women and appealing to Belgian miners' 'manliness' — initially did little to change most Belgian men's attitudes toward their female co-workers, though the newspaper dutifully reported the international meetings and resolutions in which the anti-women feelings were expressed. Gradually, however, the tone of the Belgian papers' editors began to change; by 1913–14 the increasing number of articles supporting the removal of all women from mine work (though the language was considerably less violent than that employed by the Germans or Austrians) suggested that the Belgians were beginning to adopt the attitudes of their misogynist neighbors.[65]

The second piece of evidence for the Belgian public's ignorance of the *hiercheuses* is a prize-winning book published in 1985 which purports to tell the story of coal mining in Wallonia and in France's Nord and Pas-de-Calais coal fields, from its origins in the twelfth century to the closing of the last Belgian coal mine in 1984. *Les geules noires* (the 'black jaws'), written by two male journalists, glorifies coal miners — their courage, their inventiveness, their stolidity, their strength — in the manner common to authors from Victor Hugo to George Orwell. Yet throughout the book, the authors' complete lack of awareness of women's contribution to Belgian coal production is apparent. Only three times do women miners appear at all; in each case, the context underscores the authors' indifference to their existence. In the first instance, the authors note in passing that women and children were 'for a long time' forbidden to work underground in the mines of Liège. Although this statement is quite wrong — Lucie Dejardin's mother had worked underground in a Liège mine before the births of her many children in the final quarter of the nineteenth century — it is significant both because it never occurred to the authors to check the accuracy of their belief, and because they have followed a time-honored method of denigrating women by identifying them not as adult workers but rather as half of the single term, women-and-children.[66]

The second occasion occurs in the authors' lexicon of mining terms. Here, only one occupational category – '*hiercheur*' – includes an indication ('-euse') that women sometimes did the work as well. Despite this brief suggestion, however, the *hiercheuses* themselves appear only once, toward the end of the book, when the authors are writing about pit ponies. At one point they note that before the arrival of ponies (which they imply was general, throughout Belgian mines by the middle of the nineteenth century, though of course this too is incorrect) the work of pushing the wagons to the surface was done by '*hiercheurs (ou les hiercheuses)*'. Even the pit ponies receive more of the authors' attention – to the extent of a sentimental poem memorializing the ponies' hard lives.[67] Despite the existence of many poems about the female miners, not to mention the hundreds of paintings and sculptures of them, these authors' indifference is total. This attitude suggests the extent to which the *hiercheuses* have nearly vanished from public view, despite their portraits in every public museum. Thus are lost from the collective memory of most Belgians (excluding, perhaps, those from mining cities like Charleroi or Liège, or Mons) these women who, when the conflict between industrial prosperity and bourgeois morality was at its height a century ago, had provoked so much heated public dispute.

Notes

*   This article owes much to the research assistance of Enrique Garcia, as well as to the help (especially with the translations of what is very awkward French) of Timothy J. Reiss. Research was funded by the Fulbright Foundation, the National Endowment for the Humanities and the American Council of Learned Societies.

1   Antonio Gramsci. *Selections from the prison notebooks*, ed. Quintin Hoare and Geoffrey Nowell Smith (New York, 1971), pp. 296–7.

2   Dorinda Outram, 'Le langage mâle de la vertu: women and the discourse of the French revolution', in Peter Burke and Roy Porter (eds), *The social history of language* (Cambridge, 1987), pp. 120–35.

3   Dejardin quoted in E. B. Chalmers, *Lucie Dejardin: Hiercheuse et deputée socialiste* (Huy, 1952), p. 16. Henri Pirenne's words are found in *Histoire de Belgique*, VII (Brussels, 1923), 123. Good general descriptions of bourgeois family life in the nineteenth century are found in Mark Poster, *Critical theory of the family* (New York, 1980), and Mary Poovey, *The proper lady and the woman writer* (Chicago, 1984).

4   Among representative samples of the masculinity of coal are George Orwell's *The road to Wigan pier* (Harmondsworth,1972), esp. pp. 20–1, where Orwell employs heavily sexual language to describe the 'fillers' at work in a British coal mine. These men, who, in Orwell's words, arouse 'a pang of envy for their toughness' were doing the work done in Belgium by the *hiercheuses* and *chargeuses*. See also Beatrix Campbell's *Return to Wigan pier: poverty and politics in the eighties* (London, 1984). Angela John, in *By the sweat of their brow: women workers at Victorian coal mines* (London, 1984), tells the story of Britain's coal mining women (usually called 'girls' or 'lasses') and their expulsion from the pits in the middle of the nineteenth century. Women in tin mining in Cornwall also encountered a heavily gendered stereotype which effectively masked their work from public view. See Gill Burke, 'The decline of the independent bal maiden: the impact of change in the Cornish mining industry', in Angela John (ed.), *Unequal opportunities: women's employment in England, 1800–1918* (Oxford, 1986), pp. 179–206. One further example of the extent to which the British generally began to think of miners solely as men is an 1869 translation of a Belgian book by the Belgian L. Simonin. The British version of the work,

Underground life, or mines and miners, translated and adapted to the present state of British mining', by H. W. Bristow (New York,1869), features one drawing of a group of Belgian miners, taken from a photograph. In the drawing are both male and female miners, the latter dressed in their *hiercheuses* uniforms with hats that show them to have been Charleroi miners. The caption reads, 'Pitmen *and their wives*' (emphasis mine).

5 See Kathleen Gales and P. H. Marks, 'Twentieth-century trends in the work of women in England and Wales', *Journal of the Royal Statistical Society*, series A, cxxxvii, (1974), 60–70. One might note here that in France, few women ever worked underground in coal, despite Zola's portrait of them in *Germinal*. See Rolande Trempé, *Les mineurs de Caimaux, 1848–1914* (Paris, 1971), pp. 133ff. Trempé notes that many other industrializing nations followed Britain's lead in restricting women's mine work to the surface. These included Germany (1878–1881), Austria (1884), France (1874), Sweden (1891), and two of the states of the US, in 1879 and 1883.

6 The term '*hiercheur*' or '*hiercheuse*' originally referred only to male or female workers whose job it was to push coal wagons in and around coal mines. The term dates from the eighteenth century. As the nineteenth century wore on, however, the term came to include all women working underground, as well as those who worked transporting the coal on the surface. See *Trésor de la langue française: dictionnaire de la langue du XIXe et du Xe siècle (1799–1960)*, IX (Paris, 1981), 775.

7 On the POB's commitment to mass art education, see Walter Debrock, 'De Kinderen van het proletariaat en de kunst', in Jaal Brepoels, *et al.* (eds), *Eewige dilemma's: honderd jaar socialistische partij* (Louvain, 1985), esp. p. 235. See also Paul Aron, *Les Ecrivains belges et le socialisme (1880–1913)* (Brussels, 1985). Louis Pierard, himself a socialist, published many studies of painters and of art in this period with the socialist party press, *Editions labor.* See also *De Arbeid in de kunst van Meunier tot Permeke, Stad Antwerpen, 26 april – 30 juni, 1952*, Museum voor Schone Kunsten (Antwerp, 1952).

8 A discussion of the pre-Raphaelite view of lower class women is found in Linda Nochlin, 'Lost and found: once more the fallen woman', in Norma Broude and Mary Garrard (eds), *Feminism and art history: questioning the litany* (New York, 1982), pp. 221–46. Among Belgian artists who depicted mother-saints and 'fallen women' were some who also painted the *hiercheuses*. Meunier's '*Maternité* ', for example, commissioned by the Belgian government as part of his *Monument du Travail*, is one example of the former. His 'Mater Dolorosa' is another. Felicien Rops and his student Armand Rassenfosse were frequently drawn to portray the latter. The best study of the manipulation of the female figure in the creation of national identity is Maurice Agulhon's *Marianne into battle: Republican imagery and symbolism in France, 1789–1880* (Cambridge, 1981).

9 See Mikhail Bakhtin, *Rabelais and his world* (Bloomington, 1984), p. 21, and Jane Harrison, *Prolegomena to the study of Greek religion* (New York, 1955), and *Epilegomena to the study of Greek religion and Themis* (New York, 1962). See also Patricia J. Hilden, 'Women in Hellenistic religion: a study of the cults of Demeter, Dionysus and Isis', unpublished paper, March, 1975.

10 Demetrius C. Boulger, *Belgian life in town and country* (New York and London, 1904), p. 262.

11 These figures are a composite of those found in *Eléments d'enquête sur le rôle de la femme dans l'industrie, les oeuvres, les arts and les sciences en Belgique* (Brussels, 1897), and Royaume de Belgique, Office du Travail, *Revue du Travail* (Brussels, 1896), pp. 1130–2; pp. 1092–3, and Le Père G.-C. Rutten, *Nos Grèves houilleres et l'action socialiste* (Brussels, 1900), p. 21, Hyack Kuborn, *Rapports sur l'enquête faite au nom de l'Academie royale de médecin de Belgique par la commission chargée d'étudier la question de l'emploi des femmes dans les travaux des mines* (Brussels, 1864), p. 14; Henri Marichal, *L'Ouvrier mineur en Belgique: ce qu'il est, ce qu'il doit être* (Paris, 1869), pp. 12, 20; Royaume de Belgique, Ministère de l'Intérieur, *Enquête sur la condition des classes ouvrières et sur le travail des enfants*, vol. II (Brussels, 1846); *L'Ouvrier mineur*, jan–mars 1905, juin 1906, juillet 1906, sept. 1906, dec. 1906, sept.–oct. 1907.

12 Throughout the nineteenth century mine owners and mining engineers repeatedly complained about the indiscipline of their work force, despite the argument of Hubert Watelet that by 1841 the Borain mine workers had succeeded in creating a disciplined proletariat. See Watelet, *Une Industrialisation sans développement. Le Bassin de Mons et le charbonnage du Grand-Hornu du milieu du XVIIIe au milieu du XIXe siècle* (Ottawa, 1980), pp. 270, 365–6. It is true that the social relations of coal production were generally those of industrial capitalism, but the proletariat's discipline was less than perfectly established. See complaints in *Revue du Travail* throughout the 1890s.

13 See Michael Hiley, *Victorian working women* (Boston, 1980), p. 100.

14 These *botresses* were famous all over Belgium, but particularly in their home city of Liège, where today several public sculptures feature them, and where the Musée de la vie wallonne sells tiny plaster figures of *boteresses*. Camille Lemonnier, in *La Belgique* (Paris, 1888) described these women in language similar to that used in the rhetoric about women miners. '*La créature hommasse et parcheminée, la puissante et musculeuse femelle virilisée par vie*', p. 651. One popular saying at the time maintained 'One good Fleming is worth two Walloons, but one *boteresse* is worth two Flemings'. Other local occupations included that of an ambulant merchant (the option chosen by Lucie Dejardin's mother, in preference to returning to the mines where she had worked as a young woman). Other work in mining regions is described in Françoise Dehousse *et al.*, *Leonard Defrance: L'oeuvre peinte* (Liège, 1985).

15 Quoted in *Royaume de Belgique, Enquête … 1846*, p. 423.

16 Ibid. p. 427.

17 These walled convents existed (and continue to exist) all over Flanders, where they provided a retreat from the world for women whose families were wealthy enough to build them a house or apartment in one of them.

18 Dr Peetermans, in *Enquête … 1846*, p. 158.

19 This usage was not uncommon. An 1872 work by Alexandre Dumas *fils* was titled *L'Homme-Femme*. It dealt with the oppression of women in marriage. In the same period, various German sexual pathologists, including Krafft-Ebbing and Magnus Hirschfeld, coined the term 'das Mann-Weib' to refer to the 'masculine' lesbian. See Gudrun Schwarz, '*Viragos' in male theory in nineteenth-century Germany*, in Judith Friedlander *et al.*, *Women in culture and politics: a century of change* (Bloomington, 1986), pp. 128–43. I am grateful to Timothy J. Reiss for these references.

20 Quoted in *Enquête … 1846*, pp. 260–1.

21 Many French-speaking Belgians were familiar with the work of the eighteenth-century Frenchman, Cabanis, whose book, *On the relations between the physical and moral aspects of men*, ed. George Mora (Baltimore, 1981), contains these words: 'Man must he strong, audacious, enterprising, and woman weak, shy, secretive. Such is the law of nature', p. 234, Michelet's widely-quoted remarks began: 'L'Ouvrière, mot impie, sordide…' See *La Femme* (Paris, n.d.), p. 22.

22 Simone de Beauvoir remarked on the persistence of these ideas into the twentieth century in her 1949 book, *The second sex*. In it, she wrote: 'I can only suppose that in such misty minds there still float shreds of the old philosophy of the Middle Ages which taught that the cosmos is an exact reflection of a microcosm – the egg is imagined to be a little female, the woman a giant egg'. See the edition trans. by H. M. Parshley (New York, 1974), p. 15.

23 On the subject of what he has termed the 'spermatic economy' in nineteenth-century America, see G. J. Barker-Benfield's *The horrors of the half-known life: male attitudes toward women and sexuality in nineteenth-century America* (New York, 1976).

24 Hyack Kuborn, *Rapport sur l'enquête faite au nom de l'Académie Royale de Médecin de Belgique par la commission chargée d'étudier la question des femmes dans les travaux souterrains des mines* (Brussels, 1868), p. 81.

25 Ibid.

26 Ibid. pp.8–9.

27 Ibid. and p. 46.

28 See Edna Bay, 'The royal women of Abomey', unpublished PhD dissertation, Boston University, 1977. I am grateful to Dr Bay for this information.

29 Kuborn, *Rapport*, p. 46. In *Larousse de la langue Française: lexis*, ed. Jean-Pierre Mevel *et al.* (Paris, 1979), 'virago' is defined as 'a woman of masculine allure'. See also Gill Burke, 'Independent bal maiden', and Claire Moses, *French feminism in the nineteenth century* (Albany, New York, 1984), pp.123–26.

30 Ibid. pp. 46–7. Marchienne and Chatelineau were the sites of two of the biggest and most violent mining strikes.

31 H. Marichal, *L'Ouvrier mineur*, p. 36. (It is interesting to compare these words with Marichal's view of male workers. Of them he wrote: 'by his nature left to himself, the Belgian *ouvrier* has a simple composition, and far from finding him inclined to disorder, one might rather reproach him for his insouciance, his indifference to everything that is of public interest'.

32 M. Le Docteur Vleminckx, *Lettre a l'Académie Royale de Médecine à l'occasion de la publication de l'enquête ordonné par M. le Ministre des travaux publics sur la situation des ouvriers dans les mines et les usines métallurgiques de la Belgique, 26 mars 1870*, pp. 11–12.

33 See note 29 above.

34 Quoted in D.-A. Van Bastelaer, *La Question du travail des femmes et des enfants dans les houillères en présence de la statistique officielle. Discours prononcé dans la séance du 6 novembre 1969 de l'Academie Royale de Médecine de Belgique pendant la discussion du rapport de M. Kuborn* (Bruxelles, 1869), pp. 30, 32.

35 Many historians have taken up this subject, including Louis Chevalier, in *Labouring classes and dangerous classes in Paris during the first half of the nineteenth century* (London, 1973). The Belgians, however, were less prone to this fear of industrial workers, and less prone to conflate them with the criminal or dangerous classes. Part of the reason lay in the fact that it was rural, agricultural Flanders, rather than industrial Wallonia that produced the vagabondage elsewhere associated with the urban poor. In other words, there was no equivalent in industrial Belgium to 'outcast London'. There was, on the other hand, a very substantial 'outcast Flanders'. On this see Edouard Ducpetiaux's *Mémoire sur le paupérisme dans les Flandres* (Bruxelles, 1850).

36 Discussions of such fears are found in Klaus Theweleit, *Male fantasies*, I: *Women, floods, bodies, history* (Minneapolis, 1987), 201ff. And Wolfgang Lederer, *The fear of women* (New York, 1968), pp. 44ff.

37 The first and most prominent of Belgium's social scientists included Edouard Ducpétiaux (whose studies began to appear during Belgium's 'hungry forties') and A. Quêtelet, who was one of Belgium's first demographers, whose work also began to appear in the 1840s.

38 C. Wouters and P. Deneubourg, *Réflexions sur le travail des femmes dans les mines* (Mons, 1870), p. 2 (This book opens with the promise, '*la vérité, rien que la vérité!*').

39 Martin Schoenfeld, *Nouvelles recherches sur l'état sanitaire, moral et social des houilleurs pendant la période actuelle de salubrité des mines en Belgique. Discours et études sur le travail des filles dans les charbonnages* (Charleroi, 1870), p. 22.

40 Ibid. pp. 79, 73, 72.

41 Ibid. p. 53. His statements of women's right to equality are very similar to those of the French socialist leader, Jules Guesde, speaking at a workers' congress in the 1870s. Guesde's words are quoted in Hilden, *Working women and socialist politics in France: a regional study, 1880–1914* (Oxford, 1986), p. 177.

42 *L'Ami du peuple*, (ADP) 21 Sept. 1873. (I owe this reference to Enrique Garcia.)

43 *L'Union des charbonnages, mines, et usines métallurgiques de la province de Liège, no. 1: du travail des femmes dans les mines. Rapport présenté par une commission spéciale et approuvé par le comité permanent de l'union des charbonnages... de la province de Liège... séance du 10 mars 1869* (Liège, 1869).

44 Ibid. p. 24.

45 Ibid. p. 14.

46 Victor Hugo, Alexandre Dumas *et al.*, *Guide Touriste en Belgique* (Bruxelles, 1845).

47 *L'Union des charbonnages...*, p. 6.

48 The socialist leader Jules Destrée summed up developments in this period: 'the workman,' he wrote, 'took his place in art and was recognized as the equal of the ancient gods'. Quoted in Emile Cammaerts, *The treasure house of Belgium: her land and people, her art and literature* (London, 1924), p. 118.

49 Marice Le Blond, in Bazalgette, Bouyer *et al.*, *Constantin Meunier et son oeuvre* (Paris, 1955), p. 76.

50 Meunier's work is discussed in Armand Behets, *Constantin Meunier: L'homme, l'artiste, et l'oeuvre* (Brussels, 1942); Lucine Christophe, *Constantin Meunier* (Antwerp, 1947); Louis Pierard, *Constantin Meunier* (Brussels, 1937). Many of Meunier's drawings, paintings and sculptures are collected in the Musée Constantin Meunier in Ixelles, Belgium.

51 A photograph of this figure is found in Bazalgette *et al.*, *Meunier*, n.p. I would like to thank Drs Bonna Westcoat and Irena Grudzinska-Gross for their interpretations of Meunier's work.

52 Another important factor in shaping Belgian public opinion was the reaction to women industrial workers elsewhere prevalent in Europe. As both socialism and unions internationalized into Europe-wide federations, the views of miners from more misogynistic countries, particularly Germany and Austria, began to circulate amongst Belgian mining leaders. A close reading of the Belgian miners' federation paper, *L'Ouvrier Mineur* from 1903 to 1914 shows quite clearly the differences between the attitudes of Belgian miners and those of their European co-workers. The latter were rabid and persistent in their denunciation of Belgians for allowing women to work in mining. Some speeches implied that the Belgian men were 'weak' because they appeared not to mind women working with them. Most of these speeches were reported, but without comment. Marcel van der Linden has written about this process of internationalization from a rather different perspective in 'The national integration of European working classes, 1871–1914', in *International Review of Social History*, XXXIII (1988), pp. 285–311.

53 For many of these pictures I am grateful to the *Institut de la patrimoine artistique*, Brussels. Many are also found in *Art et société en Belgique: 1848–1914*, catalogue of an exhibition at the Palais des Beaux-Arts de Charleroi, 11 Oct.–23 Nov. 1980. In this exhibition, pictures of bourgeois life are strikingly absent. It is also interesting to note that the cathedral of St. Bavo in the textile city of Ghent has one stained glass window dedicated to women textile workers. It depicts women's work in the mills.

54 *Eléments d'enquête sur le rôle de la femme dans l'industrie, les oeuvres, les arts, et les sciences en Belgique* (Brussels, 1897).

55 Again, these insights come from Dr Bonna Wescoat.

56 I am extremely grateful both to Mme Nadine Dubois at the Musée de la vie Wallonne in Liège, as well as to Mme Veronique Vercheval at the Musée de la photographie in Mont-sur-Marchienne (Charleroi). In both places I received a good deal of help finding information about Gustave Marissiaux. I also owe thanks to Prof. Jacques Dubois of the Université de Liège, for his unfailing advice and help. See also *La Photographie en Wallonie, des origines à 1940*, Musée de la vie Wallonne, Liège, 19 octobre au 29 avril 1980.

57 Until this time, Belgium's women miners were among the few women workers whose working clothing was distinctive. The *boteresses*, the women dock workers, the ambulant merchants, the glassworkers usually carried some sort of distinctive tool (e.g. the large straw baskets of the boteresses), but their dress was generally indistinguishable from that of other women of their class and region. Although Marissiaux's photographs suggest that Liège area mining women had discarded their trousers, many photographs from the 1930s, as well as some twentieth-century drawings show women mine workers still wearing trousers, though they were no longer knee-length, and no longer white. These 'uniforms' also characterized Britain's mining women in the nineteenth century. As Beatrix Campbell notes in *Return*, p. 100 '... their very strength, and their androgynous uniform was (*sic*) invoked in the campaign to abolish their right to work ... during the 1890s'.

58 This method was not confined to the *hiercheuses*. One police spy reported that although a *Parti ouvrier* meeting had attracted fifty women from Dison in April, 1893, they were 'mainly recruited from Verviers houses of prostitution'. Report found in Liège, Archives de l'Etat, Sûreté publique, XXI. A. 43, 'Division Commissariat de police à bourgmestre', 14 avril 1893.

59 Needless to say, perhaps, this process of 'pre-modernizing' industrial scenes was yet another means of diluting the reality of Belgium's industrial problems. Of course in present-day Belgium, where there are no longer any working mines, the slag heaps have begun to sprout plant life. Indeed, some municipalities have sponsored tree-planting on the slag heaps – both to alter the grim sky-line with trees and to keep the slag from sliding. In some areas, the sky-line suggests that Belgium is naturally more hilly than it originally was.

60 C. Malva, *Un Mineur vous parle* (Lausanne, n.d.), p. 128.

61 N. Dethier, *Centrale syndicale des travailleurs des mines de Belgique: 60 années d'action, 1890–1905* (n.p., n.d.), p. 21. Two mining engineers, writing in the 1930s, also recalled, 'Feminine personnel has from time immemorial been employed among us in the coal mines and in the sale of coal'. See Paul Fourmarier and Lucien Denoel, *Géologie et industrie minérale du pays de Liège* (Paris and Liège, 1930).

62 See reports in *Revue du travail*, 1900, pp. 309, 421.

63 Quoted in Malva, *Un Mineur...*, p.51.

64 Evelyn Thayer Eaton. *The Belgian leagues of christian working class women* (Washington, D.C., 1954), p. 50.

65 See note 52 above.

66 Michel Delwiche and Francis Groff, *Les Gueles noires* (Brussels, 1985), p. 26.

67 Ibid. pp. 81, 149.

Chapter 17

Rachel G. Fuchs and Leslie Page Moch

■ 'PREGNANT, SINGLE, AND FAR FROM HOME:
MIGRANT WOMEN IN NINETEENTH-CENTURY PARIS',
American Historical Review, 93 (4), October 1990, pp. 1007–1031

JULIETTE SAUGET SET OUT FOR PARIS at the age of seventeen in the company of an elder, married sister who resided there. Born in 1886 into an impoverished woodcutter's family, Juliette left home as a gesture of solidarity with another sister, whom her father had struck in anger. In Paris, her married sister advised her to work as a domestic servant, because Juliette needed lodgings as well as a job. In her first position, she complained one night at supper that the seventeen-year-old son of the family had come to her room with the intention of having sexual relations with her. The family laughed in reply, so she felt she had to leave. This incident marked the beginning of a series of jobs: first in Paris, then in Amiens—the capital of her home province, where other of her siblings resided—then back in Paris. Eventually, she developed a social life at the public, outdoor dances in Paris. At age twenty-four, she became pregnant.[1]

The story of Germinie Lacerteux is better known, for this fictionalized account of a domestic servant who worked in the home of Edmund and Jules Goncourt appeared in a popular novel of the 1860s. Emile Zola, in his introduction to one of the many editions of *Germinie Lacerteux*, calls our attention to the plight of this "whole bleeding corner of humanity."[2] The character Germinie was born some fifty years earlier than Juliette Sauget, in eastern France. The youngest daughter of poor weavers, she and her sisters struggled to make ends meet after the deaths of her mother, father, and elder brother. At the age of fourteen, Germinie followed her elder sisters to Paris, where she worked as maid to the mistress of a café. Before the year was out, an old waiter raped and impregnated her. After bearing a stillborn baby, Germinie returned to domestic service. Eventually, she met and courted the son of a neighborhood shopkeeper. Germinie wanted nothing more than to marry, but instead she again became pregnant.

Neither Germinie Lacerteux nor Juliette Sauget married the father of her children. Both the woman and the character had come to Paris following siblings who had worked as servants. Their story was far from unusual for single migrant women in the nineteenth century. During this century of mass migration, men and women, predominantly single, left rural areas for the cities of the European continent and for the New World in unprecedented numbers. Frequent movement in and out of cities made this an especially mobile age.[3] Women traveled farther from home than ever before. In France, each generation of nineteenth-century women was more mobile than the last; by the generation born in the 1890s, women were more likely than men to leave their home districts. Migration streams of workers from the countryside to cities came to include, and even be dominated by, women.[4]

Despite its importance, female migration in Europe and the aspects of migrant life unique to women are only now being explored. The major studies of migration on the European continent have emphasized male labor migrants. Consequently, migration has been defined in terms of the male experience, and differences between male and female migration patterns are not well understood.[5] Upon arrival in the city, men and women found different jobs, and, oftentimes, men and women from the same villages moved to different locations to take employment. Women moved and lived in familial contexts more often than men; they moved to marry or, if single, to live with relatives, with their employer's family, or in supervised employer dormitories.[6] Finally, although both male and female newcomers to the city were subject to exploitation in dangerous and ill-paying jobs, only the women were at risk of pregnancy. This was the biological manifestation of their economic and social vulnerability, and pregnancy was particularly devastating for a woman who did not marry. Aware of this situation, families, the church, private philanthropies, and municipal agencies tried, in different ways, to protect migrant women.

Like contemporaries of Juliette Sauget and Germinie Lacerteux, today's historians see a clear link between migration to the city and sexual vulnerability—that is, a connection between leaving home and the loss of social protection. Research on out-of-wedlock births seeks to explain the "illegitimacy boom" in West European cities between 1750 and 1850 in terms of women's poverty, geographic mobility, occupational instability, and absence of social protection.[7] Louise Tilly, Joan Scott, and Miriam Cohen have pointed out that, while these women may have expected to marry their partners, the circumstances of migrant women's lives rendered them powerless. Cissie Fairchilds suggests that the increase in illegitimacy resulted from changes that limited women's security and familial protection, especially in the late eighteenth century, when poor women increasingly left home at an early age. Some migrated to the city, where their wages were insufficient. They frequently changed jobs, which made them susceptible to economic appeals and threats, vulnerable to seduction. Gradually, many eighteenth-century female servants realized that their only chance for male companionship was outside of marriage. George Alter has demonstrated that, in the nineteenth-century textile town of Verviers, similar social and economic pressures acted on women to deprive them of leverage in courtship and the marriage market.[8]

Illegitimate births were common in many, but not all, large European cities from the nineteenth into the twentieth century. In France, they were recorded most frequently in Paris.[9] At the beginning of the nineteenth century, almost 40 percent of all reported births in Paris and the surrounding area were illegitimate. By mid-century, that proportion declined to approximately 25 percent of the total reported births, where it remained until the end of the century. In the 1880s, when 29 percent of Parisian babies were illegitimate, the figure for Vienna and Prague was 50 percent, 45 percent for Rome, 40 percent for Stockholm, 38 percent for Moscow, and 31 percent for Budapest. By contrast, only 4 percent of London's babies were born out of wedlock.[10]

Out-of-wedlock births were not an urban phenomenon alone; rural illegitimacy was high in some regions. In fact, historians, anthropologists, and demographers have emphasized the variety of contexts that produced high rates of illegitimacy: these have included local courtship culture in the Zurich highlands, marriage law in southern Germany, international emigration patterns in Portugal and Italy, and economic downturns in the English midlands.[11] Scholars have urged that pregnancies of single women be investigated in light of the particular circumstances that gave rise to them, rather than forcing a mechanistic, unitary framework on a phenomenon that occurred under a great variety of conditions.

We investigate the pregnancies of unmarried women in the context of migration to nineteenth-century Paris in order to illuminate the social and demographic context in a large city. Like most large cities on the Continent, Paris housed more women than men at the end of the nineteenth century, when its inhabitants numbered 3.8 million and its sex ratio was 89 for the city proper (that is, there were 89 men for every 100 women).[12] Its population became more female because French administration and Parisian commerce offered jobs for women in the expanding service sector and in the garment industry supported by the middle-class. The expansion of the bourgeoisie in Paris increased demand for domestic servants, the female workers who played a key role in both the history of migration and the nineteenth-century city.[13] Such women, if they did not enter a well-established urban milieu, could have sexual relations but could not muster the resources to compel men to marry them. French law explicitly forbade the single mother to search for the father of her child or to hold him responsible for any child support. Their physical vulnerability and geographical mobility placed women at the heart of the processes that transformed the continent of Europe between 1815 and World War I—on the move away from home, out into the world, susceptible to the vagaries of social and economic fortune both at home and away.[14]

This article explores the complex connections between urban migration and illegitimate births in nineteenth-century Paris by looking at four issues: the link between the process of migration and single women's pregnancies, the extent to which single migrant status shaped women's occupational and sexual experience, the role of single mothers in the changing patterns of migration to Paris, and the connections between the migration of single women, networks of wet nurses, and traffic in foundlings. To do so, we investigate women's productive and reproductive behavior, their vulnerability and agency, as well as gender relations and the political and social constraints on poor women in a nineteenth-century metropolis. Such issues have significance beyond the nineteenth-century Parisian world because they advance historians' understanding of women's role in the larger drama of urban life.[15]

INFORMATION ABOUT PREGNANT MIGRANT WOMEN in the city is sparse. They appear briefly in accounts by French social reformers and agents of public welfare programs in the last decades of the century.[16] We can observe them in shelters for the homeless at the end of the century in Paris. We see others being refused public assistance because they had been in Paris for less than a year before they delivered a child. Such shreds of data can be augmented by the court records of women accused of abortion or of killing their newborn. Their trial records offer a rare glimpse into the individual lives of poor migrant mothers and personalize institutional admissions records.[17]

The greatest number of single mothers in public records over the course of the century were patients in the free, state-run maternity hospital for the destitute called La Maternité, where 2,000–4,000 women delivered their babies annually—an estimated total of 200,000 women between 1830 and 1900. Hospital admissions officers recorded the woman's birthplace, address in Paris, age, and occupation; these records constitute this study's major source and allow us to sketch out a portrait of the single mother in Paris.

Women in La Maternité were among the poorest of mothers. Most women preferred midwife-assisted delivery, and until the 1880s hospitals were more dangerous than home delivery with a midwife. Consequently, women in La Maternité tended to be those who could not pay a midwife's fee or did not have a room of their own in which to have a baby; they were therefore unlikely to be married or live in a consensual union.[18] The vast majority were single migrants in Paris. At the turn of the century, migrant women were 82 percent of the single mothers in La Maternité, yet they made up only 63 percent of the women of childbearing age in the city of Paris. The average age of a single migrant mother was twenty-four years.[19] Her experiences suggest the links between migration, urban life, and illegitimacy for single women.

MUCH SCHOLARLY WORK ON THE BOOM OF ILLEGITIMATE BIRTHS in European cities between 1750 and 1850 assumes that migrant women in the city were villagers with an urban future. Yet migration often involved more than a single move from a town or village to a capital city like Paris. Records such as urban censuses obscure the fact that many Europeans moved more than once, that many were temporary workers in the city and that some, like Juliette Sauget, returned to their home region. Others moved to the city by stages, going from home village to provincial town to a great city like Paris.[20]

Moreover, the relationship between migration and pregnancy is not unidirectional, with migration preceding pregnancy. Although single women were vulnerable to pregnancy in the city, pregnancies in the provinces did not always result in marriage. Instead, failed relationships and pregnancies caused many women to migrate to Paris, where they hoped to deliver their babies in the anonymity of a large city.[21] A small proportion were doubtless from elite provincial families and took great care to disguise their purpose in the city by the use of private homes for unwed mothers, pseudonyms, and incognito birth registrations.[22] They successfully elude the historian. The arrival of the more numerous and more dependent poor pregnant women concerned the public assistance authorities, for, by the late nineteenth century, about 250 new mothers per annum who had been in Paris less than one year requested aid.[23] In hopes of discouraging these arrivals, in 1852 the public assistance hospitals barred such newcomers from La Maternité and other public hospitals unless they were in hard labor or presented a medical emergency. The welfare institutions of Paris did not want to be inundated by paupers from the countryside, who, they feared, would abandon their infants. It is unclear how many new arrivals knew about the one-year residency rule, but evidence from infanticide trials suggests that some pregnant newcomers who had been denied admission to La Maternité did not return with the onset of labor. Unable to afford a midwife, they delivered alone in their rooms.[24]

Most mothers in the hospital had established prior residency. Demographer Etienne van de Walle concluded that, "in the instance of Paris at least, there exists abundant statistical evidence that mothers of illegitimate children were almost always domiciled in the city at the time of delivery."[25] Thus, although there is no way of knowing exactly where they conceived or how long they had been in Paris, it is certain that the thousands of migrant women who delivered in the public assistance hospitals had been in the city for at least several months before their pregnancy.

This assertion is borne out by the sole direct evidence on the length of time migrant women lived in Paris before delivery: the records of a program to send pregnant women who applied to La Maternité to a welfare midwife. During the 1869–1880 period, these records noted how long each woman had resided in Paris. The vast majority of these women (who are like those in La Maternité in every other respect—age, occupation, and birthplace) had resided in Paris at the time of conception. Only 22 percent had lived in Paris less than nine months before delivery.[26] 1n 1889, Emile Levasseur estimated that a quarter of all the city's illegitimate babies were conceived outside the city.[27]

Those women who arrived in Paris pregnant often were desperate. In the absence of systematic data about them, we offer two emblematic cases gathered from court records. In her early twenties, Marie Gérard, had already left her small-town home in northern France when she became pregnant. While working as a domestic servant in the provincial capital of Reims in 1880, Gérard had a sexual relationship with another worker in her employer's house—a carter with whom she planned marriage. The father of her child married another woman without warning after Gérard became pregnant. Humiliated and demoralized by her inability to enforce his promise of marriage, Gérard could no longer face working with her former lover. Unable to return to her family in her condition, she chose to hide her pregnancy in Paris, where she sought domestic work.[28]

Anna Bordot, daughter of a poor, pious family in the Auvergne in central France, had worked as a domestic since the age of fourteen. In her mid-twenties, in 1875, she was courted by an Alsatian brewery worker in her hometown. Her suitor did not inspire her parents' trust, but after eight months they gave their approval to her marriage. This permission achieved, Bordot "abandoned" herself to him six weeks before the wedding. The Saturday before the nuptials, her fiancé disappeared, taking the trunk that contained her hard-earned trousseau. This humiliation was followed by her realization that she was pregnant. Bordot had one thought: to hide her condition. She took the train to Paris, where she found work as a domestic.[29]

The pregnant newcomer faced the problem of survival in Paris: where to stay, how to find others in the city who would, and could, help her. When public assistance officials interrogated hundreds of post-partum migrant women not eligible for assistance because they had lived in Paris less than a year, these women described their survival strategies.[30] Just over a quarter of them had worked as domestic servants for wages that the authorities explicitly recognized as extremely low. A slightly smaller group (22 percent) stayed with friends and relatives until delivery, and the same proportion lived en garni—in the cheap, crowded lodgings clustered around the railroad stations and in the central portions of the city that rented beds to the poor. A few more found small apartments or rooms to rent. Only one in thirteen was accompanied by the father of the child. Those who arrived near term—about one in seven—could stay in the Asile Michelet shelter for the pregnant homeless. Some went to shelters upon arrival, others just before delivery, and many more after their children were born; some women had several stints in the shelters. One in twenty arrived so late in her pregnancy that she went directly to the hospital to deliver.[31]

If we consider these alternatives from the perspective of the women being interviewed rather than the interviewers, both the people who met them at the station and the choices facing the newcomer—pregnant or not—appear in a different light. A relative or compatriot met some new arrivals; others had to find lodgings and a job on their own, and two kinds of strangers awaited the lone woman descending from the train in nineteenth-century Paris: procurers and employees from servant employment bureaus. In a study of Parisian prostitution, Alain Corbin wrote about procurers who recruited at railroad terminals. Their victims related harrowing tales in court. Recruiting employment bureaus could also be exploitative; some charged a stiff fee from the servant in exchange for temporary lodgings and job placement.[32] Fortunately, religious or philanthropic organizations also exhibited a genuine concern for new arrivals, such as the Maison Protestant de Convalescense and the two houses of the Catholic Soeurs de la Croix, who welcomed migrant women and servants who were ill or between positions. They had been established to help young women from Brittany but took in other migrants as well.[33] After 1900, about 3,900 arrivals per year sought refuge in one of the temporary shelters for women established by municipal, departmental, and private philanthropic organizations around 1900.[34]

The more fortunate of the pregnant new arrivals were part of a migration stream from their homeland to Paris and, like Juliette Sauget, were met at the station by a compatriot with whom they could lodge until they secured a position.[35] This was the case for shepherdess Jansette Michel, age thirty, whose brother and cousin were part of the migrant group that formed a link between Paris and the alpine highlands of Savoy. She surprised and displeased her father by departing for Paris in 1874, keeping secret her impregnation by a man of fifty-seven—a close friend of her family and her godfather. Michel joined her brother when she arrived in Paris; she then lived with a cousin who was puzzled by her tears and suffering. After ten weeks as an economic burden on her relatives, she escaped from family observation and dependency by taking a job as a domestic cook.[36]

Most single women who gave birth in Paris probably did not arrive pregnant but conceived their children in Paris. Like Juliette Sauget, migrant women became pregnant as a result of sexual relations that were part of the urban household, neighborhood, and municipal life. The particular vulnerability of single women to pregnancy is somewhat surprising, in light of research on chain migration, which indicates that people moved to cities where they had opportunities or contacts who could help them. Indeed, research on French cities reveals that the experience of moving into the growing nineteenth-century city did not produce the dislocation and anomie that scholars once thought.[37] Findings from La Maternité show that these interpretations of migration should be modified to take account of the women's different experiences of migrant community protection and sponsorship. Women with kin in Paris, like Juliet Sauget and Jansette Michel, were welcomed to the city by relatives who could sponsor them, help them find work, and provide them with material aid.[38]

It was not possible, however, for the migrant community to prevent seduction or to bring partners to marriage once pregnancy occurred. An explanation is found in a close examination of the dynamics of migrant groups in the city. Compatriots could not protect women migrants from pregnancy out of wedlock or from the dangers of delivery in La Maternité, because female migrants, especially domestic servants, often lived apart. Even in the *garni* of Paris, however, where young migrant women did live in local communities, they were liable to seduction by their poor countrymen—some of whom were married men leading the single life in Paris. Court cases reveal that the married cousin or the countryman who worked in the neighborhood or lived in the same rooming house seduced young female migrants.[39] In either case, the migrant community had little power to force marriage on an impoverished or already married man, even less to enforce marriage with a worker from another region or a member of the middle class. The powers of a migration system—even one operating on close family ties like that of Juliette Sauget—were severely limited. Migrant networks could help newcomers get started but could not protect them from exploitation.[40] Many single women were left vulnerable to pregnancies outside of marriage.

Despite the difficulties of life in Paris for pregnant women and single mothers, few chose to return home. Whether a woman became pregnant in Paris or at home, then came to Paris to hide her "fault," as Marie Gérard and Anna Bordot testified they did, she could not return home unless she successfully hid the birth and abandoned the infant. Child abandonment, however, became increasingly difficult after 1852.[41] Starting in 1888, public assistance authorities in Paris tried to encourage a few hundred women each year who had sought public welfare to return home with their babies by offering to pay their food and train fare in a "repatriation" program. Neither the city nor the surrounding *département* wanted to bear the cost of aiding indigent mothers from the rest of France, nor did they want to support their abandoned children. But the free ticket home was evidently not tempting, for fewer than 20 percent of those offered "repatriation" accepted the offer, despite the threat of ineligibility for Parisian public assistance.[42]

The case history of La Maternité patient Jeannette Pazy illustrates the migrant woman's dilemma. Pazy, a day laborer from the Nièvre, southeast of Paris, left home pregnant at age twenty-three; she worked on the outskirts of Paris as a domestic for two months before delivery, first in one location, then another. When she went into labor, Pazy hastened to La Maternité, where she bore a son on October 17, 1857. While at the hospital, she asked for welfare for herself and the baby or, in absence of that, assistance in abandoning her infant. The director of the hospital informed her that because she had not lived in the area for a year, the only form of assistance to which she was entitled was free transportation home; she could not even leave her baby at the Paris foundling home. Pazy's mother had died, and only her father remained at home. Lacking family support, without money for a wet nurse, despairing of welfare or the possibility of legal abandonment, Pazy took what she thought to be her only recourse. She did not leave the city, but, within hours of her discharge from La Maternité, she left the infant near the entrance to the foundling hospital across the street.[43]

MIGRANT WOMEN WERE LIKELY TO APPEAR AT THE DOOR of La Maternité because the Parisian poor of both sexes were predominantly migrants. Months or even years in Paris did not guarantee them economic security. Migrants in disproportionate numbers filled the welfare rolls and the shelters for the homeless near the end of the century. They made up three-quarters of the indigents receiving aid from the many welfare bureaus of the city in the 1880s and 1890s—despite the fact that one year of residence in the city was required to qualify for aid. Female migrants made up over three-quarters of those who found refuge in the four shelters for homeless women operated jointly by private philanthropy and public assistance in Paris during the 1890s. About a quarter of them had been in the city over two years, and about 10 percent had arrived in Paris less than two months before.[44]

Single migrants who gave birth in the capital city lived in a variety of domestic arrangements: alone in their rooms, as domestics in their employers' home, with friends or relatives, or in consensual relationships. Consensual unions were common in nineteenth-century Paris but their exact numbers are unknown. Emile Levasseur estimated that, in 1880 and 1891, 27 to 33 percent of Paris's illegitimate births were to couples in stable consensual unions. In 1884, he argued, about half the Parisian children born out of wedlock were the fruit of consensual unions, a quarter were from countrywomen who entered Paris to give birth anonymously, and a quarter were "the real product of Parisian immorality."[45] Programs of aid to poor mothers reported in 1895 that 45 percent were living alone, 23 percent lived with parents or family, and only 2 percent admitted cohabiting (it is estimated that many more were cohabiting than reported).[46]

According to a municipal inquiry, there was one consensual union for every four married couples in mid-century Paris. Michel Frey's research, which is centered on this report, argues that consensual unions were founded on sexual attraction but grounded in women's economic, legal, and physical vulnerability. They were perceived by the women as failed courtships. Frey concluded that "illegitimacy and *concubinage* are not in contradiction to marriage in the working class. The two are linked and it is the *non-realization of marriage* that determines the position of the *concubine*."[47] Single female migrants, entering Paris poor, had little hope of a lifelong relationship and legal marriage. Whether migrant mothers lived with a man or not, they lacked the economic or social clout to marry the partners of their choice. Not only were there social and economic obstacles to marriage but French regulations required visits home and multiple fees to obtain notarized certificates of birth and parental consent (or evidence of the death of parent).[48] Single mothers were not simply victims, however, for some were sexually active by choice. Both Juliette Sauget and Germinie Lacerteux were willing sexual partners with the fathers of their babies; both the man who impregnated Juliette Sauget and the old waiter who raped Germinie Lacerteux made marriage offers that were refused. But neither woman could protect herself from pregnancy: they lacked access to safe or efficacious methods of birth control and abortion.[49]

Most single migrant mothers who gave birth at La Maternité worked at one of the occupations open to females in the city. The largest number were in domestic service, which was ever more prevalent as the century progressed, 33 percent in La Maternité in the period before 1870 and 46 percent in the subsequent thirty-year period. One in seven was a seamstress (*couturière*). During the first half of the nineteenth century, 6 percent worked in the other needle trades (sewing white goods, lingerie, garments, shoes, gloves, or ornamental trim), a proportion that declined to 3 percent by 1900. Together, seamstresses and women in the needle trades constituted almost one-fifth of the single women giving birth at La Maternité. Unspecified day labor was the next most important occupational category, ranging from 16 percent before 1870 to 8 percent at the end. Other single mothers at La Maternité worked as laundresses, linen menders, or cooks.[50]

Single mothers' employment patterns resemble those of all the women working in Paris and of migrant women in particular. By the turn of the century, over 336,000 women from the provinces of France had jobs in Paris; they worked at a great variety of occupations, from schoolteacher to laundress. Most, however, worked at traditional female occupations in the needle trades or services. All in all, 33 percent were domestics of one kind or another, 43 percent worked in the city's industries, and another 19 percent worked in commerce. Native-born Parisian women were more likely to work in the multiple industries of the city (including the needle trades) and to seek out better-paying jobs in commerce. Only 6 percent of women born in the *département* were domestics: 73 percent worked in industries and 15 percent in commerce.[51] Across nineteenth-century Europe, domestic servants came from the countryside, a smaller town, a village, or a foreign land; they were rarely natives of the city in which they served. Over 90 percent of the servants in Berlin, Moscow, St. Petersburg, and Paris—and the clear majority in London were migrants by the end of the nineteenth century.[52] Service offered the newcomer housing, a domestic atmosphere, and protection from the life of the streets; consequently, parents who sent their daughters to town were willing to allow them to enter this relatively private and protected situation.[53]

But there was a less protected side to domestic service, as we have seen. Servants like Juliette Sauget were notoriously vulnerable to sexual advances both from members of the employer's family and from other servants in the household and apartment building. In a study of female workers that had nine editions between 1863 and 1891, Jules Simon described the servants' sexual vulnerability: "Many of them find a seducer in the same house where they serve. A lackey, a coachman have only too many occasions to do ill to the servants who spend the most part of their free time with them, far from all supervision; and sometimes it is the master himself who corrupts the morals of a poor girl, doubly seduced by his authority and by his fortune."[54] Alexandre Parent-Duchâtelet's investigation of Parisian prostitution, first published in 1836, also links domestic service to sexual exploitation; next to the unemployed, servants were the women most likely to move into prostitution. Often, it was a pregnancy and subsequent dismissal from her post that pushed the servant into prostitution.[55]

Servants' sexual vulnerability was accentuated by their housing arrangements and the structure of employment. Parisian apartment buildings typically housed all the servants in small rooms along one hallway; sometimes, two women shared a room. These rooms were under the eaves of the mansard roof on the building's top floor. On errands for the household, servants met the shopkeepers and workers of the neighborhood. At public dances and other large gatherings, they came in contact with strangers.[56] Neither employers, other servants, neighborhood tradesmen, nor strangers at public dances were interested in protecting the chastity of female servants. What is more, they were vulnerable to seduction and rape, not only because they were poor but also because they generally lived apart from their compatriots; many slept in an unlocked room to which others had access. Domestic service, the largest single profession in the nineteenth-century city, offered a double-edged sword of sexual protection and exploitation.[57]

Thus domestic servants appeared at the doors of La Maternité, as well as at the public shelters of Paris, in disproportionate numbers. Domestic service was the occupation of more than one-third of all single women who gave birth in Paris's maternity hospitals during the 1880s and 1890s. Seamstresses and day laborers (predominantly in the needle trades) together made up another third.[58] Over half of the pregnant women who were without a residence in Paris and temporarily housed in Asile Michelet, the municipal shelter for homeless women in their last month of pregnancy, listed their occupation as domestic servant.[59]

The social and sexual situation of the female garment worker was more autonomous but still precarious. The housing of young women who worked in the needle trades, either sewing at home alone or in sweatshops, was no more luxurious than that of servants. In fact, the cramped, cold, and dim single rooms to rent were often the same sort of attic rooms that housed servants.[60] But this housing allowed young workers greater independence from their employers and co-workers than servants had.[61] However, garment and textile workers' extremely low salaries (exacerbated by seasonal unemployment), in combination with the freedom to change residence without losing employment, led more needleworkers than servants into consensual unions. According to contemporary observers and scholar Michel Frey, needleworkers' low salaries created a "blurred boundary" between consensual unions and prostitution.[62]

The story of Marie Renard illuminates the particular problem of domestic service. Renard came to Paris from the distant Savoy in the Alps at age sixteen because her parents had died—her mother when she was eleven, her father when she was fifteen. They had both previously worked in Paris, and her designated guardians, an aunt and uncle, lived in the city. She stayed with her aunt and uncle for about ten days until they found her a position as a domestic servant with a family virtually around the corner from their dwelling. Renard soon asked her employers for a key to her room to protect her from the advances of their seventeen-year-old son; it was denied. The young man entered her room and asked to share her bed. She testified that she tried to prevent him from doing so, but he forced himself on her, and sexual relations continued after this occasion. Marie Renard became pregnant within four months of her arrival in Paris.[63]

Like many young women who came to the city, Renard had no parents to advise or protect her. According to nineteenth-century marriage records, single migrant women were more likely to have lost one or both of their parents than were the native-born women.[64] The death of a parent—especially the father—was likely to disrupt life at home and lead to the departure of young women. A father's death was devastating to the economic and social protection a young migrant woman could marshal. With a mother's death, young women lost a personal advisor as well as a social and economic sponsor. Once in the city, orphaned women were more likely to stay.[65] While the death of a parent did not alone determine that a single woman would bear a child in the city, it was one in a series of disabilities that robbed women like Marie Renard of social power in the urban marriage market. Women without parents were at greater risk of having illegitimate children.[66] The connection between pregnancy and the process of migration for single women in the context of this metropolis will emerge from an examination of the origins of Paris's single mothers.

IN THE PERIOD FROM 1830 to 1900, women from points progressively more distant from Paris bore children at La Maternité. From 1830 through 1848, they reflected in a general way the *départements* that sent people to the capital. In the middle of the century, 1852–1869, women born in more distant provinces came to La Maternité. By the last decades of the century (1880–1900), a dramatic shift had occurred, and many more women were émigrés from the west of France. (See Maps 1, 2, and 3, which divide France into twenty-one regions, for hospital registrations by regional subdivisions, the French *départementes*.)

During the hospital's first two decades, 1830 through 1848, migrant women at La Maternité generally reflected the *départements* that sent people to Paris.[67] Sixteen percent came from the Ile-de-France; 14 percent from Picardy, nearby to the north of Paris; 11 percent from Lorraine; 10 percent from Burgundy, and 9 percent from the populous Nord.[68] (See Map 1.) Women from the nearest regions worked in the needle trades as well as in domestic service; by contrast, almost all of the women from Burgundy and Lorraine were domestic sevants.[69] Very few mothers came from the south or the west of France.

More distant provinces sent women to La Maternité during the prosperous middle of the century, 1852–1869. Picardy and Lorraine still dominated (with 10 percent each). Burgundy and the Centre, southwest of Paris, sent the next highest proportion of women (9 percent each) followed closely by the Ile-de-France (with 8 percent). Fewer women came from the Champagne-Ardennes, northeast of Paris, and the Nord (6 percent each). (See Map 2.) Their occupational pattern remained the same.[70]

By the last decades of the nineteenth century (1880–1900), the pattern had changed dramatically. Brittany, in the far west of France, which before this time had produced less than 3 percent of the women at La Maternité, now was the most common birthplace for single migrant mothers (12 percent), followed by the Centre (11 percent), Burgundy and Picardy (8 and 7 percent, respectively), Alsace (7 percent), the Nord and Ile-de-France (6 and 5 percent), and Lower and Upper Normandy (5 and 4 percent).[71] As the general migration trends shifted from east to west, Lorraine and Champagne-Ardenne sent few (only 4 and 2 percent respectively). (See Map 3.) [72]

A comparison between the origins of the women in La Maternité and all migrant women in Paris reveals three distinct patterns. Of the twenty-two regions of France, the majority

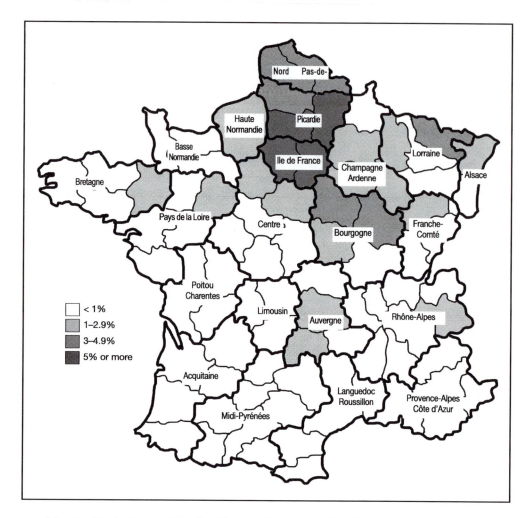

Map 1. Birthplaces of Single Migrant Mothers in La Maternité, 1830–1848

SOURCES: Daniel Courgeau, "Three Centuries of Spatial Mobility in France," *UNESCO Reports and Papers in the Social Sciences,* 51 (1982), 53; Archives de l'Assistance Publique, l'Hôpital Port Royal, Registres des Entrées, 1830, 1837, 1838, 1847, 1848.

(fourteen)—such as Burgundy—sent women to La Maternité in about the same proportion as they contributed to the population of Paris.[73] For example, 9 percent of the women in Paris were born in Burgundy, as were 9 percent of the single mothers who delivered in La Maternité in the 1890s. Five other regions sent disproportionately few women to the hospital for the indigent.[74] The area surrounding Paris, for example (Ile-de-France) supplied 12 percent of the city's population but only 6 percent of the mothers in La Maternité. Finally, three regions sent more women to the hospital than might be expected, given their numbers in Paris: the north of France, Alsace, and Brittany.[75] The *départements* of the Nord provided 5 percent of Paris's migrant women and 6 percent of the single mothers in La Maternité; the figures for Alsace are nearly equal to these. Brittany, by contrast, furnished Paris with only 5 percent of its migrant women; but 15 percent of the single mothers in La Maternité came from that region.

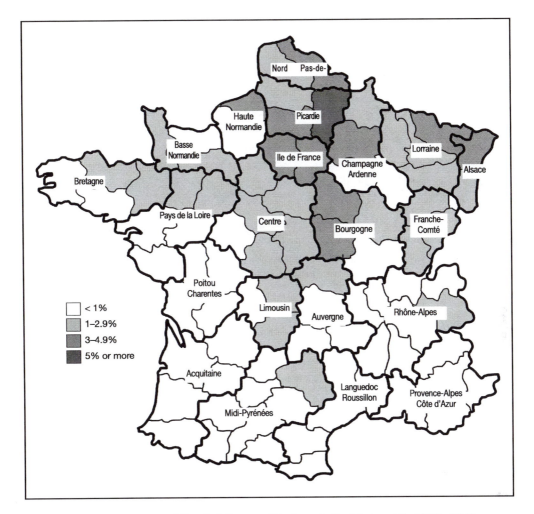

Map 2. Birthplaces of Single Migrant Mothers in La Maternité, 1852–1869

Sources: Daniel Courgeau, "Three Centuries of Spatial Mobility in France," *UNESCO Reports and Papers in the Social Sciences,* 51 (1982), 53; Archives de l'Assistance Publique, l'Hôpital Port Royal, Registres des Entrées, 1852, 1855, 1860, 1865, 1869.

The data from exemplary regions' histories of migration to Paris, the composition of their streams of migrants to the city, and illegitimacy figures for home areas help establish the connection between these patterns and migration to Paris. Single women least likely to deliver babies in La Maternité were from areas with long histories of migration to the capital, such as Picardy, Champagne-Ardennes, and the Loire region—and were, like those from the Ile-de-France, close to home and had many compatriots. Most of these provinces had histories of low illegitimacy rates.[76] For example, the Auvergne in central France had sent men to Paris since the eighteenth century. Their legendary hard work, miserliness, and business acumen afforded them success in business and starring (albeit sometimes unsavory) roles in Honoré de Balzac's *Comédie humaine.* Auvergnat women were part of a distinct and well-established group in the city. This migration stream included equal numbers of men and women; the sex ratio of the Auvergnat group in Paris was 100 in 1901 compared with

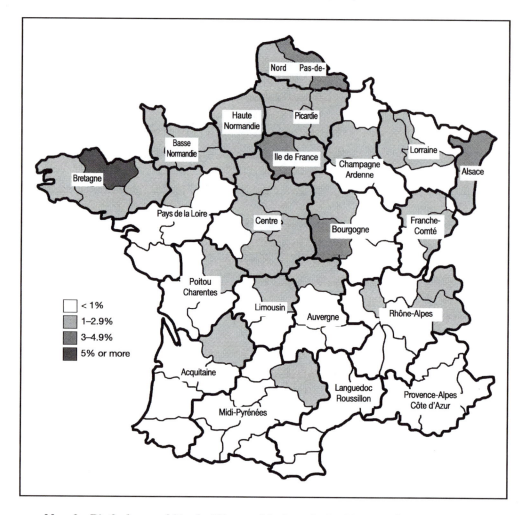

Map 3. Birthplaces of Single Migrant Mothers in La Maternité, 1890–1900

SOURCES: Daniel Courgeau, "Three Centuries of Spatial Mobility in France," *UNESCO Reports and Papers in the Social Sciences,* 51 (1982), 53; Archives de l'Assistance Publique, l'Hôpital Port Royal, Registres des Entrées, 1890, 1895, 1900.

89 for the entire city. The Auvergnat women numbered over 34,500. Fifty-nine percent were in the labor force; of these, only 23 percent were domestic servants, and about the same proportion (25 percent) were in the needle trades.[77]

Single migrants most likely to deliver in La Maternité came from regions with different home traditions and migration histories. For example, during the nineteenth century, in the Nord, the textile and mining industries produced industrial cities with levels of human misery unmatched in most parts of France. The Nord's longstanding high rates of illegitimacy increased. By the turn of the century, migrants from the Nord in Paris were likely to be women, even more likely than the population as a whole, because the sex ratio of this group was 79. These 34,000 women were extremely poor and often lacked local kin. Fifty-six percent were in the labor force; of these, 21 percent were domestics, and even more (30 percent) were in the needle trades.[78] The women of Alsace had been victimized by the vagaries of international politics. The Franco-Prussian War and subsequent absorption of Alsace into the German empire resulted in a massive migration to Paris for many single Alsacian women. As foreigners, they found the bureaucratic prerequisites for marriage even more difficult to meet.[79] It is hard to ascertain the status of the 32,750 Alsacian women in Paris at the turn of the century; 51 percent of them were in the labor force, but, because Alsace was not a part of France at the time, they are not included in the detailed occupational portrait provided by the census. It is clear that illegitimacy was relatively high in Alsace before the break with France and that it remained higher than in most of France during this period.[80]

In the home areas of the Nord and Alsace, the high rates of illegitimacy suggest that sexual vulnerability in the city was aggravated by regional circumstances that simultaneously pressured single women to be sexually active and depressed their expectations of marriage.[81] On the other hand, women from these areas produced only a few more children in La Maternité than their total numbers suggest (4.5 percent of female population versus 6.1 percent of women in La Maternité for the north; 4.3 percent of female population versus 6.1 percent of women in La Maternité for Alsace.) This appearance may be a statistical artifact of the age structure and martial status of migrant women as a group from the north and Alsace. The women of Brittany stand out in this trio of home areas because their appearance in La Maternité was so much greater than their presence in Paris (5.4 percent of female population versus 14.5 percent of women in La Maternité). This proportion is particularly striking because illegitimacy rates in Brittany itself were low throughout the nineteenth century; whatever role high rates of illegitimacy at home may play in the behavior of women after they leave home, those rates are not relevant for Breton women, whose home area was devout and conservative. Several factors set Breton women apart, such as the history of migration between their province and Paris and the structure of their migrant group. Breton migration to Paris was relatively late; very few came to Paris before 1850, a stream began in the 1870s, and, by the 1890s, Bretons were flooding into the city in the thousands. As a consequence, its people had among the least well-placed web of contacts.[82] Bretons' sparse education and rural background did not prepare them for urban professions or for sophisticated occupations in Paris; one urban chaplain declared succinctly in 1898 that the Breton immigrant was "the pariah of Paris."[83]

These pariahs were most likely to be women. Unlike long-established migration streams that originated with male labor, such as the famous masons and construction workers from the highlands of central France, the majority of Breton immigrants were women. The sex ratio of Bretons in Paris was a very low 69; the sex ratio of the group from the Côtes-du-Nord—the area that supplied many Bretons to Paris—was 64. There were over 41,500 women from Brittany in Paris, of whom over two-thirds were in the labor force. Of Breton women who worked, married and single, nearly 40 percent were domestics, but only half that proportion worked in the needle trades. Brittany supplied turn-of-the-century Paris with over 11,000 servants, more than any other province—and these were among the poorest, least sophisticated, and most vulnerable of the city's domemestics.[84] As a group, Breton women in Paris represent the extreme case. Their appearance in La Maternité suggests that they were indeed the least fortunate.

A FURTHER ANALYSIS OF THE ORIGINS AND OCCUPATIONS of single mothers in Paris reveals another side of the connections between migration and pregnancy, that of the traffic in wet nurses, foundlings, and mothers' milk. The wet-nursing industry that persisted in France until

World War I links illegitimacy and the city. First, it drew unmarried pregnant women to Paris in hopes of obtaining the relatively lucrative job of wet nurse after their babies were born. Second, a two-way traffic joined single mothers in Paris with the provinces, because thousands of their infants were sent out to rural wet nurses. Many single mothers in the metropolis did not keep and nurse their infants; rather, they chose one of two other options: they turned over their infants to the state-run foundling home, which sent the foundlings out to wet nurses, or they sent their infants to a rural wet nurse whom they chose themselves. In the course of the century, an estimated 300,000 foundlings were sent out to rural wet nurses, and another one million Parisian babies went to the provinces under private auspices. The foundlings who survived to adulthood played specific roles in the politics, social hierarchy, and labor force of their rural homes.[85] The infants born in the city, then, affected both the rural and urban social fabric. Their existence in the countryside, as well as the itineraries they traveled, reinforces broader observations of two-way migration streams between nineteenth-century Paris and rural areas.[86]

Foundling children, traveled by wagonloads to wet nurses in the countryside, where sometimes over half met an early death. In the 1830s, these children went to wet nurses predominantly in *départements* north of Paris or in the Morvan region of Burgundy southeast of Paris.[87] By the 1860s, the main route of this traffic led to the Morvan—primarily to the *département* of the Nièvre—and some infants were taken to the north of France, as before. Foundlings also traveled farther from Paris, however, going south and west.[88] This trend continued in the 1880s, when the Nièvre stood out as the area receiving the major share of foundlings, followed by the north of France. Areas to the west and south of Paris, toward Brittany and toward the Auvergne, received many foundling children for the first time.[89] Throughout the century, the wagons carrying babies out of Paris traveled many of the same roads and rivers, then railroads, that poor single women took to Paris. This shift over the century went from the areas near Paris to the east and north to more distant areas to the south and west.[90]

Foundlings were only part of this traffic. Many mothers did not abandon their babies but sent them out to nurse in some of the same regions that nursed foundlings, particularly the Morvan.[91] Others sent their infants to the region surrounding the city. Like domestic servant Germinie Lacerteux, they could not nurse their infants and work at the same time, but they wanted to have their infants close enough so they could visit. Lacerteux's Sunday outings consisted of a train ride, then a walk, to visit her infant daughter lodged with a wet nurse about forty miles east of Paris.[92] Areas that received nurslings from mothers in Paris, like those that received foundlings, were pockets of poverty in the countryside. The wet nurse's wages served as a supplement to meager agricultural incomes for the marginal population of the country—the same population that sent poor single women to become domestic servants in the city.

Mothers of the Morvan are emblematic of the traffic in misery that linked migration, illegitimacy, and wet-nursing.[93] They were a quarter of the wet nurses who sought a nursling in Paris, generally to take back to their cottages.[94] Single women who delivered a baby in the Morvan often left the infant in their home village, then went to Paris, where they sought jobs as live-in wet nurses for bourgeois women. In the spring of 1901, 302 women from the *département* of the Nièvre alone were engaged in this service for elite families; thus this one *département* (among the eighty-six that sent women to work in Paris) supplied one-seventh of the city's wet nurses.[95] After weaning the infants in their care, many women of the Morvan stayed on in Paris to work as domestics. In this way, over the years, hundreds of single mothers from the Morvan traveled to Paris. Conversely, tens of thousands of illegitimate and abandoned children, as well as nurslings of artisans, were shipped out to married women who recently had a baby in the Morvan. One historian has noted that the "wet-nursing in the Morvan was rooted in the tradition of long-distance labor migrations from a remote and poor region ... The tradition was transposed from men to women, from masonry, forestry, and harvesting to wet-nursing, by ... the capital's insatiable demand for cheap, safe, and reliable infant care and feeding."[96] A two-way traffic of adults joined the Morvan to Paris, and the majority of people in this migration stream, like that from Brittany, were women by the turn of the century.[97] These very *départements* of the Morvan that received tens of thousands of Parisian infants also sent out single women to seek employment in that capital city, many of whom (like Jeannette Pazy) ended up in the wards of La Maternité.[98]

The Morvan's engagement in a two-way traffic of poor mothers and infants was not unique. Northern France provided a similar exchange; the ten *départements* of this region provided one-fifth of the wet nurses who took on nurslings in Paris near the end of the century—generally to take back to their cottages. These areas also were the source for one-fifth of the single mothers in La Maternité in the 1890s.[99] The *départements* that provided the greater proportion of live-in wet nurses for Paris at the turn of the century were the same ones that sent migrant women to Paris and to La Maternité—Côtes-du-Nord and Morbihan in Brittany, Nièvre in the Morvan, the Nord and Pas-de-Calais in the north.[100] Poverty was the source of these migration streams.

These live-in wet nurses may well have been migrant women who chose this post-partum occupation in Paris, opting not to return home. Scattered evidence suggests that some single women gave birth to an infant whom they abandoned or put out to nurse, then found work as a resident wet nurse in Paris. Those who did go home may have made the trip to bring their baby to a local wet nurse, or to a parent, only to return to Paris without their infant to work as a well-paid and privileged wet nurse for members of the Parisian bourgeoisie. Elite families invested money and energy to hire a healthy wet nurse for their offspring and, in some cases, contracted to hire single mothers even in advance of their delivery.[101]

In sum, many single mothers in Paris became welfare or charity recipients and appeared on the registers of the shelters for the homeless, the maternity hospitals, or the local welfare bureaus. They were an expense to the city and region, whose officials wanted them either to return home or to become economically independent members of urban society. In nineteenth-century Paris, administrators tried to repatriate recently arrived mothers, but few women returned home. They stayed on, and their babies were a burden to both the mothers and the government. Under the auspices of one or the other, infants were shipped out of Paris to be cared for elsewhere—often in the same regions that sent women to Paris. The interrelationships among migration, illegitimacy, and poverty are, in part, elucidated by this two-way traffic in misery.

INFORMATION FROM PARIS provides insights into the urban lives of migrant women who had children out of wedlock. Some of the children born in the nineteenth-century city had been conceived elsewhere, but most were not. Neither domestic servants nor migrants who did not belong to a well-established urban milieu could muster the resources to compel men to marry them. In addition, the market for wet nurses encouraged poor, unmarried women who had just delivered to come to the city. That the poor women at La Maternitié were most often single migrants in domestic service supports the argument that the women most likely to bear children out of wedlock lacked the social and economic resources needed to persuade a partner to marry or attract a marriageable mate. By the end of the century, the most visible pregnant mothers were part of new migration streams that offered weak networks of contacts in Paris. Yet, although better-established migrating groups might help single women find housing and jobs, even they could not protect them from pregnancy, partly because the single most important occupation for female migrant newcomers separated them from their compatriots.

The lives of single migrant women illuminate a complex of noneconomic motives and by-products of migration that merit further exploration. Although pregnancy is biologically unique to women, the vulnerability of the female migrant is related to the broader context of gender relations in nineteenth-century Paris.[102] The employment opportunities of this capital city placed female migrants in positions that denied them both protection from sexual relations and the earning power to underwrite a marital relationship. The nation's civil code assigned no fiscal, moral, or social responsibility to the fathers of children born out of wedlock, unless the father legally recognized the child. The pregnancy and the child were solely the legal responsibility of the single mother. Although the law remained unchanged for the entire century, the state, concerned by France's declining birth rate and high infant mortality, often intervened. It saw women not as members of the polity—for, indeed, they were not—but as mothers of children who were valued resources of the state.[103]

Single pregnant migrants were integral to the process of urbanization and geographic mobility. Pregnancy motivated some migrations and was the result of others. These women's experience enriches our understanding of migration, urbanization, and life in the metropolis. Likewise, the complex patterns analyzed here echo in other cities and other times.

A note on the population samples

Several other public hospitals for the indigent in Paris delivered babies, but the annual numbers of deliveries in each was in the hundreds, not in the thousands as in La Maternité (except for a few years when the Hôtel-Dieu admitted over 1,000). Further, La Maternité was the only hospital just for childbirth. At the beginning of the century, approximately one-tenth of all births and one-third of all illegitimate births in Paris took place in this hospital; by the end of the century, the proportion of births had fallen to approximately 5 percent and the proportion of illegitimate births to 20 percent because more hospitals and other alternatives had developed for the pregnant poor. To reconstruct the population of that hospital, we collected a random sample of approximately 100 women per year from those admitted for the years 1837, 1838, 1852, 1855, 1860, 1865, 1869, 1875, 1880, 1885, 1899, 1895, and 1900. The year 1852 was selected to pinpoint the effect of bureaucratic and legislative changes, and 1869 rather than 1870 was selected because 1870 was a year of war and civil disturbance during which the hospital was closed for almost a year. A sample of fifty women admitted during the years 1830, 1847, and 1848 was gathered to test the effects of political and economic crises on hospital admissions. All references to the demographic characteristics of the population at La Maternité are based on these data. The single migrants were never married, therefore neither widowed nor divorced. It is impossible to ascertain if they were in common-law marriages.

In order to discover how women at La Maternité differed from those in other hospitals, we took a sample of 400 women who delivered at the Hôtel-Dieu from 1850 through 1865. These women were similar to La Maternité patients in age, occupation, marital status, and origin. We chose this hospital because, during those years, it was second to La Maternité in the number of deliveries. From 1802 through 1862, the total number of deliveries at the Parisian public hospitals was 155,105 for La Maternité, 22,363 for the Hôtel-Dieu, 21,957 for La Clinique (for which the records are not available), 15,719 for St.-Louis, 5,022 for Lariboisière, and 3,979 for the Hôpital Saint-Antoine. See Stéphane Tarnier, *Mémoire sur l'hygiène des hôpitaux de femmes en couches* (Paris, 1864).

We also sampled 809 of the 25,958 women who delivered their babies with a welfare midwife paid for by public assistance between 1869 and 1900 (the last year for which records are available). The women who gave birth at La Maternité, the Hôtel-Dieu, and with welfare midwives were all similar in terms of age, occupation, marital status, and department of origin. The records of private hospitals and midwives are not available.

Acknowledgements

We wish to thank the National Endowment for the Humanities for support of our individual research. We also thank Gay Gullickson, Elizabeth Pleck, Louise Tilly, Nora Faires, and James Farr for comments on an earlier version. Rachel Fuchs wishes to thank the Department of History at Purdue University for its hospitality during the time this article was in preparation.

Notes

1   Marthe-Juliette Mouillon, "Un Exemple de migration rurale: De la Somme dans la capitale: Domestique de la Belle Epoque à Paris (1904–1912)," *Etudes de la région parisienne*, 44 (1970): 1–9.

2   Emile Zola, "Edmond and Jules Goncourt," in Edmond Goncourt and Jules Goncourt, *Germinie Lacerteux* (Paris, 1910), viii.

3   Abel Châtelain, *Les Migrants temporaires en France de 1800 à 1914*, 2 vols (Lille, 1976); Steve Hochstadt, "Migration and Industrialization in Germany, 1815–1977, *Social Science History*, 16 (1981): 445–468; Dirk Hoerder, ed., *Labor Migration in the Atlantic Economies* (Westport, Conn., 1985). Although population records suggest that mobility reached unprecedented levels in the period between 1850 and World War I, the absence of comparable data for the earlier period makes it impossible to know for certain. German migration statistics reveal an extremely high population turnover for the period 1880–1914. For example, up to 60 percent of the population of West German industrial cities of Essen and Bochum, and up to 30 percent of the administrative centre Cologne, left or entered the city every year in the last half of the nineteenth century; James Jackson, Jr., "Migration in Duisburg, 1867–1890: Occupational and Familial Contexts," *Journal of Urban History*, 8 (1982): esp. 244–245; see also Hochstadt, "Migration and Industrialization in Germany, 1815–1977." For the mobility revealed by Belgian and Italian population registers, see George Alter, *Family and the Female Life Course: The Women of Verviers, Belgium, 1849–1880* (Madison, Wis., 1988), chap. 2, David Kertzer and Dennis Hogan, "On the Move: Migration in an Italian Community, 1865–1921," *Social Science History*, 9 (1985): 1–23.

Migration was not measured directly in France or England. High population turnover is measured only indirectly in French records; censuses and urban marriage records indicate that a high proportion of the urban population was born in the provinces. National trends are described in Châtelain, *Los Migrants temporaires en France de 1800 à 1914*; Yves Tugault, *La

Mésure de la mobilité: Cinq études sur les migrations internes (Paris, 1973), 30–37; Daniel Courgeau, "Three Centuries of Spatial Mobility in France," *UNESCO Reports and Papers in the Social Sciences*, 51 (1982); Philip Ogden and Paul White, eds, *Migrants in Modern France: Population Mobility in the Later 19th and 20th Centuries* (London, 1989); see also Louis Chevalier, *La Formation de la population parisienne au XIXᵉ siècle* (Paris, 1950). Only a few case studies and specialized public assistance records suggest the actual volume of movement in France; see Michael Hanagan, "Nascent Proletarians: Migration Patterns and Class Formation in the Stephanois Region, 1840–1880," in *Migration in Modern France*, 74–96. Some public assistance records that suggest the volume of movement into and out of Paris are the annual reports of Assistance Publique. See Administration Générale de l'Assistance Publique à Paris, Service des Enfants Assistés de la Seine, *Rapport presenté par le Directeur de l'Administration générale de l'Assistance publique à M. le Préfet de la Seine* (Montevrain, 1877–1904).

4 For the gender composition of migration streams, see Châtelain, *Les Migrants temporaires, passim*; Pierre Guillaume, *La Population de Bordeaux au XIXᵉ siècle* (Paris, 1972), 251–254; Leslie Page Moch, *Paths to the City: Regional Migration in Nineteenth-Century France* (Beverly Hills, Calif., 1983); Jean-Pierre Poussou, *Bordeaux et le sud-ouest au XVIIIᵉ siècle* (Paris, 1983), 104–114. For exemplary studies of women and migration, see Caroline Brettell, "Hope and Nostalgia: Portuguese Migrant Women in Paris" (Ph.D. dissertation, Brown University, 1978); and *Men Who Migrate, Women Who Wait: Population and History in a Portuguese Parish* (Princeton, N.J., 1986).

5 See, for example, Lenard R. Berlanstein, *The Working People of Paris, 1871–1914* (Baltimore, Md., 1984); Chevalier, *La Formation de la population parisienne;* Jan Lucassen, *Migrant Labour in Europe, 1600–1900* (London, 1987), Hochstadt, "Migration and Industrialization in Germany, 1815–1977," 445–68; Steve Hochstadt, "Migration in Preindustrial Germany," *Central European History*, 16 (1983): 195–224; Leslie Page Moch, "The Family and Migration: News from the French," *Journal of Family History*, 11 (1986): 193–203. Studies of Old Regime migration are especially likely to ignore female migration altogether; see Jean-Pierre Bardet, *Rouen aux XVIIᵉ et XVIIIᵉ siècles* (Paris, 1983); and Abel Poitrineau, *Remues d'hommes* (Paris, 1983). Two recent exceptions are Poussou, *Bordeaux et le sud-ouest au XVIIIᵉ siècle*; and William Sewell, Jr., *Structure and Mobility: The Men and Women of Marseille, 1820–1870* (Cambridge, 1985).

6 Gay Gullickson, *Spinners and Weavers of Auffay: Rural Industry and Sexual Division of Labor in a French Village, 1750–1850* (Cambridge, 1986); Moch, *Paths to the City*, chap. 2; Louise Tilly and Joan Scott, *Women, Work and Family* (New York, 1978), 108.

7 Edward Shorter, "Female Emancipation, Birth Control, and Fertility in European History." *AHR*, 78 (June 1973): 605–40; Edward Shorter, John Knodel, and Etienne van de Walte, "The Decline of Non-marital Fertility in Europe," *Population Studies*, 25 (1971): 375–93. Illegitimacy in Germany was highest in the Southeast (esp. Bavaria and Saxony) with rates at the turn of the century higher than in French *départments*, except for the *département* of the Seine where Paris is located. Only Austria, Hungary, and Portugal had higher rates of illegitimacy. Illegitimacy rates were lower in western provinces of Germany at the turn of the century. See John Knodel, *The Decline of Fertility in Germany* (Princeton, N.J., 1974), 75–77; Etienne van de Walle, *The Female Population of France in the Nineteenth Century* (Princeton, 1974), 181–182.

8 Alter, *Family and the Female Life Course*, chap. 5; Cissie Fairchilds, "Female Sexual Attitudes and the Rise of Illegitimacy: A Case Study," *Journal of Interdisciplinary History*, 8 (1978): 627–667; Louise Tilly, Joan Scott, and Miriam Cohen, "Women's Work and European Fertility Patterns," *Journal of Interdisciplinary History*, 6 (1976): 447–476.

9 The index for illegitimacy in nineteenth-century Paris is the percentage of illegitimate births of all live births. This ratio, though imprecise, is the only computation possible because of the lack of age-specific data on single women. In France, the urban *départements* surrounding the cities of Strasbourg, Marseille, Bordeaux, Lyon, and Paris stand out as the ones with the highest rates of illegitimacy; in addition, the industrial *départements* of the north have high illegitimacy rates; Etienne van de Walle, "Illegitimacy in France during the Nineteenth Century," in Peter

Laslett, Karla Oosterveen, and Richard M. Smith, eds, *Bastardy and Its Comparative History* (Cambridge, 1980), 264–277.

10 Emile Levasseur, *La Population française*, 3 vols. (Paris, 1889–92), 2: 400–401; Adna Weber, *The Growth of Cities in the Nineteenth Century* (1899; rpt. edn, Ithaca, N.Y., 1965), 405.

11 For illegitimate birth rates in German cities and rural areas, see Weber, *Growth of Cities in the Nineteenth Century*, 332–333, 335; John Knodel and Steven Hochstadt, "Urban and Rural Illegitimacy in Imperial Germany," in *Bastardy and Its Comparative History*, 301–2. For a comparison of regional illegitimacy rates in Europe, see Shorter, Knodel, and van de Walle, "Decline of Non-marital Fertility in Europe," 386–392. Rudolf Braun, "Early Industrialization and Demographic Change in the Canton of Zurich," in *Historical Studies of Changing Fertility* (Princeton, N.J., 1978), 289–334; Brettell, *Men Who Migrate, Women Who Wait*, chap. 5; Donna Gabaccia, "Migration and Women in 19th-Century Italy" (unpublished paper, Mercy College, 1988); Gullickson, *Spinners and Weavers of Auffay*, chap. 9; Frances Kraljic, "Round Trip Croatia, 1900–1914," in *Labor Migration in the Atlantic Economies* (Westport, Conn., 1985), 412–413; David Levine, *Family Formation in an Age of Nascent Capitalism* (New York, 1977), chap. 9; Susan Cotts Watkins, *From Provinces into Nations: Demographic Integration in Western Europe, 1870–1960* (Princeton, 1990), chap. 2.

12 Weber, *Growth of Cities in the Nineteenth Century*, 289.

13 *Ibid.*, 278–279, 284, 289, 371, 374–376; Abel Châtelain, "Migrations et domesticité féminine urbaine en France, XVIIIᵉ siècle-XXᵉ siècle," *Revue d'histoire économique et sociale*, 47 (1969): 506–528; Theresa McBride, *The Domestic Revolution: The Modernization of Household Service in England and France, 1820–1920* (New York, 1976).

14 See, for example, Danielle Delhome, Nicole Gault, and Josiane Gonthier, *Les Premières institutrices laïques* (Paris, 1980); Olwen Hufton, "Women without Men: Widows and Spinsters in Britain and France in the Eighteenth Century," *Journal of Family History*, 9 (1984): 355–376; Martine Segalen, *Love and Power in the Peasant Family*, trans. Sarah Matthews (Chicago, 1983). Article 340 of the French Civil Code, in effect throughout the nineteenth century, forbade *recherche de la paternité*.

15 This article does not focus on all illegitimate births; rather, it focuses solely on the kind of illegitimacy that illuminates the nexus of gender and migration to the large city. For a general view, see Laslett, *et al.*, *Bastardy and Its Comparative History*; Shorter, Knodel, and van de Walle, "Decline of Non-marital Fertility in Europe." For an excellent local urban study, see Alter, *Family and the Female Life Course*. Rural illegitimacy was significant in some areas of Europe, and village out-of-wedlock conceptions were produced by the departure of migrating males; see Brettell, *Men Who Migrate, Women Who Wait*, chap. 5; Donna Gabaccia, "Migration and Women in 19th-Century Italy"; Gullickson, *Spinners and Weavers of Auffay*, chap. 9; Kraljic, "Round Trip Croatia, 1900–1914," 412–413.

16 For example, see Rachel G. Fuchs, "Morality and Poverty: Public Welfare for Mothers in Paris, 1870–1900," *French History*, 2 (1988): 288–311; and "Preserving the Future of France: Charity and Welfare in Nineteenth-Century Paris," in *The Uses of Charity: The Poor on Relief in the Nineteenth-Century Metropolis*, ed. P. Mandler (Philadelphia, 1990), 92–122.

17 Archives de la Ville de Paris et Département de la Seine (hereafter, AD Seine), D2 U8 Dossiers Cour d'Assises. Court records are used here for their illustrative value. We attempted to identify and eliminate outright lies or strategies that women and their attorneys employed in an attempt to secure an acquittal or conviction with attenuating circumstances. The stories used in this article are all corroborated by witnesses and letters. While the cases of infanticide and abortion brought before the courts do not present a broad picture of pregnant migrants in Paris, they offer valuable glimpses into the lives of individual women. There are no memoirs and autobiographies by single mothers. By agreement with the appropriate authorities, we use no actual names.

18 The hospital was particularly dangerous during the 1850s and 1860s, when epidemics of puerperal fever struck. In 1869, hospital authorities instituted a program of paying midwives to deliver women who could not be admitted to La Maternité because of overcrowding or epidemics of puerperal fever.

19 This figure compares the birthplaces of single French women admitted to La Maternité in the decade 1890–1900 with the birthplaces of women aged fifteen to forty-four listed in the 1901 census. Ninety-eight percent of the women who gave birth in La Maternité in this decade were aged fifteen to forty; 62 percent of the migrant women in Paris were of this age group; Ministère du Commerce, de l'Industrie, des Postes et des Télégraphes, *Résultats statistiques du recensement général de la population effectué le 24 mars 1901*, 4 vols (Paris, 1906), 1: 312. The majority (63 percent) of women who gave birth in La Maternité in the nineteenth century were between twenty and twenty-seven years of age; 11 percent were teenagers; 14 percent were between twenty-eight and thirty-one, and the remainder were over thirty-one years old. During the 1890s, 72 percent of the women who gave birth at La Maternité were single.

After 1853, La Maternité may have had fewer migrant women because women not in "imminent peril of delivery" were required to prove they had lived in Paris for at least one year. The Hôtel-Dieu had no such requirement, and admissions there rose by 19 percent (196 cases) in the next year, a rise credited by the Hôtel-Dieu administrators to La Maternité's restrictions on immigrant deliveries; Archives de l'Assistance Publique, Fosseyeux 151, Notes relatives au Service des accouchements de l'Hôtel-Dieu.

The birthplace information in the hospital records provides a history of migration of women to La Maternité that can be put in the context of the history of all migration to Paris. Birthplace data for all Parisians made available with the 1901 census allows a precise comparison of the origins of women in La Maternité with all women in Paris at the end of the century. This census also gives an occupational profile of migrant women and a more detailed portrait of women in Paris from each *département* of France. A study of migrant women who did not become pregnant or of migrants who married is beyond the scope of this article.

20 Sydney Goldstein, "The Extent of Repeated Migration: An Analysis Based on the Danish Population Register," *Journal of the American Statistical Association*, 59 (1964): 1121–1132; James Jackson, Jr., and Leslie Page Moch, "Migration and the Social History of Modern Europe," *Historical Methods*, 22 (1989): 27–36; Jackson, "Migration in Duisberg"; Hochstadt, "Migration and Industrialization in Germany"; Kertzer and Hogan, "On the Move: Migration in an Italian Community"; Paul White and Robert Woods, "Spatial Patterns of Migration Flows," in *The Geographical Impact of Migration* (London, 1980), 21–41.

21 For examples from the eighteenth century, see Alain Lottin, "Naissances illegitimes et filles-mères à Lille au XVIIIᵉ siècle," *Revue d'histoire moderne et contemporaine*, 17 (1970): 302; Poussou, *Bordeaux et le sud-ouest*, 163.

22 One family's efforts were preserved in correspondence; see *Marthe: A Woman and a Family: A Fin-de-siècle Correspondence*, trans. Donald Frame (New York, 1984), 10, 16–17, 49–50. Letters reveal the care taken to conceal the pregnancy and the labor invested in finding a suitable spouse for the mother after the child's birth.

23 L'Assistance Publique, *Rapport*, 1888: 15–16; 1889: 41; 1892: 6–8; 1893:, 27–28; 1894: 22–24; 1895: 2–4. See also Rachel G. Fuchs, *Abandoned Children: Foundlings and Child Welfare in Nineteenth-Century France* (Albany, N.Y., 1984).

24 Rachel G. Fuchs, *Poor and Pregnant in Paris: Strategies for Survival in the Nineteenth Century* (New Brunswick, N.J., forthcoming), chaps. 4, 6, and 8.

25 Fewer than 5 percent of the single mothers who gave birth in Paris in 1880 had a legal residence elsewhere; *Annuaire statistique de la ville de Paris*, 1880: 185, also cited in van de Walle, "Illegitimacy in France," 276. The data from La Maternité put the figure at under 2 percent. One might suspect that the proportion of migrant mothers at La Maternité is artifically low because of the one-year residency requirement. But this requirement seems to have made little difference,

because only 15.8 percent of women who delivered at the Hôtel-Dieu (where it was not enforced) were born in Paris. (Records from La Maternité proper do not reveal how long migrant patients had resided in Paris; they note only birthplace.)

Of the mothers in La Maternité *who subsequently abandoned* their babies, an 1844 inquiry showed that two-thirds had arrived in Paris pregnant; the one-year residency requirement was instituted the next year and reinforced in 1852. A. Boicervoise, *Rapport au Conseil général des Hospices de Paris sur le service des enfants trouvés du département de la Seine* (Paris, 1845), 24–5. For the Hôtel-Dieu, see Archives de l'Assistance Publique, Fosseyeux 151, Notes relatives au Service des Accouchements de l'Hôtel-Dieu, n.a., November 16, 1853.

The question remains whether or not women falsified information about residency in order to gain admission. It is unlikely that this was possible (or even necessary, given the ease of admission if they were in labor): several weeks before the expected date of delivery, women had to supply the hospital admissions authorities with certificates from the *arrondissement* mayor testifying that they were Paris residents and indigent; prior addresses in Paris and statements from their landlords (or employers, in the case of domestic servants) were also required. Hospital authorities often verified such residency claims. See Archives de l'Assistance Publique, l'Hôpital Port Royal, Registres des Correspondance, 1856–1897.

26 Archives de l'Assistance Publique, l'Hôpital Port-Royal, Femmes en Couches Envoyées chez les sage femmes, 1869–1880. Data are based on a random sample of 400 women sent to a welfare midwife by L'Assistance Publique for the years 1869 through 1880, the only years in which length of residency in Paris was recorded.

27 Levasseur, *La Population française* (Paris, 1891), 2: 34.

28 AD Seine, D2 U8 (12D) Dossiers Cour d'Assise, Dossier September 12, 1881. Her employer in Reims secured her a position with one of his relatives in Paris.

29 AD Seine, D2 U8 (48) Dossiers Cour d'Assise, Dossier June 9, 1876.

30 Data on where migrant women stayed between their arrival in Paris and delivery is based on information for the 563 women who delivered in Paris less than one year after arrival in 1894 and 1895 and were offered repatriation; L'Assistance Publique, *Rapport*, 1894: 23–24; 1895: 3–4. These are the only years for which data exist.

31 L'Assistance Publique, *Rapport*, 1895: 4.

32 Alain Corbin, *Les Filles de noce: Misère sexuelle et prostitution aux 19ᵉ et 20ᵉ siècles*, (Paris, 1978), 109; AD Seine, D2 U8 Dossiers Cour d'Assise, cases of "Detournement d'une mineur," 1867–1889; Dossier (62) July 3, 1877; Dossier (49) June 20, 1876. Anne Martin-Fugier, *La Place des bonnes: La Domesticité féminine en 1900* (Paris, 1979), 43–101.

33 AD Seine, D2 U8 (37) Dossiers Cour d'Assise, Dossier April 13, 1875.

34 Fuchs, "Preserving the Future of France"; *Annuaire statistique de la ville de Paris* (1900), 581.

35 For the important role of chain migration and migration streams, see Chevalier, *La Formation de la Population parisienne;* Charles Tilly, "Migration in Modern European History," in *Human Migration: Patterns and Policies*, W. McNeill and R. Adams, eds (Bloomington, Ind., 1978), 48–74; and works on the present such as Janice Perlman, *The Myth of Marginality: Urban Poverty and Politics in Rio de Janeiro* (Berkeley, Calif., 1976); Michael Piore, *Birds of Passage: Migrant Labor and Industrial Societies* (Cambridge, 1979).

36 AD Seine, D2 U8 (27) Dossiers Cour d'Assise, Dossier May 7, 1874.

37 Chevalier, *La Formation de la population parisienne;* Moch, *Paths to the City;* Sewell, *Structure and Mobility.*

38 In addition to materials on Paris (Chevalier, *La Formation de la population parisienne*) and on France (Moch, *Paths to the City;* Sewell, *Structure and Mobility*), see Grace Anderson, *Networks of Contact: The Portuguese and Toronto* (Waterloo, 1974); and Mark Granovetter, *Getting a Job* (Cambridge, Mass., 1974).

39 AD Seine, D2 U8 (153) Dossiers Cour d'Assise, Dossier October 25, 1883; D2 U8 (285) Dossier October 14, 1891. See also Châtelain, *Les Migrants temporaires en France*, 1062.

40 For a Parisian example, see Jeanne Bouvier, *Mes mémoires; ou 59 annés d'activité industrielle, sociale et intellectuelle d'une ouvrière, 1876–1935* (Paris, 1983), 35–98.

41 Fuchs, *Abandoned Children*, chap. 2; Fuchs, "Legislation, Poverty, and Child Abandonment in Nineteenth-Century Paris," *Journal of Interdisciplinary History*, 18 (1987): 55–80.

42 L'Assistance Publique, *Rapport*, 1888: 15–16; 1889: 41; 1892: 6–8; 1893: 27–28; 1894: 22–24; 1895: 2–4.

43 Archives de l'Assistance Publique, l'Hôpital Port Royal, Registres de Correspondance, November 16, 1857. Because names of hospital patients in Paris cannot be revealed within 150 years of admission, we have assigned a pseudonym to this patient.

44 France, Préfecture de la Seine, Service de la Statistique Municipale, *Annuaire statistique de la ville de Paris* (Paris, 1880–1900), 1889: 716–725; 1893: 84–85; 1894: 576–579; 1895: 614–619; 1896: 554–555; 1897: 518–519; 1899: 534–535, 569–571; 1900: 546–547, 580–583. The four shelters together housed over 5,800 women in 1899, and over 6,100 in the following year.

45 Levasseur, *La Population française*, 2: 34; quote is from Weber, *Growth of Cities in the Nineteenth Century*, 405. Maternity hospital records are silent on women's domestic arrangements.

46 Fuchs, "Morality and Poverty," 301; van de Walle, "Illegitimacy in France," 269.

47 Michel Frey, "Du mariage et du concubinage dans les classes populaires à Paris (1846–1847), "*Annales: Economies, sociétés, civilisations*, 33 (1978): 803–829, emphasis in the original.

48 Gérard Jacquemet, *Belleville au XIXe siècle: Du faubourg de la ville* (Paris, 1984), 341–342; Katherine Lynch, *Family, Class and Ideology in Early Industrial France: Social Policy and the Working-Class Family* (Madison, Wis., 1988), 88–100; Fuchs, *Poor and Pregnant in Paris*, chap. 4.

49 Only after World War I were effective birth control measures available to indigent or working women. Until then, couples relied on *coitus interruptus*. Once pregnant, women could attempt abortion, but these poor migrant women rarely had the money or the information network to lead them to a midwife, doctor, or other abortionist. Most often, they resorted to a concoction usually of white wine, absinthe, and rue—a mixture that worked as a purgative rather than as an abortifacient. See AD Seine, D2 U8, for the dossiers of the women tried for abortion or infanticide in the Cour d'Assise, and the accompanying doctors' reports; see also Angus McLaren, "Abortion in France: Women and the Regulation of Family Size, 1800–1914," *French Historical Studies*, 9 (1978): 462–485.

50 These data concern only the single women (excluding widows) who gave birth in La Maternité. For a complete statistical analysis and explanation of these changes, see Rachel G. Fuchs and Paul E. Knepper, "Public Policy and Women in the Paris Maternity Hospital during the Nineteenth Century, "*Social Science History*, 13 (1989), table 4.

51 Ministère du Commerce, *Résultats statistiques du recensement*, 1: 329; 4: 295, 305. Published census data do not isolate migrant single women as a category; rather, the census provides information on single women (migrant and native-born) and on migrant women (married and single). In 1901, women working in a combination of all industries in Paris (either in the industrial establishments or alone in their rooms as *femmes isolées*) outnumbered domestic servants. This was true for all women in Paris, but native-born women from the *département* of the Seine working in industry outnumbered native-born women in domestic service by 12 to 1. However, migrant women working in industry outnumbered migrant women in domestic service by only 1.3 to 1. Single (but not necessarily migrant) women in Paris working in industry outnumbered domestic servants by only 1.7 to 1. Domestic service employed almost as many single and almost as many migrant women as all industries combined.

52 Gareth Stedman Jones, *Outcast London: A Study in the Relationship between Classes in Victorian Society* (Oxford, 1971), 136–139; Weber, *Growth of Cities in the Nineteenth Century*, 375; David Ransel, *Mothers of Misery: Child Abandonment in Russia* (Princeton, N.J., 1988), 164; Ministère du Commerce, *Résultats statistiques du recensement*, 1: 329.

53 Châtelain, "Migrations et domesticité féminine urbaine en France," 506–528; Martin-Fugier, *La Place des bonnes*; McBride, *Domestic Revolution*; Tilly and Scott, *Women, Work and Family*.

54 Jules Simon, *L'Ouvrière* (Paris, 1891), 229–30.

55 Alexandre Jean-Baptiste Parent-Duchâtelet, *De la prostitution dans la ville de Paris* (Paris, 1836), 1: 72.

56 McBride, *Domestic Revolution*, chap. 3; Martin-Fugier, *La Place des bonnes*, 125–147, 287–328.

57 John Gillis, "Servants, Sexual Relations, and the Risks of Illegitimacy in London, 1801–1900, "*Feminist Studies*, 5 (1979): 142–173; McBride, *Domestic Revolution*, chap. 6. Anna Clark explicated the vulnerability of domestic servants in *Women's Silence, Men's Violence: Sexual Assault in England, 1770–1845* (London, 1987), 28, 90–109.

58 Préfecture de la Seine, Service de la Statistique Municipale, *Annuaire statistique de la ville de Paris*. See, for example, 1880: 199; 1881: 231; 1882: 163; 1883: 215; 1884: 171; 1885: 191. The remaining third consisted of laundresses, lingerie workers, linen menders, cooks, cleaning women, and female workers in a variety of occupations, such as sewing machine operators.

59 *Annuaire statistique de la ville de Paris*; 1894, 1895, and 1900 are the only years for which such data are available for the shelters; see especially 1894: 576–579; 1895: 614–619; 1900: 582.

60 For a description of the single seamstress's housing in turn-of-the-century Paris, see *Bouvier, Mes mémoires*, 82–90.

61 Simon, *L'Ouvrière*, 229.

62 Frey, "Du mariage et du concubinage dans les classes populaires à Paris (1846–1847)," 817; Bouvier, *Mes mémoires*, 90. Contemporary social observers, feminists, and novelists are unanimous in regarding marriage as a necessity for economic survival and social status, while deploring this necessity; see Othenin d'Haussonville, *Salaires et misères de femmes* (Paris, 1900), 3–124; Emile Zola, *L'Assommoir* (1877); Maria Vérone in *La Fronde*, January 14, 1903.

63 AD Seine, D2 U8 (83) Dossiers Cour d'Assises, Dossier March 24, 1878.

64 Moch, *Paths to the City*, notes that over half the fathers of migrants' brides (and 35 percent of the fathers of native women) had died before their daughters' marriages in Nimes at the turn of the century.

65 Alter, *Family and the Female Life Course*, 183–184, 131; Lottin, "Naissances illegitimes et filles-mères à Lille au XVIIIᵉ siècle," 305. The only person for Renard to return to, her brother, did not want her, even when she expressed a desire to marry someone who had been interested in her. Of the seventy-six women tried for infanticide in Paris between 1867 and 1891, fifteen had a deceased parent explicitly mentioned in court testimony; in ten cases, the mother's death was noted. The body of court testimony suggests that in many more cases, one or more parent was deceased; AD Seine, D2 U8 Dossiers Cour d'Assises.

66 Alter, *Family and the Female Life Course*, table 5.5, 127, 131. Janet Potash noted that such women were more likely to abandon their child as well; Janet R. Potash, "The Foundling Problem in France, 1800–1869: Child Abandonment in Lille and Lyon" (Ph.D. dissertation, Yale University, 1979), 277–278.

67 Chevalier, *La Formation de la population parisienne*, 285. Unfortunately, a specific assessment of birthplace by gender is not available for Parisian residents in this period.

68 This analysis follows a current division of French regions; see Courgeau, "Three Centuries of Spatial Mobility in France," 53. The analysis of twenty-two regions included Corsica, which does not appear on the maps because no women from Corsica appeared in La Maternité. These figures reflect the birthplace of all single migrant women in La Maternité for each time period, excluding those few who were foreign born. The Ile-de-France includes the *départements* of the Seine-et-Oise and the Seine-et-Marne. Picardy consists of the *départements* of the Aisne, Somme, and Oise.

69 Burgundy includes the *départements* of the Cote-d'Or, Nièvre, Saône-et-Loire, and Yonne. Lorraine includes the *départements* of the Meurthe-et-Moselle, Meuse, Vosges, Moselle, and

Meurthe; and the region of the Nord includes the *départements* of the Nord and Pas-de-Calais. Forty-six percent of the women from Lorraine and Burgundy were domestic servants, compared with 26 percent from other regions.

70 Over 40 percent of the women from Burgundy and over 50 percent of the women from the Centre and Champagne worked as domestic servants. The Centre includes the *départements* of the Cher, Eure-et-Loie, Indre, Indre-et-Loire, Loir-et-Cher, and Loiret. Champagne includes the *départements* of the Marne, Haute-Marne, Aube, and Ardennes.

71 Brittany includes the *départements* of Côtes-du-Nord, Finistère, Ille-et-Vilaine, and Morbihan; Alsace includes the *départements* of the Bas-Rhin and Haut-Rhin. Half the women from the Nord, Alsace, and Lorraine were domestic servants.

72 Ministère du Commerce, *Résultats statistiques du recensement*, 1:312. Turn-of-the-century information can address the question of how typical of migrants the single mothers in La Maternité were and whether some migrant women were more likely than others to appear at this hospital for the indigent. The 1901 census data, which gives information on the birthplaces of women residing in Paris, permits comparison of the origins of the single mothers in La Maternité with those of all migrant women in Paris, although data on the age and marital status of migrant women from particular provinces is not available. But women usually migrated at childbearing age, and migrant women in Paris were more likely to be at childbearing age than native-born residents of the city.

73 This analysis is based on a comparison of the birthplaces of all women in Paris (married and single), according to the 1901 census, with the birthplaces of all women in the Maternité sample, 1890–1900. Census data do not differentiate between married and single migrant women in Paris. The regions that sent the same proportion of women to Paris as to La Maternité (within 1.5 percentage points) are Lorriane, Upper and Lower Normandy, Centre, Burgundy, Franche-Comte, Rhône-Alpes, Limousin, Poitou-Charentes, Aquitaine, Mid-Pyrénées, Languedoc-Rousillon, Provence-Côte d'Azur, and Corse.

74 These are Picardy, Champagne-Ardennes, Ile-de-France, Loire, and Auvergne. This is despite the high proportion of single migrant women coming from Picardy and Champagne in the data presented above and on Map 3.

75 *Départements* of the Nord, Pas-de-Calais, Côtes-du-Nord, Ille-et-Vilaine, and Morbihan.

76 See van de Walle, "Illegitimacy in France."

77 A. Bonnefoy, *Les Auvergnats à Paris* (Paris, 1933); Chevalier, *La Formation de la population parisienne*, 204–213.

78 See Yves Blayo, "Illegitimate Births in France from 1740 to 1829 and in the 1960s," in *Bastardy and Its Comparative History*, 279; Chevalier, *La Formation de la population parisienne*, 161–162, 208, 285; van de Walle, *Female Population of France in the Nineteenth Century*, 181–182.

79 Chevalier, *La Formation de la population parisienne*, 208.

80 Van de Walle, "Illegitimacy in France," 272–276; Knodel, *Decline of Fertility in Germany*, 77; Knodel and Hochstadt, "Urban and Rural Illegitimacy in Imperial Germany," 293; see Watkins, *From Provinces into Nations*, chap. 2.

81 In her comparison of foundlings in Lille and Lyon, Potash suggested that illegitimacy was not only more prevalent but also more acceptable in areas such as the Nord; "Foundling Problem in France," 194, 207, 215. Although foreign migrants may have compounded the high illegitimacy rates of the Nord and Alsace, native-born workers may have been more likely to bear children out of wedlock; see Claude Hélène Dewaepenaere, "L'Enfance illegitime dans le département du Nord au XIXᵉ siècle," in *L'Homme, la vie et la mort dans le Nord au 19ᵉ siècle*, ed. Marcel Gillet (Lille, 1972), 151–153. The importance of regional practices fits findings for Germany; see Knodel and Hochstadt, "Urban and Rural Illegitimacy in Imperial Germany," 308–309.

82 Philippe Ariès, *Histoire des populations françaises et leurs attitudes vers la vie* (Paris, 1971), 72.

83 Chevalier, *La Formation de la population parisienne*, 211.

84 Châtelain, "Migrations et domesticité féminine," 525; *Résultats statistiques du recensement*, 4: 304–305, 476–477; Emile Zola, *Piping-Hot*, trans. Percy Pinkerton (New York, 1924).

85 For a complete discussion of women's options and child abandonment, see Fuchs, *Abandoned Children*, chaps. 2 and 5, esp. 67–69, 170–184; Fuchs, "Legislation, Poverty and Child Abandonment in Nineteenth-Century Paris," 55–80. For an excellent discussion of wet-nursing, see George Sussman, *Selling Mothers' Milk: The Wet-Nursing Business in France, 1715–1914* (Urbana, Ill., 1982), chaps. 5–7, esp. 110–117, 169. Abandoned babies who survived infancy tended to stay, and reach adulthood, in those *départements* where they had been sent as infants. For the political and economic role of abandoned children in the countryside, see Nancy Fitch, "'Les Petits Parisiens en Province': The Silent Revolution in the Allier," *Journal of Family History*, 11 (1986): 131–55.

86 See footnote 4, above.

87 *Départements* to the north include the Nord, Somme, Pas-de-Calais, and Aisne, in that order; those in the Morvan are the Nièvre, Yonne, and Côte-d'Or, followed by the Saône-et-Loire. The Loir-et-Cher, Eure-et-Loir, Sarthe, and Loiret also took foundlings but in fewer numbers than the aforementioned *départements*.

88 The Morvan, centered in Burgundy, included the *départements of* the Nièvre, Yonne, Côte-d'Or, and Saône-et-Loire. *Départements* receiving infants in 1866, in order of importance, are the Nièvre, Yonne, Côte-d'Or, Saône-et-Loire, Pas-de-Calais, Nord, Aisne, and Loir-et-Cher.

89 In 1886, the Nièvre was followed by the Pas-de-Calais; the Loir-et-Cher and the *départements* of the Morvan received about.an equal proportion of abandoned infants and a similar proportion to prior decades. The Sarthe, Allier, Ille-et-Vilaine, and Puy-de-Dôme for the first time received considerable numbers of abandoned children.

90 Fuchs, *Abandoned Children*, 171–175.

91 Sussman, *Selling Mothers' Milk*, 137, 151. Data are derived from the surviving mayoral registers in which parental declarations of placement with a wet nurse were recorded. Registers exist only for the first, third, and tenth *arrondissements* and give the mother's name, that of the father, and their address. AD Seine, V bis 1Q7, V bis 3Q7, and V bis 10Q7, *Registres de déclarations de placement des enfants en nourrice, en sevrage ou en garde*. A random sample of 545 entries was collected, with a similar proportion for all three *arrondissements*. These three *arrondissements* are socially and economically heterogeneous; see Chevalier, *La Formation de la population parisienne*, 81–6. For other use of these data, see Sussman, *Selling Mothers' Milk*, 169–171. On wet-nursing and the rural economy, see James R. Lehning, "Family Life and Wetnursing in a French Village," *Journal of Interdisciplinary History*, 12 (1982): 645–56; and Fitch, "'Les Petits Parisiens en Province.'"

92 Goncourt and Goncourt, *Germinie Lacerteux*, chap. 21; Germinie Lacerteux's infant daughter was in the village of Pommeuse near Coulommiers, southeast of the town of Meaux in the *département* of the Seine-et-Marne. Many Parisian mothers listed in the mayoral registers sent their nurslings there.

93 Châtelain, *Les Migrants temporaires en France*, 2: 1069–1070; Sussman, *Selling Mothers' Milk*, 152–158.

94 *Statistique de la ville de Paris* (1889), 889–91.

95 There were 460 live-in wet nurses from the four *départements* of the Morvan; *Résultats statistiques du recensement*, 4: 303–304.

96 Sussman, *Selling Mothers' Milk*, 157–158.

97 *Résultats statistiques du recensement*, 4: 476–477.

98 For a similar traffic between Moscow, St. Petersburg, and the Russian countryside, see Ransel, *Mothers of Misery*, chap. 11.

99 Northern France refers to the ten *départements* of the Aisne, Eure, Eure-et-Loir, Nord, Oise, Pas-de-Calais, Seine-et-Marne, Seine-et-Oise, Seine-Inférieure, and the Somme. Wet nurses

from these areas who sought nurslings in Paris are recorded in the *Statistique de la ville de Paris* (1889), 889–891.

100 The exceptions to this list are the Haute-Vienne in the Limousin to the south and the Saône-et-Loire in the Morvan, from which as many women were wet nurses as from the Saône-et-Loire, but few entered La Maternité. Two *départements* of the Morvan, the Côte-d'Or and the Yonne, did not send live-in nurses but rather received nurslings at rural cottages. The Nièvre itself supplied 14 percent of the live-in nurses, and the Côtes-du-Nord in Brittany supplied 8 percent of the total; see *Résultats statistiques du recensement*, 4: 303–04.

101 For example, see AD Seine, D2 U8 (52) Dossiers Cour d'Assise, Dossier September 6, 1876; (62) Dossier June 25, 1877; (61) Dossier June 23, 1877; (135) Dossier July 25, 1882; (147) Dossier June 8, 1883. For the pay, attention, and gifts to a prospective wet nurse by an elite family, see *Marthe*, 12–13, 23, 27.

102 Joan Scott, "Gender: A Useful Category of Historical Analysis," *AHR*, 91 (December 1986): 1053–75.

103 Fuchs, *Poor and Pregnant in Paris*, chap. 2; Karen Offen, "Depopulation, Nationalism, and Feminism in Fin-de-Siècle France," *AHR*, 89 (June 1984): 648–676.

Judith R. Walkowitz

■ from 'MALE VICE AND FEMINIST VIRTUE:
FEMINISM AND THE POLITICS OF PROSTITUTION IN
NINETEENTH-CENTURY BRITAIN', *History Workshop Journal*,
13, Spring 1982, pp. 80–89

[…]

PAST GENERATIONS OF FEMINISTS attacked prostitution, pornography, white slavery, and homosexuality as manifestations of undifferentiated male lust. These campaigns were brilliant organising drives that stimulated grass-roots organisations and mobilised women not previously brought into the political arena. The vitality of the women's suffrage movement of the late 19th and early 20th centuries cannot be understood without reference to the revivalistic quality of these anti-vice campaigns, which often ran parallel with the struggle for the vote. By demanding women's right to protect their own persons against male sexual abuse and ultimately extending their critique of sexual violence to the 'private' sphere of the family, they achieved some permanent gains for women.

Nonetheless, judging by the goals stated by feminists themselves – to protect and empower women – these campaigns were often self-defeating. A libertarian defence of prostitutes found no place in the social purity struggle; all too often prostitutes were objects of purity attacks. Feminists started a discourse on sex, mobilised an offensive against male vice, but they lost control of the movement as it diversified. In part this outcome was the result of certain contradictions in these feminists' attitudes; in part it reflected their impotence to reshape the world according to their own image.

In Great Britain explicitly feminist moral crusades against male vice began with a struggle against state regulation of prostitution. Parliament passed the first of three statutes providing for the sanitary inspection of prostitutes in specific military depots in Southern England and Ireland in 1864. Initially this first Contagious Diseases Act, as it was obliquely entitled, aroused little attention inside or outside of governmental circles. Public opposition to regulation did, however, surface in the 1870s, when a coalition of middle-class nonconformists, feminists, and radical working men challenged the Acts as immoral and unconstitutional, and called for their repeal. The participation of middle-class women in repeal efforts shocked many contemporary observers, who regarded this female rebellion as a disturbing sign of the times. The suffrage movement was in its infancy, and respectable commentators looked on with horror and fascination as middle-class ladies mounted public platforms across the country to denounce the Acts as a 'sacrifice of female liberties' to the 'slavery of men's lust' and to describe in minute detail the 'instrumental rape' of the internal examination. One troubled member of Parliament was moved to remark to Josephine Butler, the feminist repeal leader, 'We know how to manage any other opposition in the House or in the country, but this is very awkward for us – this revolt of women. It is quite a new thing; what are we to do with such an opposition as this?

Under the leadership of Josephine Butler, the Ladies National Association (LNA) was founded in late 1869 as a separatist feminist organisation. A 'Ladies Manifesto' was issued, which denounced the Acts as a blatant example of class and sex discrimination. The Manifesto further argued that the Acts not only deprived poor women of their constitutional rights and forced them to submit to a degrading internal examination, but they officially sanctioned a double standard of sexual morality, which justified male sexual access to a class of 'fallen' women and penalised women for engaging in the same vice as men.

The campaign also drew thousands of women into the political arena for the first time, by encouraging them to challenge male centres of power – such as the police, Parliament, and the medical and military establishments – that were implicated in the administration of the Acts. Rallying to the defence of members of their own sex, these women opposed the sexual and political prerogatives of men. They rejected the prevailing social view of 'fallen women' as pollutants of men and depicted them instead as victims of male pollution, as women who had been invaded by men's bodies, men's laws, and by that 'steel penis', the speculum. This entailed a powerful identification with the fate of registered prostitutes.

Mid-Victorian feminists treated prostitution as the end result of the artificial constraints placed on women's social and economic activity: inadequate wages, and restrictions of women's industrial employment forced some women on to the streets, where they took up the 'best paid industry' – prostitution. They also saw prostitution as a paradigm for the female condition, a symbol of women's powerlessness and sexual victimisation. Feminists realised that the popular sentimentalisation of 'female influence' and motherhood only thinly masked an older contempt and distrust for women, as the 'The Sex', as sexual objects to be bought and sold by men. The treatment of prostitutes under the Acts epitomised this more pervasive and underlying misogyny. 'Sirs', declared Butler, 'you cannot hold us in honour so long as you drag our sisters in the mire. As you are unjust and cruel to them, you will become unjust and cruel to us...'

As 'mothers' and 'sisters' feminists asserted their right to defend prostitutes, thereby invoking two different kinds of authority relationships. A mother's right to defend 'daughters' was only partially an extension and continuation of women's traditional role within the family. It was also a political device, aimed at subverting and superseding patriarchal authority: it gave mothers, not fathers, the right to control sexual access to the daughters. But it also sanctioned an authority relationship between older, middle-class women and young working-class women that, although caring and protective, was also hierarchical and custodial. In other contexts, feminist repealers approached prostitutes on a more egalitarian basis, as sisters, albeit fallen ones, whose individual rights deserved to be respected and who, if they sold their bodies on the streets, had the right to do so unmolested by the police.

This was the radical message of the repeal campaign. It was linked to an enlightened view of prostitution as an irregular and temporary livelihood for adult working-class women. The regulation system, feminists argued, not prostitution as such, doomed inscribed women to a life of sin by publicly stigmatising them and preventing them from finding alternative respectable employment. 'Among the poor,' declared Josephine Butler, the 'boundary lines between the virtuous and vicious' were 'gradually and imperceptibly shaded off' so that it was 'impossible to affix a distinct name and infallibly assign' prostitutes to an outcast category. In fact, the young women brought under the Acts lived as part of a distinct female subgroup in common lodging houses, among a heterogeneous community of the casual labouring poor. They were both victims and survivors. The 'unskilled daughters of the unskilled classes', their lives were a piece with the large body of labouring women who had to eke out a precarious living in the urban job market, for whom sexual coercion was but one form of exploitation to which they were subjected. But prostitutes were not simply victims of male sexual abuse: they could act in their own defence, both individually and collectively, while prostitution itself often constituted a 'refuge from uneasy circumstances' for young women who had to live outside the family and who had to choose among a series of unpleasant alternatives.

Through their agitation, feminist repealers established a political arena that made it possible for prostitutes to resist, 'to show the officers', in the words of one registered woman, 'that we have some respect for our own person'. LNA leaders and their agents descended upon subjected districts like Plymouth and Southampton, agitated among registered prostitutes and tried to persuade them to resist the regulation system. Feminists knew they were dealing with an ambiguous social underground – with lodging-house keepers who made profits out of renting rooms to prostitutes and with 'fallen' women who would 'rise' again.

[...]

After the suspension of the Acts in 1883, Butler and her circle turned their attention to the agitation against the foreign 'traffic in women' and the entrapment of children into prostitution in London. When Parliament refused to pass a bill raising the age of consent and punishing traffickers in vice, Butler and Catherine Booth of the Salvation Army approached W. T. Stead of the *Pall Mall Gazette* for assistance. The result was the 'Maiden Tribute of Modern Babylon', published in the summer of 1885.

The 'Maiden Tribute' was one of the most successful pieces of scandal journalism published in Britain during the 19th century. By using sexual scandal to sell newspapers to a middle-class and working-class readership, Stead ushered in a new era of tabloid sensationalism and cross-class prurience. New typographical and journalist techniques were introduced to sell an old story, the seduction of poor girls by vicious aristocrats, one of the most popular themes of nineteenth-century melodrama, street literature, and women's penny magazines. The 'Maiden Tribute' resembled popular fiction and drama in that it contained a criticism of the vicious upper classes; but, as in the case of melodrama, this class criticism was immediately undercut by sentimental moralism, prurient details, and a focus on passive, innocent female victims and individual evil men that diverted attention away from the structural issues related to prostitution.

In lurid and prurient detail, the 'Maiden Tribute' documented the sale of 'five pound' virgins to aristocratic old rakes, graphically describing the way the 'daughters of the people' had been 'snared, trapped and outraged either when under the influence of drugs or after a prolonged struggle in a locked room'. The series had an electrifying effect on public opinion: 'By the third instalment mobs were rioting at the *Pall Mall Gazette* offices, in an attempt to obtain copies of the paper'. An enormous public demonstration was held in Hyde Park (estimated at 250,000) to demand the passage of legislation raising the age of consent for girls from 13 to 16. Reformers of all shades were represented on the dozen or so demonstration platforms. For one brief moment, feminists and personal rights advocates joined with Anglican bishops and socialists to protest the aristocratic corruption of young innocents.

Recent research delineates the vast discrepancy between lurid journalistic accounts and the reality of prostitution. Evidence of widespread entrapment of British girls in London and abroad is slim. During the 1870s and 1880s officials and reformers uncovered a light traffic in women between Britain and the continent. All but a few of the women enticed into licensed brothels in Antwerp and Brussels had been prostitutes in England. Misled by promises of a life of luxury and ease as part of a glamorous demimonde, they were shocked and horrified at the conditions enforced upon them in licensed state brothels, a sharp contrast to what they had experienced in England. In most cases, then, it was the conditions of commercial sex and not the fact that deeply upset the women. Stead's discussion of child prostitution contained similar misrepresentations and distortions. There undoubtedly were some child prostitutes on the streets of London, Liverpool, and elsewhere; but most of these young girls were not victims of false entrapment, as the vignettes in the 'Maiden Tribute' suggest; the girls were on the streets because their other choices were so limited. 'Since sexuality in western culture is so mystified,' notes Gayle Rubin, 'the wars over it are often fought at oblique angles, aimed at phony targets, conducted with misplaced passions, and are highly, intensely, symbolic.' The 'Maiden Tribute' episode strikingly illustrates both this mystification and its political consequences. Shifting the cultural image of the prostitute to the innocent child victim encouraged new, more repressive, political initiatives over sex.

Why then did feminist reformers endorse this crusade? Why did they ally with repressive moralists and anti-suffragists who were as anxious to clear the streets of prostitutes as to protect young girls from evil procurers and vicious aristocrats? Like the image of the instrumental violation of registered women under the CD Acts, the story of aristocratic corruption of virgins 'generated a sense of outrage with which a wide spectrum of public opinion found itself in sympathy'. Feminist repealers undoubtedly believed they could manipulate this popular anger for their own purposes, first to secure the full repeal of the CD Acts (they were finally removed from the statute books in 1886) and then to launch a sustained assault on the double standard. They were also attracted to the radical message in Stead's exposé of aristocratic vice. The disreputable performance of MPs during the debates over the age of consent confirmed feminists' worst suspicions about 'the vicious upper classes'. During the debates, old rakes like Cavendish Bentinck treated prostitution as a necessary and inevitable evil, while others openly defended sexual access to working-class girls as a time-honored prerogative of gentlemen. One member of the House of Lords acknowledged that 'very few of their Lordships ... had not when young men, been guilty of immorality. He hoped they would pause before passing a clause within the range of which their sons might come'.

Feminists felt obliged to redress the sexual wrongs done to poor girls by men of a superior class, but they registered the same repugnance and ambivalence toward incorrigible girls as they had earlier toward unrepentant prostitutes. For them as well as for more repressive moralists, the desire to protect young working-class girls masked impulses to control the girls' sexuality, which in turn reflected their desire to impose a social code that stressed female adolescent dependency. [...]

Another sub theme of feminist discussion was that females of all classes were vulnerable to male sexual violence.

[...]

What was the outcome of the 'Maiden Tribute' affair? The public furore over the 'Maiden Tribute' forced the passage of the Criminal Law Amendment Act of 1885, a particularly nasty and pernicious piece of omnibus legislation. The 1885 Act raised the age of consent for girls from 13 to 16, but it also gave police far greater summary jurisdiction over poor working-class women and children – a trend that Butler and her circle had always opposed. Finally, it contained a clause making indecent acts between consenting male adults a crime, thus forming the basis of legal prosecution of male homosexuals in Britain until 1967. An anti-aristocratic bias may have prompted the inclusion of this clause (reformers accepted its inclusion but did not themselves propose it), as homosexuality was associated with the corruption of working-class youth by the same upper-class profligates, who, on other occasions, were thought to buy the services of young girls.

Despite the public outcry against corrupt aristocrats and international traffickers, the clauses of the new bill were mainly enforced against working-class women, and regulated adult rather than youthful sexual behaviour.
[…]

While the social purity movement served middle-class interests, it is a common error among historians to assume that working-class support for social purity was ephemeral or that both before and after the summer of 1885 social purity remained an almost exclusively middle-class movement. Middle-class evangelicals may have predominated in the National Vigilance Association, but the values of social purity seem to have penetrated certain portions of the working class.
[…]

But sexual restraint could also serve women's interest. In a culture where women were often the victims of sexual coercion yet blamed for crimes committed against them, and where it was difficult even to conceive of female sexual agency as long as women lacked agency in other vital areas, defenders of women's rights could and did regard the doctrine of female passionlessness and male sexual self-control as a significant advance over traditional assumptions of a dangerous and active female sexuality. Whatever its drawbacks, this sexual strategy resulted in some permanent gains for women: it made it possible for women to name incest and rape as crimes against their person (rather than as crimes against the property of men). Most particularly, though the Incest Act of 1908, young women were offered legal recourse against sexual violence by male family members for the first time. By insisting that women had the right to refuse the sexual demands of husbands, and by widely propagandising this view in the early decades of the 20th century, feminists within social purity laid the foundation for a new egalitarian code of marital relations still to be fully realised in the contemporary era. In feminist hands, desexualisation could empower women to attack the customary prerogatives of men. [sic] it could also validate a new social role for women outside the heterosexual family. The 'New Women' of the late-19th century, as Carroll Smith-Rosenberg has noted, strove to achieve social autonomy, but at the cost of sexual identity, to legitimise their social and economic independence at the 'price of donning the mask of Victorian [sexual] respectability'.

Since middle-class women elaborated these ideas, it is hard to know what working-class women thought of them. Labouring women did participate in mothers' meetings, and they may have found the moral authority imparted to desexualised women attractive, as it reinforced the power of mothers and female collectivities. In the dense urban neighbourhoods of late-Victorian and Edwardian England, where female neighbours shared space and services, and where female relatives sustained the bonds of kinship, social and sexual norms were often articulated at 'street level' through hierarchical female networks. The mothers of Plymouth, Lancaster and Salford, for example, enforced incest taboos, socialised their daughters into a fatalistic and dependent femininity, and increasingly shunned 'bad women' (often at the instigation of purity agencies). On the whole, the activities of neighbourhood matriarchs sustained social hierarchies and divisions, particularly along generational and sex lines. Female sexual respectability in these neighbourhoods was purchased at a high price, with little promise of social independence. The 'New Woman' option was simply not available to working-class daughters: they could not aspire to a future outside heterosexual domesticity – for working-class women, such a future could only forebode a life of hardship and homelessness. As a result, the contradictory nature of the power imparted to women through 'passionlessness' appears even more apparent for working-class women. However much this doctrine mitigated the powerlessness of dependent wives, it left working-class women alienated from and ignorant of their own sexuality and body, and unable to control reproduction – a disabling condition, to judge from the depressing letters collected by the Women's Co-operative Guild in their volume, *Maternity*.

Social purity presented working men with a different set of implications and opportunities; it could bolster their authority as responsible patriarchs if they were willing to submit themselves to a certain domestic ideology. In general, sexual respectability became the hallmark of the respectable working man, anxious to distance himself from the 'bestiality' of the casual labouring poor at a time when increased pressure was being placed on the respectable working class to break their ties with outcast groups.

[…]

Although some feminists still maintained a national presence in the purity crusade, all in all, by the late 1880s feminists had lost considerable authority in the public discussion over sex to a coalition of male professional experts, conservative churchmen, and social purity advocates. On the other hand, social purity left a permanent imprint on the women's movement through the First World War. Both the 16-year campaign against state regulation, and later sexual scandals such as the 'Maiden Tribute', ingrained the theme of the sexual wrongs perpetrated against women by men on later feminist consciousness. After the 1880s, the 'women's revolt' became 'a revolt that is Puritan and not Bohemian. It is an uprising against the tyranny of organised intemperance, impurity, mammonism, and selfish motives.' On the whole this attack on male dominance and male vice involved no positive assertion of female sexuality. Although a small minority of feminists like Olive Schreiner and Stella Browne were deeply interested in the question of female pleasure, they were far removed from the feminist mainstream, where the public discussion of sexuality and male dominance was still couched within the terms of a 'separate sphere' ideology, implying that women were moral, 'spiritual' creatures who needed to be protected from animalistic 'carnal' men, and demanding, in the words of Christabel Pankhurst, the Edwardian militant suffragist, 'votes for women', and 'chastity' for men. Moreover, the obsession with male vice again sidetracked early twentieth-century feminists into another crusade against white slavery (1912), while obscuring the economic basis of prostitution. It even prompted the most progressive women of the day to advocate raising the age of consent to 21. Finally, it led to repressive public policies. Commenting on the enforcement of the White Slavery Act of 1912, Sylvia Pankhurst remarked, 'It is a strange thing that the latest Criminal Amendment Act, which was passed ostensibly to protect women, is being used almost exclusively to punish women'. As late as 1914, first-wave feminists were rediscovering that the state 'protection' of young women usually led to coercive and repressive measures against those same women.

These then are the early historical links between feminism and repressive crusades against prostitution, pornography, and homosexuality. Begun as a libertarian struggle against the state sanction of male vice, the repeal campaign helped to spawn a hydra-headed assault on nonmarital, nonreproductive sexuality. The struggle against state regulation evolved into a movement that used the instruments of the state for repressive purposes. It may be misleading to interpret the effects of these later crusades solely as 'blind' repressive attacks on sexuality; in many ways they clarified and identified whole new areas of sexuality. According to Michel Foucault, this elaboration of new sexualities was a strategy for exercising power in society. By ferreting out new areas of illicit sexual activity and sometimes defining them into existence, a new 'technology of power' was created that facilitated control over an ever-widening circle of human activity. But power is not simply immanent in society; it is deployed by specific historical agents, who have access to varying sources and levels of power. The reality of a hierarchy of power severely impeded feminists' efforts to use purity crusades to defend and empower women. Through rescue and preventive work, feminists and other women were certainly implicated in the regulation and control of sexuality. But there were others whose access to power was more direct. Rescue work, mothers' meetings, and moral suasion by no means carried the same authority as a morals police under the CD Acts, male vigilance committees, or an emerging 'science of sexuality' controlled by male professionals. The feminist challenge to male sexual prerogatives was a major historic development, one necessary precondition for the ideology of egalitarian heterosexual relations: but when they tried to use the powers of the state to protect women, particularly prostitutes who had been the original objects of their pity and concern, feminists usually came face to face with their own impotence.

Chapter 19

Lorraine Coons

■ ' "NEGLECTED SISTERS" OF THE WOMEN'S MOVEMENT: THE PERCEPTION AND EXPERIENCE OF WORKING MOTHERS IN THE PARISIAN GARMENT INDUSTRY 1860–1915', *Journal of Women's History*, 5 (2), Fall 1993, pp. 50–74

THE NINETEENTH-CENTURY NOTION of "woman's proper place," given its connotation of economic dependency, its vision of the ideal home, and the role of woman as mother and educator, is clearly a bourgeois creation.[1] Only then and only among the middle and upper classes did there exist this hierarchical division within the family between wage earner and spender. When we refer to "woman's proper place" in this context, we are identifying an ideal held by bourgeois society alone. The difficulty arose when nineteenth-century middle-class reformers sought to extend this image of women to the working classes.

In the pre-industrial age, there was no incompatibility between women's productive and reproductive functions. Remunerative work was performed within the confines of the household, thus women could satisfy both responsibilities—nurturer of the family and co-breadwinner. Industrialization brought special challenges for working mothers. While their productive and reproductive responsibilities continued, women found it increasingly difficult to reconcile these two incompatible functions. The significant change coming with industrialization was not so much in the nature of the work but in the locale. This separation of workplace and home posed the greatest challenge to women attempting to balance their varied responsibilities. Even the most progressive feminists of the late nineteenth century accepted the narrowly defined roles assigned to the mother of the family. Rather than question tradition, they sought to adapt to it.

Within the confines of the bourgeois notion of "proper place," a woman was expected to retire from the active labor force after the birth of her first child to assume her newly assigned roles of wife, mother, and housekeeper. This was one of Napoleon's most powerful legacies. Article 213 of his *Code Civil* clearly defined the respective roles of each spouse: "The husband owes protection to his wife, the wife obedience to her husband."[2] This conventional attitude had complex and underlying religious, political, and socioeconomic roots.

These attitudes encouraged the revitalization of home industry in the garment trades which was made possible by the impact of economic modernization on certain industries in the late nineteenth century. Mothers, faced with the added responsibility of acting as co-breadwinner, could now fulfill their economic obligations without violating society's norms. This article analyzes the concept of the "proper sphere" for working-class mothers in late nineteenth- and early twentieth-century French society and its link to the regeneration of home industry in the Parisian garment trades.

Women's involvement in homework was restricted to those trades which were an extension of their work in the home, and thus clothing manufacture had a special appeal. Under this rubric, women were employed in the fabrication of lace, artificial flowers, hosiery, tapestries, and were engaged in embroidery and the millinery trade.[3]

By the first quarter of the twentieth century, however, homework had degenerated into a source of exploitive "sweated" labor. Rather than change the attitudes about the married woman's "proper place," legislators sought to reform homework. The second part of this article focuses on the women's response, first to late nineteenth-century attitudes about woman's "proper place" and then to early twentieth-century concerns about the dangers of home industry to working-class mothers. With minor exceptions, women's rights activists, too, supported the retention of homework. Their idea of improving the system included protective labor legislation and unionization while the attitudes remained securely in place.

Industrialization did not open up new opportunities for women in the workforce. It likewise failed to change traditional attitudes which continued to restrict women's growth and development well into the twentieth century. When confronted with the problem of outside employment for mothers of the working class, feminists, both bourgeois and militant alike, generally subscribed to the middle-class notion of a "woman's proper place."[4] In their call for equal rights, feminists were championing the cause of the single woman. Once a mother, she became a "neglected sister" of the feminist movement and was expected to retreat to her separate sphere. Rights for women of the working classes, thus, ended at the moment of conception of their first child.

Securing woman's "proper place"

In a largely agrarian economy, women labored alongside their husbands in agricultural tasks. During the winter season, they also engaged in piecework. Thus they fulfilled the three intrinsic responsibilities of a woman: production, reproduction and child care. With the coming of the industrial age in France, women found a new marketplace for their labor, which complicated their domestic situation. The question of a woman's "proper place" became an issue for both middle- and working-class society only when traditional attitudes clashed with the effects of economic modernization.

The crisis in the quality of motherhood became the key issue in the debate. Throughout France and elsewhere in Europe, depopulation was a grave concern for lawmakers and reformers alike. While middle-class women opted for smaller families, working-class mothers consciously restricted the size of their own because of economic realities. The annual number of births in France plummeted between 1896 and 1906 from 834,173 to 806,847.[5]

The family was seen as a microcosm of French society and woman as central to its well-being. The future of the Republic, then, was directly linked to the continued health and growth of the family unit. The insistence upon motherhood as the natural occupation of women thus served the interests of the state.[6] Reformers and physicians sought to place the responsibility for the deterioration of the working-class family on the women themselves.

A "cult of domesticity" was widely promoted throughout France and the rest of Europe— a bourgeois ideology imposed upon working-class women to keep them at home.[7]

Motherhood received a boost in status; it became the duty and *raison d'être* of women and their ultimate reward as well. All of this required instruction. The domestic sciences gained a prominent, respected place in the field of female education. Blaming motherhood rather than the social order proved expedient and more economical. It was far easier to educate individuals and expand social services than to tackle the insurmountable problem of poverty. Banning the employment of mothers became the preferred solution even for those who had recognized the impact of environmental factors.[8]

The issue of work was not so much a class consideration as it was one of gender, affecting bourgeois and working-class women alike. For the rising bourgeois, it was a question of social status. No respectable middle-class businessman could permit his wife to engage in an occupation other than motherhood without risking a loss in social standing in the community. Her proper place in the home assured him his privileged place in society.

Working-class males, fearful of wage competition, willingly subscribed to the bourgeois ideal of "woman's proper place" for economic considerations. The resentment of workers is clearly expressed in the proceedings of workers' congresses as early as 1867. Small tailors were being slowly displaced by the new ready-made clothing manufacturers who were steadily gaining ground and respectability. These entrepreneurs sought to tap the abundant, cheap supply of women's labor. The tailors saw women as an economic threat and, thus, were among the most vocal in their opposition to women's work outside the home.

Irenée Dauthier, a Parisian saddler and outspoken delegate at a session of the Workers' Congress held in Paris in October, 1876, was concerned about the problems resulting from exposing women to the excesses of factory work:

> Her health, her physical strength, do not permit her to prolong this existence for long, because if this state of affairs continues, family life will soon disintegrate and indifference will replace affection in the household.[9]

Dauthier lamented the fact that women were forced to engage in tasks contrary to their delicate natures. By subjecting them to strenuous factory work, Dauthier contended, both their health and ultimately that of the nation would be jeopardized. Dauthier included working mothers with nuns and prison inmates as a detrimental source of competition for their husbands.[10]

Delegates to workers' congresses held in Marseille in 1879 and in Le Havre in 1880 repeatedly called for a living wage which would be sufficient for the man to support his family. One delegate summed up public opinion thus: "We would prefer that the married woman confine herself to house-keeping, and ... that the man should support the woman."[11]

The remarks of Keufer, a delegate to the fourth National Workers' Congress held in November 1880, also reveal a deep-seated fear that men's wages would further decrease should women remain in the active labor force. "If the woman must work, let her look for an occupation that will not remove her from the home," he said. "She will earn a little less maybe, but there will be nevertheless great benefits to be gained from her remaining at home."[12]

Many agreed with Keufer's endorsement of homework, seeing it as a viable means for women to reconcile their dual responsibilities and allowing them the flexibility to coordinate domestic and economic activities. The woman's place within the home insured the continuity and stability of the family which in turn seemed to guarantee the future well-being of France. As Marilyn Boxer has demonstrated, home industry was endorsed as a solution not only to the woman question but to the social question as well. It signified a return to the family-based corporate order of the past.[13] Home and work were thus reorganized under one roof for this purpose. By the end of the nineteenth century, home industry had been revitalized and was estimated by government records to be employing over one-fifth of the total active female population of France.

Theory versus practical application: women's experience in home industry

During the first half of the nineteenth century, the manufacturing of clothing was a small, independent, simple domestic industry. By the 1850s, large department stores attracted numerous customers with their moderate prices, the new system of buying on credit, and the abundance and wide selection of ready-made garments.[14] Despite the creation of some garment factories by mid-century, subcontractors (intermediaries) who distributed the orders for the *grands magasins* relied heavily on homework. While the factory absorbed many industries by the end of the century, garment manufacture retained its traditional character.

Home industry continued to act as the principal employer of women well into the twentieth century. 1896 government figures show that of the 33 percent of women who worked (6,382,658), one-fifth (1,450,000) were involved in home manufacture, 650,000 of whom were employed in the clothing industry.[15] By 1906, 36 percent of French women worked, 850,000 of whom were engaged in home industry in the clothing trades.[16] Women's increased participation in home industry can be further illustrated by the findings of an 1896 French government inquiry which revealed that of the 131,000 persons occupied in the linen trades, a subdivision of the garment industry, throughout France, 83,000 (nearly two-thirds) were "isolated" (largely home) workers. [17]

In an effort to conserve production, manufacturers avoided expanding their establishments to meet the demands of the peak season. Instead, they tapped a vast reserve of homeworkers as a complementary labor force, thus explaining the revitalization of the industry in the late nineteenth century. Other manufacturers began to parcel out simple finishing and accessory tasks to homeworkers which required little skill and brought the women very little revenue.

Of the total active female population in 1896, 52 percent of single women worked, while 38 percent of all married women were part of the labor force.[18] The *Office du Travail* made the following tabulations based on results from an early twentieth-century investigation of homeworkers engaged in the linen trades.[19]

Branch of Garment Industry	Single	Married	Divorced/ Widowed
Undergarments (women /children)	16	50	33
Undergarments (men)	22	53	24
House Linens	18	51	30
Work done in *oeuvres d'assistance*	17	48	34

Each group above reflects the average distribution per one hundred workers in Paris. Such studies indicate that homework was largely a married woman's domain. By grouping married, widowed, and divorced women together, these findings further imply that homework became the overwhelming option of women once they began a family. Of the 510 women questioned in this study, 258 were married and 169 were widowed or divorced, while only 83 were single. Well over half of the women responding to the question about family were working mothers.[20]

Homework in the clothing trades, and its long string of abuses, became an excellent example of the "sweating system," a phrase coined by the English writer Charles Kingsley. The dramatic increase in the number of women involved in home manufacture in the garment industry and the accompanying deterioration of their material condition prompted the *Office du Travail* as well as other government agencies and social reformers to conduct investigations during the early twentieth century.

Sweated trades were characteristically associated with the clothing industry. Here, a vast supply of homeworkers were easily assembled. Since they were not concentrated in one workplace, homeworkers had no cohesion and were prime candidates for exploitation by the manufacturers. For some women, homework provided only an accessory wage, but for many working mothers, it was the family's sole means of financial support. Many women were widowed, others had been abandoned by their husbands; some had none. The idea that most women worked for an accessory wage, a notion advanced by government investigators and social reformers, was a myth. Numerous findings of government and private investigations of home industry conducted in the early twentieth century reveal that the vast number of women were single-handedly supporting their families. The accessory wage theory provided an easy way out for government officials and others who chose to ignore the reality of the working-class woman's experience in home industry.

The economic pluses of home industry were all on the side of the manufacturers. By relying on homeworkers, businessmen drastically cut their production costs. They saved on expenses incurred in running factories (machinery, electricity, heating), and on providing necessary work supplies (threads, needles, and so on) which became the responsibility of the homeworker. They were not bound by any governmental legislation regulating work hours or wages. In fact, there was little in the way of government regulation for any type of female labor before 1892.[21] The use of homeworkers enabled manufacturers to amass great profits. Homeworkers themselves derived no benefits. Hours were long, earnings low, and working conditions unsanitary at best. Much of their time was wasted in transit because they had to pick up the work from the contractors. The practice of *le trucking* (partial payment in goods rather than in cash) was not uncommon among the contractors who often ran businesses on the side, obliging their workers to purchase items at their shops at highly inflated prices. A law passed on December 7, 1909, requiring employers to pay their employees in cash wages, contributed to the eventual disappearance of the *le trucking* system.

An investigation of homework in the artificial flower industry conducted by the *Office du Travail* between 1910 and 1913 revealed that three-quarters of women workers in the provinces and just under one-half in Paris earned a daily wage of one to two francs.[22] This does not reflect prolonged periods of seasonal unemployment. In Paris, only 22 percent of women flowermakers had steady work. 23 percent reported being out of work between three and five months, while 18 percent were without work as many as seven months of the year.[23]

Many statesmen and reformers justified the visible inequality in wage scales between the sexes by insisting on the limitation of women's physical and mental capacities. In an investigation of the *Office du Travail* determining cost-of-living figures for both sexes, wage differentials were explained by the fact that physiologically, women required less food than men. Women were also thought to have fewer vices than men, such as smoking or drinking, and thus required less money for living expenses.[24]

The exploitation of workers by the intermediaries, or *marchandage*, was a form of subcontracting used in numerous industries, especially in the linen trades and the ready-made clothing industry. After deducting a customary 35 percent commission from the price paid by the department store, contractors distributed the orders among homeworkers. Some contractors chose to work through intermediaries who likewise retained a sizeable commission, usually another 35 percent, leaving the worker with only one-third of the total price paid by the department store for the finished garment. At that rate, the woman had to pedal at her machine from 7:00 A.M. until 11:00 P.M. to earn forty francs a month.[25]

Jeanne Bouvier's investigation of home industry

In her autobiography, *Mes Mémoires*, Jeanne Bouvier, a seamstress who became active in her trade union in 1898 and rose to a position of leadership in the French labor movement, recounts her own experience as a homeworker. Once, she and a neighbor spotted a small notice: "We are looking for workers to sew plackets on corsets." Together they eagerly took on a large quantity of work:

> We got up early and went to bed late. When the work was finished, we returned to the employer with the completed work and were told that of the 11 francs 50 we should have been paid, approximately 4 francs remained after deducting the cost of the ribbon … We worked two days, the both of us, from 5AM until 10PM.[26]

Bouvier was elected to serve on the *Conseil Supérieur du Travail* in 1909. In 1913, she was commissioned by the Labor Minister to undertake a comprehensive investigation of home industry. Bouvier went "undercover," posing as a hosiery worker seeking employment from establishments that promised high wages to able-bodied workers, provided that they first purchase one of the company's machines. In each case, the companies were perpetrating frauds. One such hosiery manufacturer was the *Union Ouvrière*, which had won both the gold and bronze medals at the *Exposition Internationale des Arts du Travail* in 1912. The company offered free lessons to persons purchasing their machines. In brochures intended to lure prospective customers, the *Union Ouvrière* included names and addresses of satisfied clients who boasted of daily earnings of three to four francs. The frequent inclusion of the name of a clergyman or nun further guaranteed the company's good standing. Company catalogs promised to change the worker's life, but Bouvier's investigation revealed that no such noble intentions dominated their thinking; they were in business to sell machines, not to establish charity workshops. Letters Bouvier received from workers revealed that many shared a common experience which in no way lived up to the promises of the brochures or newspaper advertisements.

One letter from a knitter, Mme. Maupertuy, implicated the *Union Ouvrière*. When she tried to return the inferior machine she had purchased, the company refused to refund her money. Instead, they offered to exchange her machine for a bicycle.[27] Bouvier recorded her personal experience with the *Union Ouvrière*, which confirmed the stories she had heard from other women, in a report to the *Conseil Supérieur du Travail*. One acerbic exchange with the company follows: (Letter to Bouvier from B. Arnold of the *Union Ouvrière*, dated May 3, 1913, rejecting her work.)

We are confirming your conversation this morning when you delivered your finished work to us which did not conform to the specifications of your work card.

We are very surprised, in fact, that you gave us an article so easy to make as a scarf, without even taking into account the dimensions and weight that were indicated to you. ....[28]

In response, Bouvier informed M. Arnold that the wool given her was of such poor quality that she could not work with it. She concludes, challenging them:

I will bring them back to you Saturday morning ... if you refuse them I will appeal to the Conseil des Prud'hommes to settle the question by asking them to send an expert to my home to assist me in redoing the scarves to see if he finds the wool workable.... The expert will be able to state in his report that it is impossible to obtain the wages your workers had quoted me when I made inquiries; they lied because they were paid off....[29]

Endorsements by respected members of Parisian society surely improved business for many such companies. Noting her own experience, Bouvier continues:

I wrote to four persons indicated as references: two priests, one nun, and a municipal guard. This last one represented authority while the others were spokesmen of God who said: "You will not be deceived." It seemed to me that their testimony should be a sure guarantee.[30]

In her report, Bouvier suggests that clergymen were often duped by the companies who took them on a tour of their establishments, showing them the finest quality machines which would certainly bring the worker the wages the company promised. The prohibitive cost of such machines, however, made them virtually inaccessible to the workers, who settled for inferior quality machines which brought drastically lower earnings.

Bouvier's report also revealed that the companies' enticing brochures "accidently" neglected to mention additional expenses, i.e., 150 to 200 francs *caution* (security deposit) required upon purchase of a machine, the fact that all raw materials had to be bought from them at greatly inflated prices, and payment of an additional *caution* of 10 francs per kilogram of material, even when that material might only cost 3 francs 50. Bouvier discovered that in instances where the company agreed to take back the machine, the worker rarely was reimbursed in cash but instead offered an exchange for some other machine of much less value than the one returned (as in the case of Madame Maupertuy). Bouvier spoke of other instances wherein employees of these companies would appear at the door of the desperate worker under a different guise and offer to buy the machine at a greatly reduced price, often 20 to 30 percent less than the rate she paid. In this way, a company could recycle their machines, making an immense profit in the transaction.

Exploitation of homeworkers was the key issue connected with the economic deprivations suffered by these women; exploitation manifested itself in all forms: by the contractors and intermediaries, by the manufacturers, by the women themselves, in *le trucking* system, and over the question of competition. Each in their own way and all collectively contributed to the economic plight of the workers. Their material condition, in terms of earnings, was more critical than that of their factory co-workers who were beginning to group together to protect their own interests. Homeworkers had no one to plead their case and became the "orphans" of the industry. Their earnings suffered on two counts: first, they were women, and even worse, they were homeworkers for whom no regulation of the trade applied.

Bourgeois women's activism

Efforts to enforce government regulation of homework in England, Australia, New Zealand, Germany, and the United States gained the attention of French social reformers and legislators who took an active interest in obtaining limited reform of the industry. As early as 1888, the debate on home industry occupied sessions of the Chamber of Deputies. By the early 1900s, the evils associated with home manufacture, particularly in the garment industry, concerned several prominent social reformers, moralists, writers, government agencies, and secular and church groups. Numerous doctoral theses dealt with different aspects of the problem of home industry in France. In 1904, the Association for the Legal Protection of Workers submitted its own proposal for an investigation of home industry.[31] Interestingly, however, no one proposed a minimum wage at that time.

The role played by women activists from diverse social backgrounds in attempting to reform home industry is particularly significant. In December 1902, Henriette-Jean Brunhes, a bourgeois feminist, organized the French equivalent of the American Consumers' League, *La Ligue Sociale d'Acheteurs* (LSA), which focused its attention on the working classes in general and the homeworkers in particular. The LSA was entirely bourgeois in its orientation and approach and in the kinds of solutions it proposed. For the LSA, the basic evil of home manufacture was the grossly inadequate earnings of the women which were determined by the public's demand for *luxe d'imitation*. Thus the organization resolved to launch a "war against cheapness," to educate consumers to understand that by paying less for items, they were indirectly contributing to the social problems afflicting the nation. They published a number of bulletins and tracts, issued a series of postcards depicting the plight of the homeworkers, and even introduced an academic course, *L'Education de l'acheteur par l'enquête*, into the curriculum of the College Libre des Sciences Sociales in 1903.

Other bourgeois women were actively involved in using their privileged position to improve the material condition of the homeworkers. In 1908, Gabrielle Duchêne, one of the prominent "ladies of the leisure class," established *Entr'Aide*, by far the most effective and successful of the clothing cooperatives. Enraged by employer exploitation of home-workers, Duchêne resolved to begin her own cooperative to ensure equitable earnings for women by eliminating the intermediary. Duchêne personally operated the store, selling the merchandise made by the forty women she employed. Like the LSA, she launched her own war against *camelote* (cheap, shoddy merchandise) by educating the consumer to shop for quality rather than bargains. In its advertisements, *Entr'Aide* appealed to the consumer-worker: "Purchase from Entr'Aide—in so doing you permit the workers to live by the fruits of their labor. It will be a demonstration of an act of solidarity and at the same time be a good deed."[32]

Duchêne's active role met with muted criticism from bourgeois feminists who felt that her actions were beneath her social station. Better to be president of a "Society for Abandoned Dogs" than to occupy oneself with operating a store which sold and manufactured under-garments. To sponsor organizations to benefit the workers was considered acceptable; to participate in their actual operation was totally out of character for a woman in Duchêne's social position. By transcending class barriers, Duchêne became something of an embarrassment to the bourgeoisie. She later became an active member of the council of the *Syndicat de la Chemiserie-Lingerie* and, together with Jeanne Bouvier, co-founded the French section of the International Homework Office in Paris in 1914.

Feminists' campaign against *Le Sweating*

Socialist feminists, like their bourgeois counterparts, sought ways of improving the life of the working mother while stopping short of denouncing home industry. Outspoken feminists (both relational and individualist) seem to have conformed to traditional, patriarchal attitudes about "woman's proper place" once she became a mother. For them, motherhood was part of a woman's normal life cycle. Such perceptions would contribute to the longevity of home manufacture. Feminists, however, did not agree with the male objection to mothers' work outside the home on the grounds of women's physical frailty or intellectual inferiority. For them the real question was one of a woman's priorities in life. Once of age, a woman would naturally marry and assume her new responsibilities.

Some women did challenge custom in arguing that a woman should be able to choose both her occupation and workplace. As early as 1868, Maxime Breuil, in a discourse on women's work, accused Roman Catholic popes in their Christian family dogma of seeking to confine women to their homes by advancing the argument that the mother's presence was indispensable to the education of the child:

> Let the woman alone to do as she wishes; she will raise her children properly if she is well enough prepared; but it is not by her submission to conventional roles that she will arrive at being a prudent and able guide for them, it is rather through the development of all her own potentials that she can hope to help them develop themselves; she needs something more to fulfill herself other than the routine chores of housework to which you wish to condemn her....[33]

Women delegates at the 1878 Workers' Congress held in Lyon hinted at the need for a redefinition of women's roles. Marie Finet, a seamstress and member of the *Chambre Syndicale des Femmes de Lyon*, supported the right of a woman to work, even when her labor was not needed to supplement the family income:

> Woman has a right to enlightenment: in the name of the interests of the nation, she should emerge from the state of servitude.... If she does not carry arms for the defense of the country, she gives birth to those who do.[34]

Where this work was to be executed, however, Finet did not specify. Although she called for a reconstitution of the family based on equality between the sexes, Finet also believed that a woman, once a mother, should retire from the work force to take up her newly assigned role.

At the Socialist Workers' Congress held in Marseilles in 1879, Hubertine Auclert,[35] who by today's standards would be considered a militant socialist-feminist, ardently campaigned for women's suffrage and was intolerant of women who relied on their husbands' income to support them. Men, she contended, should not have to assume the full financial responsibility for the family. "Every woman who can work but finds it more convenient to be housed and fed by her husband," she wrote, "is, from my point of view, nothing more than a kept woman!"[36]

Auclert was no less harsh on men who saw a clear-cut sexual division of domestic responsibilities. She expressed such revolutionary ideas in penned notes on the *Difficulté du travail féminin*:

> All unproductive functions which one attributes to women in the home are, in society, filled by men for money wages (for money, men sweep streets, are cleaners, shine shoes, sew, mend and darn, are chefs …, are dishwashers…).
>
> The repugnance of men for domestic chores is not inherent to their sex, it comes simply from the fact that from birth, one treats the little boys as lords and masters; after their mothers there are the sisters who become their servants.[37]

Auclert believed that housework, like recreation, should be shared by both husband and wife. Such comments place her in the forefront of the women's movement of the next century.

Nevertheless she recognized the limitations of women, once married with children, and made no value judgments on their lifestyle. Auclert perceived housework to be a full-time occupation like all other productive work for which women should be equally compensated. To these ends she campaigned for old-age pensions for "retired" housewives, advancing the argument that the woman who "devotes her life to raising her children" is entitled to a pension as much as another "who works in the factory, putting sugar cubes into boxes."[38] In order to qualify for a pension, under the terms of the government's pension law which she opposed, women "must abandon their children, to sell their labor at the workshop, where thirty years of assiduity will procure for her a pension."[39] Such a reckless law, she argued, helped to decrease the already dangerously low birthrate, freeing women from maternal duties in order to guarantee their own security in old age. Auclert's attitude is shared by other leading French feminists of her age. This "maternal role" was not inconsistent with mainstream feminist thinking—it was simply assumed.

Auclert is an interesting, colorful, complex figure whose revolutionary feminism must not be underestimated because of her traditional stand on the duties of wife and mother. Her ideas on shared responsibilities within the home and on housewives' pensions remain revolutionary in our own day.

Her position on married women's work outside the home is less clear. She seems to accept, along with everyone else, the given that the mother of the family should remain at home. She circumvents the issue by pushing for financial provisions for mothers. On the highly sensitive issue of employment for married women, Auclert was confronted with centuries of an entrenched tradition which was not in her power to change and which she, herself, did not challenge on this point. Auclert, along with middle-class reformers, feared that the stability of the family would be jeopardized should the mother leave the home to find outside employment. Thus, she had to make some necessary alterations in her thinking.

Another socialist-feminist who was outspoken on the question of women's work and wages was Paule Mincke. Mincke joined the separatists from the fourth National Workers Congress at Le Havre in November 1880 in forming their own National Socialist Workers' Congress. There she echoed the sentiments expressed by Auclert and others:

Men have created crèches for their women's children.... But this reflects their egoism; in so doing they may fully benefit from the work of the mothers. The place of women is at home, provided that the father will earn enough to feed and raise his family....

The woman who has no provider, father, brother, or husband must fatally come to find a necessary replacement, a lover, since it is impossible for her to support herself by her work.[40]

Mincke thus concedes the point that under the existing political and economic system, the welfare of a woman depends exclusively on the ability of finding a male protector. She, too, agreed that the place of the woman once married was within the home. It was not by choice, she insisted, but rather out of necessity that a mother left her home to "close herself up for many horrible hours in these infernal factories and workshops where the air is foul and the atmosphere is suffocating."[41]

Mincke was not opposed to women's work in general. She realized that economic realities forced mothers to seek outside work, but her solution was homework. Mincke arrived at this conclusion differently than did male workers and bourgeois reformers who shared a similar view. Rather than the traditional arguments against outside work, such as economic competition, fear of moral laxity, and the intellectual inferiority of women to men, Mincke's objections focused on the artificial separation of the mother from the warmth and security of her family and home.

Even the social revolutionary, Louise Michel, had an opinion on the position of working-class mothers.[42] In a rich and wonderfully detailed biography by Edith Thomas, Michel's position on women's work becomes clear. In the newly constituted society following the social revolution which she envisioned, working-class women would not be forced to seek outside employment. Their mission would be to educate their daughters. Perhaps this is one reason Michel chose to remain single throughout her life.

Another interesting figure is Aline Valette, schoolteacher turned socialist-feminist, who came to be identified with Jules Guesde's *Parti Ouvrier Français*.[43] Valette insisted upon the primary importance of a woman's maternal role and was intolerant of those women who neglected their domestic responsibilities. In 1883, she published a successful homemaker's guide, *La Journée de la petite ménagère*, which went through thirty-four editions in ten years. It outlined the extensive program of housework which, if conscientiously adhered to, guaranteed to keep a woman secured permanently in traditional roles. Valette, like her socialist and bourgeois counterparts, lamented the present state of the economy which pushed women into the labor force to supplement their husbands' insufficient wages. Such work should be temporary, she wrote, in anticipation of "the happy era when women will be returned to their biological role of creator and educator of the species."[44]

In one of her last articles, published in July 1898, Valette stated that society, as it was evolving, was preparing for a revolution and that if blood were to be shed, the bourgeoisie could thank themselves, for they were to blame for the disintegration of the working-class family.[45] Never wavering from the position that motherhood was the ultimate ideal toward which socialism would carry women, she was, in the words of Guesde, the "only woman who has understood socialism."[46]

French women generally agreed with French men that married women's work outside the home was potentially harmful by threatening the continuity of the family. As the basic unit of society, the family was a microcosm of the French nation. The woman was the pivotal member in the family, holding the structure together. Once she deserted the home to work in industry, the family (and ultimately the nation) would be in jeopardy. This fear increased after the Franco-Prussian war. As early as 1879, Hubertine Auclert had insisted on this central social role of women when she appealed for support of women's rights at the Workers' Congress in Marseille, warning that "the woman who is poorly nourished ... who weakens herself, loses along with her own health, the health of the generation."[47]

Karen Offen has argued that French republican feminists underscored "the centrality of their roles as mothers-of-citizens" in order to justify reforms in the position of women in the family and society.[48] While accepting many of the traditional values of their male counterparts, such as the veneration of motherhood, the feminists hoped to turn it to their advantage. Although they ardently championed the cause of equal rights for all women, it is clear from the writings of even the most enlightened and visionary of the late nineteenth-century French feminists, that women, once married and with child, had moved into a different category, where different standards applied to their new situation. Although women's rights activists challenged the centuries-old traditional attitudes about single women, they were largely in accord with their male opponents when the focus shifted to married women and mothers. Motherhood was seen as a sacred institution which no one dared challenge, even outspoken critics like Finet, Auclert, Mincke, and Michel. They, too, were products of a male-dominated society which for centuries had preached that motherhood was woman's highest and most natural vocation. This idea was firmly embedded within French society, of which Finet, Auclert, Mincke, Michel, and others were themselves a part.

The revitalization of home industry in the late nineteenth century was thus welcomed as the best means both of accommodating working-class mothers and, in the long run, serving the interests of the state. By the early twentieth century, however, it had become clear that homework was not living up to those expectations. Just as bourgeois social reformers had to rethink their position, so, too, did feminists have to analyze their position.

Among the outspoken opponents of home manufacture was the militant feminist Stephanie Bouvard, secretary-general of the *Chambre Syndicale des Ouvrières Fleuristes, Plumassières et Métiers Similaires* in Paris. Bouvard and her colleagues referred to the bourgeois feminists as "natural adversaries" who were under the influence of the Church. She called for the total suppression of homework as a means of liberating women:

> The work of the woman at home is an obstacle to her emancipation; instead of coming to our meetings, enriching and educating herself, the woman remains at home.... If we encourage woman's work in the home, we lose an important means of emancipation. I myself am witness to this, having once been obliged to do work at home. I tell you quite frankly, it bored me! [49]

Referring to home manufacture as the *bête noire* at the Women's Work Congress in 1907, she blamed women homeworkers directly for the depressed wages of factory workers: "Homework has disastrous consequences; we Parisians consider that the woman who remains at home should not work, and if she must work, let her do so in the factory or workshop."[50]

Bouvard's ideas more closely resemble the attitudes of her male co-workers than the majority of women represented at the 1907 congress. Male delegates to workers' congresses in the immediate years preceding World War I were again impassioned over the subject of competition as they had been in the 1860s and 1870s. This time, however, the focus had changed; women were still the culprits, but now the delegates blamed the homeworkers. By having been instrumental in removing women from the factory (wherein they would have been subject to the same governmental regulation), union members were indirectly responsible for the exploitation of the homeworkers. Their solution this time was to get women back into the factories and workshops as quickly as possible or at least put an end to the practice of homework.

The same argument was still being used, only this time the target had changed. At a meeting in 1914 of the *Syndicat des Travailleurs de l'Habillement*, section of dressmakers and tailors of women's clothing, one delegate, Mme. Despuech, expressed the familiar complaint that homework brought about the destruction of the family: "The woman … no longer has the time to look after the household or the children; the husband then looks for relief at the cabaret."[51] Whether she worked within or outside the home, the woman seemed to have failed in meeting her domestic responsibilities.

Debates surrounding the question of government regulation of home industry reflected a real polarization in French society which transcended all class lines and political affiliations. Bourgeois reformers were in both camps, some strongly advocating legislation, others defending the economic principle of *laissez-faire* which excluded government intervention. Male factory workers were generally hostile to the industry as a whole and pushed for its total suppression. Others proposed less radical solutions which stopped short of governmental regulation.

Women, too, were largely divided. Generally, bourgeois feminists sought limited solutions, like the LSA's "war on cheapness" to improve the material lot of the workers. They also supported moderate, prudent government legislation and the formation of Christian-sponsored women's unions. Working-class women took several stands on the issue. While militant feminists like Bouvard clung to the uncompromising position of total suppression, some of her colleagues adopted a more moderate position. The co-secretary of the *Chambre Syndicale des Ouvrières Fleuristes, Plumassières, et Métiers Similaires* and member of the *Conseil Supérieur du Travail*, Ms. Blondelu, disagreed with Bouvard:

> Personally, I don't condemn homework. Besides it is impossible to suppress it. There are many women who have good reasons to stay at home and who must however earn a living—due to reasons of age, health, of responsibilities to their children….[52]

Blondelu endorsed legislation which would ensure such a woman a just, daily minimum wage. While awaiting government action, Blondelu encouraged the extension of cooperatives for production and consumption like Duchêne's *Entr'Aide* and her own *L'Oeuvre des Artisans Parisiennes*.

Other working-class feminists pushed for unionization. For women like Louise Saumoneau, a dressmaker and co-founder of *Le Groupe Feministe Socialiste* (GFS) in Paris's Latin Quarter in 1899, the only viable means of improving the lot of the homeworkers was through association. By admitting homeworkers into the unions, the threat they posed to factory workers would be eliminated. Her group disagreed with Bouvard's extreme solution of total suppression, while at the same time opposing exceptional protective legislation which singled out women homeworkers. Such legislation would prove harmful to women, GFS co-founders Saumoneau and Elizabeth Renaud insisted, since it would perpetuate the false notion of female inferiority. They argued that to be truly effective, the law had to be applied universally.

The bourgeois government alone was not to blame for enacting legislation which handicapped women, the GFS contended; so were the socialist parties themselves. By supporting "protective" legislation that restricted women's work in the 1890s, socialists hoped to achieve a dual purpose: returning women to their homes (liberating them from the factory) and raising men's wages (liberating them from the role of co-breadwinner) so that French family life might once again be restored. While French feminist groups were calling for equal work, equal pay, and equal access to employment opportunities in the early 1900s, socialists were winning votes by supporting legislation which shielded women from some of the worst working conditions while at the same time restricting them from some of the best. One such example was the 1900 Colliard-Millerand law which basically prohibited night work for women, making them less competitive for jobs. This law directly affected women proofreaders working for Marguerite Durand's newspaper, La Fronde. Since such work frequently required overtime, this law closed another source of employment to women.[53]

Saumoneau and the GFS urged all women workers, including the isolated homeworkers, to band together and join the unions—the only means by which genuine reform could be attained, they contended. Interestingly enough, the GFS, like the bourgeois feminists, regretted the unfortunate situation created by the new industrial age in which mothers "are forced to abandon their children to go out and earn enough to feed their families."[54]

Even the homeworkers' position on legislation was guarded at best. Working-class women expressed their concern about homework by attending a Women's Work Congress held in Paris in March 1907, where the problems of home industry were discussed. Chaired by Marguerite Durand, editor and publisher of the short-lived newspaper, La Fronde, delegates included women workers (both factory and homeworkers) from all trades. The proposal for inspections of family workshops, a common practice in England and Germany, was discussed. Such inspections were intended to eliminate the excessively long hours of home-work. But the congress was hostile to the idea, viewing government inspection as a violation of privacy. Durand expressed the workers' opinion: "If we are to accept a law which obliges us to stop working at 6 PM, this will be a vexation for everyone."[55]

Many women resented any interference in their personal affairs. They were also generally hostile to the proposal of government inspection of family workshops. This paranoia of strangers "snooping around" in their personal affairs necessarily limited the power of law enforcement. Although no concrete solutions were proposed, the Congress did clarify most women workers' position on homework. Congress members were almost unanimous on the most expedient means of remedying the problem of homework: unionization and prudent government legislation rather than the total suppression of the industry, as called for by many of their male co-workers/union members. Furthermore, they feared that employers, forced to abide by wage guidelines, would boycott home industry entirely. Thus, homeworkers actively sought the retention of the industry and opposed any proposal that would place restrictions or limitations on their work. They called for a higher, more equitable, daily wage but not at the expense of the work itself. They asked that a minimum wage, if one were to be established, be fixed at as low a rate as possible so that manufacturers would continue to employ homeworkers.

The 1915 Homework Law

In 1909, Albert de Mun, a prominent Catholic social reformer, submitted a proposal for a law which would authorize the Office du Travail to set up an elected representative committee of employers and employees to establish a minimum hourly wage in all occupations which employed homeworkers. The next year the *Conseil Supérieur du Travail* set forth its own proposal, modifying the Mun proposal to concern itself exclusively with women homeworkers in the garment industry. A revised version of the proposed bill was submitted in 1911, debated and voted on in the Chamber of Deputies in 1913, further expanded and discussed before the Senate, and finally ratified on July 10, 1915.[56]

This law applied exclusively to women homeworkers in the garment industry, thereby ignoring the suggestion of the revolutionary feminists and the homeworkers' unions that any legislation should apply to both men and women and to all branches of home industry to avoid a potential source of competition.

The *Conseil Supérieur du Travail*'s definition of a minimum wage was adopted:

The wages payable to a woman employed as a homeworker ... shall not be less than the average wages payable by the hour or the day to an unskilled worker in the locality in question.[57]

By fixing the minimum wage by region, the possibility was left open for employers to contract work out to women in the provinces where it would be lower than in the urban centers, creating a problem for Parisian homeworkers.

Labor inspectors were still not allowed into the homes of the workers. This stipulation reflected the legislators' bending to pressure from the homeworkers' overwhelming hostility to any invasion of their privacy. Such limitations rendered the government inspectors virtually powerless. Thus, government reform was moderate, measured, and by and large ineffective.

Although Jeanne Bouvier, Gabrielle Duchêne, and other women activists served on the *Conseil Supérieur du Travail* which drafted this bill, they had little input in its formation. After decades of debates and detailed examination of countless proposals by diverse individuals and groups, the homework bill was little more than a watered-down version of a constructive reform measure. Bourgeois, feminist, and workers' groups all had different ideas on what would constitute acceptable legislation. Legislators found it difficult to reconcile these diverse proposals and accommodate all groups involved. Bending to pressure, the legislators passed a law which, after all the discussions, debates, and publicity, failed to make a visible difference in the material condition of the homeworkers. In fact, the law worked against them in the long run, because it specifically singled out women and homework in the garment industry.

Earlier "protective" legislation for women had proved to be a double-edged sword. Women labor activists saw the possibility of the 1915 legislation taking the same turn as its predecessors and unsuccessfully tried to alter its course. By its sheer ineffectiveness, the 1915 Homework Law did little to change the workers' situation.

The failure of legislation convinced women like Saumoneau, Duchêne, and Blondelu that the one avenue left for bringing some tangible improvement to the material condition of the homeworkers was unionization. Even Bouvard had to reconcile herself to the reality of the continued presence of homework in the garment industry. Constructive measures had to be taken to educate these women, helping them to develop a consciousness of themselves as workers having specific interests and goals. As Auclert had earlier advised, instead of fighting the homeworkers, unions should open up their ranks to them so that their interests would be identified with those of the union. As "orphans" of the industry, they were isolated workers with no one to look out for their material welfare. Legislation having failed, unions needed to push for their "adoption."

Conclusion

Motherhood was considered a sacred institution which was tied directly to the continued stability of the French family, the basic unit of society. If the sanctity of motherhood was defiled, there was little hope for the future of the French nation. Unable to challenge tradition on this point, female labor activists, joining male social reformers, sought to improve the economic position of married women homeworkers. Very few condemned the institution of homework itself. For most, it served a useful purpose—allowing working mothers to coordinate their domestic and economic responsibilities under the same roof. The myth that women worked largely for pin money persisted.

As long as French society (including women themselves) accepted the premise that "woman's proper place" was the home, homework would continue to be the only acceptable alternative for working-class mothers in search of an income. Homeworkers would remain left behind in the women's movement as "neglected sisters." Efforts were channeled into making homework an economically viable occupation, whereas the redefinition of women's roles which Breuil, Finet, Bouvard, and others had called for quietly faded into the background, not to resurface for another half-century.

Notes

1 Joan Wallach Scott and Louise Tilly, "Women's Work and the Family in Nineteenth-Century Europe," *Comparative Studies in Society and History* 17, no. 1 (1975): 41.

2 *Livret de Famille* (Nouvelle Modèle 1898, Copoix-Prisque, ed.).

3 Chambre du Commerce et de l'Industrie, *Enquête sur les conditions du travail en France, pendant l'année 1872—Département de la Seine* (Paris: Chambre du Commerce, 1875), 38–84.

4 In using Karen Offen's categories of relational feminists and individualist feminists (one insists on the distinct nature of the sexes and the idea of the complementary couple while the other, more radical group focuses on the demands for women's natural rights and autonomy) it still seems clear that on the question of the mother of the family, there was a consensus on the notion of "woman's proper place." For a discussion on relational vs. individualist feminists, see Karen Offen, "Liberty, Equality, and Justice for Women: The Theory and Practice of Feminism in Nineteenth Century Europe," in *Becoming Visible*, eds Bridenthal, Koonz, Stuard (Boston: Houghton Mifflin Company, 1987), 335–362.

5 Director of the *Office du Travail*, Arthur Fontaine's figures for 1925 cited in Charles Poisson, *La Salaire des femmes* (Paris: Librairie des Saints-Pères [1906–07]), 3.

6 For an excellent discussion of French republican fears of depopulation in the late nineteenth century, see Karen Offen, "Depopulation, Nationalism, and Feminism in Fin-de-Siècle France," *American Historical Review* 89 (June 1984): 648–676.

7 Anna Davin, "Imperialism and Motherhood," *History Workshop Journal* 5 (1978): 9–65. Davin, writing about the experience of English working-class women in the same context, argues that the ideology of motherhood transcended class. The fear of women from the middle and upper classes shirking their maternal responsibilities to pursue new and fulfilling careers translated to the working class in the concern that working-class mothers were largely ignorant of the duties of motherhood. Thus, one means to combat the rapidly declining birthrate was to elevate the status of motherhood. Davin explains that while a powerful ideology of motherhood emerges in the twentieth century as a response to these problems, "it was firmly rooted of course in nineteenth-century assumptions about women, domesticity and individualism."

8 *Ibid.*, 26.

9 *Séance du Congrès Ouvrier de France—Session de 1876* (Paris: Sandoz and Fischbacher, 1877), 74. The Congress, recognizing that woman's work was necessary for the financial upkeep of the household, reluctantly accepted the idea of women working, but only on the condition that they do so at home.

10 *Archives de la Préfecture de Police*. BA33, *Congrès Ouvrier à Paris, 1876* (séance du 3 octobre), "Le Travail des Femmes", 6–7.

11 Cited in Michelle Perrot, "L'Eloge de la ménagère dans le discours des ouvriers français au XIXème siècle," *Romantisme*, nos. 13–14, (1976): 111.

12 *4ème Congrès National Ouvrier de France, 5ème jour* in *Le Petit Havre*, November 19, 1880. See also discourse of Vallet of l'Union Syndicale de Paris, *Compte-Rendu*, November 21, 1880. Michelle Perrot's analysis of workers' reactions to women's work outside the home at the 1879 Congrès Ouvrier confirms this tendency among male workers, see *Romantisme*: 110–119.

13 Marilyn J. Boxer, "Protective Legislation and Home Industry: The Marginalization of Women Workers in Late Nineteenth—Early Twentieth-Century France," *Journal of Social History* 20 (Fall 1986): 45–65.

14 Madeleine Guilbert and Vivianne Isambert-Jamati, *Travail féminin et travail à domicile (Enquête sur le travail à domicile de la confection féminine dans la région parisienne)* (Paris: CNRS, 1956), 16.

15 *Ibid.*, 187. The *Bulletin de l'Office du Travail*, June 1901, p. 400, estimated that in 1896, there were 1,565,000 homeworkers. Georges Mény has revised the general statistics and arrived at the more plausible figure of 1,450,000.

   Within the category of clothing trades are found the following subdivisions: laundresses, hosiers, hat-makers, shoemakers, costumers, dressmakers and seamstresses, furriers, used clothes dealers, linen workers, milliners, and tailors. See Chambre du Commerce et de l'Industrie, *Enquête sur les conditions du travail en France, pendant l'année 1872—Département de la Seine*, 38–84.

16 Chambre du Commerce et de l'Industrie, *Rapport: Salaire de ouvrières à domicile dans l'industrie du vêtement*, Jean Morel, Sénator (III 5–14, dossier 1913).

17 Direction du Travail, *Résultats Statistiques du Recensement des Industries et Professions*, vol. 1, *Région du Paris* (Paris: Imprimerie Nationale, 1899), 207. See also Direction du Travail, *La Petite Industrie (Salaire et durée du travail)*, vol. 2 (Paris: Imprimerie Nationale, 1896), 573.

18 T. Deldycke, H. Gelders, and J.M. Limbor, *La Population active et sa structure* (1969), 185, cited in Scott and Tilly, 40.

19 Direction du Travail, *Enquête sur le travail à domicile dans l'industrie de la lingerie*, vol. 5, *Résultats Généraux* (Paris: Imprimerie Nationale, 1911), 33. For an analysis of government investigations of home industry, see Lorraine Coons, *"Orphans" of the Sweated Trades: Women Homeworkers in the Parisian Garment Industry (1860–1915)* (New York: Garland Publishing Co., 1987); and Judith Coffin, "Social Science Meets Sweated Labor: Reinterpreting Women's Work in Late Nineteenth-Century France," *Journal of Modern History* 63 (June 1991): 230–270.

20 *Ibid.*, vol. 1, *Paris*, 731–732.

21 For a discussion of 1892 and 1900 government legislation to "protect" women workers, see Marilyn J. Boxer, 45–65. Boxer sees this legislation as playing a central role in the marginalization of the female labor force and in contributing to make "the working-class family a facsimile of its bourgeois counterpart."

22 Cited in Dr. B. Roussy, *Education domestique de la femme et rénovation sociale* (Paris: Delagrave, 1914), 92.

23 Direction du Travail, *Enquête sur le travail à domicile dans l'industrie de la fleur artificielle*, vol. 1, *Paris* (Paris: Imprimerie Nationale, 1913), 140–142.

24 Käthe Schirmacher, "Le travail des femmes en France," in *Musée Social—Mémoires et Documents* (Paris: Arthur Rousseau, 1902), no. 6, 338.

25 Baronne Georges Brincard, "Le Travail à domicile pour les mères de famille", *Bulletin des Ligues Sociales d'Acheteurs*, 2ème trimestre (1905): 64.

26 *Bibliothèque Historique de la Ville de Paris*, Fonds Marie-Louise Bouglé, sous-fonds Jeanne Bouvier, Box 9, *Mes Mémoires* (manuscript original), 89.

27 *Ibid.*, Box 19.

28 *Ibid.*, *Travail à Domicile—Enquête sur le travail à domicile (1913–1914)*.

29 *Ibid.*, Box 17, *Correspondance*. (This is a draft of a letter. It is not clear whether the letter was ever sent).

30 The following observations were made in Bouvier's report, *Enquête 1913–1914 sur le tricotage et la bonneterie à Paris*, Box 9 (dossier vert)—BHVP.

31 Marcelle Richard, "Le Travail à domicile," *Bulletin des groupes féministes de l'enseignement laiquiée* 55 (April 1930): 26. The Association proposed: 1. that an official investigation of the hygiene, work hours, and earnings of workers engaged in home industry should be undertaken, 2. that employers should furnish the work inspectors with the names and addresses of the intermediaries and workers they employ, 3. that wage books should list fixed payments for different operations and the actual wage earned by the woman.

32 *Bibliothèque de Documentation Internationale et Contemporaine*, Fol. Res. 353, *Dossiers Duchêne*, "L'Entr'Aide, Paris (1908–1918)—textes divers."

33 Maxime Breuil, *Deux discours sur le travail des femmes* (Paris: Armand le Chevalier, 1868), 15. We know nothing of Breuil's activities other than these recorded speeches which I found at the Bibliothèque Marguerite Durand. She is one of the few women who could be classified as an individualist feminist following Karen Offen's analysis.

34 Excerpted from *Le Rappel*, February 1, 1878, and *Ordre*, February 5, 1878.

35 Auclert, an orphan, born in 1851, came to Paris at age 22 in search of work and in 1876 founded the society, Le Droit des Femmes. She represented this group along with a cooperative association, Les Travailleurs de Belleville, at two workers' congresses held in Marseille in 1879 and Le Havre in 1880. She is the subject of a study by Steven Hause, *Hubertine Auclert* (New Haven: Yale University Press, 1987).

36 *Séance du Congrès Ouvrier Socialist de France*, 3rd session, Marseille (Marseille: J. Doucet, 1879), 156.

37 *Bibliothèque Historique de la Ville de Paris*. Fonds Marie-Louise Bouglé, sous-fonds Hubertine Auclert, box 13.

38 *Le Féminisme*, March 22, 1908.

39 *Ibid.*

40 *Le Petit Havre*, November 19, 1880.

41 *Paule Mincke—communarde et féministe 1839–1901* (preface, notes, and commentary by Alain Dalotel) (Paris: Syros, 1981), 119, 125.

42 Schoolteacher turned anarchist by her personal involvement in the Paris Commune of 1871, Michel dreamed of a future society in which mothers of the working class would have their dignity restored. Michel had gained notoriety as a famous *petroleuse*, one of the women accused of setting fire to government buildings in Paris during the bloody suppression of the Commune in May 1871. Throughout the remainder of her life, Michel preached the coming of the social revolution.

43 As a good socialist, Valette subordinated her feminism to the party. The two proved incompatible in France, and in making a choice she identified herself more with the cause of socialism than women's rights. See Charles Sowerwine, *Sisters or Citizens: Women and Socialism in France since 1876* (Cambridge: Cambridge University Press, 1982).

44 Quoted in Charles Sowerwine, 61.

45 *La Fronde*, "Le Travail des femmes: évolution pacifique?", July 3, 1898, quoted in Sowerwine, 65.

46 Charles Verecque, in *La Femme Socialiste*, December 1932, quoted in Sowerwine, 63–64. Verecque was a young Guesdist who began to write on women's issues in 1893.

47 *Séance du Congès Ouvrier Socialist de France*, 156.

48 Karen Offen, "Depopulation, Nationalism, and Feminism in Fin-de-Siècle France": 673–676.

49 2ème Congrès International des Oeuvres et Institutions Féminins, *Compte Rendu des Travaux*, vol. 3 (Paris: Imprimerie Typographique Charles Blot, 1902), 486.

50 Congrès Féminin du Travail, session of March 23, 1907.

51 *Archives Nationales. F713740, Réunion Syndicale des Travailleurs de l'Habillement*, April 27, 1914.

52 *Archives Nationales, F713881, Ministère du Travail et de la Prévoyance Sociale—Circulaire* (Grève-Juillet, 1913, Ouvrières de l'Habillement à domicile à Rennes).

53 For a comprehensive discussion of government legislation concerning women workers and its implications, see Mary Lynn Stewart, *Women, Work, and the French State: Labour Protection and Social Patriarchy (1879–1919)* (Montreal: McGill-Queen's University Press, 1989) which includes the text of the labor laws of 1892 and 1900, 203–204.

54 Louise Saumoneau, *Principes et action féministes socialistes* (Publications in "La Femme Socialiste", n.d. [1919], 3–4.

55 Congrès Féminin du Travail, *Rapports—1907 Rapport Général*, session of March 26, 13. See Marilyn J. Boxer for an excellent discussion of the 1915 Homework Law, footnote #31: 63–65.

56 *Bibliothèque historique de la ville de Paris*, Fonds M. L. Bouglé, "Articles des Journaux—Thèmes (T)", 'France, Governmental Project. Draft of a bill ... Wages of women...'.

57 Conseil Supérieur du Travail. *Session de 1910—Salaire Minimum pour les ouvrières à domicile. Procès-verbaux des séances de la commission pérmanente/Documents* (Paris: Imprimerie Nationale, 1910).

PART FOUR

Twentieth Century

THE TWENTIETH CENTURY WAS TO SEE the continuation of many of women's concerns of the nineteenth century: motherhood, work, sexuality as Abrams demonstrates. At the same time it was also punctuated by issues traditionally seen as men's : war, revolution and citizenship. The demands for citizenship by late eighteenth-century reformers such as Wollstonecraft were gradually realised with the British suffrage movement providing an example for much of Europe.

Anderson and Zinsser discuss women's struggle to win the vote throughout Europe. This occurred at different times in different countries according to socio-political environment. Thus women in Catholic nations had a longer battle to achieve enfranchisement, while those in the Nordic countries fared much better. With the extension of the suffrage came a move for the establishment of welfare states. However there was an inherent problem in social policy: whether it should be gender neutral or based on the model of the male breadwinner and woman homemaker. Koven and Michel explore these tensions. Claudia Mitchell's study of Madeleine Pelletier illustrates the way in which this French feminist developed a theory of sexual difference. Darrow continues this with her account of the gender typification of war heroism and nursing.

War was not the only upheaval taking place in the first quarter of the twentieth century. The Russian Revolution of 1917 once again impacted on the debate about female and male roles in society and the economy. The roles of motherhood and of working women in Soviet Russia and the ways in which these were redefined to accommodate the needs of the state are discussed in articles by Waters and Koenker. Hagemann's article deals with workplace tensions which arose from different expectations of women's roles and Summerfield continues this theme.

The Second World War, while again relying heavily on female labour did not lead to a lasting emancipation of women. At the end of the war, women were still expected to resume their place in the domestic sphere. In the final article, Teo shows how the worst excesses of men's oppression of women continued in occupied Germany.

Chapter 20

LYNN ABRAMS

■   'MARTYRS OR MATRIARCHS? WORKING-CLASS
WOMEN'S EXPERIENCE OF MARRIAGE IN GERMANY
BEFORE THE FIRST WORLD WAR', *Women's History Review*,
1 (3), 1992, pp. 357–376

For a worker marriage almost always becomes a misery.
And for the woman worker? A Martyrdom.
(Alice Salomon, "Stumme Märtyrerinnen", 1909)

ABSTRACT The German family before 1914 has commonly been portrayed as patriarchal and authoritarian. Paternal authority was sustained by ideological conservatism, a discriminatory civil law code and an economic framework which treated husbands as breadwinners and wives as dependants. Such a model, it has been suggested, may have legitimised male violence within the home. It is easy to depict working-class women as martyrs at the hands of their violent husbands, yet domestic power relations were complex. Marital disputes occurred in a context of poverty and contested resources and male violence against women reflected conflict over resource allocation and shifting gender roles within marriage. The image of female dependency ignores women's ability to establish relative power within the household based on control of consumption. Escape from such situations was difficult for women owing to restrictive divorce laws and the precarious female employment market but female support networks provided temporary refuge and women's resilience allowed them to resist incursions into their territory. These women were not matriarchs but neither were they martyrs to a patriarchal, authoritarian model of marriage.

I

For the prominent social worker and feminist, Alice Salomon, marriage was nothing less than a tyranny for the working-class wife. "She lives like a prisoner, or like an old dog", she remarked, and for such a woman happiness means merely "that she does not receive any beatings and that she isn't deceived by her husband".[1] Salomon was in no doubt that the patriarchal authoritarian marriage was the predominant model amongst the working class and that women suffered at the hands of their husbands. In nineteenth-century Germany paternal authority within the family was sustained by ideological conservatism which alluded to the family as the fundamental basis of the moral, economic and political order. In practical terms this was supported by a civil law code which imprisoned women within the ideology of separate spheres and rigid gender roles and an economic framework which treated husbands as breadwinners and wives as dependants. Thus, men were able to maintain their patriarchal status within the family with reference to their legal rights and by claiming special privileges by virtue of their role as breadwinner. And, as a recent study of marriage relations in Britain has argued, "taken to the extreme this pattern of male authority and female responsibility could legitimize male violence within the home".[2]

The pre-First World War German family, then, has commonly been portrayed as the paradigm of the patriarchal-authoritarian model. Equality of the sexes, the proclaimed slogan of bourgeois emancipated society in the nineteenth century, was nothing more than an illusion. Despite evidence of emancipatory and democratic trends in German society – notably the existence of an exceptionally strong labour movement and feminist movement before the First World War – there is sparse evidence to suggest that at the level of the most fundamental social and economic unit – the family – patriarchal-authoritarian power structures had even been threatened let alone overturned by 1914.[3] Indeed, one is left with the overriding impression that the second half of the nineteenth century saw "an extraordinary increase in the paternalistic power sphere whereby the wife and mother had never before had such an oppressed and dependent position within the family".[4]

The search for evidence of women's emancipation from this oppression has traditionally been focussed upon politics and the economy: the public sphere treated as separate from the private. Power or emancipation continues to be predicated upon production. Research on women's changing role in the economy has, hitherto, attempted to equate women's power and emancipation with participation in the active, external economy. The fact that the majority of married women were engaged in unskilled, poorly paid, domestic out-work coupled with some evidence of women's active (and equal?) contribution to the household economy in the eighteenth century, simply reinforces this view.[5] Producers and not consumers, it is argued, brought resources to families. Thus, we are left with the fairly convincing argument that increased dependency on male wages led to a decline in women's status and a loss of power within the household in industrial society.[6] Women were in no position to challenge the patriarchal-authoritarian model upon which power relationships within the family were based.

In this paper I suggest that the debate be broadened to encompass areas of women's lives in which at least their potential for power was located. Instead of equating emancipation with economic and political change we might focus on the household, the family and the neighbourhood and women's efforts to maintain power in traditional areas, to resist incursions into their spheres of influence and to resolve abuses of power by re-establishing the boundaries of that power. By using gender as a category of analysis we can reconstruct the dynamics of working-class society along alternative lines, emphasising the powers of consumption as much as those of production; focussing on the strategies women articulated in the "private" sphere as much as acknowledged "feminist" actions in the public sphere.[7] This approach has already been successfully employed by historians of women and working-class communities in England. Ellen Ross and Nancy Tomes have graphically and movingly demonstrated that although working-class women were trapped within the economic stringencies of the precarious household economy and the strict definition of gender roles within marriage, they established a degree of power within the family by resisting incursions into their sphere and asserting their authority to maintain and reinforce their role.[8] Most never became matriarchs but they certainly were not martyrs. While it is incontrovertible that the position of working-class women in Germany before the First World War was determined by their legally defined role within marriage, their marginalisation in the labour market and their struggle for survival within a culture of poverty, it would be a mistake to view these women as universally oppressed, resigned, unwilling or unable to escape the cycle of poverty and oppression. Women contested the balance of power within marriage and challenged the power of husbands, gaining them respect and status within the community. The illusion of matriarchy was better than the reality of slavery.

II

Conservative family ideology in Germany was underpinned by the ideas of philosophers such as J. G. Fichte and W. H. Riehl who argued that marriage was a relationship determined by nature and reason incorporating the natural (i.e. different) roles of the man and woman.[9] This notion of the polarisation of the sexes was widely disseminated in Germany ascribing notionally equal yet different roles to men and women on the basis of nature or God-given destiny.[10] Clearly, this value-system served to reinforce patriarchal authority not just in the purely ideological sense but in practical terms too. The Prussian law code or *Allgemeines Landrecht* (ALR) of 1794, and particularly the unified German code, the *Bürgerliches Gesetzbuch* (BGB) of 1900, acknowledged and upheld the man's authority within the family. "The man is the head of the household; and his decision is final in household matters" stated the ALR.[11] Thus, a married woman was not permitted to take a job or sign a contract without her husband's permission, any money she earned was legally the property of her husband and any decisions with regard to the care and education of the children rested with him. Moreover, in the realm of sexual morality, the French *Code civil* which remained in force in the Rhineland – including the Düsseldorf district – until 1900, reinforced the double standard, subordinating women to a strict code of sexual conduct.[12] Women were not merely imprisoned by the ideology of separate gender roles but were legally defined and treated as second-class citizens.[13] "Marriage as a legal institution represented for women a legal prison in which access to full majority and unlimited legal autonomy in almost all areas of political, social and commercial life was barred", writes Blasius, and from which, it should be added, escape was extremely difficult.[14]

Inequality of the sexes within marriage was paralleled by even greater inequalities without. Whereas in theory divorce should have provided an escape route, divorce law discriminated against women. Although the divorce clauses of the ALR were not especially *frauenfreundlich* (woman-friendly) it was at least possible for women to make a case on the grounds of wilful desertion and until 1900 and the tightening up of divorce law, a couple could divorce by mutual consent (*beiderseitiger Einwilligung*). However, following the implementation of the BGB throughout Germany, divorce law was used to bolster the notion of the indissoluble marriage. It was hoped that couples would think twice; "If the spouses know that the marriage cannot be easily dissolved ... the couple will reconcile themselves to one another".[15] Henceforward divorce was based on the *Schuldprinzip* or guilt principle. While certain specific reasons constituted clear grounds for termination of the marriage contract – adultery, unnatural intercourse, attempted murder, mental illness and wilful desertion – other so-called "relative" reasons were open to interpretation in the courts, including mistreatment or failure to fulfil marital duties as laid down in the marriage contract. Since the vast majority of divorce petitioners were women and their claims were based upon these "relative" reasons, women's access to divorce was somewhat curtailed.[16]

Married women, then, found their role within marriage circumscribed by the prevailing ideology of the family which was supported in practice by the civil law code. A women's position within the household was now primarily defined by her status as wife and mother. Access to power and status derived from the productive economy was effectively sealed off. Ute Gerhard cites the 1850s as the watershed in this respect when, following a period of labour surplus, women were excluded from economic life and bound to their dependent familial role.[17] A man's new status as sole breadwinner gave him power within the household; the majority of married women with children who were unable to take outside employment found their power limited to within four walls. Under the BGB a woman was entitled to take employment without requiring the permission of her husband and her earnings were legally her own. However, in the heavy industrial towns of the Ruhr and Rhineland, the powerhouse of German industrialisation in the second half of the nineteenth century, opportunities for outside employment for married women were limited. In Düsseldorf and the surrounding district, the focus of this study, in spite of its rather more mixed economy, metal was king and jobs for women were to be found in traditional areas of female employment such as textiles, the clothing and cleaning trades and, of course, domestic service and agriculture in the still predominantly rural outlying district. Of the just over 20,000 females registered as employed in Düsseldorf town in 1895 (excluding live-in family helpers which included wives of farmers in the outlying rural areas), around half were engaged in these sectors and the vast majority of those, 85%, were single women.[18] By 1907 the number of employed females had risen to just over 27,000 but still only 3246 married women (11.8% of all working women) were registered as working.[19] Indeed, more than 300 factories in the city refused to employ married women.[20] Still, compared with neighbouring coal and steel towns a comparatively high proportion of Düsseldorf women were employed. The vast majority of married women, then, were denied an independent economic role in the formal sense although, as the tensions and conflicts between spouses makes clear, women assumed a greater economic role than was formally recognised and admitted, especially by their husbands.

In the rest of this article I want to examine the factors that determined and reinforced the balance of power within German working-class marriages before the First World War. I shall suggest that despite the limitations on women's power within the household women learned to adjust their expectations of marriage and preserve their limited power within artificially constructed boundaries. Indeed, I shall argue that it was the very limitation of women's scope for independent power that explains their tenacity in guarding their territory. Few married working-class women really opposed the cultural values within which they lived and worked but at certain times in their lives they resisted incursions into their social, economic and physical space by their husbands. Violence within marriage was not always a one-way process, inflicted by the man on the woman. Physical violence and verbal abuse served to dissipate tensions and re-establish spheres of responsibility while representing a contest for control within marriage. These women were not sacrificial martyrs to the patriarchal-authoritarian prerogative yet neither were they matriarchs, either within their own homes or communities.

III

"Love could not fill empty stomachs".[21] An observer of factory workers in 1911 noted. "For he who has to attend to his work the whole day, a clever wife to run the household is particularly necessary …".[22] The bourgeois, notion of equality within marriage based upon mutual dependence and complementary roles, was translated into Prussian civil law before 1900 thus: "He the husband is bound to guarantee his wife support in accordance with rank". (sect 185), and "The wife is responsible for the maintenance of the man's household according to his status and rank" (sect 194).[23] Yet these words found little resonance within working-class households. For although many working-class wives were obliged and did their best to fulfil their part of the bargain they were unable to force their husbands to reciprocate. Such an ideal marriage relied upon trust and openness and required sufficient financial support yet many working-class marriages were founded upon deceit, inequality and poverty. The pressures on working-class marriages were immense. Distress, illness, poverty, imprudence, infirmity, accidents, not to mention drink, violence, unemployment and death placed great financial and emotional strains upon couples leading to confrontations over money and household duties – the prime bargaining issues – sometimes resulting in violent incidents.

Money and alcohol featured prominently in marital disputes and contests for control within marriage. German men were unwilling to disclose their earnings to their wives. A bricklayer who was seen working on a building site by his doctor is reported to have hurried over to say "Don't tell my wife that I have got work, otherwise she'll not give me any money and she'll have it all".[24] At least his wife was given some housekeeping, unlike the invalid wife of a Düsseldorf man who, on applying for help from the city poor fund in 1914, explained that although her husband earned 4 Marks a day and had savings of 76 Marks "he does not care for his family but he cooks solely for himself and says he is not obliged to care for his wife and children".[25] Problems were also caused by workers spending their wages on drink before they got home. "After the men had got their wages they were often drunk, and their wives sat at home without any money", reported a miner's wife from a village near Duisburg. "Many ran straight to the pit and caught hold of their husbands so they didn't end up in the pub".[26] Alternatively the wives worked in concert with employers. It was the practice at the Düsseldorf glassworks to pay the housekeeping allowance direct to the wives who then provided their husbands with pocket-money. "This control, which is a thorn in the side of the schnapps-sellers, will prevent these people giving credit. Often the woman has had the housekeeping money torn out of her hands in order for the growing schnapps debt to be paid".[27] Indeed, the purchase of alcohol on credit was a common practice amongst working men. Needless to say, the accumulation of debt could ruin a family. The son of one such addict reported in 1850 that when "the father is drunk he sells not only the indispensable things in the house but even the shirt from his back to quench his momentary thirst for the poisonous spirit".[28] Johann D. turned to drink shortly after his marriage. He neglected his business, spent all day in local taverns and sold his house, his land and eventually all the furniture to the value of around 3000 Thalers to finance his addiction.[29] "Alcohol was a real problem", wrote a woman in her memoirs; "Most men didn't earn enough to get drunk and still have enough to pay the rent and feed their family".[30] Men derived their position of power within the family from their position in the labour market. Women were only able to curb flagrant abuses of this power. Rarely were they in the position to benefit positively from improvements in their husbands' industrial working conditions. They were always on the defensive, fighting a rearguard action to, at best, alleviate the deprivation of their everyday life.

IV

Against this context of married women's ideological and legal discrimination and economic oppression, an analysis of marital conflict, separations and divorce may suggest some ways in which women negotiated the boundaries of their lives. Intervention by the police and local authorities in the lives of the working classes in German towns and cities in this period was not uncommon and recourse to the authorities was becoming increasingly common in instances of domestic strife, producing a wealth of material which the historian may access: here I have used primarily Düsseldorf police reports on instances of marital conflict, desertion, domestic violence, and violations of the criminal law, as well as divorce case files from Düsseldorf and the neighbouring rural district of Cleve. Careful reading of the stories constructed by individuals and corroborated statements by witnesses suggests the patriarchal-authoritarian family model would appear to have been thriving in lower-class communities before the war in Germany.

The vast majority of cases that were brought to the attention of the authorities allegedly involved mistreatment and serious violence by the husband against the wife and children, frequently accompanied by excessive alcohol consumption. Men appear to have taken advantage of their economic primacy and abused women's position within the household by using threatening and often violent behaviour. Indeed, before 1900 wife-beating was not a criminal offence; the Prussian law permitted "moderate bodily chastisement".[31] In these circumstances women can easily be interpreted as sacrificial martyrs or passive victims of unprovoked violence. For instance, in November 1833 Anna B. described how her husband had repeatedly beaten her during their nine-year marriage, citing a number of specific cases. For example, during the previous autumn Matthias "mistreated his wife without any reason, dragged her by the hair, hit and wounded her on the forehead so deplorably with a pipe-bowl ...", and on 9 August he jumped out of bed, picked up a sabre which was standing in the bedroom and threatened to hit his wife with it and luckily only wounded her on her arm.[32] The case of Johanna L., wife of baker Johann, is perhaps extreme but not untypical of the position of women within unhappy marriages:

> As early as 4 to 6 weeks after the marriage L. accused his wife of having had forbidden relations with another man before the marriage; he insulted her: whore, liar, beast etc, hit and shoved her with his fists ... and tore the clothes from her body – these insults and cruelty were repeated all day until late in the evening and the night. Besides he smashed and demolished the furniture in the house, ripped up his wife's clothes, threw her out of bed and threw the bedding into the lobby and threatened to throw her out of the house.[33]

Johanna was awarded a divorce in view of the severity of the abuse she had suffered at the hands of her husband. But hers was by no means an isolated case. The wife of a Düsseldorf milkman, Wilhelm S., endured 18 years of marriage during which her husband mistreated her almost every day so that she often had to seek medical help. "When he came home at night I often had my death before my eyes". He only provided her with 2 Marks a day to feed their six children and on occasions beat them too. The family lived in one room furnished with one bed and two chairs. Because they did not possess a cooker they lived mainly on bread.[34] This family was clearly living in great poverty as a consequence of the failure of Wilhelm to fulfil his financial obligations, although there is no suggestion here of alcohol abuse. However, drink and violence were inextricably linked in many cases brought before the authorities. Frau Anton H., also of Düsseldorf but living in nearby Duisburg, was a victim of this dangerous combination. "I was forced to leave my husband because he has not worked for two years and is addicted to drink so that when I am at home my life is no longer safe, at night he threw a burning petrol lamp and threatened me in bed with an open razor knife …".[35] And in 1900 Charlotte R., aged 24, told the Düsseldorf police: "I left the house with my 4-year-old child as it is impossible to live together with my husband any more. He is an alcoholic and cares only for himself, he always comes home drunk in the evening. As a result I found it necessary to go out washing and cleaning so that I can live with my child. I have repeatedly been mistreated by my husband and abused in the most common ways so that finally I have left him …".[36]

Domestic conflict was not entirely arbitrary; that is, fights and violence often occurred in circumstances in which one or other partner could be accused of not fulfilling their assigned role within marriage or where the authority of one partner was questioned or threatened. The historian David Sabean has recently categorised two forms of domestic violence: systematic chastisement and reactive striking out. Both served to reinforce or maintain the household hierarchy, yet here in the Rhineland, as in Sabean's village in Württemberg, reactive violence as a symbolic demonstration of patriarchy appears to have become more common in comparison with the more systematic use of physical power.[37] Violence frequently centred on the allocation of resources within the household and the balance of power therein. For instance, failure of the husband to provide financially for his wife and children, often owing to alcohol addiction or profligate expenditure on drink, was a trigger for taunts and arguments; failure of the wife to carry out her household duties to the approval of the husband could similarly be used as a pretext for violence. Might not these domestic tensions reflect a shifting balance of power between the spouses as women in particular exerted their control within the household, economically and socially? The fact that women were consistently more willing than their husbands to break up a marriage, in rural and urban areas, suggests this may have been the case.

Historians writing about working-class married women in nineteenth-century England have vividly portrayed strong, resilient women who challenged male supremacy within the household.[38] A woman needed to be assertive; her tenacity in preserving her locus of power was essential if the family was to survive. Undoubtedly German women exhibited similar survival strategies to their British cousins in making ends meet. They supplemented household income by engaging in home-work, by taking in lodgers and finding outside employment. A survey carried out at the turn of the century calculated that male income as a proportion of total household income varied between 50% and 90% with the rest being made up by women and, to some extent, children.[39] Married women engaged in a considerable amount of "invisible" employment illustrated by the fact that the Reich employment statistics list the vast majority of married women as "family helpers". It is no exaggeration to say that "Within the family mothers and not fathers were the central authorities who guaranteed the internal support and continuity in the general fluctuation of the urban-industrial world".[40]

Day-to-day control of the household finances – meagre as they were – and care of the children must have been scant recompense for the material deprivations endured by lower class women and a rude awakening to those who had expected an escape from the slavery of paid, full-time employment which in any case provided many single women with a camaraderie and independence they were never to experience during their married lives.[41] Moreover, oral evidence and material gathered from police and court reports suggests self-preservation prompted women to perpetuate the illusion that the man was the head of the household. "Harmony within the working-class family was all too frequently achieved at the cost of the woman", writes Karen Hagemann. "If the woman is the stronger person in a normal family, stronger in spirit, character and ability, and if her weaker husband recognises this ... the woman remains at the level of a second-class citizen", noted an early observer of women's position in the family.[42] As long as men remained in full-time employment their patriarchal prerogative was rarely challenged since it was justified by the wage packet they brought home. But a man who became unemployed lost the justification for his power and consequently might resort to reinforcing his power by other means, possibly psychological and physical violence. Certainly if a man lost his job he simultaneously lost his self-respect and the ability to provide for his wife and family according to the terms of the marriage contract. Of course not all unemployed men turned to drink but it was said that during bad times, "the pubs are full, where the unemployed deaden the cold and hunger with spirits and try to forget their misery".[43] The reversal of roles was threatening and destabilising and men sought to re-establish the balance of power by resort to an overt display of male privilege.[44]

In these circumstances men appear to have exerted their moral and physical authority in areas in which they may have felt threatened by their wives' power, that is with regard to the running of the household and the rearing of children. We should not be surprised, then, that mealtimes often precipitated violent incidents between spouses. Mealtimes were not only economically exposing occasions, the meal table was also a focus for the reciprocal duties of husband and wife. On 2 January 1841 Catherina H. was busy in the kitchen preparing a meal for some guests. Her husband flew into a rage and started to be abusive. He then took a stick of sausages which was hanging above the oven and started to throw them piece by piece at her feet so that sausages flew all over the kitchen.[45] He was not always so restrained. Some months later he jumped up from the table after the midday meal and hit his wife on the head with his clenched fist so that she fell to the floor unconscious and was left with a swelling and a terrible headache for eight days afterwards.[46] In another divorce case Theodore J. related how her husband Gerhard had thrown the food she had prepared into her face and then forced her to prepare a meal in the middle of the night and take it to him in bed.[47] One of the witnesses to the case, a local pastor, described how when he called at the house that evening he found food lying all over the room and Theodore complaining that when she had prepared roast meat sausage and other things her husband had flung the leftovers around the room.[48] It is not surprising perhaps, that conflicts often arose at mealtimes when the household finances were subject to implicit scrutiny. When Eduard L. returned home to his wife and children and sat down at the kitchen table to find there was no alcohol for him to drink, she responded to his complaints by throwing an empty pan at him. He reacted, according to his statement to the police, by saying he would no longer pay for milk and rolls when he did not have the right to drink, whereby his wife became abusive and he grabbed the teapot out of her hands and threw it to the floor. This argument escalated into a full-scale fight between the couple.[49] Various household implements were to be found in the kitchen which were invariably hurled towards the other partner, thrown to the floor, or brandished as a threat. Wilhelm S. threw a water container at his wife, hitting her head; Johann G. hurled a similar implement at his wife causing severe injuries; Gerhard J. used to chase his wife around the table threatening her with a knife.[50]

The case of Elisabeth and Rüttgerus H., which reached the divorce court clearly demonstrates the way in which marital conflict was firmly located within the household economy. Their two-year marriage had never been harmonious and Rüttgerus had, on occasions, physically and verbally abused his wife. The situation became intolerable, however, when Rüttgerus "took away the running of the household from his wife and transferred it to the daughter of his first marriage since when he had ceased to say a friendly word to his wife … banished her from his table and forced her to eat alone in her room" and then deprived her of all food and drink so that she had to beg for food from friends and neighbours. Elisabeth subsequently filed for divorce on the grounds that her husband was failing to fulfil his duties according to the terms of the marriage contract in that he was guilty of not providing the necessities of life.[51]

The running of the household was traditionally the woman's sphere and thus we should not be surprised that husbands aiming to assert their authority attempted to weaken women's authority in this area.[52] Carl G. subordinated his wife to his mistress, forcing her to ask the mistress for the key to the cupboard when she wanted to eat.[53] When the widow O. married Wilhelm S. in 1849 she could not have been prepared for her husband's behaviour as it was described in the divorce papers some two years later:

> The marriage was only 14 days old when S. began to be coarse, to insult his wife and treat her in the most offensive way; he spoke of her contemptuously; he called her dumpling (Knödel), bore (Stockfisch) and so on, withdrew from all domestic life, inhabited his particular bar, at the most spoke a couple of words with his wife about food and drink; treated her like a servant …[54]

Husbands also banished their wives from their bedrooms: Engelbert H. ordered Catherina to move out of the common bedroom taking her belongings with her saying she could "go and lie where she liked" adding she would never again be allowed to sleep with him.[55] When Margarethe B. returned home having fled her husband's violence she found him in the marriage bed with his brother. She was regularly thrown out of the house and it is reported that on one occasion she spent three nights sleeping in the fields until the local pastor intervened.[56]

Pregnancy also acted as a trigger for violence suggesting men may have resented the arrival of another mouth to feed but it also highlighted men's sensitivity regarding the solidarity amongst women and children.[57] Theresa E. filed for divorce against her husband on the grounds that he had beaten her while she was pregnant placing the unborn child at risk, and furthermore he had beaten her while she was breastfeeding her child.[58] Similarly the husband of Justine G. beat her while she was pregnant making it necessary for her to flee to her parents.[59] And Elisabeth S. had been thrown down the stairs by her violent husband when she was heavily pregnant.[60]

V

The level and duration of violence tolerated by these women appears to have been quite high and those women who took their cases to the divorce courts had often endured violent relationships for many years. Wilhelmina W. finally divorced her husband Wilhelm after 30 years of marriage and six children.[61] Elisabeth S. married her husband in 1836, filed unsuccessfully for a divorce after years of mistreatment in 1846, and finally escaped in 1860;[62] and Carolina B. endured 24 years of "serious injuries and mistreatment" which had been repeatedly dismissed by the local police as "domestic conflict".[63] Clearly the options for women in this position were limited. Women were more likely to verbally abuse or scold their husbands. It was alleged that Frederika G. had a quarrelsome nature and that she frequently crudely insulted her husband and "called him by the most scandalous swearwords, a bad sort, swine, scoundrel and so on".[64] Some women fought back with physical violence. The wife of Eduard L., in response to his taunts, threw a lid in his face and wounded him on the cheek. "Then she took my walking stick from the wardrobe stand and hit the handle so hard against the floor that it flew into two pieces … my wife tried to hit me with the stick. When I had the stick in my hands she forcibly grasped my clothing and tried to rip my suit from my body".[65] But few women appear to have reacted in this way. More often they fled the house, took refuge with neighbours or friends or deserted their husbands either temporarily or for good. Female support networks were crucial in these circumstances. Mothers, sisters and other female relatives were the most likely port in a storm if they lived locally but female neighbours could usually be relied upon to come to the aid of a battered or neglected woman.[66] When Theodore Th.'s husband injured his wife and his 11-month-old child who she was holding at the time she called the neighbours for help.[67] And when Valentin Z. began to beat his wife on the back and repeatedly hit her in the face with his fist, throwing her to the floor, she eventually succeeded in "escaping his murderous hands by fleeing to a neighbour's house".[68] Male neighbours and relatives appear to have kept their distance from these disputes although local officials and churchmen intervened in an official or mediatory capacity. It was not until the end of the century that women in the main cities were provided with a more formal female support system. Under the auspices of the *Bund Deutscher Frauenvereine* (BDF) a number of legal advice centres were established to provide women with free advice concerning the problems they faced in their everyday lives, including marital problems.[69]

A woman might choose to leave her husband and maybe sue for a legal separation (separation from bed and board) or divorce. There were legal obstacles to women wishing to sue for divorce and the future for a divorced woman with children was bleak. Few women were prepared to abandon their children and some who did found themselves being sought by the police at the request of their husbands. Josef P., in fear of losing his job after his wife left him with four children to care for asked the Düsseldorf police to compel her to return.[70] A divorce law which aimed to make people try harder to make their marriages work almost certainly had little impact on the working-class and more likely had an adverse effect. The numerous cases of marital conflict dealt with by Düsseldorf officials, many of which never reached the divorce court, and the nature of the divorce cases processed show that many working-class marriages were unhappy, some were violent, and the divorce laws merely exacerbated an already tense and sometimes dangerous situation. Before 1900 Blasius points out that "legal decisions, in fact, often resulted in relief from the social, psychological or physical constraints of a disturbed family life",[71] whereas after 1900 the still fairly low divorce rate suggests many working-class couples were denied such relief.[72] Consequently informal separation was common, yet divorced or separated women remained marginal in an industrial labour market which valued male labour and maintained its adherence to the patriarchal family model.

Once a woman had gained her freedom, however, and unless she had been able to extract a fair maintenance payment from her former husband, her financial problems were likely to be severe. A woman was only legally entitled to maintenance if judged to be the innocent partner in a divorce case and even then if the former husband remarried or was in receipt of insufficient earnings he was not obliged to pay. Women who simply deserted their husbands had no grounds for financial redress yet many women took this road perhaps in the knowledge they would be unlikely to win a divorce case in the court. The wife of Wilhelm S. resorted to requesting official help in coercing her estranged husband, who was living intermittently with a widow, to increase his payments to support her and their three children. Owing to her poor eyesight she was afraid of having to rely on poor relief if the police could not persuade her husband to pay at least 10 Marks per week maintenance rather than the 3 to 4 Marks he was currently paying.[73] Women were resourceful in these circumstances; after all, they had been used to "making ends meet". Some certainly managed to live an independent existence like Elisabeth H. who left her husband of nine years in 1909, taking her three young children with her. It was reported that the children were well cared for, and she managed to pay the 28 Marks monthly rent for her three-room apartment with an income of 18 Marks from her husband, by renting out a spare room, and taking in washing.[74] But many women in the industrial towns lacked the support networks of family and neighbours and for them often the only way to survive was remarriage (impossible for many who were unable to get a divorce) or cohabitation with another man. Taken together, the remarriage rate and the number of cohabiting couples suggests women in this period were not rejecting marriage and the family as an institution *per se*. The marriage rate remained more or less stable at around 8 marriages per 1000 population between 1865 and 1914.[75] The plight of the single mother was highlighted by the case of Hermann I., prosecuted by the Düsseldorf police for illegally cohabiting with a widow. In his defence he stated that it was extremely difficult to find accommodation at a reasonable price and he was doing his best to support the widow and her six children.[76] For a single woman, either legally divorced, informally separated or even widowed, the speedy formation of a new marital relationship was often the only form of re-insurance for the future.

VI

German working-class women were imprisoned within a straitjacket consisting of a conservative family ideology, a discriminatory civil law code and a labour market that marginalised their economic contribution. Upon marriage men and women entered into a contract that relied on the notion of mutual dependency for its success. There is little evidence to suggest the working-class marriage was challenging or departing from this model before 1914. And yet the catalogue of incidents related above suggests this ideal of mutuality and harmony based upon divided responsibility was a field of contest owing to the fact that the ideal was shot through with contradictions. The male prerogative as head of the household was based upon the husband's ability and willingness to provide for the material needs of the family. Many men were either unable or unwilling to fulfil their side of the bargain. The female role of dependency belies women's staking out of a position of relative power within the household based upon the control of consumption. When violence erupted it was often in situations where the fragile balance of power was perceived to be threatened. The threat and reality of physical and verbal violence backed up the sexual division of labour within the household;

it reinforced a weakened male prerogative and returned a woman to her rightful place. It would, therefore, be misleading to portray these women as universally oppressed, resigned and passive martyrs. Rather they were resilient and adaptable. Women's scope for independent power was limited and yet it was precisely this restricted field of play that determined women's tenacity in guarding their territory. They only resorted to the law when men's abuse of power became untenable.

Women's power within the household was, on the whole, illusory. It could always be challenged by husbands both formally in the courts or informally behind closed doors. Yet a married woman possessed a certain amount of status and respect and access to female support networks from which single and particularly divorced and separated women were largely excluded. A married woman's position within the household was almost certainly more secure and invested with more power than her position in the patriarchal, authoritarian labour market. Perhaps then, it is not surprising that women's toleration levels appear to have been so high and separation or divorce were so frequently followed by cohabitation or remarriage. Matriarchs they were not but German working-class women before World War I preferred the illusion of matriarchy to the reality of martyrdom.

Acknowledgement

The research on which this paper is based has been supported by a grant from the Deutsche Akademische Austauschdienst, to whom I am very grateful. Thanks are due to the participants at the Women's History Conference held at Lancaster University in March 1991 where this paper was originally presented, and to the editors of this collection, Penny Summerfield and Penny Tinkler, for their helpful suggestions.

Notes

1 A. Salomon (1909), Stumme Märtyrerinnen, *Die Frau*, 16, p. 272.

2 P. Ayers and J. Lambertz (1986) Marriage relations, money, and domestic violence in working-class Liverpool, 1919–39, in J. Lewis (Ed.) *Labour and Love: Women's Experience of Home and Family, 1850–1940*, p. 197 (Oxford). For a more general application of the argument that the basis of wife-beating is social, economic, political and psychological power rather than pathological aggression see L. Gordon (1988) *Heroes of Their Own Lives: The Politics and History of Family Violence* (London).

3 This conclusion is also reached by Karen Hagemann (1988) "Der Sozialismus fängt im Hause an". Familienalltag im sozialdemokratische Milieu, 1900–1933, unpublished paper, Anglo-German Conference on Working-Class Culture, Lancaster University 1988, an argument pursued further in K. Hagemann (1900) *Frauenalltag und Männerpolitik: Alltagsleben und gesellschaftliches Handeln von Arbeiterfrauen in der Weimarer Republik* (Bonn).

4 Weber-Kellermann, cited in U. Gerhard (1978) *Verhältnisse und Verhinderungen. Frauenarbeit, Familie und Rechte de Frauen im 19. Jahrhundert*, p. 149 (Frankfurt am Main).

5 See B. Franzoi (1985) *At the Very Least She Pays the Rent: Women and German Industrialization, 1871–1914* (London); R. Dasey (1981) Women's work and the family: women garment workers in Berlin and Hamburg before the First World War, in R. J. Evans and W. R. Lee (Eds) *The German Family*, pp. 221–255 (London); and, on the role of women in the proto-industrial economy see H. Medick (1976) The proto-industrial family economy: the structural function

of household and family during the transition from peasant society to 1983 industrial capitalism, *Social History*, 3, pp. 291–316.

6 P. Stearns (1972) Working-class women in Britain, 1890–1914, in M. Vicinus (Ed.) *Suffer and Be Still: Women in the Victorian Age*, pp. 100–120 (Bloomington); L. Oren (1974) The welfare of women in laboring families: England, 1860–1950, in M. S. Hartman & L. Banner (Eds) *Clio's Consciousness Raised: New Perspectives on the History of Women*, pp. 226–244 (London); J. Scott and L. Tilly (1975) Women's work and the family in nineteenth century Europe, *Comparative Studies in Society and History*, 17, pp. 36–64.

7 For a plea for this approach to be applied to the history of women in Germany see Jean Quataert's review of R. J. Evans (1991) *Comrades and Sisters, European History Quarterly*, 28, pp. 138–139.

8 E. Ross (1982) Fierce questions and taunts: married life in working-class London, 1870–1914, *Feminist Studies*, 8, pp. 575–602; N. Tomes (1978) A Torrent of abuse: crimes of violence between working-class men and women in London, 1840–1875, *Journal of Social History*, 11, pp. 328–345. See also C. Chinn (1988). *They Worked All Their Lives: Women of the Urban Poor in England, 1880–1939* (Manchester).

9 W. H. Riehl (1855) *Die Familie* (Stuttgart). For a wide-ranging discussion of European family ideology see M. Mitterauer & R. Sieder (Eds) (1982) *The European Family: Patriarchy to Partnership from the Middle Ages to the Present* (Oxford). Also K. Hausen (1981) Family and role-division: the polarisation of sexual stereotypes in the nineteenth century – an aspect of the dissociation of work and family life, in R. J. Evans and W. R. Lee (Eds) *The German Family*, pp. 51–83 (London).

10 Hausen, *Family and Role Division*, pp. 57–58.

11 W. Hubbard (1983) *Familiengeschichte. Materialen zur deutschen Familie seit dem Ende des 18. Jahrhunderts*, p. 50 (Munich).

12 See Ursula Vogel (1992) Whose property? The double standard of adultery in nineteenth-century law, in C. Smart (Ed.) *Regulating Womanhood: Historical Essays on Marriage, Motherhood and Sexuality*, pp. 147–165 (London).

13 Or as Dirk Blasius has described it, as a type of *Unperson* (non-person). D. Blasius (1988) Bürgerliche Rechtsgleichheit und die Ungleichheit der Geschlechter: das Scheidungsrecht im historischen Vergleich, in U. Frevert (Ed.) *Bürgerinnen und Bürger*, p. 68 (Göttingen).

14 Blasius, Bürgerliche Rechtsgleichheit, p. 68.

15 M. Weber (1908/9) Das Problem der Ehescheidung, *Die Frau*, 16, p. 581.

16 In the Rhineland the number of women divorce petitioners was consistently higher than the number of men. In Krefeld, for instance, 1908: 76% women; 1910: 66%; 1914 64% [HStAD, Landgericht Krefeld: Rep 8/281]. In the rural district of Cleve between 1837 and 1870, 47 of a total of 60 separation and divorce cases were filed by women (78%) [HStAD, Rep 7]. While in Hamburg women presented the overwhelming majority of petitions, never below 75% between 1825 and 1878, but accounted for around half of petitioners in cases that reached the court Stadtarchiv Hamburg: Präturen 211–6; Stadtarchiv Hamburg: Niedergericht 211–5].

17 Gerhard, *Verhältnisse und Verhinderungen*, p. 149.

18 *Statistik des Deutschen Reichs*, Vol. 108 (1895), pp. 85–91.

19 *Statistik des Deutschen Reichs*, Vol. 207 (1907) pp. 477–481. It is important to note, however, that the apparent dramatic increase (78%) in the number of female workers in 1907 compared with 1895 is partly ascribed to different census recording which picked up women who worked in domestic industry, see Franzoi, *At the Very Least*, pp. 18–20.

20 Franzoi, *At the Very Least*, p. 169. In textile centres the level of female employment was considerably higher, see Dasey, Women's work and the family.

21 P. Borscheid (1986) Romantic love or material interest: choosing partners in nineteenth century Germany, *Journal of Family History*, 11, p. 167.

22 K. Keck (1911) Das Berufsschicksal der Arbeiterschaft in einer badischen Steinzeugfabrik, *Schriften des Vereins für Sozialpolitik*, 135, pp. 135–136.

23 Hubbard, *Familiengeschichte*, p. 50.

24 H. Ludwig (1896) Die Ehe im vierten Stande, *Die Frau*, 4, p. 50.

25 Stadtarchiv Düsseldorf (StAD), III 4778: Frau Ramloch to Düsseldorf Städtische Armen-verwaltung, 15 July 1914.

26 Duisburg Autorenkollektiv (1979) *Und vor Allen Dingen das is' Wahr! Eindrücke und Erfahrungen aus der Filmarbeit mit alten Menschen im Ruhrgebiet*, p. 120 (Duisburg).

27 Hauptstaatsarchiv Düsseldorf (HStAD), Regierung Düsseldorf (RD) 8971: Glasfabrik Gerresheim, 19 December 1885.

28 Stadtarchiv Bochum, Landratsamt 1175: Wattenscheid, 1 November 1850.

29 HStAD, Rep 7/225: Königliche Landgerichts-Präsidenten, Cleve, 25 March 1850.

30 P. and R. Knight (1974) *A Very Ordinary Life*, cited in J. Fout (1984) The women's role in the German working-class family in the 1890s from the perspective of women's autobiographies, in J. Fout (Ed.) *German Women in the Nineteenth Century* (London).

31 With the implementation of the BGB in 1900 wife-beating was made illegal but only "*Grosse Mißhandlung*" (severe mistreatment) was a sufficient ground for divorce and even then it was left to the discretion of the judge to decide whether the degree of severity warranted divorce.

32 HStAD, Rep 7/240: Ehescheidungs-Sache, Bletschen gegen Bletschen, 20 November 1833.

33 HStAD: Rep 7/268: Ehescheidungsklage – Johanna Cath. Bongartz gegen Johann Langen, 1850.

34 StAD, III 4778: wife of Wilhelm Starkhoff to Düsseldorf police, 22 August 1911.

35 StAD, III 4778: Anton Heiden to Düsseldorf police, 26 October 1902.

36 StAD, III 4778: Charlotte Rupp to Düsseldorf police, 10 November 1900.

37 D. Sabean (1990) *Property, Production and Family in Neckarhausen, 1700–1870*, pp. 133–134 (Cambridge).

38 Ross, Fierce questions and taunts, p. 577; Tomes, A torrent of abuse, pp. 332–333. See also Chinn, *They Worked All their Lives*, and E. Roberts (1984) *A Woman's Place: An Oral History of Working-class Women, 1890–1940* (Oxford).

39 U. Knapp (1984) *Frauenarbeit in Deutschland. Vol 2: Hausarbeit und geschlechtsspezifischer Arbeitsmarkt im deutschen Industrialisierungsprozess*, p. 261 (Munich).

40 Knapp, *Frauenarbeit in Deutschland*, p. 268.

41 There is some evidence to suggest that women were keen to return to the work in which they had been engaged before their marriage; "… wie schon erwähnt wurde, sie vermisst in ihrer stillen Wohnung, vor allem wenn sie keiner Kinder hat, die "Ereignisse" des Fabriksaals, das Zusammensein mit den andern, das sie seit dem 13. oder 14. Jahre gewöhnt und greift auch ohne direkte Notwendigkeit aus "Langeweile" wieder nach den früheren Beschäftigung", M. Bemays (1910) Auslese und Anpassung der Arbeiterschaft der geschlossenen Grossindustrie, *Schriften des Vereins für Sozialpolitik*, 133, pp. 220–221, Clf. J. Stephenson and C. Brown (1990). The view from the workplace: women's memories of work in Stirling. c. 1910–c. 1950, in E. Gordon and E. Breitenbach (Eds) *The World is Ill Divided: Women's Work in Scotland in the Nineteenth and Early Twentieth Century*, pp. 7–28 (Edinburgh).

42 A. Rühle-Gerstel cited in Hagemann, *Der Sozialismus*, note 29, p. 15.

43 J. Schiller (1846–97), in W. Herzberg (Ed.) (1985) *So war es: Lebensgeschichten zwischen 1900 und 1980*, p. 94 (Leipzig).

44 See Pamela Haag (1992) "The ill-use of a wife': patterns of working-class violence in domestic and public New York City, 1860–1880, *Journal of Social History*, 25, esp. pp. 462–471, on men's use of violence to enforce privileges embedded in the marital contract, particularly concerning control of the household economy.

45 HStAD, Rep 7/255: Die Ehescheidungs-Sache Röding v. Hülsken, 1844.

46 Ibid.

47 HStAD, Rep 7/253: Ehescheidungssache Janssen v. Janssen, 1842.

48 HStAD, Rep 7/254: Ehescheidungssache Janssen, witness statement, 1842.

49 StAD, III 4778: Eduard Lichte to Düsseldorf police, 7 September 1914.

50 HStAD, Rep 7/261: Ehescheidung Katharina Stegmann v. Wilhelm Spicker, 1846; Rep 7/230: Ehesache Ackersmann Johann Heinrich Grote zu Reeserschanz, 1819; Rep 7/254: Ehescheidungssache Janssen v. Janssen, 1842.

51 HStAD: Rep 7/225, report to Präsidenten des Königl. Landgerichts zu Cleve, 23 July 1844.

52 See Haag, The "ill-use of a wife", pp. 464–465.

53 HStAD, D 8941: Frau Carl Gerhards to Königliche Regierung zu Düsseldorf, 24 July 1898.

54 HStAD, Rep 7/270: Ehescheidungsklage Pieper v. Spiegelhoff, 21 February 1851.

55 HStAD, Rep 7/255: Ehescheidungs-Sache Röding v. Hülsken, 8 February 1844.

56 HStAD, Rep 7/247: Ehescheidungs-Sache Boll v. Boll, 27 September 1838.

57 See E. Ross (1983) Survival networks: women's neighbourhood sharing in London before World War I, History Workshop, 15, pp. 4–27.

58 HStAD Rep 7/267: Ehescheidungsklage – Theresa van Ihsum gegen Martin Eirman, 11 December 1848.

59 HStAD Rep 7/279: Ehescheidungsklage – Justine Anna Deenen gegen Alexander Goohsens, 5 June 1856.

60 HStAD Rep 7/278: Ehescheidungsklage, Schreiber gegen Schreiber, 7 February 1856.

61 HStAD Rep 7/280: Ehescheidungsklage der Wilhelmina Jansen, Ehefrau des Ackerers Wilhelm Weill, 10 April 1856.

62 HStAD Rep 7/278: Ehescheidungsklage, Schreiber gegen Schreiber, 7 February 1856; Rep 7/285: Ehescheidungsklage Schreiber gegen Schreiber, 16 May 1859.

63 StAD Rep 7/266: Ehescheidungsklage – Carolina Bego gegen Wilhelm Bego, 2 November 1848.

64 HStAD, Rep 7/468: Ehescheidung – Ackerer Friedrich Gembler zu Pfalzdorf, 22 December 1870.

65 StAD, III 4778: Eduard Lichte to Düsseldorf police, 7 September 1914.

66 Cf. Ross, Survival networks; R. Phillips (1980) Gender solidarities in late eighteenth century urban France: the example of Rouen, Histoire Sociale – Social History, 13, pp. 325–337; Haag, The "Ill-use of a wife", pp. 468–470.

67 HStAD, Rep 7/239: Theodore Disch gegen R. Theloh, Trennung von Tisch und Bett, 2 March 1833.

68 HStAD, Rep 7/241: Ehescheidungs – Sache Regina Ludewig wider Valentin Zillig, 16 October 1834.

69 See A. Irmer (1989) For Better, For Worse: Married Women and the German Civil Law, 1900–1914. MA Dissertation, University of East Anglia; R. Schade (1989) Frauen helfen Frauen: Camilla Jellinek und die Rechtsschutzstelle für Frauen und Mädchen e.V. in Heidelberg, Feministische Studien, 2, pp. 135–143.

70 StAD, III 4778: Josef Poscher to Düsseldorf Police Inspector, 10 October 1902.

71 D. Blasius (1984) Scheidung im 19. Jahrhundert: zu vergessenen Traditionen des heutigen Scheidungsrechts, Familiendynamik, 9, p. 365. This was a problem also acknowledged by contemporaries, see M. Weber (1908/9) Das Problem der Ehescheidung, Die Frau, 16, pp. 577–587.

72 Prussian divorce rate per/100,000 population: 1905: 18.5, 1911: 24.2, 1920: 58.9. In the Rhineland 1905: 13.5, 1911: 20.7, 1920: 46.5. The lower rates in the Rhineland were probably due to the predominantly Catholic population in that region, Statistisches Jahrbuch für das Deutsche Reich, 28 (1907), p. 22; Vol. 34 (1913), p. 27; Vol. 42 (1921–2).

73 StAD, III 4775: Frau Schüller to Düsseldorf Oberbürgermeister, 13 March 1893.

74 StAD, III 4778: police report on cast of Conrad Hubner, 4 February 1909.

75 Statistisches Jahrbuch für das Deutsche Reich, Vol. 37 (1916) p. 6.

76 StAD, III 4776: Hermann Israel to Düsseldorf police, 14 June 1899.

Chapter 21

Bonnie Anderson and Judith Zinsser

■ from 'ASSERTING WOMEN'S LEGAL AND POLITICAL
EQUALITY', *A History of their Own: Women in Europe from Prehistory
to the Present*, volume II, Penguin, London, 1990, pp. 367–370

[…]

IN THE FIRST QUARTER of the twentieth century, women won the vote in nations
most similar to England. In Scandinavia, feminists allied with liberals, socialists, and
nationalists, and when those groups attained power, women won the franchise But winning
the vote showed the limits of equal rights feminism. Before the twentieth century, with its
focus on winning the vote, equal rights feminists had tried to keep the issue in perspective.
Women's suffrage, stated Millicent Fawcett in 1886, "will be a political change, not of a
very great or extensive character in itself, based upon social, educational and economic
changes which have already taken place." Because of the bitterness of the struggle for the
vote, this perspective was lost. Liberalism argued that once people were enfranchised, they
possessed the means to work out their own liberation. Equal rights feminism, strongly tied
to and influenced by liberalism, tended to the same view. Both liberalism and equal rights
feminism declined when the vote alone proved incapable of liberating groups which remained
economically and culturally subordinated.

Rights of citizenship – the vote, the right to serve on juries, the right to hold political
office – in fact meant relatively little to most women. In addition, these were the kinds of
rights which, when won, were often taken for granted. Equal rights feminists, who had
fought so hard for the vote, sometimes became disillusioned when elections failed to make
a major difference in the lives of most women. "Nowadays, when it is often difficult to
persuade women to come out and vote," wrote Hannah Mitchell, active in the WSPU
before World War I,

> I wonder whether these women, like all electors today, who have had the vote handed
> to them on a gold plate, so to speak, would not have been just as well left among the
> "infants, imbeciles, and criminals" [who had also been denied the vote under English
> law].

Prior to women's suffrage, many equal rights feminists believed that women's vote would change the world. "Women's suffrage spreads culture!" asserted a 1908 manifesto of the German Suffrage Union, ten years before German women won the vote.

> *Women's suffrage* encourages peace and harmony among different peoples.
> *Women's suffrage* effectively promotes abstinence and thus prevents the ruin of a people through alcohol.
> *Women's suffrage* opposes the exploitation of the economically and physically weak, it takes pity on children and tormented animals.

These hopes did not materialize. Women did not vote in a separate bloc as women or feminists – they voted much as men of their classes did. In Sweden, for instance, a "Woman's List" of candidates for the Stockholm City Council in 1927 received only 0.6 percent of the vote.

Catholic nations resisted women's suffrage, and in Catholic nations, equal rights feminists remained disparaged and ignored. In 1934, the French feminist Louise Weiss complained that "peasant women remained open-mouthed when I spoke to them of the vote. Working-class women laughed, women clerical workers shrugged their shoulders, bourgeois women rejected me, horrified." Fear among liberal and left-wing male politicians of hordes of Catholic women voting for Catholic and conservative parties delayed women's suffrage. In Catholic nations women did not vote until after the Second World War.

In addition to having relatively little impact on the lives of most women, equal rights feminism succeeded only in those nations where class and political boundaries could be easily crossed. In both England and Scandinavia, feminists worked with liberal *and* socialist parties, and equal rights organizations united middle-class *and* working-class women. Elsewhere, political and economic disparities led to the development of two separate women's movements. One was an equal rights movement: middle-class, liberal, and focused on the vote, especially for women of property in societies where male suffrage .was not yet universal. The other women's movement was socialist: composed of working-class women and those who identified with them, and focused primarily on issues of the economy and overturning capitalism. In France, Russia, Italy, Austria, and Germany, the two women's movements bathed each other, and the feminist unity achieved in England proved impossible in most other European nations.

Equal rights feminists and feminist socialists differed sharply on issues and tactics. First, they divided bitterly on the issue of protective legislation limiting women's working conditions and hours, even in England. "If every demand raised by these women [the equal rights feminists] were granted today," declared Eleanor Marx (1856–1908), Karl Marx's youngest daughter, in 1892,

> we working-women would still be just where we were before. Women-workers would still work infamously long hours, for infamously low wages, under infamously unhealthful conditions … Has not the star of the women's rights movement, Mrs. Fawcett, declared herself expressly in opposition to any legal reduction of working hours for female workers?

Millicent Fawcett's husband, Henry, a Liberal Member of Parliament, first opposed laws limiting working women's hours in 1873. Obsessed with literal equality, thinking in terms of the professions rather than factories, condescending toward the working class, equal rights feminists backed "equality" for women workers. This meant opposing all attempts made to restrict women's labor in industry, everything from shorter hours to prohibitions against night work and labor in mining. Equal rights feminists clashed with labor unions and socialist parties, and in most cases, this policy of opposing protective legislation for women led to or exacerbated the split between themselves and feminist socialists. In England, feminism had largely overridden such class divisions; elsewhere it could not. Feminist socialists repudiated a cross-class alliance; so did equal rights feminists.

Equal rights feminists and feminist socialists also differed on tactics. In Germany, for instance, the *Bund Deutscher Frauenverein* (*BDF*, the League of German Women's Associations) not only refused to link up with more activist or left-wing groups, they also repudiated the tactics which had given the English equal rights movement widespread appeal: rallies, marches, demonstrations, resistance both nonviolent and violent. "Through the imitation of men's revolutionary violence women themselves destroy the possibility of taking a place in public life," declared the *BDF* in 1913. Socialists marched, therefore marches must be avoided. In 1912, propertied Munich suffragists organized a procession of eighteen private coaches, the very emblem of nineteenth-century wealth. Trimmed in the suffragist colors of green, purple, and white, these horse-drawn carriages in an automobile age embodied the limits which class could place on feminism.

Indifferent to socialism and economic issues important to women, and satisfied with what seemed to be the full achievement of women's legal and political equality, some equal rights feminists embraced new causes once the vote had been won. Emmeline Pankhurst joined the Conservative party and worked for child welfare. Christabel Pankhurst became an evangelical Christian. More often, however, politically active women turned to socialism to solve women's problems. The novelist Virginia Woolf (1882–1941) was one: in her 1929 feminist essay *A Room of One's Own,* she declared that to create equally to men, a woman needed £500 a year and a room of her own. "The news of my legacy [an aunt left her an independent income] reached me one night about the same time that the act was passed that gave votes to women," she remembered. "Of the two – the vote and the money – the money, I own, seemed infinitely more important." Woolf became active in Labour women's groups. Adela and Sylvia Pankhurst devoted themselves to socialism and attempted to transform the capitalist economy, an issue which they saw as far more important to most women than the vote. In this move, Virginia Woolf and Sylvia and Adela Pankhurst joined the many thousands of women, a few of them middle- and even upper-class in origin, who believed that socialism offered the best hope for feminism and its demands for women.

Chapter 22

Seth Koven and Sonya Michel

■ 'WOMANLY DUTIES: MATERIALIST POLITICS AND THE ORIGINS OF WELFARE STATES IN FRANCE, GERMANY, GREAT BRITAIN AND THE UNITED STATES, 1880–1920', *American Historical Review*, 95, 4, October 1990, pp. 1076–1108

[B]y no possible means could middle-class women with nothing but brains and brawn have taken part in any one of the great movements which, brought together, constitute the historian's view of the past.

Virginia Woolf, *A Room of One's Own*

[M]aternity is repudiated or denied by some avant-garde feminists, while its traditional representations are wittingly or unwittingly accepted by the "broad mass" of women and men.

Julia Kristeva, "Stabat Mater"[1]

THE EMERGENCE OF LARGE-SCALE STATE WELFARE PROGRAMS and policies coincided with the rise of women's social action movements in France, Germany, Great Britain, and the United States in the late nineteenth and early twentieth centuries.[2] Despite their concurrence, historians have, until quite recently, studied these two great historical trends separately. But a new and voluminous body of scholarship in welfare-state history and women's history has uncovered the deep and intricate connections between them. Women's reform efforts and welfare states not only coincided in time, place, and sometimes personnel but also reinforced and transformed one another in significant and enduring ways. Women in all four countries succeeded, to varying degrees, in shaping one particular area of state policy: maternal and child welfare. It was in this area, closely linked to the traditional female sphere, that women first claimed new roles for themselves and transformed their emphasis on motherhood into public policy. During the years 1880 to 1920, when state welfare structures and bureaucracies were still rudimentary and fluid, women, individually and through organizations, exerted a powerful influence on state definitions of the needs of mothers and children and the designs of institutions and programs to address them.

In this period, women in France, Germany, Great Britain, and the United States developed grass-roots organizations as well as national and international lobbying groups to press for maternal and child welfare benefits. Many, but by no means all, used their authority as mothers to campaign for the expansion of women's rights in society. While resisting these demands for expanded citizenship rights, male bureaucrats, politicians, and propagandists encouraged women in their welfare work. Since the turn of the century, the din of male voices—Catholic and Protestant, liberal, socialist, and conservative—demanding that women take up their sacred duties has, ironically, obscured women's own initiatives in this area. The subsequent rejection of motherhood and maternalism as incompatible with female emancipation has led some historians to minimize women's influence on the formation of welfare states; this essay offers a reevaluation of the early history of "maternalist" politics and welfare states.

Maternalists not only concerned themselves with the welfare and rights of women and children but also generated searching critiques of state and society. Emilia Kanthack, a midwife and lecturer on infant welfare in St. Pancras, London, observed that "the chain reaches farther and farther back—from baby to mother, from mother to father, from father to existing social conditions swaying the labor market, which in turn result from economic conditions of supply and demand."[3] Some maternalists believed that their values should be applied universally to transform the very foundations of the social order. As early as 1885, French feminist Hubertine Auclert posed the choices confronting the French people in stark terms: the state could either devour its citizens, like the Minotaur (*état minotaur*), to satisfy its martial appetites, or mother its citizens to health and productivity in peace (*état mère de famille*).[4] In 1904, German utopian feminist Ruth Bré exalted motherhood as the fundamental, life-sustaining social labor and called for the radical restructuring of society on the basis of matriarchal family units.[5]

Late nineteenth and early twentieth-century maternalists envisioned a state in which women displayed motherly qualities and also played active roles as electors, policymakers, bureaucrats, and workers, within and outside the home. Before 1919, women in all four countries lacked full citizenship rights and necessarily operated in the interstices of political structures. The same men who applauded women's work on behalf of children were often openly antagonistic to women's aspirations to use their welfare activities to promote their own political and economic rights. The interests of children—the nation's future workers and soldiers—came before the rights of mothers. Even groups of men ostensibly committed to raising women's status, like the fledgling Labour Party in Great Britain and the Parti Ouvrier Français in France,[6] expected women to subordinate their gender-specific demands to male-controlled political and economic agendas. That the women and movements we explore in this essay ultimately lacked the political power to refashion the state according to their own visions does not diminish the importance of those visions, their accomplishments, or their legacy.

Our account focuses primarily on the political initiatives of middle-class women who were free from domestic drudgery and had the educational and financial resources to campaign for social welfare programs and policies. In the name of friendship and in the interests of the health of the family and the nation, these reformers claimed the right to instruct and regulate the conduct of working-class women. The shared concerns of family brought together different groups of women, but, at the same time, conflicts over control of the workplace and household divided them along class, race, and ethnic lines.[7]

Other patterns also characterized maternal and child welfare in the four countries under consideration here. First, the growth of welfare bureaucracies between 1880 and

1920 led to the expansion of care-taking professions dominated by women: social work, health visiting, and district nursing. Both as professionals and as volunteers, women entered into new relationships with the state, which, in turn, sharpened their political awareness and expanded the rank and file of a wide range of women's movements and movements of women.[8]

Second, maternalist discourses—often competing—lay at the heart of debates about the social role of women, children, and the family among philanthropists, legislators and bureaucrats, employers and workers, men and women. The invocation of maternalism by so many different social actors compels us to reevaluate its meanings and uses. We apply the term to ideologies that exalted women's capacity to mother and extended to society as a whole the values of care, nurturance, and morality.[9] Maternalism always operated on two levels: it extolled the private virtues of domesticity while simultaneously legitimating women's public relationships to politics and the state, to community, workplace, and marketplace. In practice, maternalist ideologies often challenged the constructed boundaries between public and private, women and men, state and civil society.[10]

Finally, in all four countries, women were usually the first to identify the social welfare needs of mothers and children and respond to them through a wide array of charitable activities.[11] States relied on the initiatives of private-sector, largely female organizations and, in many instances, subsequently took over the funding and management of their welfare programs.[12] Such activities thus constituted an important (but often overlooked) site of public policy and, ultimately, state formation. Yet a comparative examination of maternalists' achievements in the four countries leads to an awkward and disconcerting conclusion: the power of women's social action movements was inversely related to the range and generosity of state welfare benefits for women and children. "Strong states," defined as those with well-developed bureaucracies and long traditions of governmental intervention, allowed women less political space in which to develop social welfare programs than did "weak states," where women's voluntary associations flourished.[13]

For example, the United States, with the most politically powerful and broadly based female reform movements and the weakest state, yielded the least extensive and least generous maternal and child welfare benefits to women. To a lesser degree, the same pattern prevailed in Great Britain. Germany, with the strongest state, had politically ineffective women's movements but offered the most comprehensive programs for women and children; the experience of France was similar. While the degree of state strength affected the extent and character of women's movements, it cannot explain their subsequent political successes and failures. Female reformers using maternalist arguments alone could seldom compel states to act. They were more likely to be effective when their causes were taken up by male political actors pursuing other goals, such as pro-natalism or control of the labor force. The decades before World War I were supercharged with nationalist agendas and anxieties concerning depopulation, degeneration, and efficiency, as states vied for military and imperial preeminence. These issues, and then the war itself, prompted legislators to establish many programs that might not have received state support under other conditions.[14] But the programs, in turn, owed their very existence to the models, organization, and momentum created by female activists.

IN SEEKING TO UNCOVER THE AFFINITIES and reciprocal impact of women's movements and welfare states, we need first to look at the existing theoretical and empirical literature on these subjects. From the late 1880s, men and women throughout Europe and North America vigorously debated the proper role of the state in regulating the lives of its citizens. In the name of widely divergent causes, they lobbied the state to stand between them and the callous forces of the market. The impulse behind state welfare policies was sometimes conservative, as in Bismarck's introduction of social insurance in 1881; sometimes liberal or radical, as with the social reforms that accompanied the rise to prominence of British radical Lloyd George after 1906. In France and the United States as well, the "rediscovery" of poverty in the late nineteenth century by social scientists and policymakers focused attention on the breakdown of social and familial institutions in the great cities of the industrial world. Not surprisingly, many turned to the state as the sole institution with the resources needed to restore the health of the nation and to remedy the ills of modernity afflicting the family and its members.

The vast historiography of welfare states mirrors the complexity of its subject and the diversity of views expressed by contemporaries. Historians working outside a feminist perspective have offered a range of explanations for the emergence of welfare states: the process of modernization, the rise of new social forces and groups, and the internal dynamics and momentum of the state itself. Modernization theorists see the welfare state as a response to economic development, industrialization, and labor force differentiation.[15] They naturalize the welfare state as a logical response to the increasing complexity of a mature industrial society. Society-centered theorists fall into two categories. Social-democratic analysts attribute welfare-state development to the efforts of working-class leaders who translated their newly won political power into state programs designed to enhance the social and economic conditions of the workplace and home.[16] Neo-Marxists take a much less benign view. They point to the rise of professionals and corporate managers seeking to stabilize and control the work force. State welfare in such accounts is seen as a kind *of* bribe intended to coopt the legitimate (conflictual) political aspirations of the working class.[17] Finally, state-centered theorists stress the initiatives of bureaucrats and the imperatives of governmental machinery in explaining the expanded scope and role of the state in the twentieth century.[18] Some also advocate what they call an "institutional-political process perspective," in which "political struggles and policy outcomes are presumed to be jointly conditioned by the institutional arrangements of the state and by class and other social relationships."[19]

Each of these models explains important aspects of the emergence of state welfare programs and policies, but none pays sufficient notice to the impact of organized women's movements and gender issues on the process.[20] In all four countries, factors such as the "anomie" of modernity, the social consequences of rapid industrial and urban growth, and the growing power of class-based movements threatened the foundations of bourgeois civil societies and created political climates that were receptive to social welfare initiatives. Without this long-term change in attitudes toward the relationship of the state to civil society, women's successes in shaping social welfare programs and in lobbying for a variety of legislative enactments would not have been possible. However, though a necessary condition, the shift toward collectivist policies and greater state intervention in regulating home and workplace does not account for the forms of women's organizations and their causes.

From the perspective of women's history, the operative concepts and definitions of nonfeminist models seem too restrictive. For example, most nonfeminist theorists define the welfare state in terms of work-related pensions, general medical care, and old-age benefits, without examining the ways in which their models either include or exclude women or affect relationships between men and women in families. They pay little attention to the aspects of state welfare policy that most directly and explicitly affected women, namely, sex-based protective labor legislation and maternal and child welfare programs. Like the policymakers themselves, they take as their paradigm the regularly employed male wage earner. All too often, this paradigm renders women workers invisible, for it ignores differences and variations in their labor patterns created by domestic and family responsibilities.[21] Employers' and politicians' perceptions of these responsibilities produced distinctions in their treatment of male and female workers and in the social policies devised to ensure workers' welfare. Nonfeminists have also overlooked the role of women in shaping policy. Despite abundant historical evidence pointing to women's presence in the early stages of welfare-state formation, state-centered theorists have, until recently, restricted their inquiries to the period when state welfare structures had already emerged and to the male-dominated administration of the official state and the political parties vying for its control.[22] By construing the geographical and chronological boundaries of welfare-state development so narrowly, they fail to capture those women's activities in the voluntary or civic sector that often preceded state formation.[23]

Similarly, modernization and society-centered theorists obscure women's impact on state development by taking male patterns of political activity as the norm. Women were absent from or marginal to male-dominated parties, trade unions, and fraternal associations. In nineteenth-century France and Germany, they were prohibited by law from joining political parties. Disenfranchisement made clear the limits of female citizenship within the boundaries of the official, male-controlled state.[24] Yet these forms of exclusion did not render women inactive as workers or as political lobbyists. Without access to the venues for political mobilization restricted to men, women came together in other ways and around other issues. In the United States and Great Britain, for example, women formed cross-class labor organizations to promote the growth of women's trade unionism and represent the interests of women workers.[25] In France at the turn of the century, some women built upon their traditionally close ties with the church to establish Social Catholic organizations and lobbying groups including L'Action Sociale de la Femme founded by Jeanne Popinel Chenu and the Maisons Sociales established by Mercedes Le Fer de La Motte.[26] Arenas of mobilization clearly affected the types of policies each group sought to promote. In the United States, for example, Julia Lathrop, Grace Abbott, and other "federal maternalists" sought to translate the ethos of the settlement house into a distinct political mode and agenda.[27] Voluntary organizations and the many institutions they spawned for women and children figured importantly in women's political education by training them to create and work through bureaucracies, research and write policy statements, and raise funds and prepare budgets.

In drawing out the gender implications of supposedly sex-neutral policies, women's historians and feminist theorists have necessarily adopted new approaches to the study of the welfare state and redefined the state itself. However, just as nonfeminist scholars have ignored the impact of welfare states on gender relations (and vice versa), many feminists have also been one-sided, focusing exclusively on the state's instrumentality in perpetuating patriarchy. Some argue that state welfare programs are intended primarily to regulate women's productive and reproductive lives. Capitalist states use welfare policies to impose a "family ethic" on women, just as they use other measures to impose a "work ethic" on men.[28] Elizabeth Wilson's provocative study *Women and the Welfare State* (1977) claimed that "the difference between the policeman's and the social worker's role ... illustrates the difference between the directly repressive State and the ideological repression of the State. In either case, the function of police and social welfare agencies is to repress." The welfare state defined woman as "above all Mother," which, Wilson asserted, equals "submission, nurturance and passivity." Many other feminists concur with Wilson that welfare states situated women as clients and dependents in order to limit them to their "primary task" of "reproducing the work force."[29] Despite its insights into the power of welfare states to control behavior, such scholarship tends to produce narratives of loss and victimization, in which women appear as passive, disorganized, and helpless in the face of the encroaching male power of the state.[30] It obscures women's roles as autonomous actors and agents, in large part because here, too, the political process is conceived as a male domain.[31] If, under patriarchy, motherhood always entails dependency on a husband or father, or on the state serving in *loco patris*, it is difficult to conceive that claiming maternal identity could help women gain autonomy and political power.[32]

Recently, scholars have begun to revise social welfare history, insisting on clients' activism, even at the individual level, within the penumbra of the state. For example, Linda Gordon, in her study of family violence, while clearly aware of the discriminatory aspects of many policies, stresses the ways in which female clients of both voluntary and state agencies shaped policies and institutions to suit their own needs.[33] The history of middle-class women's activities on behalf of women and children, like that of Gordon's working-class heroes, does not support the equation of motherhood with dependence or the depiction of women as victims. Many middle-class women viewed motherliness not as their special burden or curse but as a peculiar gift that encouraged them and justified their efforts to gain some measure of personal and political autonomy.

THE ROOTS OF MATERNALIST MOVEMENTS lie in the early nineteenth century, when women in Western countries began to organize in the name of social reform, reclamation, and moral purity. Essential to this mobilization was the rise of domestic ideologies that stressed women's differences from men, humanitarian concerns for the conditions of child life and labor, and the emergence of activist interpretations of the gospel (which varied from country to country and included evangelicalism, Christian Socialism, Social Catholicism, and the social gospel).[34] Women's moral vision, compassion, and capacity to nurture came increasingly to be linked to motherliness. Once embedded within an ideological and political framework, these private qualities became the cornerstone of the public, political discourses we identify as maternalism.

Such discourses linked religious activism and domesticity to one another in a curiously unstable matrix of mutually reinforcing yet contradictory values. On the one hand, women were enjoined to cultivate their womanhood within the home; but, on the other, they were urged to impress Christian values on their communities through charitable work. Inevitably, the practice of some women's lives as charitable workers conflicted with the dictates of domesticity. Maternalist discourses were marked not only by national histories but also by their specific political and rhetorical contexts. Maternalism was and remains an extraordinarily protean ideology capable of drawing together unlikely and often transitory coalitions between people who appeared to speak a common language but had opposing political commitments and views of women.

Maternalism grew out of a variety of nationally specific constructions of domesticity.[35] In the United States, for example, nineteenth-century women activists could draw on a rich legacy of domestic ideologies that historians have named "the cult of true womanhood" and "republican motherhood" in constructing maternalist visions of women and the state.[36]

Working in organizations that were sex-segregated by choice, female reformers initially sought to avoid any association with politics, which, they feared, would compromise their putative moral purity and hence undermine the rationale for their womanly mission.[37] But some quickly realized that they would be more effective if they could mobilize the powers of the state on their own behalf. As Mary P. Ryan notes, in the 1820s and 1830s female moral reformers in New York City "were not averse to seeking either police power or state funds to support their cause."[38] By mid-century, the women's reform movement had become increasingly sophisticated, shifting tactics from "moral suasion" to direct political action. This trend gained impetus during the Civil War and especially Reconstruction, as benevolent women worked with the federal government to bring aid to former slaves through the Freedmen's Bureau.[39] Yet, even as they moved further onto the political stage, women continued to claim for themselves a kind of moral superiority rooted in their differences from men. As late as the Progressive Era, the noted reformer Florence Kelley insisted that women possessed special insights into issues of social justice and social welfare and were, at the same time, entitled to special protection.[40]

Not all American maternalists believed it was the federal government's responsibility to aid and protect women. The noted Boston Brahmin and anti-suffragist Elizabeth Lowell Putnam called upon her home state to pass pure milk laws but opposed any form of federal programs on behalf of women and children. She claimed that the U.S. Children's Bureau, established at the behest of women activists in 1912, "is merely a clever way, because appealing, of granting power to the federal government and taking it away from individual states, which is the great way in which the Soviet government works in getting control of its people, particularly the young—by putting the many in the control of the few."[41]

The British case also illustrates the ways in which women joined notions about their motherly social tasks to different political agendas. Although Millicent Garrett Fawcett, a leading constitutional suffragist, was committed to John Stuart Mill's vision of formal equality between the sexes, she believed that women's private and voluntary philanthropy and welfare work was "the most womanly of women's duties."[42] Her adversaries, the women who signed the "Appeal against Female Suffrage" of 1889, also believed that social reform and reclamation were women's special province. The signatories, who included such prominent female leaders as Beatrice Webb and Mary Augusta (Mrs. Humphry) Ward, contended that the parliamentary franchise would pollute women by implicating them in the violent business of wars and empire. They urged women, however, to extend their housekeeping out into the municipal arena by seizing opportunities to serve in local government as elected and appointed officials and social welfare organizers and workers.[43]

While it is not surprising to find anti-suffrage women invoking a maternalist vision of women's sex-specific social obligations, it is noteworthy to find such views in the writings of leading socialist feminists and Labour party women.[44] In 1907, Margaret MacDonald, a founder of the Women's Labour League, appealed to that "great majority of women whose first duty and responsibility is to their home and children but who are learning that they cannot thoroughly fulfill their charge without taking part in the civic life which surrounds and vitally affects their home life."[45] MacDonald's plea was part of a larger platform that included women's suffrage, women's freedom to chose to work inside or outside the home, higher wages for male heads of households, and extensive benefits for mothers.

In the French Third Republic, anxieties over depopulation and the perception of military weakness in the aftermath of crushing defeat in the Franco-Prussian War made the contest to control maternalist political rhetoric exceptionally intense. Maternalism took many forms among French women, depending on whether it was linked to conservative Catholic ideologies, the philanthropic traditions of the active-but-small Protestant minority, republicanism, socialism, or one of the late nineteenth-century variants of feminism. Until the 1880s, two groups of Catholic women had traditionally dominated the care of mothers and children within their communities: Catholic nuns and well-to-do Catholic lay women.[46] Bonnie Smith's study of the bourgeoises of the Nord argues that these women saw charity as an organic and natural extension of their domestic roles as mothers and as Catholics.[47] Subscribing to an anti-modern, anti-capitalist world view, these *dames patronnesses* established crèches, kindergartens, and maternal aid societies. Such women lived very public lives but refused to see themselves as engaged in politics. While they, like Auclert, valued motherliness, they were hostile to her support of suffrage and rejected as godless the radical republicanism of another feminist, Marguerite Durand.[48]

In the 1880s, the leaders of the Third Republic, as part of their struggle against the church, actively sought to undermine the hold of Catholic women on social welfare. Abandoning the moralistic prejudices against unmarried mothers that had characterized the work of Catholic maternalists, advocates of this new, modern ideology recognized all mothers and children as vital resources for the Republic.[49] Their efforts not only increased intervention by male professionals pursuing scientific, bureaucratic initiatives but also created an opening for women committed to advancing motherhood within a context of republican ideology and female emancipation.[50] This did not, however, lead to professional opportunities for women, for male republicans continued to stress the importance of women's contributions as "the natural agents of ... charity."[51]

Catholic women, though marginalized during this period, continued to promote maternal and child welfare, reemerging as a vocal and potent political group in the early twentieth century with La Ligue Patriotique des Femmes Françaises (the Patriotic League of French Women). Unlike their Catholic predecessors, league women felt compelled to enter politics, even as they sought to uphold women's traditional subordination to men.[52] At approximately the same time, a cadre of elite, moderately feminist Protestant French women laid the foundations for the interdenominational Conseil National des Femmes Françaises (National Council of French Women) by recruiting members from associations "that concerned themselves with the lot of women or of children."[53] Thus French women who openly opposed one another on fundamental issues such as suffrage or married women's wage labor often found themselves in agreement over the need to expand and improve maternal and child welfare.

Maternalism was perhaps the most significant thread tying together the disparate women's movements in Germany from the 1880s until the 1920s. Ann Taylor Allen cogently argues that the "overwhelming majority of feminist leaders during the nineteenth century" embraced the concept of "spiritual motherhood." Allen aptly insists that, "far from the reactionary affirmation of traditional subservience which some feminist historians have denounced, the nineteenth-century glorification of motherhood was initially a progressive trend."[54] Shortly after the 1848 Revolution, Henriette Breymann, a leader of the kindergarten movement, wrote, "I foresee an entirely new age dawning for women when she will be the center of the home and when she ... will bring to the broader community a quality which until now has been entirely lacking—the spirit of motherhood in its deepest meaning and in its most varied forms."[55] Breymann linked her vision of women to liberal reforms in the education of women and children.[56]

Breymann could not have predicted the varied meanings and forms "motherhood" would take in Germany over the next seventy years. By the end of the century, maternalist women had linked it to sex reform, socialist reconstruction of the state and society, suffrage, and a wide range of state welfare policies and programs. Alice Salomon, who, along with Jeannette Schwerin, pioneered the development of professional social work in Germany, literally built on the foundations laid by Breymann by establishing the first Soziale Frauenschule (Social Work School for Women) in Breymann's Pestalozzi-Fröbel Haus in Berlin.[57] Salomon demanded the vote and aggressively pushed for state intervention: "We asked not for privileges, for preferential laws, but for an adjustment to women's greater vulnerability arising from specific organic functions imposed upon them by nature."[58] Salomon's maternalism was inextricably bound up with her consensual vision of social relations. The daughter of a wealthy, assimilated Jewish family, she envisioned a motherly state that aimed not to transform class relations but to transcend the conflicts between classes through the bonds of motherhood.

Socialist women, while divided among themselves, denounced Salomon and the bourgeois feminist movement as collaborators with an exploitative system.[59] Women's emancipation could never be achieved, nor the rights of mothers and children secured, without transforming the relationship between working-class clients and middle-class female social reformers. Lily Braun, a renegade from the aristocracy and a leader of the ethical-socialist Bund für Mutterschutz (League for the Protection of Motherhood), enunciated a passionate brand of maternalism that challenged the male-centered foundations of her society. Braun insisted that women—as women, not only as socialists and workers—had essential contributions to make to society. She argued that just as women received "the seed" from men in creating life, so, too, male-dominated societies needed to receive the seed of women's distinctive gifts to civilization.[60] Although Bebel's *Woman under Socialism* was the bible of socialist women, and the Sozialdemokratische Partei Deutschlands (SPD) was the most powerful political advocate for women's emancipation in pre-World War I Germany, Braun believed that even the German socialist movement was implicitly part of the "hitherto purely masculine culture" she sought to feminize.[61]

Activist women in all four countries regarded motherhood as empowering, not as a condition of dependence and weakness. They saw the home—domestic and maternal duties—as the locus of their power within the community. Yet, although maternalism offered women a common platform that transcended differences in religious affiliation, political inclinations, and nationality, their commitment to it could not conceal conflicts among them. When Alice Salomon traveled to London for the Quintennial Meeting of the International Council of Women in 1899, she happily anticipated sharing the platform on "Protective Labor Legislation for Women" with Beatrice Webb, the renowned Fabian socialist and expert on social welfare and social policy. Expecting Webb to be "a romantic figure," she found her "detached, unemotional, typically a scholar." More shocking, Salomon discovered that Webb "thought in different categories from feminists and social workers."[62] Salomon's revelation underlines an important point: maternalist women, while actively seeking to improve the conditions of women, were not necessarily feminists—some, in fact, deliberately refused to so define themselves.

Maternalism proved a fragile foundation on which to build coalitions. Women were divided among themselves on many key issues, and they lacked the political power to maintain control over maternalist discourses and policies. Although male politicians used maternalist rhetoric, it was often merely a cloak for paternalism. Their interests seldom lay in promoting women's rights or even strengthening the family as a goal in itself. From the mid-nineteenth century onward, legislators passed a variety of measures that singled out women for special protection by the state. Protective legislation limited or prohibited women's labor force participation by dictating hours, wages, and working conditions.[63] Despite the humanitarian and maternalist language that accompanied the passage of such bills, "limiting legislation" effectively diminished women's earnings by barring them from employment without compensatory benefits. As feminist scholars have noted, the men who led the campaigns for limiting legislation such as the Mines Act of 1842 in Great Britain and the 1892 labor legislation in France "protected" women in order to reduce the threat of competition from female workers, shore up the family wage, and compel women to remain within their homes.[64] Female activists, by contrast, typically demanded "redistributive" welfare measures that compensated women for lost wages and provided direct medical and social services. Such measures left open the possibility of maternal employment. For working women, the differences between "limiting" and "redistributive" welfare measures were stark. Limiting legislation buttressed the gender-based, dual labor market, while redistributive forms mitigated some of its worst consequences.[65]

By the early twentieth century, many male politicians had become aware of the inefficacy of limiting legislation, and they too began to call for redistributive measures. But they tended to do so not for women themselves but on behalf of infants, the race, and the nation. Emile Rey, during debates in the French Sénat over mandatory maternity leaves, echoed Frédéric Le Play's conservative prescriptions for women even as he argued for radically redistributive policies.[66] He insisted that the French state should offer non-contributory and universal allowances to all needy women, not just those who were wage workers, for performing the labor of producing and nurturing children. But Rey was not motivated by generous concern for women. Instead, he wished to prevent those who were not already employed outside the home from abandoning the *foyer* for the workshop merely to gain benefits. Rey equated women's work outside the home with "immorality."[67]

Did it make sense for women to support men like Rey, who, despite their explicit paternalism, promised to redistribute substantial resources to mothers? In 1915, American feminist Katharine Anthony advised her fellow feminists to heed the example of their German counterparts and take a pragmatic or opportunistic approach to maternalist politics. The great expansion of benefits to mothers in Germany, she confessed, "relied in great measure upon good masculine reasons which the masculine mind will understand. The spectacle of official diplomacy working out official reasons for granting a feminist demand is an exhibition from which watchful feminists may learn a great deal, if indeed it doesn't make them too furious to think."[68] What were the implications of the trade-off suggested by Anthony between gaining feminist demands in the area of child and maternal welfare and accommodating the "masculine mind"? Were the stakes of conceding control over maternalist discourses to men higher in terms of women's long-term political power than Anthony imagined? What were the tangible results of women's activism on their political identities, on maternal and child welfare policies and programs, and, more generally, on the state itself?

IN BRITAIN, FRANCE, GERMANY, AND THE UNITED STATES, female maternalists used their private voluntary associations to develop social welfare programs for working-class women and their children. But just as women's movements varied in strength, so too did the extent and influence of their voluntary associations. Theda Skocpol and other state-centered theorists have argued that weak states—that is, those with decentralized or undeveloped bureaucracies (less rationalized, in Weberian terms)—will produce or be accompanied by strong private sectors.[69] Skocpol, along with Kathryn Kish Sklar, advances an important and suggestive corollary: it is also in such situations that women's quasi-state social welfare activities burgeon.[70] During periods preceding the build-up of the state administration and in social spaces outside of government—in civic, confessional, and voluntary arenas—women's groups mobilize resources and work effectively to pursue social goals.

Skocpol highlights the strength of the British state and labor movement in comparison to those of the United States.[71] However, when placed within a broader framework of welfare policies and programs, the American and British states both appear relatively weak compared to those of France and Germany—and the political prominence of American and British women appears greater. In the United States, where organized labor had little political power, Sklar argues that female activists "used gender-specific means … to ameliorate class inequities."[72] American women claimed the political space occupied by state agencies, churches, and bureaucrats in France and Germany to transform their voluntary charity into a shadow welfare state, an entity that Sara Evans has dubbed "the maternal commonwealth."[73]

In contrast to the loose, decentralized "state of courts and parties" that characterized the American polity in the last quarter of the nineteenth century,[74] the private-sector maternal commonwealth became increasingly centralized during this period. The Woman's Christian Temperance Union, under the dynamic leadership of Frances Willard, was the first national organization to emerge in 1874. Soon, other scattered, unaffiliated, benevolent organizations, some of them hitherto unknown to one another, began forming national leagues: the General Federation of Women's Clubs (GFWC, 1890), the National Federation of Day Nurseries (NFDN, 1895), and the National Association of Colored Women (1896), among others. While the NFDN was devoted to a single form of benevolence, the others served as umbrella organizations that created more affiliates and stimulated the development of a range of activities in cities and towns across the country.[75] Although independent and firmly based in the private sector, women's organizations frequently lobbied local and state governments for improved services to needy and dependent groups, and many received public funding for the services they themselves offered. The more progressive groups turned to state governments for permanent support. The GFWC, along with the National Congress of Mothers, was a key player in campaigns for mothers' and widows' pensions during the first two decades of the twentieth century.[76] By 1920, forty states had passed such measures.[77]

While local chapters drew thousands of family-based married women into political activity during this period, single, educated women of the same and subsequent generations were attracted to the newly established urban settlement houses, which offered them myriad opportunities to participate in reform. Institutions like Hull House, in addition to providing direct services to neighborhood populations, served as staging areas for campaigns on a range of maternalist issues, particularly protective labor legislation and health programs. These campaigns soon moved from the local to the state level. With the establishment of the U.S. Children's Bureau in 1912, Hull House and its informal affiliates across the country gained a base in Washington and adapted their political strategies accordingly.[78]

The very existence of the Children's Bureau testifies to the unusual power and vigor of women's higher education and women's movements in the United States and, more generally, to their authority as social policy experts.[79] But their bureaucratic power was isolated and did not translate readily into a federal program of redistributive maternal and child welfare benefits. In 1919, the bureau undertook a comprehensive international study of maternity benefits. Bureau chief Julia Lathrop noted poignantly that the report had been compiled "in the hope that the information might prove useful to the people of one of the few great countries which as yet have no system of State or national assistance in maternity—the United States."[80] In 1921, Congress did pass the bureau-sponsored Sheppard–Towner maternal and infant health bill but refused to renew it in 1929. Another bureau-supported measure, the Child Labor Amendment, passed Congress in 1924 but could not garner adequate state support for ratification. Ironically but not surprisingly, the absence of federal redistributive infant and maternal welfare laws in the United States coincided with the presence of the only female-controlled state bureaucracy in the world. Despite these affronts to the Children's Bureau and its maternalist allies, American women became entrenched in several branches of the federal bureaucracy, on state boards of charity, and in local and state welfare agencies, where they were able to campaign successfully for state-level maternalist policies.[81]

Although the British state was somewhat stronger and more centralized than its American counterpart, both societies shared an enduring distrust of centralized government and a traditional reliance on local and private forms of welfare provision. Women's voluntary associations in Great Britain were also extraordinarily broad-based and influential.[82] But British women never matched the success of their American counterparts in gaining an exclusive foothold in the central state, even though both the Majority and Minority Reports of the Poor Law Commission of 1909 called for the creation of a children's ministry, which, presumably, would have been run by female activists.[83] Throughout the nineteenth century, British women reformers developed welfare programs in the private sector. Many of these women saw voluntary activities as a means to test new ideas free from the constraints of public scrutiny and interference.[84] Armed with proof of their success, they then lobbied for public subsidies and legislative support on the municipal or state level.[85]

Women's settlements in England, like their more celebrated American counterparts, also functioned as "borderlands" between the state and civil society where women developed social welfare programs and policies.[86] For example, Mrs. Humphry Ward, in conjunction with the Women's Work Committee of the Passmore Edwards Settlement House, established influential programs for handicapped children as well as after-school and recreation programs for the children of working mothers.[87] Ward was quite clear about the role that women's voluntary associations should play in shaping public policy. Addressing the Victoria Women's Settlement in Liverpool at the turn of the century, she sketched her vision of women's settlements and voluntary associations in England.

> These irregular individualistic experiments are the necessary pioneers and accompaniments with us of all collective action. We don't wait for Governments; we like to force the hand of Governments ... [W]e like to fling our irregular forces on the enemy ... to make a hundred mistakes, before we call up the regular battalions and dream of a final decision.[88]

Ward's child welfare schemes drew increasing subsidies from the London County Council in the years before World War I. Ultimately, it was the strains of war, with its double demand for women's labor as mothers and factory workers, that led the president of the board of education, H. A. L. Fisher, to approve a national and state-funded system of after-school recreation programs based on Ward's model in 1916.[89]

The maternal and child welfare scheme developed in the Yorkshire textile town of Huddersfield illustrates the close links between women's voluntary associations and the state, partnerships between activist male doctors and politicians and women, as well as women's increasing power as paid and unpaid officials. Championed by the mayor, Benjamin Broadbent, and headed by a progressive male Medical Officer of Health, Dr. Samson G. H. Moore, the scheme was explicitly modeled on French precedent and provided the blueprint for the Notification of Births Act of 1907.[90] The Assistant Medical Officers of Health who oversaw the system were salaried medical women who saw their positions as "steppingstones" to careers in the expanding area of maternal and child welfare.[91] Each district in the town was in turn supervised by one to three unpaid Lady Superintendents. Approximately one hundred "Lady Helpers" followed up on the official visit by the Assistant Medical Officers of Health and Lady Superintendents by offering personal advice and assistance to mothers.

In Huddersfield and elsewhere, the expansion of public welfare was accompanied by increasing power and opportunities for women, who were enlisted to execute policies. By the 1890s, an estimated 500,000 British women were engaged in public social welfare work, 20,000 in salaried positions like the Assistant Medical Officers of Health in Huddersfield.[92] In the years before World War I, these numbers continued to grow. Barbara Hutchins, a feminist and early historian of female labor, argued that the expansion of state and public welfare services was made possible by and in turn encouraged the growth of women's professions, which then opened up new social and political opportunities for women.[93] While some working-class mothers resented the intrusion of both volunteers and professionals, their presence did not automatically lead to greater social control on the part of the middle class. In Huddersfield, for example, it was, at least in theory, up to the client to decide whether or not to admit the visitors. The Lady Helpers were told, "A very simple formula defines the position—not to cross the threshold unless an invitation is given to enter, not to sit down unless a seat is offered, to remember that every room of a cottage has as much right to privacy as any lady's drawing room."

Compared to British and American women, French women's power to shape social policy was more circumscribed. To an extraordinary degree, the French regarded family matters as a public concern, far too important in the eyes of men to be left to women. Male politicians often initiated social welfare policies for women and children, and typically they headed private as well as public social welfare agencies. In an important study of women and protective labor legislation in France, Mary Lynn Stewart concludes that "feminists played a peripheral role in the campaign for hours standards."[95]

On the grass-roots level and in a wide range of organizations, however, French women did participate in public and private social welfare provision. Their activities in voluntary associations, unlike those of their British and American counterparts, were more often subsidized by public funds and regulated by government officials from the central state (in the case of parochial activities, the church provided funds), as well as from progressive *départements* such as the Seine and communes such as Villiers-le-duc. Well into the twentieth century, French women were far more likely to participate in maternalist activities than join feminist organizations, even though maternalism did not necessarily further their emancipation as a sex. While some historians estimate that feminists before the turn of the century probably numbered no more than a few thousand,[96] the conservative Ligue Patriotique rapidly became the most powerful organization for women in the country, with over 400,000 members by World War I.[97] Léonie Chaptal, along with other committed Social Catholic women, established anti-tuberculosis clinics in the slums of Paris and developed pioneering childbirth and infant-care programs. The Paris branch of the Maternité Mutuelle, like so many other maternal and child welfare agencies in France, was established by a man but relied on a large corps of well-to-do patronesses to implement its directives.[98]

Pointing to the reduced infant mortality rates resulting from the organization's excellent services to employed working women, legislators cited the Maternité Mutuelle of Paris as a model for the kinds of programs envisioned by the Strauss Law of 1913.[99] This measure, which mandated a four-week post-partum period for working mothers to rest and care for their infants, also stressed the importance of creating an army of "women of good standing in their communities" to offer person-to-person advice to working mothers about the virtues of breastfeeding and proper infant hygiene.

German women in the late nineteenth century, like those of the other three nation states, drew on a legacy of private charitable work in maternal and child welfare. But their freedom to initiate policy was profoundly limited by a strongly entrenched state bureaucracy and a system of education that made it difficult for women to acquire necessary skills and training.[100] The precocious development of state welfare programs under Bismarck and the mandarin workings of the exclusively male civil service that it sheltered narrowed the range of issues and power available to German women.[101]

Yet the work of Christoph Sachsse suggests that the middle-class German woman's movement played a key role in establishing the programmatic foundations of *Sozialfürsorge* (social relief), which, unlike alms and private charity, was based on the social rights of citizens and was preventive in aim.[102] As a wide range of new social problems confronted the rapidly expanding urban centers of Germany, middle-class feminists called for female emancipation based on women's motherly roles as welfare providers in society. They not only organized the national Bund Deutscher Frauenvereine (League of German Women's Associations) but also initiated policies and programs through organizations like the Mädchen-und-Frauengruppen für Sozialhilfsarbeit (Girls' and Women's Groups for Social Assistance Work).[103]

The socialist women who founded the Bund für Mutterschutz (The League for the Protection of Motherhood) called for a new sexual ethics and for birth control to give women direct control over their reproductive labors. The Bund demanded a wide range of redistributive state programs including maternity insurance,[104] extended terms of indemnified and mandatory leave from work before and after parturition, child care, and legal advice for mothers. It even succeeded in its campaign to have state maternity rights extended to unmarried mothers.[105]

WHILE BY NO MEANS EXHAUSTIVE, these examples demonstrate that women in all four countries contributed substantially to the development of private, voluntary, maternal and child welfare programs, some of which served as models for state programs and others of which were themselves taken over by the state. But there were important and enduring differences among women's gains in terms of tangible benefits and political power, differences highlighted by two sets of comparisons. The first examines concrete benefits such as the provision of state-subsidized crèches, maternity leaves and nursing bonuses. The second evaluates women's success in achieving power within state and local bureaucracies as inspectors and officers of health.

A comparative survey of day nurseries and crèches in France, Germany, and Great Britain undertaken in 1904 revealed striking contrasts. In Great Britain, all of the day nurseries responding to the survey were charitable undertakings that relied entirely on private subscriptions. While not included in the survey, the United States presented a similar picture. In France and Germany, a majority of the crèches and *Krippen* were subsidized by a combination of local, state, and private resources, with the exception of parochial charities staffed, funded, and controlled by churches.[106]

By the turn of the century, the sixty-six crèches in Paris alone received £1,468 from the minister of the interior, £67,045 from the Ville de Paris and £1,376 from the Conseil Général des Départements. While we do not have fully comparable statistics for Germany, the evidence strongly suggests that *Krippen* and "waiting schools" (generally for children between two and six years old) were even more widespread and better funded than in France. In Berlin, as in Paris, there were sixty-six crèches in 1904, although the population of Paris was nearly 30 percent greater. By contrast, London, with more than twice the population of Berlin, had only fifty-four crèches, none of which were publicly subsidized or licensed.[107] New York City, with a population almost equal to London's, had ninety-two day nurseries, but these, too, lacked public support or regulation.[108] Outside the capital cities, the differences were even more marked. There were only nineteen provincial crèches in all of England, compared to 322 in France. In the United States, by 1916, there were approximately 700 nurseries in operation, but only a few received partial funding from municipal subsidies.[109]

With public funding came greater regulation. In both France and Germany, state and municipal-level authorities established detailed requirements for the management of all crèches and *Krippen*—both public and private—including minimum room temperatures, daily registers, and guides to weighing children and preparing pure milk. The French women who ran the crèches were closely supervised by officers of the ministry of the interior, who had the right to inspect nurseries to ensure that they conformed with codes.[110] By comparison, in Britain and the United States, standards were largely the concern of voluntary authorities. In Britain, regulation was left up to individual managers, while in the United States, where only a few states and cities required nurseries to obtain permits, the National Federation of Day Nurseries urged members to meet certain standards.[111]

The British and American women who ran and staffed day nurseries were free from the scrutiny of male officials, but they also had to make do with less generous funding. As a result, their nurseries tended to be less well staffed. French crèches, for example, had large female staffs including directors, wardens, cooks, and laundry maids, who were assisted by well-to-do women, appointed by the mayor to serve as managers or *dames patronnesses*. Doctors, almost always men, visited the crèches daily and helped set up Schools for Mothers. The appointment of salaried crèche personnel typically required official approval by the prefect or mayor.[112] In Britain and the United States, women in similar positions were either privately employed or volunteers, and the slender budgets of the charitable nurseries kept staff wages and numbers to a minimum. It might be argued that American and British women had more autonomy in the field of child care—as elsewhere—but they also had to make do with scantier public subsidies and other kinds of governmental support.

The inability of American and British maternalists to gain more generous benefits for the women and children of their countries appears all the more ironic when one compares their bureaucratic and political power to that of women in France and Germany. In these latter countries, women had trouble gaining footholds in the state itself, even at the lowest levels of the civil service. Denied *Beamte* status (full membership in the civil service, which carried permanent job security) because they lacked the necessary qualifications, German women inspectors were viewed as little more than functionaries and had no police authority.[113] British women factory inspectors had full powers to prosecute offenders and did so themselves.[114] Their reports were published separately and often commended for their particular thoroughness and insight,[115] while those of German women inspectors were usually published under name of the (male) head inspector.[116] The position of French *inspectrices* resembled that of their German counterparts: they were often denied powers to investigate conditions or to enforce codes, and their authority and discretionary powers were severely limited. Because of educational and other bureaucratic requirements, they were unlikely to be promoted.[117]

German and French women's restricted avenues to the civil service also denied them political leverage, with the result that they had little voice in the legislative process.[118] Nonetheless, concrete measures were passed on their behalf. British and American women were far more vocal. They served as expert witnesses and members of public boards and commissions, and used their positions as factory, health, and school board inspectors to organize female workers and more generally promote women's trade unionism. In addition to highly visible positions within the Children's Bureau, American women worked not only as factory inspectors but as statisticians and analysts in state labor bureaus, where they gathered data vital to their public reform campaigns. Even though they succeeded in establishing public programs at the municipal and state level throughout the 1910s and 1920s, they did not gain permanent federal entitlements for women and children until the 1930s.

In the development of maternal and child welfare legislation in the four countries, Germany and France repeatedly led the way in the range and amount of benefits they provided mothers and children.[119] From 1883 onward, German women received assistance (*Wochengeld*, or confinement money) from the state to compensate for their lost earnings during mandatory maternity leaves. The length of these leaves and the categories of women eligible to receive them were expanded several times between 1880 and World War I, eventually reaching eight weeks and covering agricultural laborers as well as factory workers. Beginning in 1893, French women had the right to free medical treatment during confinement and, after 1911, paid maternity leave and a nursing bonus.[120]

British women received fewer benefits, and what they had often took the form of limiting rather than redistributive protective legislation. From 1891 until 1911, Britain alone prohibited postnatal employment for four weeks, but it offered no compensatory payments. In 1911, the wives of insured workers and women insured in their own right were finally granted a lump-sum payment, usually 30 shillings at confinement, to address this hardship. Initially, the benefit was paid to the husband, but after strenuous lobbying by groups including the largely working-class Women's Cooperative Guild, mothers gained direct control over these funds.[121] Confusion and skepticism over what constituted genuine incapacity to work due to pregnancy intensified deeply engrained objections to public support for maternal welfare in Britain. For several years after the Insurance Act was passed, the Approved Societies charged with administering it, fueled by the anxieties of their male rank and file as well as a looming fiscal crisis caused by an actuarial miscalculation of the extent of women's perinatal illness, usually denied women's claims for sickness benefits during pregnancy.[122]

The United States provided neither federal maternity benefits nor medical care for mothers and children. Under the Sheppard–Towner Act of 1921, public health nurses could offer maternal and infant health education but no direct services. The United States was, however, the first country to offer widows' and mothers' pensions (albeit only at the state level until 1935).[123] Since payment levels in most states were calculated to support children but not their mothers, these early pension plans did not prohibit maternal employment; this restriction came later, when the federal government took over provisions as Aid to Dependent Children under the Social Security Act of 1935.[124]

Although British and American maternalists were often stymied in attempts to use their bureaucratic positions to institute and control maternal and child welfare programs in their own countries, they sometimes had the peculiar experience of seeing them taken up in France and Germany. With some bitterness, Margaret McMillan, a British child-welfare advocate, noted that "Germany never despised any advance in English social life." In 1896, McMillan had spearheaded "an agitation for school baths" in Bradford, where she sat as an elected Independent Labour party representative on the school board. As she tells it, "A leaflet on Hygiene and Cleanliness was sent out into the schools. It had been carefully and tactfully written. England ignored the whole effort, but not so Germany. She [Germany] had the leaflet translated and circulated in her schools, and she started to build school baths by the thousand."[125] While British women had the political and social space and power to develop innovative schemes like school baths, German bureaucrats transformed isolated pioneering efforts into widespread and publicly financed programs.[126]

Once established, the German and French state welfare systems, through direct programs and indirect subsidies, offered mothers and children more and better resources than did those of the United States and Britain. However, French and German women generally had much less control than did their British and American counterparts over the formulation and administration of policy. In all four countries, women often lost control over maternalist discourses when they were debated in male-dominated legislatures or became linked with other causes.[127] This sequence of events was most dramatic in Germany. The middle-class feminists who established the first Soziale Frauenschule on the moral and non-partisan foundations of "spiritual motherhood" endured the transformation of their schools into tools of national socialism. The Prussian ministry of education decreed in 1934 that Salomon's Frauenschulen should be renamed Schulen für Volkspflege (Schools for Training Officials for the People's Welfare), with the aim of planting "the ideas of National-Socialism deeply in the mind of the "students" through instruction in subjects such as race theory and "Adolph Hitler and the history of the National-Socialist Party."[128]

A REVIEW OF CURRENT RESEARCH DEMONSTRATES THAT welfare-state development was deeply influenced by female activists and their philosophies, commitments, and experiments in social welfare. Maternalist women put an unmistakable stamp on emerging welfare administrations. But their success was always qualified by prevailing political conditions and tended to be inversely proportionate to the strength of women's movements. Without maternalist politics, welfare states would surely have been less responsive to the needs of women and children, for maternalists raised issues—or highlighted them in specific ways—that seldom occurred to male politicians. Indeed, many men felt that only women could identify and respond to these needs. Yet women activists were compelled to rely on male politicians to gain state support for their programs and often had to wait until a national crisis such as war or class conflict created an opening for their initiatives.[129]

To different degrees, depending on the availability of political space in the four nations we have examined, maternalism served women as an important avenue into the public sphere. Female reformers demonstrated that a strong commitment to motherhood did not necessarily limit or weaken their political participation but instead transformed the nature of politics itself. Paula Baker's observation about the United States holds true for France, Germany, and Great Britain: by identifying and insisting on issues of gender-based needs, women challenged the male monopoly on public discourse and opened it up to discussions of private values and well-being.[130] It was not the case that male political actors, unsolicited, instigated state encroachments on family life; rather, female political actors demanded that states take up the concerns of women and children.[131]

Nevertheless, for female activists and clients alike, the political process that culminated in the passage of protective and welfare legislation for women and children functioned, in an exaggerated fashion, as a Weberian "iron cage": they found dissonance between means and ends, their own motives and ultimate policy outcomes. The translation of maternalist measures into state policy meant that poor and working-class women, initially at a disadvantage because they lacked direct representation in philanthropically based social services, were even further removed from the sites of policy making. As social work and related health fields became professionalized and services moved into state-run agencies, middle-class women carved out niches for themselves within the state. In these new positions, however, women frequently found themselves at the bottom of organizational hierarchies, their voices diminished in policy discussions with male bureaucrats, physicians, and politicians. To offset their liability to marginalization, the younger generation of American activists consciously jettisoned maternalism, which they characterized as unsystematic and unscientific.[132]

In the United States and Great Britain, women used their authority as experts in maternal and child welfare to forge political identities. These identities, in turn, helped some to build a wide range of women's political and social action organizations and movements.[133] By the end of World War I, significant groups of women in both countries achieved full citizenship rights. But, because their positions in mainstream political parties and within the central government remained peripheral for decades, female activists could not make legislative gains on their own. The need for male political allies often forced them into difficult compromises and concessions.

French and German women were even weaker politically. Though granted more generous benefits, they were unable to convert welfare programs into political currency. In France, maternal and infant legislation existed in what was otherwise a political wasteland for women, who were, legally, appendages of their husbands until after World War II. German women won employment rights and the vote after War I, but these gains were vitiated during the Weimar Republic and under the Third Reich. Abetted by conservative women's organizations, the Nazi regime perverted the meaning of maternalism as it condemned women to producing children for the state.

Despite these outcomes, the weight of the new research compels revision of historical conceptualizations of maternalist activities, state development, and the relationship between them in the late nineteenth and early twentieth centuries. When viewed from the perspective of maternalist politics, women's charitable institutions and organizations take on new significance as components of networks of benevolence as well as sites of state welfare program and policy formulation, experimentation, and implementation. Women's campaigns for maternal and child welfare emerged at approximately the same time in all four nation states, sometimes in concert with one another, and drew attention to the special needs of women and children in an industrializing world. Joining humanitarian appeals to thorough research and investigation, they contributed to the political momentum needed for reform. Maternalist women not only played important roles in promoting the growth of publicly funded welfare programs but were quick to exploit the new opportunities that statutory agencies offered them. The interactions between women's movements, states, and national political cultures from 1880 to 1920 affected the subsequent course of both women's history and the history of welfare states. The traces of these interactions remain distinctly perceptible today.

Acknowledgements

This article grew out of a series of conferences on Gender and the Origins of Welfare States held at the Harvard Center for European Studies in 1987–1988; we are grateful to the participants in those meetings, as well as to our fellow organizers, Frances Gouda, Jane Jenson, and Jennifer Schirmer. We would also like to thank Anna Davin, Jane Lewis, Adele Lindenmeyr, Karen Offen, Susan Potter, Sonya Rose, and Theda Skocpol for valuable suggestions on the manuscript. The Committee on States and Social Structures of the Social Science Research Council has generously provided support for this project.

Notes

1 Virginia Woolf, *A Room of One's Own* (London, 1929), 67; Julia Kristeva, "Stabat Mater," in Susan Rubin Suleiman, ed., *The Female Body in Western Culture: Contemporary Perspectives* (Cambridge, Mass., 1985), 99.

2 This observation holds true for many advanced industrial societies. We focus on these four because the rich secondary literature for each permits meaningful comparisons.

3 Emilia Kanthack, *The Preservation of Infant Life* (London, 1907), 28.

4 Hubertine Auclert, "Programme électoral des femmes," *La Citoyenne*, August 1885, as cited in Edith Taïeb, ed., *Hubertine Auclert: La Citoyenne, 1848–1914* (Paris, 1982), 41. Karen Offen explored this theme in "Minotaur or Mother? The Gendering of the State in Early Third Republic France" (unpublished paper).

5 Ruth Bré outlined her vision in *Das Recht auf Mutterschaft* (Leipzig and Berlin, 1904). For a discussion of this work and its relationship to the socialist Bund für Mutterschutz (League for the Protection of Motherhood), see Ann Taylor Allen, "Mothers of the New Generation: Adele Scheiber, Helene Stocker, and the Evolution of a German Idea of Motherhood, 1900–1914," *Signs*, 10 (Spring 1985): 418–438.

6 For example, Theresa McBride argued that "the consensus of male trade unionists before 1914 was that women's work was a necessary evil, and that women undercut male wages by increasing the competition for jobs"; "French Women and Trade Unionism: The First Hundred Years," in Norbert Soldon, ed., *The World of Women's Trade Unionism: Comparative Historical Essays* (Westport, Conn., 1985), 37. On the paternalistic attitudes of leading British trade unionists such as Ben Tillet, see Sheila Lewenhak, *Women and Trade Unions: An Outline History of the British Trade Union Movement* (London, 1977), 91. On the strained relationship between the Labour party and the Women's Labour League, especially during its formative years, see Christine Collette, *For Labour and for Women: The Women's Labour League, 1906–1918* (Manchester, 1989), 35. On women and the Parti Ouvrier Français, see Marilyn J. Boxer, "Socialism Faces Feminism: The Failure of Synthesis in France, 1879–1914," in Boxer and Jean H. Quataert, eds, *Socialist*

Women: European Socialist Feminism in the Nineteenth and Early Twentieth Centuries (New York, 1978), 79; Charles Sowerwine, *Sisters or Citizens? Women and Socialism in France since 1876* (Cambridge, 1982); and Steven Hause with Anne R. Kenney, *Women's Suffrage and Social Politics in the French Third Republic* (Princeton, N.J., 1984), chaps. 2–3. For an account of the relationship between women and earlier forms of socialism in France, in particular Saint-Simonism, see Claire Goldberg Moses, *French Feminism in the Nineteenth Century* (Albany, N.Y., 1984), chap. 3. On a similar phenomenon in England in the 1830s, see Barbara Taylor's analysis of the ways in which Owenite men, ostensibly in the vanguard of women's rights, ultimately undermined their initiatives, in *Eve and the New Jerusalem: Socialism and Feminism in the Nineteenth Century* (New York, 1983), chap. 4.

7   Scholars like Jane Lewis have rightly pointed out that interpersonal forms of welfare are often based on the assumption that the individual is morally culpable for her or his poverty; see Lewis, *The Politics of Motherhood: Child and Maternal Welfare in England, 1900–1939* (London, 1980), 18–19. The female founders of social work rejected this equation, at least in theory. While they complained about working-class mothers' neglect of their children, reformers were often acutely aware of the burdens faced by working women. The opening of Carolyn Steedman's autobiographical *Landscape for a Good Woman: A Story of Two Lives* (New Brunswick, N.J., 1987), highlights the class-divided nature of social welfare as women's work in Britain. The psychological violence a female health visitor inflicted on Steedman's mother becomes Steedman's own "secret and shameful defiance"; 2. Racial and ethnic divisions between reformers and clients were most common in the United States, although most minority groups made concerted efforts to care for "their own." On the black maternal and infant health movements, see Darlene Clark Hine, *Black Women in White: Racial Conflict and Cooperation in the Nursing Profession, 1890–1950* (Bloomington, Ind., 1989), chaps. 4, 7. On cultural conflict between German and East European Jews, see Elizabeth Rose, "Americanizing the Family: Class, Gender, and Ethnicity in a Jewish Settlement House," paper presented at the Eighth Berkshire Conference on the History of Women, Rutgers University, New Brunswick, New Jersey, 1990.

8   By women's movements, we mean those expressly aimed at shaping and changing the conditions of women's lives, sometimes but not always sympathetic with the goals of political feminism. By movements of women, we refer to organizations and campaigns initiated and managed by women that did not seek to change women's status.

9   Our definition is similar to those that Karen Offen gives for "familial feminism" in "Depopulation, Nationalism, and Feminism in Fin-de-Siècle France," *AHR*, 89 (June 1984): 654, and for "relational feminism" in "Defining Feminism: A Comparative Historical Approach," *Signs*, 14 (Autumn 1988): 119–157. In the latter article, she writes, "Relational feminism emphasized women's rights *as women* (defined principally by their childbearing and/ or nurturing capacities in relation to men). It insisted on *women's* distinctive contributions in these roles to the broader society and made claims on the commonwealth on the basis of these contributions"; 136. We prefer to use the term "maternalism" for this set of ideas. See Nancy Cott's caution against conflating all forms of women's activism under the umbrella term of feminism or one of its variants in "What's in a Name? The Limits of 'Social Feminism, or, Expanding the Vocabulary of Women's History," *Journal of American History*, 76 (December 1989): 809–29; and Cott, "Comment on Karen Offen's 'Defining Feminism: A Comparative Historical Approach,'" *Signs*, 15 (Autumn 1989): 203–205.

10 We have used the categories public and private to highlight their permeability. Other feminist scholars have pointed out that the strict gender division between public and private that many social theorists take as a given is, in fact, a social construction. For the evolution of this dichotomy, see Jean Bethke Elshtain, *Public Man, Private Woman: Women in Social and Political Thought* (Princeton, N.J., 1984), chap. 4; and Joan Landes, *Women and the Public Sphere in the Age of the French Revolution* (Ithaca, N.Y., 1988).

11   See Nancy Fraser, "The Struggle over Needs: Outline of a Socialist-Feminist Critical Theory of Late Capitalist Political Culture," in *Unruly Practices: Power, Discourse, and Gender in Contemporary Social Theory* (Minneapolis, Minn., 1989), 161–187; for a specific comparative case study, see Jane Jenson, "Paradigms and Political Discourse; Protective Legislation in France and the United States before 1914," *Canadian Journal of Political Science*, 20 (June 1989): 235–258.

12   States also relied on other forms of private-sector welfare initiatives, including those emanating from churches and business. On the role of business in the French welfare system, see Laura Lee Downs, "Between Taylorism and *Dénatalité*: Women, Welfare Supervisors, and the Boundaries of Difference in French Metalworking Factories, 1917–1995," in Dorothy O. Helly and Susan M. Reverby, eds, *Connected Domains: Beyond the Public-Private Dichotomy* (Ithaca, N.Y., forthcoming).

13   We use the terms "strong" and "weak" states here to designate domestic, policing, and welfare mechanisms, not external functions such as the financing and waging of war. See John Brewer, *The Sinews of Power: War, Money, and the English State, 1688–1783* (New York, 1989), xvii–xxii. In the British case, the term "limited" state may be more apt than "weak". While the British state lacked "a strong bureaucratic stratum with powerful interests of its own, a strong set of popular expectations of the role of the state or a sense of popular identification with it," Pat Thane argues that it did nonetheless possess "highly effective central government institutions." See Pat Thane, "Government and Society in England and Wales, 1750–1914," in F.M.L. Thompson, editor, *The Cambridge Social History of Britain*, Vol. 3 (Cambridge, 1990): 1.

14   Deborah Dwork captured the irony of this political fact in the title of her book, *War Is Good for Babies and Other Young Children: A History of the Infant and Child Welfare Movement in England, 1898–1918* (London, 1987). On Britain, see also Anna Davin, "Imperialism and Motherhood," *History Workshop*, 5 (1977): 9–65. Alisa Klaus offers a useful comparison of the impact of similar ideologies in "Depopulation and Race Suicide: Pronatalist Ideologies in France and the United States," in Seth Koven and Sonya Michel, eds, *Gender and the Origins of Welfare States in Western Europe and North America* (forthcoming); see also Offen, "Depopulation, Nationalism, and Feminism." On the inadequacy of provisions in Germany, see Karin Hausen, "The German Nation's Obligations to the Heroes' Widows of World War I," in Margaret Higonnet, *et al.*, eds, *Behind the Lines: Gender and the Two World Wars* (New Haven, Conn., 1987), 126–140.

15   See, for example, Gaston V. Rimlinger, *Welfare Policy and Industrialization in Europe, America and Russia* (New York, 1971); and Peter Flora and Arnold J. Heidenheimer, eds, *The Development of Welfare States in Europe and America* (New Brunswick, N.J., 1981).

16   For a comprehensive discussion of this group of theorists, see Michael Shalev, "The Social Democratic Model and Beyond: Two Generations of Comparative Research on the Welfare State," *Comparative Social Research*, 6 (1985): 315–351.

17   For the United States, see, for example, Edward Berkowitz and Kim McQuaid, *Creating the Welfare State: The Political Economy of Twentieth-Century Reform*, 2nd edn (New York, 1988); and Gwendolyn Mink, *Old Labor and New Immigrants in American Historical Development* (Ithaca, N.Y., 1986), esp. part 3.

18   See Hugh Heclo, *Modern Social Politics in Britain and Sweden* (New Haven, Conn., 1974); Roger Davidson, "Llewellyn Smith, the Labour Department, and Government Growth, 1886–1909," in Gillian Sutherland, ed., *Studies in the Growth of Nineteenth-Century Government* (Totowa, N.J., 1972), 227–62; and Peter Evans, Dietrich Rueschemeyer, and Theda Skocpol, eds, *Bringing the State Back In* (New York, 1985).

19   Margaret Weir, Ann Shola Orloff, and Theda Skocpol, "Understanding American Social Politics," in Weir, Orloff, and Skocpol, eds, *The Politics of Social Policy in the United States* (Princeton, N.J., 1988), 3–27.

20   To be sure, most of these models were first developed before women's history and gender studies emerged as full-blown fields. But their failure to consider women's relationships to welfare states is still surprising, given the availability of dramatic data on past and continuing

gender differentials in poverty rates, and the prominence of women in charity and social welfare work.

21 For the impact of these factors on British working-class women, see Sonya Rose, *Gender, Labor, and Capital: The Creation of a Segregated World of Work and Its Consequences in Nineteenth-Century Britain* (forthcoming); on American working women, Alice Kessler-Harris, *A Woman's Wage: Symbolic Meanings and Social Consequences* (Lexington, Ky., 1990).

22 Strongly indebted to Max Weber, state-centered theorists have assimilated his restrictive definition of the state: "[L]ike the political institutions historically preceding it, the state is a relation of men dominating men, a relation supported by means of legitimate [that is, considered to be legitimate] violence"; "Politics as a Vocation," in *From Max Weber*, ed. and trans. by Hans Gerth and C. Wright Mills (New York, 1946), 78. Although Weber was using the word "men" generically here, he was, in fact, describing a bureaucracy and political system occupied exclusively by men.

23 Heclo's otherwise fine study, *Modern Social Politics in Britain and Sweden*, illustrates the drawbacks of such an approach. It forces women's work in creating and implementing policies in the private sector and in partnership with municipal and public authorities into the category "lobbying" or "interest" groups and thus devalues the political meaning of these activities and understates their impact. By explicitly taking gender into account, Theda Skocpol has begun a major recasting of state-centered theory; see her *Protecting Soldiers and Mothers* (forthcoming); and Skocpol and Gretchen Ritter, "Gender and the Origins of Modern Social Policies in Britain and the United States" (forthcoming).

24 In this sense, women were following the pattern of disenfranchised Englishmen in the eighteenth and early nineteenth centuries who turned to charitable and civic work to gain political expertise and power. See John Brewer, "Commercialization and Politics," Part 2, in Neil McKendrick, John Brewer, and J. H. Plumb, *Birth of a Consumer Society* (Bloomington, Ind., 1982), 227; and R. J. Morris, "Voluntary Societies and British Urban Elites," *Historical Journal*, 26 (1989): 95–118. For men's charity work and voluntary associations, see also Lenore Davidoff and Catherine Hall, *Family Fortunes* (Chicago, 1989), chap. 10; on men's associations more generally, 73. For a comparative perspective, see Ira Katznelson, "Working-Class Formation and the State: Nineteenth-Century England in American Perspective," in Evans, Skocpol, and Rueschemeyer, *Bringing the State Back In*, 270–74. According to Katznelson, it was "in the voluntary organizations created in the 'free space' of communities separated from work spaces [that] English workers learned to put claims to their employers and to the state in a rhetoric and idiom of class"; 270.

25 See Elizabeth Payne, *Reform, Labor and Feminism: Margaret Dreier Robins and the Women's Trade Union League* (Urbana, Ill., 1988).

26 Henri Rollet, *L'Action social des catholiques en France: 1871–1914*, 2 vols. (Paris, 1958), 2: 34–36, 116–125. For a firsthand account of a visit to a Maison Sociale, see L. J. Charles, "Visites de la Société Internationale," *Revue philanthropique*, 7 (April 1906): 779–785. The Maisons Sociales in Paris, like women's settlements in the United States and Britain, were residential communities of single women located in poor urban districts. But, unlike their Anglo-American counterparts, the French women saw themselves as agents of Christian benevolence and "apostolic zeal," not as pioneers of scientific social work and shapers of public policy. And while several residents sought diplomas in household management or nursing, they lacked the collegiate credentials of most Anglo-American settlement workers.

27 See Molly Ladd-Taylor, "Hull-House Goes to Washington: Mothers, Child Welfare and the State," paper presented at the meeting of the American Historical Association, Cincinnati, Ohio, December 1988.

28 Mimi Abramovitz, *Regulating the Lives of Women: Social Welfare Policy from Colonial Times to the Present* (Boston, 1988), 36–40. For more theoretical arguments along these lines, see Mary McIntosh, "The State and the Oppression of Women," in Annette Kuhn and AnnMarie Wolpe, eds, *Feminism and Materialism: Women and Modes of Production* (London, 1978), 254–289; and

Zillah R. Eisenstein, ed., *Capitalist Patriarchy and the Cast for Socialist Feminism* (New York, 1979). For a cogent critique of this position, see Jane Jenson, "Gender and Reproduction: Or, Babies and the State," *Studies in Political Economy*, 20 (Summer 1986): 9–46.

29 Elizabeth Wilson, *Women and the Welfare State* (London, 1977), 14, 7–8. See also Abramovitz, *Regulating the Lives of Women*. For Wilson's personal views on motherhood, see her "in a Different Key," in Catherine Gieve, ed., *Balancing Acts: On Being a Mother* (London, 1989).

30 Gillian Pascal made a similar critique of reifying or monolithic feminist theories of patriarchy in *Social Policy: A Feminist Analysis* (London, 1986). A parallel criticism has been made of Marxist social control theorists who set up a binary opposition between bourgeois and working-class culture that assigns thrift and sobriety to the former, leaving, by implication, shiftlessness and insobriety to the latter.

31 Nonfeminists simply take this for granted, while some feminists make it the explicit point of their critique.

32 Carole Pateman calls this "Wollstonecraft's Dilemma." While viewing women's political participation in a patriarchal state as problematic, she points out that women's growing economic importance has drawn attention to the inequities of their political status and believes that women can achieve equality if there is a shift from welfare states to welfare societies; Pateman, "The Patriarchal Welfare State: Women and Democracy," in Amy Gutman, ed., *Democracy and the Welfare State* (Princeton, N.J., 1988), esp. 250–260. For a more pessimistic view, see Catherine McKinnon, *Toward a Feminist Theory of the State* (Cambridge, Mass., 1989).

33 Women exerted what Linda Gordon, borrowing from Elizabeth Janeway, calls "the powers of the weak" to use these agencies as resources to enlist middle-class visitors and social workers as their allies in efforts to protect themselves and their children; see *Heroes of Their Own Lives: The Politics and History of Family Violence* (New York, 1988), 251. Gordon has also written that "[w]elfare not only replaced men as the object of women's dependence; it also subverted women's dependence on men"; "What Does Welfare Regulate?" *Social Research*, 55 (Winter 1988): 630.

One of the first historians to focus on client activism was Barbara Brenzel in *Daughters of the State: A Social Portrait of the First Reform School for Girls in North America, 1856–1905* (Cambridge, Mass., 1983), although she did not use this approach as consistently as Gordon does. A fine study by Alisa Klaus shows that women actively sought information from the U.S. Children's Bureau; see *Every Child a Lion: The Origins of Infant Health Policy in the United States and France 1890–1920* (Ithaca, N.Y., forthcoming). Other recent studies reveal the extent to which working-class women used and affected policies in receiving private charity and public welfare in Germany, France, and Britain. See, for example, Jean Quataert, "Women's Work and the Early Welfare State in Germany: Legislators, Bureaucrats and Clients before the First World War," in Koven and Michel, *Gender and the Origins of Welfare States*; and articles by Lynn Lees, Rachel Fuchs, and Ellen Ross in Peter Mandler, ed., *The Uses of Charity* (Philadelphia, 1990).

34 Dorothy George linked this phenomenon, which she called the "new humanitarianism," to her optimistic assessment of early industrial capitalism in Britain. See *England in Transition: Life and Work in Eighteenth-Century England* (London, 1931). On the impact of evangelicalism on women's position, see Jane Rendall, *The Origins of Modern Feminism: Women in Britain, France and the United States, 1780–1860* (New York, 1984), chap. 3.

35 Although maternalist ideologies bore identifiable national characteristics, they also shared commonalities as a result of activist women's long history of international collaboration. That between British and American women began at meetings of the World Anti-Slavery Society in the 1840s and continued through the Woman's Christian Temperance Union, the International Council of Women, the Charity Organization Society, and the settlement house movement. See Daniel Rodgers, "The Transatlantic Origins of the American Welfare State," paper presented at the Charles Warren Center, Harvard University, December 2, 1987.

36 The term "cult of true womanhood" was first used by Barbara Welter in her essay by the same name, "The Cult of True Womanhood, 1820–1860;" *American Quarterly*, 18 (Summer 1966): 151–174. For the ideology of republican motherhood, see Linda Kerber, *Women of the Republic: Intellect and Ideology in Revolutionary America* (Chapel Hill, N.C., 1980), chap. 5.

37 Maternalist ideologies were closely linked to new notions of respectability, which, according to George Mosse, arose with the nationalisms of late eighteenth and early nineteenth-century Europe. See Mosse, *Nationalism and Sexuality: Middle-Class Morality and Sexual Norms in Modern Europe* (Madison, Wis., 1985), chap. 1.

38 Mary P. Ryan, *Women in Public: Between Banners and Ballots* (Baltimore, Md., 1990), 100.

39 Lori D. Ginzberg, "'Moral Suasion Is Moral Balderdash': Women, Politics, and Social Activism in the 1850s," *Journal of American History*, 73 (December 1986): 601–622; and Ginzberg, *Women and the Work of Benevolence: Morality, Politics, and Class in the Nineteenth-Century United States* (New Haven, Conn., 1990), chaps. 5–6.

40 See Florence Kelley, "Should Women Be Treated Identically with Men by the Law?" *American Review*, 3 (May–June 1923): 277.

41 Elizabeth Lowell Putnam, "Note on the Children's Bureau," (n.d. [1929?]), box 3, folder 57, Elizabeth Lowell Putnam Papers, Schlesinger Library, Radcliffe College. Putnam's remark draws attention to the fact that anti-Soviet backlash was particularly strong in the United States and contributed to the overall hostility to federal welfare measures.

42 Mrs. Henry [Millicent Garrett] Fawcett, *Some Eminent Women of Our Times* (London, 1889), 1; see also Fawcett, "The Appeal against Female Suffrage: A Reply," in *Nineteenth Century*, 26 (July 1889): 86–96.

43 "An Appeal against Female Suffrage." *Nineteenth Century*, 25 (June 1889): 781–788. On the anti-suffrage women, see Brian Harrison, *Separate Spheres: The Opposition to Women's Suffrage in Britain* (London, 1978). Local government, perhaps the most important political arena open to British women, was also a stronghold of a "civic maternalist" ideology; see Seth Koven, "Civic Maternalism and the Welfare State: The Case of Mrs. Humphry Ward," paper presented at the Seventh Berkshire Conference on the History of Women, 1988; and Patricia Hollis, *Ladies Elect: Women in English Local Government 1865–1914* (Oxford, 1987).

44 These included Independent Labour party spokesperson Margaret McMillan and leaders of the Women's Cooperative Guild, the largest maternalist organization in Britain, Margaret Llewellyn Davies and Margaret Bondfield.

45 Women's Labour League, *Annual Report* (1907), 9.

46 Olwen Hufton, "Poverty and Charity: Revolutionary Mythology and Real Women," in *Women and the Limits of Citizenship in the French Revolution*; and Claude Langlois, *Le Catholicisme au feminin: Les Congregations françaises à supérieure générale au XIXᵉ siècle* (Paris, 1984), parts 2–3. For a discussion of the early context of Social Catholicism, see Katherine A. Lynch, *Family, Class, and Ideology in Early Industrial France: Social Policy and the Working-Class Family, 1825–1848* (Madison, Wis., 1988).

47 Bonnie Smith, *Ladies of the Leisure Class: The Bourgeoises of Northern France in the Nineteenth Century* (Princeton, N.J., 1981), chaps. 4, 8; see also Margaret H. Darrow, "French Noblewomen and the New Domesticity, 1750–1850;" *Feminist Studies*, 5 (1979): 41–65.

48 Their views of Durand were colored partly by her socialist-feminist politics, partly by her illegitimate birth. See Hause with Kenney, *Women's Suffrage and Social Politics in the French Third Republic*, 33–6.

49 Feminists like Marie Deraismes linked women's emancipation to the protection of the family and the Republic; see Moses, *French Feminism*, chap. 9.

50 Moses, *French Feminism*, chaps. 8–9; Hause with Kenney, *Women's Suffrage and Social Policy*, chap. 2.

51 Klaus, "Depopulation and Race Suicide." According to Klaus, the republicans claimed that women's "feminine attributes would enable them to personalize an increasingly bureaucratic welfare system, thus healing the alienation of the working class from the bourgeoisie. In addition,

physicians and politicians often voiced the hope that such voluntary activity would restimulate the maternal instinct of bourgeois women and girls"; (forthcoming).

52 The league's first president, Baroness de Brigode, great-granddaughter of Lafayette, asserted, "Next time we will check the color of the ballots a bit more carefully, for it affects our children's future"; Anne-Marie Sohn, "Catholic Women and Political Affairs: The Case of the Patriotic League of French Women," in Judith Friedlander, *et al.*, eds, *Women in Culture and Politics: A Century of Change* (Bloomington, Ind., 1986), 242.

53 Hause with Kenney, *Women's Suffrage and Social Policy*, 38.

54 Ann Taylor Allen, "Spiritual Motherhood: German Feminists and the Kindergarten Movement, 1848–1911," *History of Education Quarterly*, 22 (1982): 319–20.

55 Henriette Schrader-Breymann, quoted in Allen, "Spiritual Motherhood," 323–24.

56 Not all of her contemporaries were so progressive. One, Amalie Sieveking, saw her motherly work as entirely compatible with women's traditional place in society. See Catherine M. Prelinger, "Prelude to Consciousness: Amalie Sieveking and the Female Association for the Care of the Poor and Sick," in John C. Fout, ed., *German Women in the Nineteenth Century: A Social History* (New York, 1984); and Prelinger, *Charity, Challenge, and Change: Religious Dimensions of the Mid-Nineteenth-Century Women's Movement in Germany* (Westport, Conn., 1987), chap. 4.

57 See Alice Salomon, *Sozialfrauenbildung* (Leipzig, 1908).

58 Alice Salomon, "Character Is Destiny." typescript autobiography, 66–67. The Leo Baeck Institute in New York City has a copy of this manuscript, but we must thank Irmela Georges for sending a photocopy from Berlin. Originally written in English, the autobiography has been translated into German and published as *Charakter ist Schicksal. Lebenserinnerungen* (Basel, 1983).

59 For socialist women in Germany, see Jean Quataert, *Reluctant Feminists in German Social Democracy, 1885–1917* (Princeton, N.J., 1979).

60 Lily Braun, "The Female Mind," in Alfred G. Meyer, ed. and trans., *Selected Writings on Feminism and Socialism by Lily Braun* (Bloomington, Ind., 1987), 188.

61 Braun's simultaneous embrace of maternalism and socialism earned her the vituperation of Clara Zetkin, who refused to call herself a feminist because it suggested that women's battle for emancipation could be separated from the struggles of the proletariat to overthrow capitalism. For Braun's response to Zetkin's charges, see her "Left and Right," in Meyer, *Selected Writings*. Jean Quataert discusses the Zetkin-Braun controversy in "Unequal Partners in an Uneasy Alliance: Women and the Working Class in Imperial Germany," in Boxer and Quataert, eds, *Socialist Women*, 130–135.

62 Salomon, "Character Is Destiny," 67.

63 These campaigns were led by men like Lord Shaftesbury, Richard Waddington, and Gustave Dron, whose ostensible motives were benevolent and humane, although the consequences of their work were economically damaging for women and ultimately reinforced male control over workplace and family structures. On Waddington and Dron, see Mary Lynn Stewart, *Women, Work and the French State: Labour Protection and Social Patriarchy, 1879–1919* (Kingston, 1989), 31–36.

64 See Jane Humphries, "Protective Legislation, the Capitalist State and Working Class Men: The Case of the 1842 Mines Regulation Act," *Feminist Review*, 7 (1981): 1–33, for the response of working-class miners, men and women, to this legislation in England. On women's strikes against the implementation of protective laws in France, see Stewart, *Women, Work and the French State*, 202; on working women's resistance to protective laws in Germany, see Jean Quataert, "Social Insurance and the Family Work of Oberlausitz Home Weavers in the Late Nineteenth Century," in Fout, ed., *German Women*, 270–289.

65 Examples of redistributive legislation include the 30 shillings maternity allowance in Britain that was part of Lloyd George's 1911 social insurance scheme, the 1913 Strauss Law in France, and the various state-level mothers' and widows' pension measures passed in the United States from 1906 on.

66 On the byzantine debates and political machinations over this issue, see Mary Lynn McDougall [Stewart], "Protecting Infants: The French Campaign for Maternity Leaves, 1890s–1913," *French Historical Studies*, 13 (Spring 1983): 79–105; and Jenson, "Gender and Reproduction." The debate can be followed in the minutes of the Sénat, *Journal officiel*, March 9 and December 3, 1912. As McDougall noted, while France was late in passing a mandatory maternity leave, it was not from lack of interest in the issue or from lack of a tradition of state intervention in maternal and child welfare; 79–80.

67 Emile Rey, Minutes of the Sénat, *Journal officiel*, March 8, 1912.

68 Katharine Anthony, *Feminism in Germany and Scandinavia* (New York, 1915), 132.

69 The concepts of "strong" and "weak" states were first introduced in J. P. Nettl, "The State as a Conceptual Variable," *World Politics*, 20 (1968): 559–592; see also the critical discussion by Peter B. Evans, Dietrich Rueschemeyer, and Theda Skocpol, "On the Road toward a More Adequate Understanding of the State," in Evans, Rueschemeyer, and Skocpol, *Bringing the State Back In*, 350–351.

70 In so doing, Skocpol and Sklar are expanding the concept of the private sector, which, in this context, is usually thought to include business, trade unions, and (male) voluntary associations. See Skocpol, *Protecting Soldiers and Mothers*; and Kathryn Kish Sklar, "Explaining the Power of Women's Political Culture in the Creation of the American Welfare State, 1890–1930," in Koven and Michel, *Gender and the Origins of Welfare States*. Other state-centered scholars continue to ignore gender, even when it is germane to their analyses; see, for example, Stephen Skowronek, *Building the New American State: The Expansion of National Administrative Capacities, 1877–1920* (New York, 1982); and Abram de Swaan, *In Care of the State: Health Care, Education, and Welfare in Europe and the USA in the Modern Era* (Oxford, 1988).

71 Skocpol and Ritter, "Gender and the Origins of Modern Social Policies."

72 Sklar, "Explaining the Power of Women's Political Culture."

73 Sara Evans, *Born for Liberty: A History of Women in America* (New York, 1989), chap. 6.

74 The phrase is Skowronek's; see *Building a New American State*, part 2.

75 The Women's Christian Temperance Union's motto in the 1880s was "Do Everything"; see Ruth Bordin, *Women and Temperance: The Quest for Power and Liberty* (Philadelphia, 1980), 98.

76 See Skocpol, "An Unusual Victory for Public Benefits: The 'Wildfire Spread' of Mothers' Pensions," *Protecting Mothers and Soldiers*, chap. 7.

77 U.S. Children's Bureau, *Laws Relating to "Mothers' Pensions" in the United States, Canada, Denmark and New Zealand*, U.S. Children's Bureau Publication no. 63 (Washington, D.C., 1919).

78 Ladd-Taylor, "Hull-House Goes to Washington"; Robyn L. Muncy, "Creating a Female Dominion in American Reform, 1890–1930" (Ph.D. dissertation, Northwestern University, 1987), chap. 2.

79 Lela Costin, *Two Sisters for Social Justice: A Biography of Grace and Edith Abbott* (Urbana, Ill., 1983); Ellen Fitzpatrick, *Endless Crusade: Women Social Scientists and Progressive Reform* (New York, 1990); and Muncy, "Creating a Female Dominion," chap. 3.

80 Julia Lathrop, Letter of Transmission, in H. Harris, *Maternity Benefit Systems in Certain Foreign Countries*, U.S. Children's Bureau Publication no. 57 (Washington, D.C., 1919), 2.

81 On the next generation of women in government, see J. Stanley Lemons, *The Woman Citizen: Social Feminism in the 1920s* (Chicago, 1973); Susan Ware, *Beyond Suffrage: Women in the New Deal* (Cambridge, 1981); Ware, *Partner and I: Molly Dewson, Feminism, and New Deal Politics* (New Haven, Conn., 1987); and Muncy, "Creating a Female Dominion," chap. 4. Muncy notes that, at the urging of the Children's Bureau, by late 1921 forty-five states had established child hygiene divisions; forty-two were directed by women, and all were largely staffed by female public health nurses and other officials; 119.

82 See Anne Summers, "A Home from Home—Women's Philanthropic Work in the Nineteenth Century," in Sandra Burman, ed., *Fit Work for Women* (London, 1979), 33–63, for a study of the class tensions between middle-class women philanthropists and their clients in England and of the role of philanthropy in shaping women's sense of power and public identity.

83 For a reassessment of these reports and their best-known women authors, Beatrice Webb and Helen Bosanquet, see Jane Lewis, "The Place of Social Investigation, Social Theory, and Social Work in the Approach to Late Victorian and Edwardian Social Problems: The Case of Beatrice Webb and Helen Bosanquet," in Martin Bulmer, Kevin Bales, and Kathryn Kish Sklar, eds, *The Social Survey in Historical Perspective* (Cambridge, forthcoming).

84 For example, Elizabeth Fry's voluntary work in the 1820s and 1830s for the insane and for criminal women and Mary Carpenter's institutional experiments in juvenile reformatories in the 1840s and 1850s paved the way for parliamentary legislative reforms. Josephine Butler's campaign for the repeal of the Contagious Diseases Act was sparked by philanthropic concern for the exploitation of working-class prostitutes but ultimately mobilized women of all classes in exposing the state's role in sanctioning sexual double standards; see Judith Walkowitz, *Prostitution and Victorian Society* (Cambridge, 1980).

85 See Madeline Rooff's *Voluntary Societies and Social Policy* (London, 1957). Rooff, writing before the emergence of modern feminist scholarship, did not explore the implications of the preponderance of female actors in the histories she recounts. The Charity Organization Society (which was always a mixed sex organization) was an important exception to this model in its rejection of state interference.

86 See Martha Vicinus, *Independent Women, Work and Community for Single Women, 1850–1920* (London, 1985), chap. 6; Seth Koven, "Culture and Poverty: The London Settlement House Movement, 1870 to 1914" (Ph.D. dissertation, Harvard University, 1987), chap. 6; and Koven, "Borderlands: Women's Voluntary Associations and the Welfare State in Great Britain," in Koven and Michel, *Gender and the Origins of Welfare States*. On one men's settlement, see Standish Meacham, *Toynbee Hall and Social Reform: The Search for Community* (New Haven, Conn., 1987).

87 Ward was best known as the author of many celebrated and debated novels, including *Robert Elsmere* (London, 1888). A founder of Somerville College and settlement houses in London, Ward inherited a strong tradition of public service as granddaughter of Thomas Arnold and niece of Matthew Arnold.

88 Typescript, Liverpool Speech, delivered at Victoria Women's Settlement (n.d. [ca. 1899]), Passmore Edwards Settlement Papers, Mary Ward House, London. Eleanor Rathbone was beginning her own career at the settlement at the time Ward gave this speech, although it is not known whether she was in the audience.

89 See Janet Ward Trevelyan's account of this in *Evening Play Centres for Children* (New York, 1920), 56–57; for the effects of the war on other maternal and child welfare programs in Great Britain, see Dwork, *War Is Good for Babies*. Wartime demands increased the scope of welfare benefits elsewhere, but the topic is too large to take up here. In England, France, and Germany, a wide array of measures quickly passed into law, some designed specifically to insure women on the basis of their status as soldiers' wives. On the ambiguities of women's wartime gains in Germany and England respectively, see Anthony, *Feminism in Germany*, 32; and Susan Pedersen, "Gender, Welfare, and Citizenship in Britain during the Great War," *AHR*, 95 (October 1990): 983–1006. In the United States, the war had the effect of increasing the maternalists' political domain through the establishment of the Woman's Committee of the Council of National Defense; see Muncy, "Creating a Female Dominion," 112–115.

90 A local Act of Parliament, the Huddersfield Corporation Act of 1906, was the first statute of its kind in Great Britain; notification was not made mandatory on a national basis until 1915.

91 While Broadbent explicitly claimed that the scheme offered important new opportunities for women, ironically, the Vigilance Committee of the National Federation of Women Doctors blacklisted the posts in 1909 because the salaries were too low and because they feared that the work too closely resembled that of nurses. See Medical Women's Federation Collection, SA/MWF/C57, Contemporary Medical Archives, Wellcome Institute, London.

92 Louisa Hubbard, "Statistics of Women's Work;" in Angela Burdett-Coutts, ed., *Women's Mission: A Series of Congress Papers on the Philanthropic Work of Women by Eminent Authors* (London, 1893), 364.

93 See Barbara [Elizabeth] Leigh Hutchins, *Conflicting Ideals: Two Sides of the Woman's Question?* (London, 1913). On the expansion of health and welfare professions for women, see Dwork, *War Is Good for Babies*, 154–160.

94 S. G. H. Moore, *Report on Infantile Mortality*, County Borough of Huddersfield, 4th edn (1916), 115.

95 Stewart, *Women, Work and the French State*, 96. For an alternative interpretation, see Klaus, *Every Child a Lion*, chap. 3, which addresses a range of issues and movements that are marginal to Stewart's study. Klaus describes women's maternal and child welfare activities, including the Société de Charités Maternelles and its conflicts with officials of the Third Republic.

96 See Hause with Kenney, *Women's Suffrage*, 28–29.

97 Sohn, "Catholic Women," 237.

98 Pierre Budin's famous *Consultations de nourrissons* followed this pattern as well. See "Allocution de M. Paul Strauss," Assemblé générale de la fondation Pierre Budin, March 4, 1911, in *Revue philanthropique*, 29 (June 15, 1911): 199.

99 Minutes of the Sénat, *Journal officiel*, March 8, 1912.

100 See works by James C. Albisetti, "'The Reform of Female Education in Prussia, 1899–1908: A Study in Compromise and Containment," *German Studies Review*, 8 (February 1985): 11–41; "Could Separate Be Equal? Helene Lange and Women's Education in Imperial Germany," *History of Education Quarterly*, 22 (Fall 1982): 301–17; and *Schooling German Girls and Women: Secondary and Higher Education in the Nineteenth Century* (Princeton, N.J., 1989).

101 See Fritz Ringer, *The Decline of the German Mandarins: The German Academic Community, 1890–1933* (Cambridge, Mass., 1969), esp. chap. 3.

102 See Christoph Sachsse and Florian Tennstedt, *Geschichte der Armenfürsorge in Deutschland*, 2 vols. (Stuttgart, 1980, 1988), vol. 2: *Fürsorge und Wohlfahrtspflege 1871–1929*; Sachsse, *Mütterlichkeit als Beruf* (Frankfurt, 1986); and Young Sun Hong, "Femininity as a Vocation: Gender and Class Conflict in the Professionalization of German Social Work," in Geoffrey Cocks and Konrad H. Jarausch, eds, *German Social Work, 1880–1950* (New York, 1990), 232–237.

103 Sachsse, "Social Mothers, Feminism and Welfare State Formation in Germany, 1890–1929," in Koven and Michel, *Gender and the Origins of Welfare States*.

104 See Lily Braun, *Die Mutterschaftsversicherung* (Berlin, 1906).

105 Anthony, *Feminism in Germany and Scandinavia*, 139.

106 The role of confessional groups in the funding and management of maternal and child welfare is an area that needs much more investigation, particularly in Germany, where some states were Protestant, others Catholic.

107 Mrs. Townshend, "The Case for School Nurseries," Fabian Tract 145 (September 1909), in Sally Alexander, ed., *Women's Fabian Tracts* (London, 1985). Townshend also investigated the Ecoles Maternelles in France, which served children too old for nurseries but too young for school. These Ecoles also were staffed by salaried women and funded jointly by public funds and private contributions. See also "Report on Crèches," July 8, 1904, the Public Control Committee, London County Council, Greater London Record Office, which was based in part on the same statistics. An excellent social history of the impact of inadequate provisions can be found in Anna Davin, *Little Women: The Childhood of Working-Class Girls in Late Nineteenth-Century London* (forthcoming), esp. chap. 4, "Caretakers or Schoolchildren?"

108 Association of Day Nurseries of New York City, *Annual Report* (1910).

109 Emily D. Cahan, *Past Caring: A History of U.S. Preschool Care and Education for the Poor, 1820–1963* (New York, 1989), 13.

110 For example, see the proposed texts for a presidential decree and ministerial order adopted by the High Council for Public Assistance, *Revue philanthropique*, 1 (May 15, 1897): 117–119. According to the law of June 27, 1904, *inspectrices* were allowed to visit and inspect crèches. See also Hélène Moniez, "Lettre Ouverte à M. le Ministre de l'Interieur," *Revue philanthropique*,

18 (April 1906): 666, 671; and on female inspectors more generally, "Le Rôle de la femme dans le contrôle des services d'Assistance," *Revue philanthropique*, 14 (February 1904): 422.

111 Dr. S. Josephine Baker, director of the Division of Hygiene of the New York City Department of Health, complained that because of the lack of regulation, "the day nursery, in a number of instances, has come to be looked at as a commercial proposition, maintained for gain, and sometimes to the actual detriment of the children who are cared for"; "Day Nursery Standards," in U.S. Children's Bureau, *Standards of Child Welfare*, U.S. Children's Bureau Publication no. 60 (Washington, 1919), 219–233.

112 It is important to recognize that the degree of official control, even in France and Germany, varied locally. See the response of officials from Elberfeld, Germany, in Moore, *Report on Infantile Mortality*, 93–98.

113 See Jean Quataert, "A Source Analysis in German Women's History: Factory Inspectors' Reports and the Shaping of Working Class Lives, 1878–1914," *Central European History*, 16 (June 1988): 99–121. Quataert focused on the role of inspectors in imposing bourgeois behavioral norms on the working class, but she also considered the roles of male and female inspectors.

114 See Mary Drake McFeely, *Lady Inspectors: The Campaign for a Better Workplace 1893–1921* (Oxford, 1988), esp. chap. 7, on the inspectors' prosecutions of offenders.

115 See Gertrude Tuckwell Collection (Brighton, Sussex, Harvester Press Microform, 1981), for large numbers of newspaper clippings praising the reports of the women inspectors. Praise could be double-edged, as is clear from the report in the *Glasgow Herald* on May 20, 1910: "It is not many years since there was none but harsh criticism on the woman inspector and her 'narrow, fidgety, ways.' The change of opinions must arise from the fact that employers of labour have got accustomed to women as factory inspectors, or that the women take themselves less seriously and use their powers with more discretion than before." The piece ended on the "amusing note" that "men inspectors now admit women to the annual dinner, but they do not permit them to smoke on these occasions." It is important, however, not to overstate the power of British women in the civil service, for they still faced considerable obstacles well into the twentieth century. See Meta Zimmeck, "Strategies and Strategems of Women in the Civil Service," *Historical Journal*, 27 (1984): 901–924; and "The 'New Woman' in the Machinery of Government: A Spanner in the Works?" in Roy MacLeod, ed., *Government and Expertise: Specialists, Administrators and Professionals, 1860–1919* (New York, 1988), 185–202.

116 Quataert, "Source Analysis," 103–105.

117 Stewart, *Women, Work and the French State*, 89–93.

118 See Klaus, "Depopulation and Race Suicide."

119 For extraordinarily comprehensive and useful data about maternal and child welfare bills, their implementation and policy implications, see International Labour Office, Studies and Reports, esp. *The Law and Women's Work: A Contribution to the Study of the Status of Women* (Geneva, 1939), Series I, no. 4; *Women's Work under Labour Law: A Survey of Protective Legislation* (Geneva, 1932), Series 1, no. 2; and the *International Survey of Social Services* (Geneva, 1933), Series M, no. 11.

120 French women were also given a nursing bonus for the first twelve weeks. In addition to a maximum of eight weeks of paid pre-partum and post-partum maternity leave, they received half a franc per day of nursing for four weeks.

121 The guild was also responsible for the initial inclusion of a maternity benefit in the 1911 Insurance Act. Under the leadership of Margaret Llewelyn Davies, the guild was the largest and most politically adept organization representing working-class mothers in England. Davies claimed, "The Guild has … made a notable contribution to breaking down class and sex disabilities in public life"; *Life as We Have Known It* (1931; rpt. edn, London, 1977), xiv. The lobbying of women's groups like the Women's Cooperative Guild and Women's Labour League forced the government to acknowledge the sex-based distribution of resources within the

family and to pay mothers directly. On internal economies of working-class families in Britain, see Ellen Ross, "Labour and Love: Rediscovering London's Working-Class Mothers, 1870–1918;" in Jane Lewis, ed., *Labour and Love: Women's Experience of Home and Family, 1850–1940* (London, 1986), 73–98.

122 This miscalculation was, in fact, an artifact of women's own underreporting of illness during the period when they were not covered and felt compelled to work, no matter what the state of their health. Once benefits were available, they acknowledged their illnesses more openly. See Margaret Bondfield, *The National Care of Maternity: A Scheme Put Forward as a Basis for Discussion* (London, 1914), 9. On the attitudes of male trade unionists and friendly societies to the emergence of welfare legislation, see Pat Thane, "The Working Class and State Welfare in Britain, 1880–1914;" *Historical Journal*, 27 (1984): 877–900. Also see Sonya Rose, "Gender Antagonism and Class Conflict: Exclusionary Strategies of Male Trade Unionists in Nineteenth-Century Britain," *Social History*, 13 (May 1988): 191–208.

123 However, as Susan Pedersen points out, the criteria for mothers' and widows' pensions were more restrictive than those for the "endowment for motherhood" envisioned by British feminists (but never passed in its original form). While the endowment would have granted universal support to mothers of young children, American mothers' and widows' pensions, as well as the British version that was eventually passed in 1925, predicated payments on the absence of a male breadwinner. According to Pedersen, "[M]aternalist, 'separate but equal' ideology was pressed into service in the creation of policies encoding dependence, not the value of difference"; "The Failure of Feminism in the Making of the British Welfare State," *Radical History Review*, 43 (1989): 105.

124 See Molly Ladd-Taylor, "Mothers' Pensions: Payment for Childrearing or Charity for Children?" paper presented to the Conference on Women's History and Public Policy, Sarah Lawrence College, June 1989.

125 Margaret McMillan, *The Camp School* (London, 1919), 18. The French system of Gouttes du Lait (milk depots) and crèches were the envy of George McCleary, one of England's leading experts and bureaucrats in infant and maternal welfare in the early twentieth century; see his *The Early History of the Infant Welfare Movement* (London, 1933).

126 This incident suggests that the exchange between Britain and Germany did not always follow the usual pattern, which went in the opposite direction: see, for example, E. P. Hennock, *British Social Reform and German Precedents: The Case of Social Insurance, 1880–1914* (New York, 1987).

127 A striking example of such a turnabout is described by Susan Pedersen in "Gender, Welfare, and Citizenship." On the campaign for the endowment of motherhood, see Hilary Land, "The Introduction of Family Allowances: An Act of Historic Justice," in Phoebe Hall, Land, Roy Parker, and Adrian Webb, eds, *Change, Choice, and Conflict in Social Policy* (London, 1975), 157–231; and John Macnicol, *The Movement for Family Allowances, 1918–1945* (London, 1980).

128 See Alice Salomon, *Education for Social Work: A Sociological Interpretation Based on an International Survey* (Zurich, 1937), esp. 21–36.

129 On the impact of class on French welfare policy, see Klaus, "Depopulation and Race Suicide."

130 Paula Baker, "The Domestication of Politics: Women and American Political Society, 1780–1920", *AHR*, 89 (June 1985): 620–647.

131 For a critical interpretation of this development in the context of the United States that holds female activists responsible for state incursions into the family and the private sphere, see Christopher Lasch, *Haven in a Heartless World: The Family Besieged* (New York, 1979).

132 This shift was led by Julia Lathrop, Grace and Edith Abbott, and Sophonisba Breckinridge; see Muncy, "Creating a Female Dominion," 102–103. In *Heroes of Their Own Lives*, Linda Gordon labels early maternalist efforts as feminist, insofar as they were linked to a comprehensive critique of male domination in society (32–34), and argues that "[t]he decline of feminist influence in social work, particularly after World War I, meant not only the decreased visibility

of family-violence problems altogether but also their redefinition in ways that were disadvantageous to victims [women and children]"; 292. While her conflation of maternalism and feminism seems problematic (see n. 9 above), the transformation in social welfare that she identifies is striking.

133 For the divisions among American activists on linkages between maternalism and feminist issues such as suffrage, see Nancy F. Cott, *The Grounding of Modern Feminism* (New Haven, Conn., 1987).

Chapter 23

Claudine Mitchell

■ 'MADELEINE PELLETIER (1874–1939): THE
POLITICS OF SEXUAL OPPRESSION', *Feminist Review*, 33
Autumn, 1989, pp. 72–92

I N APRIL 1939 A WOMAN PHYSICIAN, aged sixty-four, was arrested in France
for practising abortion, and sentenced to prison. A few lines appeared in small print in
the socialist press:

For the Doctoresse Pelletier

The pioneer propagandist of our ideas, a founder member of *Social War*, is still incarcerated, a victim without a defendant. (File Pelletier)

In the oppressive climate of 1939 no one seems to have bothered to take any action, and
Pelletier died in prison, eight months later, on 29 December 1939. Thus ended her forty
years of militancy in the French feminist and socialist movements.

Pelletier was one of the most significant feminist thinkers in France before de Beauvoir.
She broke with nineteenth-century feminism to develop a cultural theory of sexual difference.
To articulate the case for sexual equality, nineteenth-century feminists had extolled the
social value of women's traditional roles and celebrated feminine virtues against masculine
vices. This was the wrong track, Pelletier thought, since it confined women to their traditional
roles by rooting femininity in biology. If, on the contrary, it could be proved that femininity
and masculinity were the products of culture, then feminism could make advances by
attacking cultural phenomena.

At the turn of the century Pelletier set out to investigate the social forms which
constructed and maintained sexual difference, thus laying the foundations for a wealth of
future work in sociology. Pelletier has never been given credit for this work, either by postwar feminists or by the American historians who have recently rediscovered her, only to
perceive her as an 'extraordinary failure'. The purpose of this study is to retrieve the feminist
framework Pelletier created.

It is first necessary to give some account of the historical circumstances in which and in
response to which Pelletier's thinking developed. In order to survive intellectually, she had

to move in and out of existing political structures, using them, challenging them, questioning their boundaries. Her feminist theories were closely bound up with her political activism in the socialist movement; her theory of sexual oppression emerged from the criticism she made of the political system and of the ineffectiveness of the feminist movement in influencing political machinery. Her writings of the 1920s and 1930s, for example, focused on the politics of the family – an emphasis which emerged from reflexions on the Russian Revolution.

Pelletier wrote extensively. For forty years she contributed articles to the feminist press; between 1908 and 1919 she ran her own paper, *La Suffragiste*, composed of short articles designed mostly to recruit and encourage feminist militancy. Before 1911, Pelletier wrote continuously for the socialist press, the two major papers being *Guerre Sociale* and *L'Humanite*; in the 1920s, she wrote mostly for the anarchist press, less frequently for the feminist papers *La Fronde* and *La Voix des Femmes*, and occasionally for medical journals. The bulk of her theoretical writings were published as pamphlets. I have traced thirty essays, each dealing with specific issues: religion, morality, war, education, sexuality, the family, women's rights to employment or women's political rights. They share one theme in common: oppression, class and sexual oppression. The argument is always concise; rigorous at times, didactic or experimental at others. They are combative works which acquire their full meaning only in the political context which generated them.

Until 1919, Pelletier's pamphlets were published mostly through the feminist organization she directed (*La Suffragiste*) and, after the war, mostly by anarchist and left-wing organizations. She wanted her articles to be republished in book form; her first series of essays on sexual oppression was reprinted in 1908 as *Women in Struggle for their Rights* and others in 1911 as *The Sexual Emancipation of Women*. In the changed political climate of the 1930s, and as a result of her work on abortion, she had difficulty finding a publisher; her later essays on sexuality were not finally published until 1935, under the title *Rational Sexuality*.

Pelletier was also the author of three novels, one autobiographical; another science fiction; and three short plays. She saw all of these as means to propagate her views amongst a wider audience. In the 1970s, with the emergence of a strong abortionist movement in France, her essay *The Right to Abortion* was reprinted together with three other essays (Maignien, 1978: 123–40). There is nothing else of Pelletier's writings in print today.

Pelletier's theory of sexual oppression

The right to abortion

The repression of abortion in France was an interwar phenomenon. Until 1914 abortions were frequent and virtually unpunished, though outlawed by Article 317 of the Penal Code. There was even a campaign in favour of abortion: Pelletier herself contributed evidence to a medical commission set up in 1911 to seek legalized abortion. Movements for free abortion throughout this period had clear political colours; their foremost advocates were left-wing working-class intellectuals. From 1911, for example, the Neo-Malthusian Workers Federation organized co-operatives where their members, mostly trade unionists and anarchists, could learn about contraceptive methods and buy contraceptive devices. Pelletier was one of their frequent speakers, and in 1913 they republished, as a pamphlet, her essay *The Right to Abortion*. A classic statement on the subject, it went through several reprints in the 1920s and again in 1935.

The issue at stake in Pelletier's publication is women's right not to bear children. Abortion is envisaged as a method of birth control, a last resort for unwanted pregnancy at a time when contraceptive methods were unreliable and insufficiently available amongst the working class. Abortion is presented as a sad experience, but nevertheless as an improvement on the drama of unwanted pregnancies recurrent in the nineteenth century. Here, Pelletier has in mind the tragedies of suicide, infanticides, the fate of maids or daughters who were thrown out in the street, and women who had to turn to prostitution for survival.

Pelletier's work developed socio-economic pro-abortion arguments which were already well known to the intellectual working class. Birth control, she maintained, was part of the requirement of living in a modern capitalist state. If, for the petite bourgeoisie, birth control was a means of acquiring good housing and providing their children with good education, for the working class it was a means of surviving with dignity. The patriotic argument of the Natalists – that France's vitality depended on a high birthrate – was presented by Pelletier as a class position – one that represented the interests of the wealthy, who used the working class as a pool of labour to bolster the economy.

Pelletier also directed attention to the way abortion was already practised within the working class. She spoke from direct observation of northern industrial France, where abortion was carried out by unqualified women who had acquired basic knowledge of the operation, but had no sense of hygiene. Working-class women learned to operate on themselves using domestic utensils, and by douching with soapy water; in some cases, they aborted several times a year. In these conditions, abortion was highly dangerous; women risked permanent injuries and often fatal infections.

Pelletier argued that it was repressive law that made abortion dangerous. If practised before the third month of pregnancy under proper medical care, abortion was a simple technical operation. But she also raised another argument, unfamiliar in 1911; the question of women's rights over their own bodies. She argued that, since the pregnant woman was one person not two, no one had the right to oblige her to continue carrying in her womb a fertilized ovum she did not want. To deny her this right was to deny her the status of a person. To solve the question of the civil status of the foetus, Pelletier reminded her readers that the existence of the individual in law was from the moment of natural birth. At the moment of natural birth the child was an individual who had a right to protection, and infanticide was a crime. But the state did not have to legislate on the status of foetus, for it was part of the mother's body. Pelletier thus posited the right of a woman over her own body to be an absolute right. Against the communists, she maintained that the freedom of the individual was absolute: that the state should serve the individual, not vice versa (Pelletier, 1919). And in *The Right to Abortion* she tackled the further issue of women's right to sexual pleasure. Contrary to dominant views, the sexual act, she said, had to be conceptualized as separate from the reproductive function. The aim of the sexual act was not conception but pleasure. Man's right to sexual pleasure was recognised; there was no just grounds to deny it to women. Indeed, for Pelletier, such denial indicated a general form of oppression of women through sexuality. Women's sexuality, she suggested was regimented and organized in matrimony and its counterpart, prostitution. It was a question of human right to separate the sexual act from maternity by the proper use of contraceptive methods, including abortion.

Even if the salary of a woman allows her to bring up one or two children on her own, maternity, if it is not to be a servitude, must not be imposed on her. It must be left to each woman to decide if and when she wants to be a mother. (Maignien, 1978: 127)

Members of her audience, particularly in the 1930s, thought she was advocating sexual freedom for its own sake. Pelletier's perspective was different. She wanted an end to a social order which placed sexuality at the core of women's subjection.

Pelletier on sexual difference

Pelletier's argument on abortion stood as the symbol of a larger crusade on behalf of women. But her work in other areas is of equal significance to her feminist framework. Crucially, she introduced to feminist thought new ways of thinking about sexual difference. Pelletier argued that sexual difference was the product of culture, and that all forms of social relations were determined by it. The acquisition of gender identity, she argued, was the result of socio-conditioning, a complex experience that could not be reduced to biology:

> It is from their parents and the entire social milieu that children receive their psychological gender. (Pelletier, 1908a: 2)

In opposition to the nineteenth-century notion of femininity and masculinity as consisting in a set of fixed attributes inherited at birth and determining the persona, Pelletier proposed the notion of 'psychological gender'. She saw gender identity as constructed through psychological processes, and set out to demonstrate her case in her essay of 1908 'The Sociological Factors of Feminine Psychology' (Pelletier, 1908a: ch. 7). Here she drew attention to the unequal treatment which girls and boys received from their parents, to the devaluation of the mother, and to discrepancies between the intellectual and sexual education of young men and women. She also focused attention on language as the transmitter of ideological assumptions about femininity and masculinity and their respective value. The nineteenth-century feminists had spoken of 'a hierarchy of the sexes'. Pelletier added the notion of 'norm': society made man the norm to which the entire social order was related.

If this important work has been overlooked, then this is almost certainly in part because of the style in which it was written. Pelletier's method consisted of calling attention to the ordinary events of people's daily life, giving examples common enough for her readers to carry out an analysis of their own experiences. Thus the first section of her essay, examines the psychological processes which make girls internalize a sense of inferiority, passivity and subservience. Rather than theorizing, Pelletier draws attention to the series of prohibitions which punctuate a girl's existence, and the linguistic formulae in which they are articulated. She points out that a girl's body is the subject of constant restrictions which sap her energy and paralyse her willpower. She emphasizes that the sole explanation given to girls as to why they should restrict their physical activities is a purely formulaic one: 'Little girls don't do that'. Girls who persist in their behaviour, she suggests, are dubbed 'garçon manqué' ('failed boy' – the French idiom is more telling than its English equivalent, 'tomboy'). Such formulations convey a fixed notion of femininity; and failure to conform to that notion carries moral sanctions.

Pelletier's work on sexual difference also deals with issues of class. She uses the example of working-class girls being made to serve their brothers to demonstrate the inculcation of female subordination in working-class families. Meanwhile, middle-class girls were encouraged to focus on the presentation of self – on dress, cleanliness, demeanour, manners. This led to subservience of another kind: the female body was made an object of servitude, the female psyche subjected to men's evaluation.

Sexual difference was internalized, Pelletier thought, through domestic uses of language, in which repeated reference was made to sexual difference and women's inferiority. She cites the example of parents quarrelling, and children witnessing their mothers being devalued with such phrases as 'You speak like a woman', or 'You don't earn money', or 'You with your small wage'. In such idioms, children could already perceive money as a symbol of masculine power.

Pelletier's essay 'The Sociological Factors of Feminine Psychology' also contained a critique of girls' education (Pelletier, 1908a). Like many nineteenth-century feminists, Pelletier argued that the so-called difference in intelligence between men and women was purely the result of education. Since the beginning of state secondary education for women in the 1880s, feminists had denounced the curriculum discrepancies which existed between boys' and girls' schools. What worried Pelletier was not so much content, as teaching methods. For her, the aim of secondary education was to develop intelligence and give respect for learning by stimulating genuine inquiry. She took as a crucial example the way philosophy was taught. Instead of philosophy, girls were taught 'morality'. Rigid dogmas were inculcated which narrowed their outlook and stultified their intelligence. Part of these moral dogmas led women to seek achievement not in great deeds, but in the small actions of daily life.

Pelletier also drew attention to the way everything in women's secondary education was subordinated to the idea of matrimony as the goal of a woman's life. In the last section of 'The Sociological Factors of Feminine Psychology', she denounced the refusal to give to young women any proper form of sexual education. Instead girls were isolated from experience by prohibitions and surveillance, in a system which produced fear of the unexplained, of men, of their 'rights' and of sexuality.

In her later work – her essay, *The Feminist Education of Women*, published in 1914 – Pelletier began to propose ways of preventing the female body being constructed as the locus of women's subjection. Examining childhood games as well as the intellectual and sexual education of the child and teenager, she proposed a method of education that might construct the female psyche positively. 'Positive education' meant for Pelletier, the acquisition of what was necessary to take active part in the public sphere: assertiveness, intelligence, willpower, stamina, ambition, energy.

Sexuality

Alongside her work on the notion of 'psychological gender', Pelletier's other major contribution to feminist thinking was her analysis of the agencies which regimented sexuality and made it the locus of woman's oppression. She posited the sexual act to be 'a physiological function', 'a natural law', 'an instinct'. This enabled her to claim that sexuality was as legitimate an object of scientific study as any other natural law, at a time when the discussion of sexuality was viewed as immoral. It also enabled her to break away from the moral, legal and religious language that had predominated amongst nineteenth-century feminists. Pelletier considered that all the forms of affectivity or subjectivity that were attached to sexuality were a product of culture; indeed she believed that the very idea of sexuality as the centre of human life was a cultural construct (Pelletier, 1930–3: 8; 1926a: 13). Thus, unlike many intellectuals of the period, Pelletier, at least in her published work, was not interested in the subconscious. Her field of investigation was, to use her own words, the interaction between the sociological and the psychological. Her argument began instead with a reflection on moral language. In her 1911 essay, 'One Moral for the Two Sexes' (Pelletier, 1911: ch. 1, pp. 1–11; 1935: ch. 5), she invited her readers to ponder the meaning of the term 'honest' when applied to women, as in the expressions '*honnête fille*' or '*honnête femme*'. The term, she said, did not refer to general codes of conduct, but to a very specific sphere: sexuality. An 'honest' woman was one who was a virgin until she was married, and remained 'faithful' after marriage. The notion of 'honesty', though formulated as a moral principle, legitimated forms of surveillance, suggested Pelletier, which regimented women's lives. The pressure of moral principles, as well as the exercise of parental and fraternal authority, meant that women's every action was strictly controlled. Married women, for example, were called upon by their husbands to give account of how they spent time in their home. Even spinsters, Pelletier argued, were subject to the tyrannical absurdity of men's law. Though the virginity of the ageing spinster was no longer of any value, she remained subject to sanctions if she attempted to move freely in public spaces.

Pelletier further exposed the irrationality surrounding sex itself. One case she cited was the attitude to women's sexual initiation, the subject of an article Pelletier wrote entitled 'Devirginization' (Pelletier, 1935: 10–14). Since the breaking of the hymen was painful, and since the first experience of sexual intercourse could be traumatic for a woman unprepared for it (as they still frequently were), it would be rational, Pelletier suggested, to prepare women intellectually for 'deflowering' – and, to prevent the pain by prescribing ointment or even asking doctors to cut the hymen painlessly.

As Pelletier pointed out, virgin brides already had recourse to deceits such as using rabbits' blood or red ink to simulate blood, or making the date of their wedding coincide with that of their menstrual cycle. Did this not indicate, Pelletier asked, that the hymen membrane had become the very symbol of women's oppression?

Pelletier also considered the law to be an agency of the sexual oppression of women. A case she cited was the law on adultery which had engaged the energy of nineteenth-century feminists. While men did not feel compelled to respect marital fidelity, and while wives were called upon to forgive adultery, women's adultery was condemned as a crime (Pelletier, 1912a). The law was presented as a means to protect illegitimate children; Pelletier, by contrast, argued that the law was men's way of securing their paternal rights:

> The moral discredit which falls on the seduced woman is in fact a form of material depreciation; the loss of her virginity makes of her a thing that is no longer new … a damaged product that is more difficult to sell.
>
> Paternal pride is no more than a sense of ownership. Man, the sovereign master of his wife, retains sole right to give her children; another man's child would be tantamount to theft of his own property. (Pelletier, 1935: 27, 29)

To demonstrate that the sexual act had been culturally constructed as men's appropriation of the woman's body, Pelletier also called attention to linguistic attitudes to sex. In legal terms, the sexual act in matrimony was conceived as 'man's right' and 'woman's duty'. In colloquial usage too, man's participation in the sexual act was (and indeed still is) depicted in the active transitive form, 'l'homme baise' (the man fucks), while women's participation was presented in the passive form: 'la femme est baisée'. (There was further ambiguity in this use of the passive form, since to be *baisé* also means to be conned.) Pelletier pointed out the double-bind for women: while slang depicted women's sexuality as something appropriated by man, the polite form depicted it as a gift to men from women.

Alongside morality, the law, and the common language of sexuality, Pelletier had a further target: the family. In 'Feminism and the Family' (c.1910), she presented the family as the institution which made of woman's sexuality a state of dependency and subordination. She argued that in matrimony, as in prostitution, women's bodies were exchanged for money, the symbol or the key to man's power (Pelletier, 1911: 6–9; 1935: ch. 7, 89; 1928; various undated leaflets). Pelletier defined the family as the agency of woman's servitude. It was within the family that woman's consciousness was constructed as subservient. It was also through their confinement in the institution of the family that women were prevented from intervening in the public sphere. The family was governed by authoritarian principles which oppressed both women and children. Cohabitation always implied woman's literal servitude, since they had to serve their husbands. Maternity too, Pelletier argued, enslaved women in menial domestic tasks – with the exception of women in the wealthy classes, who exploited other women as domestic servants. These bourgeois women did however suffer another kind of servitude: moral servitude. Their role was to please, and their anxious desire to retain their husbands' affection was, suggested Pelletier, another form of subjection.

Thus morality, the law and the family were analysed by Pelletier as the cultural agencies which made women's sexuality the locus of their oppression. In her work on those agencies, she outlined a field of enquiry, formulated important concepts and produced a methodology for a study of sexual oppression. Her manipulation of language to expose sexual oppression was perhaps the most innovative of her feminist strategies. To attack deep-rooted beliefs, Pelletier used short, polemical sentences designed to shatter the reader's emotional attachment to particular ideologies. She never prepared her readers or attempted to convince them of her viewpoint; she started with an attack in the form of a paradox, a baffling statement, or a distinctly working-class sarcasm. She only used short sentences to present her controversial views in the form of statements of facts. Pelletier destroyed cultural stereotypes with formulations that were equally stark and truncated. Her staccato texts were punctuated by sentences that sounded like slogans:

'Maternal love is a luury'

'Woman is a machine to fabricate the male'

'The natalists believe in a barbarian form of birth control – war'

This, then, is the feminist framework into which Pelletier's argument for the 'right to abortion' must ultimately be integrated.

Feminism and party politics

What then of Pelletier's socialism? In little over a decade she moved from the optimistic quasi-religious faith in socialism which had animated the left in the mid nineteenth century to the uncertainties more characteristic of our own era. The process was accelerated for her by the problematic position of feminists in the French socialist movement as well as the general bewilderment caused by the First World War and the Russian Revolution.

Pelletier first entered the political arena in 1906. Born into a poor and uneducated working-class family, she left home, prepared for her baccalaureate and entered the Faculty of Medicine, where she graduated in 1899. Though the faculty had been open to women since the 1870s, the proportion of working-class students was infinitesimal. Pelletier first decided to dedicate herself to the bettering of the conditions of the deprived by working for the Assistance Publique and was the first woman doctor in this institution. She next selected work with the mentally ill, but a clause in the conditions of eligibility for examination – examinees were required to have voting rights and to have undertaken military service – eliminated all women. The Feminist paper *La Fronde* helped her to stage-manage an impressive campaign to open the Faculty of Psychiatric Medicine to women and she won her case in 1906.

Between 1906 and 1913 Pelletier operated within recognized political bodies, in which she rose to positions of relative significance. She was the leader of the Parisian-based feminist group, Solidarity, and was a member of the French Socialist Party. During this period she took active part in nine National Congresses of the Party and two International Congresses, was a socialist candidate in the legislative elections of 1910 and 1912, and was nominated to the Executive of the Party in 1910.

At this time, Pelletier saw the French feminist movement as lacking any political force. It was, she observed, a plurality of competing groups each organized around a personality or a handful of narrow objectives without any significant following. She also realized that her working-class background and her politics would make it difficult for her to get on with the bourgeois and Catholic women who far outnumbered the socialist feminists (Pelletier, 1908b; c.1919: 8–47; 1933: 90–189).

Nevertheless, Pelletier believed a French feminist movement could be organized, beyond political allegiances, around three areas: around reforms of the law which legitimized sexual subordination; around access for women to all forms of employment and public service; and thirdly, around the recognition of women's political rights (Pelletier, 1908a: 41–50). To achieve these goals feminists should infiltrate official political parties, establish themselves in positions of power and influence party policy (Pelletier, 1908a: ch. 3, republished in Maignien, 1978: 145–56).

When Pelletier entered the French Socialist Party her ambition was to win votes for women. By 1913 she had already lost faith that such goals could be realized in the prevailing circumstances (Pelletier, 1912b).

I have tried to bring feminism to the proletariat, I have utterly failed ... (Pelletier to Arria Ly, 6 October 1911).

The working class will be the last to accept it, they will come to it when we have our political rights, not before. (22 August 1911)

Pelletier's activism as a leader of Solidarity was condemned by the French feminist body represented at the 1908 June Congress of Women's Civil and Political Rights. The issue at stake was street action. The period 1904–1908 was a rare period of pre-war French feminist history when a few women, notably Pelletier, considered appropriating some of the British suffragettes' tactics to pressurize the government. The events were few and unspectacular (Hause and Kenny, 1984: 48–50, 78–81, 102–05). In June 1906 Pelletier threw suffragists' hand bills on deputies' heads from the gallery of the National Assembly, and during the elections of June 1908 she threw a small stone at the window of the polling station. The members of Solidarity objected that she might hurt someone. The event was viewed by the press as appalling violence, and the government took steps to ensure the women could not be turned into heroic martyrs. When, in June 1908, two marches were organized, Pelletier and a few colleagues found it difficult to persuade a hundred or so women to go on to the streets, with visiting British suffragettes. Those who did follow suggested that they should make amends for their involvement in political action by publicly proclaiming their belief in women's traditional role (Pelletier, c.1919: 20–8;1933: 106–10).

Pelletier's experience as leader of Solidarity led her to the conclusion that the problems which paralysed the French feminist movement were not separate from the question of women's oppression. She observed that women seemed unable to pursue any course of action which did not conform to existing codes of femininity. The narrow intellectual education women received, she said, left them ill-equipped to theorize their positions. These, Pelletier thought, were some of the reasons which made women unable to act efficiently in the political sphere (Pelletier, 1908a: ch. 2).

Her experience in the Socialist Party led her to similar conclusions – though she did succeed in making the Socialist National Congress of 1906 pass a motion on women's suffrage. The deputies were to introduce the issue to Parliament the following year; in the end, however, the motion was to no effect. It took the deputies three months to nominate a subcommittee which happened to include no feminist sympathizers and which, in the event, never met (Sowerwine, 1982: 110–28). In 1907 Pelletier made the National Congress vote on the same resolution, which again was not carried. French women had to wait until 1945 to be granted their political rights.

The bad faith of socialist politicians in respect of women's suffrage was symptomatic of the general attitude of the French socialists to feminism. Though the Workers' Party had officially passed a resolution in support of suffragism at the Congress of 1879, the general opinion was that feminism was a bourgeois diversion. At the 1907 National Congress, Pelletier's suffragism was thus opposed by a Madame Gauthiot on the grounds that it was 'one of these numerous diversions' (Sowerwine, 1982: 116). The dominant doctrine was that women's liberation would be achieved only through trade-unionist struggle and the revolution. Thus, after the 1906 National Congress, Pelletier concluded that the French Socialist Party tolerated feminism only as long as it could serve the Party.

Feminists and trade unionists were also in regular conflict over the issue of women's employment. When, in 1914, Pelletier wrote articles arguing for women to take up jobs vacant on the labour market, her trade unionist colleagues accused her of 'patriotic collaboration with the bourgeoisie' (Pelletier, c.1919: 20–8; 1933: 106–10).

Feminism and socialism

In the first decade of the century the question which preoccupied socialist women was whether or not they should ally themselves with feminists, whom they mistrusted as 'bourgeois'. The issue was raised at the first congress of socialist women held in Stuttgart in 1907, under the presidency of Clara Zetkin. It was decided that there should be a complete separation from bourgeois feminists. Pelletier was the only person to oppose this decision, arguing that it was necessary to have a feminist movement sufficiently autonomous from the Party to concentrate on the issue of women's rights. In her article 'The question of Women's Vote' which was an answer to the International Congress, she stated:

> If a woman has, like a man, the right to be a socialist, she cannot, without betraying her own cause, sacrifice feminism to a masculine political party, whatever it be ... Feminism is logically neither bourgeois or socialist for it is not a class party but a sex party. (Pelletier, 1908h: 15)

In this article, Pelletier developed the argument that class oppression and women's oppression were of a different kind. The main problem for women was that, bound to their oppressors within the family, they could not develop the group identity which was necessary for revolt.

The combative position of Pelletier on the more revolutionary left wing of the Party was another hindrance to her furthering the cause of feminism. In 1917 she dissociated herself from the left-wing section of Guesdes on the question of the trade unions which they wanted to control, accusing them of integrating the working class within the capitalist state rather than preparing them for the revolution. She became a leading figure of the Insurrectionist group created by Gustave Herve who was, she thought for a time, a genuine revolutionary force (Pelletier, 1910). However, the Insurrectionists were antiparliamentarian, and Pelletier's commitment to antiparliamentarism was used by socialist politicians to weaken her suffragist arguments. It was a feminist issue which brought her collaboration with the Insurrectionists to an abrupt end in 1910. The antisuffragists had always used the argument that women in France did not have to do military service, unlike men. It had therefore become a feminist strategy to ask for a form of military service for women, and Pelletier wrote to that effect in *La Suffragiste*. Thereupon Herve, of the antimilitarist Insurrectionists, insisted that Pelletier retract her argument in *Social War*. She refused and resigned.

The conflicts between feminism and socialism and the political tensions within the French Socialist Party ultimately defeated Pelletier. Yet she was not convinced that the root of the problem was a question of doctrine. What she noted in her unpublished memoirs was the opposition to her as a woman. When she had joined anarchist groups in the 1890s she had felt ostracized as a woman because she did not want to follow the codes of sexual behaviour which the left regarded as those of the liberated. Later, she felt equally ostracized in the Socialist Party as a single woman claiming independent ideas and seeking a position of relative power. The conflicts between feminism and socialism were, Pelletier concluded, instances of a more general phenomenon of sexual oppression. Thus, in 1908, she described the problematic position of feminists in the Socialist Party as a problem of incommunicability between two radically different systems of thought:

> The poor faint voice of women's claims. They listened to it with a distracted ear because no one understood what women said. They spoke an unknown and bizarre language which came from very far away: the voice of the other sex (Pelletier, 1908a: 34).

The language of the dominant culture presented as natural the fact of women's subordination to men. It could not assimilate the language of the feminists, since they challenged the institutions and systems of beliefs which made sexual oppression the very structure of the social order. For Pelletier this was also a problem of psychology: of men's incapacity to think of women as autonomous beings and women's incapacity to think of themselves other than in a relationship of dependency for men.

Feminism, concluded Pelletier, had to work upon what she called 'mentalities': people's sense of identity, the agencies which moulded gender and class identity, and the cultural processes which perpetuated them. Feminism had to become a cultural struggle.

Pelletier and communism

In 1920, the French Communist Party allied itself to Moscow; Pelletier became a member. Yet with the end of Lenin's government, she became disillusioned with the ideal of revolution. Revolution killed and oppressed like war, and inevitably ended up in dictatorship. She also came to doubt whether it was possible to mobilize the proletariat for revolution; for culture, she wrote, was controlled by the bourgeoisie, and the bourgeois leaders of the working class would always use the proletariat to maintain their privileges.

Pelletier also rejected the idea of progress through reform, as proposed by the moderates; she saw it as producing an endless swing between conservative and progressive governments. Reforms, she argued, depended on imposing socialist views on those who were against them, and the bourgeoisie would always ensure that social reforms did not last for ever (Pelletier, 1926a). Social progress, she concluded, depended on a constant cultural struggle that would bring about a democratic state willing to suppress social inequalities by transforming the agencies which perpetuated class and sexual oppression (Pelletier, 1931: 23).

The politics of the family

In her essay 'Feminism and the Family' of 1911 Pelletier put to feminists a categorical and embarrassing question: could sexual equality ever be achieved without a fundamental re-ordering of society? Could women become autonomous beings without financial independence from men? Was it possible to reconcile maternity and women's employment? At the time of Pelletier's essay, socialist feminists such as Hubertine Auclert were arguing that feminism would succeed in transforming the nuclear family into an egalitarian unit, with men and women sharing domestic and parental duties. Maternity would be regarded as a highly valued social function and mothers would receive a state salary. There would be a modification of the marital law and matriarchy would be established.

Pelletier spoke from a different position. With her direct experience of the conditions of existence of working-class people, Pelletier's socialism involved a commitment to the abolition of private property, to the collectivization of the means of production and the reorganization of the economy at state level. But more than that, Pelletier did not subscribe to the dominant conviction in the French Socialist Party that women's emancipation would come out of trade unionism or the revolution. She was not satisfied either with her Marxist colleagues' attempt to explain psychology only in terms of the material conditions of existence (Pelletier, 1931: 12). She believed that there was a sex and class 'mentality' which was transmitted in culture, most particularly within the family. She brought to bear on French Marxism a conviction, developed through her involvement in nineteenth-century anarchist circles, that to obtain a truly egalitarian society the family had to be abolished. Pelletier's perspective was a feminist one: since the nuclear family institutionalized the sexual oppression of women, the only way to achieve sexual equality was through its disintegration. The upbringing of children and domestic labour would be taken over from individual women and assumed by the collectivity.

In the wake of the Russian Revolution it was hardly possible for French socialists to discuss these issues in the abstract, and Pelletier restated her position in a schematic article of 1926, *Capitalism and Communism*, where she assessed the merits and failure of Bolshevist Russia. One had to recognize, Pelletier wrote, that the first experience of communism had caused much unhappiness and that the Bolsheviks had in many ways failed communism. The Bolsheviks had had to resort to dictatorship in order to survive: yet there had been no real need for the authoritarian economic programme they implemented. By restricting individual liberties, economic dictatorship had stifled individual initiative and become self-destructive. Bureaucracy had got out of hand, and the soviet ceased to function as the government of the proletariat.

By putting the majority at the mercy of a few, Pelletier concluded, Bolshevism had paved the way for personal dictatorship and corruption.

Yet, Pelletier went on to argue, the Bolsheviks had accomplished enough social reforms for it to be impossible to use the Russian Revolution as an argument against socialism. In particular, the Russians had made great progress towards sexual equality:

> The Bolshevist code, which frees women from all the fetters of matrimony, has realized all the ideas which have been discussed in various groups for over a century and are still considered a utopia here. It is truly deplorable that millions of people had to be massacred to achieve this. (Pelletier, 1926a: 7–9)

After she visited Russia in 1921 as a delegate to the International Conference, Pelletier reported signs of relative sexual equality. Women proved freely in public spaces: most of them preferred freedom of movement to fashionable looks – which indicated to her that they no longer lived for men alone; women were in employment throughout the Soviet administration, and former peasants and working-class girls occupied fairly senior posts. There were women in the army, and the risky and responsible job of propaganda in the army was entrusted to women. The Women's Section of the Communist Party was given prestigious status and was very active. An effective propaganda network ensured that even women in the remotest villages were kept informed of ideas and developments.

These were the positive signs. Yet the Women's Section of the Party had been politically marginalized. Its work was confined to traditional roles – education and social welfare. Women were noticeably absent from key administrative and political functions. Nevertheless, concluded Pelletier, if in practice sexual equality had not yet been achieved, the Russians had taken the measures which could make it possible. The reform of the legal system had inscribed equality into Soviet law; and true equality, argued Pelletier, would gradually be achieved through the suppression of matrimony and the entry of all women into production (Pelletier, 1922; pp. 144–8, 216–21).

During her stay in Moscow Pelletier met Alexandra Kollantai, and she concluded that their positions on the family had enough in common for her to present her views as close to those of Bolshevist feminism (Pelletier, 1922: 143). For her, Bolshevist feminism meant the abolition of the family, legalized abortion, the collective upbringing of children and collective housekeeping. Pelletier continued to advocate this kind of feminism even after 1931, when she had stated that the Bolsheviks had failed in their sexual ideals as they had in many others (Pelletier, 1931: 16). Bolshevist feminism had become for her a way of upholding a belief in socialism. As a result, her position in the French Left became insecure; for French socialists dreaded the idea of the destruction of the family. Her position in the French Communist

Party, as in the feminist movement, remained one of painful isolation because of her views on the family.

Arguments for the transformation of the family

In what sense, then, did Pelletier see the family as detrimental to social progress? First, it was, she argued, through the agency of the family that people were placed in fixed social positions. The family regimented life-cycles according to rigid patterns from which individuals had little chance of escape. According to Pelletier, the family was essentially a financial institution of the bourgeois order, and it was to safeguard their privileges that the bourgeoisie celebrated the family and denounced its disintegration as the greatest of upheavals.

Pelletier's position on sexuality also permitted her to argue logically for the suppression of matrimony. If, as she believed, the sexual act did not automatically give one person property rights over another, then sex was a matter of private concern on which the state had no right to legislate.

Though the family was an oppressive agency, Pelletier went on to argue, it did protect its members. It offered assistance to the sick and the elderly, and, for the present, was indispensable to children. But was it not unjust, Pelletier asked, to sacrifice half of the present generation to the next generation? The state had already begun to take charge of the care of the sick and elderly and of a portion of children's education. The evolution of society, she concluded, was towards a greater role for the state in these areas (Pelletier, n.d.a).

Pelletier's writings on the family anticipated by ten years her encounter with Kollontai, whose *Communism and the Family* she had read in 1920. The Russian experience helped Pelletier concretize her ideas about collective housekeeping and the collective upbringing of children. During her stay in Russia, Pelletier visited institutions for abandoned children, and was impressed by the adult education system developed at Sorlov University (Pelletier, 1922: ch. 2). In 1926 she published a series of three articles on education in Russia, which praised the Russian system for its attempt to develop individuals who had a clear consciousness of their role in society. Thus, for example, education in the Soviet Union did not consist of passive listening; instead children studied themes which made them actively explore the various orders of knowledge and their relation to contemporary society. Children were regarded as members of society whose present task happened to be to acquire an education. The way schools were organized developed their sense of responsibility and gave them a sense of identity in society (Pelletier, 1926b). Thus, in her pamphlet *The Educator State* of 1931, Pelletier argued that the French state institution for abandoned children should experiment with such progressive pedagogical methods and provide models for the collective upbringing of children. And in another pamphlet of the 1930s, *Love and Maternity*, she argued for the 'de-individualization of childcare'. According to Pelletier, the progress of medicine, hygiene and child psychology ensured that the young child's basic needs were satisfied. Amongst the reforms she advocated was the replacement of breast-feeding by the use of pasteurized milk, and throwaway nappies – practical campaigns designed to ease the burden of working-class women. She also turned her attention to the question of nurseries. The women of the bourgeoisie she argued, had long ago discharged the burden of childcare on to other women; the women of the working class, concluded Pelletier, would come to understand that such institutions were equally to their advantage.

Pelletier believed, like Kollantai, that the affective energy invested in the family could be redirected towards the community. Individual identities however were not to be submerged within the state (Pelletier 1919; 1926: 143). People, she thought, might come to live in communes where the state was not to regiment sexual relationships (Pelletier, c.1933a).

Conclusions

To write about Pelletier is to wrestle with history. De Beauvoir, who reinvented in 1949 the concept of woman as 'the other' did not acknowledge Pelletier's first formulation. In the *History of French Feminism*, published in 1977, Albistur and Armogathe had only eight words for Pelletier. Their readers learn only that she travelled to Russia and reported that sexual equality had not been achieved (1977: 574).

Pelletier's activism between 1906 and 1912 has been recorded in the 1980s by four American historians. They all conclude that she failed completely in her endeavour. Marilyn Boxer, while claiming for Pelletier a place in 'the sisterhood of great socialist women', concludes an article subtitled 'the extraordinary failure of Madeleine Pelletier' with the following lines:

> She failed on all counts ... Pelletier found herself caught in a double, double bind: between reform and revolution, between feminism and socialism ... unable to reconcile the conflict, unwilling to forsake feminism in socialism or socialism in feminism, Pelletier finally withdrew from party politics. In the last decades of her life she turned on the one hand to fictional worlds where total resolution was possible and, on the other, to the reality of women's lives, where the radical act of abortion could solve immediate problems. (1981: 65, 67)

Whether Pelletier's belief in socialism is only 'a fictional world' is a legitimate question, but an inadequate assessment of her work. Historians like Boxer have failed to understand that their intellectual categories – 'suffragism', 'women in socialism' are too narrow to grasp the work of the French socialist feminists. They have failed to see that Pelletier challenged the dichotomy socialism/feminism as a manifestation of sexual oppression.

The interesting aspect of Pelletier's work is not the ineffectiveness of her attempt to influence the machinery of politics, but the analysis she made of it and the ideas she articulated to overcome the problem. She decided that feminism had to be a cultural struggle carried out in the order of language. That decision might be viewed as a retreat to a supposedly cosier world of intellectual speculation; but surely it was more than this? Though her antifamily position was Pelletier's distinctive mark, she stated in 1931 that it would be wrong to abolish the family in the present patriarchal society, for this would be done at the expense of women. If the upbringing of children were to cease to be individual women's responsibility, the State had to assume the entire upbringing of children at the same time. But it was very doubtful, she wrote, that collective education could ever be realized. The ideology of parental love was too strong for parents ever to agree to hand their children over to the state: besides it was unlikely that any state could ever finance such a project (Pelletier, 1931: 18–19).

Pelletier believed that the evolution of society towards sexual equality was an irreversible process. The gradual involvement of women in production, the political rights which women were bound to be granted sooner or later, the relative sexual emancipation of the post-war period would progressively alter women's consciousness and make the agencies of women's oppression disintegrate. It was the task of feminists to keep that process alive. They had to think ahead, to ensure that all women, and in particular the more oppressed women of the working class, benefited from it.

Pelletier wanted her writings to act as a stimulus for feminist thinking. The introduction she wrote to *The Feminist Education of Women* is indicative, I think, of the perspective she had on her entire work. She explained that her book was not prescriptive; it did not offer a series of recipes to be followed to the letter. She wanted it to be a focus of discussion and reflection. Individual mothers, she hoped, might take up one aspect or the other, modifying it to suit their own situation and adding to it ideas she had not foreseen. Should a rich feminist decide to give some money to the cause of feminist education, added Pelletier, it would be more useful for her to use the money to propagate the idea of feminist education rather than set up a school according to Pelletier's pedagogical principles.

Even within a capitalist regime her ideas had, she thought, some measure of applicability. For instance, she forecast that shortages of domestic labour would accelerate the technologization of housework. It was the task of feminists to ensure that this be done to the advantage of working-class women. The capitalists, who wanted to keep control of women's labour, would be interested in the nursery system. The feminists had to think out the practical means of freeing women from their everyday servitude.

Secondly, Pelletier thought of socialism as a dynamic process. In 1931 she stated that the establishment of a social democracy was not an historical impossibility. Whether it came or not, it was the task of feminist socialists to devise methods that would prevent the family and the education system from continuing to mould class and gender identities by positioning the working class and women as inferior.

Thirdly, Pelletier believed her writing to be an active form of' socialist militancy which could act on the present political situation. She saw her role in the socialist movement as that of 'propagandist'. She often worked with a left-wing organization which called itself 'the Group of Propaganda by the Brochure', and the Socialist Party did accredit her with that status when they wrote: 'Pelletier, the old propagandist of our ideas'.

I have argued that Pelletier came to see socialism as a constant struggle in the order of culture. The unifying principle of her publications is their common strategy: to undermine capitalism by identifying and unmasking the ideologies which she saw as fundamental to its perpetuation. Religion, morality, patriotism, the education system, the family are presented by her as the agencies of class and sexual oppression. In that perspective, Pelletier's 'antistyle', and the violence of her writings, can be seen as functional. Pelletier's tactics consisted in attacking dominant ideologies in specific areas, focusing on crucial examples whose examination could challenge the entire structure of capitalist patriarchy.

Note

Claudine Mitchell wrote a doctoral dissertation on Art and Politics and teaches at the Universities of Leeds and Sheffield where in 1984 she created a course, 'Women and Art'. She would like to thank Simone Blanc and the librarians of the Bibliothèque Marguerite Durand and Erica Carter for their assistance.

References

Albistur, Maité and Armogathe, Daniel (1977) *Histoire du Féminisme Français* Paris. Des Femmes.

Boxer, Marilyn (1981) 'When Radical and Socialist Feminism Were Joined. The Extraordinary Failure of Madeleine Pelletier' in Slaughter and Kern (1981).

Hause, Steven and Kenny, Anne (1984) *Women's Suffrage and Social Politics in the French Third Republic* Princeton: Princeton University Press.

Maignien, Claude (1978) editor *Madeleine Pelletier* Paris: Syros.

Pelletier, Madeleine to Arria Ly, correspondence, 56 letters, 1908–1934, Bibliothèque Historique de la Ville de Paris.

Pelletier, Madeleine to Hélène Gousset and Hélène Brion, correspondence, 19 letters, 1912–1939, Bibliothèque Marguerite Durand, Paris.

Pelletier file, Bibliothèque Marguerite Durand, 79 rue Nationale, Paris.

Pelletier, Madeleine (1908a) *Women in Struggle for their Rights* Paris: Giard.

Pelletier, Madeleine (1908b) 'Question of Women's Suffrage' *La Revue Socialiste* Paris.

Pelletier, Madeleine (1910) 'Guedism or Herveism *La Suffragiste* No. 17, June 1910, pp. 1–4.

Pelletier, Madeleine (1911a) 'Abortion and Depopulation' *La Suffragiste* No. 20, May 1911, pp. 13–15.

Pelletier, Madeleine (1911b) *The Sexual Emancipation of Women* Paris: Giard.

Pelletier, Madeleine (1912a) 'The Half Emancipated' *La Suffragiste* No. 24, January 1912, pp. 1–3.

Pelletier, Madeleine (1912b) 'Feminism and the Working Class' *La Suffragiste* No. 30, July 1912, pp. 1–4.

Pelletier, Madeleine (1913) *The Right to Abortion* Paris: Du Malthusien. 1911 version reprinted in Maignien (1978).

Pelletier, Madeleine (1914) *The Feminist Education of Women* Paris: Giard, republished in Maignien (1978: 63–15).

Pelletier, Madeleine (1919) *Individualism* Paris: Giard.

Pelletier, Madeleine (c.1919) *The Diary of a Feminist* unpublished MS.

Pelletier, Madeleine (1922) *My Adventurous Journey in Communist Russia* Paris: Giard, 218 pp.

Pelletier, Madeleine (1926a) *Capitalism and Communism* Ermont: Le Vegetalien.

Pelletier, Madelcine (1926b) 'Education in Russia' *La Fronde*, 2–4 June.

Pelletier, Madeleine (1928) 'Prostitution' *Revue de L'Anarchie* No. 20, November 1928, re-published in 1935: ch. 7.

Pelletier, Madeleine (1931) *The Educator State* Paris: Voix des Femmes.

Pelletier, Madeleine (1932) *The New Life* Paris: Figuiere.

Pelletier, Madeleine (c.1933a) *Celibacy Superior State* Paris: Brochure Mensuelle, republished in 1935; ch. IX.

Pelletier, Madeleine (c.1933b) *Wormen's Right to Work* Paris: Brochure Mensuelle, republished in Maignien (1978: 159–76).

Pelletier, Madeleine (1933) *The Virgin Woman* Paris: Bresle.

Pelletier, Madeleine (c.1930–3) 'Love and Maternity' *Brochure Mensuelle*, No. 71, Paris.

Pelletier, Madeleine (1935) *Rational Sexuality* Paris: Sphinx.

Pelletier, Madeleine undated (n.d.a) 'Feminism and the Family' Paris, (16 pp.) republished in 1911; ch. II.

Pelletier, Madeleine undated (n.d.b) 'The Disintegration of the Family' Paris, (after 1926).

Slaughter, Jane and Kern, Robert (1981) editors *European Women on the Left* Westport, CT: Greenwood.

Sowerwine, Charles (1982) *Sisters or Citizens* Cambridge: Cambridge University Press.

Chapter 24

Margaret H. Darrow

■ from 'FRENCH VOLUNTEER NURSING AND THE MYTH OF WAR EXPERIENCE IN WORLD WAR I', *American Historical Review*, 101, 1, February 1996, pp. 80–106

I N THE LATE NINETEENTH CENTURY, the European powers and the United States shared a similar conception of gender and war and a rhetoric that elevated the relationship between them into the Myth of War Experience, as Historian George Mosse has called it: war was noble, chivalric, and, above all, masculine. By transforming weak and callow youths into ardent, resolute men, war saved the nation from degeneracy and restored it to its virile tradition. In France, the discourse of the War Myth had become the signature tune of the nationalist Right in the 1890s, but in the decade of war scares that preceded the actual declaration of war in 1914, it played across the whole political spectrum – and it left French women immobilized, frozen out of the discussion of the envisioned war. The only relationship the War Myth admitted between women and war was a hostile one, that of opponents to war, anti-militarists, pacifists, and spies. It is significant that today, the two women many French people associate with World War I are Hélène Brion, jailed for pacifism, and Mata Hari, executed for spying. This was the discourse that French women and their allies had to address before and during the war to claim a war experience for women.

The difficulty almost all commentators displayed in relating women to the war is evident in their ambivalent views of all the possible postures women could take toward the war, from the most traditional, of waiting, praying, and grieving, to the most radical, of donning uniforms and serving in the military. Although commentators trivialized female munitions workers by calling them 'munitionnettes,' many worried that they were, in fact, war profiteers, working not for their country's defense but for the scandalously high wages, which they then wasted on luxuries. Women who did charity work for soldiers, refugees, or war orphans might merely be filling their social calendars with a pretense of usefulness. Women who 'adopted' soldiers by correspondence mainly were interested in flirtation. Not even war widows were blameless; their mourning could be insincere – a mere fashion statement – or worse, excessive. A truly patriotic widow would make sure her display of grief did not damage morale.

Of all these activities, volunteer nursing offers us the best example of the pervasive unease with any connection between women and the war. If it were possible to conceive of a feminine sphere consecrated to the French masculine war effort rather than hostile to it, the nurse offered the best possible parallel to the soldier. In the iconography of posters and postcards, the begrimed, bloody, unshaven *poilu* is paired with the clean, solicitous nurse, white-robed and veiled: the masculine and the feminine in wartime guise. [...] The French government rewarded the valor of nurses with decorations; nurses were even sanctified if they died in the line of duty. Thus, of all the French women involved in World War I, nurses would seem to have been the most worthy, if not to stand level with the soldier in the national pantheon, at least to be included in the tableau in a supporting role.

In fact, the intrusion of the nurse into the war story barely survived the war itself. While the stone and bronze of war memorials and the pages of fiction and popular memoirs commemorate the trench fighter, nurses have disappeared from the national memory. Although praised at the time – Maurice Donnay compared Noëlle Roger's work *Les carnets d'une infirmière* (1915) to *Uncle Tom's Cabin* – the personal accounts of war nursing published during and immediately after the war soon went out of print and today are difficult to find. When I tell French librarians and archivists that I am researching women in France during World War I, they frequently begin to talk about the Resistance. World War II produced legends of female heroism; World War I did not. Since the volunteer nurses of World War I had the best chance to create a story of women's war experience, the fact that no such story entered the culture is significant. By examining the way commentators conceived of nursing and the way that nurses themselves understood their wartime service, we can begin to understand why women's own contributions to the war failed to find a place in French memory.

[...]

[...] It [Women's war service] was to be patriotic, it was to be national, and it was to call forth devotion and self-sacrifice equivalent to men's. But it was to be feminine: supportive and nonviolent. For the vast majority of commentators, nursing the wounded best fit the bill.

[...]

Previous to the Red Cross's successful publicity campaigns, nursing was not popularly imagined as patriotic – it was not even considered especially feminine. The work of nursing was unpleasant, manual labor, most akin to that of a maid-of-all-work. Nurses scrubbed wards, emptied bed pans, boiled bandages, and carried coal, as well as washing and feeding patients and changing dressings. Both men and women performed this work. Nor did people think of nursing as benevolent service to the sick. Working-class men and women did it for pay – and very low pay at that – while nuns labored in self-mortifying service to God.

The new ethos of nursing, [...] took *over* the nun's vocation, turned it from God to *la patrie*, and characterized it as distinctly feminine. [...] First of all, Red Cross promoters cast volunteer nursing as a national service for women parallel to military service for men. M. Levasseur, writing about the Red Cross in 1899 in *Le petit parisien*, maintained, 'When the whole nation rises up to defend the soil and patrimony of France, the two sexes have an equal duty with different functions: the men to combat and the women to the ambulance!' Louis Lespine, in his 1914 instruction manual for Red Cross organizations, claimed that volunteer nurses 'are also a voluntary reserve of the national army.' Dr. César Legrand, another Red Cross activist, even raised the possibility of nurse heroines, women killed in battle.

Secondly, in the new ethos, nursing was to be a vocation, requiring the spirituality, self-abnegation, and perfect submission to authority of a nun. Inevitably, this was the main message of Catholic social activists such as Witt-Guizot, but Red Cross publicists made use of this aspect as well. In her 1914 book, *La croix-rouge française: Le rôle patriotique des femmes*,

Andrée d'Alix claimed that a Red Cross nurse – *une vrai* – required difficult training, not only in science and medical practice but especially in self-mastery and self-abnegation [...]

Thirdly, the Red Cross portrayed nursing as naturally feminine, the extension and embodiment of motherhood.

[...]

If femininity so perfectly prepared women for wartime nursing, could it admit them to that preserve and testing ground of masculinity, the battlefield? The Military Medical Corps firmly believed it could not; the statute of 1913 relegated women to service in hospitals in the rear. But Red Cross promoters were not so sure. For example, while Dr. Legrand admitted that current military plans denied any possibility of Red Cross nurses on or near the battlefield, he speculated that if a war should prove lengthy, the rigid exclusion of women from front-line medical units might be difficult to maintain. He counseled Red Cross committees to fall in with the army's current regulations but to be prepared – even to hold back funds – in anticipation of 'a new mission.'

Nursing, promoted as women's wartime service, was envisioned as feminine devotion nationalized, militarized, and even combat-ready but still held back from the masculine, military war experience.

[...]

Despite the enduring contradiction, when France declared war on Germany, nursing was the main way that French women could imagine themselves participating.

[...] Nonetheless, nursing war wounded remained conceptually and rhetorically (if not numerically) the quintessential feminine war service. As Léon Abensour wrote in 1917, 'Whoever thinks of French women in 1914 sees a young nurse draped in a white or blue veil, very gay despite her monastic headdress displaying the blood-red cross'. [...] Nonetheless, wartime literature failed to resolve the contradictions of pre-war discourse. For most commentators, volunteer nursing was the ultimate feminine war service, yet whether it was *military* service, whether the nurse was truly engaged in the masculine war, remained in dispute. [...] For example, Louise Zeys, a feminist journalist, called attention to the joint mobilization of soldiers and Red Cross volunteers: "During the night of the first of August, all the nurses on *active duty* received their mobilization orders [...] [T]hey joined the military trains that carried our troops toward the East, and in compartments reserved for nurses in *uniform* they were acclaimed by all as new comrades. Weren't they going to campaign together?"

[...]

Much less controversial, although much more difficult to integrate into the masculine experience of war, was the depiction of the nurse as simultaneously mother and nun and definitely all woman, repeating and expanding the themes that had emerged before the war. Religious imagery, of course, arose easily from the history of nursing. Of the previous models, the poor working women and the nun, only the nun embodied any of the qualities that volunteer nursing wished to project. Red Cross uniforms copied nuns' habits with their coifes and impractical long veils in a conscious effort to appropriate to their wearers not only the qualities of nuns – selflessness, devotion, and asexuality – but also the respect and privileges society accorded them, for example, the ability to travel alone and to associate closely, even intimately, with men not of their immediate family, without jeopardizing their reputations or their caste. [...]

[...]

The most popular image of all was the nurse as mother and the *petit poilu* as her infant. A song of the period, 'Adieux à l'hôpital,' explained,

There we found rest
and to bandage our booboos [bobos]
women's hands …
Goodbye to you, the good Mama
whose devotion is without limit.
Sweet nurse
now when everything is black
soften the despair
like a mother!

From nun to mother, the image of the volunteer nurse rested on essential womanhood [...]
[…]

But although devotion and motherhood were values beyond criticism, some aspects of femininity as embodied in volunteer nursing drew attacks. If, to Red Cross supporters, femininity translated into self-sacrifice and conservation of the social order, to Red Cross critics femininity spelled frivolity, fashion, sexuality, romantic adventure, and gender chaos. The Red Cross, critics claimed, licensed women to pursue selfish desires, obviously at odds with France's wartime interests, under a hypocrite's veil of patriotic devotion.

The nun, secularized and trained, was the model of the 'true' nurse; her opposite, the society lady, was the favorite example of the rival image, the false nurse
[…]

If the ideal volunteer was trained as a nurse and obedient as a nun, fashionable women who rushed to volunteer ('les élegantes de la premiére heure') were both ignorant and independent. Used to getting their own way, they refused to subordinate themselves to a doctor's authority. For Dr. Lejars, the perfect nurse was silent and anonymous – and society ladies were neither. Their conception of nursing was to give out smiles and treats to handsome young officers – no dirty, coarse, or painful duties. [...] Although none of the serious commentators accused 'false' nurses of treason, such stories appeared so frequently in newspapers and novels early in the war that British General Walter Kirk suspected all 'secretive females with fancy Red Cross outfits' in the war zone of being 'an obvious means of access for hostile agents.'

The key failing of the society lady as a nurse, however, was her sexuality. When represented as a nun or a mother, the nurse was asexual – and so was her patient; the soldier became a soul to be saved or a child to be nurtured. The fashionable woman, by contrast, brought sexuality with her; her patients were, first and foremost, men. Thus she exploded the neat gender sequestration that the war rhetoric had ordained, that masculinity was locked in solitary combat on the battlefield while femininity waited in abeyance at home.
[…]

Behind these criticisms lurked the fear that nursing spelled the end of sexual innocence for young women. [...] As Dr. Toulouse sermonized, 'The war came, and the most sheltered young woman enrolled in the nursing corps. The mystery of the other sex, which had been strictly kept from her, was brusquely revealed in the beds of pain of wounded soldiers … The young woman now knows. She is warned, she no longer lowers her eyes like before, and she sees clearly ahead of her, in the world and in life.' Toulouse did not entirely condemn this eventuality, even though he regretted it. But, for others, French soldiers' demonstrations of manliness in the trenches would come to nothing if wartime female emancipation cast France back into the pit of gender chaos. What was the point of the war at all if women's war experience undermined men's?

[. . .]

Critical evaluations of nurses were not confined to a few misogynists and conservatives; they pervaded the wartime literature that explored women's relationship to the war. Commentator after commentator, republicans, socialists, and feminists, as well as clerics and conservatives, in chapters usually titled 'White Angels,' followed their eulogies to nurses' devotion and feminine healing powers with doses of criticism. Some commentaries quickly dismissed 'abuses' as insignificant, but in others, the depiction of the 'false nurse' – ambitious, frivolous, wanton – claimed as much or more space than that of *la vraie*. Without doubt, the volunteer nurse, although held up as the best symbol of feminine support for the war, was a disturbing figure

[. . .]

Volunteer nurses suppressed the sisterhood of nursing in their memoirs in order to insist that they were fighting the same war as the soldiers, the masculine war, the trench-fighters' war. Their accounts focused almost all the attention on the relationship between the nurse and the wounded soldier, not as a romantic or erotic tie but as comrades in arms and accomplices in suffering, in league against the brutal enemy and the callous authorities. But, even then, nurses could not risk claiming an equal experience to the soldiers', an equal sacrifice to the national cause; since masculinity had to triumph, it was not a camaraderie of equals that they depicted but the nurse as the soldier's disciple. Exhausted or frightened or sick as she was, it was his suffering that caused hers. Antelme wrote, 'You know, those agonies, they tear the soul, and to know your impotence to stop that suffering, that is the worst of all.' As her emotional anguish reflected his physical pain, so, too, did her war experience reflect his. Rather than commemorating a unique feminine experience, in account after account memoirists subordinated the nurse's story to the soldier's.

Chapter 25

Elizabeth Waters

■ 'THE MODERNISATION OF RUSSIAN MOTHERHOOD 1917–1937', *Europe-Asia Studies,* 44 (1), 1992, pp. 123–135

I N A FAMOUS SPEECH delivered during the first five-year plan in 1931, Stalin exhorted his people to greater efforts in the construction of socialism.

> To slacken the pace would mean to lag behind; and those who lag behind are beaten.... Russia ... was ceaselessly beaten for her backwardness ... For military backwardness, for cultural backwardness, for political backwardness, for industrial backwardness, for agricultural backwardness.[1]

The phraseology had a novel bluntness, but the underlying message-that the country must modernise if it were to maintain its status in the Western community of nations—went back to Peter the Great. In Stalin's Russia, catching up and overtaking the West meant above all achieving higher levels of production, but it was also recognised that before the workers and peasants could transform the economy they themselves must be transformed: the new Soviet Man must be neat and efficient, literate and cultured, hygienic and healthy. The health of the next generation, of infants and young children, had from early in the 19th century been a matter for national concern, and campaigns for modern mothering dated from that era. Enlightenment propaganda aimed to inculcate the ideas of modern medicine on pregnancy, childbirth and infant care current across the industrialising world from Paris to New York and Sydney. In post-revolutionary Russia, this transmission of knowledge was effected through clinics, public lectures and the mass publication of popular literature, the same methods of propaganda employed elsewhere. Also, as elsewhere in the Western world, both before and since, the campaign for modern mothering was coordinated by the medical profession, which presented itself as the guardian and practitioner of the new knowledge and instructed mothers to turn to doctors rather than to wise women for advice and aid.

As well as these similarities, this modernisation of Russian motherhood exhibited a number of special characteristics. It was rather late in starting, and slow to get off the ground. At the end of the 19th century, child care manuals were circulating in the cities and urban clinics had opened their doors, but not until the 1920s and 1930s did the new medical knowledge begin to make an impression on the villages, and even then changes were sporadic and uneven. Because of the sharp gulf, historically, between society and the people in Russia, and the small size of the middle class, this shift from traditional to modern was resisted with unusual vigour. It took place at a time of revolutionary upheavals, at a time when ideas of freeing women from the 'cross' of motherhood were proclaimed, a circumstance which might have been expected to place the doctors, who were not radical socialists by any means, in opposition to the regime, and to some extent it did. However, the tradition of public service to which the obstetricians and gynaecologists subscribed predisposed them to take in their stride the notion of state-organised and communally oriented care. Moreover, the more radical ideas of social restructuring—the withering away of the family and the household—were shelved in the early 1920s as the New Economic Policy was introduced and the discipline of the market accepted. This moderation of Bolshevik aims made possible an alliance between the medical profession and the party based on their shared belief in the need for modernisation, an alliance further cemented by the party's willingness, once the principle of state control had been asserted, to allow doctors a certain amount of autonomy. Like other alliances made in the 1920s, though, this one did not survive the first five-year plan. When the country, with Stalin at the helm, plunged towards industrialisation, all professional groups, including the doctors, lost status and social influence. While the messages on mothering remained. constant in content, their context was transformed: it was politicised, and harnessed in the cause of economic targets. The regime in the 1930s expected women to reproduce and produce for its convenience, with only the barest of welfare provisions.

Ironically, it was in these years of extreme hardship for mothers that their image was adopted by the political iconographers. In a society living under extraordinary pressure, in constant flux, the sense of continuity offered by the maternal image, its suggestion of intimacy and solace, had therapeutic possibilities. With the disappearance, one after the other, of those institutions mediating between the family and the government—political factions, voluntary organisations, (relatively) independent unions and press, and the *zhenotdel* (women's department)—the iconic conflation of mother and motherland, family and state served to humanise and legitimise the party.

Enlightenment propaganda: content and form

Mothercraft was coordinated in the post-revolutionary period by a subdepartment for the Protection of Motherhood and Infancy (usually known by its abbreviations, Okhmatmlad or OMM) under the Commissariat of Health. By 1925 it was operating over 200 clinics in the Russian Republic (RSFSR)[2] for pregnant women and around 400 for mothers with young babies.[3] Women were advised to make regular visits from the time they discovered their pregnancy until the child was two years old, when it became the responsibility of the regular health clinics. Okhmatmlad had its own publishing house and between 1926 and 1927 brought out more than 170 titles, in a total of over 1.5 million copies.[4] The written word could not be relied upon solely in a country with a high female illiteracy rate, and was complemented by radio programmes, slide shows and public talks, and most importantly by the posters that decorated the clinics and the *zhenotdel*, and the women's corners and displays in clubs and libraries, and that were the subject of frequent special exhibitions.

These posters covered all aspects of modern mothering in a manner designed to be striking, comprehensible and persuasive.[5]

'Look After the Mother', a poster produced in the 1920s for a peasant audience, comprised two scenes of pregnant women doing heavy work—carrying wood and a pail, and bringing in the harvest—and one of a mother engaged in feeding livestock, a task considered appropriate to her condition. The husband is told he must free his wife from unsuitable work, such as lifting weights. 'The master of the house', the text notes wryly, 'looks after his mare and his cow, but not his pregnant wife'.[6]

If the medical profession had something to say on the responsibilities of family members to the mother, it focused mainly on the numerous and weighty responsibilities of the mother to the child. These included providing the right environment—a room that was clean, full of light and well ventilated. 'Sun is the baby's best friend', advised one poster.[7] 'Cleanliness is the guarantee of health', taught a second.[8] Breast feeding was another of the mother's responsibilities. 'Nature has its iron laws', wrote one doctor, 'and punishes for the slightest failure to observe them. Breast feeding of the baby by the biological mother is one of these iron laws of nature which cannot be broken without serious consequences'.[9] The consequences were graphically spelled out in a poster entitled 'Mothers, Breast Feed Your Babies', which featured a bottle-feeding mother, inset against a cemetery, and a breast-feeding mother beneath a scene of healthy little children playing games.[10]

Just as infants could be endangered by their mothers' ignorance of the rules of feeding, they could be put at risk if sleeping arrangements were incorrect. 'How to look after your baby' included, as one of its five panels, a picture of a hanging cradle and a text below, enumerating its dangers, 'The cradle is very harmful. The cradle stupefies the baby. Do not rock [the baby] either in a cradle or in your arms'. Another panel warned the mother against taking the infant to bed with her because of the risk of accidently smothering it, or of passing on infection. In the final panel a baby sleeps peacefully in a neat and clean crib, illustrating the moral of this story, reiterated by the text: 'Buy a linen basket and your baby will have a cheap and healthy bed!'[11]

'How to look after your baby' also included instructions on swaddling, a practice still customary in Russian towns, as well as in the countryside. Strips of cloth were wrapped around the baby, restricting its movement, and thus keeping it out of mischief, and saving the mother from having to tend it constantly or worry for its safety. While swaddling was not linked by the doctors to high rates of infant mortality, it was thought to prevent normal physical development and hence occupied a prominent place in the list of 'don'ts'. 'Do not swaddle the baby and do not dress it in a bonnet indoors', the poster commanded. 'Do not wrap it up tightly either in winter or summer. The swaddling bands prevent the child from breathing and growing and encourage various rashes. Dress the child so that it can move its arms and legs freely.' The text is not essential for comprehension. The chubby-faced infant clad only in a short vest, content and comfortable in its cot, was designed to warm a mother's heart, just as the drawn and distressed face of the swaddled mite was guaranteed to prick her conscience. This same contrast between pleasure and misery, between the baby who cries and the baby who smiles, is employed by the artist, A. Komarov, in another poster, this time exclusively devoted to the theme, 'Do not swaddle infants and do not dress them in a bonnet'.[12]

In their attempts to gain and hold attention, the posters used a variety of techniques. Babies were shown in a number of life-threatening situations: Komarov, for example, drew a baby, alone in a rough-hewn sailing boat, buffeted between rocks that were labelled with incorrect mothering practices: 'stuffy, stale air', 'dark room', 'poor care', 'dirty environment' and 'cow's milk'.[13] They were shown making demands on their mothers in a series of posters of babes and toddlers holding banners and demonstrating for correct care; in one case, animated and militant, they are attending a meeting to listen to a nightgowned peer making a speech, and waving placards that proclaim, among other things, 'midwives, not wise women', 'mother's breast', 'protection from flies', and dry, clean, nappies'.[14]

Texts were didactic and authoritarian in style, a characteristic of all enlightenment propaganda produced in this period (and indeed of the literature on mothering produced in other Western countries also). The tone adopted by G. N. Speransky in his popular *Azbuka materi*, which went through several editions in the 1920s, was typical. 'If they tell you that without swaddling-bands the legs will be crooked, don't believe it', he wrote; 'it's absolute rubbish'.[15] His comments on such matters as breast feeding and diet were equally short and sharp. It was not that the medical profession lacked arguments, rather it appears to have felt that Soviet mothers should be prepared to take on trust whatever advice it saw fit to offer.

The medical profession had emerged in 19th-century Russia, recruiting from the small, educated elite, and its members were often critics of tsarism, anxious to do something to change their society. It was not uncommon for men and women who had been active in radical movements to choose a career in medicine and a job in the countryside, with the aim of improving the lot of the peasants. For all their good intentions, perhaps precisely because of them, the doctors never doubted that they had a right to teach, to enlighten, to remake the lives of 'the people'. Mothering, the enlightenment propaganda emphasised, was not a matter of intuition, or something the woman would pick up as she went along; it was a craft that had to be learned, and learned from those who knew best. As experts on the subject of modern medical knowledge, the doctors felt that it was their task to teach and command, and the duty of women to listen and obey. Because their own lives and experiences were so removed from those of their patients, they tended to dismiss with contempt traditional methods of mothering. This high-handed approach was no doubt also fuelled by a sense of isolation. In the 1920s only 5% of births were attended by trained medical personnel, such was the shortage of doctors. And whereas in other Western countries urbanisation, print culture and education had created fairly favourable conditions for the wide reception of modern mothering among all sections of the population, and middle-class women especially were willing converts to its cause, Russia was still rural and unschooled, and the pool of educated women from whom help could be expected was tiny.

Moreover, the system of traditional care was still well entrenched. Every Russian village had its *babka*, a woman wise in magic spells and herbal medicine (znakharstvo), who attended at childbirth and gave advice to young mothers. The medical profession remained combative in the face of this formidable resistance to its messages. One doctor called for a 'struggle against znakharstvo, which still holds our Russian woman firmly in its tenacious paws',[16] another wrote of the necessity of 'completely destroying the remnants of darkness and superstition'.[17] In the 1920s and 1930s, as the regime was consolidated and the villages were gradually caught in. the orbit of state institutions, the opportunities for organising such a struggle improved. All methods of propaganda were pressed into service. Short stories cast the *babka* as villain, plays examined the fatal influence she could have on the young and unsuspecting, and posters illustrated the positive benefits that accrued from avoiding her. One poster contrasts a rude peasant but with a bright and shining hospital, and the wise woman's ignorance—she is old, gnarled and clutching a new born baby in a dirty rag—with the doctor's expertise. 'Give birth in a hospital, the wise woman ruins your health', reads the text.[18] The damage the wise woman can do to health is the focal point of another poster: leaning on a stick, a peasant woman hobbles painfully about her business, clearly a victim of the wise woman, who lurks in the background, old, unclean and menacing. Modern medicine is represented by a young woman clad from head to foot in whites who points to a notice which reads 'hospital' and to a row of neat and spotless beds. The written text confirms the message of the visual images: 'With the wise woman's help you will soon give up the ghost. Without the midwife you will suffer pain'.[19]

Doctors and the party: the making and the breaking of an alliance

If this bid to transform the social relations of motherhood-the replacement of traditional healers by professional experts—was typical for countries travelling the path of modernity, it occurred for the first time against the background of a political revolution that identified itself as socialist, a coincidence that was not without impact on the manner in which the messages about mothering were conveyed. Bolshevik enlightenment propaganda in the immediate post-revolutionary years made reference to the emancipation of women and the triumph of the October revolution over exploitation and oppression. A poster produced in Saratov in 1920 linked the provision of child-care facilities with the creation of a socialist society. In its top left-hand corner, a bloated, top-hatted capitalist greedily clasps to his bosom the chains of women's unfortunate destiny, while, his victims huddle below, in the shadow of a reformatory, a brothel and various nightspots, which signify the system of social and sexual oppression under which they live. On the right-hand side of the poster we are shown the socialist future, a world of creches and nurseries, in which women, unfettered and joyful, gather under a banner proclaiming, 'All hail the 3rd Communist International'.[20]

The first head of the administrative board of Okhmatmlad, Alexandra Kollontai, was well known for her radical views on women and the family. She was confident that the revolution would usher in equality and freedom for women, and would provide the most favourable conditions for the 'combination of work and motherhood'. While capitalism forced women to work right up until childbirth in conditions of poverty and neglect, and to experience motherhood as a 'cross', socialism, she promised, would do everything in its power to assist women with their mothering, and would accord them the high status that was their due. Motherhood, Kollontai emphasised, was a social rather than a private matter, and child care ought to be communal rather than domestic.[21] During the period of 'war communism' such views had considerable currency. A resolution passed in 1918 at the First Congress of Worker and Peasant Women advocated a system of social education for children from birth to 16 years of age.[22] The following year, at the First Congress on the Protection of Childhood, one delegate argued that the state alone was able to create the necessary educational environment for the development of the communist personality,[23] an opinion echoed by V. Golubeva, a *zhenotdel* organiser, in her paper at the first Okhmatmlad conference in 1920.[24] Nadezhda Krupskaya remembered how during the civil war she and her colleagues in the Commissariat of Enlightenment believed social upbringing to be both 'essential' and 'feasible'.[25] Another educationalist, Anna Kalinina, described how her department 'sought out' children for communal institutions and 'carried out propaganda among the parents'.[26]

There were some who worried that parents were usually assumed to be female: 'We organise talks at clinics and schools for women only, instead of for parents', wrote an Okhmatmlad organiser, 'invite only wives, and not husbands or parents to the abortion commissions, organise child care circles for 'future mothers' and for 'girls', and do not encourage boys to be involved in these activities'.[27] The young communist paper, *Komsomol'skaya pravda*, criticised the idea that wives must take all the responsibility for looking after their babies, and their husbands none at all.[28] *Rabotnitsa* on one occasion appealed to men to take a greater part in child care,[29] and on another published a short fictional piece about a man who stayed home to look after his baby, supported by alimony from his ex-wife.[30] Early *zhenotdel* leaders, in particular Inessa Armand and Alexandra Kollontai, were careful to use ungendered words when referring to the child minders of the future, or to include men as well as women in their number.[31] This challenge to sexual stereotyping, though, was weak and hesitant, and found no broad support among party activists, let alone enthusiasm among the masses.

Nor were efforts to substitute public for private child care successful. To be sure, communal alternatives to family upbringing grew in number at a rate initially undreamed of by even their most enthusiastic supporters. The number of children in homes rose from just under 30000 in 1917 to 400000 in 1920, and to over half a million in 1922.[32] However, the homes were crowded with children who had been deserted and orphaned by war and revolution and their aftermath, who came out of necessity; they fell far short of the ideals of cleanliness, comfort and communist socialisation. The lofty purpose of child care institutions—the education of citizens for a new world—was not quite forgotten, but the mundane issues of everyday crisis management held centre stage: instructions during the civil war noted the importance for the emancipation of women of the 'combination of motherhood and work', but then turned to the question of fixing water mains and to the need for the 'closest attention' to 'the struggle against flies'.[33]

In the economic and social environment of NEP—the streamlined industry, the high female unemployment, the reduction of welfare budgets—talk of emancipating women through the transformation of the family and the socialisation of child care was seen as increasingly inappropriate. There was neither the political will nor the funding for the construction of a comprehensive network of communally run services to replace the private household. The family was recognised to be, for the time being, the safest and best environment for the child, and with the relegalisation of fostering and adoption in the mid-1920s the children's home became the last resort, even for the orphan. The creche and the nursery, too, were luxuries beyond the party purse. Manuals on mothering in the 1920s rarely mentioned the public alternatives to family care. Even the journal *Okhrana materinstva i mladenchestva*, designed primarily for Okhmatmlad organisers, was devoting almost half of its pages to the purely medical aspects of motherhood and infancy by 1927.

The Bolshevik rejection of the more radical aims of 'social upbringing' further disposed the medical profession to make peace with the regime. Especially as the doctors' were themselves inclined, by and large, to favour a certain measure of public care. They believed most women to be ignorant and in need of tutelage, and had few qualms about intervention in the families of 'the people'; they viewed the creche and the nursery as excellent channels for the dissemination of modern ideas on mothering. While the doctors may have thought it right that their own wives should stay at home, they took it for granted that most women would work outside the family. Domesticity was not as universal an ideal as it was elsewhere in the West.

A second bone of contention between the doctors and the Bolsheviks had been the question of power. In the first months after the October revolution the party's position was insecure, and it took what measures it could to pre-empt oppositional challenges. As early as December 1917 one of the pre-revolutionary mothercraft organisations, the Council of Children's Shelters, was abolished,[34] and the All Russian Guardianship (Vserosiiskoe Popechitel'stvo), a charitable body set up by tsarist directive in 1913 to supervise child welfare, was ordered to hand over its property and equipment to the recently formed Okhmatmlad.[35] These moves to deprive the medical profession of its organisational role aroused deep resentment.

Over this issue, too, an acceptable compromise was soon reached. The Bolsheviks had no option but to rely on the expertise of the 'bourgeois specialists' (there was no other kind available), and were willing to recognise, in return for cooperation, a certain amount of professional autonomy. Doctors were invited to sit on committees and draft proposals; their learned societies, disrupted by the uncertainties of the civil war, resumed activity. Business for the medical profession proceeded much as usual. An issue of *Zhurnal akusherstva i zhenskikh boleznei* in 1927 dedicated to A. V. Markovsky was accompanied by a photograph of the professor, smart in jacket, tie and pin-striped trousers, very much the gentleman-physician.[36] The journal *Okhrana materinstva i mladenchestva*, honouring the 25 years of service to the profession of another eminent specialist with a biographical essay, saw no need to mention the October revolution or the Soviet regime, so little apparently did the political upheavals impinge on medical careers.[37]

However, a few years later the alliance between the party and the doctors came to an end. In 1931 the January issue of *Okhrana materinstva i mladenchestva* appeared under a new editor and with a fresh orientation. The previous leadership was criticised for its 'isolationism' (*otorvannost*) and 'its distance from the basic tasks of socialist construction' and its 'rather apolitical approach'.[38] From now on, it was stated, the journal would take a greater interest in the political issues of the day, and reject the (alleged) narrow-mindedness, sentimentality and elitism of the old editorial board. As evidence of this determination to change direction, the format of the journal was altered, social and political articles, of which there were far more than before, were placed first, while medical matters were dealt with briefly, and at the back. In these years of cultural revolution the whole range of enlightenment propaganda came under scrutiny. Posters were examined closely for ideological errors, certain mothering manuals were denounced as 'bourgeois' and their withdrawal from circulation advised.[39] The methods and relationships of mothering remained unchanged; it was their political context that underwent restructuring. The state was intent on establishing its control, and did so without too much difficulty, through a mixture of bullying, intimidation and inter-vention. The professional organisations of gynaecologists and obstetricians, as well as their editorial boards, came under attack, and one of the most serious blows to the profession's power and prestige, paradoxically, was the vast expansion and dilution of its ranks by an ill-educated, and largely female, student body.

There was, during the period of the first five-year plan, a resurgence of interest in the creche and the nursery. The promise of rapid industrial development and communist construction encouraged the re-emergence of the utopian ideas of the post-revolutionary years, including predictions about the withering away of the family and the household. This time round, though, the interests of the economy were given a priority they had not had before, as the posters of the time clearly demonstrated. One, issued in 1930, proclaimed the message: 'By strengthening the protection of motherhood and childhood, we help the working woman to be an active constructor of socialism', and illustrated it with a large red woman in factory clothes, a kerchief round her head and a hammer in her hand, against a distant background of creche buildings.[40] This lack of proportion—large working women, small communal facilities—is a feature of a number of posters of the period; so too is the productionist bent of their slogans:

> By organising creches, children's playgrounds, factory kitchens, canteens and mechanised laundries we will provide 1 600 000 new working women for the completion of the five-year plan.

> The broad development of the network of creches, nurseries, canteens and laundries guarantees the participation of women in socialist construction.[41]

These posters did not hide the fact that the creche was the means to an end; the provision of child care would increase the number of women working in the economy and their productivity in factory and field. Also, child care provision would make it possible for women to have more children, a crucial consideration for a government that kept a worried eye on the birth rate. 'Children are our future', claimed a poster produced shortly after abortion was banned in 1936; it depicted a woman sitting at home with a baby on her lap and a child at her side and advised its audience 'not to deprive themselves of the joys of motherhood'.[42] Women were to be both workers and reproducers, whatever the cost—and the cost to maternal and infant health, to the psychological and social well-being of the mother and child, in the 1930s, was very high indeed.[43]

Motherhood and nation

Soviet political iconographers, in their attempts to provide a population ravaged by rapid industrialisation, forced collectivisation and famine and the purges with a sense of self, with the cement of identity and unity, began to employ images of motherhood. Historically, maternity had a firm place in the Russian visual lexicon. Icons of the Mother and Child were, in the pre-revolutionary period, regularly carried with armies, taken on demonstrations and used to decorate the home and the work place, as well as the church. In the posters on mothering produced after October 1917 there were some echoes, suitably secularised, of the composition and style of the Orthodox *Bogomater'* and the Catholic Madonna: women held their babies close to their bodies or sat them on their laps; often mother and child were positioned against a blank or ornamental background, or isolated by distance from society.[44] These posters, though, had limited circulation and were mostly confined to female spaces, to the walls of maternity clinics, *zhenotdel* offices and 'women's pages'. In public and political iconography women and children were conspicuous by their absence. Despite its professed commitment to women's emancipation, the bolshevik regime saw change in terms of factory and production, reference points that were primarily masculine; the hero was the male industrial worker and it was his image that stood for revolution and socialism.

At the time of the first five-year plan, this male hegemony was challenged. The state, in need of an increasing supply of workers, elevated maternity to an issue of national resonance. Posters on Okhmatmlad were displayed in public places;[45] mothers and children featured for the first time on postage stamps; women participated in gymnastic parades, wearing narrow, mid-calf skirts, and holding aloft bouquet-bearing children.[46] In search of unifying symbols the state twinned motherhood and nation. A political poster produced in the mid-1930s shows a mother and girl-child cowering helplessly before the Nazi menace; the two figures, painted in a realistic style, draw attention to the dangers which individual women and children face, but they clearly also represent the nation that has to be defended against fascism. During the Great Patriotic War this conflation of family and state and their representation by motherhood became commonplace. The middle-aged woman holding up in urgent entreaty a copy of the 'military oath' in Iraklii Toidze's famous war poster 'Rodina-mat' zovet'[47] is both real mother and motherland. 'Za rodinu-mat', another of the most ubiquitous posters of the period, depicts five soldiers in battle-like poses beneath the towering figure of a woman, draped in red, with a banner raised in her right hand, her free arm round a small (male) child; she combines the qualities of both the martial female heroines of Russian folklore and the maternal stereotype. She is *Matushka-Rossiya* personified.[48] Viktor Koretsky's '*Voin krasnoi armii, spasi!*'[49]—a mother and (male) child threatened by an enemy bayonet—evokes, in its realism, the loved ones left behind and, in its composition, the Mother of God, symbol of faith and nation. Gigantic reproductions of this poster were pasted up in Soviet streets, as if it were an icon affirming the holy nature of the struggle against Germany.[50]

The shift of Soviet ideology towards traditional themes, particularly Russian nationalism, is often dated to 1941, and certainly the frequent depiction of motherhood in poster art during the war attests to their growing importance; but the appropriation by public iconography of mother and child began earlier, as the Stalinist regime sought to bolster its legitimacy through a semblance of patriarchal stability.

The modernisation of motherhood

Over the past 15 years a substantial sociological and historical literature on the impact of modern medicine on motherhood and infant welfare has been published.[51] While earlier work in the field chronicled the development of the medical profession and listed its achievements, the more recent literature has examined critically the benefits and drawbacks of modern mothering and its wider significance for society and culture. The transformation of motherhood from a social into a medical event has been described, following the emergence, beginning from the 18th century, of the medical profession and its successful claim to supervise birth and infant care. In many cases, control passed as a result of this process from women to men—from female healers, friends, relatives, neighbours, and from mothers themselves, to male doctors; everywhere decision making passed from individuals and their communities to the experts. Modernisation thus comprised not only new knowledge about the birth process and a set of instructions on mothering but also, and more importantly, a range of new social relationships.

In Russia, by the end of the 19th century, gynaecologists and obstetricians were already well organised in the cities. Lectures were held and manuals published to preach the virtues of modern mothering; in major urban areas the medicalisation of childbirth was far advanced, with over 60% of births in St Petersburg and Moscow taking place in maternity shelters and wards by 1914. The Bolsheviks, when they came to power, criticised the tsarist regime for the timidity and inadequacies of its reforms, and condemned the philanthropy and class inequalities of the past, but they did not make fundamental changes to the programme of modernisation embarked upon by the pre-revolutionary doctors. The Soviet government was happy to sponsor campaigns that exhorted women to bath their children with soap and water and buy them cribs to sleep in, happy to see wise women denounced. The official notion of modernisation, in this instance, fitted well with the one subscribed to by the professional intelligentsia. Bolshevik socialism, even in its Utopian moments, provided few resources for prefiguring contemporary criticisms of the medicalisation of motherhood and contemporary concern with the mother's loss of control over the processes of pregnancy and birth and the father's lack of participation in parenting. The Bolsheviks shared the faith of their era in technology and expertise; and at the same time, and again in tune with their times, they paid homage to nature and did not question the maternal instincts of women or seek to emancipate them from their monopoly on the nurturing role.

The Bolsheviks set out to do things bigger and better, but not differently. The modernisation of motherhood after 1917 continued along pre-revolutionary lines and it conformed to patterns of development observable everywhere in the Western world. Modernisation in the Russian context did have its specificities. The country was vast and rural, which put brakes on the spread of the new knowledge on mothering, both before and after 1917. The professional classes were tiny and isolated, and inclined as a consequence to accept collective, state-orchestrated solutions to the problems of maternal and infant welfare. And finally, the weakness of civil society and of democratic political traditions in Russia propelled the state, rather later than was fashionable in most Western countries, to employ motherhood as a political icon.

Australian National University

This article is based on a paper presented to the First Meeting of the International Federation for Research in Women's History at the 17th International Congress of Historical Sciences, Madrid, August 1990. I would like to thank Susan Gross Solomon and Elizabeth Wood for comments on this earlier version.

My research on motherhood in post-revolutionary Russia, has been made possible by a British Council Scholarship to the USSR in 1981–83 and a place on the Australian National University exchange with Moscow University in 1989–90. I am also grateful for grants from the ANU Faculties' Research Fund in 1989 and 1990. I would like to thank the curators of poster collections at the Hoover Institution, Stanford University, the State Lenin Library, Moscow, the State History Museum, Moscow, the State Museum of Revolution, Moscow and the State Saltykov-Shchedrin Library, Leningrad, for their generous assistance.

Notes

1 Quoted in I. Deutscher, Stalin: A Political Biography (Harmondsworth, Penguin, 1972), p. 328.
2 Okhmatmlad had branches in all the republics of the USSR and the process of modernisation was in many respects uniform across the country. However, there were cultural differences, which need to be addressed separately. The focus here is on the RSFSR and Russian motherhood.

3   V. P. Lebedeva and G. N. Speransky, *Kniga materi (kak vyrastit' zdorovogo i krepkogo rebenka i sokhranit' svoe zdorov'e)* (Moscow, 1926), p. 103.

4   *Katalog no 3* (Moscow, 1928), p. 4.

5   For a discussion of enlightenment propaganda see my 'Teaching Mothercraft in Post-Revolutionary Russia', *Australian Journal of Slavonic and East European Studies*, 1, 2, 1987, pp. 29–56. The instructional images of Soviet motherhood posters are analysed in my 'Child care Posters and the Modernisation of Motherhood in Post-Revolutionary Russia', *Sbornik. Study Group on the Russian Revolution*, 13 (1987), pp. 65–93.

6   Hoover Institution Archives (Hoover) RU/SU–1639; State Saltykov-Shchedrin Library, Leningrad, otdel estampov, (SSSL), P1Md925/8–8.

7   Hoover, RU/SU–905.

8   Hoover, RU/SU–916.

9   A. N. Antonov, *Okhrana materinstva i mladenchestva. Posobie dlya vrachei*, vol. 1, issue 1 (Leningrad, 1929), p. 17.

10   Hoover, RU/SU–918.

11   Hoover, RU/SU–964. A small number of posters on methods of mothering has been published in E. M. Konyus, *Puti razvitiya sovetskoi okhrany materinstva i mladenchestva (1917–1940)* (Moscow, 1954). For 'How to Look After Your Baby', see p. 203.

12   Hoover, RU/SU–6a.

13   Hoover, RU/SU–1101. A. Komarov's poster was designed for an OMM exhibition; it is reproduced in Konyus, p. 133.

14   Hoover, RU/SU–1102. This poster was also designed by Komarov for an OMM exhibition. See Konyus, p. 132.

15   G. N. Speransky, *Azbuka materi* (Moscow, 1924 (2nd edition)), p. 37.

16   B. S. Ginzburg, *Sud nad mater'yu podkinuvshei svoego rebenka* (Moscow, 1924), p. 44.

17   N. Alfeevskaya, *Babka i delegatka. Instsenirovka dlya klubnykh postanovok i zhivykh gazet* (Moscow, 1927), p. 7.

18   State Lenin Library (SLL), P2 iX 1, no. 4429.

19   Konyus, p. 204.

20   *Ibid.* p. 100.

21   For Alexandra Kollontai's ideas on motherhood and socialism see *Rabotnitsa-mat'*, St Petersburg, 1914, and *Obshchestvo i materinstvo*, Petrograd, 1916; both were reissued after the revolution. Also see her *Sem'ya i kommunisticheskoe gosudarsvo* (Moscow, 1920).

22   A. Kollontai, *Kak i dlya chego byl sozvan pervyi vserossiiskii s"ezd rabotnits* (Moscow, 1923), pp. 10–22.

23   *Pervyi vserossiiskii s"ezd deyatelei po okhrane detstva 2 fevralya 1919* (Moscow, 1920), p. 13.

24   *Materialy pervogo vserossiiskogo soveshchaniya po okhrane materinstva i mladenchestva. Moskva, 1–5 dekabrya 1920* (Moscow, 1921), p. 58.

25   N. Krupskaya; 'K voprosu o detdomakh'; *Na putyakh k novoi shkole*, 7–8, 1924, p. 6.

26   A. D. Kalinina, *Desyat' let raboty po bor'be s detskoi besprizornost'yu* (Moscow, 1928), p. 29.

27   Voronina and Farmakovskaya, 'Formy kul'turno-prosvetitel'noi raboty yaslei v bor'be za novyi byt', *Okhrana materinstva i mladenchestva*, 8 (1929), p. 27.

28   *Komsomol'skaya pravda*, 13 August 1926.

29   'Rabochim nado pomoch' svoim zhenam', *Rabotnitsa*, 13 (1925), p. 17.

30   'Zapiski ottsa', *Rabotnitsa*, 32 (1929), p. 13.

31   I. Armand, 'Osvobozhdenie ot domashnego rabstva', in *Kommunisticheskaya partiya i organizatsiya rabotnits* (Moscow, 1919), pp. 31–34, and Kollontai, Sem'ya ..., p. 13.

32   I. Danyushevsky and V. Vasil'eva, 'Sostoyanie detskoi besprizornosti i detuchrezhdenii i ocherednye zadachi v etoi oblasti', in S. S. Tizanov, V. L. Shveitser and V. M. Vasil'eva, eds, *Detskaya besprizornost' i detskii dom. Sbornik* (Moscow, 1926), p. 184.

33   'Instruktsiya po organizatsii uchrezhdenii i raspredeleniyu raboty ukhazhivayushchego personala', in *Sputnik po okhrane materinstva i mladenchestva* (Moscow, 1921), pp. 32–34.

34 *Sobranie uzakonenii i rasporyazhenii*, 1917–1918, 11, article 165.

35 Konyus, p. 96. For a discussion of the relations between Okhmatmlad and the pre-revolutionary mothercraft organisations see also *Otchet po otdelu okhrany materinstva i mladenchestva s 1 maya 1918 goda po 1 maya 1919 goda* (Moscow, 1919), pp. 7–12.

36 For the dedication and photograph, see the last two unnumbered pages of *Zhurnal akusherstva i zhenskikh boleznei*, 1927, book 4.

37 'V. O. Mochan (K 25-letiyu vrachebno-obshchestvennoi deyatel'nosti)', *Okhrana materinstva i mladenchestva*, 3, 1925, pp. 163–164.

38 'Ot redaktsii', *Okhrana materinstva i mladenchestva*, 1, 1931, pp. 1–2.

39 V. S. Vail', 'Ustarevshie massovye knizhki po okhrane materinstva i mladenchestva', *Okhrana materinstva i mladenchestva*, 8, 1932, p. 33.

40 Hoover, RU/SU–1695.

41 State Historical Museum, izo., folder 20, 77958/73071; SSSL, P1Md 925/6–4.

42 Konyus, p. 309.

43 In the early 1930s infant mortality rates increased, the number of foundlings rose and the proportion of working women provided with creche and nursery places for their children fell. See B. S. Ginzburg, *Rodovspomozhenie i aborty v zapadnoi Sibiri* (Tomsk, 1931), p. 7; 'Ocherednye zadachi po okhrane materinstva i mladenchestva', *Kommunistka*, 13, 1929, p. 20; 'Zadachi okhrany materinstva i mladenchestva v svyazi s vovlecheniem novykh zhenskikh kadrov v proizvodstvo', *Okhrana materinstva i mladenchestva*, 3–4, 1931, p. 5.

44 Two posters produced for 'Motherhood and Infancy Protection Weeks' in 1923, one in Moscow, the other in Georgia, show mothers and children against a plain background, unrelieved, or in the Georgian case broken only by stylised flowers and the branch of a tree. See Konyus, p. 168. The emblem of Okhmatmlad featured in the foreground a mother with a baby on her lap and a toddler at her side, and far in the distance the urban skyline of the socialist future. *Ibid.* p. 171.

45 W. A. Rukeyser, *Working for the Soviet. An American Engineer in Russia* (London, Cape, 1932), p. 83.

46 For a photograph of such a parade see G. Shudakov, *Pioneers of Soviet Photography* (New York, Thames & Hudson, 1983), p. 155. It was taken in Red Square by Ivan Shagin in 1937, the year after the ban on abortion was introduced, and contrasts sharply with one from 1930 by the photographer Arkadii Shaikhet of determined women gymnasts in shorts and t-shirts, striding out unencumbered.

47 *Plakaty velikoi otechestvennoi voiny, 1941–45* (Moscow, 1985), p. 19.

48 *Ibid.* p. 135.

49 *Ibid.* p. 71.

50 *Ibid.* pp. 64–65.

51 See Nancy Schron Dye, 'History of Childbirth in America, *Signs*, 1, 1980, pp. 97–108; Judith Walzer Leavitt, 'Under the Shadow of Maternity: American Women's Responses to Death and Debility Fears in Nineteenth Century Childbirth', *Feminist Review*, 1, 1986, pp. 129–154; Barbara Ehrenrich and Deidre English, *For Her Own Good: 150 Years of the Experts' Advice to Women* (London, Pluto Press, 1979); Ann Oakley, *Women Confined Towards a Sociology of Childbirth* (Oxford, Martin Robertson, 1980); J. Lewis, *The Politics of Motherhood: Child and Maternal Welfare in England 1900–1939* (London, Croom Helm, 1980); E. Shorter, *A History of Women's Bodies* (New York, Basic Books, 1982); Ann Oakley, *The Captured Womb: A History of the Medical Care of Pregnant Women* (Oxford, Blackwell, 1984); Philippa Mein Smith, *Maternity in Dispute. New Zealand 1920–1939* (Wellington, Dept. of Internal Affairs, 1986).

Chapter 26

Diane P. Koenker

■ 'MEN AGAINST WOMEN ON THE SHOP FLOOR IN EARLY SOVIET RUSSIA: GENDER AND CLASS IN THE SOCIALIST WORKPLACE', *American Historical Review*, 100 (5), December 1995, pp. 1438–1464

RUSSIAN WORKERS have carried a heavy burden. Branded by conservative historians as uncultured, irrational, and manipulated by Machiavellian political actors, they were long portrayed by cruder spokespersons for Soviet dogma as "men of marble," heroic fighters for proletarian independence, the repository of progress and virtue. Within the last twenty years, new generations of scholars in the West and in the USSR have combined to challenge these extreme stereotypes, and they have looked broadly at the experience of workers at work, at home, and in politics. Nonetheless, in rescuing workers from their enemies and their friends, in attempting to valorize Russian workers on their own terms, historians have tended to emphasize a new ideal type: the intelligent, autonomous skilled worker, a rational actor in a complicated world, a person who valued dignity and self-worth, one who prized solidarity and equality. These values and this image of workers underlay organized labor movements before 1917 and helped to shape the course of the revolution and the building of socialism that followed.

This focus on heroic and independent figures has tended to blur aspects of working-class culture and life that appear less heroic and less worthy. These model workers themselves condemned elements of worker behavior that did not conform to their image of true class consciousness, elements that are now receiving new attention by historians of Russian workers: drunkenness, violence, anti-Semitism, and misogyny.[1] It is time to reconsider the extent to which the working-class culture that "made the revolution" was an exclusively masculine culture, one that deliberately and consistently excluded women from participation and devalued women's contributions to the common cause.

Women, to be sure, were a highly visible *category* in revolutionary Russia, particularly in the official Communist project. Communist leaders argued that the emancipation of women was a prerequisite for the emancipation of all. Throughout the 1920s, organizational work among women occupied a distinct and mandated place on the agendas of every public institution. Some activists believed that women, as the most oppressed of all proletarians, could be mobilized as a lever to liberate the rest of society.[2] One path to mobilization was to reveal to women the reality of their enslavement to men and the necessity of breaking free of patriarchal domination. Another path was wage labor. Participation in the work force by women was widely assumed to be the necessary and sufficient condition for the elevation of their consciousness and for their empowerment in society.

This essay is an attempt to rethink the history of the Russian working class by focusing on gender conflict at the point of production, on how gender relations conditioned work culture and shop-floor culture in the first decade and a half of Soviet power. It is an attempt to engender Russian working-class history by demonstrating that the shop floor in Russian industry was not gender-neutral but was in fact a gender battleground.[3] It will argue that common, garden-variety misogyny, ubiquitous in prerevolutionary workplaces, carried over into the socialist period, despite official policies and official protests by men and by women. It will also suggest that initial official attempts to inculcate new attitudes toward women on the shop floor soon failed and that divisions between men and women in Soviet work places became more distinct, not less, by the eve of the First Five-Year Plan.

The perspective from the shop floor rather than from party or union headquarters is an important one. Such an approach provides an especially valuable entry into the shop-floor culture and mentalities of workers in socialist Russia and permits a consideration of the construction of social identities, of "class" identities, in the socialist project. Historians of the working class are conditioned to look for antagonisms between workers and managers on the capitalist shop floor: the explosiveness of these antagonisms has provided scholars with much raw material for understanding class relations in capitalist societies. In the USSR, by contrast, the official ideology of productivism tended to mute local conflict and hide the shop floor from view. The self-styled proletarian state sought to blur conflicts and differences between workers and their managers, who were now by origin or ascription members of the same class as the men and women they employed. A focus on the conflicts provoked by the presence of women at work reopens the shop floor to historians and provides important new understandings of the ways in which Soviet workers constructed their new culture and new society. Such a focus will also help to illuminate the experience of women workers, who are too often visible only as statistical aggregates or economic categories, in the context of family and home, or in political activism.[4] In short, a specific focus on the battle between the sexes on the shop floor helps to provide a new approach for the study of gender and class under developing socialism.

The experience of workers in the printing industry offers an especially vivid picture of this shop-floor battle. Women had made significant inroads into the printing industry labor force since the revolution. Their share of the Moscow printing labor force in 1923, for example, was 25 percent of the industry's 12,700 workers, five times the level it had been during 1912. In Petrograd, women comprised 35 percent of the 10,000 printers there during 1923. By contrast, the proportion of women in other skilled industries after the revolution (metal work, leather, wood) hovered around the pre-war level of 5 to 10 percent.[5] Moreover, in most printing enterprises, such women worked alongside men as unskilled assistants rather than in segregated departments; they were segregated by skill level rather than by space. Proud of their craft and conscious of their long history of labor activism, workers in the printing industry produced a rich collection of labor writing before and after the 1917 revolution in which their work, their organizations, and their lives received extensive self-examination. The following discussion of the role of gender is based on a careful reading of hundreds of items (on many topics) contributed to the printers' union press from 1918 to 1930: monthly union journals, factory newspapers, and the national press, as well as on materials from the archives of the printers' union and individual factories.

The evidence presented here represents, therefore, a thorough review of the public discourse on women in the industry.

Almost all the evidence about shop-floor relations between men and women, in this industry and others, is mediated through Communist sources. It is often difficult to separate the prescriptive reports from the descriptive, difficult to determine when an account represents the party's voice and when it expresses the "authentic" voice of the shop floor. Indeed, as workers learned to "speak Bolshevik," in the phrase coined by Stephen Kotkin, it is difficult to separate the voices.[6] In evaluating reports of conflicts on the shop floor, one must be perpetually aware that the reports submitted by workers were selected for publication to inculcate values and prescribe behaviors. Even archival accounts may have been sent up the line worded so as to meet with political approval. Both the morally positive fables of comradely egalitarianism and the condemnatory accounts of verbal and physical assaults by males on their female co-workers were reported for a purpose. But since there is no reason to assume that each and every report was manipulated and fashioned by higher authorities for some unified higher goal, the way in which relations between men and women were reported is very much part of this story.

MEN AND WOMEN marched together into the brave new world of socialism still burdened with the weight of deeply ingrained attitudes about gender roles in the workplace. In her seminal study of women workers in prerevolutionary Russia, Rose Glickman writes, "On the shop floor, abuse and sexual harassment were commonplace in a woman worker's experience." The dimensions of this experience became evident only after a workers' press emerged following the Russian revolution of 1905. Women complained about male hostility on the shop floor, that they were treated like prostitutes, unnatural comrades, and viewed as a lower order of being. Attitudes may have been slowly changing after the 1905 revolution, as "conscious workers" began to write publicly about the need for cultural improvement among the working class. The call for new attitudes about social relations came heavily laden with the discourse of class struggle: only "bourgeois morality" tolerated the indignities that female workers suffered at the hands of men.[7] Such analysis may well have drawn piquancy from the liberal discourse examined by Laura Engelstein, who argues that sexuality acquired political content as a result of the 1905 revolution. Nonetheless, the male voices of proletarian gender equality remained isolated ones. Women continued to complain in the press up to 1914 about the daily hostility they endured in the workplace from foremen and co-workers alike. Male labor activists perhaps believed that such bad manners would become transformed under socialism, but they made little effort to include women in their organizations or in their culture.[8]

Public (male) attitudes about women workers in the printing industry did not change dramatically with the triumph of the proletarian dictatorship over bourgeois morality after 1917. Women workers continued to receive scorn and hostility from their male co-workers, but now in addition to traditional complaints about women's innate inferiority (their lack of physical strength, their inability or refusal to learn skills, their disorderliness), women workers were criticized on revolutionary grounds as well. According to their critics, they resisted calls to raise their consciousness: they preferred shopping over factory meetings and gossip over Lenin study circles.

It is significant that the public call for women's equality produced such strident claims about their inequality: in attempting to change attitudes, the public press reinforced old stereotypes. On work grounds, men objected to women because they were less "craftsman-like" (*iskusstnyi*) than men. Women did not have the strength to press books and cut cardboard in the bookbinding departments. "You can't make a worker from your old lady [*baba*]," said one. Women were more often sick, they gave birth, they nursed infants—in a word, "they were trash [*khlam*]."[9] Women were depicted as being uninterested in learning advanced skills.[10] "They'll just get married and quit work," said one union leader. Women just want to go home after work; they refuse to learn skills, said another. "Why the devil should we train a woman? She'll get married and her husband will support her." Women were reportedly incapable of thinking about their jobs when they were not at work. Because they could not understand complicated machines, women had too many accidents and damaged the machinery as well as themselves.[11] It appeared that women were always fighting with one another. Two squabbling women at one shop in Moscow so interfered with production that one had to be reassigned to another shop by the union leadership. In Leningrad, a worker anonymously complained that one could not enter the brochure department of the print shop, without observing constant tears and hysterics, especially concerning work assignments: "from morning to night women workers insult each other, and the most outstanding is the Young Communist League member Savinkova, who gives no one mercy, who swears at everyone."[12]

Women like this, argued the male-dominated workers' press, were incapable of acquiring class consciousness and therefore of participating in building the revolutionary society. Young women in the print shop cared mainly about dressing well and dancing; they remained under the spell of their aunts and godmothers. Women were too fond of gossip, of comparing notes on who was seeing whom, discussions that dominated their free time. In a small town in Tver' province, women came to factory meetings only to gossip and munch on sunflower seeds and walnuts, refusing to pay attention to the agenda item about the all-union trade union congress; in Leningrad, they slept through factory committee discussions or else thumbed their noses at the proceedings. In Khar'kov, a worker named Tulina committed the incredible gaffe of rejecting a decoration with Lenin's portrait on the day of his funeral, saying, "To the devil with him."[13] What more was there to say?

To what extent did women share these attitudes ascribed to them? The records of women themselves, while scattered, produce a fascinating plurality of voices, as Soviet women workers attempted to define in practice what it meant to be a worker, what it meant to be a woman, and what it meant to be a woman worker in a socialist society. The dominant female voice in these records is that of the women activists. These were full-time paid organizers employed by the trade unions or the party, women who took a regime perspective and who usually accepted the idea that women workers were still insufficiently interested in public life as well as in the life of production.[14] These activists frequently described the mass of women workers in words such as "a stagnant swamp, impossible to budge."[15] Women workers, lamented the activists, shunned meetings and organizations, to their personal detriment, since such meetings publicized the availability of socialist benefits: maternity leave and child care. "You comrades don't go to meetings, and therefore you don't know anything. I told you already, we discuss all of this at meetings," chastized a Moscow organizer.[16]

In the second half of the 1920s, a minority view in the trade-union press attempted to depict women as serious, attentive, and interested in raising their skills. Women were better teachers than men: sober and punctual, they took their production responsibilities seriously. Women were good workers, they did not take unexcused absences, they treated their work stations like their children. But even the positive portrayals of women carried a formalistic flavor. The proof of their activism was generally the number of voluntary organizations they belonged to: the Friends of Children, the Society to Help Political Prisoners, the cooperative, the mutual aid fund, and the club.[17] Women did appear to gravitate toward their own separate sphere, and this sphere was defined more by issues of everyday and family life, less by issues of work and production. Women factory committee members were encouraged to join subcommittees dealing with children, housing, health and safety, medical care, and culture. Questions of everyday life (*byt*) were most likely to draw women to factory meetings and to induce them to speak up. In Leningrad, women workers in the engraving plant came to all the meetings, and they were reportedly "not just furniture" there but were active, although "of course," they were mostly interested in questions of daily life.[18]

But if the public side of private life was acceptable territory for the mobilization of women, the private side of private life constituted a much more criticized area of women's interest. Men and women organizers alike believed that women workers were far too interested in gossip, which they conducted largely during work breaks in the women's washroom. Two female apprentices received a tongue-lashing in their Moscow factory newspaper for preferring each other's company to learning their trades: they were inseparable, they pulled proofs together, they even went to the washroom together, where they spent entirely too much time discussing last night's dates with their boyfriends. The brochurist who signed her article as V. complained in her factory newspaper that her fellow women workers did not take advantage of the freedoms they had won. They discussed and argued about subjects "we don't, as women workers, need. Our heads are occupied almost entirely with what we observe, who is going with whom, who is chasing whom; does he love her, does she love him? Why do we need such conversations? Nature takes care of this without any conversations."[19]

Some historians might argue that such behaviors confirm the male and activist view of women, even at work, as being primarily oriented toward home and hearth, toward traditional family roles. Leslie Tentler described similar behaviors among women workers in the United States and concluded that their interests were fundamentally private, not public. The workroom culture in which many young women found themselves, she says, "communicated to most of them very conservative ideas about their identities and destinies as women." Other scholars, however, suggest that "gossip" could serve as a tool of consciousness and even political mobilization, and that young women's concern with dress, cosmetics, and dating served to define their autonomous, independent role in society and their relations with authority. Susan Glenn demonstrates how the early-twentieth-century factory was a school of urban culture for young immigrant Jewish women. "The female gang at work served as a mediating force to funnel into the still somewhat unfamiliar territory of mixed-sex socializing."[20] The washroom here and in Russian print shops, served as a women's club, where they not only applied their cosmetics, smoked cigarettes, and discussed boyfriends, free love, and civil marriage but also defined their roles within production as well. Soviet organizers did not see the washroom in this way: organizers at the Leningrad Pechatnyi Dvor plant in 1924 complained that they could not convince women to come to general meetings, even though at other times, women gathered in groups and carried on a continuing debate about raising their pay grades and improving their wages—even "in the washroom, during work time! ... You will not improve your position with *empty conversation*; you need to go to meetings."[21]

Such behaviors, coded negative by men and by women activists, were not so different from the behaviors of men. Men took smoke breaks in the washrooms, and their drinking rituals occupied an important part of their shop-floor culture. They did not smoke and drink silently. Print-shop culture was a highly verbal one, especially in the relatively noise-free typesetting departments: joking, laughter, and teasing, labeled *zvon* in the printers' jargon, were all important components of working life, and had been so since well before the revolution.[22] A short story "from life" published in the union journal in 1926 described the daily shop-floor banter. Typesetting an article on "the women's question" or a textbook in anatomy would invariably set the discussion off on the theme of the sex life of one or another worker. "The laughter starts with general questions and ends with intimate details of family life—but all are devoted to sexual questions": who is sleeping with whom, paternity, and prostitution.[23]

Women's public attitudes about men were no less critical than men's views about women. In her study of the debate over the marriage laws in 1926, Wendy Goldman compiled a litany of complaints by women about their men: the new marriage law was needed to protect women because men were unfaithful, selfish, pleasure-seeking, and drunk.[24] At work, the rudeness and despotism of foremen toward women workers was an endemic complaint. Women associated with the printing industry publicly chafed under the arbitrariness and authoritarian behavior of their husbands, and they lamented their economic dependence on them. Waiting for their husbands on paydays, printers' wives lamented how one husband promised to buy his children sandals but spent his money on drink instead; another regularly spent his last kopeck on drink instead of flour for his family.[25] Aniuta, a fictional printer in a 1924 short story, mused that if it were not for the need to support her three children, she would leave her hostile and unhelpful husband and never see him again. A Moscow woman printer's political activism angered her husband; but, even after many beatings, she refused to denounce him to their factory committee for fear he would turn her out of her home.[26]

Moreover, women workers—both activists and rank-and-file workers—criticized the obstacles that men placed in their path to activism. One husband refused to agree to his wife attending a meeting: "What do you mean I should wash the diapers, baby-sit, and make the soup? The hell with that! I won't let you out to the meeting. I won't care for the kids myself." Another woman was told by her husband that she could join the Communist Party if she wanted to, but he would abandon her: he needed a non-party wife. A Khar'kov woman printer brought her husband to a comrades' court in 1924 (a "very ordinary" case) for regularly beating her up, most recently after Lenin's funeral because the husband felt she was grieving too much over the loss.[27]

To be sure, many women held onto traditional views about men and about gender roles. Such women received public criticism in the party and trade-union press. Even women who had emancipated themselves from the church and who regularly attended meetings, wrote one woman organizer, still believed that men should not be expected to do "women's work." Older women were seen as a deep repository of traditional prejudices. One woman cited her neighbor, a serious, proper, and moral woman who disapproved of young women's haircuts, boyfriends, cigarettes, and books. Grandmothers who refused to mind their daughters' children when the mothers stayed late at meetings needed to be reeducated.[28]

Such attitudes and predispositions carried over from prerevolutionary times, but they were now given new focus and urgency by the official socialist commitment to the emancipation of women. The trade union and factory committees devoted at least lip service to mobilizing women: official policy reserved a spot on each factory committee for a woman and a youth representative (they were rarely elected otherwise). Women trainees were assigned to work in the various factory subcommittees, although more frequently in cultural and labor protection work than in the powerful rates and conflicts commissions. Special meetings for women workers were held within print shops, and city-wide women's conferences encouraged women in the nation's two largest cities to discuss the issues that concerned them. The union press devoted special sections to contributions from women correspondents, and to articles about women. In 1924, a special journal, *The Woman Printer* (*Pechatnitsa*), was published to mark that year's International Women's Day. But the real task of women's emancipation would be carried out not in the pages of legal, party, or trade-union journals but in actual relations between men and women in the workplace, the family, and the public sphere.

Workplace relations were often conflictual, and the remainder of this article will address three interrelated areas of contention in shop-floor relations between men and women. The first area of relationships produced the most serious conflicts: this was the overt, aggressive, and militant masculinity of shop-floor culture, with its attendant harassment of women workers verbally, physically, and sexually. A second area of conflict concerned the issue of women's acquisition of advanced skills. Women's claim to parity on the shop floor depended, in the long run, on their ability to perform the same tasks as men, and the union and the regime officially supported this goal. But, in practice, women found their efforts to upgrade their skills blocked at every turn, by the pressures of daily life and especially by men's attitudes. One reason, I will argue, is that "skill" itself was considered a male attribute: it had more to do with gender than with training, and this is why men so steadfastly sabotaged women's efforts to climb the ladder of production success. A third set of relationships concerned the gender inequality rationalized by the concept of the "family wage." This area produced less conflict along gender lines. Women and men generally accepted the fairness of hiring and firing decisions based on family-wage needs, not on those of individuals, especially after 1925. This attitude, however, was conditioned by circumstances, and it need not signify women's acceptance of a traditional subservience to men. Discussions of the issue reveal additional ways in which gender structured work relations in socialist Russia.

THE PRINT SHOP was normally a place of banter, teasing, swearing, practical jokes, and even cruelty. Drinking was a normal part of the work day, particularly in typesetting departments, where all kinds of ruses were employed to sneak out and bring back vodka to share among the boys. Printers competed with one another to invent "three-story" or "seven-story" obscenities. Sexual innuendo and braggadocio were common currency in shop-floor culture.[29] This was true not only among Russian printers. Men's relationships with one another on the shop floor, as Cynthia Cockburn has pointed out, were mediated through the "coinage" of women, in which women, as abstract sex objects, were handled and routinely besmirched. Paul Willis has argued that the construction of a masculine shopfloor culture is an important mechanism of resistance and self-assertion. "Discontent with work is turned away from political discontent and confused in its logic by a huge detour into the symbolic sexual realm."[30] Neither discontent with work nor political discontent disappeared in Russia with the triumph of the socialist state; in fact, the printers' union consistently voiced opposition to Communist policies until the union was forcibly silenced in a series of repressive measures beginning in 1918 and lasting until 1923. At the same time, the socialist state's urgent need for production was transforming the workplace in the early 1920s from egalitarian experimental republics of the civil war era to regimented sites of order, discipline, production, and submission.[31] Printers might well react by reasserting their traditional masculinity, threatened by the dramatic increase in the number of women working in the industry and by the state's official discourse of gender equality.

Women were seen as intruders into the male club, and the comrades made their attitudes quite clear. Reports of hostility between the sexes, presumably with both prescriptive and descriptive intent, were especially common during the years 1920–1924, as the new socialist workplace contract was being defined and the state was attempting to carry out its promise to emancipate women. A man named Chusov, a "socialist" at Moscow's Third State print shop, declared in 1920 that all the shop's troubles were the fault of women, and he wished he could expel them all. A correspondent in the union journal wrote that it was a rare day when the men in the composing room were not drunk and insulting the women. "Vulgar" insults toward women were the most common occurrence for a factory committee member at the Krasnaia Nov' shop in Moscow. Elsewhere, women dared not open their mouths to ask a question, for fear of being insulted.[32] Some might argue that such printers were treating women like one of the boys, since insults and pranks were commonly directed against other men and not just toward women. But underlying much of the hostility toward women was a distinct sexual consciousness. A short story in the union journal described the arrival at work of the young compositor Tania, just recently married. Teased for simply arriving on time when she was still on her honeymoon ("How was it, Tania?" "Was it good?"), she decides not to notice the usual congratulations on her newly married state. The teasing moved on to other targets, and Tania was left alone. "When banter [zvon] is not malicious, but truthful, friendly, making fun of the abnormal events of production and daily life, it lifts your mood, and strange as it may seem, it even accelerates the tempo of work." Tania understood this kind of banter and joined in. But when it turned against a young fellow trying to quit smoking, Tania defended him, and the teasing came back to her. The pretext by mid-morning was a page of corrections in a book on geography. "Correct the geography, Tania; you will become knowledgeable, [and] you can screw all around Europe with your husband …" "And your husband through I-taly—" with a pun on another verb for copulation, talit'. The factory committee chairman would not take Tania's complaint seriously and instead just smiled at her smarmily, "Why Tania, you've gotten prettier …"[33]

Even where the obscenities and swearing were not directed specifically at women, many complaints were registered about the uncomfortable atmosphere created by men's language. At the Thirty-Ninth State print shop in Moscow, men spoke around women "as they would among themselves," and it made the women blush. At the Sixteenth State print shop, a male worker wrote to the factory newspaper that women bookbinders had to pass through the Linotype department to reach their workroom. Passing through this "filter," they were subject to such noise and whistles that it even made the correspondent blush. A 1923 story in the newspaper recounted how a printer's daughter had decided to become a printer, too. Her daddy was so affectionate and kind at home, she was sure that the print shop would be a wonderful place in which to work. But when she arrived, she discovered, to her embarrassment and dismay, that all the men—including daddy—were foul-mouthed and rude.[34] Sometimes, men's hostility took physical form. In Sevastopol, workers refused to permit a woman to come to work in place of a sick comrade—they insulted her, and one of them threw a metal composing stick at her. At the Third State print shop in Moscow in 1923, railing at a woman was not enough for the factory committee chairman and member of the Moscow Soviet, so he punched her in the nose, causing her to be sent to the doctor. When the union tried to have this fellow removed from office, he was defended by his workers—both male and female. One worker said, "I've lived with my wife for twenty years, and I hit her in the snout when I feel like it. You mean I should not have the right to do this?" The normality of such practices is confirmed by the constant refrain of union officials, who repeatedly vowed to eliminate the "antagonism between men and women."[35]

Insults, obscenities, and violence were mere skirmishes in the battle of the sexes, a prelude to plotting and scheming to exercise power over women. Where did the normal—if uncomfortable—sexual banter on the shop floor end and manipulative pressures to trade job security for sex begin? Favorable job assignments were frequently attributed to a woman's "pretty face." In the all-important assignment of pay grades, supervisors enjoyed great latitude. A Communist named Stogov "not only assigns grades, but simply will fire someone because he doesn't like her mug," whereas another woman would be asked to stay, "because her mug he likes."[36]

Complaints about overt propositions and manipulative sexual relations apppeared in the record throughout the 1920s. At the Third Goznak Factory, the status of a woman in production in 1923 was determined not by her work ability but by personal relations. The factory committee room in the evenings there became a place of assignation; some women workers "discreetly" disappeared for a half hour or more, claiming "pressing business" with the factory committee. When the committee room became too crowded, the "business" would be conducted in the private dining room of a nearby restaurant. And if a woman were to refuse her summons to "pressing business," another would be called and the first one fired "in the interests of production."[37] In Samara during 1928, women reported constant verbal harassment from their male co-workers and a continual devaluation of their skill grades. There was only one way to get ahead: "You're a pretty woman," the foreman would say. "Spend the night with me and I'll promote you to the 6th pay grade. If you don't, I'll find an excuse to fire you."[38]

Many women may have participated willingly in these affairs. Employment was increasingly insecure in the printing industry. By 1926, layoffs had reached alarming proportions, and women constituted a disproportionate share of the unemployed, but pressure to lay off women first was constant throughout the decade.[39] It is not surprising that some women sought non-production paths to job security. One of the more widely reported incidents came to light in a public disciplinary trial at the First Model print shop in Moscow in 1924. Two cases were on the docket, and over a thousand workers came to listen. These were show trials, explicitly designed to illustrate appropriate social (and socialist) behaviors. In the first case, a foreman was accused of hitting an apprentice and spitting in his face. The foreman pleaded not guilty—saying that was how he was trained, and how else should he train an apprentice? (He was given a suspended sentence of six months' exclusion from the trade union.) In the second case, forty-year-old Dubov, an assistant foreman in the press department, was accused of making "vile suggestions" to a woman worker assigned to him. If women refused his frequent advances, they were assigned to another department or to more difficult jobs. In the case at hand, he had made advances toward a "middle-aged" forty-year-old worker, Ivanova, offering her candy if she accepted and threatening to transfer her if she refused. Dubov denied his guilt; claiming Ivanova herself initiated the "dirty conversations" and provoked him to proposition her. A second witness, however, a young woman, testified that Dubov had proposed she visit him at his apartment twice a week. He would give her five rubles. Another woman was offered money to live with him secretly, without his wife knowing. "'I'll give you twenty rubles,' he said. 'You won't have to work.'" Until Ivanova brought charges against him, the younger women said they were too ashamed to report Dubov's advances. The trial of Dubov lasted until two in the morning. One witness in his behalf denied hearing any of the vile suggestions; another claimed that such jokes during work with women were a common occurrence and that the women themselves took an active part. "Passing by, you can't help but pinch a pretty worker." The court concluded that Dubov had abused his position of authority, expelled him from the trade union for six months, and requested the union dismiss him from work without compensation. Equally interesting was the factory reaction to the verdict. The decision was met "coldly;" and most workers, including women, believed it was too strict. The women themselves were considered guilty of encouraging Dubov by joining in the "indecent conversation." Ivanova should be punished for her foul mouth, said one account.[40]

Indeed, women had trouble having their complaints taken seriously. In Voronezh, a young female worker claimed that Ionov, a foreman, while drunk, forced her down to the cellar. But she could not prove that Ionov, who was generally rude to the women in the shop, had done the deed, and she herself was found guilty of violating labor discipline for leaving her work. When another woman filed a formal complaint with the factory's conflict commission about verbal abuse, the women's representative who advised this course of action was removed from her post, and the commission never acted on the initial complaint.[41]

The vulnerability of women to such incidents and pressures was due to their sex, and this was something they could not change. They could, one supposes, try to fit into this shop-floor culture. They could acquire the knack of three-story swearing, tell indecent jokes, and become one of the boys, but this left them open to the charge of inviting sexual relations. They could remain quiet and aloof, not daring to complain to their factory committee, losing confidence in the power of the workers' state to intervene on their behalf. There were certainly more reports in the union record of passive and apathetic women than of sexually assaulted ones. They could develop their own shop-floor culture. A woman typesetter, Sorokina, wrote to the union journal about how her father had forced her to work in the print shop and about how unpleasant she found the work. She kept thinking she would find a better job elsewhere, but meanwhile she made friends with other daughters of workers, and this not only caused her to stay on but to become active in the struggle for the rights of women workers in her shop. Women workers at the Leningrad Pechatnyi Dvor print shop were rebuked for their lack of "consciousness": they would not come to regular meetings but instead would gather on their own (outside union control) and in the washroom to discuss how to raise their pay grades. To the shop's union organizers, this was "empty conversation," but for women in an aggressively masculine work environment, this may have been the most effective way to mobilize.[44] Women's gravitation to organizations devoted to daily life indicates the influence of their domestic burden, but it provided them as well with a comfortably separate space in the workplace away from the hostility of men. Most frequently of all, women blamed their vulnerability on their own lack of economic value to the enterprise, on their lack of skills. If only they could acquire proper training, they could contribute more to the enterprise, they could earn higher wages, and they would be less vulnerable to cutbacks and layoffs in the industry, to the whims of male supervisors who could easily replace them. In the struggle to acquire skills and challenge the gendered definition of skill, however, women's efforts to liberate themselves from dependence on capricious foremen and misogynist factory committees foundered on the same male attitudes that had propelled them to embrace skill-raising strategies in the first place.

THE MARXIST PROJECT of the emancipation of women and the Soviet project of productivism dovetailed neatly when it came to promoting women's occupational training. The measure of social worth was productivity, and the Soviet economy under the New Economic Policy could not afford to employ marginally productive individuals. To guarantee a place in the competitive socialist work force, therefore, women had to offer more to the enterprise than the willingness to perform menial, repetitive tasks. They needed to acquire skills. Otherwise, they were of more value to society at home cooking soup and laundering diapers than occupying a niche in the factory order. At the same time, organizers still believed that women at home would remain outside the politically and socially mobilized sphere of society, and they would remain "forces of darkness" and inertia in their private spaces. Socialist mobilization, therefore, needed to bring women into the workplace, where they could be more readily organized: women could be empowered only through waged work.[43]

The relationship between skill and productivity also concerned incentives. During the civil war, under an economic regime that came to be known as War Communism, workers' remuneration was generally independent of skill level or productivity. All workers in "essential" industries received the "reserved" ration; all others received less, with corresponding declines in output as these workers absented themselves in order to scrounge for food for their families. The transition from War Communism to the New Economic Policy brought a return to skill-based wages: each occupation was subdivided into pay grades, ranging from 1 to 24. Differentials between the lowest and highest grades were meant to be big enough to motivate workers to improve their skills. In 1921, women began to speak of the importance of attaining skilled positions on the wage grid, while at the same time, the printers' union congress adopted a resolution to *exclude* women from a number of specialties in the profession.[44] This institutional discrimination was reversed in 1923, another example of the broad-based and officially supported effort in that year to promote the equality of women. The official slogans for International Women's Day (March 8) in 1923 included the question of increasing women's production skills, and the printers' union central committee publicly reversed its "incorrect" decree of 1921 that denied women full participation in the industry. The problem, argued the union leadership, was that the average pay grade for men was 9, and for women 7, and women would be displaced from production if they did not improve on these levels.[45]

The notion of "skill" is complicated and contested. Where economists might argue that skill is the accumulation of human capital, acquired through education and training, sociologists would say that skill is a social artifact, a construction based on status and wage levels rather than pure "know-how."[46] Feminist critics would add that skill is defined by men as an exclusively masculine attribute, but I will return to this point.[47] To one Russian woman printer in 1923, however, "simple" work was a job that did not require apprenticeship, one that an adult worker straight from the countryside could easily learn. The basic attributes of "skill" were "responsibility, accuracy, complexity, craftsmanship, difficulty, injuriousness, intensity, severity, and danger."[48] For most Russian printers, as for other skilled workers, there were two traditional paths to skill. One was through apprenticeship, which began in the teenage years and lasted about four years. Apprentices were assigned to skilled instructors, or to skilled craftsmen, who taught them their craft and initiated them into the rituals of the trade.[49] A second method of acquiring skills was the less formal method of "training up." An inexperienced worker began doing menial tasks in the print shop and, by observing the tasks performed around him or her, acquired enough know-how to begin to perform a task, moving up gradually to machine helper and then to machine operator. Quite commonly in the 1920s, a woman would begin to work in a print shop as a floor sweeper, advance in the press section to the job of carrier, taking printed sheets off the press, and then to press feeder and general helper. In the binding department, she might begin as a sweeper or carrier, move next to the job of folder, and then move up to more complex assembly. In typesetting, the upward path started with the distribution of used type back to the typecases, then to composing straight text, the simplest kind of work. Ultimately, she might train up to work on the Linotype machine, but this was extremely rare. A worker's progress up the ladder of skill was measured by the pay grade and rewarded with pay. In both trajectories, through apprenticeship or training up, the most important element was close collaboration between the trainee and a senior skilled worker, who would share his knowledge and correct the trainee's mistakes. To supplement these traditional methods, printers' unions in the major cities organized vocational schools. Apprenticeship was also formalized into "factory training schools" in the shops themselves, and, in 1923, official union policy reserved 25 percent of apprenticeship entry positions for young women.[50] There were ceremonial promotions: every March 8, to mark International Women's Day, a few women in each print shop were selected for promotion and special training in more advanced skills.

Discussion of the factors impeding the acquisition of skills by women occupied a prominent place in the women's pages of the union's periodical press, beginning in 1923. One lamentable cause, cited by men and women alike, was that many women themselves had no interest in learning new skills and raising their pay grades. During the civil war, they had grown accustomed to the idea that they could earn the same wage whether skilled or unskilled: why bother to train?[51] Such women came to the print shop planning to work for three or four years until they married and thus chose to learn the simplest jobs rather than the entire craft. Conditioned to see themselves as contributors to the family wage and temporary sojourners in the work force, they were content to take jobs at low pay rates and skill levels, not realizing that their lack of versatility would target them for layoffs as economic pressures mounted.[52]

In some of these cases, women asserted—and activists agreed—that their domestic burden was to blame. Women at one meeting explained their reluctance to take on more demanding work or extra work activities because of their double burden: "During all these meetings, she trembles inside." She knows that at home await her husband—maybe "half or totally famished"—her nearly orphaned children, a washtub of dirty linen, mending, unwashed dishes, and more.[53] A factory newspaper featured "a day in the life" of several women workers. One named Borisova described her routine: up at 6 a.m., she wakes her children, dresses them, readies them for school. She drinks some tea and straightens up the one-room apartment. At 8 a.m., she arrives at work for her eight-hour shift. Returning home, she is greeted by a "whole heap" of work: she cooks, hurries to the cooperative to shop, washes linen for herself and three children, mends their clothes. She has no time for public meetings or for supplementary training in her job.[54] The "eight-hour shift" is passed over as unworthy of further description: for Borisova, this was *not* the focus of her day.

In other cases, it was women's allegedly "delicate physical characteristics" that impeded true equality and skill acquisition. Night work for women was officially prohibited in the 1922 Labor Code, although exceptions were granted for industries like printing, where 50 percent of work was done at night. (Many of the reported cases of sexual assault occurred during night shifts; perhaps women who worked at night were considered to be outside the protection of the law.) In June 1923, the presidium of the union's central committee resolved that women should not be permitted to work in particularly harmful departments: typecasting, because it required work with hot metal; in the stereotype departments, where hot metal was poured into matrices; in zinc-engraving departments, where poisonous materials were involved; in engraving departments; and on the Monotype typesetting machine.

These were constructed "hazards." On the one hand, they were no less harmful for men, but, on the other, machine typesetting work in other countries was considered to be especially appropriate for the "weaker sex."[55]

Most frequently of all, however, women cited the hostility of men or the indifference of male-dominated factory committees for their lack of training. At one print shop, women were not allowed to work on the presses because "they are not capable of thinking about production matters when not at work." Low-skilled women were dismissed and not trained because men said, "We don't want to work with women; it's uncomfortable for us." Women were not given access to the experience they needed to train up: if a foreman steps away from the shop floor, reported one woman, he hands over his supervisory role to an apprentice with two years' experience rather than to a woman with fifteen or twenty years on the job. The heroine of a short story in a collection published by women printers begged her foreman to teach her to operate the printing press. No, he said, not worth it—better that women should stick to supplying the press with clean paper. "If you all become masters, what will our brothers do?"[56]

Again and again, in 1923, 1924, and after, women reported the same story. Training required women to work alongside a senior, experienced man. But the standard male attitude was negative: you'll get married and quit work. So most workers refused to instruct them. Such craftsmen were happy to train a man; but, for women, the output quota would be declared unreachable, there was not enough paper to allow for the inevitable wastage, or the machinery was "not appropriate." Even when trained, women were directed to "women's jobs": to the auxiliary skills of feeding and removing paper from the press, rarely to typesetting or work on the press itself.[57]

A rejection of official policies for gender equality in the printers' trade union was evident by 1924, just a year after the loud official proclamation of women's equality within the industry. Grigorii N. Mel'nichanskii, a leader of the All-Union Council of Trade Unions, admitted to printers in late 1924 that the policy of mobilizing women was in trouble. "I know that you in your conferences discuss the question, and you adopt resolutions about involving women more in our work. But I also know that many comrades, after discussing these questions at official meetings, when they go off to the side, they begin to mock them, to smile, to snigger; they say, all the same, nothing will come of such work."[58]

By the beginning of 1926, the practice of reserving one factory committee place for a woman had been abandoned; mainstreaming women and youth into regular union activities was now the norm. This retreat from tokenism was supposed to ensure that "fewer, but better" women would serve on the committees.[59] At the same time, perhaps not coincidentally, union leaders launched an assault on the status of women folders as skilled workers. Women in this occupation were not in fact skilled, union men decided, and should be paid at the same level as common day laborers. A woman delegate to a 1926 Leningrad union congress denounced this view: "We, so-called unskilled hand folders, can do whatever is needed—we sew bindings, we fold, we can do any of the work and we can do all of it." These women, who had worked side by side with men for eight years, were told they had no skills: "This is very insulting."[60]

Raising women's skills on the shop floor was official union policy, but men's attitudes help explain why affirmative action was practiced often in a purely formal way. Every March 8, women complained, a few of them were ceremoniously promoted from menial jobs to positions on the skill ladder, with little regard to whether they were suited for the new work. The factory administration of the Ninth Mospoligraf print shop found a "suitable candidate," Khriapinskaia, for training as a press feeder; on March 8, it awarded her the opportunity to train on each press for a week at a time. But the male pressmen went to the factory committee and protested; Khriapinskaia remained untrained, having learned only the obscenities "that were liberally poured upon her." Women climbed up the skill ladder with the greatest difficulty, and most of them remained huddled at the bottom levels of the pay grades, from which they were all too easily declared superfluous and thrown onto the unemployment rolls. By March 8, 1928, women, who represented 24 percent of printers' union members, constituted 45 percent of the registered unemployed. In October 1929, they were 30 percent of union members and at least 60 percent of the unemployed.[61]

Increasingly, factory committees and managers responded to the requests to advance women by promoting them to positions *outside* the shop: to cooperatives, factory cafeterias, kindergartens, and medical clinics.[62] Such positions fulfilled some of the promise of socialism—economic independence and work in the public sphere—and they allowed women to escape the oppressive atmosphere of the skilled workshop. But even such successes reinforced a gendered division of labor in which men operated machines and produced goods and women provided public domestic services.

There were some notable and exceptional successes, heroic women who learned advanced skills and even became instructors themselves. But more commonly reported toward the end of the 1920s was an opposite effect: demotion (*zadvizhenie*). At the Moscow Krasnyi Maiak print shop, women who had worked in the press department since almost the time of the revolution found themselves pushed out by the administration from the press department to common labor. One delegate from the Central print shop in Moscow reported that women were regularly promoted but then returned to "sweeping snow," the common metaphor for the most menial of factory jobs. Even one of the most capable of women workers and leaders fell victim to the demotions of the later 1920s: Elizaveta Iaunzem, a skilled typesetter, had been a party member since 1919, a factory committee activist and Moscow Soviet member since 1922. When a shop needed a new assistant director, Iaunzem was chosen over two men, one who was "not very practical" and the other who was a "blockhead." Iaunzem served for two years, but when her shop was liquidated, she found herself out of a job, and as the union paper reported in October 1927, "lives to this day on the doorstep of the labor exchange"; in other words, she remained unemployed. The union's explanation for this evident callousness toward a gifted woman administrator was that sufficient enterprises did not exist for Iaunzem to find a new assistant director's post. She had been offered positions managing various lesser departments, but she had refused them, preferring to improve her typesetting skills. In early 1928, perhaps because of the publicity given to her case, the union had sent her to learn the Linotype at its vocational school in Moscow.[63] Iaunzem's marginalized career exemplifies the precarious position of women in the printing industry. If skilled women workers were the only ones who could be worthy of their male comrades' respect, most women—those without the party and union connection of an Iaunzem—found the path to respect and equality effectively barred.

IN THE CONTEXT of such prevailing hostilities toward women's entry into the masculine realm of work, conflicts over firing women first, especially when their husbands were already employed, might seem to be yet another' example of Soviet misogyny. The ideal of a male-earned wage sufficient to support a family—the "family wage"—has been seen as an example of the dual patriarchy of capitalism, in which women are subordinated both in the family and in the workplace. It has been alternatively explained as a form of working-class resistance against capitalist exploitation.[64] Other historians have suggested that the family-wage ideal illustrates the domestic ideology of women workers, their acceptance of separate spheres and separate roles; that is, women workers accepted the morality of the family wage because their primary sphere was domestic and their work strategies needed to be optimized according to domestic and family needs, not individual goals.[65] The issue of the family wage, or the problem of "doubles" (*dvoiniki*) as it was known in the Soviet lexicon, is actually more complex than a struggle between classes or between sexes. Examining some of the arguments about "doubles" in the workplace provides additional insight into the role of gender in the workplace and women's efforts to define their socialist identities. In particular, the timing of the debate about the female wage must be seen in the context of women's overall experience in the workplace. The frontal assault on inequality at work had clearly failed by 1925. The debate over the family wage perhaps reflects an adjustment and adaptation by women to the gendered realities of Soviet working-class society.

The family wage was never codified, but it was applied in practice during the earliest months of the revolution. Faced with growing unemployment in March 1918 due to the contraction of industry and the return of soldiers from the army, a congress of labor commissars endorsed the idea that employment should be based on a "family minimum": when the combined family income raised the family wage over that minimum, one of the family members should be fired. The person fired should be the family member least necessary to the enterprise. In nearly all cases, this was a woman.[66] Women workers reacted angrily to this practice, and they protested. In January, two hundred of them had gathered at the Kushnerev print shop in Moscow to demand the right to work. They had heard that women would be fired because they were less skillful (*iskusstnyi*) and because their husbands worked. The women had worked hard in the men's place during the war, they complained, but now, "they want to take from us the right to a share of bread, the right that belongs to every citizen. They want to deprive us of that right and throw us in the street."[67]

By the early 1920s, official policy had become strictly egalitarian. The printers' trade union insisted that women were to be hired and fired only because of their personal abilities or lack of them, and it consistently overruled factory committees that fired women because of their family ties. Such discrimination, it insisted in 1923, was a survival of the "old psychology," the old workplace practice. "We should never place [a woman] in dependence on the work of her husband, since this enserfs her materially and therefore morally, turning her into a slave." Even with the growth of severe unemployment after the middle of the decade, striking especially hard in Leningrad, union voices still defended a woman's absolute right to work. Work in production liberates women, claimed a woman activist at a union congress in 1928: women should not have to be dependent on men, "since there is not one woman who is guaranteed against being left alone, without the help of a man or a husband." A male union official concurred: "There is no place in this worker-peasant state for women to be regarded as some lower form of existence. It is nobody's business whether she has a husband or not."[68] A secondary consideration in opposing the family-wage ideal was the effect the policy had on the family itself. First of all, it was difficult to enforce a policy against hiring both members of a married couple in a culture in which common-law marriage was a normal occurrence. Secondly, the ease of divorce in the Soviet family code led to fictitious divorces, which also confused those employers trying to identify a "double." And, in some cases, discrimination against two-earner families produced genuine family dissolutions.[69]

Official policy notwithstanding, women bore the brunt of the layoffs that accompanied the economic crisis in the industry. At one Moscow print shop in 1924, the rates and conflict commission upheld the firing of nineteen women: twelve were dismissed because their husbands were already employed, five because other family members were employed, and two because of their inadequate skills. At the same time, ten men were dismissed, four because their fathers or other family members had jobs, one because he had income from a plot of land in the country, four because of poor skills or work habits, and only one because his wife worked.[70]

The voices that surfaced in the debate over firing doubles expressed ambiguous understandings about the right and obligation to work. Some workers tended to reject the union's (and regime's) position that the right to work was the right of every Soviet citizen. Rather, the right to work was intimately connected to the right to subsistence. The Kushnerev women protesters in 1918 demanded the "right to a share of bread," not the right to a job for its own sake. Women's right to work was couched most often in terms of their personal need or the need of their families. Single unemployed women whose only alternative was prostitution ought to have jobs, said one woman. Another said, to loud applause, "When people are offered work, first priority should be given to single women who are the most needy." By 1929, 52 percent of the female union members were listed on the rolls of the unemployed, but only 15 percent of these women were married; one of these unemployed women argued that women with children should receive priority for jobs over married women; because they most needed the income. In the good old days of socialist idealism, in fact, wrote a woman contributor to her factory newspaper, married, better-off women, those without children, "imbued with consciousness," voluntarily gave up their positions so that those who were truly needy would have work.[71]

The goal was social justice rather than individual rights: by firing "doubles," the state would not reduce unemployment but would spread its effects evenly among families. When the union intervened to lay off six men instead of six women at one Moscow shop, 110 workers at the Krasnyi Maiak plant wrote the union journal in protest: "The man is the chief support of the family." These women were not needy; they were either childless, their children were grown, or their husbands were skilled workers. "We don't want children starving for lack of a breadwinner when other families have multiple incomes."[72] Among the unemployed printers who gathered to express their grievances in the second half of the 1920s, women joined men in arguing for the firing of doubles as one solution to the unemployment crisis. Like U.S. women facing the challenge of the Depression, Soviet women and men seemed to share the notion that "work was the prerogative of those who must support themselves and their families."[73]

Nonetheless, the right to work was still special, and it was better than the dole. Women's (and men's) reactions to the family-wage problem thus reflected a fusion of public and private spheres, of the identity provided by family and the identity offered by work. The unemployed worker Petrova said, "We have to insist on our demand to the union about the recognition of our right to work and to existence. We don't want a hand-out—give us work!" And there were alternative ways to achieve social justice: removing doubles from the workplace was only one of many strategies proposed for spreading the cost of economic dislocation. Printers endorsed work-sharing, through a ban on overtime and a reduced work week. They demanded that workers with ties to land be removed from the work rolls before women.[74] They demanded that the number of apprentices in the industry be reduced. And increasingly toward 1928 and 1929, what aroused their ire more than the dual-income family was the practice of party members and union officials placing their own family members into scarce positions in the printing industry. One unemployed man complained that a foreman at a Leningrad print-shop had found jobs there for his wife and two sons, and the union did nothing to correct this. A Novgorod woman complained she had been laid off in 1926 because she had married, but her position was taken by the wife of the local newspaper editor. A Leningrad official who spoke loudly in favor of the right of all women, even doubles, to hold a job nonetheless denounced the practice of nepotism: "It is another matter when an entire family is hired at an enterprise through nepotism; we have to fight strictly against this."[75]

The battle between the sexes was relatively muted in this debate about the employment of husbands and wives facing growing unemployment. Was this because male workers had learned by the second half of the 1920s to conceal their misogynist views in public? Or had women learned through bitter experience that, as women, they could no longer expect equal treatment in the socialist economy? Given the consistent hostility to women in the printing industry, unemployed women printers perhaps shifted the discourse away from equal rights for men and women, which emphasized difference, and toward the solidarities of class. Women and men, in arguing for employment based on need, for the sharing of jobs and of incomes, were placing social needs, class needs, above individual needs, whether one was a man or a woman. The attacks on nepotism reinforced this emphasis on class solidarity, placing a class-based sense of social justice above family loyalties. The family-wage debate (and the entire discussion on unemployment, which deserves further study) thus marks an important watershed in the formation of the Soviet working class: the class that would face the challenges of the Five-Year Plan was for this moment so fundamentally differentiated by gender that appeals to essential gender equality may have seemed pointless.

THE FIRST DECADE OR SO of Soviet power was a period in which the search for new social forms and new social identities produced a rich canvas of social experimentation and conflict in virtually every field of human endeavor. In the sphere of relations between men and women, it would appear that those relations in the printing industry deteriorated between 1920 and 1930. Some women had emerged from the revolution and civil war with a feisty sense of equality, and the trade-union press fairly bubbled in the early 1920s with news by and about women. Much of this news documented the deep-seated hostility toward the participation of women in the hitherto masculine world of work. In the second half of the 1920s, such activity diminished, and the union seemed to drop women as a special project. By 1926, the trade-union press in general turned away from the cultural and social concerns that had characterized it earlier, and the special women's pages disappeared. By 1929 and 1930, women's issues were raised only in the obligatory March 8 issues of the journal *Pechatnik*. At work, women found their efforts to obtain skills and gain parity with men increasingly blocked.

Among other factors, the economic crisis and resulting chronic unemployment surely contributed to this increasing marginalization of women in the printing industry toward the end of the 1920s. The industry came under tremendous pressure to reduce its costs and improve efficiency throughout the 1920s, but as it did so, the demand for skilled printers fell dramatically.[76] As competition for scarce jobs became keener, it is not surprising that men would close ranks to protect the marketability of the skills they had mastered. Aspiring male workers fell victim to this contraction as well as women: the union successfully fought to reduce its quota for apprentices after 1926. Technological rationalization proceeded slowly in the printing industry, which remained last in line for imports of new technology from Western Europe; but, even here, mechanization was also beginning to erode the old privileged positions of skilled workers, as old tasks were replaced or subdivided by the introduction of machines. Given the control that men exercised on the shop floor, it is no surprise that they arranged for women to be deskilled before men were. The women folders were merely the most visible of those affected.

We must also look at the bargain struck between the Communist regime and its working class in this first decade of Soviet power. A new socialist system of labor relations was being forged in the first half of the decade of the 1920s, one in which labor-management conflict could no longer be understood as a manifestation of class conflict. State-appointed "red" directors assumed the reins of power in Soviet factories, and many of them were veterans of the labor movement, workers themselves by origin. If workers had grievances about their conditions and social positions, it was not possible to base their grievances on their political disenfranchisement or economic exploitation: the USSR was, after all, a proletarian state. Different scapegoats had to be found: not managers, who were "ours," but petty traders ("Nepmen") and shopkeepers, who were "other"; not political leaders, who were "ours," but agents of foreign class enemies, who were "other."[77] Women were both "ours" and "other." Official policy stressed the inclusion of women in the working family and utilized examples of male hostility to try to educate workers about the new position of women in society. But unofficial reality—harassing women on the shop floor in the many forms indicated here—provided a safety valve, a culturally if not politically acceptable target for male frustration and anger.

We may find here an explanation for the evident shift in official policy toward women workers that took place around 1925. The year marked roughly the success of economic recovery and a repositioning of economic policy toward more rapid economic development. The debates that would produce the First Five-Year Plan were already filling the press. The new efficiency drive, with its emphasis on cost-effectiveness and more stringent quality control, hit workers hard.[78] Piecework rates and tighter supervision were reintroduced to raise labor productivity, and the very success of these policies threw thousands of printers out of work.

In exchange for these sacrifices, the regime offered workers the opportunity for new kinds of participation: a mass draft into the Communist Party (the "Lenin levy") that began in 1924; an organized campaign to promote workers into positions of authority and leadership; and the introduction of "production conferences" at work, in which rank-and-file workers would help engineers and managers solve day-to-day problems.[79] Women benefited very little from any of these forms of worker participation: relatively few joined the party, the little upward mobility they experienced propelled them into gender-specific activities, and they were notably absent from production conferences in the printing industry.[80] Perhaps their exclusion was also part of the bargain that the state made with male workers in exchange for the increased intensity of work.

One might also speculate on the need for men to reassert their masculinity and control at precisely the moment when the USSR was embarking on the radical economic transformation of the First Five-Year Plan. The traditional male enclave with its discourse of sexual conquest might serve as an anchor of stability as the Communist Party led these workers into the uncharted waters of industrial expansion. As party leadership increasingly and forcefully asserted its mastery over the rest of society through the mechanisms of political denunciations and purges, such workers needed to reassert their mastery over the subordinates closest at hand, and resistance to women could serve as a surrogate for resistance to management.[81] Women workers were now denounced for their femininity, which was seen to be incompatible with production values. As part of a general campaign against "petty-bourgeois proclivities" of young women (the fox-trot, plucked eyebrows, cosmetics, and dyed hair), one male worker presented the case of Marusia Vorobeva, a twenty-nine-year-old worker who liked the fox-trot and had quit the Komsomol. Now she has dyed her hair: "will the five-year plan be better fulfilled if she is a redhead?"[82] And perhaps it is no accident that the trade-union record links "Trotskyite-opportunist opposition" in 1930 with the support of women.[83] If women supported the opposition, then the manly thing was to rally round the Communist Party leadership, the Stalin leadership.

Some women accepted their exclusion from the male world of class and carved out their separate sphere of activism within a gendered public space: in child care, medicine, public catering, education, and other "domestic" concerns. Some women defined their class culture differently from party norms: why should not the fox-trot and cosmetics—living freely and looking good—mean "modern," not "bourgeois"? But these attempts by some women to develop a new class-gender identity had to evolve against the backdrop of the enduring masculine character of shop-floor culture in Russia. It was male workers as men and not as Communists who defined female characteristics and male characteristics in work. Women were represented as partial workers, incomplete and transient. They were never taught the whole job. Men, who knew the whole job, retained the power of control on the shop floor and managed to confine women to the margins of shop-floor life. A job was "skilled" because men said it was.[84] And in the Soviet Union, the socialist trade union gave them the authority to say so.

What did socialism bring to Russian women as workers? Theirs was a state officially committed to the liberation of women, to the inclusion of women in the polity, to eradicating the economic differences between women and men by supporting women's participation in the work force and by providing public services for women and the family. These ideals would continue to animate women workers and male activists alike, and surely the battle between the sexes in the workplace would be renewed as women poured into the labor force with the five-year plans and again during the war years. But this was a state also committed to the privileging of class over gender, and as long as class was defined in masculine terms, as in the workplace, then Soviet women were left with few possibilities for resisting and transforming these attitudes.

Notes

An earlier version of this article was presented at the 1991 annual meeting of the American Association for the Advancement of Slavic Studies. Thanks to Jim Barrett, Barbara Engel, Laura Engelstein, Leslie Reagan, Lewis Siegelbaum, and Elizabeth Wood for helpful readings and suggestions. I am grateful for research support from IREX in 1989 and 1993, the Fulbright-Hays Faculty Research Abroad Program of the U.S. Department of Education in 1989 and 1993, the National Council for Soviet and East European Research in 1989, and the Midwest Universities Consortium for International Affairs in 1991.

  1 Daniel Brower, "Labor Violence in Russia in the Late Nineteenth Century," *Slavic Review*, 41 (Fall 1982): 417–431; Charters Wyan, *Workers, Strikes, and Pogroms: The Donbass-Dnepr Bend in*

Late Imperial Russia (Princeton, N.J., 1992); Laura Lynne Phillips, "Everyday Life in Revolutionary Russia: Working-Class Drinking and Taverns in St. Petersburg, 1900–1929" (Ph.D. dissertation, University of Illinois, 1993); Rose L. Glickman, *Russian Factory Women: Workplace and Society, 1880–1914* (Berkeley, Calif., 1984); Mark D. Steinberg, *Moral Communities: The Culture of Class Relations in the Russian Printing Industry, 1867–1907* (Berkeley, 1992).

2 Gregory J. Massell, *The Surrogate Proletariat: Moslem Women and Revolutionary Strategies in Soviet Central Asia: 1919–1929* (Princeton, N.J., 1974), xxii–xxiii.

3 For similar calls to reevaluate U.S. and German labor history, see Ava Baron, ed., *Work Engendered: Toward a New History of American Labor* (Ithaca, N.Y., 1991), especially Baron, "Gender and Labor History: Learning from the Past, Looking to the Future," 1–46; and Kathleen Canning, "Gender and the Politics of Class Formation: Rethinking German Labor History," *AHR*, 97 (June 1992): 736–768.

4 See, for example, Gail Lapidus, *Women in Soviet Society: Equality, Development, and Social Change* (Berkeley, Calif., 1978), chap. 2; Michael Paul Sacks, *Women's Work in Soviet Russia: Continuity in the Midst of Change* (New York, 1976); Wendy Z. Goldman, *Women, the State, and Revolution: Soviet Family Policy and Social Life, 1917–1936* (Cambridge, 1993); Richard Stites, *The Women's Liberation Movement in Russia: Feminism, Nihilism, and Bolshevism, 1860–1930* (Princeton, N.J., 1978); Carol Eubanks Hayden, "Feminism and Bolshevism: The Zhenotdel and the Politics of Women's Emancipation in Russia" (Ph.D. dissertation, University of California, Berkeley, 1979); Elizabeth Wood, "Gender and Politics in Soviet Russia: Working Women under the New Economic Policy, 1918–1928" (Ph.D. dissertation, University of Michigan, 1991).

5 *Statisticheskii ezhegodnik goroda Moskvy i moskovskoi gubernii* (Moscow, 1927), vyp. 2: 46, 70; *Pechatnik*, 7 (June 1923): 11.

6 Stephen Kotkin, "Coercion and Identity: Workers' Lives in Stalin's Showcase City," in *Making Workers Soviet: Power, Class, and Identity*, Lewis H. Siegelbaum and Ronald G. Suny, eds (Ithaca, N.Y., 1994), 274–310.

7 Glickman, *Russian Factory Women*, 142, 203–208, 276–277; Steinberg, *Moral Communities*, 243–244.

8 Laura Engelstein, *The Keys to Happiness: Sex and the Search for Modernity in Fin-de-Siècle Russia* (Ithaca, N.Y., 1992), 215–253; Glickman, *Russian Factory Women*, 203, 276–277.

9 *Pechatnik*, 1–2 (1918): 19; *Pechatnik*, 2 (January 15, 1925): 17; *Moskovskii pechatnik*, 4–5 (January 1926): 10; *Pechatnik*, 7–8 (March 10, 1927): 5; *Pechatnitsa* (March 8, 1924): 19.

10 For example, in *Moskovskii pechatnik*, 9 (July 12, 1925): 20; 5 (February 8, 1925): 11; 7 (February 22, 1925): 12; 11 (March 22, 1925): 9; 10–11 (March 1926): 11; Tsentral'nyi Gosudarstvennyi Arkhiv Moskovskoi Oblasti (hereafter, TsGAMO), f. 699 (Moscow union of printers), op. 1, d. 570, l. 279 (factory committee protocols of the Sixteenth State print shop, 1924); *Pechatnik*, 2 (January 15, 1925): 17; 26 (November 20, 1925), 10.

11 *Pechatnik* 15 (August 1, 1925): 14; 10 (April 7, 1927): 10; Tsentral'nyi Gosudarstvennyi Arkhiv Sankt Peterburga (hereafter, TsGA SPb), f. 4804 (Leningrad Trade Union of Printers), op. 9, d. 104, l. 82 (protocols of meetings of women workers, 1925); *Pravda*, June 8, 1923; *Moskovskii pechatnik*, 8 (June 16, 1923): 2.

12 Gosudarstvennyi Arkhiv Rossiiskoi Federatsii (hereafter, GARF), Moscow (formerly Tsentral'nyi Gosudarstvennyi Arkhiv Oktiabr'skoi Revoliutsii), f. 5525 (All-Union Trade Union of Printers), op. 5, ed. khr. 64, l. 98 (protocols of the Moscow province union board of directors, 1923); *Zorkii glaz* (newspaper of the Zinov'ev print shop, Leningrad), 27 (June 1, 1925).

13 *Pechatnik*, 7 (March 12, 1929): 7; *Moskovskii pechatnik*, 19 (March 27, 1924): 15; *Nasha zhizn'* (newspaper of the Sixteenth State print shop, Moscow), 40 (April 30, 1925): 4; *Pechatnik*, 48 (November 27, 1926): 8; *Zhizn' pechatnika* (newspaper of the First Model print shop, Moscow), 11 (36) (June 1, 1926): 1; *Pechatnik*, 7 (April 1, 1925): 17; TsGA SPb, f. 4804, op. 9, d. 104, l. 81; *Moskovskii peehatnik*, 22 (May 15, 1924): 21; *Pechatnik* 9 (May 1, 1925): 12; 5 (March 15, 1924): 16.

14 Elizabeth Wood's study of conflicts between the party and trade union over organizing women illuminates this activist perspective: "Class and Gender at Loggerheads in the Early Soviet State: Who Should Organize the Female Proletariat and How?" in *Gender, Class, and Labor in Modern Europe*, Laura Frader and Sonya O. Rose, eds (Stanford, forthcoming).

15 GARF, f. 5525, op. 4, ed. khr. 119, l. 8 (protocols of general meetings of women workers, 1922). Similar sentiments were expressed by a women's organizer at the First State print shop in Petrograd in 1921: Tsentral'nyi Gosudarstvennyi Arkhiv Istoriko-Politicheskikh Dokumentov (hereafter, TsGAIPD) (former Leningrad Communist Party Archive), f. 435 (Communist faction of the Leningrad branch of the printers' union), op. 1, d. 29, l. 164 (party collective meetings at the First State print shop, 1920–1921).

16 TsGAMO, f. 699, op. 1, d. 285, ll. 4–5 (protocols of women's meetings in the Krasnopresnenskii district, Moscow, 1922).

17 *Pechatnik*, 19 (October 1, 1925): 12; *Pechatnik*, 8 (March 25, 1929): 22; TsGA SPb, f. 4804, op. 9, d. 104, l. 82; *Pechatnik*, 15 (August 1, 1925): 7; 41 (October 9, 1926): 9; 7–8 (March 10, 1927): 28; *Moskovskii Pechatnik*, 17 (April 1926): 10.

18 *Moskovskii Pechatnik*, 2 (February 15, 1921): 10; *Pechatnik*, 4 (March 1, 1924): 17; other mentions of this theme can be found in *Moskovskii Pechatnik*, 9 (March 1926): 12; 5 (February 8, 1925): 11; and *Leninskii zakaz* (Moscow, 1969), 141–142.

19 *Nasha zhizn*, 4 (49) (June 19, 1926): 3; *Zhizn'pechatnika*, 11 (36) (June 1, 1924): 1.

20 Leslie Woodcock Tender, *Wage-Earning Women: Industrial Work and Family Life in the United States, 1900–1930* (New York, 1979), 60; Susan A. Glenn, *Daughters of the Shtetl: Life and Labor in the Immigrant Generation* (Ithaca, N.Y., 1990), 156. See also Susan Porter Benson, " 'The Customers Ain't God': The Work Culture of Department-Store Saleswomen, 1890–1940," in *Working-Class America*, Michael H. Frisch and Daniel J. Walkowitz, eds (Urbana, Ill., 1983); Kathy Peiss, *Cheap Amusements: Working Women and Leisure in Turn-of-the-Century New York* (Philadelphia, 1986); Christine Stansell, *City of Women: Sex and Class in New York* (New York, 1986). On how "gossip" aids in political mobilization, see Temma Kaplan, "Female Consciousness and Collective Action: The Case of Barcelona, 1910–1918," *Signs*, 7 (Spring 1982): 545–566.

21 *Pechatnyi Dvor* (newspaper of the Pechatnyi Dvor print shop, formerly First State print shop, Leningrad) (May 19, 1924): 2, italics mine.

22 *Zvon* is defined as "rumor," while *spletnia*, the term used when women engage in the practice, is defined as "unfounded rumor." S. I. Ozhegov, *Slovar' russkogo iazyka* (Moscow, 1973).

23 *Moskovskii pechatnik*, 32–33 (August 1926): 15–16. For prerevolutionary examples, see Steinberg, *Moral Communities*, 78–79; and Maxim Gorky's short story about bakers, "Twenty-Six Men and a Girl" (1899), in *The Collected Short Stories of Maxim Gorky*, Avrahm Yarmolinsky and Moura Budberg, eds (Secaucus, N.J., 1988).

24 Wendy Z. Goldman, "Working-Class Women and the 'Withering Away' of the Family: Popular Responses to Family Policy," in *Russia in the Era of NEP: Explorations in Soviet Society and Culture*, Sheila Fitzpatrick, Alexander Rabinowitch and Richard Stites, eds (Bloomington, Ind., 1991), 135–139.

25 TsGA SPb, f. 4804, op. 10, d. 66, l. 52 (Pechatnyi Dvor factory committee, 1926); op. 7, d. 92, l. 6 (protocols of general meetings of women workers, 1923); *Pravda*, July 14, 1923; July 17, 1923.

26 *Iskry* (factory newspaper of the Evgeniia Sokolova print shop, Leningrad) (September 10, 1928): 5; *Moskovskii pechatnik*, 11 (March 22, 1925): 9; 33 (November 7, 1924): 4.

27 *Moskovskii pechatnik*, 2 (February 15, 1921): 10; 11 (March 22, 1925): 9; 18 (May 8, 1925): 12; *Pechatnitsa* (March 8, 1924): 17, 18; *Pechatnik*, 10 (May 15, 1925): 10; 5 (March 15, 1924): 16.

28 *Moskovskii pechatnik*, 10 (August 12, 1923): 19; *Pechatnitsa* (March 8, 1924): 19, 20.

29 See Steinberg, *Moral Communities*, 74–79.

30 Cynthia Cockburn, *Brothers: Male Dominance and Technological Change* (London, 1983), 186; Paul Willis, "Shop-Floor Culture, Masculinity, and the Wage Form," in *Working-Class Culture*, J. Clarke, C. Critcher and R. Johnson, eds (New York, 1979), 196.

31 On this process in the printing industry, see Diane P. Koenker, "Labor Relations in Socialist Russia: Class Values and Production Values in the Printers' Union, 1917–1921," in *Making Workers Soviet*, 59–93. See also William Chase, *Workers, Society, and the Soviet State: Labor and Life in Moscow, 1918–1929* (Urbana, Ill., 1987).

32 *Pravda*, October 24, 1920; *Moskovskii pechatnik*, 6 (May 1, 1921): 16; 15 (January 7, 1924): 16; 23 (June 1, 1924): 13; 12 (March 1926), 5; TsGAMO, f. 699, op. 1, d. 438, l. 5 (protocols of the Krasnyi Proletarii factory committee, November 1923).

33 *Pechatnik*, 4 (February 1, 1928): 31.

34 *Pravda*, August 30, 1922; *Nashazhizn'* (September 19, 1923): 1; (October 26, 1923): 1; (December 1, 1923): 3. Other examples can be found in GARF, f. 5525, op. 4, d. 119, l. 15.

35 *Pechatnik*, 2 (January 20, 1929): 15; *Moskovskii Pechatnik*, 8 (June 10, 1923): 19; GARF, f. 5525, op. 6, ed. khr. 71, l. 147 (protocols of meetings of the Leningrad printers' union board of directors, May 20, 1924); *Moskovskii Pechatnik*, 28 (August 15, 1924): 16.

36 TsGAMO, f. 699, op. 1, d. 285, l. 4; another example is reported in *Pechatnik*, 9 (August 1923): 17.

37 *Moskovskii Pechatnik*, 10 (August 12, 1925): 17. Other examples can be found in TsGAMO, f. 699, op. 1, d. 266, l. 90 (Moscow factory committee protocols, 1922); d. 570, l. 61; *Nasha zhizn'*, 5 (79) (March 27, 1928): 4; 15 (89) (October 24, 1928): 4; *Pechatnik*, 24–25 (September 1, 1928): 19.

38 *Pechatnik*, 5 (February 12, 1928): 19.

39 William Chase, "Moscow and Its Working Class, 1918–1928: A Social Analysis" (Ph.D. dissertation, Boston College, 1979), 390–392; *Pechatnik*, 50–51 (December 20, 1926): 23.

40 *Pravda*, March 23, 1924; *Zhizn' pechatnika*, 4 (30) (March 1, 1924): 1; 7 (32) (April 1, 1924): 3; *Moskovskii pechatnik*, 20 (April 15, 1924): 17; *Zhizn' pechatnika*, 8 (33) (April 16, 1924): 4.

41 GARF, f. 5525, op. 2, ed. khr. 56, l. 15 (protocols of printers' union comrades-disciplinary courts, 1920); *Moskovskii pechatnik*, 34 (December 5, 1924): 22.

42 *Moskovskii pechatnik*, 6 (May 1, 1921): 9; *Pechainyi Dvor* (May 19, 1924): 2.

43 An early statement of this policy in the printers' union is reported in *Pravda*, February 15, 1920. Another argument can be found from 1924: TsGA SPb, f. 4804, op. 8, d. 95, l. 13ob (factory committee protocols at the Pechatnyi Dvor print shop, 1924).

44 *Vserossiiskii pechatnik*, 11 (1921): 8; *Pravda*, January 16, 1921; *Tret'ii s"ezd soiuza rabochikh poligraficheskogo proizvodsiva: Protokoly i postanovleniia (izvlechenie iz stenogramma)* (Moscow, 1921), 91.

45 *Pravda*, June 8, 1923; *Pechatnik*, 6 (May 16, 1923): 31; 3 (February 1923): 37.

46 Charles More, *Skill and the English Working Class, 1870–1914* (New York, 1980), 9–24.

47 Sian Reynolds, *Britannica's Typesetters: Women Compositors in Edinburgh* (Edinburgh, 1989), 138; Helen Hardin Chenut, *La construction sociale des métiers masculins et féminins dans la Bonneterie Troyenne 1900–1939* (Paris, 1987); Ava Baron, "Contested Terrain Revisited: Technology and Gender Definitions of Work in the Printing Industry, 1850–1920," in *Women, Work, and Technology: Transformations*, Barbara Drygulski Wright, *et al.*, eds (Ann Arbor, Mich., 1987), 58–83.

48 *Zhizn' pechatnika*, 16 (July 15, 1923): 2. The Russian terms are: *otvetstvennost', tochnost', slozhnost', iskusstvo, trudnost', vrednost', intensivnost', tiazhest', opasnost'*.

49 *Istoriia Leningradskogo soiuza rabochikh poligraficheskogo proizvodstva* (Leningrad, 1925), 1: 62. Apprenticeship was generally regarded to be longer than necessary for teaching skills alone; it was also a socialization process and a way to exploit cheap labor. See also Steinberg, *Moral Communities*, 68–74; and Cockburn, *Brothers*, 45–46, 59–60.

50 *Pechatnik*, 6 (May 16, 1923): 31.

51 *Pechatnik*, 6 (May 16, 1923) : 3. See also Goldman, *Women, the State, and Revolution*, 122–126, for similar discussions by women in other industries.

52 *Pravda*, September 14, 1923; *Moskovskii pechatnik*, 8 (July 1923): 13; 5 (February 8, 1925): 11; *Pechatnik*, 23 (August 25, 1927): 14; 2 (January 9, 1926): 11; *Moskovskii pechatnik*, 11 (March 22, 1925): 9; 2 (January 15, 1925): 14; 18 (February 27, 1924): 24; TsGAMO, f. 699, op. 1, d. 570, l. 27; *Moskovskii pechatnik*, 10 (August 12, 1923): 20; 9 (July 12, 1923): 21.

53 *Moskovskii pechatnik*, 10 (August 12, 1923): 19; the double burden was also catalogued in *Zhizn' pechatnika*, 6 (31) (March 8, 1924): 1; and TsGAMO, f. 699, op. 1, d. 395, l. 55 (protocols of meetings of active women workers, 1923).

54 *Nasha zhizn'*, 25 (March 8, 1925): 4. See also *Pechatnitsa* (March 8, 1924): 17; *Moskovskii pechatnik*, 22 (May 15, 1924): 20; *Pechatnik*, 26 (November 20, 1925): 10; *Moskovskii pechatnik*, 9 (March 1926): 11; *Pechatnik*, 7 (March 12, 1929): 4.

55 "Kodeks zakonov o trude RSFSR Izd. 1922 g.," in *Deistvuiushchee zakonodatel'stvo o trude*, E. Danilova, ed. (Moscow, 1927), 1: 14 (Article 130); GARF, f. 5525, op. 5, ed. khr. 118, l. 3 (protocols of general meetings of women, 1923). In Scotland, the Monotype had been considered "preeminently suited for females" because keyboarding and typecasting were in fact separated (Reynolds, *Britannica's Typesetters*, 70).

56 *Pravda*, June 8, 1923; October 17, 1923; TsGAMO, f. 699, op. 1, d. 395, l. 84; also *Moskovskii pechatnik*, 8 (June 16, 1923): 14; TsGAMO, f. 699, op. 1, d. 849, l. 84 (protocols of the Sixteenth State print shop factory committee, 1926); *Pechatnitsa* (March 8, 1924): 9.

57 *Pechatnik*, 15 (August 1, 1925): 14; 10 (April 7, 1927): 10; *Moskovskii pechatnik*, 8 (June 16, 1923): 15; 9 (July 12, 1923): 21–22; 7 (February 22, 1925): 12; *Pravda*, January 4, 1924; *Moskovskii pechatnik*, 38–39 (October 14, 1925): 29; *Pechatnik*, 7–8 (March 8, 1928): 4.

58 Tsentral'nyi Komitet Soiuza Rabochikh Poligraficheskogo Proizvodstva SSSR, *Stenograficheskii otchet V s"ezda soiuza rabochikh poligraficheskogo proizvodstva SSSR, 20–24 dekabria 1924 goda* (Moscow, 1925), 17

59 GARF, f. 5525, op. 8, ed. khr. 1, l. 20 (protocols of the Sixth All-Union Congress of the Trade Union of Printers, December 1926); *Moskovskii pechatnik*, 1 (January 1926): 11. Wood discusses some other factors in this shift, in "Class and Gender at Loggerheads."

60 TsGA SPb, f. 4804, op. 10, d. 4, ll. 508, 517–18, 567 (Leningrad Province Congress of the Printers' Union, March 1926); *Moskovskii pechatnik*, 14 (April 1926): 3; TsGA SPb, f. 4804, op. 10, d. 4, l. 567–68.

61 *Pechatnik*, 12–13 (May 1, 1927): 33; 8 (March 25, 1929): 22; 7 (March 12, 1929): 17; 7–8 (March 8, 1928): 4–5; 6 (1930): 4.

62 *Pechatnik*, 29–30 (October 25, 1929): 17; TsGAMO, f. 699, op. 1, d. 1059, l. 15 (protocols of the Fourth Moscow Province Conference of the Printers' Union, October 26, 1928); *Pechatnik*, 6 (1930): 4.

63 *Pechatnik*, 35 (December 18, 1927): 11; TsGAMO, f. 699, op. 1, d. 1141, l. 21 (protocols of the Eighth Moscow Province Congress of the Printers' Union, 1927); *Pechatnik*, 7 (March 1, 1929): 5; 29–30 (October 25, 1927): 17; 5 (February 12, 1928): 1.

64 Heidi Hartmann, "Capitalism, Patriarchy, and Job Segregation by Sex," *Signs*, 1 (Spring 1976, Suppl.): 137–70; Jane Humphries, "Class Struggle and the Persistence of the Working-Class Family," *Cambridge Journal of Economics*, 1 (1977): 241–258.

65 See especially the discussion in Alice Kessler-Harris, "Gender Ideology in Historical Reconstruction: A Case Study from the 1930s," *Gender and History*, 1 (Spring 1989): 31–49; Margaret Hobbs, "Rethinking Antifeminism in the 1930s: Gender Crisis or Workplace Justice? A Response to Alice Kessler-Harris," and Kessler-Harris, "Reply to Hobbs," *Gender and History*, 5 (Spring 1993): 4–15, 16–19. See also Martha May, "The Historical Problem of the Family Wage: The Ford Motor Company and the Five Dollar Day," *Feminist Studies*, 8 (Summer 1982): 399–424; and Maurine Weiner Greenwald, "Working-Class Feminism and the Family Wage Ideal: The Seattle Debate on Married Women's Right to Work, 1914–1920," *Journal of American History*, 76 (June 1989): 118–149.

66 Report in *Biulleten' Moskovskogo Obshchestva Tipo-Litografov*, 2–3 (April 15–28, 1918): 13.

67 *Pechatnik*, 1–2 (January 31–February 13, 1918): 19.

68 *Moskovskii pechatnik*, 12 (October 29, 1923): 24; GARF, f. 5525, op. 10, ed. khr. 41, ll. 71, 73 (protocols of the First Oblast Congress of the Leningrad Union of Printers, February 1928). There were other male voices of support at this congress as well (for example, see l. 84).

69 *Pechatnoe delo*, 15 (January 31–February 13, 1918): 14; TsGA SPb, f. 4804, op. 11, d. 158, ll. 184, 220ob (protocols of meetings of Leningrad province unemployed printers, 1926–1929); TsGAMO, f. 4660, op. 1, d. 31, l. 5 (protocols of meetings of Moscow province unemployed printers, 1929).

70 TsGAMO, f. 699, op. 1, d. 564, ll. 77–78 (protocols of the factory committee of the Krasnyi Proletarii print shop, Moscow, 1924).

71 TsGA SPb, f. 4804, op. 11, d. 158, l. 159; TsGAMO, f. 699, op. 1, d. 1110, l. 9 (protocols of meetings of unemployed Moscow printers, 1928); TsGAMO, f. 4660, op. 1, d. 31, l. 6; *Zorkii glaz*, 3 (33) (March 8, 1927): 1.

72 TsGA SPb, f. 4804, op. 8, d. 95, l. 13ob; *Moskovskii pechatnik*, 12 (October 29, 1923): 24.

73 This view, based on letters sent to government officials during the Depression, is discussed in Kessler-Harris, "Gender Ideology," 40; one dissenting opinion labeled as "sovietization" the granting or denial of employment as a dole (39).

74 TsGA SPb, f. 4804, op. 11, d. 158, l. 168; op. 10, d. 4; GARF, f. 5525, op. 8, d. 1; TsGA SPb, f. 4804, op. 11, d. 158, l. 167; village ties: TsGAMO, f. 699, op. 1, d. 564 (protocols of the factory committee of the Krasnyi Proletarii print shop, Moscow, November 1924); TsGA SPb, f. 4804, op. 11, d. 158, l. 220ob; TsGAMO, f. 4660, op. 1, d. 31, l. 10. Similar sentiments were expressed in the United States during the Depression (Kessler-Harris, "Gender Ideology," 41).

75 TsGAMO, f. 4660, op. 1, d. 31, l. 4; TsGA SPb, f. 4804, op. 11, d. 158, l. 102; *Pechatnik* 4 (February 1, 1928): 20; GARF, f. 5525, op. 10, d. 41, l. 73. Other examples can be found in TsGAMO, f. 4660, op. 1, d. 31, ll. 5, 10, 52ob, 83.

76 Unemployed union members argued in 1927 that the industry's economic problems would be solved if the government introduced freedom of the press, but such outbursts were met with cries of "Shame!" TsGA SPb, f. 4804, op. 11, d. 158, l. 141 (meeting of Leningrad unemployed printers, February 24, 1927).

77 For more detailed discussions of both labor-management relations and of the consciousness of printers in this period, see Koenker, "Labor Relations in Socialist Russia," in *Making Workers Soviet*; and "Class and Consciousness in a Socialist Society: Workers in the Printing Trades during NEP," in *Russia in the Era of NEP*, 34–57. See also Sheila Fitzpatrick, "Ascribing Class: The Construction of Social Identity in Soviet Russia," *Journal of Modern History*, 65 (December 1993): 745–770.

78 Leon Trotsky excoriated the workers in the printing industry for the miserable quality of their output in 1926 (*Moskovskii pechatnik*, 32–33 [August 1926]: 20–21). Is it just coincidence that the same issue of the journal printed the most explicit story yet about the sexual content of workplace culture? In other words, printing the story might have been meant to compensate for Trotsky's criticism of printers' manliness, as defined in "competence." See Baron, "Contested Terrain Revisited," 71–75.

79 See the discussion in Lewis H. Siegelbaum, *Soviet State and Society between Revolutions, 1918–1929* (Cambridge, 1992), 180–187; see also Chase, *Workers, Society, and the Soviet State*; and John Hatch, "The 'Lenin Levy' and the Social Origins of Stalinism: Workers and the Communist Party in Moscow, 1921–1928," *Slavic Review*, 48 (Winter 1989): 558–577.

80 Examples of their "lack of interest" in production conferences appear throughout the record of the printers' union, for instance, GARF, f. 5525, op. 10, ed. khr. 41, ll. 62, 68 (1928); op. 11, ed. khr. 53, l. 53 (protocols of the presidium of the Moscow printers' union, 1929).

81   Public purge hearings begin to appear in the print-shop factory press in 1928 and 1929, and the entire union leadership was replaced in 1929 for "right deviationism."

82   *Pechatnyi Dvon*, 14 (99) (June 5, 1930): 3. More work needs to be done to understand on their own terms some behaviors negatively coded "feminine" and "petty-bourgeois" in socialist Russia, including dancing, cosmetics, and sexuality. See Kathy Peiss, "'Charity Girls' and City Pleasures: Historical Notes on Working-Class Sexuality, 1880–1920," in *Passion and Power: Sexuality in History*, Kathy Peiss and Christina Simmons, eds (Philadelphia, 1989). For some approaches for Russia, see Anne E. Gorsuch, "Soviet Youth and the Politics of Popular Culture during NEP," *Social History*, 17 (May 1992): 189–201; and Anne Bobroff, "Russian Working Women: Sexuality in Bonding Patterns and the Politics of Daily Life," in *Powers of Desire: The Politics of Sexuality*, Ann Snitow, Christine Stansell and Sharon Thompson, eds (New York, 1983).

83   TsGAMO, f. 4660, op. 1, d. 121, l. 194 (protocols of the Second Moscow Oblast Congress of the Printers' Union, December 1930). Not long before this congress, peasant women had been in the forefront of opposition to collectivization, as shown by Lynne Viola, "*Bab'i bunty* and Peasant Women's Protest during Collectivization," *Russian Review*, 45 (January 1986): 23–42. Russian historians should pursue further the ways in which political opposition may have been coded in gendered terms.

84   I owe this discussion to Cockburn, *Brothers: Male Dominance and Technological Change*, a study based on interviews in the London typesetting industry, and to Reynolds, *Britannica's Typesetters*. Russian women printers recognized the monopoly position of men in defining skill when they demanded that one of theirs, a folder, be elected in 1926 to the union board of directors in order to defend their position in the skill hierarchy (TsGA SPb, f. 4804, op. 10, d. 4, ll. 508, 930).

Chapter 27

Karen Hagemann

■ 'MEN'S DEMONSTRATIONS AND WOMEN'S PROTEST: GENDER IN COLLECTIVE ACTION IN THE URBAN WORKING-CLASS MILIEU DURING THE WEIMAR REPUBLIC', *Gender and History*, 5, 1, 1993, pp. 101–119

O N 12 NOVEMBER 1918, only a few days after the outbreak of revolution in Germany, the 'Council of Peoples' Deputies', the new national government, proclaimed universal, equal suffrage for men and women. When Germany's women were allowed to vote for the first time on 19 January 1919,[1] it was the culmination of a long, hard fight by large segments of the women's movement, particularly its middle-class radical and socialist wings.[2] The Weimar Constitution would also guarantee women 'equal citizenship'. Against the will of most women parliamentarians, however, this equality was modified by the word 'fundamental', a harbinger of other disappointments to come. In her first parliamentary speech, Marie Juchacz, National Women's Secretary of the Social Democratic Party (SPD) and Deputy to the National Assembly, expressed the hopes of many women that formal civil equality would lead to economic, social and political equality.

> Political equality has given my sex the possibility to fully develop its powers. ... I would like to say here that the Woman Question, as things stand now in Germany, no longer exists in its old sense, that it is solved. We need no longer struggle for our rights with assemblies, with resolutions, with petitions. Political struggle, which will always exist, will play itself out in other forms from now on. We women now have the opportunity to let our powers have an effect within the framework constructed by ideology and by freely-chosen party groupings.[3]

This optimism soon proved premature, however. Women remained disadvantaged in all areas of the economy, society and politics during the Weimar Republic.[4] The formal equality guaranteed by the constitution did nothing to change the structural causes of their dependent and subordinate position in society. Women who wanted to take advantage of their newly-acquired equal rights and opportunities could only do so by adapting to norms and structures tailored by and for men. In the recently conquered field of 'high' politics, women paid for their integration into the system of parliamentary democracy by disciplining their political behavior. Their sphere of social action[5] was increasingly diverted into the male-controlled realms of parties and parliaments, where women were tolerated only in circumscribed areas designated as 'female'. Men conjured up the danger of growing competition and conflicts between the sexes, which formal political equality potentially increased since women now had the right to equal consideration in filling parliamentary posts and junctions. Men sought to ward off this danger by transposing the old sexual division of labor onto the terrain of party and parliamentary politics which was now open to women. Thus women remained excluded from large segments of the political arena.

These tendencies were intensified by the 'militarization'[6] and 'brutalization'[7] of political life, which were more pronounced in Germany after 1918 than in the other war powers.[8] The violence-laden and militant rhetoric of pre-war politics, with its friend/enemy dichotomy, had already laid the essential social-psychological preconditions, but the decisive impetus came during the war itself. The masculine military mentality lived on into postwar society, expressing itself not only in general admiration for all things military but also in an increased readiness to resort to physical violence to solve both private and public conflicts.[9] Social crises, particularly, a level of mass unemployment unknown before 1914, fundamentally challenged male identity, strongly defined as it was around waged labor.[10] Together with seemingly threatening changes in gender relations, especially in marriage and the family,[11] men felt compelled to put on a show of strength. The 'militarization' of politics was also a reaction to democratization. Right-wing supporters were not the only ones to fear that the new conditions would thrust women into the traditional 'male domain' of politics. Thus men increasingly sought to create 'women-free' space in the political arena—in 'self-defense'.

Against the background of socio-economic and political crisis, one can distinguish four phases of political 'militarization' during the Weimar Republic: the revolutionary period (1918–19) with its armed confrontations between adherents of soviet socialism and representatives of the new state; the inflation-ridden postwar years (1920–23) with their right-wing assassinations and attempted coups and uprisings of the extreme left; the period of relative economic stabilization (1924–28), a phase of general formation in paramilitary units with a growing number of violent clashes between political opponents in public, particularly in the streets; and the years of economic crisis (1929–33), in which these 'violent clashes' gradually escalated into armed conflicts around the control of public space.[12] This development went hand-in-hand with political radicalization. The parties of the extreme right and left, particularly the National Socialist Party (NSDAP) and Communist Party (KPD) which were also those most frequently involved in violent political conflict, enjoyed increasing influence, primarily among male voters, over the course of the Weimar Republic.[13]

The paramilitary 'Protection and Defense Leagues', decidedly 'masculinist' organizations,[14] greatly promoted the escalation of political violence. The 'Protection and Defense Leagues' activities were particularly instrumental in bringing a 'manly-military' stance into everyday politics. Although the leagues originated on the Right, their example was soon followed so that by the mid-1920s such groups existed all across the political spectrum. Uniforms, parades in military formation and violent clashes increasingly became an integral part of political life, which excluded women.[15]

The exclusion of women from large segments of politics thus took on a new quality under conditions of 'equal citizenship'. Formally integrated into the newly constituted system of parliamentary democracy, in reality women were increasingly relegated to 'specifically female' areas of the political arena and saw their opportunities for autonomous social action reduced. This article investigates this process using the example of 'collective actions'[16] in the urban working-class milieu. The analysis centers on gender-specific protest and demonstration behavior in public, particularly in streets and public squares. Here the differences in form and content of men's and women's social action are particularly apparent.

The study focuses on Hamburg, the largest German city after Berlin and the most important trade and service center and industrial site in northern Germany. Since the Wilhelmine period, Hamburg had been considered a stronghold of the workers' movement, whose massive influence could be seen, for example, at election time. In March 1919, in the first democratic town council elections, the SPD received an absolute majority of 50.5% and the Independent Social Democratic Party (USPD) garnered 8.1%. Until 1932 the SPD captured the majority of votes. Only after 1924 did it experience serious competition from the left. Disappointed in the party's 'conservative defensive policy', workers increasingly turned to the Communist Party (KPD), which gathered 21.9% of the vote in the September 1931 town council elections while the SPD's share fell to 27.8%.[17]

This article first describes the development of the Weimar workers' movement's male-dominated demonstration culture. It then interprets the picture that emerges as a reflection of gender relations in the workers' movement. Finally, it discusses 'specifically female' forms of collective action in the Weimar workers' milieu.

During the Weimar Republic, in contrast to the pre-war period, demonstrations were a fact of everyday life in which all elements of the political spectrum participated. They took five basic forms: outdoor public rallies, which began as processions to the meeting place; culturally-flavored parades; marches in military formation; organized street demonstrations as we know them today; and spontaneous protest demonstrations. Demonstrations fulfilled several functions. Vis-à-vis outsiders, their chief purpose was to occupy public space physically and demonstratively, to take a political position, articulate protest and, recruit new members. They offered participants political identity and identification through the concrete sensuous experience of belonging to a mass of like-minded people, coming together to embrace the political slogans of the hour. They were thus intended at once to strengthen solidarity and to mobilize their constituents.

The workers' movement, too, frequently called its adherents out into the streets to demonstrate the size and power of its 'troops'. Aside from May Day, which remained the workers' movement's most significant 'day of struggle and celebration', the most important occasions for demonstrations were: Anti-war Day, commemorating the beginning of the First World War; Revolution Days, with which the KPD observed the anniversary of the Russian October Revolution and the SPD the declaration of the Republic; Constitution Day, with which the SPD and other republican organizations celebrated the signing of the Weimar Constitution; as well as regional, national and international meetings, festivals and congresses of workers' organizations.[18] During the second half of the Weimar Republic, demonstrations also became central elements of SPD and KPD election campaigns. In the escalating political conflicts of the Republic's final phase, expressive militant demonstrations of the 'popular masses' were favored instruments of agitation.

The sole source of information on gender-specific participation in workers' movement demonstrations, the few existing contemporary photographs, indicate that although more women took part in demonstrations than before the war, their numbers still lagged behind their representation in labor organizations. In 1928, women made up 21% of the 867,671 SPD members and 17% of the 130,000 KPD members. In Hamburg, as in most large cities, they represented a significantly higher percentage of members. Here in the same year women were 26% of the 48,186 SPD and 23% of the 10,211 KPD members. Men dominated in visual representations. The photographs show men of all ages, mainly in all-male groups. In contrast, most women demonstrators appear to be under thirty and were usually in male company, i.e. on the arms of fathers, sweethearts or husbands. The age of the women attending demonstrations diverged markedly from the average age of female members of both labor parties. The majority of women Social Democrats and Communists were housewives and mothers between thirty and fifty. In the Hamburg SPD, the only local party for which gender-differentiated figures on age exist, 79% of female members in 1929 were over thirty years old. In the KPD, whose membership was in general much younger than that of the SPD, the percentage of women members under thirty was presumably somewhat higher. In 1927, 72% of all women Social Democrats and 79% of all women Communists in Hamburg were listed as housewives who did not work outside the home. Women under thirty made up the majority of the small group of women in full-time employment in both parties.[19]

Women's participation seems to have been greatest at demonstrations with a holiday atmosphere. Parades and marches with cultural and festive offerings apparently appealed most to working-class women. Such events allowed them to bring their children, the care of whom often prevented women's attendance at other kinds of demonstrations. The participation of women and children was especially great at the May Day parades which became increasingly important forums in the 1920s for both working-class parties to demonstrate the breadth and variety of workers' culture. The percentage of women at military-style marches, in contrast, was miniscule; men had the events to themselves.

It was only in the last years of the Weimar Republic that both labor parties organized women's blocs with their own banners at demonstrations, usually during election battles. They also began to hold women's open-air election rallies which began as processions from different neighborhoods, 'reinforced' by members of children's and youth groups, and workers' sport and choral clubs marching in formation. Both types of demonstrations were specifically intended to appeal to women and win their votes. In the final phase of the Weimar Republic, the SPD and KPD women's organizations staged their own women's marches and street demonstrations for the first time. In order to articulate women's interests effectively and publicly during a time of radicalized political conflict, they had to resort to forms of action previously reserved mainly for men. Most autonomous women's demonstrations were organized for International Women's Day, the annual high point of both labor parties' activities for women. In the last years of the Weimar Republic these demonstrations focused on the battle for abortion rights, along with the struggle against militarism and National Socialism.[20]

Abolition or reform of the misogynist abortion law had been a central demand of the social democratic and communist women's movements since the beginning of the Weimar Republic. Family planning and birth control were of paramount importance in the everyday lives of working-class women, holding out the promise of not only an improved financial situation but also less work and better health. Ignorance about sure methods of birth control and lack of financial means limited the success of their efforts, however, and abortion remained a last resort for many. According to physicians' estimates, the number of illegal abortions rose continually from the beginning of the Weimar Republic to some 800,000 annually at the end of the 1920s. In the face of this development, public debate over the abortion law, §218, became ever more polarized. The campaign to decriminalize abortion reached its apex in the early 1930s. The struggle for a fundamental reform of abortion law, as a battle for 'women's right to self-determination', became the focal point of social democratic and communist women's politics. It went hand-in-hand with the struggle against the Right, since conservative Christian, German nationalist and National Socialist circles were the most vehement supporters of the prohibition on abortion. This development was accompanied by more radical forms of action; alongside petitions and resolutions, information and protest meetings, the women also organized demonstrations.[21]

Male dominance at demonstrations is hardly surprising. After all, the physically demonstrative appropriation and occupation of space belonged to men's everyday behavioral repertoire, serving to demonstrate and secure their power in both the private and public spheres. Military-style marches in particular, which became increasingly common in the mid-1920s, strike the viewer as veritable rituals of masculinity. The dominant body language at these demonstrations, characterized by a 'resolute gaze', 'raised fist' and 'march step', was a masculine one.[22] The wearing of uniforms emphasized not only the demonstrator's own manliness but also his membership in a masculinist brotherhood.

The place where these actions occurred also corresponded to that part of urban space in which men moved as a matter of course. In the working-class milieu, the most important sites of public male activity, aside from the workplace as the center of men's lives, were pubs, streets and public squares. At the same time, these places' central significance as a spatial basis of working-class culture only increased during the 1920s. After all, the 'militarization' of politics demanded an escalating battle for the street as a struggle for control over public space, i.e. political influence. This battle was fought out in working-class neighborhoods, where people spent a great deal of everyday life outside their crowded lodgings.[23] Growing numbers of unemployed men, in particular, began to spend most of their time in the street.

Aside from their homes (which represented the primary workplace for most women, regardless of age, marital status or occupation), the main women's spaces in working-class neighborhoods were courtyards, marketplaces and shops. To be sure, women could only reach them via the streets. Unlike men, however, women mainly used public thoroughfares with a definite purpose: as workers, housewives or mothers to go from one workplace to another, to do errands and shopping, to take their children to school or out to play, etc. Even in the 1920s, women who wanted to appear 'respectable' could not move alone in their 'free time', without visible purpose, through men's public space without attracting attention and disapproval. Unlike men, they required an escort even for leisure activities. Contrary to the popular image of the 'New Woman', who demonstrated her independence through dress, leisure and sports, during the Weimar Republic most women's autonomous sphere of movement remained extraordinarily circumscribed.[24] Thus even working-class women had to overcome significant internal and external constraints if they wanted to move in public space outside the roles and tasks accorded them by society. This made it difficult even for politically organized working-class women to attend demonstrations or labor movement meetings alone.

For working-class women of the older generation in particular, whose attitudes had been shaped in the Wilhelmine period, these constraints were strengthened by the notion that politics was 'a male affair', which persisted despite 'equal citizenship'. If they participated in politics anyway, they usually found it difficult to act publicly together with men. They were less accustomed to such collaboration than women of the younger generation, who were familiar with it from the workplace or the labor movement. Thus older women in particular preferred to take part in politics through women's indoor meetings. The type of gathering that most appealed to them was the 'women's leisure hour' (Frauenfeierstunde), as the above-average number of participants suggests. At these events women were treated to an 'artistic program' including recitations, singing and music presented on a 'cheerfully decorated stage'. A short, impressive speech on a women's topic formed the evening's centerpiece.[25] The SPD in particular made increasing use of such women's evenings from the 1920s on, in place of the traditional public women's meetings centered on a lecture and discussion. The introduction of the 'women's leisure hour' belonged to a new conception of women's agitation which sought to fulfill the needs of so-called 'indifferent' women by bringing more 'diversion and relaxation' into their 'laborious and care-worn lives'.[26] From the mid-1920s on, the KPD also increasingly changed its public meetings for women to include an extensive and varied cultural program alongside the usual political lectures.[27]

The younger generation of women active in the workers' movement in the 1920s appears to have regarded 'equal citizenship' more as a 'self-evident right'. Accordingly, these women participated to a greater extent not only in the workers' organizations' 'general' meetings but also in demonstrations. On the whole, however, only a relatively small proportion of younger women took part. Most of the two labor parties' 'general' meetings were oriented towards the needs and interests of the majority of members, men. Their usual format consisted of a speech and discussion, only very rarely dealing with women's issues. The usual meeting places, pubs, with their masculine atmosphere redolent of beer and tobacco smoke, put women off. The meeting times chosen, weekday evenings and Sunday mornings, made it virtually impossible for women with household responsibilities to attend. As a result, even in large cities like Hamburg the proportion of women at the SPD's 'general' party meetings rarely exceeded 10%. Figures for the KPD were probably equally small.[28]

Changes in demonstration culture in the 1920s served to increase male domination of these events. 'Troops' of uniformly dressed men walking in military formation gained in significance as politics became militarized. The founding of the SPD-linked republican Reichs Banner Black Red Gold (Reichsbanner Schwarz-Rot-Gold) and the communist Red Front Fighters' League (Roter Frontkämpfer Bund, RFB) in 1924 decisively promoted this development. These proletarian Protection and Defense Committees quickly won mass influence; the Reichs Banner had some one million members nationally in the second half of the 1920s and the RFB some 100,000. In Hamburg alone there were c.18,000 'Reichs Banner comrades' and 4,500 'RFB fighters'.[29] With them a new culture of demonstration took hold in the labor movement, characterized by uniform-dress, military march discipline and the carrying of banners and red flags.

This style, intended to express discipline, comradeship, strength and readiness for battle, appealed to young men in particular. In their eyes it symbolized not only 'powerful manliness' but also 'rationality', and thus corresponded to the general trend towards a 'rationalization' of all areas of work and life. For broad segments of politically organized working-class youth, 'functionalism' and a 'new objectivity' became key concepts in a new culture of everyday life. Daily confrontations with a variety of social and economic problems, especially unemployment which hit the younger generation particularly hard, formed the social-psychological background to this realistic and critical stance. For young men, the loss of employment meant the loss not only of a central area of male identity but also of all prospects and hopes for the future. Because of gender-specific expectations, young women, in contrast, could at least hope for security in marriage, seeking their happiness in family life.[30] As expressions of new 'objective-functionalist' attitudes, disciplined military-style public appearances and uniform clothing came more and more to characterize the communist and social democratic worker's youth movements—primarily movements of young men—

from the mid-1920s on. Girls had little influence on the form and content of politics in either organization, although they made up a greater percentage of members here than in the 'mother parties'. In 1929 the Socialist Worker Youth (Sozialistische Arbeiterjugend, SAJ) had 55,958 members nationally, with girls making up 36% of the total. The figure was probably similar for the Communist Youth League (Kommunistischer Jugendverband, KJVD), with a national membership of 20,000. In the same year the SAJ had some 1,800 members in Hamburg, of whom 47% were female. A total of 1,150 young people were members of the Hamburg KJVD.[31]

The growing regimentation of proletarian demonstration culture also affected women, to be sure, but only those active in the workers' youth organizations and the Red Women's and Girls' Federation (Roter Frauen und Mädchenbund). The female members of these 'sister organizations' to the Red Front Fighters' League, which the KPD founded in 1925, also demonstrated in uniform dress.[32] On the whole, however, women appear to have had greater misgivings than men about this trend toward uniformity and militarization. The increasing violence of political confrontations in the later phase of the Weimar Republic apparently discouraged them in increasing numbers from participating in 'general' events organized by the labor movement. Social democratic women's organizations reacted to this development by organizing women-only meetings, both indoor public assemblies and open-air rallies, for the first time. These were intended to protect women from the violent confrontations with political opponents which had become common.[33]

The image of political participation offered by proletarian demonstration culture reflects gender relations in the Weimar labor movement. In theory, both the SPD and the KPD supported women's equal economic, social and political rights. In practice, however, women did not enjoy equality in any of the labor organizations. The male majority's attitude to the so-called 'Woman Question' was characterized by a 'modernized version of proletarian antifeminism'.[34] Women's policy and women's agitation interested the male majority in the Weimar labor movement primarily from three standpoints: the necessity to win women as voters; as supporters of men's economic social and political struggle; and as dutiful housewives, devoted mothers and socialist educators, who assured the reproduction of the working class and workers' movement.[35] 'Women's problems', the contemporary term used to describe the structural issues standing in the way of female emancipation, were thus taken up not for women's own sake but only when they were thought to have significant consequences for male workers. Accordingly, the suggested remedies were seldom immediately and primarily aimed at improving women's situation. Labor organizations only supported women's interests where they seemed conducive to the reproduction of the working-class family and the development of the movement. In practice, women were only accorded those rights which male interests deemed unavoidable.

In most working-class organizations, women exercised little influence on the form or content of politics. This was particularly true for the labor parties. Nowhere was women's representation in party office commensurate to their proportion of membership. The composition of delegates at party conferences, the highest resolution-making, bodies, for example, clearly demonstrated the power relations between men and women in the party. On average, women comprised only 13% of delegates at SPD national party conferences and the figure was similar in other higher party offices. Most male members and functionaries could not conceive of a woman as first or second chairman on even the lowest level of the party bureaucracy. Only when women were doing so-called 'spadework'—leafletting, door-to-door recruitment, and collecting membership dues or donations—did male comrades welcome women's work for the party.

The hierarchical sexual division of labor in the workers' movement served to magnify discrimination against women. Social and educational work in the broad sense were seen as women's 'natural' spheres of activity. At the beginning of the Weimar Republic, the SPD even cemented this political division of labor with a new gender-specific concept of emancipation.[36] Positing women's 'equal worth' but 'natural difference', it sought to broaden systematically women's specific cultural influence'.[37] Women's task was to balance the 'all-male politics of reason' with a politics 'imbued with understanding feeling'.[38] As 'born nurturers and protectors of human life' women were destined to be interested in social policy and welfare work as well as the education of both children and adults. Here they could best exercise their 'feminine cultural contribution'.[39] This emancipation strategy, which had much in common with the concept of 'organized motherhood'[40] propagated by the moderate wing of the middle-class women's movement since the 1890s, rested on a dichotomous notion of gender. Women were mainly viewed from the standpoint of their biological sex, while men were described in terms of their cultural and social capabilities and activities.

This 'gender-specific emancipation strategy'[41] was intended as a corrective to an outdated socialist theory of emancipation. The leaders of the SPD women's organization believed that with equal political rights a central precondition for women's emancipation had been achieved. Economic and social equality could, they thought, be won through parliamentary means. To be sure, they still saw the 'Woman Question' and the 'Social Question' as inseparable. The old principle that the 'full emancipation of the female sex' could only be realized by a socialist revolution, however, was no longer deemed valid, just as employment outside the home was no longer regarded as a necessary precondition for women's individual and social emancipation. The 'socialist theory of emancipation' had already come under increasing fire in the SPD in the Wilhelmine period, but it was not until the Weimar Republic, when the labor movement splintered and the SPD became a reformist party supporting the government, that an official revision became necessary and possible. The KPD, whose policies toward women continued to be determined by the old socialist concept of emancipation, officially rejected the 'gender-specific emancipation strategy'. In practice, however, a similar political division of labor existed in the communist workers' movement.

The consensus on men's and women's 'natural' and hence 'appropriate' tasks in economy, society and politics crossed party boundaries. Most women members of both working-class parties supported a gender-hierarchical division of labor in politics resting on a dichotomous notion of gender they shared with broad segments of the Weimar population. This political division of labor also corresponded to the working and living conditions of the mass of women party members, which led them to view household and family as the center of their lives. Their approach to social action, like that of most working-class women, accordingly tended to be oriented towards everyday life and their actions largely spontaneous, conducted outside organizational structures.[42]

The female social network of family, friends and neighbors represented working-class women's most important form of everyday self-help. This network helped women face problems of hunger and poverty, of physical and mental distress, supported them in caring for children, the ill and the elderly, and also provided advice on birth control. This form of female solidarity at once decisively expanded women's sphere of action and limited it with strongly milieu-specific norms and a high degree of social control.[43]

During the early years of the Weimar Republic, protest forms[44] also took their cue from structures and methods of action already present in working-class social networks, and women responded to food shortages and inflationary prices with demonstrations against hunger, 'market riots' and looting. Such subsistence-oriented street protests, described collectively as 'food riots' and largely dominated by working-class women, occurred in almost all large German cities between 1920 and 1923.[45] Many of the participants had probably already experienced this form of protest during World War I, when for the first time in many years shortages of basic goods were so severe that food riots broke out.[46]

Subsistence-oriented protests had a much longer tradition than organized street demonstrations.[47] Women had always been the main participants in these actions since the shops and marketplaces where most subsistence unrest took place were their central public arena as well as the most important centers of consumption, where housewives made most of their daily food purchases. Every shortage or price rise had an immediate effect on women's housekeeping, since it was their duty to stretch a small and fluctuating income to meet the needs of all household members. Women were particularly sensitive to food shortages and inflated prices and they could express their outrage over abuses directly in shops or marketplaces. Here a large group of women could gather quickly, loudly expressing their anger and dissatisfaction. Expecting local government to ensure adequate provisions and 'fair prices', they frequently addressed their demands to the municipal authorities as well as to traders and suppliers. Spontaneous market and street demonstrations publicly underlined their demands. Conflicts could escalate rapidly if their demands were not met. In such cases women did not hesitate to use force. They threatened traders, overturned market stalls, destroyed fittings and looted shops.

The attitude the Weimar labor movement adopted toward these forms of women's protest was everywhere the same: it tried to keep the actions under control and prevent the outbreak of further 'unrest'. Autonomous actions in the working-class milieu—actions outside and independent of the labor movement, actions organized by women—had no place in the political concepts of the SPD, USPD or KPD. They rejected such actions as 'unpolitical' and 'harmful' and claimed that 'riots' were provoked by reactionary spies'. They urged workers not to let themselves be seduced into rash actions by 'hired lackeys' and to see to it that their wives and children 'stayed home'.[48] At the same time the labor parties, in concert with the free trade unions, sought to discipline autonomous protests through organized actions such as the price control commissions they established in many cities.

This form of protest all but disappeared once the currency and the supply of basic goods were stabilized and only a few such actions occurred during the Depression years.[49] With the decline of subsistence-oriented street protest, a form of social action that had offered women a relatively large autonomous sphere of action disappeared from the German scene. This development went hand-in-hand with a transformation in the Weimar labor movement's political culture and in political behavior in the working-class milieu. The establishment of parliamentary democracy increasingly channelled political action into the formal structures of male-dominated parties, trade unions and parliaments. The initial hopes that working-class women had placed in political equality after the November Revolution soon gave way to disappointment. More and more women withdrew in resignation from any form of political activity. This withdrawal was more marked among women than among their male class comrades, whose disappointment in the crisis-ridden development of the Weimar Republic was more likely to express itself through political radicalization.

Women's average electoral participation sank from 82% in the National Assembly elections of January 1919, only 0:1% lower than men's, to only 62% in the Reichstag election of May 1924, while men's participation fell far less, to 74%. Women did make more use of their voting rights in the elections that followed, but their participation continued to lag significantly behind men's until the end of the Weimar Republic. At the Reichstag election of September 1930, in which an extraordinarily high percentage of the electorate participated, 78% of eligible women voted, but 84% of eligible men. Gender-specific electoral participation probably followed a similar trend in Hamburg as elsewhere in the country.[50]

The level of women's organization in trade unions and political parties, which had risen significantly during and after the November Revolution, also fell in the early 1920s. Female membership in the free trade unions, which reached its Weimar apex in 1920 with 1,710,761 nationally, had declined, with fluctuations, to 617,968 in 1931. In the same period the proportion of women fell from 22% to 14% of total members. In the SPD the number of women members declined from 207,007 to 130,000 between 1920 and 1923 and the proportion of women fell from 18% to 10%. In the years that followed the party managed to recoup its membership losses, however. In 1931 the SPD had 228,000 female members representing 22% of the total, the highest figure it achieved during the Weimar Republic. Developments in Hamburg were similar. Here the number of women organized in the free trade unions declined from 61,871 in 1920 to 28,940 in 1929, a fall in their representation from 23% to 14%. Female membership in the SPD declined from 16,332 to 9,621 between 1920 and 1924, or from 21% to 20% of total membership. By 1929 their numbers rose again to 12,858, and women made up 26% of party members.[51]

Even women's strike participation, which because of methodological problems with strike statistics is very difficult to determine, appears to have declined dramatically in the years immediately following the war. In the early years of the Weimar Republic the willingness to strike reached hitherto unknown proportions all over Germany. In the greater Hamburg area, for example, the number of strikers rose steadily between 1919 and 1923, from 23,464 to 116,036. The proportion of women among strikers, however, declined from 35% to 5%. It remained extremely low throughout the Weimar Republic in comparison to women's participation in the labor force, which was 30% in the mid-1920s. Only in 1927, when employees of all the large Hamburg textile factories, who were 63% female, walked out, did the percentage of female strikers (30%) even approach the level of 1919.[52]

Most working-class women were not only not interested in participating in political activities organized by unions, parties and parliaments but also lacked the time and energy. Even politically engaged male workers were extremely reluctant to take on housework and childcare in order to allow their female relatives to participate in politics. Despite their double or triple burden of employment, home and family, however, more working-class women were willing to organize politically, at least in the early years of the Weimar Republic, than had been before the war. The experiences of the First World War and the November Revolution had apparently had a politicizing effect. Thus women's representation in the free trade unions rose from a national average of 10% in 1914 to 22% in 1919 and in the SPD from 16% to 20%. In the Hamburg free trade unions it rose even more sharply in the same period, from 9% to 24%, and in the SPD from 17% to 24%.[53]

Working-class women, particularly the housewives and mothers who represented the majority of SPD and KPD members, organized primarily out of family-oriented motivations, seeking a better present and future for their children. The focus of their engagement mirrored the reasons for their political activities: they were particularly concerned with all issues affecting household and family in the broadest sense, and were active in organizations which addressed these problems. Alongside the SPD and KPD women's organizations, these included the proletarian welfare organizations Worker's Welfare (Arbeiterwohlfahrt) and International Workers' Aid (Internationale Arbeiterhilfe), the children's organizations Friends of Children (Kinderfreunde) and Young Spartacus (Jungspartakus), the consumer cooperatives and the sexual reform leagues. For working-class women, engagement in these areas was at once political work and self-help. The common forms of activity—women's evenings with a lecture and discussion, craft evenings, sewing circles, soup kitchens, children's holiday games and hikes, self-help courses on the theory and practice of birth control—continued their everyday forms of action in the women's social network, allowing them to use their specific qualifications as housewives and mothers. As in the everyday context of the women's social network, where party membership was of little importance, working-class women's organized self-help also extended beyond party boundaries, although only among the rank and file.

This (self-)relegation to 'female' areas of politics had an ambivalent effect. On the one hand, it gave working-class women a satisfying and meaningful sphere of social activism without having to compete with men. On the other hand, in practice it restricted not only their political sphere of action but also their political influence. In the long run the (self-) relegation to 'specifically female' tasks also strengthened traditional gender roles and thus fostered discrimination against women. The gender-specific division of labor in politics, which increased in all political camps after women achieved 'equal citizenship', favored a gender-hierarchical structuring of the political arena in society as a whole. Both sexes operated in very separate, hierarchically ordered spheres of political action, with women on the margins and men at the center of political power. The male monopoly over politics thus remained essentially unchallenged by parliamentary democracy.

* * *

The analysis of gender-specific demonstration and protest behavior in the working-class milieu during the Weimar Republic shows that the differences between men's and women's forms of social action resulted largely from men's and women's everyday experiences. The fact that the urban spaces through which both sexes moved, as well as the ways in which they appropriated space, diverged in broad segments of everyday life, and the fact that male and female public self-presentations were perceived and evaluated differently, served to magnify the differences.

Social action by working-class women traditionally took up the problems and structures of women's everyday life in the household and family. This held true for both the old forms of subsistence-oriented protest and the new forms of women's action within the labor movement. Unlike these newer forms, though, the older forms had still given relatively broad scope to women's autonomous actions. The 'modernization' of protest behavior was also a 'disciplining', directing social protest more and more into the orderly structures of the labor movement. In the process, the space for autonomous women's protest around everyday problems disappeared. This tendency increased after women achieved 'equal citizenship'. Their sphere of social action became increasingly restricted to trade unions, parties and parliaments.

At the same time, the concrete space available for women's social actions narrowed. The main site of subsistence-oriented protest, the marketplace, had been a central element of women's public arena, to be sure, but at the same time it belonged to the male public sphere of streets and squares and was thus open. The 'modernization' of women's social action meant its increasing restriction to an indoor women's public. It was not until the end of the Weimar Republic that the 'female segment' of the body politic expanded its demonstration and protest behavior by organizing women's street demonstrations, in a bid for broader and deeper political influence in a male-dominated society. This radicalization resulted, above all, from women's disappointment over continuing discrimination despite formal 'political equality'. More and more women within the parties came to recognize that by limiting themselves to a 'female sector' of the political arena, to 'female forms' of political action in a broader political system shaped by men, they had perpetuated and reinforced both their own powerlessness and the restrictions placed upon them. Nowhere did this become clearer than in the years that followed the collapse of the Weimar Republic.

Notes

This article is based on research for my *Frauenalltag und Männerpolitik. Alltagsleben und gesellschaftliches Handeln von Arbeiterfrauen in der Weimarer Republik* (J. H. W. Dietz, Bonn, 1990). A different German version of the article was published as 'Frauenprotest und Männerdemonstrationen. Zum geschlechts-spezifischen Aktionsverhalten im großstädtischen Arbeitermilieu der Weimarer Republik', in *Massenmedium Straße. Zur Kulturgeschichte der Demonstration*, ed. Bernd-Jürgen Warneken (Frankfurt/New York, 1991), pp. 202–225. I am grateful to Pamela Selwyn for translating the article into English. I also wish to thank Anja Baumhoff, Karin Hausen, Jan Lambertz and Lyndal Roper for their stimulating comments and criticism.

1 On gender-specific voting behavior in the Weimar Republic, see Helen L. Boak, 'Women in Weimar Germany. The "Frauenfrage" and the Female Vote', in *Social Change and Political Development in Weimar Germany*, ed. Richard Bessel and E. J. Feuchtwanger (London, 1981), pp. 155–173; idem., '"Our Last Hope". Women's Votes for Hitler—A Reappraisal', in *German Studies Review*, 12 (Fall 1989), pp. 289–310; Brian Peterson, 'The Politics of Working-class Women in the Weimar Republic', *Central European History*, 10 (1977), pp. 87–111.

2 See Richard J. Evans, 'Women's suffrage and the left', in *Comrades and Sisters. Feminism, Socialism, and Pacifism in Europe 1870–1945* (Sussex/New York, 1987), pp. 66–92; idem., *The Feminist Movement in Germany 1894–1933* (London, 1976), pp. 71–108.

3 Cited in 'Die erste Parlamentsrede einer Frau in Deutschland', *Die Gleichheit*, 12 (14 March 1919).

4 On women during the Weimar Republic see, among others, Helen L. Boak, 'The Status of Women in the Weimar Republic' (University of Manchester, PhD, 1982); Renate Bridenthal, et al. (eds) *When Biology Became Destiny. Women in Weimar and Nazi Germany* (New York, 1984); Renate Bridenthal and Claudia Koonz, 'Beyond kinder, küche, kirche. Weimar women in politics and work', in *Becoming Visible. Women in European History*, ed. Renate Bridenthal, et al., 2nd edn (New York, 1987), pp. 33–65; Ute Frevert, *Women in German History. From Bourgeois Emancipation to Sexual Liberation* (Oxford, 1989), pp. 168–204; Hagemann, *Frauenalltag*.

5 I define as 'social action' all efforts and actions in private and public spaces which aim to transform individual and social conditions.

6 James M. Diehl, *Paramilitary Politics in Weimar Germany* (Bloomington/London, 1977), pp. 3–23.

7 George L. Mosse, *Fallen Soldiers. Reshaping the Memory of the World Wars* (New York/Oxford, 1990), pp. 159–191.

8   Aside from Germany, one can observe similar tendencies particularly in its ally Austria. See Gerhard Botz, *Gewalt in der Politik. Attentate, Zusammenstöße, Putschversuche, Unruhen in Österreich 1918–1933* (München, 1976).

9   See Mosse, *Soldiers*, pp. 159–91.

10 See Marie Jahoda, Paul F. Lazarsfeld and Hans Zeisel, *Die Arbeitslosen von Marienthal. Ein soziographischer Versuch über die Wirkungen langandauernder Arbeitslosigkeit* (Leipzig,1933; repr., Frankfurt, 1980).

11 See Frevert, *Women*, pp. 168–204.

12 See Diehl, *Politics*, pp. 23–198; Eve Rosenhaft, *Beating the Fascists? The German Communists and Political Violence 1929–33* (Cambridge, 1983); Anthony McElligott, 'Street politics in Hamburg, 1932–3', *History Workshop*, 16 (1983), pp. 83–90.

13 See Jürgen Falter, Thomas Lindenberger and Siegfried Schumann, *Wahlen und Abstimmungen in der Weimarer Republik. Materialien zum Wahlverhalten 1919–1933* (Munich, 1986).

14 See Klaus v. See, 'Politische Männerbund-Ideologie von der wilhelminischen Zeit bis zum Nationalsozialismus', in *Männerbande-Männerbunde. Zur Rolle des Mannes im Kulturvergleich;* ed. Gisela Völger and Karin Welck (Cologne, 1990), vol. I, pp. 93–102.

15 See Diehl, *Politics*, pp. 96–198 and pp. 293–296.

16 Following Tilly, I define 'collective action' as 'joint action in pursuit of common ends' or, in a more recent formulation, 'people banding together on their shared grievances, hopes and interests.' Charles Tilly, *From Mobilization to Revolution* (Englewood Cliffs, 1978), p. 84; idem., *The Contentious French* (Cambridge, 1986), p. 3.

17 See Falter, *Wahlen*, p. 94; on the history of the workers' movement in Hamburg see Ulrich Beuche, *et al.* (eds), *'Wir sind die Kraft'. Arbeiterbewegung in Hamburg von den Anfängen bis 1945* (Hamburg, 1988).

18 See W. L Guttsman, *Workers' Culture in Weimar Germany. Between Tradition and Commitment* (New York/Oxford/Munich, 1990), pp. 238–245.

19 See Hagemann, *Frauenalltag*, pp. 566–573; Bauche, *Arbeiterbewegung*, pp. 233–270.

20 See Renate Wurms, *Wir wollen Freiheit, Frieden, Recht. Der Internationale Frauentag. Zur Geschichte des 8. März* (Frankfurt, 1980).

21 See, among others, Atina Grossmann, 'The New Woman, the New Family, and the Rationalization of Sexuality. The Sex Reform Movement in Germany, 1928 to 1933 (Abortion, Birth Control, Sterilization)' (Rutgers University, PhD, 1984); idem., 'Abortion and economic crisis. The 1931 campaign against Paragraph 218', in Bridenthal, *Women*, pp: 66–85; Hagemann, *Frauenalltag*, pp. 197–203 and pp. 268–305; idem. (ed.) *Eine Frauensache. Alltagsleben und Geburtenpolitik 1919–1933* (Pfaffenweiler, 1990); Cornelie Usborne, *The Politics of the Body in Weimar Germany. Women's Reproductive Rights and Duties* (London, 1992).

22 See Gottfried Korff, 'Rote Fahnen und geballte Faust. Zur Symbolik der Arbeiterbewegung in der Weimarer Republik', in *Transformationen der Arbeiterkultur*, ed. Peter Assion (Marburg, 1976), pp. 86–107.

23 See James S. Roberts 'Wirtshaus und Politik in der deutschen Arbeiterbewegung', in *Sozialgeschichte der Freizeit. Untersuchungen zum Wandel der Alltagskultur in Deutschland*, ed. Gerhard Huck (Wuppertal, 1980), pp. 23–139; Eve Rosenhaft, 'Working-class life and working-class politics. Communists, Nazis and the state in the battle for the streets, Berlin 1928–32', in Bessel, *Change*, pp. 207–240; McElligott, *Politics*.

24 See Lynn Abrams, 'From Control to Commercialization. The Triumph of Mass Entertainment in Germany 1900–25?', in *German History*, 8 (1990), pp. 278–293; Hagemann, *Frauenalltag*; Detlev J. K. Peukert, *Jugend zwischen Krieg und Krise. Lebenswelten von Arbeiterjungen in der Weimarer Republik* (Köln, 1987), pp. 189–244.

25 Aus der Arbeit des Frauenaktionsausschusses, in *Hamburger Echo*, 25 March 1928.

26 Marie Juchacz, in *Protokoll über die Verhandlungen des Parteitages der SPD* (Pr.Pt.SPD), held in Berlin 1924 (repr., Glashütten, 1974), pp. 226–227.

27 See Johanna Piiper, *Die Frauenpolitik der KPD in Hamburg 1928 bis 1933* (Köln, 1988), pp. 53–6.

28 See Hagemann, *Frauenalltag*; pp. 583–600.

29 See Diehl, *Politics*, pp. 244–258 and 295–296; Bauche, *Arbeiterbewegung*, p. 187 and p. 247.

30 See Detlev J. K. Peukert, 'The lost generation. Youth unemployment at the end of the Weimar Republic', in *The German Unemployed. Experiences and Consequences of Mass Unemployment from the Weimar Republic to the Third Reich*, ed. Richard J. Evans and Dick Geary (London/Sydney, 1987), pp. 172–193.

31 Martina Naujoks, *Mädchen in der Arbeiterjugendbewegung in der Weimarer Republik* (Hamburg, 1984), p. 170; Hagemann, *Frauenalltag*, p. 568; Bauche, *Arbeiterbewegung*, p. 261; see also Peter Stachura, *The German Youth Movement 1900–1945. An Interpretative and Documentary History* (London, 1981), pp. 94ff.

32 Karen Hagemann and Jan Kolossa, *Gleiche Rechte—Gleiche Pflichten? Ein Bilder-Lese-Buch zu Frauenalltag und Frauenbewegung in Hamburg* (Hamburg, 1990), p. 156.

33 See Hagemann, *Frauenalltag*, p. 546.

34 Ulla Knapp, *Frauenarbeit in Deutschland*, vol. II: *Hausarbeit und geschlechtsspezifischer Arbeitsmarkt im deutschen Industrialisierungsprozeß* (München, 1984), p. 490.

35 See also in the following: Hagemann, *Frauenalltag*; idem., '"Equal but not the same". The social democratic women's movement in the Weimar Republic', in *Bernstein to Brandt. A Short History of German Social Democracy*, ed. Roger Fletcher (London, 1987), pp. 133–143; Silvia Kontos, *Die Partei kämpft wie ein Mann. Frauenpolitik der KPD in der Weimarer Republik* (Frankfurt, 1979); Renate Pore, *A Conflict of Interest. Women in German Social Democracy 1919–1933* (Westport, 1981).

36 See Hagemann, *Frauenalltag*, pp. 528–551.

37 Marie Juchacz, *Praktische Winke für die sozialdemokratische Frauenbewegung*, ed. Executive Committee of the SPD (Berlin, 1920), p. 4.

38 Clara Bohm-Schuch, in *Pr.Pt.SPD* held in Kassel 1920 (repr., Glashütten, 1973), p. 62.

39 Sophie Schöfer, in *Pr.Pt.SPD* held in Görlitz 1921 (repr., Glashütten 1973), p. 11.

40 Irene Stoehr, '"Organisierte Mütterlichkeit". Zur Politik der deutschen Frauenbewegung um 1900', in *Frauen suchen ihre Geschichte. Historische Studien zum 19. und 20. Jahrhundert*, ed. Karin Hausen (Munich, 1983), pp. 221–249.

41 See also: Richard J. Evans, *Sozialdemokratie und Frauenemanzipation im deutschen Kaiserreich* (Berlin, Bonn, 1979); Heinz Niggemann, *Emanzipation zwischen Sozialismus and Feminismus. Die sozialdemokratische Frauenbewegung im Kaiserreich* (Wuppertal, 1981); Jean Helen Quataert, *Reluctant Feminists in German Social Democracy 1885–1917* (Princeton, 1979); Jacqueline Strain, 'Feminism and Political Radicalism in the German Social Democratic Movement 1890–1914' (University of California, Berkeley, PhD, 1964); Werner Thönnessen, *The Emancipation of Women. The Rise and Decline of the Women's Movement in German Social Democracy 1863–1933* (London, 1973).

42 See also in the following: Hagemann, *Frauenalltag*; for Spain: Temma Kaplan, 'Female consciousness and collective action. The case of Barcelona, 1910–1918', *Signs*, 7 (1982), pp. 545–66.

43 See for England: Ellen Ross, 'Women's neighbourhood sharing in London before World War One', *History Workshop Journal*, 15 (1983), pp. 4–27.

44 Following Tarrow I define 'protest' as a 'disruptive collective action that is aimed at institutions, elites, authorities, or other groups on behalf of the goals or the actions of those they claim to represent'. Sidney Tarrow, *Struggle, Politics, and Reform. Collective Action, Social Movements, and Cycles of Protest* 2nd edn (Ithaca, N.Y. 1991), pp. 11–12.

45 See also in the following: Ute and Eckhard Brockhaus, 'Die Lebensmittelunruhen in Bremen Ende Juni 1920', in *Autonomie*, no. 2 (1976), pp. 24–39; Kontos, *Partei*, pp. 208–32; Anthony McElligott, 'Petty complaints, plunder and police in Altona, 1817–1920. Towards an interpretation of community and conflict', in Assion, *Transformationen*, pp. 111–125; Robert

Scholz, 'Ein unruhiges Jahrzehnt. Lebensmittelunruhen, Massenstreiks und Arbeitslosenkrawalle in Berlin 1914–1923', in *Pöbelexzesse und Volkstumulte in Berlin. Zur Sozialgeschichte der Straße*, ed. Manfred Gailus (Berlin, 1984), pp. 79–123; for the USA: Dana Frank, 'Housewives, socialists, and the politics of food. The 1917 New York cost-of-living, protests', *Feminist Studies*, 11 (1985), pp. 255–285.

46 See Volker Ullrich, *Kriegsalltag. Hamburg im Ersten Weltkrieg* (Cologne, 1982), pp. 51–72.

47 See also: John Bohstedt, 'Gender, household and community politics. Women in English riots 1790–1810', *Past and Present*, no. 120 (August 1988), pp. 88–112; Natalie Zemon Davis, *Society and Culture in Early Modern France* (Stanford, 1975); Carola Lipp (ed.) *Schimpfende-Weiber und patriotische Jungfrauen. Frauen im Vormärz und in der Revolution 1848/49* (Moos, Baden-Baden, 1986); E. P. Thompson, 'The Moral Economy of the English Crowd in the Eighteenth Century', *Past and Present*, no. 50 (Feb. 1971), pp. 76–136.

48 Die Teuerungsunruhen, *Hamburger Echo*, 28 June 1920; Arbeiter laßt Euch nicht provozieren!, *Hamburger Volkszeitung*, 29 June 1920.

49 See Matthias Schartel; 'Ein Kampf ums nackte Überleben. Volkstumulte und Pöbelexzesse als Ausdruck des Aufbegehrens in der Spätphase der Weimarer Republik', in Gailus, *Pöbelexzesse*, pp. 125–167.

50 Separate counts of male and female votes were by no means made for every election, so that the statistics on gender-specific voting behavior are very incomplete. Hagemann, *Frauenalltag*, pp. 552–561.

51 Hagemann, *Frauenalltag*, pp. 468–483 and pp. 562–570. No gender-differentiated yearly membership figures exist for the KPD.

52 Hagemann, *Frauenalltag*, p. 26 and pp. 483–490. Figures on strike behavior in Germany during the Weimar Republic are not broken down by gender.

53 Hagemann, *Frauenalltag*, p. 469 and p. 571.

Chapter 28

Penny Summerfield

■   " 'THEY DIDN'T WANT WOMEN BACK IN THAT JOB!':
THE SECOND WORLD WAR AND THE CONSTRUCTION OF
GENDERED WORK HISTORIES", *Labour History Review*, 63, 1,
Spring, 1998, pp. 83–104

THE SECOND WORLD WAR caused considerable shifts in the employment of
women, at least on a temporary basis, but the effects of these changes on women's
personal work histories have not been systematically studied.[2] This is partly because of the
character of most research into the history of work, which typically uses large scale samples
and standard questionnaires in order to produce comparable and generalisable conclusions
about trends in employment patterns in relation to changes in the industrial structure. It is
widely acknowledged that individual work histories, particularly those of women, are
extremely complex.[3] The detailed accounts given by female interviewees, describing in full
their meandering and fractured work histories, have to be simplified and schematised to
make them suitable for quantitative analysis.[4] In such analyses wartime employment may
figure as just another twist in an already over-complicated story to be smoothed away in
order to create a general picture. Oral history research, on the other hand, is designed to
tap, in depth, an individual's experiences of a working life, and is conducive to the
presentation of a relatively small number of cases in all their complexity.

This article is based on an oral history project conducted by myself and two researchers
in the early 1990s, and concerns the relationship of the Second World War to women's
work histories. The forty-two women interviewed were drawn primarily from over 300
responses to a short piece in a popular women's magazine, *Woman's Weekly*, asking women
with memories of wartime training and work to contact us. We interviewed ten women in
each of the four categories produced by constructing a matrix of manual and non-manual,
military and civilian types of war work. The women were drawn from all over Britain, and
in addition we interviewed two Black women who had migrated from the Caribbean to
work in the women's auxiliaries to the Armed Forces. The median date of birth of the
forty-two women was 1922, so most were young adults during the war. Using a series of
prompts together with some direct questions, we invited the women to talk in as much
depth as they wanted about their working lives in general, and their experiences of work
during the war in particular. Most of the interviews lasted for at least ninety minutes and
they rendered a set of very detailed personal work histories.[5]

The status of such personal testimony in relation to history has, however, been questioned by some feminist scholars. In particular, post-structuralists such as Joan Scott and Judith Butler detect an essentialist naivety in the focus of women's history on uncovering women's 'experience' in order to understand the working of gender in the past.[6] Post-structuralists emphasise instead the ways in which gender identities and relations are constructed by discourse. This tension between historical approaches which prioritise discourse, and those which prefer an emphasis on experience, requires further discussion. Out of the seeming impasse between the two approaches came the particular method of interpreting oral history accounts used here.

The debate about experience and discourse has particular relevance to the Second World War. Marxist feminists of the 1970s and early 1980s broadly believed that paid work (even when it was exploitative and alienated) and socialised forms of domestic work, were the route away from the patriarchal oppression of women in the home, and towards women's participation in their own right in class struggle. Frustration, incomprehension and the use of such concepts as 'collusion' and 'false consciousness' therefore greeted the absence of evidence that women wanted these things, even at times when they were apparently within their reach. One such time was thought to be the end of the Second World War. Where was the evidence of women taking mass militant action to retain both wartime work and the socialised forms of domestic labour (such as nurseries) which helped break down their identification with unpaid work in the home? Denise Riley, in her book *War in the Nursery* (1983), confessed to having expected to find such evidence. She posed the question of whether there was a historical method which could be used to discover 'why and how people produce particular formulations about what they want'.[7] Her answer was negative. Contemporary wartime surveys were unreliable because they used loaded questions which produced ambiguous answers. Riley did not trust personal accounts, such as autobiographies or oral histories, either.

> The trouble with the attempt to lay bare the red heart of truth beneath the discolourations and encrustations of thirty-odd years on, is that it assumes a clear space out of which voices can speak – as if, that is, ascertaining 'consciousness' stopped at scraping off history. That is not, of course, to discredit what people say as such, or to imply that considering the expression of wants is pointless. The difficulty is that needs and wants are never pure and undetermined in such a way that they could be fully revealed, to shine out with an absolute clarity, by stripping away a patina of historical postscripts and rewritings.[8]

This formulation led Riley to her later theoretical position, informed by post-structuralism, on women's history. She argued against the use of 'women' as a category, the record of whose experiences might reveal women's consciousness and agency. Instead the object of study should be the discourses within which gender has been constructed by powerful sources, and which defined women and men and controlled the parameters of possibility in their lives. 'To speak about the individual temporality of being a woman is really to speak about movements between the many temporalities of a designation. And as this designation alters historically, so do these myriad possibilities assume different shapes.'[9]

But why should the historian dismiss women from history, individually and collectively, in favour of public discourses produced by powerful institutions? Is it not arrogant to proclaim that individuals' interpretations of their personal histories are worthless because they have been determined by larger ideological forces?[10] There is surely a relationship between discourse and experience. Rather than seeing as a problem what Riley called the 'discolourations and encrustations' that affect memory over time, and being halted by the impossibility of removing the 'patina of historical postscripts and rewritings', why not accept them as part of personal history and seek to identify and understand them? This indeed is the approach taken by scholars who make a special study of subjectivity (although it has been applied to auto/biography rather than oral history). They seek to unite understandings of discourse with understandings of individual consciousness. For example, the Australian cultural sociologist Bronwyn Davies theorised the relationship between women and subjectivity in the following way:

> When I talk about the experience of being 'a woman', I refer to the experience of being assigned to the category female, of being discursively, interactively and structurally positioned as such, and of taking up as one's own those discourses through which one is constituted as female.[11]

Furthermore the outcome is unstable and contradictory:

> The discourses through which the subject position 'woman' is constituted are multiple and contradictory. In striving to successfully constitute herself within her allocated gender category each woman takes on the desires made relevant within those contradictory discourses. She is however never able to achieve unequivocal success at being a woman.[12]

These are helpful formulations of the relationship between subjectivity and discourse, which can usefully be applied to accounts gathered through oral history. When collecting the work histories on which this paper is based, through oral interviews, the three researchers were not only asking women to remember such things as the jobs they took at different points in their lives and why they left them, but also inviting recall of the understandings of a woman's relationship to paid work occasioned by the discourses in which they were represented at the time, and have been since. We need not fall into the trap identified by Riley of assuming that there ever could be 'a clear space out of which voices can speak' nor do we have to concern ourselves exclusively with discourse. Rather, we can ask how discursive constructions of the relationship between women and work during the lives of those interviewed were used by women to understand and explain their work histories. In short we can find out what, culturally, has gone into the making of gendered work histories.

There were four major formulations of the relationship between women and work over the period of the interviewees' lives, from the First World War to the 1990s. One powerful representation emanating from sources directly located in concerns about employment, was of the marginality of women to paid work. Another, coming from sources concerned with education and training, emphasised opportunity in women's working lives. Both of these representations span the entire period of my interviewees' lives. A third, intersecting with both of them, emerged in the 1950s when it was given authoritative expression by Alva Myrdal and Viola Klein. It conceptualised women's relationship to paid work and to the home as the 'dual role'. Since the 1970s, popular feminist analysis of women's inter-related oppression at work and at home, has challenged all three and yet in various ways it has drawn on them all.

The discourse of marginality

In the period from the 1920s to the 1970s women were persistently represented as marginal to the workforce. Repeated government reports and policy documents, as well as more popular writing, declared that 'women's work' did not demand skill or strength, it required the exercise of 'feminine' characteristics such as dexterity or maternal qualities, and it was located in woman-employing niches in industries, services or professions. The explanation of the association between women and such work lay in what were usually referred to as 'natural and conventional' factors. These were the temporary place of paid work in a woman's life cycle, and its unimportance to a woman relative to domestic concerns, because of her prior orientation to marriage and motherhood, which biologically, socially and morally dominated her life. Married women who worked were depicted as engaged in irksome toil. They were 'doing double employment, paid and unpaid: running a home in the hours left over from factory or domestic or casual employment'.[13]

The demand for labour in the Second World War caused a temporary shift in representations of women and work. Wartime recruitment campaigns emphasised that women's patriotic duty was to release men from industry, and from military offices and workshops, to fight. Emphasis was placed (for example by the Ministries of Labour and of Information) on women, including married women, moving into the so-called 'essential industries', those seen as vital to the production of the means to fight the war. The popular construction of women's war work was that it was men's work, temporarily taken on by women to help in an emergency.[14]

However, this wartime disruption was not accompanied by any striking alteration to the marginalising discourse of women and work, whatever the source – including those from which one might have expected a challenge. For example in 1945 Gertrude Williams, an economics lecturer at Bedford College, London University, published a book called *Women and Work* in a series aimed to stimulate popular discussion of important issues, but her arguments were remarkably conventional. She made four main points. Firstly, the war had changed women's working lives temporarily, but most women would want to withdraw 'when the men were free to take up their usual occupations again'.[15] Secondly she represented the sexual division of labour as the natural order: women did different work from men because they were made differently and because their primary bio-social function was to bear and rear children within marriage.[16] Thirdly, women necessarily occupied a marginal position to the labour market, working in undemanding jobs while unmarried because they would withdraw or work only temporarily or on a part-time basis, after marriage. Training, the acquisition of skill, and the assumption of managerial responsibilities were irrelevant to them: 'Marriage and the expectation of marriage, are the dominant factors in moulding the pattern of a woman's life'.[17]

Pronatalism imbued Williams' account of wife and motherhood. Married women might want or have to work, but it was not good for their children. Echoing the medical and psychological orthodoxy of the 1940s she asserted that 'as a substitute for the home the nursery school leaves ... much to be desired'.[18] Exceptions were swept away. A 'small handful of professional women' worked from interest rather than necessity, but even their effectiveness was undermined by marriage and children: 'There are of course exceptions, but the majority of women find that, despite domestic assistance in housework, their capacities can no longer be so narrowly canalised when they have children and that much of the vitality and strength that a man can put into his work necessarily goes into the unique relationship with the growing family'. This text was positioned beneath an appealing picture of two babies in high chairs endearingly chewing rusks.[19]

Williams' fourth point represented a new development which still marginalised women. While she was adamant that married women should stay at home and rear children while young, Williams also argued that confinement in the home was bad psychologically and in terms of citizenship, for older women. When a woman's children were grown up, and no longer draining her creative energy, she should work part-time. This was the only way to prevent the home becoming a 'prolific breeding-ground of neuresthenic unhappiness'.[20] Herein lay the postwar future for women: as mothers they must devote themselves to their children, but as older women they should return to paid work in unskilled jobs with little responsibility. Views such as Williams' of the nature of women's present and future prospects, were part of a powerful set of messages popularly communicated from many media at the end of the war and thereafter.[21]

The discourse of opportunity

There was however an alternative story to this strong representation of the marginality of women to paid work. Throughout the period 1920 to 1970 educational and training literature, and popular versions of it, referred to the opportunities at work available to girls and women as a result of investment in education. Contrary to the monolithic story of the marginality of women to paid work, in which all were marginalised whatever their social class or education, in this account the female sector of employment was highly differentiated and offered a range of opportunities.

Official literature concerning the education of girls in the interwar period was, as Felicity Hunt has argued, two-faced. On the one hand it advocated the domestic norm, for which domestic training was surely the logical preparation. On the other there were several reasons to stress the benefits of either a more intellectual education or specific types of vocational training, even if girls had 'deficits' caused by biology and social function, which meant that identical provision to that of boys would never be appropriate.[22] These benefits included both the cultural advantages of educated wives and mothers and the idea of education and training for girls as an insurance against spinsterhood, widowhood or a husband's failure to fulfil the role of breadwinner.

Such views were popularised in magazines targetted at schoolgirls and young women workers in the period 1920–1950. Penny Tinkler has analysed the magazines' involvement in the construction of a range of opportunities for girls from different social classes. Papers aimed at elementary schoolgirls omitted the future working lives of their readers, which were assumed to lie in the routine unskilled 'meantime' jobs central to the discourse of marginality, and unlikely to offer girls an 'attractive identity'.[23] But magazines addressed to working-class girls at work offered them guidance on how to survive in an uncertain labour market, and communicated a strong work ethic, praising girls for training and taking work seriously. They addressed girls who might have taken vocational courses at school or after, in skilled trades such as millinery, upholstery, dressmaking, office work and catering. Nevertheless, Tinkler writes that papers of this type, like *Pam's Paper*, tended to portray work, particularly through fiction, 'as a means to find a husband or develop skills useful to the potential wife and mother' at which point in their lives it was assumed that they would become marginal to the labour market.[24]

In contrast magazines for secondary schoolgirls, such as *Miss Modern* and *Girls' Own Paper*, constructed a picture of the relationship between education and employment for middle-class, or upwardly mobile, girls. This was consistent with the approach of the headmistresses of girls' secondary schools from the 1920s to the 1970s. Tinkler sums up their philosophy as one in which marriage remained a legitimate goal, but greater emphasis was placed on the idea that 'women should develop their skills and utilise these and their talents in the service of the community'.[25] Rather than suggesting that girls might undertake a variety of jobs while awaiting marriage, in the same way as the magazines for working-class girls, these papers presented their secondary schoolgirl readers with a range of possible careers, in professional and skilled occupations. Above all, teaching was consistently presented to girls as an opportunity for a satisfying and worthwhile career.[26] Tinkler argues that this advocacy of women's work opportunities was qualified in two ways. Firstly, the magazines emphasised the compatibility of the careers they advocated with femininity. Secondly, at least one magazine (*Miss Modern*) consistently cautioned girls against revelling too much in the independence that training and work would give them. The price they would pay would be unmarriageability and loneliness.[27]

The idea that women's biological and social functions must be fulfilled within the social institution of marriage was not challenged in the discourse of opportunity. Indeed, this notion of femininity shaped the female sector of employment delineated within the discourse, in that the careers within this sector were identified with a caring and maternal role and were mostly subject to the marriage bar.[28] But women's universal marital destiny was seen as a postponed moment of closure for the girl seeking education and training, rather than as removing opportunity from work at the start. At the end of the Second World War, in some renderings of this version of women and careers, marriage was not seen as a necessary closure at all. In tension with the pronatalism which (as we have seen) was central to the account of marginality in 1945, were the dictates of new ways of conceptualising the postwar labour market. The official removal of the marriage bar from teaching and the civil service in 1944 and 1946, for example, prepared for a postwar labour shortage in some professions and industries, which would necessitate a continuation of the wartime participation of married women. A contributor to *Girls' Own Paper* in November 1945 placed this approach within the discourse of opportunity in a way that challenged the discourse of marginality.

> I would like to see almost every girl married. Even more fervently I would like to see her equipped for a career. Both offer different ways of enriching and fulfilling her individuality. Marriage and motherhood can, of course, be a whole-time job, and the most selfless career in the world. But motherhood should be regarded as a temporary one, for the sake of the children as well as the parents.[29]

The discourse of the 'dual role'

The idea that married women, including mothers of children, could and should participate in the labour market gained momentum in the 1950s but was controversial, because it was in tension with the account of women's bio-social priorities in the discourse of marginality. The book published by Alva Myrdal and Viola Klein in 1956, *Women's Two Roles*, endeavoured to settle the controversy at the same time as telling a story of women's paid work in terms of opportunity. The discourse of the dual role, to which they contributed, accepted the married woman worker as someone who had a permanent place in the labour market. Her 'dual role' was not the irksome and ill-advised toil envisaged in the discourse of marginality. In the modern context of domestic technology and companionate marriage women could undertake paid work and run homes, without damage to either, and could thereby make a significant contribution to society. These arguments were based on the idea of the importance of both domesticity and participation in paid work for women. Myrdal and Klein had in mind women who would choose and train for 'careers' or 'vocations' rather than those who would take unskilled jobs. They advised women to choose 'occupations which they will be able to continue after marriage or resume after an interval of a few years' and this meant the types of work defined within the discourse of opportunity as specially suitable for women.[30] Above all jobs like teaching were advocated, because they were 'so easy to combine with marriage and motherhood that, metaphorically speaking, a woman can practise them almost with one hand at the cradle'.[31]

The feminist challenge

In the 1970s, more radical challenges to the assumption that women's social functions as wives and mothers must dominate their lives emanated from the women's liberation movement.[32] The idea of equal opportunities took on new meanings. The exclusion of women from areas of work deemed unsuitable for them was challenged and the barriers to women's chances of promotion (the glass ceiling) were explored and their causes debated. The dual role was seen as intolerable, reconceptualised as the double burden, as it was in the discourse of marginality. But rather than being seen as an unfortunate by-product of flouting the natural order, it was depicted as a consequence of dual oppression. The origins of the double burden in male exploitation within the family and its implications for the labour market were questioned and challenged. The concepts of masculinity that were inexplicit within and yet central to the discourse of women's marginality to work, were exposed and questioned. Why should men not take responsibility for housework and child care? Why should it be assumed that women had to do so, and that this debarred them from more skilled and responsible types of work? They had done them in the war, hadn't they?

Women interviewed in the 1990s about their wartime selves and the 'choices' they made about training, work, marriage and childbearing in the 1940s, remembered events which took place in the context of the discourses outlined above, and within a timeframe when the challenges to these discourses launched by the feminist understandings of women and work of the 1970s and 1980s were widely available (kept alive by resistance to them, and by the ensuing publicity). It is now time to explore the relationship to these discourses of women's own accounts of their place in the labour market. I have chosen, as a focus, my interviewees' end-of-war work histories, because for most this was a moment of disruption and transition which drew from them both description and interpretation of the place of paid work in their lives as a whole. In accounts of the end of the war, the story of wartime work intersected with longer work histories revealing a variety of ways in which individuals drew on discursive constructions of women's work, so as to render their lives coherent.

Regretful return to marginality

The first types of account to consider are the work histories told as stories of marginalisation from which war work figured as an escape. In these accounts bitter regret was expressed that the end of the war signalled a return to marginality after a period in which the narrator felt that she had done socially valued as well as personally satisfying work.

An account of this sort came from Felicity Snow, a wartime air mechanic in the WAAFs. Her story of a limited education as the daughter of hardworking parents who ran a café, of leaving school at fourteen and being channelled by parents and teachers into office work, speaks of the marginal woman worker, with no special interest in her low status occupation or in training or education which would improve her position in the labour market. The war transformed her work history, however, which she now told in heroic terms. Felicity volunteered as soon as she was old enough and sought a mechanical, military, man's job. Giving up this hard but, to her, deeply satisfying skilled job, which she described as 'very open and free' at the end of the war, was the cause of regret: 'You were demobbed and you came out back into civilian life and found it very hard to start with, because you missed the comradeship, and you missed the freedom'.[33] She applied with a WAAF friend to join the Police Force and the friend was not accepted, so the two of them found jobs as telephonists at General Post Office. Felicity thus drifted back into clerical work. She vividly reconstructed the loss of freedom in her new job describing how she resented being confined to a chair in the General Post Office, 'plugged into the telephone operator's position'. She described making herself adjust out of a robust sense of 'reality' although this did not remove her sense of loss: 'there was no openings for flight mechanics: not in that way, not in those days, 1946 ... they didn't want women back in that job'.[34]

Reflecting on the end-of-war removal of a valued opportunity, Felicity commented on what she might have done had she had her life over again 'These days I probably would have gone into engineering as a career, but in those days there was nothing whatever in that way, no openings for women in those days at all'.[35] These comments, based on (mis)perceptions of the changed possibilities for women in the labour market by the early 1990s, constitute tokens of earnest placed within her testimony to give it the conviction she wanted it to carry. They call upon the discourse of feminine opportunity, though as the projection of a fantasy. Engineering to this day has an uncertain status as suitable work for women in this discourse of opportunity.[36]

Felicity remembered her wartime work opportunity as a welcome interlude in a career which before and after the war followed a marginalised pattern. The wartime opportunity was impossible to retain because of the inevitable regendering of the labour market at the end of the war: 'they didn't want women back in that job'.[37] Among the forty-two women interviewed there were a number who constructed similar stories. Their accounts of satisfying war work and deep regrets about giving it up throw into sharp relief their constructions of otherwise marginal working lives.

Among those work histories with a similar figuration of meanings there was a subset in which it was not the end of the war in itself, but pregnancy that ended the woman's war work. As we have seen, the construction of women as marginal to the work force was given a special gloss by the pronatalism of the end of the war. Pronatalism reinstated motherhood, undertaken exclusively and not combined with paid work, as a highly socially approved role. But in the case of these accounts it was far from welcomed. Beryl Bramley, for example, told a pre-war work history of drifting into hairdressing after failing the exams for her preferred career of librarianship. The war offered her a new chance, and her account shifted gear as she outlined her progress within the new set of opportunities. She moved from rivetting in an aircraft factory to training and working as a member of the Aeronautical Inspection Directorate, and had more plans to make use of wartime opportunities by joining the Air Transport Auxiliary. But the account came to an abrupt end with a bitter story about giving up war work. It was 1944 and Beryl was about to leave her Aeronautical Inspection Directorate job at the Preston New Road components factory to train to be a pilot in the Air Transport Auxiliary:

> I was just going into that, and found out that I was pregnant. So after I'd been sick on the trains several times and wandered along the Promenade also being sick and utterly wretched, I went and told the chief inspector, and he said 'oh well never mind' he said, 'you go and have the baby' he said 'and then after six weeks your mother can have it and you can come back'. I said 'you don't know my mother!' I could just imagine my mother's face when I told her 'would you mind looking after this while I go back to work?' So that was the end of it, that's why I say it's rather boring because the rest of the war there was just – horrible really because I couldn't do anything obviously because I had the baby, and I must admit that I was always a bit resentful'.[38]

Beryl could not remember finding anything to salvage from the wreck of her plans in rearing a family. This form of feminine fulfilment was not satisfying to her; but she did not feel that she could defy the conventions surrounding motherhood for someone from her social milieu, in order to pursue her ambitions across the gender boundary. She focused on motherhood, rather than the removal of women from wartime men's work, as the barrier to her occupational progress. Such progress remained alive in her account as a foregone possibility: 'I sometimes think that I would have had a very rewarding career, if I hadn't had any children'.[39] She did return to paid work after the war, but it was subordinated to family. She described meandering in and out of the labour market, in a number of welfare and retailing jobs, never finding the satisfaction she had experienced in her war work.

Such accounts as Felicity's and Beryl's are the ones celebrated in popular feminist representations of women's participation in the war effort of the last twenty years, such as the American film *Rosie the Riveter* released in 1982.[40] This film told a story of women in the USA enthusiastically taking up war work across the gender boundary. They found that they were good at it and could earn high wages, and would have liked to have stayed in it, but come the end of the war they were dismissed and expected to 'return home' much against their will.

Welcome return to marginality

These were not, of course, the only types of account. There was an opposite version in which an understanding of the self as a marginalised woman worker was a comfortable identity, and found expression in a story about wanting to return to 'meantime' women's work, intrinsically unimportant and subordinate to the prospect of matrimony and motherhood. The end of the war, in these accounts, was represented as a let out, an end to a period of enforced war work, possibly in a masculine environment, which the woman had tolerated on sufferance. Demobilisation was both an opportunity to return to women's work, and above all a chance to fulfil feminine expectations by getting married and having a family. This interpretation of the meaning of the end of the war for women was the standard one in the 1940s, projected by a great deal of mid-1940s film, literature and (as we have seen) commentary.

The 'take up' of this discourse can be illustrated from the account of respondent Evelyn Mills, who remained in the same occupation, clerical work, throughout the war, but was required to move to 'essential work'. She told her complete work history in terms that were consistent with the model of the marginal woman worker. She spoke of disliking school, of leaving as soon as she could at the age of fourteen, and of taking up whatever paid work was available locally. After working in a laundry, she moved to a building contractor's office where she collected rents and did some book-keeping. She was called up by the State in 1942 and went to work reluctantly as a duplicator-operator at the Admiralty. She spoke with relief about obtaining a discharge from this job on grounds of ill health after two years, and returning to her old job at the builder's. Marriage was now a high priority for her. She married in 1946, and although she did not stop doing paid work, she constructed herself as now having a different relationship to the labour market. She took part-time and temporary jobs as a married woman, as well as, at times, working from home. Evelyn expressed the relationship between herself as a wife and as a worker in terms which are almost precisely those which Williams used: 'I didn't want a job with any responsibility, you know, like a wages clerk or a bookkeeper or anything like that. Once I was married. Those sort of jobs, if they're short of staff or if you've got a day's holiday, you've still got to make up and do your work, and I thought, I can't work in that way so much now I'm married, because you've got other ties'.[41]

Continuation in war work: marginality

The third type of account is of women who did continue with their 'masculine' work after the war. There were just two women for whom this was the case in the sample. One was an engineering draughtswoman and the other a bench fitter and gauge setter in an engineering works. While the draughtswoman told her wartime and immediate postwar work history as a story of the pursuit of opportunity and the experience of marginalisation (in which opportunities ceased on the birth of her first child in 1948), the bench fitter's narrative drew on the discourse of marginality. In fact Elizabeth Little's account could belong to a work history in which the wartime venture into the male sphere of work was no more than a brief interlude, undertaken reluctantly, in a life which otherwise conformed contentedly to the norms of feminine marginality, that is a combination of episodic women's work with prioritisation of the family. However the dynamics of gender in the workplace disrupted this narrative, without displacing the marginal place of paid work in her life. Before the war Elizabeth was a grocery shop assistant. Wartime call-up led to her training for work as a bench fitter then a gauge setter for Reyrolles, an engineering company in north-east England. Her job as a dilutee was classified as 'men's work' and her shop steward insisted that she should receive equal pay under the 'Extended Employment of Women Agreements', which also meant that she was made redundant at the end of the war.[42] Although she said 'I was sorry really when I finished there', Elizabeth was far from outraged by the fact that 'they didn't want women back in that job'. She spoke of quietly accepting it: 'you just took it in your stride, you knew it was going to happen sort of once the war finished, yes, and you expected just to go back to your normal work'.[43] In the event, however, she could not 'go back to her normal work' because she could not get a job as a grocery assistant. Instead she was sent by her family to help in an uncle's betting shop in London. Her career sounded very much like the meandering one of the marginalised woman worker.

However on her return to the North East in 1946, Elizabeth became a beneficiary of the gender restructuring of engineering, in which the sectors labelled women's work were expanding. One of the male toolmakers from Reyrolles sought her out and asked her to work with him at Reyrolles' Hebburn factory, in a store room. She fell in with this, and later moved into work similar to her wartime work in the gauge room, with a woman friend from the war. 'I knew what was going on in there, I quite liked it'.[44] Elizabeth thus re-entered her wartime firm and resumed a job similar to her war work, although she did not now receive equal pay with men as her job had been reclassified as women's work. Her return was not prompted by any enthusiasm on her part for the opportunities opened up by the war, nor was she seeking to pursue a job unusual for a woman.

On the contrary, she emphasised that the new work at Reyrolles was specially designed for women: 'the department that I was looking after the store for; that was all women'.[45] But she was resuming a work opportunity to which wartime conscription had introduced her, and for her, it was not the case that 'they didn't want women back in that job'. She maintained her career in engineering for five years (1947–1952), then it was fractured when her family sent her to look after a widowed cousin's children. She subsequently married the cousin. Elizabeth did not return to the gauge room, in spite of the fact that 'I just seemed to enjoy it all'.[46] Marriage and motherhood deflected her from her war-initiated career, although they did not end her participation in paid work. Her subsequent employment fitted around the family. In the 1960s she ran a pub with her husband and in the 1970s she worked once more in a grocer's shop. Elizabeth's account was of a life within which work was marginal to her central role in the family. She told a work history which was determined by family demands, intersected in wartime by those of the state and after the war by those of the men seeking to staff an industrial sector which had been reclassified in gender terms.

Pursuit of opportunity outside war work

The fourth type of account depicted the war as an interesting and not unwelcome interruption to a work history told in terms of opportunity. However the narrator did not expect or want to continue with war work afterwards. For her the disruption at the end of the war represented a chance to take a new career direction, or to improve upon an old one. The account of Nadia Beale is an example. Nadia, from British Honduras (now Belize), was in the process of qualifying as a teacher in 1943, when she patriotically signed up for the Auxiliary Territorial Service (ATS) in which she became a clerk. Although this act fractured a promising career, it ultimately paid off handsomely. Nadia's account as a whole was a story of achieved self-esteem, rather than the more troubled life review visible in other accounts, including that of the other Black woman in the sample. Its central theme was that Nadia was a 'coloured' colonial entering a welcoming and tolerant 'mother country' in which she could realise her childhood dreams. Nadia vividly reconstructed the excitement she felt about the 'big experience' of leaving the West Indies to join the war effort. She described enjoying life as a clerical worker in the ATS in Britain, while stressing what it did for her, in terms of expanding her horizons and providing a stepping stone to other things, rather than emphasising what she was doing for the war.[47] When she was demobilised in 1947 she obtained a place at St Hild's College, Durham to acquire a British teacher's certificate. She went back to British Honduras as a qualified teacher in 1949, but was struck by how small the country now seemed, culturally and in terms of professional opportunities, and became determined to leave again: 'I thought, mm, no way am I going to stay here'.[48] Her opportunity came through marriage. She told a romantic story of a relationship with a Welshman which developed from a single meeting when he was visiting the Caribbean with the Royal Navy in 1950. They corresponded for three years 'then he asked me if I might get married' and sent for her to join him in Ceylon, where he was posted.[49] They returned to Britain as a married couple in 1955.

Nadia cast her view of the relationship between paid work and marriage at this point in her life in terms of the widely legitimated feminine career fracture. Life as a married woman was preferable to life as a working wife: 'I wasn't going to work any more, he was going to look after me, you know, I thought no way now, I was, have finished with teaching, forget it'[50] But in the early 1960s, after the birth of their three children, her husband left the Navy, money was short and Nadia was ready for a change. Although she said she liked being a housewife, she also 'had itchy feet'. 'I began to move out, you know, from domesticity then'.[51] She was recruited to a local primary school suffering a shortage of teachers when it was discovered that she was qualified. Problems about the care of her underschool-age daughter were swept away. The school head suggested she should bring her to school with her half-time, and send her to a nursery for the other half of the day. Nadia had put her daughter's name on a nursery waiting list and went to see the nursery head when offered the job: 'she said well why didn't you tell me you were a teacher ... I would have taken her from then ... And I used to take her to the nursery on my way to school, because the nursery wasn't very far, and then my husband would pick her up at lunchtime for me if it was necessary, but I used to be able to walk down and bring her back with me to school. And that's why I came back into teaching'. It felt, said Nadia, 'like I had never left'.[52] She presented the dual role, in the context of a companionate marriage, as unproblematic. She described taking further training thereafter and pursuing a highly successful career; to which her husband adapted, rather than requiring Nadia to fit in with his career plans. Nadia became a primary school headteacher before her retirement in 1985.

Rejection of wartime opportunities

The last type of account discussed here is one in which work histories, including war work, were constructed as stories of opportunity rather than marginality. However in returning to her pre-war work or training the narrator described actually rejecting opportunities to continue with wartime occupations which were (in peacetime) unusual for women. While women like Felicity Snow and Beryl Bramley reconstructed pasts which, if lived over again, would have embraced a continuation of the kinds of work they had done in the war; these women had that chance and turned it down. One was offered a continuation of her job on a centre lathe in an engineering works; another was offered funding to go to university and train as a personnel manager by the company which had employed her during the war as a progress chaser; and a third was offered work on aircraft design and construction with a private company (de Havillands) after working as an aircraft rigger in the Women's Royal Naval Service. In these accounts it was not the case that 'they didn't want women back in that job' and yet all the narrators rejected offers, in spite of their confessed enthusiasm for the work during the war. The testimony in each account is fascinating, but just one will be discussed here, that of Wilma Harrison.

Wilma described her early work history in terms of opportunity and progress. She had trained enthusiastically at a trade school as an upholsteress and embroiderer before the war and worked for Eventide Bedding Company from 1937 to 1942. Her decision to return there at the end of the war involved her turning down an offer of continued employment from her wartime boss at a South London engineering firm. She rejected this invitation even though, after going into engineering cautiously, she took great pride and interest in the work of cutting and grinding metal to precision measurements and spoke of the trust her bosses had in her. Nevertheless, she described herself as 'a bit depressed' by the work at the end of the war. The ostensible reason was that she believed that people doing the same work for other companies were earning far more than her. Reading from some notes, she said 'I wanted out of there as quick as possible. Not that the work was not interesting, but low pay and long hours. I was released at the beginning of 1946'.[53] She presented her return to Eventide Bedding Company as 'a challenge', rather than as being consigned to marginality. She was given work on internally sprung mattresses, by a trusting boss who wanted her to find 'a quicker way of doing it'. Accomplishing this, she taught other workers her method, moved on to the cutting side of the business and became a chargehand.[54]

Wilma's story was of having a strong preference for work she regarded as feminine, but which still offered opportunities. However she interpolated into her post-war work history a startlingly romantic, if brief, vignette of her courtship. It was worthy of the kind of magazine construction of women's work as the path to attracting Mr Right. Wilma's future husband worked in a cardboard firm next door to Eventide. He 'used to go up and down in the lift and he used to see me cutting, and he fell in love with me in me white overall'.[55] They married in May 1947 and their daughter was born in January 1948.

Yet the reason Wilma gave for preferring the bedding to the engineering company did not seem totally satisfying to her. The fact that she read out the statement about leaving engineering from notes which she had made before the interview, the only point at which she did this, suggests that she was taking refuge in the authority of the written word to protect herself from challenging inquiry. Later Wilma struggled to construct an account of the relationship between paid work and marriage and motherhood, as if she was using the opportunity of the interview to try to work out her own feelings. She recalled her ambivalence about moving in and out of paid work as a wife and mother and emphasised the difficulties of managing the two roles. Rather than the equilibrium model of Myrdal and Klein, she evoked the double burden and the advantages of being supported by a man's wage, of the discourse of marginality. 'Women do put themselves – too much on themselves, make life much harder for themselves, than they need to ... I have had to go out to work, and I've had to keep a family, and I think, you know, you realise that when you can sit back, it's nice'.[56] She presented a view of the propriety of masculine precedence which was central to the discourse of marginality: 'I've always been of a mind that women should give way to the men. I think men do need work outside ... perhaps women do an' all ... I like to see men being the breadwinner myself'.[57] Enlarging on this she explained that she felt she could fulfil her role at home better when she was not going out to work. She could rest in the afternoon and be fresh when her daughters and husband came in 'you can listen to all their problems and things, it makes life much easier'.[58] And yet her uncertainties in respect of her assertion that men had a special need to go out to work ('perhaps women do an' all'), suggest that she was uncomfortable with the transition in the telling of her work history, from an account couched in the discourse of opportunity, to one of marginality. It was as if the latter did not completely suit the identity she wanted to construct in reviewing her life.

Conclusion

The discourses of women and work available from the 1920s to the 1990s offered the interviewees a number of models for the construction of work histories. In the middle of the 1940s, when women were experiencing 'demobilisation', these discourses were particularly contradictory. The expectation that paid work for women would be a marginal aspect of lives henceforth centred on the home, on marriage and on motherhood was central to demobilisation policy and to much of the rhetoric of post-war reconstruction. We have observed the ready 'take up' of this construction of contented marginality in some accounts, especially those of women who were relatively unenthusiastic recruits to war work. On the other hand, we have also noted the frustration with such an identity expressed by women who felt that the new types of work which the war opened up for them were thwarted at its end. In their accounts the reinstatement of the discourse of marginality contradicted the possibilities simultaneously expressed within the discourse of opportunity. Feminist discourse of the period since 1970, which included a critique of the removal of women from 'masculine' jobs in the post-war period, may have exacerbated the sense of missing out which these women expressed. Furthermore, the feminist interpretation presented women who actually had a chance to carry on with their 'masculine' war jobs in the second half of the 1940s but spurned it, with particular difficulties in composing coherent accounts of their work histories. In contrast, the discourse of opportunity provided an appropriate frame for accounts of the pursuit of careers within the conventionally 'feminine' sphere of employment. War work *per se* figured in such accounts as a temporary and readily relinquished diversion, while the changes and dislocations associated with the war enhanced the narrator's progress towards her desired career goals.

Social class did not determine a woman's take up of one or other of the discourses in which she could narrate the story of her working life. Domestic marginality and career opportunity were not neatly separated by social class. Domesticity was an approved identity for women from anywhere in the social spectrum. 'Opportunity' within a trade or profession was notionally available to any capable and hardworking woman, and was urged by educationalists as both the route to social mobility and the way to maintain middle-class social status. The idea of the dual role, and the contingent discourse of companionate marriage, were reference points for those who recalled their attempts to combine work and marriage in the post-war years. However the dual role was, as feminists of the 1970s pointed out, in practice close to the double burden. 'Women put too much on themselves' reflected Wilma Harrison. A rejection of the dual role in preference for domesticity alone meant, however, in terms of feminist discourse, an understanding of the self as the occupant of a subordinate position within an oppressive institution, hardly an identity conducive to self esteem.

The purpose of this oral history analysis has been to relate the meanings and feelings within which the work histories were framed to the discursive constructions of women's work popularly available during the narrators' lives. By identifying in this way what Riley called the 'discolourations and encrustations' of 'historical postscripts and rewritings', which she saw as contaminating the space from which women speak, and relating them to women's personal accounts, we can see how women made those discourses their own. The accounts become a window both on women's negotiations with discourse in endeavouring to give their lives coherence and meaning, and on the processes of women's active involvement in the gendered construction of work. By using an approach which does not regard work histories as revealing 'the red heart of truth' but nevertheless takes their content seriously, we can start to understand the interactions of discourse and subjectivity, the influences of culture on memory and the relationship between personal histories and public history.

Notes

1 This paper is based on material researched for my forthcoming book *Reconstructing Women's Wartime Lives, Discourse and Subjectivity in Oral Histories of the Second World War*. See in particular Chapter 6, 'Demobilisation and Discourses of Women's Work'.
2 On the effects of the Second World War on women's paid employment see P. Summerfield, *Women Workers in the Second World War, Production and Patriarchy in conflict*, 1989.
3 For example David Vincent argues that women's work histories in the first half of the twentieth century were concentrated in categories he labels 'meandering' (that is movement through numerous unconnected jobs with no apparent progression) and 'fractured' (that is career paths broken and not recovered, usually as a result of marriage). In contrast men's work histories were mostly in the 'gold watch' and 'migration' categories, of steady progression in work either for the same employer or for different employers but within the same trade or profession. See D. Vincent, 'Mobility bureaucracy and careers in twentieth-century Britain' in A. Miles and D. Vincent (eds), *Building European Society. Occupational Change and Social Mobility in Europe, 1840–1940*, Manchester, 1993, pp. 217–39. (On these career pathways specifically, see pp. 225–26.)
4 For example, Sylvia Walby used the work history method for a study of deindustrialisation in Lancashire women's lives in the period 1960–1980. This concluded that relatively few women experienced de-industrialisation personally, because of continuity in the sectors in which they worked, extending across breaks due to childbirth. This conclusion was the result of analysis focused on aggregate movements of women between industries and occupations over the period, based on a coding of the jobs women did, and whether childbirth was a reason for leaving. Walby commented that some of the 300 interviews lasted 'several hours' rendering information which could not be used in the analysis. S. Walby, 'Labour markets and industrial structures in women's working lives' in S. Dex (ed.), *Life and Work History Analyses: Qualitative and Quantitative Developments*, 1991, p. 300.
5 The interview project was resourced from an Economic and Social Research Council grant, R000 23 2048, 1990–1992, entitled 'Gender, Training and Employment 1939–1950, An Historical Analysis'. I am indebted to Nicole Crockett, Research Associate, and Hilary Arksey, Student Researcher, for their help in conducting the interviews. For a report of the findings of the project see P. Summerfield, 'The Patriarchal Discourse of Human Capital: training women for war work, 1939–45', *Journal of Gender Studies*, vol. 2, no. 2 (November 1993), pp. 189–205. Although only a few women requested anonymity when asked, they have all been given pseudonyms. For a discussion of oral history methodology, and the ethics of bestowing anonymity in particular, see P. Summerfield, *Reconstructing Women's Wartime Lives*, Chapter 1, 'Gender, Memory and the Second World War'.
6 See, for example, J. Scott, 'Experience' in J. Butler and J.W. Scott, *Feminists Theorize the Political*, 1992, pp. 22–40; J. Butler, *Gender Trouble: Feminism and the Subversion of Identity*, 1990.
7 D. Riley, *War in the Nursery: Theories of the Child and Mother*, 1983, p. 190.

8 Riley, *War in the Nursery*, p. 191.

9 D. Riley, *'Am I that name?' Feminism and the category 'women' in History*, 1988, p. 98.

10 Catherine Hall has posed this question powerfully: 'Do we really think about ourselves only as subjects interpolated in a discursive field? Is it not also vital to think about the ways in which individuals and groups are able to challenge meanings and establish new inflections which expand the terrain?' C. Hall, 'Politics, Post-structuralism and Feminist History', *Gender and History*, 3, 2, 1991, p. 210.

11 B. Davies, 'Women's Subjectivity and Feminist Stories' in C. Ellis and M.G. Flaherty, *Investigating Subjectivity. Research on Lived Experience*, 1992, p. 54.

12 Davies, 'Women's Subjectivity and Feminist Stories', p. 55.

13 M.A. Hamilton, *Women at Work: a Brief Introduction to Trade Unionism for Women*, 1941, p. 12. See also Parliamentary Papers, *Report of the War Cabinet Committee on Women in Industry*, Cmd 135, HMSO, 1919; Parliamentary Papers, Home Office, *A Study of the Factors which have operated in the past and those which are operating now to Determine the Distribution of Women in Industry*, Cmd 3508, HMSO, 1930; Parliamentary Papers 1930–1, xvii, *Royal Commission on Unemployment Insurance*, First Report, Cmd 3872; Pilgrim Trust, *Men without Work*, Cambridge, 1938.

14 See P. Summerfield, '"The girl that makes the thing that drills the hole that holds the spring …" Discourses of women and work in the Second World War' in C. Gledhill and G. Swanson (eds), *Nationalising Femininity: Culture, Sexuality and the British Cinema in World War II*, Manchester, 1995, pp. 35–52.

15 G. Williams, *Women and Work*, 1945, p. 11.

16 Williams, *Women and Work*, p. 12. 'Men have muscular strength' read the caption to one of the black and white photographs illustrating the book, and on the opposite page, '– but women have the deft touch'; over the page 'the man applies the skill' and '– the woman runs the machine'.

17 Williams, *Women and Work*, p. 19.

18 Williams, *Women and Work*, p. 104.

19 Williams, *Women and Work*, p. 118.

20 Williams, *Women and Work*, p. 127.

21 See, for example, Parliamentary Papers, 'Marriage Bar in the Civil Service', *Report* of the Civil Service National Whitley Council Committee, Cmd 6886, 1946; Parliamentary Papers, *Report* of the Royal Commission on Equal Pay, HMSO, 1946, Cmd 6937, especially para. 343 to 366; J. Newsom, *The Education of Girls*, 1948; Ministry of Education, *Half Our Future*, a Report of the Central Advisory Council for Education (England), HMSO, 1963.

22 F. Hunt, *Gender and Policy in English Education*, Brighton, 1991, pp. 138–44.

23 P. Tinkler, *Constructing Girlhood. Popular Magazines for Girls Growing Up in England*, 1995, p. 115.

24 Tinkler, *Constructing Girlhood*, p. 93.

25 Tinkler, *Constructing Girlhood*, p. 90.

26 On the construction of teaching as a particularly feminine career; see A. Oram, *Women Teachers and Feminist Politics 1900–39* (Manchester, Manchester University Press, 1996), especially pp. 15–23.

27 Tinkler, *Constructing Girlhood*, pp. 94–100.

28 On the marriage bar see for example A. Oram, 'Serving two masters? The introduction of a marriage bar in teaching in the 1920s' in London Feminist History Group (eds), *The Sexual Dynamics of History* (Pluto Press, 1983); M. Zimmeck, 'Strategies and stratagems for the employment of women in the British Civil Service, 1919–1939', *The Historical Journal*, vol. 27, no. 4 (1984), pp. 901–24; M. Zimmeck, 'Marry in Haste, Repent at Leisure: Women, Bureaucracy and the Post Office, 1870–1920', in M. Savage and A. Witz (eds), *Gender and Bureaucracy*, Oxford, 1992, pp. 65–93.

29 *Girls' Own Paper*, November 1945, pp. 6–7, quoted by Tinkler, *Constructing Girlhood*, p 114. Although, like Williams, this writer referred to views derived from post-war psychiatry of the

benefits to women's psychological health of working outside the home, she put a different gloss on them. Careers, rather than the unskilled routine jobs of Williams's version, were her objective. And she linked the personal fulfilment of 'every girl' (as well as the good of the children) with the dual pursuit of motherhood and a career.

30 A. Myrdal and V. Klein, *Women's Two Roles. Home and Work*, 1956, 1968 edition, p. 155.

31 Myrdal and Klein, *Women's Two Roles*, p. 157.

32 For this kind of writing see for example M. Wandor (ed.), *The Body Politic. Women's Liberation in Britain 1969–1972* (London, Stage One, 1972); S. Rowbotham, *Woman's Consciousness, Man's World* (Harmondsworth, Penguin, 1973); *Spare Rib, a Women's Liberation Magazine*, published from 1972 to 1992.

33 ESRC Project R000 23 2048, 'Gender; Training and Employment 1939–1950', Interview with Felicity Snow (112, 259). The figures in brackets refer to the text unit numbers added to the transcripts by the computer package (NUDIST) which we used to help index and sort the interviews by theme. Each paragraph of a transcript constituted a text unit, and the numbering system is an invaluable aid to data retrieval. Henceforth, when referring to interviews I shall cite only the name (pseudonym) of the interviewee and text unit number(s).

34 Felicity Snow (259, 263).

35 Felicity Snow (27).

36 See C. Cockburn, 'The gendering of jobs: workplace relations and reproduction of sex segregation' in S. Walby (ed.), *Gender Segregation at Work* (Milton Keynes, Open University Press, 1988); S. Heath, *'Preparation for Life'? Vocationalism and the Equal Opportunities Challenge* (Aldershot, Ashgate, 1997).

37 Felicity Snow (263).

38 Beryl Bramley (200).

39 Beryl Bramley (533).

40 *The Life and Times of Rosie the Riveter*, Clarity Educational Productions, Emeryville, California, 1982. Producer and Director, Connie Field. See P. Colman, Rosie the Riveter, *Women Working on the Home Front in World War II*, New York, 1995.

41 Evelyn Mills (292).

42 For details of these agreements see Summerfield, *Women Workers in the Second World War*, chapter 7.

43 Elizabeth Little (738, 790).

44 Elizabeth Little (744).

45 Elizabeth Little (839).

46 Elizabeth Little (718).

47 Nadia Beale (31, 33).

48 Nadia Beale (141).

49 Nadia Beale (151).

50 Nadia Beale (169),

51 Nadia Beale (221, 223).

52 Nadia Beale (175, 177),

53 Wilma Harrison (460).

54 Wilma Harrison (507).

55 Wilma Harrison (515).

56 Wilma Harrison (396).

57 Wilma Harrison (392, 396).

58 Wilma Harrison (396).

Chapter 29

Hsu-Ming Teo

■ 'THE CONTINUUM OF SEXUAL VIOLENCE IN OCCUPIED GERMANY, 1945–1949', *Women's History Review*, 5, 2, 1996, pp. 191–218

ABSTRACT This article explores male sexual violence against German women in Occupied Germany, 1945–49. Drawing upon the feminist sociological concept of a 'continuum of sexual violence', it argues that German women's experience of rape and prostitution must be seen in relation to other aspects of male sexual violence such as murder, verbal, visual and physical abuse, and sexual harassment. It seeks a historical explanation for this violence through an examination of twentieth-century Western hegemonic masculinity, arguing that National Socialist or Fascist masculinity is merely the extreme end of a right-wing, militaristic masculinity constructed around violence against and domination over women and perceived 'others' in society. Through the course of World War II this strand of masculinity became dominant and facilitated the continuation of 'war' against German women throughout the period of Occupation.

During the 1945 Battle for Berlin and in the immediate postwar period, approximately one in three Berlin women were raped by Allied troops – mostly from the Red Army – while 10,000 women in Berlin died from sexual assault.[1] Many women committed suicide after rape, some forced to do so by their fathers because of their 'dishonour',[2] while others were shot and killed by their husbands for consenting to sexual relations with Allied soldiers.[3] Many German women were verbally abused by German soldiers on the streets or in their homes for being 'Allied whores', many received threatening letters from German men, and in at least one extreme case, a woman had her head shaved by a returning POW for consorting with Allied troops.[4] Rather than facing the threat of multiple rapes by unknown soldiers each day, many women found themselves 'protectors' who supplied them with food and other basic necessities as well as luxury items in return for sex. Even after the threat of multiple rape was over, many women – both from the petit-bourgeoisie as well as the upper middleclass – continued this form of sexual relations, especially with US and British soldiers.[5] At the end of the war there were approximately 50,000 professional and semi-professional prostitutes in Berlin, but the number tripled by the end of 1946, and this did not include the huge, unquantifiable mass of amateur prostitutes and sex workers.[6] It is very clear that while the Second World War might have ended for European men on 8 May 1945, the war against German women continued long after through the period of Allied Occupation.

This article examines the war against German women in Occupied Germany, 1945–49, which took the form of rape, prostitution, murder, suicide, verbal, visual and physical abuses, and sexual harassment in the workplace and in public spaces. In the first section I address methodological concerns which affect my analysis: namely, theoretical frameworks drawn from feminist sociology which inform my account of German women's experiences of sexual violence. In particular, I explore the usefulness of the concept of a continuum of sexual violence. The next section deals with concrete examples of sexual violence while the third section examines the way in which the sociological concept of 'hegemonic masculinity' may help to explain the extent of this violence. In the concluding section I discuss briefly the relevance of my research for German history.

I

Undoubtedly one of the main difficulties in dealing with the subject of the rape and prostitution of women in Occupied Germany is the problem of how this topic should be analysed. Traditional historians separate rape and prostitution, perceiving the former as an act of sexual violence forced upon women, whereas prostitution is perceived as a choice – albeit a constrained one – deliberately made by women for "food and luxury items".[7] Feminist historians such as Ute Frevert and other social historians sympathetic to the plight of German women, such as Douglas Botting, also separate the categories of rape and prostitution. However, Frevert and Botting locate the cause of women's prostitution not in a desire for luxury items such as nylons and chocolates, but in dire socio-economic circumstances whereby they – and often their families – were on the brink of starvation.[8]

In my view there is overwhelming evidence to support Frevert's and Botting's position; nevertheless I do not believe that a historical analysis of German women's experiences during Occupation should treat rape and prostitution as separate categories. Recent feminist theorisation of male violence attempts to construct a framework of analysis which encompasses the various forms of male violence linked to continuing struggles by (mainly white) men to maintain their position as the dominant group over women (and other ethnic groups) in society.[9] Rather than separating categories of violence against women, contemporary feminist theories of male sexual violence connect all crimes against women, viewing them along a continuum, and parallels are made between the sexual abuse/exploitation of women and sexual harassment of women in the workplace. As Anne Edwards observes: "In both situations men are able to use their superior power position to treat women as objects, and primarily as sex objects, rather than as human beings".[10] While acknowledging that sexual violence is used as a means of control over women, contemporary feminist scholarship escapes accusations of ahistoricity and biological essentialism since male violence is recognised as being "a socially-produced and often socially-legitimated cultural phenomenon" rather than being the result of biological drives inherent in men.[11]

The concept of a continuum of sexual violence is useful for a study of German women's experiences in Zero Hour for the following reasons. Firstly, it can be used to conceptualise German women's sexual experiences, ranging from "consensual sex (equally desired by woman and man), to altruistic sex (women do it because they feel sorry for the man or guilty about saying no), to compliant sex (the consequences of not doing it are worse than the consequences of doing it), to rape".[12] The continuum of male sexual violence is also useful in examining the ways in which men interpret their own behaviour, ranging from those who acknowledge their sex act as rape and those who attempt to avoid viewing it as rape.[13] In Occupied Germany there were soldiers who tried to turn their acts of rape into prostitution on the part of women whereby, according to the notions of traditional historians, sexual relations are consensual. However, it is a mistake to assume that all sexual intercourse which is not defined as rape is therefore consensual. The boundary between rape and prostitution was often blurred because many women turned to prostitution to avoid rape. Furthermore, an exploration of women's alternatives to prostitution reveals that much of the type of work available to women during Occupation often involved systematic sexual harassment and the reduction of women's bodies to sexual objects to feed male fantasies. The notion of a continuum enables fluid movement between otherwise rigid categories of analysis. This model also allows the range of sexual violence to be extended to include forms of behaviour such as sexual harassment, which is often laughed off by men as 'jokes' or 'a bit of fun', but which women often find threatening.[14] It was only within a structure of male sexual violence that soldiers at the time could have made the frequently heard sexual proposition, 'May I offer you a little abuse?' and have perceived it as a very funny joke.[15]

It may be objected that such a model treats women as victims. Certainly the utility of the notion of a continuum of sexual violence also needs to be considered in relation to questions of agency and victimisation. Such issues have been particularly debated by feminist historians of Nazi Germany who have discussed the extent to which German women who lived through the Third Reich could be viewed as 'perpetrators' or 'victims' of Nazism, and who have insisted on the necessity for German women to confront their roles in the Nazi state; in the last few years this debate has focused especially on Claudia Koonz's *Mothers in the Fatherland: women, the family and Nazi politics*[16] and Gisela Bock's vituperative reaction to Koonz's analysis in *Geschichte und Gesellschaft*.[17] It is evident that German women were not merely victims but did exert agency in that they made attempts to resist or avoid rape, collectively overcame their trauma by mutual support, and utilised their relations with Allied men to ensure that they and their families survived. However, there is no doubt that they were also victims in a very real way, and that their agency was severely constrained during this period by the structures of Allied military occupation, increasing loss of economic independence, and the ever-present threat of male sexual violence. In such circumstances it is difficult to see how increased sexual activity among young women constitutes sexual emancipation, as Annemarie Tröger argues.[18] It is equally difficult to see how German women could have had the same freedom to exercise agency during Occupation as before Germany's defeat. Arguments for women's agency must never blur the fact that German women *were* victims of male sexual violence during World War II and the Occupation. To argue otherwise sets very problematic precedents for women of other countries (such as those in the former Yugoslavia during the last few years, especially in 1992–94) who experience male sexual violence in war.

Finally, some mention must be made about the nature of the sources upon which I have drawn. In the initial period after the mass rapes, women freely exchanged their own stories of rape and, in the process of doing so, collectively overcame the trauma and horror of their experiences.[19] After the first few months of occupation, rape stories became scarcer, probably for three major reasons. Firstly, women's concerns were directed towards physical survival in the context of the food, clothing, and coal shortages in the aftermath of defeat. Secondly,

German men and Allied soldiers had no wish to hear of German women's rape experiences. Thirdly, official sources are unsatisfactory because of the arbitrary nature with which rape was dealt with as a crime. In the Soviet zone, for example, accusations of rape were sometimes laughed off, and sometimes offenders were shot on the spot.[20] Official statistics of these rapes are therefore difficult to come by, although Atina Grossman managed to obtain the rough estimates quoted at the beginning of this paper by looking at affidavits of women seeking abortions because they had become pregnant through rape.[21]

By the early 1950s, however, German women's stories of Russian rape began to circulate again and were this time given a more positive reception by publishers in England and the USA. In the context of the Cold War, stories of Russian atrocities against German women made good propaganda. These stories began to appear not only in women's diaries and autobiographies but also in German and Allied men's texts, and by the 1960s Cornelius Ryan and Erich Kuby had begun collecting oral histories of German women's rape experiences.[22] These sources can be problematic because published accounts were deeply imbricated in Cold War politics from the start, constructing German women as victims of communist Russian violence, and enabling German women to view themselves as perpetual victims – first of National Socialism, then of the war, of mass Russian rape, and of defeat and the ensuing material shortages.[23] The 1970s and 1980s saw a considerable growth in published autobiographies of German women, and these made it clear that sexual violence was perpetrated not only by the Soviets but also by French, British, and American soldiers; rape and prostitution were constructed as part of women's general experience of war. These are the sources upon which I have drawn for this paper, and taken together they give a comprehensive picture of German women's experiences of Allied occupation.

II

Even before the Red Army crossed the border into East Prussia, discourses of male sexual violence against women were employed as propaganda to terrify the German civilian population and to incite greater sacrifice on the parts of both civilians and soldiers. As the Red Army fought its way across Eastern Europe in 1945 and approached eastern Germany, frightening stories of Soviet brutality, murder, looting and rape became commonplace.[24] Thus when the Soviets crossed the border into East Prussia hordes of panicking refugees streamed westwards. For those who remained the stories of Soviet violence were soon confirmed.

Renate Hoffman was the wife of a German Luftwaffe officer who was living at Greifswald Air Base near Peenemünde. When the, Soviets came in March 1945 she decided to head for Greifswald with a female friend and their children. When they passed a house on the way:

> Suddenly three Russian soldiers ... pointed their guns at us and forced us into the house. We realised right away that we had walked into a trap. And we knew what they had in store for us.
>
> We were separated. They put guns to our heads. Any attempt to defend ourselves meant certain death. The only thing you could do was to pretend you were a rock or dead. I don't want to talk about what happened next ...[25]

After raping her and her friend the three Soviet soldiers left the house and the women managed to make their way to Greifswald. To her knowledge four out of every 10 women in Greifswald had been raped, including women over 50 years old.[26]

Because the rape of German women initially occurred in conditions of battle, sexual relations and male sexual excitement came to be connected intimately with death and violence. As a well-known drill sergeant's ditty put it:

> This is my rifle, this is my gun
> This is for business, this is for fun.

However, the reasons why these men forced women to have sex at gun point go beyond simplistic explanations of sexual release after the tension of battle. Nancy Hartsock believes that to the extent that a society's image of sexual relations is governed by a dynamic of dominance/submission, other societal structures will also follow the same pattern. She identifies at least two possible modes of sexuality: hostility and domination versus intimacy and physical pleasure.[27] In Western culture sexuality has been socially constructed so that, "putting aside the obvious effects that result from direct stimulation of erotic bodily parts, it is hostility – the desire, overt or hidden, to harm another person – that generates sexual excitement".[28]

Sexual excitement in Western society has also been constructed on the fetishisation, dehumanisation and objectification of the sexual object, which is "stripped of its humanity; the focus is on breasts, buttocks, legs, and penises, not on faces".[29] This fetishisation and reduction of women to their female genitalia is obvious in the following account by Hans von Lehndorff, a senior surgeon in a Königsberg hospital. Königsberg fell to the Red Army on 9 April 1945. On entering the hospital Soviet soldiers immediately began looting the premises, destroying many valuable drugs and much equipment. Attempts to complain to Soviet officers were unavailing. Von Lehndorff wrote that to the Soviets, he was "only a hall stand with pockets, they see me only from the shoulders downward"[30], and his account makes it clear that far from stopping their men, Soviet officers condoned the rape of German women. The following acts of intercourse with nurses reinforced their dehumanisation and reduction to receptacles for penises:

> A couple of nurses who got in their way were seized and outraged from behind, and then released again, thoroughly dishevelled, before they realized what was happening. The older ones could hardly believe their senses, they went wandering aimlessly about the corridors. There was nowhere to hide, and fresh tormentors kept falling on them.[31]

Further evidence of the role that the fetishisation of women's genitalia played in male sexual violence is the fact that the age or physical condition of the victim apparently did not matter to Soviet soldiers. Von Lehndorff reported that "Eighty-year-old women were no safer than unconscious ones. (At one time a patient of mine with head injuries … had been raped over and over again without knowing anything about it)".[32] The women raped were not necessarily German either.

Although many stories of Soviet atrocities reached Berlin there was a tendency to view such rumours as Nazi propaganda, which to a certain extent they were.[33] Sometimes the behaviour of the Red Army on first arriving in a neighbourhood was unexceptionable, lulling women into a false sense of security.[34] Therefore, despite the ample warnings that

Berlin women had received in news broadcasts and from east German refugees, they were unprepared for the sexual assaults of the Red Army. Atina Grossmann places the occurrences of most of the rapes between 24 April and 5 May 1945, while Erich Kuby agrees that about 80% of all the rapes in Berlin occurred between 24 April and 3 May.[35]

The anonymous author of *A Woman in Berlin* (hereafter referred to as A.) recorded that in her sector of Berlin the rapes began on the evening of Friday 27 April. Because she understood Russian, A. was thrust into a conspicuous position as the interpreter/mediator between the Germans and the Soviets. She was given the task of asking a Soviet officer for protection – which he gave reluctantly – when two soldiers attempted to rape one of the women in the cellar where she and others from her apartment block were hiding:

> Several times I heard the expression: *'Ukas Stalina'* – by the order of Stalin. This order seems to mean that 'these things' must not happen. Needless to say they happen just the same, as the officer tries to convey to me with a shrug of his shoulders. One of the two reprimanded men contradicts. His face is distorted with anger: 'So what? What did the Germans do with our women? My own sister,' he yells, 'they …' And so on. I don't understand the words, but the meaning.[36]

This exchange demonstrates that vengeance was an excuse given by Soviet soldiers for the rapes. Women were to discover repeatedly that they were being punished for German men's crimes in the USSR. On 5 May A. visited Frau Lehrmann and Fräulein Behn, who were entertaining Russians. A 17 year-old Russian asked A. to translate "a story about how, in his native village, German soldiers had stabbed some children and seized others by their feet, smashing their skulls against a wall. Before translating this I ask him: 'Did you hear this or see it yourself?' He, grimly, to himself, 'Saw it myself – twice'".[37]

Frau Lehrmann could not believe that "our men" and "my husband" could do such things, but A. and others already considered their rapes as part of the 'bill'. In the water queues women were already saying, "Well, I don't suppose our men behaved much better over there".[38] In fact, A. told C. W. Ceram, who wrote the introduction to *A Woman in Berlin*: "None of the victims will be able to wear their suffering like a crown of thorns. I for one am convinced that what happened to me balanced an account".[39] Ceram admired her for her implacable sense of justice amidst the inhumanity of the Second World War and the occupation of Germany, but it was a justice in which German women were punished for the crimes of German men.

A.'s attitude was remarkable in light of the fact that although she often went out of her way to prevent the rape of other women, her 'cellar family' gave her no support at all. During the first evening when A. was raped, she screamed for help but all she heard was the cellar door closing "with a soft thud" as her 'cellar family' locked her outside with her two rapists.[40] The Soviet Commandant's response was to scoff at her. "That hasn't done you any harm. Our men are all healthy".[41]

In her diary A. also recorded what her friends had undergone between 27 April, when the Russians first entered her neighbourhood, and 8 May, when they left. A widow was raped twice: once by an adolescent boy and later by a Ukrainian who threatened A. and the widow's lodger, Herr Pauli, with violence unless the widow had sex with him. The janitor's daughter was raped by "two rowdy, dead-drunk Ivans". A distiller told A. how Soviet troops had depleted his alcohol supplies at his factory, then found him and two female employees hiding. The narrative was then taken over by his wife because, like so many other German men, the distiller left the room at this time, unable to continue with the account of rape:

'They queued up,' whispers his wife, while Elvira just sits there speechless. 'They waited for one another to finish' ... . She thinks there were at least twenty, but of this she isn't sure ... .

I stare at Elvira. Her swollen tongue hangs from her deathly pale face like a blue plum. 'Just let them see', says the distiller's wife. And without a word Elvira unbuttons her blouse, opens her chemise, and reveals breasts covered with bruises and the marks of teeth ... . At the memory of it I feel like retching again and again and can hardly write. We left her the rest of the vaseline. There's nothing one can say — and we didn't try. But she herself started talking. We could hardly understand a word, her lips are so swollen. 'I prayed, all the time,' she muttered. 'I prayed: Dear God, I thank You for making me drunk ...' For even before queuing up as well as after, the Ivans had forced liquor down the women's throat.[42]

Although Ruth Andreas-Friedrich was not herself raped due to the intervention of 'Andrik', a fellow 'Uncle Emil' resistance fighter and senior conductor of the Berlin Philharmonic Orchestra[43], she knew many women who had been raped. Her daughter's friend and classmate, Hannelore Thiele was raped consecutively by seven Soviets. Inge Zaun, who lived in Lein-Machnow, was raped "over and over again, sixty times". She explains:

'How can you defend yourself?' she says impassively, almost indifferently. 'When they pound at the door and fire their guns senselessly. Each night new ones, each night others. The first time when they took me and forced my father to watch, I thought I would die ... . Since their captain has taken me as his mistress, it is fortunately only one. He listens to me too and helps make sure they leave the girls her sisters alone.'[44]

Julianne Hartmann was 19 years old in 1945 and she was the first girl raped on her street when the Russians entered her neighbourhood on 14 April. A Russian forced her at gunpoint into one of her bedrooms in her house and raped her there. The only thing she had been told was 'Don't try to defend yourself', because her family and friends had already heard horror stories about the Red Army. The experience was especially terrifying for her because as "an upper middle-class child, I had never been told about the facts of life".[45]

After 3 May 1945 there were fewer rapes in Berlin. Most measures taken to prevent rapes were initiated by women.[46] In one case a woman doctor hid young girls in an air-raid shelter hospital which she pretended contained typhoid cases.[47] Women who hid in the upper storeys of big apartment blocks were generally safer because Soviet soldiers seldom ventured up the stairs of Berlin's 'skyscrapers'.[48] A.'s friend Gisela escaped by painting wrinkles on her face and covering her hair with a scarf. In A.'s neighbourhood young girls became scarcer after 30 April because "the hours at which Russians go on their hunt for women are now generally known" so the girls were locked into "safe" flats and hidden away.[49]

One of the worst consequences of the mass rapes in Berlin was suicide. To place suicide within the continuum of male violence is certainly problematic because many women undoubtedly chose of their own will to commit suicide. However, it cannot be denied that in many cases German men were partly responsible for the deaths of many women. The unpublished diary of 'Frau K.' records that on the night of 28 April 1945, "a couple was found dead in their beds. He had shot her before putting a bullet into himself". Upon burial, the sexton reported that "they were the seventeenth and eighteenth suicides since the place was first occupied".[50] Andreas Friedrich notes that after 6 May, when the Soviets entered her neighbourhood, German men were lamenting the rape of their daughters and wives:

Suicide is in the air ... .

'Honor lost, all lost', a bewildered father says and hands a rope to his daughter who has been raped twelve times. Obediently she goes and hangs herself from the nearest window sash.

'If you get raped nothing is left to you but death,' a teacher declares to a class of girls two days before the final collapse. More than half the students came to the anticipated conclusion, as expected of them, and drowned themselves and their lost honor in the nearest body of water. Honor lost, all lost. Poison or bullet, rope or knife. They are killing themselves by the hundreds.[51]

For the majority of women, however, survival was the main priority. Many opted to prostitute themselves in order to stay alive. The boundary between rape and prostitution in the immediate postwar period was extremely fluid, and the relation between the two can be better understood when viewed along a continuum of male sexual violence, where 'altruistic' sex, compliant sex, and possibly consensual sex shaded into each other, and into the very palpable threat of rape during the Occupation.

For A. there was no doubt that she was deliberately prostituting herself, but any sense of agency she might have experienced was countered by the fact that her only choices were either rape or prostitution, and she saw herself as a victim of "all men and their male desires".[52] She first entered into a regular sexual relationship with a Soviet captain in order to avoid multiple rapes by other Soviet soldiers. Anatole provided A. with food as well as protecting her. When he was transferred, she was given to a Soviet major. Her sense of 'agency' was further constrained by the fact that she was treated as a piece of property – merely a female body – to be handed on from one male officer to another. In her relationship with the major, A.'s situation changed not only to prostitution but also from what we might call 'compliant sex' to 'altruistic sex' (see the above definitions) since she also felt sorry for the disability he suffered as a result of the war. Although this relationship was complicated by her genuine liking and respect for him, and by the fact that she had turned to him for comfort at their first meeting, allowing herself to cry for the first time since the rapes, I have chosen not to categorise this as consensual sex since A. makes it perfectly clear that, given the choice, she would have preferred not to have sex with any man during that period of time.

German complicity in the continuum of sexual violence against women is demonstrated by the fact that the widow and Herr Pauli placed pressure on A. to continue in prostitution. After the major was transferred out of Berlin, Herr Pauli showed his antagonism towards A., grudging her the space she took up in the widow's apartment (her own had been bombed) and the food she was consuming, although much of it had been provided by the major in payment for her sexual services. His attitude towards A. changed when she met a potential 'client', Nikolai. Even the widow advised A. not to "let that one get away" on the pretence that they would at last have "an educated man from a good family, someone we can talk to!" A. was not deceived:

In her mind's eye the widow is already seeing the supplies rolling in; she's convinced that Nikolai has access to food stores, that he'll do something for me and indirectly for the three of us. I'm not so keen ... . I'm not in the mood for one more man, I still enjoy lying alone between clean sheets.[53]

A.'s acute awareness of her body as an object for barter was emphasised by the fact that as long as Nikolai appeared to be a potential customer, she was allowed to share the group's food without objections from Herr Pauli, but "since Nikolai ... dissolved into thin air and there's no new provider on the horizon, my stock has sunk very low".[54] Once A.'s sexual use as a woman was over, Herr Pauli forced the widow to evict A., although he knew that as a single, unemployed woman she would draw the 'Death Card' for food rations.

A. was atypical of most Berlin women because throughout her prostitution she was constantly aware of her degradation and humiliation. Unlike other women she did not seem to possess mechanisms – such as cloaking her activities in 'romance' – which helped her to cope with prostitution. It was necessary at the time and she benefited by it, nevertheless:

It goes against my nature, offends my self-respect, undermines my pride. What's more, it shatters me physically ... I'll get out of this 'profession' ... with the greatest relief as soon as I can provide for myself in a manner more pleasurable and more fitting to my pride.[55]

However, alternative work to prostitution was hard to come by, especially in the western zones. The situation in occupied Berlin was such that "Baronesses thought themselves lucky to get jobs as waitresses, company directors as lavatory assistants, colonels as gardeners or waiters".[56] Moreover, the jobs which single women could get often entailed some form of sexual exploitation or harassment – further aspects of the continuum of male sexual violence.

Marianne MacKinnon managed to get work as an interpreter, but she was viewed as a potential prostitute by the Allied officers who employed her. When Americans took over her office, the first question asked about her was: "Do you think she's an easy lay?"[57] When the Soviets moved into Tangermünde, the sexually aggressive behaviour of the officers made it clear that they expected to inherit Marianne's sexual services along with the office in which they worked.[58] When she worked as an English-speaking switchboard operator in an officers' leave centre, the English manager tried to coerce her into having sex with him. When she refused, her employment was terminated and "No reason for my dismissal was given".[59]

Other German women who were unskilled and who did not wish to engage in prostitution nevertheless found that the only jobs available to them again involved the degrading use of their bodies as sexual objects for the male gaze. Drawing on his experiences as a US officer in occupied Berlin, James McGovern described the limited work opportunities for middle-class German women in his novel *Fräulein*, where lack of alternative employment forced the heroine Erika to work as a mud-wrestler, striptease and nude dancer in the numerous nightclubs and cabaret-shows which sprang up in occupied Berlin.[60]

Considering that so many of the occupations available to German women in the immediate postwar period involved the fetishisation of their bodies in explicitly sexual terms anyway, the fact that many women chose to engage directly in prostitution is not surprising. Many women coped with prostitution and made it more palatable by dressing their sexual relations in an aura of romance, and many hoped to escape the conditions of defeated and occupied Germany through marriage to an American or British soldier.[61] Fiction from the Occupation period contains many references to German women's desire to reach the 'Golden West' through marriage.[62]

To what extent were some of these sexual relations consensual? Certainly in the first few weeks after Germany's defeat it is difficult to see how sexual relations could be termed consensual when the actuality or memory of mass rapes were ever-present. Later, as social relations stabilised, the possibility of consensual sex emerged, but not without its difficulties. On the one hand, within the framework of extreme inequality in power relations and the threat of rape during Occupation the notion of consensual sex is problematic, to say the least. Gender relations during the Occupation served to throw into glaring relief the power inequalities in heterosexual relations in 'normal' society. On the other hand, if consensual sex is simply defined as sexual relations 'equally desired by woman and man', then women *did* choose to enter into consensual sexual relations with Allied men based on mutual liking, need, desire, and the romance of escape. Can these women then be called prostitutes, and if so, how does the historian categorise these women – as professional, semi-professional, or amateur prostitutes? Allied Military Government (AMG) rules often defined non-AMG women as prostitutes if they were caught with Allied personnel, but it is virtually impossible to quantify these categories which shade into one another. Again I find the idea of a continuum useful here because it takes into account the complexities involved in any kind of sexual relation and allows for the notion that even an ongoing consensual sexual relation may sometimes have elements of altruistic and compliant sex, and conversely, what sometimes begins as altruistic sex may evolve into consensual sex.

One thing, however, was certain. Women who fraternised with Allied men were caught in a double bind. They were often the ones who most desperately needed the food and other essential supplies such as coal and clothing which could be gained by sex, but they were also the ones who most wanted to escape Germany through marriage to an Allied soldier. These women were least likely to succeed because the double standards of Western hegemonic masculinity still branded them as 'prostitutes' and therefore unfit for marriage, and many of the soldiers were married anyway. A married English private recalled his affair with an 18 year-old German girl:

> I felt a bit sick at times about the power I had over that girl. If I gave her a three-penny bar of chocolate she nearly went crazy. She was just like my slave. She darned my socks and mended things for me. There was no question of marriage. She knew that was not possible.[63]

III

Thus far, I have examined evidence of the continuum of male sexual violence from rape to compliant, altruistic and consensual sex, and sexual harassment in Occupied Germany. What I have not done is to analyse in detail *why* this outbreak of male sexual violence occurred in the aftermath of the Second World War. Male observers at the time, such as William Shirer, and traditional masculinist historians writing in the 1960s, such as John Gimbel, Ralph Willet, or Harold Zink, have never addressed this question, merely assuming that such behaviour is a regrettable but inevitable concomitance of war. Susan Brownmiller similarly offers an ahistorical explanation for the mass rapes:

> War provides men with the perfect psychologic backdrop to give vent to their contempt for women. The very maleness of the military – the brute power of weaponry exclusive to their hands, the spiritual bonding of men at arms, the manly discipline of orders given and orders obeyed, the simple logic of the hierarchical command – confirms for men what they have long suspected, that women are peripheral, irrelevant to the world that counts, passive spectators to the action in the centre ring.[64]

I find this radical feminist analysis of an innate male hatred for women unconvincing, but Brownmiller's observation is useful if we take the mental and emotional attitudes she describes to be specific to the dominant or hegemonic masculinity of postwar Europe. Only if we recognise the specific nature of this particular image of Western masculinity can we begin to understand the continuum of male sexual violence and its relation to other socio-economic and political structures in society.

Bob Connell observes that 'masculinity' is not a homogeneous phenomenon. In any society at a particular moment, there are different, competing forms of masculinity, some of which are hegemonic, others subordinated or marginalised.[65] Hegemonic masculinity is a particular model of masculinity which gains dominance in a particular society because the majority of men benefit from it, since "hegemonic masculinity is centrally connected with the institutionalisation of men's dominance over women".[66] This is the case even though the actual lives and identities of most men do not correspond to the image of hegemonic masculinity.

Hegemonic masculinity is continuously constructed against other forms of masculinities by the prevalent economic, political and gender relations in society.[67] Although aspects of the hegemonic image shift, Western culture has long associated hegemonic masculinity with the "murderous hero" – the aggressive male whose use of violence to achieve "good" goals is viewed positively.[68] Theodore Roszak points out that twentieth-century Western masculine culture glorifies violence and "toughness" in:

> the cult of the bullfight and prize ring, of battlefield heroics and barroom brawling and good red wine. At a more vulgar level, it flourishes in the sadistic fantasies of Mickey Spillane and Ian Fleming – but especially in myriad he-man pulps where endless fascination with the atrocities of war and Nazism prevails.[69]

Of course, the latter part of Roszak's observation applies to postwar Western culture. But when and how did this development in hegemonic masculinity occur? One of the sources of twentieth-century hegemonic masculinity is indubitably the legacy of European imperialism in the nineteenth century and European men's presumption of their right of sexual access to non-European and working-class women.[70] Another significant source stems from fascist masculinity of the 1920s and 1930s, described by Klaus Theweleit in *Male Fantasies*. Theweleit explores the images of masculinity glorified and propagated by the *Freikorps*, who viewed working-class women (virtually synonymous with 'communist' and 'promiscuous') as aggressive 'castrating' whores who must be violently destroyed before they emasculated men. The *Freikorps* were misogynistic; deeply hostile to and contemptuous of women who did not conform to the rigidly defined 'good woman' images of 'mother' and 'sister'.[71] This model was not only available to fascist men; it was and is a model consistently propagated by right-wing, military masculinity.

Jessica Benjamin points out that masculine identity can often only be achieved through differentiation, since those with whom men identify or to whom they relate do not provide adequate 'otherness' against which their individual selves can be defined. This is potentially problematic in masculine erotic relations because:

> In order to prove his own existence, the erotic master must dominate the other, and this must be the unwilling domination that physical violence expresses, in which the other, subject-to-become-object, is dragged, kicking and screaming, into domination. This is most often borne out heterosexually as the 'male-master', 'female-victim' system, within pornographic literature and materials.[72]

These patterns of masculine erotics are evident especially in war, where the structure of military life denies individual men affirmation of their personal identities (armies want 'soldiers', not individuals), while simultaneously; homosocial bondings in the military "operate largely by exclusion or permit great cruelty to those who lie outside the borders of the group".[73] In the case of Western society, a historically-specific strand of fascist or right-wing, military masculinity became hegemonic during the six years of the Second World War, and the onset of the Cold War at the end of the 1940s – with its attendant social angst and continual state of military awareness – merely strengthened its hegemonic position.

When we examine pulp fiction written by Western men during the Occupation and in the Cold War era, the similarities between twentieth-century 'heroes' and *Freikorps* 'heroes' become clear. Over the course of the twentieth-century, hegemonic masculinity has become fiercely heterosexual, associated with a violent response to perceived threat – whether this comes from women, other races, homosexuals, or any groups of the 'other' – and based, to a large extent, on (violent/sexual) power over women.

During and after the Second World War, there was a widespread belief among female literary writers that women were being victimised by men on their own side. Susan Gubar notes that throughout the 1940s many English and American women writers such as Dorothy Parker, Kay Boyle, and Carson McCullers wrote about:

> the vulnerability of war brides, women war workers, and female civilians who are threatened less by the enemy than by their so-called defenders, while Elizabeth Bowen composed several works about heroines who fear that ... '[t]he First War had opened a few doors but ... the Second slammed many of them shut again.'[74]

This belief was borne out in reality by the number of pornographic pictures of women warriors and war workers in barracks, the 'joking' male translation of WAAF (Woman's Auxiliary Air Force) as 'Women All Fuck', and by the number of dangerous 'practical jokes' played on WASP airplanes.[75] Clearly, male sexual violence was directed against women who had availed themselves of the limited opportunities achieved by first-wave feminism, thus making the public sphere a threatening place for women. On the other hand, women who remained in traditional docile roles which were non-threatening to men's position were rewarded with marriage – both in reality and in the pulp fiction of the time. The perpetuation of hegemonic masculinity was motivated by men's need to keep women out of the economic and political spheres, and to reassert separate spheres and domestic ideology, whereby women attended solely to their husbands' comfort at home. This is evident in Occupation novels by American GIs, such as Hans Habe's *Aftermath*, or in articles in American periodicals.

Victor Dallaire, a former correspondent of the US Army newspaper *The Stars and Stripes*, wrote an article for the *New York Times Magazine* in 1946, attacking American women.[76] According to Dallaire, it took only some WACs (Women's Army Corps) and a few days back in the USA to convince him of European women's superiority to American women. His idealised image of European femininity complemented the hegemonic masculinity in which he had a vested interest, whereas American women's assertiveness was clearly threatening to him:

> Some of us used to sit in a cabaret in the Rue Washington of Paris last summer and compare the French girls and the American WACs who visited the place. The American girls would insist on a loud and full share of the conversation with their escorts while the French girls would let the men do most of the talking, adding only a word or two now and then to show their interest. Or they would go into the appreciative peals of laughter at the right moment. The over-all impression we gathered was that the Americans looked on their boyfriends as competitors while the Parisiennes seemed to be there for the sole purpose of being pleasant to the men.[77]

Western hegemonic masculinity is characterised by domination over and competition against perceived 'others', including women. The Other could be tolerated as long as she remains in subjection, inferior and on the periphery of male spaces. However, even tentative steps towards equality provoked hostile masculine reactions and resentment against women as 'competitors'.

The language used by men – both Allied and German – during this time is extremely revealing of the aggressive ideal of masculinity and the chauvinistic attitudes towards women, and it explains how women's *bodies* were viewed as booty won in combat, the 'just' reward for men who had risked their own bodies in war. In fictional and non-fictional texts written by men during this period, linguistic references to men, specifically soldiers, are positive and emphasise qualities such as machismo, heroism, and glorified aggression – for example, Alexander Solzhenitsyn's use of the words "warrior" and "honest, openhearted soldiers" to describe three Soviet rapists.[78] However, linguistic references to women are generally derogatory, reducing them to the level of sexual objects who were the property of some man. Thus, in Solzhenitsyn's *Gulag Archipelago*, Polish women could be "chased naked around the garden and slapped on the behind" as an amusement, while German women are reduced to "two raunchy broads", one of whom was the "property" of the army Chief of Counter-intelligence.[79] In *A Woman in Berlin*, A.'s rape experiences and her encounter with two Russians in a park made it very clear that to Russian men, German women existed only as recept-acles for penises: "one of the soldiers turned to me and, in the friendliest of tones, said in Russian: "What's it matter who sleeps with you? One cock's as good as another!";[80] Richard Brett-Smith reduced the rape of German women to the "one great mistake" made by the Soviets, which "did them incalculable harm politically".[81] Again, the assumption that women are men's property is demonstrated in the rhetorical device of parallelism between "body", "valuable" and "home" in Brett-Smith's following remark, while the parallelism with "story" firmly places all these on a fictive plane of mythology, or downright lies: "Of course, if one believed *every story* one heard one could only conclude that *every female body* in the city had been raped several times over, *every valuable* looted, *every home* desecrated".[82]

Many men on both sides believed that rape was not a serious crime against women since they should be sexually accessible to men anyway. The issue had to do with male right of access rather than with the violation of women's bodies. A. records that when Herr Pauli realised that a lesbian in their house had thus far escaped rape because she dressed in a man's grey suit with a man's hat over her face, he "cracks jokes at the girl's expense, hopes for her conversion and insists that it would come close to a good deed to send her some hefty Ivans – the strapping Petka, for instance, with his lumberjack's paws".[83] Interestingly enough, this comment underlines the specifically heterosexual nature of hegemonic masculinity.

Both Allied and Axis soldiers shared in common an attitude towards women entirely consonant with hundreds of years of Western patriarchal domination, the most modern form of which is grounded in a social contract from which women are excluded. As Carole Pateman observes:

> the common law doctrine of coverture laid down that wives were the property of their husbands and men still eagerly press for the enforcement of the law of male sex-right, and demand that women's bodies, in flesh and in representation, should be publicly available to them.[84]

The sale of (white) wives is no longer an acceptable practice in Western societies, but the trade in women's bodies continues with prostitution. In the late nineteenth and throughout the twentieth centuries, prostitution became increasingly professionalised and influenced by the ideology of capitalism.[85] Pateman argues cogently that the body of a prostitute cannot be simplistically paralleled with that of a (male) worker, but the main point for us here is that men believe that it can be, and that the prostitution industry can be organised along capitalist guidelines, whereby it is part of a male-controlled:

> international sex industry that includes mass-marketing of pornographic books and films, widespread supply of strip-clubs, peep-shows and the like and marketing of sex-tours for men to poor Third World countries. The general display of women's bodies and sexual parts, either in representation or as live bodies, is central to the sex industry and continually reminds men – and women – that men exercise the law of male sex-right, that they have patriarchal right of access to women's bodies.[86]

The pervasive ideology of capitalism in twentieth-century hegemonic masculinity is demonstrated by Allied men's bragging about the bargain prices at which they had their 'frat' with German women. A popular 'frat' song began:

> Underneath the bushes
> You take your piece of frat
> You first take off your gas-cape
> And then remove your hat …

continuing through half a dozen verses and finally concluding:

> … And to your chums relate
> The total cost of all of it
> Just one chocolate date.[87]

Clearly, this is a male-centred view which perceives the 'cost' in purely capitalistic terms (high returns for low investment?), whereas the emotional and physical costs for women must surely be far greater. Such behaviour was consonant with the wholesale looting done by Allied troops after the war, where valuable German heirlooms and *objets d'art* were bought from starving Germans for ridiculously cheap prices on the black market and sent back to the USA and Britain.[88]

Twentieth-century hegemonic masculinity, then, is the common denominator in the continuum of sexual violence in Occupied Germany. I do not wish to suggest that the British and Americans committed rape and other atrocities on the same scale as the Red Army, for clearly they did not. Nor do I wish to suggest that anything the Allies did was comparable in scale to what the Germans did when they overran Eastern Europe. The point is that without the structure of Western hegemonic masculinity these particular atrocities might not have occurred or been excused, on whatever scale of violence or numbers. Much has been written about the National Socialists' glorification of aggressive Aryan manhood as personified by the image of SS-men during the Second World War,[89] but ideas and images do not arise from a vacuum. 'Fascist masculinity' or 'Nazi masculinity' should be viewed as the extreme end of Western right-wing, military masculinity, which is constructed around violence and domination. Only within such a paradigm does the general reaction of German men to the rape of German women make sense.

There are a few accounts of German men taking steps to prevent women from being raped. Ruth Andreas-Friedrich and her female cellar-mates were saved from rape by their male fellow-members of 'Uncle Emil', a socialist, anti-Nazi resistance group.[90] When Marianne MacKinnon was captured by Soviet troops on her way to Berlin she was protected from rape by a fellow prisoner, Herr Busse, who disguised her as a man.[91] Erich Kuby records that Dr Heinrich Grüber, a pastor in Berlin, was able to prevent the rape of several women by sheltering them in the church.[92] Frederich Luft prevented the rape of women in his household by pretending they were dead.[93] Berlin diarist A. gave only one account of male resistance to the Russians: when a bookseller (who was in hiding because he was a member of the NSDAP (National-sozialistische Deutsche Arbeiter Partei; i.e. Nazi party) attacked a Russian who was molesting his wife.[94]

These cases are the exception rather than the rule; most German men did nothing at all while women were raped. German men's inaction has traditionally been imputed to fear and cowardice. However, there may be other contributing factors. For over a decade, German males' identity as 'men' had been intertwined with images of aggression and victory. The end of the war could not but produce a crisis in this concept of masculinity. Their sheer inability to respond with effective violence to the threat of the invading Soviets during the Battle for Berlin, their subsequent defeat, and their disarmament meant that other roles which accompanied this specific masculine identity – such as the protection of wives, mothers and sisters – collapsed also. Significantly, A. noted that German men assumed culturally recognised forms of masculine behaviour only when they were authorised to collect firearms for the Soviet authorities:

> This is the first time in weeks that I've heard German men talking in loud voices, seen them move with any sign of energy. They strike me as almost 'masculine', or at least like something we used to call masculine. I'm afraid we'll now have to think up a new and better word for this quality.[95]

In addition to having to cope with the trauma of rape and of their male patriot's inaction, German women also had to cope with German men's violent reactions to their rape. Although Marianne MacKinnon was fortunate enough to escape rape, her fellow-prisoners were all raped on the first night of their imprisonment. On the second night, the Soviets bribed the women with soup and bread in exchange for sex. When some women agreed to compliant sex (the consequences of not engaging in sex were worse than engaging in it) the German male prisoners abused them as 'Whores! Bitches!' despite the fact that those who did not 'prostitute' themselves were subsequently raped brutally.[96] When Gerd – A.'s fiancé for whom she wrote the diary – returned to the house, she found that there was "continuous friction between him and me".[97] When she described what she and her cellar community had been through:

> then the real trouble began. Gerd: 'You've turned into shameless bitches – every one of you in this house!' And he made a grimace. 'I can't' bear to listen to these stories. You've lost your standards, the whole lot of you!'[98]

Other women faced more overt violence from German men. A female neighbour of A's who had been forced into compliant sex with a Russian was shot and killed by her husband, who later killed himself also.[99] Returning German prisoners of war (POWs) often threatened their wives with violence, beat them, or shaved their heads for 'collaborating' with the Allies. Posters viciously attacking women appeared in public places, one reading (in English): "What German women do makes a man weep. One bar of chocolate or one piece of gum gives her the name of German whore. How many soldiers gave their lives for these women!"[100] In 1946, a German woman received an abusive, anonymous letter telling her:

> You are a very filthy creature, an American whore. Don't flatter yourself by thinking you are pretty. When one looks at your rouged-up puss one thinks they are seeing a worn-out cow. Just like you the following girls are hated.[101]

There followed underneath the names of seven other German women. In an extreme case, a German POW publicly shaved a German woman's head with a pair of nail-clippers to express outrage at her "whoring".[102] These incidents taught German women that both the public and private spheres were fraught with the danger of male violence when women stepped outside the role hegemonic masculinity prescribed for them. It is hardly surprising that German women retreated into traditional roles within the private sphere in the 1950s, and it perhaps explains why these women had a vested interest in restoring hegemonic masculinity, with its implicit protection of 'good' women.

   Most men, whether Allied or German, did not wish to hear of German women's experiences. William L. Shirer, a correspondent for the *New York Herald Tribune* who visited Berlin in November 1945, flatly disbelieved the majority of rape stories he heard because "I remarked how many German women sported stylish fur coats!"[103] Less than 4 months after the worst mass rapes, Shirer complained that on the whole, German women looked "pretty well, though I am not implying, God knows, that they were ever a beautiful race".[104] He observed that:

> There is always rape when an army overruns a land ... when you consider what the Germans did to the Russian population when they overran half of European Russia –

and that the Red Army soldier may have remarked this – and taking into account that Soviet troops had been in the field constantly fighting for two to three years and that capturing Berlin was a costly operation and that some of the Russian divisions were made up of very inferior sort of material not to mention a weird assortment of Asiatic troops; then the amount of raping by Russian troops here apparently was not above the average to be expected.[105]

Shirer thus excuses the behaviour of Soviet troops as "inevitable revenge" and reinforces both the racist myth that it was the barbaric, less evolved Mongolian hordes who did the raping, and the hegemonic masculinist view (famously espoused by Havelock Ellis) that men needed regular sexual release, especially after the tensions of battle. What is not explained is the fact that in many cases, there was a significant delay between the end of battle and the beginning of the rapes.

Shirer's attitude was typical of Allied forces stationed in Germany. When George Clare's 'frat', Anita, tried to tell him about her rape experiences, he silenced her quickly, perceiving such stories as examples of the Germans' excessive and unjustified self-pity.[106] Although he did not doubt the veracity of Anita's account of the behaviour of Soviet troops, Clare adds that he "nevertheless resented her saying it. The Germans had brought it upon themselves. What right had they to complain!"[107]

Western Allied soldiers also had no desire to hear German women's complaints because, after all, they were reaping the rewards of the Soviets' raping sprees. The Red Army rapes established the pattern of power relations in Occupied Germany in terms of aggressive male dominance politically, economically, and sexually. German women were forced into compliant sex with the Soviets to protect themselves from rape, and this relationship was enthusiastically continued by British, French and American troops. After the immediate postwar months, sexual relations modulated from compliant, through altruistic, to consensual sex as relations were complicated by desire and by many German women's genuine liking of their Allied partners. However, the very nature of hegemonic masculinity made male sexual violence an underlying possibility in these relations and also constrained German women's behaviour and attitudes, for women were only granted 'affection' and 'protection' as long as they conformed to the requisite femininity demanded by hegemonic masculinity: passive servants of male desires – both sexual and nurturant. To step out of this role was to provoke violent male recriminations.

IV

To the present day, little has been written about sexual violence in war, let alone the rape of German women in the last days of the Second World War and during the Allied occupation of Germany. This paper has insisted that not only German history but Western history of the postwar era cannot be evaluated without taking into account the continuum of sexual violence in occupied Germany because of the deeply disturbing patterns of gender relations and hegemonic masculinity which were established during this period, and most significantly because German women's experiences of sexual violence have had largely unexplored lasting repercussions in subsequent German history.

Gender relations constitute one of the principal dynamics in all societies, and by its very extremity, sexual violence in war throws into sharp relief the nature of gender relations in 'normal' societies. Clearly, much more research is needed into this topic, especially in view of the systematic raping of women which accompanied the break-up of the former Yugoslavia from 1902 onwards, which suggests that a new phase has emerged in masculine hostility towards women, especially in connection with militarised masculinity.

Women's experiences of the continuum of sexual violence need to be treated seriously. To do otherwise is to affirm to a patriarchal tradition of male sex-right and the notion of men as women's sexual masters, and to succumb to the myth propagated by hegemonic masculinity that women's bodies are property to be disposed of by men. These assumptions have prevented serious analyses of German women's experiences of rape and prostitution by male historians in the past, although the material is not sparse.

Furthermore, German women's memories of Germany's defeat and occupation have had serious consequences for postwar German society. According to Alexander and Margarete Mitscherlich's 1967 Freudian study, *The Inability to Mourn*, postwar German society has not been able to come to terms with the full enormity of the crimes committed in the name of the fatherland nor to mourn the victims of Nazism because the German people effectively established defence mechanisms to avoid confrontation with the past.[108] This refusal to mourn the past and face Germans' collective guilt for the horrors of World War II is what West German intellectuals call the *unbewältigte Vergangenheit*, the "undigested" or "unmastered" past, the consequences of which have been extensively documented by the Mitscherlichs and others.[109] Among the defence mechanisms established to avoid confrontation with the past and responsibility as the guilty perpetrators of war and the Holocaust is an identification with the innocent victims. The Mitscherlichs argue that:

> To the conscious mind the past then appears as follows. We made many sacrifices, suffered the war, and were discriminated against for a long time afterward, yet we were innocent, since everything that is now held against us we did under orders. This strengthens the feeling of being oneself the victim of evil forces, first the evil Jews, then the evil Nazis, and finally the evil Russians. In each instance the evil is externalized.[110]

German women have played a crucial role in establishing these defence mechanisms — a role which has been either omitted or made invisible in the Mitscherlich's account because women have been omitted from their analysis. It was extremely easy for German women to identify with the victims of war. For the first time in history, civilian populations lived amidst the massive devastation of World War II and faced death daily as bombing raids were conducted by both sides. Even before the war's end, German women, together with other European women, had to struggle for survival, living in cellars and queuing for rations. With the defeat of Germany, living conditions deteriorated, and it was easy to blame both the war and the outcome on the 'evil Nazis'. In addition to the privations experienced during Occupation many German women justifiably felt victimised by the Soviet rapes. Ironically, prostitution and fraternisation with British and US troops also aided in the construction of defence mechanisms because they enabled many German women to shift their loyalty from Hitler to the democratic allies,[111] and this undoubtedly explains the desire of many women to leave Germany and escape to Britain or the USA through marriage. The return of German soldiers and POWs to their families probably strengthened women's identification as victims, since German men often reacted with violence to German women's sexual relations with the Allies. Moreover, German men, struggling through the trauma of defeat and expending enormous psychological and emotional energy in warding off mourning and melancholy themselves,[112] made living conditions much more difficult for many women. Women were exhausted by the struggle to ensure their families' survival, yet many men who returned home were unwilling to help either with the housework or by getting a low-paid job, adding to women's burdens by demanding women's support emotionally, psychologically, and financially.[113] These, then, were the memories which German women carried into the postwar years and possibly handed down to postwar generations. It is quite possible that memories of male sexual violence left the deepest scars, although all these memories contributed to women's – and subsequent generations' – identity as victims.

Finally, although much has been made of Germany's unmastered past in terms of Nazi atrocities and the Holocaust, little ink has been spilt over Allied men's unmastered past in terms of the sexual violence they unleashed on German women during the Occupation. Peter Merkl points out:

> A criminal who feels guilty about an act of violence is just as likely to commit his crime again as he is to repent and to sin no more … The tormentor or murderer is the tortured wretch who commits his crime because of feelings of unworthiness and self-hatred which he projects, of course, onto the victim. Once he has committed his crime, this outlet for his self-hatred may become fixed, and so he goes on committing his deed, or hardening his conscience by reaffirming and rationalising it in his mind … . Only through rehabilitation can the corroding effect of hatred and self-hatred be ended, the feeling of unworthiness alleviated, and a halt called to the endless chain of mutual revenge and retribution which allows hatred to continue to proliferate and blight ever more lives.[114]

Merkl was writing about Germany's refusal to confront the crimes of Nazism, but the same insight can be applied to twentieth-century Western hegemonic masculinity and its relation to women. As long as hegemonic masculinity continues to endorse male aggression, violence, hostility, to and domination over women and 'others', and as long as military training in boot camps continues to repress individual male identities and to construct homosocial bonds at the expense of women's dignity as human beings, degrading women's sexuality and reducing them to sexual objects, there is every likelihood that rape will accompany war – although men purportedly fight to protect women.

Acknowledgement

I am greatly indebted to Carole Elizabeth Adams, under whose supervision I wrote the BA(Hons) thesis at the University of Sydney in 1993 that has served as the basis for this article.

Notes

1 Atina Grossmann (1993) Rape and the German Occupation (Poughkeepsie, New York: conference paper at the Ninth Berkshire Conference on the History of Women, Vassar College).
2 Ruth Andrea-Friedrich (1990) Battleground Berlin. Diaries 1945–1948, tr. Anna Boerresen, pp. 16–17 (New York: Paragon House).

3 Anonymous (1955) *A Woman in Berlin*, tr. James Stern, p. 218 (London: Secker & Warburg).

4 Douglas Botting (1985) *In The Ruins of the Reich*, p. 194 (London: Allen & Unwin).

5 Annemarie Troger (1986) Between rape and prostitution: survival strategies and chances of emancipation for Berlin women after World War II, tr. Joan Reutersham, in J. Friedlander, B. Wiesen Cook, A. Kessler-Harris and C. Smith-Rosenberg (Eds) *Women in Culture and Politics: A Century of Change*, p. 98 (Bloomington: Indiana University Press).

6 Richard Brett Smith (1966) *Berlin '45: The Grey City*, pp. 101–102 (London: Macmillan).

7 See for example, Harold Zink (1974) *The United States in Germany, 1944–1945*, pp. 137–138 (Westport: Greenwood Press).

8 Ute Frevert (1989) *Women in German History: From Bourgeois Emancipation to Sexual Liberation*, tr. Stuart McKinnon-Evans in association with Terry Bond and Barbara Norden, p. 258 (Oxford: Berg); and Douglas Botting, *In the Ruins of the Reich*, pp. 190–191.

9 Anne Edwards (1987) Male violence in feminist theory: an analysis of the changing conceptions of sex/gender violence and male dominance, in Jalna Hanmer and Mary Maynard (Eds) (1987) *Women, Violence and Social Control*, p. 24 (Basingstoke: Macmillan).

10 Ibid., pp. 24–25. Edwards also argues that pornography is another area where images of (hetero)sexuality reflect and reinforce male dominance and a hegemonic masculinity which emphasises male aggression in terms of capitalism and sexuality, and the "depersonalisation, objectification and degradation of women".

11 Ibid., p. 26.

12 Liz Kelly, The continuum of sexual violence, in Harmer and Maynard *Women, Violence and Social Control*, p. 55.

13 Ibid., p. 50.

14 Ibid., p. 49.

15 Tröger, 'Between rape and prostitution', p. 112.

16 Claudia Koonz (1987) *Mothers in the Fatherland: Women, the Family and Nazi Politics* (New York: St Martin's Press).

17 Gisela Bock (1989) Die Frauen und der Nationalsozialismus: Bemerkungen zu einem Buch von Claudia Koonz, *Geschichte und Gesellschaft. Zeitschrift für Historische Sozialwissenschaft*, 15, pp. 563–579.

18 Tröger, 'Between rape and prostitution'.

19 *A Woman in Berlin.*

20 Erich Kuby (1968) *The Russians and Berlin, 1945*, tr. Arnold J. Pomerans (London: Heinemann).

21 Grossmann, 'Rape and the German Occupation'.

22 For a summary of Cornelius Ryan's research see Susan Brownmiller (1975) *Against Our Will: Men, Women and Rape*, pp. 66–69 (New York: Simon & Schuster, London: Secker & Warburg); Kuby, *The Russians and Berlin, 1945*, pp. 260–288.

23 Eric Santner (1990) *Stranded Objects: Mourning, Memory and Film in Postwar Germany*, pp. 1–5 (Ithaca, New York: Cornell University Press).

24 Jay W. Baird (1974) *The Mythical World of Nazi Propaganda, 1939–1945*, p. 246 (Minneapolis: University of Minnesota Press).

25 Johannes Steinhoff, Peter Pechel and Dennis Showalter (Eds) (1991) *Voices from the Third Reich: An Oral History*, p. 331 (London: Grafton).

26 Ibid., p. 334.

27 Nancy M. Hartsock (1983) *Money and Power: Toward a Feminist Historical Materialism*, pp. 155–157 (New York: Longman).

28 Robert Stoller, cited in Hartsock, *Money, Sex and Power*, p. 157.

29 Ibid., p. 157.

30 Hans von Lehndorff (1963) *East Prussian Diary: A Journal of Faith, 1945–1947*, tr. Violet M. Macdonald, p. 53 (London: Oswald Wolff).

31 Ibid., p. 53.

32 Ibid., p. 68.

33 Baird, *The Mythical World of Nazi Propaganda*, p. 273. See also Brunhilde Pomsel's account in Steinhoff et al, *Voices from the Third Reich*, p. 320.

34 See the account of George Clare's German girlfriend, Anita, in George Clare (1990) *Berlin Days, 1946–47*, p. 59 (London: Pan).

35 Grossmann, 'Rape and the German Occupation'; Kuby, *The Russians and Berlin, 1945*, p. 275.

36 *A Woman in Berlin*, p. 66.

37 Ibid., p. 153.

38 Ibid., p. 153.

39 C. W. Ceram, Introduction to *A Woman in Berlin*.

40 *A Woman in Berlin*, p. 66.

41 Ibid., p. 68.

42 Ibid., pp. 147, 156–157.

43 Brett-Smith's *Berlin '45*, p. 122 gives an account of conductor Leo Borchard's death which tallies with that of Andreas-Friedrich's "Andrik".

44 Ibid., p.16.

45 Steinhoff *et al.*, *Voices from the Third Reich*, p. 338.

46 Kuby, *The Russians and Berlin, 1945*, p. 275.

47 *A Woman in Berlin*, p. 187.

48 Kuby, *The Russians and Berlin, 1945*, p. 267.

49 *A Woman in Berlin*, pp. 112, 187.

50 Cited in Kuby, *The Russians and Berlin, 1945*, p. 238.

51 Andrea-Friedrich, *Battleground Berlin*, pp. 16–17.

52 *A Woman in Berlin*, p. 134.

53 Ibid., p. 212.

54 Ibid., p. 212.

55 Ibid., p. 136.

56 Brett-Smith, *Berlin '45*, p. 103.

57 Marianne MacKinnon (1987) *The Naked Years: Growing up in Nazi Germany*, p. 240 (London: Chatto & Windus).

58 Ibid., p. 251.

59 Ibid., p. 296.

60 James McGovern (1957) *Fräulein. A Novel* (London: John Calder).

61 Gordon Schaffer (1947) *Russian Zone*, p. 149 (London: Allen & Unwin).

62 See for example: McGovern, *Fräulein*, pp. 222–223; Kay Boyle (1952) *The Smoking Mountain: Stories of Postwar Germany* (London: Faber & Faber).

63 Cited in Botting, *In the Ruins of the Reich*, pp. 190–191.

64 Brownmiller, *Against Our Will*, pp. 24–25.

65 Bob Connell (1985) Masculinity, violence and war, in Paul Patton and Ross Poole (Eds) (1987) *War Masculinity*, pp. 5–7 (Sydney: Intervention Publications).

66 Tim Carrigan, Bob Connell and John Lee (c.1987) Toward a new sociology of masculinity, in Harry Brod (Ed.) *The Making of Masculinities*, pp. 86–92 (London: Allen & Unwin).

67 Ibid., pp. 88–89.

68 Connell, 'Masculinity, violence and war', p. 6.

69 Theodore Roszak (1969) The hard and the soft: the force of feminism in modern times, in Betty Roszak and Theodore Roszak (Eds) (1969) *Masculine/Feminine: Readings in Sexual Mythology and the Liberation of Women*, p. 93 (New York: Harper & Row).

70 Ronald Hyam (1990) *Empire and Sexuality: The British Experience* (Manchester: Manchester University Press) is an especially useful source with regard to this point since Hyam reproduces exactly the attitudes of imperial masculinity in his sympathetic reading of the sexual adventures of British male imperialists.

71 Klaus Theweleit (1987) *Male Fantasies I: Women, Floods, Bodies, Histories*, tr. Stephen Conway in collaboration with Erica Carter and Chris Turner (Cambridge: Polity Press).

72 Cited in Jo-Ann Pilardi (1990) On the war path and beyond: Hegel, Freud and feminist theory, in Azizah Y. Al-Hibri and Margaret Simons (Eds) *Hypatia Reborn: Essays in Feminist Philosophy*, p. 13 (Bloomington: Indiana University Press).

73 Ibid., p. 15.

74 Susan Gubar (c.1987) 'This is my rifle, this is my gun': World War II and the blitz on women, in M. Higonnet, J. Jenson, S. Michel and M. Weitz (Eds) *Behind the Lines: Gender and the Two World Wars*, p. 228 (New Haven: Yale University Press).

75 Ibid., pp. 231–255.

76 Victor Dallaire (1946) The American Woman? Not for this GI, *The New York Times Magazine*, 10 March 1946, pp. 15, 51.

77 Ibid., p. 15.

78 Aleksander Solzhenitsyn (1985) *The Gulag Archipelago, 1918–1956. An Experiment in Literary Investigation*, tr. Thomas P. Whitey and Harry Willetts, p. 21 (London: Collins Harvill).

79 Ibid., p. 21.

80 *A Woman in Berlin*, p. 188.

81 Brett-Smith, *Berlin '45*, p. 158.

82 Ibid., p. 158. My emphasis.

83 *A Woman in Berlin*, p. 140.

84 Carole Pateman (1988) *The Sexual Contract*, p. 14 (Cambridge: Polity Press).

85 Ibid., pp. 195–197.

86 Ibid., pp. 199–209.

87 Cited in Botting, *In the Ruins of the Reich*, pp. 189–190. My emphasis.

88 Brett-Smith, *Berlin '45*, p. 95.

89 Ibid., p 6; see also Theweleit, *Male Fantasies*.

90 Andreas-Friedrich, *Battleground Berlin*, p. 8.

91 MacKinnon, *The Naked Years*, p. 8.

92 Kuby, *The Russians and Berlin, 1945*, p. 276.

93 Ibid., p. 276.

94 *A Woman in Berlin*, p. 176.

95 Ibid., p. 73.

96 MacKinnon, *The Naked Years*, pp. 14–15.

97 *A Woman in Berlin*, p. 281.

98 Ibid, p. 281.

99 Ibid., p. 218.

100 Botting, *In the Ruins of the Reich*, p. 194.

101 Ibid., p. 194.

102 Ibid., p. 194.

103 William L. Shirer (1947) *End of a Berlin Diary*, p. 148 (London: Hamish Hamilton).

104 Ibid., pp. 148–149.

105 Ibid., p. 148.

106 Clare, *Berlin Days*, p. 18.

107 Ibid., p. 59.

108 Santner, *Stranded Objects*, pp. 1–4.

109 Peter Merkl (1965) *Germany: Yesterday and Tomorrow* (Oxford: Oxford University Press).

110 Cited in Santner, *Stranded Objects*, p. 6.

111 Ibid., p. 4.

112 Ibid., p. 37.

113 Frevert, *Women in German History*, pp. 262–263.

114 Merkl, *Germany: Yesterday and Tomorrow*, p. 8.

Index